89-16286

THE COLLECTED WORKS OF
L. S. VYGOTSKY

Volume 2
The Fundamentals of Defectology

(Abnormal Psychology and Learning Disabilities)

COGNITION AND LANGUAGE
A Series in Psycholinguistics • Series Editor: R. W. RIEBER

A Continuation Order Plan is available for this series. A continuation order will bring delivery of each
new volume immediately upon publication. Volumes are billed only upon actual shipment. For further information please contact the publisher.

THE COLLECTED WORKS OF
L. S. VYGOTSKY

Volume 2
The Fundamentals of Defectology
(Abnormal Psychology and Learning Disabilities)

Translated and with an Introduction by

JANE E. KNOX

Bowdoin College
Brunswick, Maine

and

CAROL B. STEVENS

Colgate University
Hamilton, New York

Editors of the English Translation

ROBERT W. RIEBER and AARON S. CARTON

John Jay College of Criminal Justice
and the Graduate Center
City University of New York
New York, New York

Bureau of Educational Evaluation
Garden City, New York
and State University of New York at Stony Brook (Emeritus)
Stony Brook, New York

PLENUM PRESS • NEW YORK AND LONDON

Library of Congress Cataloging in Publication Data

(Revised for volume 2)

Vygotskiĭ, L. S. (Lev Semenovich), 1896–1934.
The collected works of L. S. Vygotsky.

(Cognition and Language)
Translation of: Sobranie Sochineniĭ.
Vol. 1– includes bibliographies and indexes.
Contents: v. 1. Problems of general psychology.
1. Psychology. I. Rieber, R. W. (Robert W.) II. Carton, Aaron S.
BF121.V9413 1987   150   87-7219

This volume is published under an agreement with the
Russian Copyright Agency (VAAP)

ISBN 0-306-42442-8

© 1993 Plenum Press, New York
A Division of Plenum Publishing Corporation
233 Spring Street, New York, N.Y. 10013

Printed in the United States of America

FOREWORD AND ACKNOWLEDGMENTS

The *Fundamentals of Defectology* is Volume 2 of Plenum's English version of *The Collected Works of Lev Semenovich Vygotsky* and it is a translation of Volume 5 of Pedagogika's six-volume series published in Moscow between 1982 and 1984. The volume contains Vygotsky's works on defectology originally published in the 1920's and 1930's as well as some posthumous undated and hitherto unpublished manuscripts. They consist of a variety of formal and informal texts. The Soviet Editorial Collegium for the publication of Vygotsky's work collected them from a wide range of publications and Vygotsky's own archives. An "Afterword" and notes were also supplied by the Soviet Collegium. The present English version also offers an introduction by the translators.

Defectology is a term not, at present, readily found in English dictionaries and it does not designate a discipline at universities or a specialty at clinics in the English-speaking world. Yet *defektologia* in the tradition of the Soviet Union is concerned with abnormal psychology, learning disabilities, and what has been called special education in North America. We have chosen to retain *defectology* in this volume. In the title it readily signals its correspondence with the Russian volume from which it was translated. There are certain historical reasons for retaining the term which the translators describe in their introduction. Furthermore, the term is otherwise difficult to translate explicitly and elegantly.

As in the first volume, the translators contributed the bulk of the work and assumed the major responsibility for its scholarly quality. The translators for this English language series are scholars whose understanding of Vygotsky's text goes far beyond the mere comprehension of the Russian. Their work, therefore, is an effort to contribute both to Vygotskyan scholarship and to the variety of academic fields to which Vygotsky had himself contributed.

The modern view of language comprehension—in all modalities and within and across languages—argues that *both* the linguistic signals one receives *and* an understanding of the concepts underlying each message *together* contribute to comprehension. Vygotsky's own discussions (see Volume 1 of the English language series) clearly anticipated this view and accounted for it with theoretical ingenuity and subtlety. It is particularly appropriate here to seek fastidiously accurate *interpretations* or renditions of his text. Such translations must be informed by the kind of sophisticated comprehension which only scholarship in the field of the text can engender. Of course, translations by scholars of advanced standing are not a novelty in modern scholarship.

The Plenum translations of Vygotsky's texts are appearing at a moment when authentic and authoritative English versions of them are rare—a moment when the frequency of works *about* Vygotsky threatens to outstrip the availability of work *by* Vygotsky. Since seminal thinkers make their contributions by provoking further thought, admirers of Vygotsky will, of course, welcome the spate of interpretation, reinterpretation, revision, reconstruction, and deconstruction which Vygotsky's work has invited and will participate with alacrity in the activity. Yet, the translations appearing in these volumes are *not* offered as interpretations in the sense that they are new analytic works *about* Vygotsky. They are offered to serve as basic texts for readers of English who may be interested in what Vygotsky himself had to say. They are offered to scholars and students, who will make their own interpretations (in its broader sense) and who will evaluate the interpretations of others.

Having taken the view that a good translation is essentially an interpretation, the claim that this volume is an accurate and authentic interpretation of *Vygotsky's* meanings and intentions—and only of those meanings and intentions—must await hoped-for reassurances from those reviewers and critics who are qualified to make such judgments. On their part, the translators subjected their manuscripts of both the translation and their introduction to critical reading by a number of scholars and in particular they wish thank the following for their comments and discussions: James V. Wertsch (Clark University), Larry E. Holmes (University of Southern Alabama), Addison Stone (Northwestern University), Alex Kozulin (Boston University), William O. McCagg (Michigan State University), and their good friend and colleague, Victor Golod (Scientific Research Institute of Defectology, USSR Academy of Pedagogical Sciences, Moscow, and Visiting Scholar at the Russian Research Center, Harvard University) whose untimely death occurred on January 20, 1991. Although gratitude is owed these colleagues for helping to reduce the number of errors and misinterpretations which might have appeared in the volume, responsibility for those flaws which have not been eliminated must, as always, remain with the editors and translators.

The basic work of collecting, arranging, and editing Vygotsky's work from among Russian publications, personal papers, and archives was carried out for this volume and all others in the series by a collegium of Soviet scholars. The editor in chief was A. B. Zaporozhets and the members of the editorial collegium were T. A. Vlasova, G. L. Vygotskaia, V. V. Davydov, A. N. Leont'ev, A. R. Luria, A. V. Petrovskii, A. A. Smirnov, V. C. Chelemendik, D. B. El'konin and M. G. Yaroshevksii. The secretary of the editorial collegium was L. A. Radzichovskii.

In addition to their respective academic institutions, the translators would like to acknowledge the grants and fellowships that facilitated their work and gave them access to research environments that were particularly conducive to the production of a scholarly translation. These came from the International Research Exchange Board (which facilitated visits to the Soviet Union), the National Academy of Sciences, the Russian and Ukrainian Research Centers at Harvard University, and the Harriman Institute at Columbia University. Inasmuch as Vygotsky cited not only writers who are well-known to the mainstream of European and American psychology and philosophy but also many who may be obscure or completely unknown for the modern (English-language) reader, the translators have undertaken to identify correctly all names, including those not identified by the author or the Soviet editors. Thus special thanks are due not only for the support provided by the aforementioned research foundations and institutes but also to the staff of Special Collections at Milbank

Library in Teachers' College at Columbia University and to many friends, students and other associates who helped with the manuscript, in particular to Joyce Gracie, Todd Breslow, Shamu Fenyvesi, Jennifer Andich, and Wilford Saunders (Bowdoin College).

Some issues in the selection of English renditions of the technical terminology used in this volume bear mentioning. Vygotsky himself wrote extensively about the intimacy—perhaps the unity—of words with concepts, and he participated fully in the European intellectual community that gave his words their meanings and which gave scientific terms their special significance. Nevertheless he wrote at a time, with an orientation, and in a milieu which may seem a bit alien to the reader of this translation. Additional complications are encountered because intellectual progress is often manifested through the reorganization of concepts and the refinement of the meanings of terms. In psychology and philosophy, the various schools and orientations add to the complications.

Furthermore, fields which deal with human distress, like defectology, are also plagued by continuous cycles of semantic pejoration and amelioration and the coining of fussy euphemisms that reflect perhaps the emotional intensity of the mainstream person's response to these problems regardless of whether that response is brutish or, like Vygotsky's, humane and optimistic. Because (as Vygotsky's discussions of Adlerian psychology argue) the very basis of successful compensation for defects consists of encouraging the ability to surmount feelings of inferiority and the establishment of self-esteem, researchers and practitioners in defectology are also constrained by a concern for the feelings of the individuals suffering from defects.

Thus terms like *mental backwardness* (*umstvennaia otstalost'*), *feeble mindedness* (*slaboumie*) and *oligophrenia* with its three gradations of mental retardation (debility, imbecility, and idiocy) were, perhaps, appropriately descriptive and decorous in the 1920's but they can seem somewhat obsolete, unscientific or even a touch unseemly and unkind today. Faced with the dilemma of preserving the historical atmosphere or of making it more accessible to the contemporary English reader, the translators sought, wherever possible, to contribute an English terminology which, at least in the scientific community, would reflect as far as possible Vygotsky's intended meanings and his realistic acceptance of abnormalities, and which would, perforce, follow the usages already established by earlier Vygotskyan translators or scholars. Therefore, the translators frequently followed James Gallagher's usage in *Windows on Russia* (1974) and used the terms *debile*, *imbecile*, and *idiot* where a contemporary writer might have used the more euphemistic *mildly retarded*, *moderately retarded*, and *severely retarded*.

Vygotsky himself saw the issue of shifts in meaning as one of the basic technical problems in the field of defectology (see, in particular, "Diagnostics of Development and the Pedological Clinic" in this volume). He also notes, alas, that the terms *Hilfsschule* or *Sonderschule* (in German, a "helping school" or a "special school"), which may seem positive or neutral enough in their connotations, were quickly perceived as designating "fools' schools" and unfit for helping children with defects. And the contemporary reader will be aware of the fact that the guidance counselor's once carefully selected, seemingly neutral terms such as *slow* or *retarded* are eventually construed as insults for justifying brawls on American playgrounds while the teachers of children who have been thus labeled must labor valiantly not only to preserve these children's self-esteem but also to change society's perceptions of what the terms designate.

In the interest of contributing to the formation of a coherent English terminology for Russian psychological texts, this series has joined in the use of the term *conditional reflex* for the older *conditioned reflex* both in Volume 1 and in the present volume. By the time Watson adopted the Pavlovian formulation as a cornerstone for behaviorist psychology in the 1910's, Pavlov's *uslovnyi* had been mis-translated "conditioned" (as a Russian passive past participle), and the whole process was designated as "conditioning" (see Boring, 1950). At mid-century, however, Osgood (1953) suggested that "Pavlov meant that the occurrence of the reflex to a novel cue was literally *conditional* [sic] upon certain operations" and observed that in "contemporary American psychology ['conditioned'] had] become practically synonymous with 'learned. '" The fifties also saw the formulation of statistical theories of learning (see, for example, Estes, 1950; Bush and Mosteller, 1955) and an interest in the probabilistic nature of many forms of behavior. "Mathematical psychology" (see Laming, 1973, for a concise review) provided methods by which the Pavlovian findings (among others) could be interpreted in terms of equations describing their probabilities and that seemed consistent with Pavlov's attempts to constrict the sensory experience of his experimental organisms in order to enhance the likelihood of the effectiveness of his experimental stimuli. Because some types of probabilities are "conditional," the expressions *conditional stimulus* and *conditional reflex* might acquire for some students connotations suggesting dual probabilities (i.e., the probability of *A* in the context of its occurrence under the probabilistic condition *B*). Translators are now left to ponder whether such connotations were intended by Pavlov and whether Vygotsky, in his use of the terms, understood them in that way. Because at least one English-Russian dictionary (Mueller, 1959) glosses *conditioned* with *obuslovlennyi* but reserves *uslovnyi* for a "conditional sentence" (and makes a special note of "conditioned reflex"), recent translations, such as Kozulin's (1986) and the ones in this series can justify the usage of *conditional* as being more nearly correct renditions than *conditioned*. Yet eighty years of psychological writings and the students trained during those years will not disappear overnight. And new English language readers who will encounter both "conditioned" and "conditional" reflexes may be inclined to resolve whatever confusions they encounter by a process well known to students of diachronic semantics: they may adduce a useful, if unintended, distinction between the two terms. Thus, as a practical matter, those future generations of readers are owed this justification for the choice of usage in this volume.

Because there are often standard English renderings for certain terms in Western European literature (such as *sublation* for Hegel's *Aufhebung* and *damming up* for Lipps' *Stauung*), Vygotsky's Russian renderings of such terms—sometimes coinings with very telling connotations—frequently seemed to merit explanations; these have been supplied by Vygotsky himself, by his Russian editors, or by his translators. (For *sublation*, Vygotsky used *sniatie*, that is, "taking down," "reaping," or, perhaps, "relieving" and for *damming up* he used *zapruda*, which is a "dam" or "weir").

In transliterating terms and names from the text, this volume follows the compromise used by most scholars in Russian and Soviet studies: For commonly known and well-established names, such as *Vygotsky*, the usual popular English spelling has been maintained. The Library of Congress transliteration system has been used to transcribe all other Soviet names or Russian terms.

As in the previous volume, we have marked notes introduced by translators or English editors differently from those provided by the Soviet Editorial Collegium. Notes not otherwise marked are Vygotsky's.

References

Boring, E. G. *A History of Experimental Psychology*. New York: Appleton, Century, Crofts, 1950.

Bush, R.S. and Mosteller, F. *Stochastic Models for Learning*. New York: Wiley, 1955.

Estes, W. K. Toward a statistical theory of learning. *Psychological Review* **57**, 94-107, 1950.

Gallagher, J. *Windows on Russia: A Report of the United States–USSR Seminar on Instruction of Handicapped Children* U.S. Government Printing Office, Washington, D.C. 1974.

Kozulin, A. (Translator). Vygotsky, L.S. *Thought and Language* Cambridge, Mass.:MIT Press, 1986.

Laming, D. *Mathematical Psychology*. London and New York: Academic Press, 1973.

Mueller, V. K. (Compiler). *English-Russian Dictionary, Sixth Edition*. New York: E.P. Dutton, 1959.

Osgood, C. *Method and Theory of Experimental Psychology*. New York: Oxford University Press, 1953.

CONTENTS

PART III: Questions at the Forefront of Defectology

VYGOTSKY AND SOVIET RUSSIAN DEFECTOLOGY

An Introduction

Jane E. Knox   Carol Stevens

Lev Semenovich Vygotsky (1896-1934) is known to the English-speaking world as a psycholinguist, a theorist, and a founder of Soviet cognitive developmental psychology. What may be less familiar is his key role in establishing the discipline of abnormal child psychology in the USSR. The American editor and translators hope that the availability of this volume in English will serve to make this additional facet of Vygotsky's work more widely known.

His text appeared in Russian in 1983 under the title, *The Fundamentals of Defectology*. The word *defectology*, which may sound harsh to Western ears, is the current Soviet term for the discipline which studies the handicapped, their development, teacher training and methods. It was apparently introduced into the Russian language in 1912 as a term borrowed from contemporary German curative pedagogy. In Russia, the field underwent dramatic transformation in the decades following the Revolution, but its name remained unchanged. In fact, one of Vygotsky's contributions to the discipline was to help provide a strong theoretical basis for continuing to treat the psychology and teaching of the handicapped as a single, unified field.[1] This present volume, which appeared as *Volume 5* of Vygotsky's *Collected Works* in Russian, contains a selection of essays, speeches, reports, comments, and reviews, assembled and edited by members of the Scientific-Research Institute of Defectology at the Soviet Academy of Pedagogical Sciences in Moscow. The relationship of Vygotsky's activities to the current Soviet discipline and its pre-eminent research institution, the Institute of Defectology, is a topic that will be discussed in greater detail below.

With a few exceptions, the compilers of the 1983 volume chose to include in it works which Vygotsky wrote between 1924 and 1931. Although most of them appeared in the

---

[1] William O. McCagg, "The Making of Defectology," in William O. McCagg and Lewis Seigelbaum, eds., *The Disabled in the Soviet Union: Past and Present. Theory and Practice* (Pittsburgh: University of Pittsburgh Press, 1989).

contemporary Soviet press, a few essays (among them, "The Blind Child," "Difficult Children," and "Moral Insanity") are printed here for the first time. The period 1924–1931 marked Vygotsky's rise to national eminence both as a brilliant and creative psychologist and as a 'defectologist' in the new Soviet Russia, and the consolidation of his influence. It may also simply have encompassed his most prolific years.[2] But Vygotsky's star did not remain at such heights in the Soviet academic firmament. Following a period of criticism and rejection beginning in the 1930's, Vygotsky's legacy in the Soviet academy has been controversial and his contribution to the discipline hotly disputed.[3]

The controversy over Vygotsky is deeply rooted not only in the theories he propounded, but also in the historical context from which those theories emerged. We should like to discuss briefly here each of these issues in an effort to elucidate Vygotsky's ideas and clarify the nature of the contemporary debate about him.

1

Vygotsky's studies of handicapped children and their psychological development emerged as part of a burgeoning interest in special education following the Russian Revolution. Neither special education nor the study of the handicapped had been prominent in Imperial Russia.[4] World War I, the Revolution, the subsequent Civil War, famine, and uneven recovery, despite the administrative, social, and economic upheaval they brought, were accompanied by an intense intellectual ferment that helped alter that situation. A number of pre-revolutionary defectologists founded revolutionized schools, clinics, and teaching institutes to study the handicapped. The result was a proliferation of institutions affiliated, with the new Commissariat of Enlightenment (Education), which were part of the Soviet government's efforts to democratize, educate, and politicize Russian society. However, these more numerous institutions remained under the leadership of pre-war defectologists whose politics and academic perspectives could hardly be described as committedly Marxist.[5]

---

[2] Cf. Akademiia Pedagogicheskikh Nauk SSSR, *Pedagogicheskaia bibliografiia, 1924–1930* (Moscow, 1967) and APN SSSR, *Pedagogicheskaia bibliografiia, 1931–1935* (Moscow, 1980). These works cite only printed pedagogical materials. However, Vygotsky had greater research resources during this time period: see also text, below.

[3] For example, Alex Kozulin, *Psychology in Utopia* (Cambridge, Mass: MIT Press, 1984), chapter 5, esp. pp. 110–120.

[4] Although recent German studies in these areas had aroused interest in Moscow and Petersburg, less than one percent of handicapped children attended special courses even in these cities. Pre-war Germany had ten times as many children using such facilities as Imperial Russia did. McCagg, "Defectology," pp. 3, 17–19; cf. Russia. Kommissariat Prosveshchenie, *Narodnoe prosveshchenie v osnovnykh pokazatel'iakh* (Moscow, Leningrad, 1928), Table 14, p. 65. As shown here, even in the 1920's, when many more students attended special courses than under the Empire, the student population still amounted to less than one percent of the client population. For greater detail on the Tsarist period, see Mary S. Conroy, "Education of the Blind, Deaf, and Mentally Retarded in late Tsarist Russia," *Slavic and East European Education Review*, nos. 1–2, 1985.

[5] There is quite a remarkable consistency between the heads of pre-war institutions for the handicapped and those holding the same or similar posts in the early 1920's. V. P. Kashchenko and G. V. Murashev, *Iskliuchitel'nye deti: ikh izuchenie i vospitanie* 2d ed. (Moscow: Rabotnik prosveshcheniia, 1929), pp. 13–14, 22; A. B. Zalkind, *Pedologiia v SSSR* (Moscow, 1929,) p. 57; McCagg, "Defectology," p. 22.

By 1921, a new social problem had focused particular attention on special education and led to the creation of an entirely different set of institutions for special education. A tragic product of the years of war, revolution, civil strife, and famine was the creation of an army of homeless, orphaned, vagrant, abandoned, and neglected children—about seven million of them by 1921–1922.[6] Officially, the educational system took responsibility for these homeless and abandoned children. The task of housing and educating them was in itself a mammoth one. To add to the difficulties, a number of these children had special problems, ranging from physical disabilities to recidivist criminal behavior. Both the scope of this problem and the general social conditions prevailing in Russia in the early 1920's made it impossible to devote exclusive attention or significant financial resources to the needs of this population. Nevertheless, concern for these abandoned children did lead to the inauguration of a special section of the Commissariat of Enlightenment called SPON (Social and Legal Protection of Minors). Beginning in 1923 (that is, after the 1921–1922 famine had reached its peak), more of the new institutions sponsored by SPON were directed toward identifying, housing, and educating children who were physically handicapped or "difficult to educate." The net result of the general focus on education and the particular concern for abandoned children was a marked increase in facilities for studying and teaching the handicapped and training teachers for them.[7] Even these new facilities, however, were often dominated by pre-war specialists whose training and perspectives were not Marxist. This was the field of "defectology" in which Vygotsky made his mark in the mid-1920's. Not only did his career reflect the new opportunities in the field, his writings also broached the particular problems of the Russian republic of that time. For example, the chapter in this volume entitled "Moral Insanity" is a particularly direct analysis of psychological traits encountered among abandoned children; this chapter and others like it document Vygotsky's personal involvement with SPON.

It would be a mistake, however, to attribute Vygotsky's influence in defectology from 1924 to 1931 solely to the independent activities of a brilliant and committed young researcher in an expanding field. Contributing to Vygotsky's emergence were attempts by the new Bolshevik government and by individual scholars to encourage or generate Marxist schools of thought in a number of academic disciplines. Indeed, Vygotsky's activities and influence in this period seem almost to epitomize the unprecedented opportunities the Revolution could provide for young Marxist scholars.

Even before the revolutionary change of power in 1917, there can be little doubt that Vygotsky was committed to a radical political perspective. Born into a Jewish family in Byelorussia (now Belarus) in 1896, his early life was unavoidably circumscribed by the restrictions the Russian Empire imposed on its Jewish subjects. His own abilities and his family's relative prosperity helped him partially to overcome these: he was privately educated, graduated a gold medalist from a Jewish gymnasium, and entered Moscow

---

[6] Jennie A. Stevens, "Children of the Revolution: Soviet Russia's Homeless Children (*Besprizorniki*) in the *1920's,*" *Russian History/Histoire Russe*, vol. 9, pts. 2-3 (1982): 246.

[7] Stevens, "Children of the Revolution," *Russian History/Histoire Russe* vol. 9 pts 2–3 (1982): 242–264, esp. pp. 246, 253. For the status of SPON, see Russia. Kommissariat Prosveshchenie, *Narodnoe prosveshchenie v RSFSR k 1924n1925* (Moscow, 1925), Appendix I, and similar organizational charts in succeeding annual reports. On the new institutions founded by SPON, see Im. M. Bogdanov, "Statistika uchrezhdenii sotsial'no-pravovoi okhrany," in A. G. Kaleshnikov and M. S. Epshtein, eds., *Pedagogicheskaia entsiklopediia*, 3 vols. (Moscow: Rabotnik prosveshcheniia, 1927–1929), vol. 2, cols. 385–386 (Hereafter, *PedEn*, 1927–1929).

University in 1914 under the tsarist quota system, which limited Jews to three percent of that prestigious institution's student body.

Vygotsky's radical political and intellectual inclinations were evident even at this age. While pursuing his studies at Moscow University, for example, he also attended Shinyavskii University. Shinyavskii was an unofficial establishment founded by those expelled from Moscow University for anti-tsarist activities in 1911. From its inception, its faculty and student body included many who would become prominent academics in the early Soviet period. Vygotsky could receive no degree there, but he undertook broadly interdisciplinary studies in psychology, history, and philosophy. These studies proved to be his enduring interests and eventually the focus of his professional career.

Meanwhile, his formal education at Moscow University culminated in a law degree in 1917. Ironically, in the Russian Empire, this choice of profession would have permitted him to reside beyond the geographic boundaries of the Pale. Otherwise, like most other Jews in the Empire, he could have legally resided only its the western lands. However, as Vygotsky graduated, the Romanov tsars were overthrown and such restrictions were lifted. Within months of his graduation, the October Revolution brought a new Soviet government to power. After graduation, he apparently abandoned his interest in law and returned to his hometown of Gomel, which was within the Pale. There, in the years following the Revolution, he taught literature and psychology. At a local teachers' training college, he established a psychology laboratory for the study of the handicapped.[8] Since Gomel harbored one of Byelorussia's two homes for mentally retarded children, one might speculate that Vygotsky's interests in the psychology and education of the handicapped developed here, but there is no direct evidence of this.[9]

Vygotsky first appeared on the national stage in 1924, after Soviet Russia had survived its first traumatic years. The homeless and abandoned children were already a major social concern; SPON had been founded. In January, 1924, he delivered a lecture in Leningrad at the Second All-Russian Psycho-Neurological Congress. His report proved an impressive challenge to reflexology, the then-dominant perspective in psychology. Vygotsky's views attracted the attention of N. K. Kornilov and A. B. Zalkind, among others. They were seeking to create in Russia a significant Marxist school of analysis in psychology and educational psychology. Vygotsky's training and early activities might have been attractive to them; his attack on reflexology and his style of analysis certainly were. He was invited to return to Moscow State University, as his alma mater was now called, and join the Institute of Psychology. As N. K. Kornilov had recently been made director of this pre-war research institution, it was rapidly becoming a prominent center for Marxist psychology. Vygotsky's connection with the Institute, where he completed his dissertation in 1925, provided him

---

[8] James V. Wertsch, *Vygotsky and the Social Formation of the Mind* (Cambridge, Mass: Harvard University Press, 1985), pp. 3–7; McCagg, "Defectology," p. 23; Kozulin, *Psychology*, p. 112; cf. Michael and Sheila Cole, *A. R. Luria: The Making of a Mind, A Personal Account of Soviet Psychology* (Cambridge, Mass: Harvard University Press, 1979), p. 42, cited by McCagg; "Vygotsky," in *Sovietskaia entsiklopediia. Gosudarstvennoe nauchnoe izdatel'stvo. Moscow, Pedagogicheskaia entsiklopediia* 4 vols. (Moscow: Sov. entsikl., 1964-1968) (Hereafter, *PedEn*, 1964-1968) reports that Vygotsky finished the history and philosophy faculty. For greater detail on pre-Revolutionary restrictions on the Jewish population of the Empire, see Lewis Greenberg, *The Jews in Russia*, vol. 2, reprint (New Haven: Yale University Press, 1965).

[9] *PedEn*, 1927–1929, vol. 2, col. 389; *Voprosy Defektologii*, 1928, no. 4: 88. The article here indicates that a reorganization of the home took place in 1925, which strongly suggests that its foundation dates to 1924 or earlier.

with a base within the national academy, and ultimately with colleagues, supporters, and disciples.[10]

In the study of the handicapped, as in psychology, Marxist perspectives were not prominent before the mid-1920's. Vygotsky quickly emerged as an important contributor in both fields. He was not only a critic of older perspectives and methods, but also an original thinker and researcher. Briefly, what he proposed was a new, eclectic Marxist view which emphasized cultural, rather than hereditary, influences on development and which drew heavily on his own reading in Western psychology. Vygotsky's first appearances as a defectologist in the capital were important occasions for the discussion of these views. One such occasion was the Second All-Russian Congress for the Social and Legal Protection of Minors (SPON). The Congress marked a sharp break in the study of the handicapped in Russia. The Congress's closing resolutions condemned older methods, castigated them for their impotence in dealing with abandoned children, and set education for the handicapped on a new path.[11] Vygotsky's two reports to the Congress (elaborations of which appear here as Chapters 1 and 2 of Part I) bolstered and supported the SPON recommendations. Vygotsky insisted particularly that special schools should share with the general educational system the social goals set by the Soviet state: productive labor and self-sufficiency.

Vygotsky's influence as both researcher and proponent of the new perspective expanded rapidly after the Second SPON Congress. This influence is readily visible in the growing list of his institutional affiliations. It was not uncommon for academics in the 1920's to hold a number of posts simultaneously, and Vygotsky was no exception. In 1925–1926, he began organizing a laboratory for the study of abnormal children at a Medical Pedagogical Station in Moscow. Vygotsky's patron, Kornilov, had been affiliated since its foundation with Moscow State University II, an institution known as the "Red University" in the late 1920's because of its many Marxist and pro-Soviet scholars. When the University organized scientific research institutes at its pedagogical faculty in 1926–1927, Vygotsky was named associate director of the defectology section. His ascendancy in studies of the handicapped became even more marked with the onset of the cultural revolution in 1928. His was the lead article in a lengthy segment on "Institutions for Children Differing from the Norm" in the major three-volume *Pedagogical Encyclopedia* (1927–1929). His research and activities at the Moscow State University II Institute also prospered as he joined the editorial board of the defectology section's new journal, *Questions of Defectology* in 1929.[12]

---

[10] Russia. Kommissariat Prosveshchenie. *Universitety i nauchnye uchrezhdeniia*, 2d expanded ed. (Moscow, Leningrad: Ob"edienoe Nauchno-Tekhnicheskoe Izdanie, 1935) p. 397; David Joravsky, "The Construction of the Stalinist Psyche," in Sheila Fitzpatrick, *The Cultural Revolution in Russia, 1928–1931* (Bloomington, Ind.: University of Indiana Press, 1978), p. 109, fn.9, p. 269; and biographical detail on Vygotsky from works cites in footnote 7, above.

[11] A. N. D'iachkov, "Razvitie Sovietskoi defektologii za 40 let," *Spetsial'naia shkola*, no. 2: 1958. 7–8; his, ed., *Defektologicheskii slovar'* 2d expanded ed. (Moscow, 1970), p. 56.

[12] Soviet "Afterword" to this volume; *Moskovskii gosudarstvennyi pedagogicheskii institut imeni V. I. Lenina, 1872–1972* (Moscow, 1972), pp. 99–100. This source provides an excellent guide, based on the Institute's own archives, to the myriad of changing teachers' training institutions in Moscow before World War II. *PedEn*, 1927–1929, vol. 2, col. 391–398; the dates and affiliation of *Questions of Defectology (Voprosy Defektologii)* can be confirmed in the Library of Congress, *Union List of Serials*, and its editorial board in any issue of the journal. {The Soviet editors of this volume date, mistakenly, we believe, the foundation of the defectology research institute at Moscow State University II in fn. 6 p. 351. The 1926–1927 date used here from the first work cited above is confirmed in Russia. Kommissariat Prosveshchenie, *Narodnoe prosveshchenie v RSFSR k 1926–1927*, (Moscow, Leningrad, 1927), pp. 140–145, and elsewhere.}

Such benefits to Vygotsky did not proceed without cost to scholars of the old school, however. In this, as in many fields, the cultural revolution beginning in 1928 intensified the challenge of militant communists against established pre-war intellectuals. The Medical-Pedagogical Station to which Vygotsky's laboratory was attached in 1925–1926 was a case in point. It had evolved from a private pre-revolutionary school-sanitarium into a complex of "revolutionized" schools, clinics, and laboratories under the direction of its founder; there was even a pedagogical institute for special education at the same address after 1920. The entire complex served as a model-experimental institution for the Soviet educational system after 1923. The pedagogical institute was closed in the wake of the Second SPON Congress, however, since it had espoused the old methods.[13] Although the station as a whole continued to be praised for its research into teaching methods and retained the classification "model-experimental" until at least 1929, the institution underwent severe restructuring in the late 1920's. Its leadership was censured for failing to conform to the Commissariat of Enlightenment's new position on special education, and the Station was described as overemphasizing biological factors in evaluating the handicapped. This stock phrase, used to identify the old defectology, distinguished it clearly from the sociocultural emphasis espoused by Vygotsky and others of the new schools.[14] Perhaps in connection with this restructuring, Vygotsky's lab gained titular independence in 1929 as the Experimental-Defectological Institute (hereafter EDI); the particular focus of its research became oligophrenia.[15]

But 1929 and 1930 proved to be the zenith of Vygotsky's influence. The cultural revolution ended, paradoxically, in 1931–1932 with an abrupt turn to greater Party discipline and a more narrowly defined orthodoxy. Not a few of the Party's erstwhile allies in academic institutions (and the new perspectives and experimentation they had encouraged) found themselves at intellectual and political odds with the new direction. The retrenchment which followed helped complete the consolidation of Stalinism in many intellectual and educational institutions. Under its impact, some parts of the educational system were reorganized; many Soviet universities were divided into smaller, more specialized units. These smaller units were intended to provide more directly for the technical and practical needs of the first economic Plans. At the same time, however, the reorganizations housed "unruly militants" in smaller, more easily disciplined units.[16] These and other changes at the close of the cultural revolution profoundly altered the disciplines of psychology, pedology (educational psychology), pedagogy, and defectology.

The place of special schooling changed as the Commissariat of Enlightenment felt the impact of events in the early 1930's. Many of SPON's independent facilities were subsumed under the general education system after 1930 (the date by which SPON had hoped to

---

[13] "Kashchenko," *PedEd*, 1964–1968; *PedEn*, 1927–1929, vol. 2, col. 325; *Pedagogicheskii slovar' v dvukh tomakh* (Moscow: 1960), vol. 1, pp. 326, 505–506; *Sotsial'no-pravovaia okhrana detei i podrostok i detskii dom*, *Materialy ko vtoromu vse-rossiskomuy s"ezdu, 24 nov. 1924* (Moscow, 1924), p. 143ff.

[14] *NarodPros k 1926–1927*, pp. 68–77; *PedEn* (1927–1929), vol. 3, col. 330; *Voprosy defektologii* 1928, no. 3: 58. The Station's status may have endured until 1937 when the classification was eliminated. Beatrice Beach Szekely, "The Establishment of the Academy of Pedogogical Sciences of the USSR" (Columbia University, unpublished Ph.D. dissertation, 1976), p. 47.

[15] "Defektivnye deti," *Bol'shaia Sovietskaia Entsikopediia* (1939); *Defekotologicheskii slovar'*, pp. 32, 49–50; McCagg, "Defectology," pp. 25, 37; Soviet "Afterword" to this volume.

[16] Sheila Fitzpatrick, "Cultural Revolution as Class War," in Fitzpatrick, ed., *Cultural Revolution*, pp. 28–40, is a succinct summary of the period; Gail Warshofsky Lapidus, "Educational Strategies and Cultural Revolution," in Fitzpatrick, ed., *Cultural Revolution*, p. 93.

eradicate the problem of abandoned children); the institutions with which Vygotsky was associated suffered among others. In 1931, another decree emphasized that special schooling was but a part of the broad mass education system. The decree guaranteed education to all, including the handicapped. At first glance, however, the newly streamlined system was ill-equipped to fulfill that promise in special schooling.[17] In a parallel fashion, defectology research felt the blast of the Communist Party's reproaches; research institutions were closed and reorganized. Marxist and non-Marxist psychologists alike, the Party argued, had not contributed constructively to the building of socialism; furthermore, some Marxist psychologists were moving in directions that directly contradicted the practical goals of the next Five Year Plan. Under attack in the early 1930's, differences of opinion within Marxist psychology deepened; Zalkind and Kornilov's early collaboration broke down. The unanimity of Marxist psychologists at the 1928 Pedological Congress turned into acrimonious confrontations about the profession's allegiance to the Party. For the next five years, condemnations, many of them against erstwhile allies, grew both from the Party and those psychologists who chose to ally themselves with its views. In 1936, after Vygotsky himself had been dead for two years, the attacks culminated in a decree excoriating educational psychology in particular. Those studying the handicapped and those selecting students for special schools were especially singled out for criticism. The decree referred obliquely to earlier accusations against defectologists. They were too eclectic; that is, they borrowed foreign theoretical perspectives and tried to pass them off as Marxist psychology. And they were too idealistic; that is, their theories were too far separated from practical requirements. The focus of the decree, however, was the fatalism attributed to educational psychologists. Such specialists blamed a child's shortcomings either on heredity or on social environment, the decree argued. This position failed to take into account the remedial effects of institutions and individuals. Thus, educational testing (and the psychologists who designed it) were discovering problems where none existed. As a result, the special schools were being flooded with children who would respond better to "normal" schooling; no wonder the care in such schools was inadequate! The Commissariat of Enlightenment was ordered to transfer these students back to normal schools forthwith.[18]

The combined long-term effects of these conditions was first to weaken Vygotsky's influence even in those institutions where it was strongest. Moscow State University II was one of the educational institutions reorganized in 1930. The Lenin Pedagogical Institute, one of its successor institutions, lacked the former University's resources. Although the new Institute retained a defectology section, that section emphasized practical teacher training, rather than a broader research-oriented approach. The research journal *Questions of Defectology* ceased publication in 1931. The ordained emphasis on activism also affected the Experimental-Defectological Institute (EDI), where Vygotsky was replaced as director in

---

[17] Zalkind, *Pedologiia*, Appendix 1; D'iachkov, "Razvitie," p. 8–9; *NarodPros v 1930*, pp. 13–14; Stevens, "Children of the Revolution," p. 261. The 1930 report and Ia. A. Perel' and A. A. Liubimov, *Bor'ba s detskoi besprizornosti* (Moscow: 1932), pp. 9–10, both argue that the homelessness problem had "basically" disappeared by 1930–1931. There was apparently a resurgence in the numbers of homeless and neglected children in the aftermath of the First Five Year Plan. Raymond Bauer, *The New Man in Soviet Society* (Cambridge, Mass: Harvard University Press, 1952), p. 42.

[18] On psychology's disputes with the Party, see Joravsky, "Construction," pp. 105–128; Bauer, *Soviet Man*, chapters 4–7. Note Zalkind's attempt to forestall criticism of the Institute of Psychology in his *Pedologiia*, p. 62. An English translation of the decree against educational psychology (pedology) is reproduced in Szekely, "Establishment," pp. 202–205. Cf. comments on the decree by Bauer, *Soviet Man*, chapter 8.

1930 by Israel Isaakovich Daniushevskii. A man from the teaching side of the profession, Daniushevskii had once been associate director of the Children's Special Commission of the Russian Soviet Federated Socialist Republic; he had also acted as associate director of the now-dissolving SPON section. Despite his replacement as director, Vygotsky's research at EDI continued, almost until his premature death in 1934 of tuberculosis. One of his last publications was co-authored with Daniushevskii and appeared under the imprimatur of the Institute, by then named in honor of M. S. Epshtein, Associate Commissar of Enlightenment. Vygotsky also retained his supporters in the Institute of Psychology, although the Institute's influence was much diminished. A few months prior to his death, a study group there undertook to edit two of his major works.[19]

The 1936 decree against educational psychology nearly eliminated whatever influence remained to these institutions and to Vygotsky's ideas. Vygotsky's EDI, under Daniushevskii's leadership, was reorganized in 1936 under the name Scientific Practical Institute of Special Schools and Children's Homes, a title it retained until 1944. The Institute of Psychology, many of whose members had resigned under Party attacks since 1930, took the full brunt of Party outrage. There were more resignations and some arrests. At least two of the leading lights of Vygotsky's time were shot, disappeared, or were sent to labor camp. By transferring individuals and favoring other institutions, the Party deliberately moved the focus of teaching and research in child development psychology to Leningrad. Vygotsky, who had been the object of overt and deliberate attack before the 1936 decree, was no longer cited even by his closest remaining friends and disciples in the purged disciplines; they did, however, make use of some of his ideas.[20]

What really caused such an abrupt rejection of Vygotsky's ideas and influence? How much of his work survives in the contemporary Soviet discipline and institutions of defectology? It is tempting simply to conclude that Vygotsky was a random casualty of high Stalinism. That is, since Vygotsky and his ideas did not correspond well to the Party condemnations of psychology and defectology between 1930 and 1936, it is not clear why he in particular should have suffered. Accusations against his "eclecticism and idealism" are barely distinguishable from similar attacks on other intellectuals, as the Party tried to establish cultural orthodoxy in the early 1930's. Recent historical work offers less random explanations for cultural and institutional changes under Stalin in the late 1920's and early 1930's; governmental and Party pressure were not the only factors involved. Among academic disciplines, for example, the tempo and character of the move toward an orthodoxy acceptable to the Party varied considerably. In some areas, the new orthodoxy was established quite early and after an abrupt break. This was true of history and architecture, for example.[21] Major changes in a few fields were less dramatic, or even delayed. V. I. Vernadskii, for example, retained his commanding institutional and intellectual position in the earth sciences surprisingly unchallenged until his death, despite being openly critical of

[19] *Mosk. Ped. Institut*, p. 124; *Universitety*, p. 400; "Daniushevskii," *PedEn* (1964–1968); *Pedagogicheskaia bibliografiia, 1931–1935*, no. 9622, p. 331.

[20] "Daniushevskii," *PedEn* (1964–1968); Szekely, "Establishment," pp. 41–2, 45; *Universitety*, pp. 398–400. For a sample denunciation of Vygotsky, see E. I. Rudneva, *Pedologicheskie izvrashchenie Vygotskogo* (Vygotsky's Pedological Perversions) (Moscow: UchPedGiz, 1937), 37pp. Szekely, pp. 41–2, states that Zalkind disappeared, and that Pinkevich and Pistrak were either shot or sent to labor camps.

[21] George Enteen, "Marxist Historians during the Cultural Revolution," in Fitzpatrick, ed., *Cultural Revolution*, pp. 154–168, and Hugh Hudson, "The Social Condenser of Our Epoch," *Jahrbuecher fuer Geschichte Osteuropas*, vol. 34, no. 4 (1986): 557–578.

Marxism.[22] The nature of disputes within a given discipline among academics themselves provides one explanation for such differences. Early and abrupt changes happened where there were attacks from some members of a profession against others, often more established or powerful; these attacks received first tacit and then increasingly active Party support until an orthodoxy was achieved which conformed to Party goals. In the absence of internal disagreement, change was slower, less abrupt. Thus, the Party's treatment of a profession or discipline in the 1930's may have been related to the internal cohesion of that profession, as well as to the Party's goals. The presence of a generally accepted scientific paradigm in a field would be a particular inducement to such cohesion.[23]

Perhaps there are lessons to be learned here with respect to Vygotsky's treatment in the 1930's and the transmission of his ideas to the current Soviet discipline. Psychology and defectology apparently corresponded to neither extreme case described above; in any case, it is difficult to draw conclusions about the structure of these two disciplines, as studies of the institutional and professional relationships among psychologists in this period are still few in number. However, despite differences among themselves, it is clear that Soviet psychologists were quite slow to accept Party leadership in the early 1930's. Only after at least four years of increasing pressure did Pavlov and others finally agree to support a new perspective that was acceptable to the Party; Marxist Pavlovianism.[24] Meanwhile, men like Daniushevskii, Vygotsky's institutional if not intellectual heir, protected some of their colleagues through the worst of the purges. Other researchers and practitioners fled into medical institutions or worked outside the major cities.[25] Indeed, in the 1940's, the institutions and even some of the individuals Vygotsky had known in the 1920's formed a nucleus for the Defectology and Psychology institutes at the Soviet Academy of Pedagogical Sciences. With others in the profession, A. N. D'iachkov, a graduate of Moscow University II's defectology section, helped to reorganize Vygotsky's old laboratory to form the Institute of Defectology in 1943; it was, after all, the oldest facility for the study of the handicapped in the country. In 1944, the Institute's first formal director was L. V. Zankov, who had worked at the laboratory since Vygotsky's time. The Institute of Psychology, refurbished by the very same N. K. Kornilov after 1938, was transferred away from Moscow University I at the end of the war. Like the Defectology Institute, it became part of the Psychology Section of the Academy of Pedagogical Sciences. Vygotsky's colleagues and students, A. R. Luria and A. N. Leont'ev, were elected to the Academy within a few years of its foundation.[26]

The foregoing oversimplifies, however, the origins of the current Soviet Institute of Defectology. In fact, of course, its first members came from a variety of universities, research

---

[22] Kendall Bailes, "Soviet Science in the Stalin Period. The Case of V. I. Vernadskii," *Slavic Review*, vol. 45, no. 1 (Spring 1986), pp. 20–37.

[23] Robert Lewis, "Science, Non-Science, and the Cultural Revolution," *Slavic Review* vol 45, no. 2 (Spring 1986), pp. 286–292 deals primarily with the relevance of a scientific paradigm in a profession as a factor in social cohesion.

[24] Joravsky, "Construction," p. 127.

[25] McCagg, "Defectology," p. 29; "Sokolianskii," Zankov," *PedEn*, 1964–1968, and biographical data offered in the Soviet "Afterword" to this volume. Daniushevskii became a director of a "general prophylactorium" in the mid-1930's. See, V. Bronner, *La lutte contre la prostitution en URSS* (Moscow, 1936), p. 42.

[26] "D'iachkov," "Kornilov," Leontiev," Luria," and "Zankov," in *PedEn*, 1964–1968, and in *Defektologicheskii slovar'*; also, *Defektologicheskii slovar'*, p. 219; Szekely, "Establishment," pp. 60, 95.

and pedagogical institutes, and they thus constituted an institutional and intellectual heritage more mixed, less Vygotskian. Nonetheless, despite current debates over Vygotsky's ideas, and the stigma and controversy surrounding those who suffered from the purges, the current pre-eminent Soviet institutions for the study of abnormal child psychology bear both the institutional and the intellectual legacy of the turbulent 1920's.[27]

2

The text *Fundamentals of Defectology* is a selection of materials written at the peak of Vygotsky's productivity and influence. It consists primarily of theoretical and critical discussions and de-emphasizes the experimental aspects of studying "handicapped" children. This theoretical emphasis reflects, in part, the dynamic and innovative changes taking place in the 1920's at all levels of intellectual, scientific, political, and artistic life. As described in the preceding section, the years between 1924-1931 saw a reassessment of traditional views in many areas of scientific scholarship and the creation of new "revolutionary" theories in the spirit of Marxist dialectics. *Fundamentals of Defectology* constitutes Vygotsky's attempt to create a new understanding of the psychology of abnormal children and a new methodology for the development of residual strengths and other intact healthy functions. Vygotsky's work with abnormal children was conducted concurrently with research on fundamental issues relating to the language development and psychology of all children and served as a basis for solving these larger problems. In short, these papers and the ideas reflected in them represent a major contribution to the formation of modern Soviet developmental psychology.

As one might expect from his personal role in creating a Marxist school of psychology, Vygotsky addressed here what he saw as the "crisis" in that field. On the one hand, Vygotsky takes a critical stand toward the existing Western schools of psychology (behaviorism, individual psychology, etc.); on the other hand, these theories served as a point of departure for his own inquiry.

The form Vygotsky used to elaborate his fundamental theories is that of critical dialogue with his contemporaries and predecessors.[28] This approach reflects a popular concept of *dialogism*, an approach based on communication shared by leading linguists, literary critics, and Marxist theoreticians of the 1920's, such as V. N. Voloshin, M. Bakhtin, L. P. Iakubinskii.[29] Accordingly, all verbal thought, (i.e., internalized speech) represents a dia-

---

[27] For greater detail on the use of Vygotsky's ideas in current Soviet special schooling and abnormal child psychology, see Jane E. Knox and Alex Kozulin, "The Vygotskian Tradition in the Psychological Study of the Handicapped, Particularly Deaf Children," in William O. McCagg and Lewis Siegelbaum, eds. *The Disabled in the Soviet Union: Past and Present. Theory and Practice.* (Pittsburgh: University of Pittsburgh Press 1989), pp. 63–84; Jane E. Knox, "The Changing Face of Soviet Defectology: A Study in Rehabilitating the Handicapped" in *Studies in Soviet Thought,* vol 37, pp. 217–236, 1989. See also *Soviet Education: An Annotated Bibliography and Readers' Guide to Works in English,* compiled by Yushin Yoo (Westport, Conn., and London: Greenwood Press, 1980), pp. 326–330, which lists articles as well as books.

[28] For more discussion of Vygotsky's "critical dialogue" see Alex Kozulin, Introduction to *Thought and Language* (Cambridge, Mass.: MIT Press, 1986), p. xxx.

[29] V. N. Voloshin, *Marxism and the Philosophy of Language* (Leningrad, 1929); M. Holquist, ed., *M. Bakhtin: The Dialogic Imagination* (Austin: University of Texas, 1981); and L. P. Iakubinskii, "Dialogic Speech," (Moscow, 1925). For a more complete description of dialogism, see James Wertsch, "Voices of the Mind," Inaugural Lecture, Oct. 27, 1987, Department of Development and Socialism, Faculty of Social Sciences,

logic interaction with the exterior social-cultural world which, in varying degrees, is perceived, reflected upon, and responded to. Vygotsky developed his position by first stating the psychological theses of others, then criticizing them, and finally adapting or revising these views to incorporate his new perspective of cultural historicism. This dialogic method corresponds to the very core of Vygotsky's theory about psychological development and is most succinctly expressed by the statement from "The Genesis of Higher Mental Functions" so often quoted by Vygotsky scholars:

> Any function in the child's cultural development appears twice, or on two planes. First it appears on the social plane, and then on the psychological plane. First it appears between people as an interpsychological category, and then within the child as an intrapsychological category.[30]

The internalization of *interpsychological* cultural or historical processes is very much a major issue in Vygotsky's extremely interesting essay in Part III of this book "The Collective as a Factor in the Development of the Abnormal Child." Here, nearly the same statement is made, but now in reference to children with psychological and physical handicaps. Moreover, what is true for *any* child appears also to be true for this *adult* scientific researcher. Vygotsky's tendency toward dialogism both in his own thinking as well as in his theories about child psychology approaches the Hegelian-Marxist formula: thesis, antithesis, and synthesis.[31] Wertsch characterizes Vygotsky's style of inquiry in the following way: "It is important to note that Vygotsky's account of mind was a mixture of existing psychological theories and Marxist ideas and that in the end there may be less [Marxism] than he would have liked. However, this outcome in no way diminishes the importance of Vygotsky.[32]

This cosmopolitan cross-referencing to Western scholarship lost its attraction to most Soviet academics in the late 1920's. Indeed, this mode of writing served as the basis of accusations of "cosmopolitanism" leveled against numerous academics in the 1930's and 1940's, Vygotsky and his colleagues among them. In fact, although Vygotsky was credited in the 1920's with constructing a new psychology based on Marxism, his referents are eclectic and not always Marxist; indeed, he referred to foreign authors without offering ideological evaluations of them.

Many scholars have pointed out that Vygotsky's approach to psychology was above all methodological. Vygotsky's methodology implied Vygotsky the "theoretician of psychology and metapsychology." As Wertsch put it, in the opinion of some of today's leading Soviet spokesmen in this field (V. V. Davydov and L. A. Radzikovskii), many of Vygotsky's "most insightful and lasting contributions come from his work in [this] category."[33] From

University of Utrecht, The Netherlands, pp. 10–11; Caryl Emerson, "The Outer Word and Inner Speech: Bakhtin, Vygotsky, and the Internalization of Language" in *Critical Inquiry*, vol. 10, no. 2 (Dec. 1983) and T. V. Akhutina "Teoriia rechevogo obshcheniie v trudakh M. M. Bakhtin i L. S. Vygotskogo," in *Vestnik Moskovskogo Universiteta*, Series 14, *Psikhologiia*, 1984, no. 3.

[30] Vygotsky, quoted by J. V. Wertsch in "The Genesis of Higher Mental Functions," in *Concept of Activity in Soviet Psychology* (Armonk, New York: M. E. Sharp, 1981), p. 163. The same statement is made here in this book again in the essay "The Collective as a Factor in the Development of the Abnormal Child."

[31] Semyon Dobkin, "Ages and Days," in K. Levitan, ed., *One Is Not Born a Personality* (Moscow: Progress, 1983), p. 26. Dobkin, Vygotsky's school friend, wrote, "Vygotsky was at that time very enthusiastic about the Hegelian view of history."

[32] James V. Wertsch, "L. S. Vygotsky's 'New' Theory of Mind," *American Scholar* (Winter) 1988, p. 83.

Vygotsky's earliest writing, he "claimed that his intention was to bring forth a 'methodo-logical,' that is metapsychological, analysis of the crisis in psychology. His position was that of a theoretician who assesses the crisis from the 'outside' rather than that of a professional psychologist tied to some partisan point of view."[34] In trying to establish a "scientific psychology," Vygotsky believed it necessary to interrelate psychological schol-arship and concrete *practical* reality. In this respect, he bridged two camps in psychology: the cognitive-oriented German school (mainly Adler's individual psychology, "idealism," etc.) and the behaviorist-oriented American school. While not accepting the idea that psychological development comes solely from within the individual's psyche, he also rejected the notion that the human mind is a *tabula rasa*, a clean slate which simply absorbs patterns of behavior from a particular environment or from the behavior of nurturing adults.[35] Vygotsky's theories, as we shall see below, combine the two approaches.

The same can be said of his approach to the psychological study of handicapped children. Here, Vygotsky elaborated new methods which he believed were theoretically valid and appropriate for the transformation of traditional approaches, for the creation of new and necessary means of working with these children. It was the particular or individual concrete facts of a handicapped child's life (the environment, the social conditions surrounding such a child, his potential, and his limitations) that Vygotsky examines as the basis for a "new" scientific understanding of abnormal development.

Many of the fundamental laws explored in Vygotsky's better known works receive attention and unique application here. For Vygotsky, the fundamental laws governing the cognitive and psychological development of an abnormal child are identical to those laws which guide the development of normal children. These laws, summed up as follows, must serve as the basis for the pedagogical and training program of any child:

1. *There are two lines of development: the natural, "physiological," or biological and the historical, cultural.* The cultural-historical line is internalized through the use of psychological tools, the most important of which is language. This line of develop-ment is superimposed on and radically transforms natural behavior. The latter is not replaced by the former but is "sublated" (Ger. *aufgehoben*, or Rus. *sniatyi*), embed-ded in the structure of the personality as a whole.

2. interfunctional dynamics is at all times present in human development; therefore neither intelligence nor personality can be reduced to a quantitative listing of various individual functions. Vygotsky's use of "dialectical materialism" (Marxist method-ology) as a scientific basis for the new psychology, led him to emphasize the "whole" person, the "whole" mind. This approach was not unique to Vygotsky. Bakhtin, for example, wrote, that although "dialectical materialism...does indeed require that the whole personality be studied, and provides the methodological foundations for such a study... the idea of the 'whole person' is certainly not exclusive to Marxism... we know that the idea of the whole personality was the culmination point of romantic

[33] James V. Wertsch, ed., *Culture, Communication and Cognition: Vygotskian Perspective* (Cambridge: Cam-bridge University Press, 1985), p. 9.

[34] Kozulin, p. xviii.

[35] For further discussion, see the assessment of Western empirical psychology given by Vygotsky's student and colleague A. P. Luria in "Problems of Language and Consciousness," in J.V. Wertsch, ed. *Language and Cognition*, (New York: Wiley, 1981), p. 23.

idealism... of Schelling's philosophy of unity...of the teaching of Fichte... in monadology of Leibnitz."[36]

3. The interaction and association among the various higher and lower functions play a paramount role, particularly when one biological function fails. In the case of such a failure, the second line of development (with the help of numerous sociocultural tools) can enlist other biological functions to circumvent the weak point and build a psychological (mental) superstructure over it. In this way, a by-pass is created so that a "defect" does not result in an overall "defective" or abnormal personality. For example, although a blind child is physically limited, his or her remaining functions work together to overcome this impediment, processing stimuli from the outer world with the help of special means such as Braille.

At any given moment, a child is full of unrealized potentials, and these offer a wealth of creative resources on which a handicapped child, or any child, may and must build. Such is the enriched, holistic psychology of human nature which Vygotsky bequeathed to us and which demands further attention by Western psychologists, linguists, and pedagogues.

In this volume on the development of abnormal children, Vygotsky focused on the last of these three fundamental laws. He devoted particular attention to the cultural or historical line of development, which he believes had previously been underestimated or neglected. We read in Vygotsky's introduction to this volume, "The history of cultural development in a handicapped child constitutes the most profound and critical problem in modern defectology. It opens up a completely new line of development in scientific research" ("The Fundamental Problems of Defectology"). Later on, Vygotsky stated, that the "development of the remaining intact, healthy senses is not enough —this disregards the sphere of social pedagogy. What is needed is the development of certain more complicated integral active and effective forms of child experience" ("The Psychology and Pedagogy of Children's Handicaps").

In Vygotsky's view, development of the higher mental functions stems not from natural inner sources alone, but from interaction with the object-oriented and socio-cultural world of the child. "In place of biological compensation, the idea of social compensation must be advanced. The mind, particularly reason, is the function of social life" ("The Psychology and Pedagogy of Children's Handicaps"). Hence, a child who comes from a socially or culturally deprived environment may not be exposed to those more complicated forms of experience of which Vygotsky spoke. As a result, this child may be diagnosed as mentally retarded or as "a difficult-to-handle child."

As Vygotsky pointed out in several sections, particularly in the chapter devoted to "difficult children," the natural abilities of these children may be intact but their higher mental functions have not been developed. This circumstance may lead society to judge them as retarded, "primitive," and even, in extreme cases, "morally insane." Their environment has not subjected them to intense acculturation, communication, or the appropriate nurturing; as a result, their development has been stymied.

As an example of such psychologically "primitive" behavior, Vygotsky refers repeatedly to the case of a young Tatar girl, "who spoke Tatar and Russian simultaneously" ("The Fundamental Problems of Defectology," "The Difficult Child") She was first diagnosed as

---

[36] M. Bakhtin, "A Critique of Apologias of Freudianism," *Soviet Psychology*, vol.23 (Spring 1985): 15.

"psychologically abnormal." Then A. E. Petrova (1888–?), a Soviet psychologist and educator who was conducting studies on child primitivism, demonstrated that this case of primitivism was in fact conditioned by a lack of command of either language (Russian or Tatar). Thus, the little girl's mental activity diminished in those situations which demanded verbalization ("The Difficult Child").

Similarly, Vygotsky would argue, a child with a biological defect, such as a hearing loss, may not have been adequately stimulated by alternative channels or paths of development. Therefore, society may believe such a child is retarded or inferior when, by means of creative alternative paths of development, he can reach a *superior* level of development through overcompensation. The critical reader might well ask: Can such a child in fact become "superior" in his development? Vygotsky argues both here and elsewhere that he can:

> The world pours, through a large funnel as it were, in thousands of stimuli, drives and callings; inside from the narrow end as response reactions of the organism in greatly reduced quantity. The actualized behavior is but an infinitesimal part of the possible behavior. Man is full of unrealized opportunities at any given moment. These unrealized opportunities for behavior, the disparity between the broad and narrow ends of the funnel is an indisputable reality, just as real as the reactions which have prevailed.[37]

Precisely because a defect impedes development, a handicapped child can be stimulated, with the help of a talented, skilled teacher, to develop strengths which might otherwise be unrealized; in this way the child overcomes or rises above his or her primary deficiency. As an example of overcompensation or superior development, Vygotsky cited the case of Helen Keller, who responded to the demands of her tutor by using all of her capabilities to reach the upper level of her development. Vygotsky wrote that in Helen Keller's case, "her defect did not only not become a brake but was transformed into a drive which insured her development" ("Defect and Compensation").

Vygotsky therefore criticized those developmental psychologists and educators who are chiefly concerned with counting and tabulating a child's weaknesses, particularly when they used those measurements (of weaknesses) as the sole basis for placing the child in an educational program (Binet and Simon, for example). In fact, he argued, one must test for a child's strengths and talents, and these are different for every child. Vygotsky strongly rejected an arithmetic approach in favor of a more qualitative evaluation which assesses the whole personality. As L. Brown and Roberta A. Ferrara pointed out, for Vygotsky "static IQ measures do not provide direct information concerning the optimal level of performance of which the testee is capable, an optimal level that is of considerable interest for those who wish to design instruction."[38] Such intelligence tests measure only the level of learning already acquired, rather than providing a gauge of the potential for improvement; "they are good predictive but poor diagnostic tools."[39] Therefore, the main aim of diagnostic testing

---

[37] Quoted by Levitan in *One Is Not Born a Personality*, p. 130.

[38] L. Brown and Roberta A. Ferrara, "Diagnosing Zones of Proximal Development," in *Culture, Communication and Cognition: Vygotskian Perspectives*, p. 4.

[39] Ibid.

should be an assessment of what a child can do under the proper educational circumstances, rather than a tabulation of what he or she has learned to that point.

Vygotsky subsequently outlined three basic issues which the scientific researcher must examine in his study of the cultural development of a handicapped child: *"the degree of primitivism in the childhood mind; the nature of his adoption of cultural and psychological tools; and the means by which he makes use of his psychological functions"* ("The Fundamental Problems of Defectology"). The last (third) issue is closely connected with the concept of mediation which plays a very important role in Vygotsky's theory and which is often referred to by Western scholars as the theory of "Second Level Signals." In order that the child mediate, make sense of, and interact in a meaningful way with the environment, he or she must have access to and acquire a multitude of psychological tools or artificial, historically developed, cultural signs available to shape and organize the world.

Because most psychological tools are designed for the normal person with all senses and mental functions theoretically intact, special psychological tools must be developed for the abnormal child which focus on his or her other healthy functions and residual strengths. For example, the handicapped child may acquire Braille, finger spelling, lip-reading, or handsigns, all of which represent symbolic systems, which have been culturally and historically developed in response to his or her unique way of processing the world.

This diversity of tools constitutes an important issue not only for Soviet defectology, but for all of developmental psychology. Every and any child must be able to obtain "ready made" those tools historically formed by many generations. As the English psychologist Paul Arnold writes, it was important for Vygotsky, that "each child does not have to 'reinvent' his or her own mind every generation. A child can therefore, potentially obtain the most modern ideas and ways of thinking."[40] For Vygotsky, linguistic tools, whatever form they may take, determine development: "Language...together with activity leads the child's development."[41]

As noted already, Vygotsky was stating that humans master themselves from the "outside" through symbolic, cultural systems. What needs to be stressed here is his position that it is not the tools or signs, in and of themselves, which are important for thought development but the *meaning* encoded in them. Theoretically, then, the *type* of symbolic system should not matter, as long as meaning is retained. All systems (Braille for the blind and for the deaf. dactylology or finger spelling, mimicry or a natural gesticulated sign language) are tools embedded in action and give rise to meaning as such. They allow a child to internalize language and develop those higher mental functions for which language serves as the basis. In actuality, qualitatively different mediational means may result in qualitatively different forms of higher mental functioning.

Although there is no way to rank these as some kind of genetic hierarchy, one could make the argument that different mediational means are associated with different intrapsychological outcomes. Each handicapped child is different because the psychological tools on which he or she relies are different. Handicapped children are then, as Vygotsky points out, psychologically different from normal children and from each other. Such a formulation might suggest a new approach to the controversies over sign language in Western deaf education.

---

[40] Paul Arnold, "Vygotsky and the Education of the Deaf Child," *British Association of Teachers of the Deaf*, vol. 9, no. 2 (1985): 30.

[41] Quoted by Arnold, p. 29.

Vygotsky, however, repeated, here as elsewhere, that although the means of development may be different, the fundamental laws of development are *the same for both normal and abnormal children and that the educational content must be the same for both*. In the case of a handicapped child, the entire difference lies in the fact that one organ of perception takes over for another, while "the quantitative content of the reaction remains the same" ("Principles of Education for Physically Handicapped Children"). In this light, Vygotsky reintroduces a Pavlovian notion stating that, "From the point of view of physiology any educational process may be seen as a process of developing conditional reflexes in response to certain signs and signals" (*ibid.*). The human being may then be trained to respond to any external stimuli which impinge upon the eye, ear, skin, and so forth. In Vygotsky's words, "the uniqueness of this type (of education for the handicapped children) simply boils down to the substitution of one path of training for another" ("The Fundamental Problems of Defectology").

Whereas traditional pedagogical methods had previously proceeded from a purely quantitative conception of childhood development, Vygotsky proposed a new fundamental thesis, the defense of which is the sole justification for the existence of defectology as a science:

> A child whose development is impeded by a defect is not simply a child less developed than his peers; rather he has developed differently...a child in each stage of his development, in each of his phases, represents a qualitative uniqueness, i.e., a specific organic and psychological structure; in precisely the same way a handicapped child represents a qualitatively different, unique type of development. (p. 3)

Given this unique character of handicapped development, Vygotsky called for a careful reexamination of the relationship between the defect and the compensation. Modern defectology, Vygotsky felt, must proceed from the position that, although a physical or mental defect may cause limitations and obstacles to a child's development, it also stimulates compensatory processes, as in the case of Helen Keller cited above. As a result, the personality of such a child becomes "something different than simply the sum of underdeveloped functions and properties" ("The Fundamental Problems of Defectology").

In his introductory section Vygotsky reexamines the views of various German developmental psychologists (such as W. Stern, 1871–1938, T. Lipps, 1851–1914, A. Adler, 1870–1937 and others) on the relationship between deficiency and compensation. For example, W. Stern's theory of the dual role played by a defect was particularly meaningful to Vygotsky. In Stern's words, "Thanks to organic unity, in the case of failure of one faculty...another faculty undertakes the accomplishment of the task"(Stern, 1921, p.1). Then Vygotsky referred to a law of mental life, established by T. Lipps, the law of psychological damming up (*Stauung*): Energy is concentrated at the point of weakness where a delay in development has occurred; however, this energy may then overcome the weakness by proceeding by roundabout ways and, in place of delayed development, "new processes are generated due to the blockage" (Lipps, 1907, p. 8). These roundabout ways and new processes become the focal point of Vygotsky's theorization.

It was A. Adler, however, with whom Vygotsky seemed to find the most in common. Particularly important was Adler's view of the creative character of development complicated by a defect. The positive uniqueness of a handicapped child lies in the new formations created by the lapse —a uniqueness not found in a normal child. Summarizing this position, Vygotsky wrote:

> Whatever the anticipated outcome, *always and in all circumstances*, development, complicated by a defect, represents a creative (physical and psychological) process: the creation and re-creation of a child's personality based upon the restructuring of all the adaptive functions and upon the formation of new processes—overarching, substituting, equalizing—generated by the handicap, and creating new, roundabout paths for development. ("The Fundamental Problems of Defectology")

Vygotsky qualified Adler's position with his own view that compensatory processes do *not* always occur *successfully*. Two results are always possible: failure or success. This outcome depends on many factors but above all on the reserves or strengths of the child and the successful interaction with the social milieu. For Vygotsky, the effect of the defect on the child's personality and psychological make-up is "secondary," because the children do not directly sense their "handicappedness." The primary cause for this "special kind of development" is the limited restrictions put on the child by society. It is the sociopsychological realization of the child's strengths which "decides the fate of personality, not the defect itself."

Precisely at this point in Vygotsky's theory, his concept zone of proximal development (a concept he finally developed in the 1930's) was foreshadowed. Although he did not use this, now well-known, term anywhere in *Fundamentals of Defectology*, its origins are implicit here. As in his other works, Vygotsky insisted that the contemporary educator must look not only at the plateau or delay in development but at overall potential. To educate a child as blind or deaf means only nurturing that child's blindness and deafness, and not the development of the whole personality. Modern defectology must liberate the special school from "any trace of philanthropic, invalid-oriented, or religious atmosphere based on an interaction of pity and charity" ("The Psychology and Pedagogy of Children's Handicaps"). Instead, it must develop special pedagogical techniques aimed at the positive uniqueness of these children, in order to create in them the necessary sociocultural superstructure which will shore up development at its point of physical or mental weakness.

Thus, it is the second line of development which best serves the development of the higher mental processes and it requires a special pedagogue to interact with this child and develop in him or her these roundabout paths of development. According to Vygotsky, "only a scientific knowledge can create a real pedagogue in this area" ("The Psychology and Pedagogy of Children's Handicaps").

In essays of Part II, Vygotsky focused on pedagogical specialists and the techniques needed when dealing with various handicapping conditions: blindness, deafness, moral insanity, primitiveness, developmental retardation, and unmanageability. In all cases, Vygotsky insisted that the same standards of education be used for the handicapped child as for the normal child. He advocated, however, new schools which would incorporate the skills of the particular symbolic system needed to compensate the deficiency, be it Braille or some alternate means of mediation and communication. The blind or deaf child will need the use of a "different symbolic system maintaining the identical content for any instructional or educational process" ("The Psychology and Pedagogy of Children's Handicaps").

In this book, considerable attention is devoted to deafness for the reason that Vygotsky saw deafness as one of the most critical defects (more critical, for instance, than blindness)

("The Psychology and Pedagogy of Children's Handicaps"). In his view, humans are first and foremost social beings and need to communicate with one another. The primary focus of deaf education must, therefore, be on the return of speech through the use of a systematic input of all the senses, kinesthetic, auditory, visual and tactile. Vygotsky feared that sign language alone would close the deaf child off in a very narrow and confining world with only those who know the "primitive language" ("The Psychology and Pedagogy of Children's Handicaps"). Later on, he gave up the notion that sign language was a primitive language, as we shall see below.

While affirming the necessity of speech instruction, Vygotsky at the same time recognized the cruelty and inhumanity of many of the existing methods for teaching speech. He considered the classical German phonetic methods for teaching speech to be antithetical to a deaf person's nature because they were based on a dead, meaningless repetition of sounds. Such an approach emphasized classes in drilling rules or articulation, not on functional ("live"), meaningful speech. Speech was not introduced as a psychological tool to be used in interaction with others or to shape one's personal experience. Speech for all children, however, depends on communication, not on the repetition of phonetic exercises.

Vygotsky supported the method proposed by the Danish educator G. Forschhammer, who developed the manual-oral system. This system involved "a coupling of the mouth and hand movement as the deaf-mute child pronounced words" because this integrated multisensory approach to speech incorporated several channels of sensory input, tapping the wealth of the overall nervous system (see footnote 10, "The Psychology and Pedagogy of Children's Handicaps").

Vygotsky was also very much interested in a report, at the June 1925 All-German Congress on the Education of the Deaf (Heidelberg), about the new method proposed originally by the Austrian specialist in deaf education, K. Malisch. Malisch proposed that children be taught words and whole phrases which they can use for communication in their surrounding milieu. The limitation of this method was that Malisch did not reject the phonetic method. According to Vygotsky, a teacher at the Moscow Institute for the Deaf-Mute, I. Golosov, was the first Russian to make an original attempt to teach oral speech by means of entire words, approaching the natural flow of real language. This was the direction in which speech instruction must proceed.

The solution, according to Vygotsky, is to revolutionize methods of teaching speech and return to a deaf child the "live language" which the child needs and can use in daily life. Only when speech merges with the deaf child's overall behavior and experience will it become an essential and permanent ingredient in this psychological development.

While promoting the special programs, Vygotsky recognized the dilemma which the special school has posed in the past and will continue to pose: It breaks off contact with the normal world and isolates the handicapped children, putting them in a narrow, closed-off world "where everything is calculated and adapted to the defect, where everything reminds the child of the defect" ("The Psychology and Pedagogy of Children's Handicaps"). Vygotsky wrote that, in the past and particularly in Germany, special schools had created an artificial milieu which was psychologically unhealthy for children because such children, already cut off to a certain degree by their handicaps, needs "closer contact," and "deeper roots" in life. Such is the task of the modern special school which must merge more closely with public education.

In order to overcome this dilemma, Vygotsky proposed that the fundamental principle of the education for handicapped children be "active participation" in collective life based on meaningful labor and vocational training; this was a principle being broadly advocated in the Soviet educational system at the time: "Work oriented education offers the best path for entrance into life...a children's collective is an essential factor because it builds up cooperative, responsible behavior and self- organization" ("Principles for the Social Education of Deaf-Mute Children"). Vygotsky devoted an entire section in Part III ("The Collective as a Factor in the Development of the Abnormal Child") to this problem. A child develops in co-relationships with his peers. Even a young child at play develops techniques for submitting to the rules of the collective. In this section Vygotsky stressed the point that, in place of the philanthropic atmosphere of an "artificial, hospital-like, invalid oriented almshouse" (i.e., the old school), the new school must foster living skills, social behavior, initiative, leadership and collective responsibility.

To support his view Vygotsky cited the position of Nadezhda K. Krupskaia (1869–1939), V. I. Lenin's wife and an advocate of similar educational reforms in the entire Soviet system namely, the position that a new polytechnic, labor-oriented education was necessary for *all* children. Like others in the 1920's, Vygotsky sought to create the "new Soviet man."[42] In the new society the very concept of "defectiveness" must become archaic and all citizens must have a productive role based on their strengths. This was a matter not only of education of the handicapped child but of reeducation of the public ("The Psychology and Pedagogy of Children's Handicaps").

With respect to mental retardation, Vygotsky divided children into two groups: physically (biologically) retarded and socially retarded. Most cases in his view belong to the second category; such children are retarded and underdeveloped because of difficult or adverse conditions in their lives and at school. In these cases, if circumstances are changed, many a formerly "uneducable" or "unmanageable" retarded child may start to thrive, exhibiting an unrecognizable "giftedness" (for more description of this type, see "The Difficult Child," Part II). As previously stated, these materials also specifically addressed pressing social problems in the Soviet Union of the late 1920's and early 1930's.

Vygotsky, however, did devote an entire essay to the first category, the physically or mentally retarded child (see "Compensatory Processes in the Development of the Retarded Child"). As Vygotsky stated in earlier essays, ("The Fundamental Problems of Defectology," and "The Blind Child,") the compensatory process cannot be understood merely as a process of substitution of one physiological function for another. In agreeing with W. Wundt (1832–1920) Vygotsky stated that this process must be understood "as a complex restructuring of all psychological activity" ("The Blind Child"). In "Compensatory Processes in the Development of the Retarded Child," Hegel's concept of "*aufheben*" (*sniatie*) is explored with respect to mental retardation. During the compensatory process, a primary loss, most apparent in the early stages of development, is gradually "diminished in importance, by newly occurring formations acquired through more mature sociocultural development." In other words, this primary defect is not omitted but buried or embedded in the overall superstructure created by the second line of development. The child's personality develops in response to the difficulties encountered and he or she must find roundabout ways to overcome the deficiency.

The major goal in the study of mental retardation is, according to Vygotsky, the creation of a positive differential approach, that is, the identification and classification of children

---

[42] This term was later coined by Raymond Bauer in *The New Man in Soviet Psychology* (Cambridge, Mass.: Harvard University Press, 1952).

according to their various individual talents and potentials. The wealth of each retarded child's reserves and strengths must be the determining factor in establishing a program for him or her. If the educational program aims only at the primary debility, then little progress will be made because this deficiency submits only indirectly and with great difficulty to pedagogical influence. However, the reverse may be true of other physiological and psychological functions such as motor development and practical common sense (versus abstract or logical thinking), which can respond to direct influence and compensate the primary weakness.

One of the most curious passages of *Fundamentals of Defectology* is the section entitled "Moral Insanity" (Part II), a manuscript from Vygotsky's personal archive and published here for the first time. This expression for mental illness or insanity was borrowed from English terminology and originally represented the extreme view of this condition as an "organic illness." Vygotsky, however, reexamined mental illness as a type of "moral deficiency" or amoral behavior, caused primarily not by an innate organic defect, but by deficient, amoral, or impoverished "socioeconomic, cultural, and pedagogical conditions in which the child grew up and developed" (*ibid.*). Vygotsky wrote, "The problem of 'moral insanity' is posed and solved in our country as a problem of environment," The solution offered here is to normalize the environment and to provide different conditions, more auspicious for child development. Here again, education must play a large role.

Vygotsky, along with other Soviet psychologists and pedagogues of this period, were responding to the large number of juvenile delinquents, child prostitutes, and other homeless, neglected children who roamed the cities and the country side during the turbulent years of the civil war and the great famines. For Vygotsky and his colleagues, it often turned out that they were dealing with "children who possessed a heightened sensitivity" and that this "observed sensitivity had been nothing more than a defensive reaction, a self-defense, a biological defensive armor against the diseased influences of the environment" ("Moral Insanity").

Vygotsky did not deny that there may be psychopathological factors behind mental illness, but he played down their significance. Like other physical and mental handicaps, this weakness or deficiency may be overcome by developing the "whole personality," by building up the second line of cultural development so that the organic impairment diminishes in overall significance. For him psychopathy was a major factor in mental or "moral" illness ("madness") only for a negligible number of children; for whatever reason, Vygotsky did not concern himself with it in these essays.

3

Vygotsky's contribution to the field of normal and abnormal child psychology is not limited to the 1920's and 1930's. Many Soviet psychologists today credit his theories (and he is more highly regarded in some institutes than in others but at least lip service is paid to his contribution). Moreover, among Western scholars, there has been a recent upsurge in interest in Vygotsky's ideas. According to James Wertsch, Vygotsky has something to say to American psychologists, whose stumbling block is too often "reductionism;" that is, they "have too often isolated and studied phenomena in such a way that they cannot communicate with one another, let alone members of other disciplines."[43] Vygotsky's approach to child development restores an "integral holistic picture of human nature," bringing together various fields such as linguistics, sociology, psychology, physiology, and pedagogy.

More significantly, Vygotsky offers us a method which allows the experimenter or educator to see the underlying, developing psychological processes. This method speaks to another stumbling block in American education. American educators traditionally reach *down* to help the child at the level he or she has already achieved, whereas the Vygotskian school of educators and psychologists set up an experimental situation which, as Arnold points out, "artificially provokes or creates a process of psychological development."[43] Such a method intentionally provokes or disrupts behavior so that the child will be drawn forward to new levels of behavior.

For example, in the section entitled "Defectology and the Studies of the Development and Education of Abnormal Children," Vygotsky promoted the "indirect structure of development" whereby a child's spontaneous, "direct attempt to complete a task is cut off," and "the child is faced with demands for adjustment which exceed his capabilities, when he cannot cope with the task by means of a natural reaction" ("Defectology and Studies of Development and Education of Abnormal Children"). Whenever the circumstances demand more than a primitive reaction, complex cultural operations begin in a child. Such is the case when a child can no longer give a direct answer to a problem in arithmetic; he or she then turns to using the fingers, which, once "only part of the background," now take on the significance of simple operational tools.

In contrast to some of J. Piaget's experiments with young children, Vygotsky wrote, "we organize a child's performance in such a way that he encounters difficulties" ("Defectology and Studies of Development and Education of Abnormal Children"). The result is that the child begins to plan operations by reasoning them out with the help of "egocentric speech." Obstacles stimulate compensatory development. Vygotsky here gave the example of a child with a drawing task which demands a red pencil. The pencil has been removed, and the child began to talk about what he must do to improvise in this situation. Vygotsky argued that if all were made easy for the child, he would then have no need to reason out loud. Such experiments are important for very young children, language-delayed children and mentally retarded children because, for all three groups, speech turns out to be a tool for reasoning. In all three cases, speech, like the fingers in an arithmetic task, can become the organizing tool to help the child plan his or her way around the difficulty.

Vygotsky forces today's psychologists to reexamine the question of how to "break out of biology's hold on psychology" and to move into the area of higher mental operations based on cultural tools ("Defectology and Studies of Development and Education of Abnormal Children"). In the Soviet Union, Vygotsky's experiments were continually elaborated at the Institute of Defectology, Academy of Pedagogical Sciences, in order: (1) to study the inner mechanisms of language development; and (2) to intervene positively in abnormal (delayed) language development.[44]

In the West, Vygotsky's method is most widely known as the realization of a child's "zone of proximal development," or ZPD or Zoped. Contemporary Western scholars interpret this approach to mean that adults or competent peers will bring a children forward from what they can already do themselves at a primitive level of operations to reach a higher,

---

[43] Arnold, p. 31.

[44] Taped interview with V. I. Golod (Laboratory for Diagnosis of Learning Disabilities, Institute of Defectology, Academy of Pedagogical Sciences, Moscow), June 19, 1988.

more complex level. That is, they will help the child acquire the tools needed for this higher level of psychological activity so to enable independent action in the performance of the aimed-for activity.

In "Vygotsky and the Education of the Deaf Child," Paul Arnold addressed the importance of "special education," which requires teachers to understand both the child's potential and limitations and to teach to the higher level of ability. Incorporating Vygotsky's notion of zone of proximal development, Arnold wrote: "Deaf children develop more slowly than hearing children, and this suggests that their zones of potential development are wider. They need more teaching to develop. We may have too low expectations of hearing impaired children because their present level is more apparent than their potential and their potential must be forced on by teaching."[45]

The concept of the ZPD has become the focus of considerable research activity in the United States and England, as well as in the Soviet Union. Much attention is being turned to the role played by adults, teachers, and "more competent peers" in fostering child development.[46] This concept is now even being incorporated into studies of children working at the computer. Here the computer: (1) sets up a zone of proximal development for the child as it automatically responds to his or her individual strengths and weaknesses; and (2) supplies a wonderful medium for child-computer-teacher or peer-computer-peer interaction.[47] Many of the resulting publications stress the Vygotskian notion that real learning and development occur in a communicative setting, that is, among people, and not as isolated, individual acts. While such ideas speak to educators and developmental psychologists concerned with *any* children, Vygotsky's views of the role of the collective in the development of speech and language have particular relevance for today's specialists and educators of handicapped children.

In principle, Vygotsky's book addresses today's problem of mainstreaming: his view that handicapped children must not be socially cut-off or outcast from the mainstream of society, but must be accepted as full productive members of society, speaks to the question of mainstreaming. As J. Tudge correctly pointed out, Vygotsky held that "if blind, deaf or mentally retarded children were educated separately from 'normal' children, they would proceed in a totally different, and not beneficial manner."[48] Vygotsky argued that "This would lead to the creation of a special breed of people" ("The Blind Child"). Here, in fact, Vygotsky's hypothesis is absolutely contradictory to the present situation in special educa-

---

[45] Arnold, p. 31.

[46] Michael Cole, Vera John Steiner, Sylvia Scribner, and Ellen Souberman, *L. S. Vygotsky: Mind in Society* (Cambridge, Mass.: Harvard University Press, 1978); B. S. Rogoff and W. Gardner, "Adult Guidance of Cognitive Development," in B. Rogoff, J. Lave eds. *Everyday Cognition, Its Development in Social Context* (Cambridge: Cambridge University Press, 1984); B. Rogoff and J. V. Wertsch eds., *Children's Learning in the "Zone of Proximal Development"* (San Fransisco, 1984); B. S. Rogoff, and S. Radziszewsta, "The Influence of Collaboration with Parents versus Peers in Learning to Plan," paper presented at the meetings of the Society for the Research in Child Development, Toronto, April 1985, reprinted in Resources in Education (ERIC), Sept. 1985; Jonathan Tudge, "Vygotsky, the Zone of Proximal Development and Peer Collaboration: Implications for Classroom Practice,: in L. Moll, ed. *Vygotsky and Education* (Cambridge: Cambridge University Press, forthcoming).

[47] V. Trush, and V. Golod, "Computers in Defectology" (Komp'iutery v defektologii), *Information and Education* (Informatika i obrazovanie), vol.2, 1986, p. 28; Sylvia Weir, "The Computer in Schools: Machine as Humanizer" in *Symposium: Computers in Classroom Instruction. Harvard Educational Review*, vol. 59, no. 1 (1989): 65.

[48] Tudge, p. 5.

tion in the Soviet Union. For the most part, handicapped children learn in special schools, and few studies have been made of this effect on their overall psychological development as a "special breed of people."

Although Vygotsky often stated that it is necessary to erase borderlines between the special school for the blind (or other handicapped children) and public school, he never insisted that the handicapped attend the same school with normal children. Instead, he insisted on the concept of differentiation, on "special, alternative means of communication and development," and on a specially manipulated environment which would supply those psychological tools most suitable for the particular child's abilities. If handicapped children need "more teaching," "specially auxiliary means," "special teachers," and "a differentiated education" at every stage of their development, how can this happen in a mainstreamed classroom with normal children whose development proceeds in other ways? This is a question which Soviet educators and diagnosticians raise today when asked about main-streaming. This question may be complemented with another: "If the child needs a special educational environment, isn't it better (economically and psychologically) to provide it in a special school?"[49]

The Vygotskian tradition has its own controversies with respect to the education of the deaf. One of them concerns the place of sign language in the rehabilitation of the deaf child. Members of the Laboratory of Adult Education at the Institute of Defectology, who have been conducting psycholinguistic studies on the structure of sign language and its role in education of the deaf, are quick to point out and applaud the gradual change in Vygotsky's attitude toward sign language. In this collection of articles, as will be explained below, Vygotsky shifted from an initial rejection of sign languages to an eventual acceptance of it as a useful auxiliary tool for development.

Vygotsky felt that deafness was a far greater handicap then blindness because it deprived children of what they need most to interact with most other children: spoken language. Originally, Vygotsky rejected what was called *mimicry* as a viable means of instruction and communication, apparently because he first perceived gesticulated language as a natural, lower, elementary function rather than as a higher, cultural or mental function. Throughout this volume of essays, a notable evolution of Vygotsky's views on mimicry (sign language of the deaf) occurs. In an early essay, he stated that mimicry, "the natural sign language of the deaf," could not serve as an instrument of abstract, logical thought ("Defect and Compensation"). In his later speeches and essays, however, Vygotsky reformulated his position on mimicry, concluding that the full development of a deaf child dictates an expansion of the system of verbal means used in the educational process: "One must reevaluate the traditional theoretical and practical attitude toward the various individual forms of speech used by the deaf-mute, and above all toward mimicry" ("Compensatory Processes in the Development of the Retarded Child").

Recognition of "sign language" as a valid auxiliary communicative system allowed Vygotsky at later stages of his activity to determine the uniqueness of a deaf child's education as a development under conditions of "polyglossia."[50] He considered the acquisition of

---

[49] Numerous interviews with members of the Laboratory for the Education of Deaf Adults, Institute of Defectology, during joint research activity sponsored by NAS (National Academy of Sciences) and IREX (International Research Exchanges) 1986.

[50] This was a term used not only by Vygotsky himself, but by G. L. Zaitseva (Laboratory for the Education of Deaf Adults, Institute of Defectology, Academy of Pedagogical Sciences, USSR) whose research on the use of

different forms of language by all possible means to be the most productive path of development and growth and he wrote, "the maximal use of all forms of speech available to a deaf child is the necessary condition for radical improvement in his or her education" ("Compensatory Processes in the Development of a Retarded Child"). It is this later view of sign language as an *auxiliary means of language acquisition* which corresponds with today's educational approach to deaf children and as such serves as the grounds for ongoing research in the Institute of Defectology.[51]

Some Soviet Vygotsky followers, like Alexander Meshcheriakov (1923–1974), placed greater emphasis on physical, material tools in the real three-dimensional world. These tools, for Meshcheriakov, were especially important for the development of blind-deaf children, for whom tactile input becomes a major source of information and means of interaction with the surrounding world. By placing a tool in the hands of a blind-deaf child, the educator turns the child's impetuous actions into a meaningful manipulation of his or her environment, into socially organized, goal-oriented activity. The connection between manual and cognitive activity (so important for a blind-deaf child) is reinforced and expanded with the help of these tools: what is in the hands becomes what is in the mind. This principle of psychological tools became the underpinning of education at the famous deaf-blind school in Zagorsk, north of Moscow, where the children were (and still are today) immersed in a world of object-oriented activity such as farming, animal husbandry, sculpturing, clay modeling, and building.

In his book about the school, *Awakening to Life* (1974), Meshcheriakov emphasized the Vygotskian notion that object oriented activity develops the higher mental functions in deaf-blind children:

> Such forms of activity as modeling and building exercises, which by their very nature are designed to promote a child's sensorimotor development, can and must be organized in such a way that they promote the child's discovery and knowledge of objects and help him to form generalized images which reflect the phenomena of real life correctly and in depth.[52]

All in all, although Vygotsky remains a controversial figure in many psychological and pedagogical circles in the Soviet Union today, he is given enormous credit. This credit is nowhere as clearly voiced as in the "Afterword" to this volume. Here the well-known members of the Institute of Defectology (E. S. Bein, T. A. Vlasova, R. E. Levina, N. G. Morozova, and Zh. I Shif) wrote that Vygotsky "made a most important contribution to the creation of a scientific basis for Soviet defectology. His experimental and theoretical research in the field of abnormal children remains fundamental to productive work on defectological problems. Vygotsky's work helped to restructure practices in the field of special education" ("Afterword from Soviet Editorial Collegium").

---

sign language for instruction of young deaf adults is based on Vygotsky's later understanding of the importance of this form of communication. From personal correspondence to J. Knox, February 28, 1985.

[51] Ibid.

[52] A. Meshcheriakov, *Awakening to Life* (Moscow: Progress Publishers, 1979), p. 189, Russian edition first published in 1974 with the title *Vozvrashchenie k zhizni i razvitie psikhi slepoglukhonemykh detei v protsesse formirovnaiia poverdeniia.*

In the overall picture of psychological development, Vygotsky's contribution to the study of children is by no means limited to abnormal children. Many American scholars today share Vygotsky's view that a careful scientific study of abnormal children allows us to observe, in exaggerated, slow-motion form, processes which are well-known as pertaining to all children (these processes are more difficult to observe in normal children because they occur at a more accelerated pace).[53] For this reason, Vygotsky's work on abnormal children should have a broad base of appeal to American readers.

---

[53] Sylvia Weir. *Cultivating Minds: A LOGO Case Book* (New York: Harper Row, 1987), p. 5.

PART I

GENERAL PROBLEMS OF DEFECTOLOGY

INTRODUCTION:

THE FUNDAMENTAL PROBLEMS

OF DEFECTOLOGY[1]

1

Only recently, the entire field of theoretical knowledge and practical scientific work, which we conveniently call by the name of "defectology," was viewed as a minor part of pedagogy, not unlike how medicine views minor surgery. All the problems in this field have been posed and resolved as quantitative problems. Entirely accurately, M. Kruenegel[2] states that the prevailing psychological methods for studying an abnormal child (A. Binet's[3] metric scale or G.I. Rossolimo's[4] profile) are based on a purely quantitative conception of childhood development as impeded by a defect (M. Kruenegel, 1926). These methods determine the degree to which the intellect is lowered, without characterizing either the defect itself or the inner structure of the personality created by it. According to O. Lipmann,[5] these methods may be called measurement, but not an examination of ability, *Intelligenzmessungen* but not *Intelligenzpruefungen* (O. Lipmann, H. Bogen, 1923), since they establish the degree, but neither the kind nor the character of ability (O. Lipmann, 1924).

Other pedological methods for studying the handicapped child are also correct and relevant—not only psychological methods, but also those encompassing other sides of a child's development (anatomical and physiological). And here, scale and measure have become the basic categories of research, as if all problems of defectology were but problems of proportion, and as though all the diverse phenomena studied in defectology could be encompassed by a single scheme: "more versus less." In defectology, counting and measuring came before experimentation, observation, analysis, generalization, description, and qualitative diagnosis.

Practical defectology likewise chose the simplest course, that of numbers and measures, and attempted to realize itself as a minor pedagogical field. If, in theory, the problem was reduced to a quantitatively limited, proportionally retarded development, then, in practice, the idea of simplified and decelerated instruction naturally was advanced. In Germany, the very same Kruenegel, and in our country A. S. Griboedov,[6] rightly defend the notion: "A reexamination of the curriculum and methods of instruction used in our auxiliary schools is essential" (A. S. Griboedov, 1926, p. 28), since "a reduction of educational material and a prolongation of its study time" (*ibid*.),—that is, purely quantitative indicators—have constituted until this time the only distinctive features of the special school.

A purely arithmetical conception of a handicapped condition is characteristic of an obsolete, old-school defectology. Reaction against this quantitative approach to all theoretical and practical problems is the most important characteristic of modern defectology. The struggle between these two attitudes toward defectology—between two antithetical ideas, two principles—is the burning issue in that positive crisis which this area of scientific knowledge is presently undergoing.

Viewing a handicapped condition as a purely quantitative developmental limitation undoubtedly has the same conceptual basis as the peculiar theory of preformed childhood operations, according to which post-natal childhood development is reduced exclusively to quantitative growth and to the expansion of organic and psychological functions. Defectology is currently undertaking a theoretical task which is analogous to the one once performed by pedology and child psychology, when both defended the position that a child is not simply a small adult. Defectology is now contending for a fundamental thesis, the defense of which is its sole justification for existence as a science. The thesis holds that a child whose development is impeded by a defect is not simply a child less developed than his peers but is a child who has developed differently.

If we subtract visual perception and all that relates to it from our psychology, the result of this subtraction will not be the psychology of a blind child. In the same way, the deaf child is not a normal child minus his hearing and speech. Pedology has long ago mastered the idea that if viewed from a qualitative perspective, the process of child development is, in the words of W. Stern,[7] "a chain of metamorphoses" (1922). Defectology is currently developing a similar idea. A child in each stage of his development, in each of his phases, represents a qualitative uniqueness, i.e., a specific organic and psychological structure; in precisely the same way, a handicapped child represents a qualitatively different, unique type of development. Just as oxygen and hydrogen produce not a mixture of gases, but water, so too, says Guertler,[8] the personality of a retarded child is something qualitatively different than simply the sum of underdeveloped functions and properties.

The specific organic and psychological structure, the type of development and personality, and not qualitative proportions, distinguish a retarded child from a normal one. Did not child psychology long ago grasp the deep and true similarities between the many developmental processes in a child and the transformation of a caterpillar first into a chrysalis and from a chrysalis into a butterfly? Now, through Guertler, defectology has voiced the view that a child's retardation is a particular variety or special type of development, and not a quantitative variant of the normal type. These, he states, are different organic forms, not unlike a tadpole and a frog (R. Guertler, 1927).

There is, actually, complete correspondence between the particular characteristic of each age-level in the development of a child and the particular characteristics of different types of development. Just as the transition from crawling to walking, and from babble to speech, is a metamorphosis (i.e., a qualitative transformation from one form into another) in the same way, the speech of a deaf-mute child and the thought processes of an imbecile are functions qualitatively different from the speech and thought processes of normal children.

Only with this idea of qualitative uniqueness (rather than the overworked quantitative variations of separate elements) in the phenomena and processes under examination, does defectology acquire, for the first time, a firm methodological basis. But no theory is possible if it proceeds from exclusively negative premises, just as no educational practice can be based on purely negative definitions and fundamentals. This notion is methodologically central to modern defectology, and one's attitude toward this notion determines the exact position of a particular, concrete problem. Defectology acquires, with this idea, a whole system of positive tasks, both theoretical and practical. The field of defectology becomes viable as a science because it has assumed a particular method and defined its object for research and understanding. As B. Schmidt [no ref.] put it, only "pedological anarchy" can follow from a purely quantitative conception of juvenile handicaps, and programs of treatment and remediation can be based only on uncoordinated compendia of empirical data and techniques and not upon systematic scientific knowledge.

It would be a great mistake, however, to think that with the discovery of this idea the methodological* formation of a new defectology is complete. On the contrary, it has only just begun. As soon as the possibility of a particular perspective on scientific knowledge is determined, then the tendency arises to search for its philosophical foundations. Such a search is extremely characteristic of modern defectology and is an indication of its scientific maturity. As soon as the uniqueness of the phenomena being studied by defectologists has been asserted, the philosophical questions immediately arise: that is, questions of principles and methods of knowledge and examination of this uniqueness. R. Guertler has attempted to establish a basis for defectology in an idealistic philosophy (R. Guertler, 1927). H. Noell based his discussion of the particular problem of vocational training for students in auxiliary schools on the modern "philosophy of value," developed by W. Stern, A. Messer (1906, 1908), Meinung,** H. Rickert,[9] and others. If such attempts are still relatively rare, then the tendency toward some philosophical formulation is easily detected in almost any significant new scientific work on defectology.

Apart from this tendency toward philosophical formulations, absolutely concrete separate problems face defectology. Their solution constitutes the major goal of research projects in defectology.

Defectology has its own particular analytical objective and must master it. The processes of childhood development being studied by defectology represent an enormous diversity of forms, almost a limitless number of types. Science must master this particularity and explain it, as well as establish the cycles and transformations of development, its imbalances and shifting centers, and discover the laws of diversity. Further, there is the practical problem of how to master the laws of development.

This article attempts to outline critically the fundamental processes of defectology in their intrinsic relationship and unity from the point of view of those philosophical ideas and social premises, assumed to be the basis of our educational theory and practice.

---

* The term methodological means here a general method of inquiry and is closer to scientific epistemology. [Tr.]

** Possibly, a reference to Alexius Meinong (1853-1920), who was concerned with a theory of knowledge at Vienna and Graz. [Ed.]

2

The dual role of a physical disability, first in the developmental process and then in the formation of the child's personality, is a fundamental fact with which we must deal when development is complicated by a defect. On the one hand, the defect means a minus, a limitation, a weakness, a delay in development; on the other, it stimulates a heightened, intensified advancement, precisely because it creates difficulties. The position of modern defectology is the following: Any defect creates stimuli for compensatory process. Therefore, defectologists cannot limit their dynamic study of a handicapped child to determining the degree and severity of the deficiency. Without fail, they must take into account the compensatory processes in a child's development and behavior, which substitute for, supersede, and overarch the defect. Just as the patient—and not the disease—is important for modern medicine, so the child burdened with the defect—not the defect in and of itself—becomes the focus of concern for defectology. Tuberculosis*, for example, is diagnosed not only by the stage and severity of the illness, but also by the physical reaction to the disease, by the degree to which the process is or is not compensated for. Thus, the child's physical and psychological reaction to the handicap is the central and basic problem—indeed, the sole reality—with which defectology deals.

A long time ago, W. Stern pointed out the dual role played by a defect. Thus, the blind child compensates with an increased ability to distinguish through touch—not only by actually increasing the stimulability of his nerves, but by exercising his ability to observe, estimate, and ponder differences. So, too, in the area of psychological functions, the decreased value of one faculty may be fully or partially compensated for by the stronger development of another. For example, the cultivation of comprehension may replace keenness of observation and recollection, compensating for a poor memory. Impressionability, the tendency to imitate, and so forth compensate for weakness of motivation and inadequate initiative. The functions of personality are not so exclusive that, given the abnormally weak development of one characteristic, the task performed by it necessarily and in all circumstances suffers. Thanks to the organic unity of personality, another faculty undertakes to accomplish the task (W. Stern, 1921).

In this way we can apply the law of compensation equally to normal and abnormal development. T. Lipps[10] saw in this a fundamental law of mental life: if a mental event is interrupted or impeded, then an "overflow" (that is, an increase of psychological energy) occurs at the point of interruption or obstruction. The obstruction plays the role of a dam. This law Lipps named the law of psychological damming up or stowage (*Stauung*). Energy is concentrated at that point where the process met with delay, and it may overcome the delay or proceed by roundabout ways. Thus, in place of delayed developmental processes, new processes are generated due to the blockage (T. Lipps, 1907).

A. Adler[11] and his school posit as the basis of their psychological system the study of abnormal organs and functions, the inadequacy of which constantly stimulates an intensified (higher) development. According to Adler, awareness of a physically handicapped condition is, for the individual, a constant stimulation of mental development. If any organ, because of a morphological or functional deficiency, does not fully cope with its task, then the central human nervous and mental apparatus compensates for the organ's deficient operation by creating a psychological superstructure which shores up the entire deficient organism at its

---

* We recall this is the disease Vygotsky died of. [Ed]

weakened, threatened point. Conflict arises from contact with the exterior milieu; conflict is caused by the incompatibility of the deficient organ or function and the task before it. This conflict, in turn, leads to an increased possibility of illness and fatality. The same conflict may also create greater potentialities and stimuli for compensation and even for over-compensation. Thus, defect becomes the starting point and the principal motivating force in the psychological development of personality. It establishes the target point, toward which the development of all psychological forces strive. It gives direction to the process of growth and to the formation of personality. A handicap creates a higher developmental tendency; it enhances such mental phenomena as foresight and presentiment, as well as their operational elements (memory, attention, intuition, sensibility, interest)—in a word, all supporting psychological features (A. Adler, 1928).

We may not and *ought* not agree with Adler when he ascribes to the compensatory process a universal significance for all mental development. But, there is no contemporary defectologist, it seems, who would not ascribe paramount importance to the effect of personality on a defect or to the adaptive developmental processes, i.e., to that extremely complex picture of a defect's positive effects, including the roundabout course of development with its complicated zigzags. This is a picture which we observe in every child with a defect. Most important is the fact that along with a physical handicap come strengths and attempts both to overcome and to equalize the handicap. These tendencies toward higher development were not formerly recognized by defectology. Meanwhile, precisely these tendencies give uniqueness to the development of the handicapped child; they foster creative, unendingly diverse, sometimes profoundly eccentric forms of development, which we do not observe in the typical development of the normal child. It is not necessary to be an Adlerite and to share the principles of his school in order to recognize the correctness of this position.

"He will want to see everything," Adler says about a child, "if he is nearsighted; to hear everything, if he is hearing impaired; he will want to say everything, if he has an obvious speech defect or a stutter. ... The desire to fly will be most apparent in those children who experience great difficulty even in jumping. The contrast between the physical disability and the desires, fantasies, dreams, i.e., psychological drives to compensate, are so universal that one may base upon this *a fundamental law: Via subjective feelings of inadequacy, a physical handicap dialectically transforms itself into psychological drives toward compensation and overcompensation"* (1927, p. 57). Formerly, it was believed that the entire life and development of a blind child would be framed by blindness. The new law states that development will go against this course. If blindness exists, then mental development will be directed away from blindness, against blindness. Goal-oriented reflexes, according to I. P. Pavlov,[12] need a certain tension to achieve full, proper, fruitful development. The existence of obstacles is a principal condition for goal achievement (1951, p. 302). Modern psychotechnics is inclined to consider control [or self-direction] to be a function so central to the educational process and to the formation of personality as a special case of the phenomena of overcompensation (J. N. Spielrein, 1924).

The study of compensation reveals the creative character of development directed along this course. It is not in vain that such psychologists as Stern and Adler partly based the origins of giftedness on this understanding. Stern formulates the idea as follows: "What does not destroy me, makes me stronger; thanks to adaptation, strength arises from weakness, ability from deficiencies" (W. Stern, 1923, p. 145).

It would be a mistake to assume that the process of compensation always, without fail, ends in success, that it always leads from the defect to the formation of a new capability. As with every process of overcoming and struggle, compensation may also have two extreme outcomes—victory and failure— and between these two are all possible transitional points. The outcome depends on many things, but basically, it depends on the relationship between (1) the severity of the defect and (2) the wealth of compensatory reserves. But whatever the anticipated outcome, *always and in all circumstances*, development, complicated by a defect, represents a creative (physical and psychological) process. It represents the creation and re-creation of a child's personality based on the restructuring of all the adaptive functions and on the formation of new processes—overarching, substituting, equalizing—generated by the handicap, and creating new, roundabout paths for development. Defectology is faced with a world of new, infinitely diverse forms and courses of development. The course created by a defect—that of compensation—is the major course of development for a child with a physical handicap or functional disability.

The positive uniqueness of the handicapped child is created not by the failure of one or another function observed in a normal child but by the new formations caused by this lapse. This uniquely individual reaction to a defect represents a continually evolving adaptive process. If a blind or deaf child achieves the same level of development as a normal child, then the child with a defect achieves this *in another way, by another course, by other means*. And, for the pedagogue, it is particularly important to know the *uniqueness* of the course, along which he must lead the child. The key to originality transforms the minus of the handicap into the plus of compensation.

3

There are limits to uniqueness in the development of handicapped children. The entire adaptive system is restructured on new bases when the defect destroys the equilibrium that exists among the adaptive functions; then, the whole system tends towards a new equilibrium. Compensation, the individual's reaction to a defect, initiates new, roundabout developmental processes—it replaces, rebuilds a new structure, and stabilizes psychological functions. Much of what is inherent in normal development disappears or is curtailed because of a defect. A new, special kind of development results. "Parallel to the awakening of my consciousness," A.M. Shcherbina[13] tells us about himself, "was the gradual, organic elaboration of my psychic uniqueness. Under such conditions, I could not *spontaneously* sense my physical shortcomings" (1916, p. 10). But the social milieu in which the developmental process occurs place limits on organic uniqueness and on the creation of a "second nature." K. Buerklen[14] formulated this idea beautifully as it applies to the psychological development of the blind. In essence, this idea may be extended to all of defectology. "They develop special features," he said about the blind, "which we cannot observe among the seeing. We must suppose that if the blind associated only with the blind and had no dealings with the seeing then a special kind of people would come into being" (K. Buerklen, 1924, p. 3).

Buerklen's views can be elaborated as follows: Blindness, as a physical handicap, gives impetus to compensatory processes. These, in turn, lead to the formation of unique features in a blind person's psychology and to the reformulation of all his various functions, when directed toward a basic, vital task. Each individual function of a blind person's neuropsychological apparatus has unique features, often very marked in comparison with those of a seeing person. In the event that a blind person were to live only among blind people, these biological processes, which formulate and accumulate special features and abnormal deviations, would, when left alone, inevitably lead to the creation of a new stock of people. Notwithstanding, under pressure from social demands, which are identical for the seeing and the blind, the development of these special features takes a form in which the structure of a blind person's personality *as a whole* will tend to achieve a specific, normal social type.

The compensatory processes which create unique personality features in a blind child do not develop freely. Rather, they are devoted to a specific end. Two basic factors shape this social conditioning of a handicapped child's development.

First, the effect of the defect itself invariably turns out to be secondary, rather than direct. As we have already said, the child is not directly aware of his handicap. Instead, he is aware of the difficulties deriving from the defect. The immediate consequence of the defect is to diminish the child's social standing; the defect manifests itself as a social aberration. All contact with people, all situations which define a person's place in the social sphere, his role and fate as a participant in life, all the social functions of daily life are reordered. As emphasized in Adler's school of thought, the organic, inherent (congenital) causes of this reordering operate neither independently nor directly, but indirectly, via their negative effect on a child's social position. All hereditary and organic factors must also be interpreted psychologically, so that their true role in a child's development can be taken into consideration. According to Adler, a physical disability which leads to adaptation creates a special psychological position for a child. It is through that special position, and only through it, that a defect affects a child's development. Adler calls the psychological complex, which develops as a result of the child's diminished social position due to his handicap, an "inferiority complex" (*Minderwertigkeitsgefuehl*).* This introduces a third, intermediate factor into the dyadic process of "handicap compensation" so that it becomes "handicap inferiority complex compensation." The handicap, then, evokes its compensation not directly but indirectly, through the feelings of inferiority which it generates. It is easy to illustrate, through examples, that an inferiority complex is a psychological evaluation of one's own social position. The question of renaming the auxiliary school has been raised in Germany. The name *Hilfsschule* seems degrading to both parents and children. It inflicts a stamp, as it were, of inferiority on the pupil. The child does not want to attend a "school for fools." The demeaning social status associated with a "school for fools" partially affects even the teachers. They are, somehow, on a lower level than teachers in a school for normal children. Ponsens and O. Fisher [no ref] propose names such as therapeutic, training, or special school (*Sonderschule*), school for the retarded, and other new names.

For a child to end up at a school for fools means to be placed in a difficult social position. Thus, for Adler and his followers, the first and basic point of the educational process is a struggle against an inferiority complex. It cannot be allowed to develop and possess the child or to lead him into unhealthy forms of compensation. The basic idea of individual-psychological therapeutic education, says A. Friedmann,[15] is encouragement (*Ermutigung*). Let us assume that a physical handicap does not lead, for social reasons, to the generation of an inferiority complex—that is, to a low psychological estimation of one's own social standing.

---

* The Russian text has *Mindenwentigkeitsgefuehl*. Perhaps, however, the Adlerian term *Minderwertigkeitskomplex* was intended for insertion since that describes the *complex* of feelings interrelated with their attendant social status.

Thus, notwithstanding the presence of a physical handicap, there will be no psychological conflict. As a result, some people with, let us say, a superstitious, mystical attitude toward the blind have a specific conception of the blind, a belief in their spiritual insight. For them, a blind person becomes a soothsayer, a judge, a wise man. Because of his handicap, he holds a high social position. Of course, in such circumstances, there can be no question of an inferiority complex, feelings of disability and so on. In the final analysis, what decides the fate of a personality is not the defect itself, but its social consequences, its socio-psychological realization. The adaptive processes, also, are not aimed directly at making up the deficiency, which is for the most part impossible, but at overcoming the difficulties which the defect creates. The development and education of a blind child have to do not so much with blindness itself as with the social consequences of blindness.

A. Adler views the psychological development of the personality as an attempt to attain social status with respect to the "inherent logic of human society," and with respect to the demands of daily life in society. Development unwinds like a chain of predetermined, even if unconscious, actions. And, in the end, it is the need for social adaptation which, by objective necessity, determines these actions. Adler (1928), with good reason, therefore, calls his psychology positional psychology, in contrast to dispositional psychology. The first derives psychological development from the personality's social position, the second from its physical disposition. If social demands were not placed upon a handicapped child's development, if these processes were at the mercy of biological laws only, if a handicapped child did not find it necessary to transform himself into an established social entity, a social personality type, then his development would lead to the creation of a new breed of human being. However, because the goals of development are set *a priori* (by the necessity of adapting to a sociocultural milieu based on the normal human type), even the adaptation process does not occur freely, but follows a definite social channel.

Thus, a handicapped child's developmental processes are socially conditioned in two ways. The social effect of the defect (the inferiority complex) is one side of the social conditioning. The other side is the social pressure on the child to adapt to those circumstances created and compounded for the normal human type. Within the context of final goals and forms, profound differences exist between the handicapped and the normal child in the ways and means of their development. Here, precisely, is a very schematic view of social conditioning in that process. Hence, there is a dual perspective of past and future in analyzing development that has been complicated by a defect. Inasmuch as both the beginning and the end of that development are socially conditioned, all its facets must be understood, not only with respect to the past, but also with respect to the future. Along with an understanding of compensation as the basic form of such development comes an understanding of a drive toward the future. The entire process, as a whole, is revealed as a unified one, as a result of objective necessity striving forward toward a final goal, which was established in advance by the social demands of daily life. The concept of unity and wholeness in a child's developing personality is connected to this. Personality develops as a united whole, with its own particular laws; it does not develop as the sum or as a bundle of individual functions, each developing on the basis of its particular tendency.

This law applies equally to somatics and physics, to medicine and pedagogy. In medicine, the belief is becoming more prevalent that the sole determinant of health or illness is the effective or ineffective functioning of the organs and that isolated abnormalities can be evaluated by the degree to which the other functions of the organism do or do not compensate for the abnormality.

W. Stern advances the following idea: Individual functions deviate from normality, while the whole personality or organism might still belong to an entirely normal type. A *child* with a defect is not necessarily a *defective child*. The degree of his disability or normality depends on the outcome of his social adaptation that is, on the final formation of his personality as a whole. In and of themselves, blindness, deafness, and other individual handicaps do not make their bearer handicapped. Substitution and compensation do not just occur randomly, sometimes assuming gigantic proportions and creating talents from defects. Rather, *as a rule*, they necessarily arise in the form of drives and idiosyncrasies at the point where the defect prevails. Stern's position supports the fundamental possibility of social compensation where direct compensation is impossible, i.e., it is the possibility in principle that the handicapped child can, in principle, wholly approximate a normal type that might enable winning full social self-esteem.

Compensation for moral defectiveness (moral insanity),[*] when it is viewed as a *special kind of organic handicap or illness*, can serve as the best illustration of secondary social complications and their role in a handicapped child's development. All consistent, intelligent psychologists proceed from a similar point of view. In part, in *our* country the reexamination of this question and the clarification of the falsity and scientific groundless of the very concept of moral disability as applied by P. P. Blonskii[16], A. B. Zalkind,[17] and others has had great theoretical and practical significance. West European psychologists are coming to the same conclusions. What was taken to be a physical handicap or illness is, in fact, a complex of symptoms with a specific psychological orientation found in children who have been completely derailed socially; it is a socio and psychogenic phenomenon, not a biogenic disorder.

Anytime the erroneous recognition of certain *values* comes into question, as J. Lindworsky[18] stated at the First Congress on Special Education [lit."Therapeutic Pedagogy"] in Germany,[19] the reason for this should be sought, not in an inherent anomaly of the will, nor in specific distortions of individual functions. Rather, it should be sought in the view that neither the surrounding milieu nor the individual himself fostered recognition of those values. Probably, the notion of calling emotional illness *moral insanity* would never have been conceived, if first the attempt had been made to summarize all the shortcomings of values and motives met among normal people. Then, it might have been discovered that every individual has his own insanity. M. Wertheimer[20] also comes to this conclusion. Wertheimer, citing F. Kramer [no ref] and V. K. Garis [no ref], the founder of Gestalt psychology in the United States,[**] asserts that if one examines the personality as a whole, in its interaction with the environment, the congenital psychopathic tendencies in a child disappear. He emphasizes the fact that a well-known type of childhood psychopathy exhibits the following symptoms: rude carelessness, egoism, and preoccupation with the fulfillment of elemental desires. Such children are unintelligent and weakly motivated, and their physical sensitivity (for example, pain sensitivity) is considerably lowered. In this, one sees a particular type which, from birth, is destined for asocial behavior, ethically handicapped

---

[*] The text frequently writes "moral insanity" in Roman letters either as a gloss for the Russian term or even as a section heading.

[**] It is quite likely that Vygotsky intended to credit Wertheimer with founding American Gestalt psychology although the translation adheres closely to the Russian text. Of course the triumvirate which founded Gestalt psychology in Germany (Koehler, Koffka, and Wertheimer) all emigrated to the United States at about the same time. (see Boring, E. *A History of Experimental Psychology*. Second Edit. Appleton-Century-Crofts, New York, 1950. [Ed]

with respect to inclinations, and so on. While the earlier term *moral insanity* implied an incurable condition, transferring these children into a different environment often shows that we are dealing with a particularly keen sensitivity and that the deadening this sensitivity is a means of self defense, of closing oneself off, and of surrounding oneself with a biological defensive armor against environmental conditions. In a new environment, such children display completely different characteristics. Such results occur when children's characteristics and activities are examined not in isolation, but in their relation to the whole, in the dynamics of their development (*Si duo paciunt idem non est idem*). In theoretical terms, this example is indicative. It explains the emergence of alleged psychopathy, of an alleged defect (moral insanity), which was created in the imagination of the investigators. And this is why they were unable to explain the profound social unsuitability of the children's development in similar cases. The significance of sociopsychogenic factors in the child's development is so great that it could give the illusion of being a handicap, the semblance of illness, and an alleged psychopathy.

4

In the last two decades, scientific defectology has become aware of a new form of disability in children. In essence, it is a motor deficiency (M. O. Gurevich).[21] Although oligophrenia (mental retardation) has always been characterized primarily by some mental defect or another, a new form of abnormal behavior—the underdevelopment of a child's motor apparatus—has recently become the object of intense study as well as of practical and therapeutic pedagogical activity. This form of disability in children has various names. Dupré[22] calls it *debilité motrice* (i.e., motor disability, by analogy with mental disability). While T. Heller[23] calls it motor delay, and in extreme forms, motor idiocy. K. Jacob[24] and A[?]. Homburger (1926a, 1926b) label it motor infantilism and M. O. Gurevich calls it motor deficiency. The essence of this phenomenon, as implied by the various nomenclatures, is a more-or-less pronounced developmental motor deficiency, which is in many ways analogous to the mental disability of oligophrenia.

This motor disability, to a large extent, permits compensation, motor functions, and the equalization of the handicap (Homburger, M. Nadoleczny,[25] Heller). Motor retardation often and easily responds, within certain limits, of course, to pedagogical and therapeutic influence. Therefore, taken alone, motor delay requires, as in the scheme, the dual characterization: defect— compensation. The dynamics of this form of disability, like those of any other form, can be ascertained only if one takes into account the organ's positive response stimuli, namely, those which compensate for the defect.

The introduction of this new form of deficiency into the inventory of science has had a fundamental and profound significance. This is not only because our definition of disability in children has broadened and been enriched by the knowledge of vitally important forms of abnormal development in a child's motor system and the compensatory processes created by it but also, and principally, because it has demonstrated the relationship between this new form and other forms which were already known to us. For defectology (both theoretical and practical), the fact that this form of disability is not necessarily connected to mental retardation is of fundamental importance. "A deficiency of this type," says Gurevich, "not infrequently coexists with mental deficiency. Sometimes, however, it may exist independently of it, just as mental deficiency may be present when the motor apparatus is well developed" (cf. *Questions of Pedology and Child Psychoneurology*, 1925, p. 316). Therefore, motor operations are of exceptional importance in the study of handicapped children. Motor delay may combine, in varying degrees, with all forms of mental retardation, thus creating a unique picture of childhood development and behavior. This form of disability can often be observed in deaf children. Naudacher [in a report in Gurevich, *op.cit.*] offers statistics for the frequency with which this form of deficiency combines with other forms: 75 percent of all idiots, 44 percent of the imbeciles, 24 percent of the debiles, and 2 percent of normal children that were studied were found to have a motor disability.

It is not the statistical computation that is fundamentally important and decisive. Rather, it is the unquestionable proposition that motor delay *can* occur independently of any mental disability. It may be absent in the case of mental retardation and may exist in the absence of any mental deficiency. In instances of combined motor and mental deficiencies, each form has its own dynamics. Compensation for operations in one sphere may occur at a different tempo, in a different direction, than in another sphere. As a result, an extremely interesting interrelationship between these spheres is created in the process of a handicapped child's development. Given the relative independence of the motor system from the higher mental functions and the fact that it is easily guided, it is often found to play a central role in compensating for mental defects and in equalizing behavior. Therefore, when studying a child we must not demand only a twofold characterization (motor and mental) but must also establish the relation between the two spheres of development. Very frequently this relation may be the result of compensation.

In many cases, according to K. Birnbaum's view [no ref.], even real defects, embedded organically in cognitive behavior, can be compensated for, within certain limits, by training and through development of substitutional function; "motor training" which is now so highly valued. Experimental investigations and practical experience in school corroborate this. M. Kruenegel, who has most recently conducted experimental research on the motor skills of mentally retarded children (M. Kruenegel, 1927), applied N.I. Ozeretskii's[26] metric scale of motor skills. Ozeretskii set himself the task of creating a method for determining motor development graduated by age level. Research has shown that motor skills are more highly developed than mental capabilities from one to three years, for 60 percent of all the children studied. In 25 percent of cases, motor skills coincided with cognitive development and they lagged behind in 15 percent. This means that motor development in a mentally retarded child most frequently outstrips his intellectual development at one to three years and only in one quarter of the cases coincides with it. On the basis of his experiments, Kruenegel comes to the conclusion that about 85 percent of all mentally retarded children in auxiliary schools, with the appropriate education, are capable of work (trade, industrial, technical, agricultural, and so forth). It is easy to imagine the great practical significance that the development of motor skills can have in compensating, to a certain degree, for mental defects in mentally retarded children. M. Kruenegel, along with K. Bartsch, demands the creation of special classes for vocational training and for the development of motor skills for mentally retarded children (*ibid.*).

The problem of motor disability is a wonderful example of that unity in diversity which can be seen in the development of a handicapped child. Personality develops as a single entity, and as such, it reacts to the defect and to the destruction of equilibrium caused by the defect. It works out a new system of adaptation and a new equilibrium in place of the one destroyed. But precisely because personality represents a unit and acts as a single entity, its development involves the advances of a variety of functions which are diverse and relatively independent of each other. These hypotheses—the diversity of relatively developmentally independent functions, and the unity of the entire progress in personality development—not only do not contradict each other, but, as Stern has shown, reciprocally condition each other. The compensatory reaction of the entire personality, stimulated by the defect in another sphere, finds expression in intensified and increased development of some single function as, for example, motor skills.

5

The notion, expressed in the study of motor skills, that the separate functions of the personality are diverse and complex in structure, has recently pervaded all areas of development. When carefully analyzed, not only personality as a whole, but also its separate aspects reveal the same unity in diversity, the same complicated structure, and the same interrelationship of separate functions. One might say, without fear of error, that the development and expansion of scientific ideas about personality at the present time are moving in two, seemingly opposing directions: (1) discovery of its unity and (2) discovery of its complicated and diverse structure. In part, the new psychology moving in this direction has almost destroyed, once and for all, former notions about the unity and homogeneity of the intellect and that function which the Russians, not altogether accurately, call "giftedness" and which the Germans call *Intelligenz.**

Intellect, like personality, undoubtedly represents a single entity but is neither uniform nor simple. Rather, it is a diverse and complicated structural unity. Thus, Lindworsky reduces the intellect to the function of perceiving relationships, a function, which in his eyes, distinguishes humans from animals, and which gives thought unto thought. This function (the so-called intellect) is no more inherent in Goethe than to an idiot and the enormous difference which we observe in the thought processes of various people can be reduced to the life of ideas and memory (J. Lindworsky, 1923). We will return later to this paradoxically expressed, but profound idea of Lindworsky. Now, what is important to us is the conclusion which the author drew from his understanding of the intellect at the Second German Congress on Therapeutic Pedagogy. Any mental defect, Lindworsky affirmed, is based in the final analysis on one or another of the factors used in perceiving relationships. A mentally retarded child can never be presented simply as mentally retarded. It is always necessary to ask what constitutes the intellect's deficits, because there are no possibilities for substitution, and they must be made available to the mentally retarded. In this formulation we already find the notion absolutely clearly expressed that various factors must enter into the composition of such a complicated education; that, corresponding to the complexity of its structure, there is not one but many qualitatively different types of mental disability; and finally, that because the intellect is so complex, its structure permits broad compensation of its separate functions.

This doctrine now meets with general agreement. O. Lipmann systematically traces the steps through which the development of the idea of overall ability has passed. In the beginning, it was identified with any single given function, for example, memory; the next step was the recognition that ability appears in an entire group of psychological functions (attention, synthesis, discrimination and so forth). C. Spearman[27] distinguishes two factors

---

* N. E. Rumiatsev translates this word as *intelligence* [intellegentnost']. Hereafter, we will use the less-than-accurate term *intellect* for this sense. [Transl.]

in any rational activity: one is the factor specific to the given type of activity and the other is the general one, which he considers to be ability. A. Binet finally reduced the determination of ability to the mean of an entire series of heterogeneous functions. Only recently the experiments of R. Yerkes[28] and W. Koehler[29] on monkeys, and those of E. Stern and H. Bogen [no ref.] on normal and retarded children have established that not just one ability but many types of ability exist. Specifically, rational cognition coincides with a rational operation. For one and the same person, a certain type of intellect may be well developed and, simultaneously, another type may be very weak. There are two types of mental retardation—one affects cognition and the other operation; they do not necessarily coincide. ("There is," says Lipmann, "a mental retardation of cognition and a mental retardation of operations.")[*] Similar formulations by Kenman, M. N. Peterson, P. Pinter, G. Thompson, E. Thorndike[30] and others more or less recognize this (O. Lipmann, 1924). E. Lindemann[31] applied the methods of W. Koehler, which were developed for experiments on monkeys, to severely retarded children. Among them, there appeared a group of severely retarded children who turned out to be capable of rational activity. Only their ability to remember new operations was extremely weak (E. Lindeman, 1926). This means that the ability to devise tools, to use them purposefully, to select them, and to discover alternate methods—that is, of rational activity—was found to occur in severely retarded children. Therefore, we must select, as a separate sphere of research, practical intellect; namely, the ability for rational, purposeful activity (*praktische, natuerliche Intelligenz*). By its psychological nature, rational activity is different from motor ability and from theoretical intellect.

Lipmann and Stern's suggested profiles of practical intellect are based on the criteria of practical intellect, laid out by Koehler, namely the ability to use tools purposefully. This ability undoubtedly has played a deciding role in the transition from monkey to man and which appeared as the first precondition of labor and culture.

A special qualitative type of rational behavior, relatively independent of other forms of intellectual activity, practical intellect may be combined in varying degrees with other forms, each time creating a unique picture of the child's development of behavior. It may appear as the fulcrum of compensation, as the means of equalizing other mental defects. Unless this factor is counted, the entire picture of development, diagnosis, and prognosis will certainly be incomplete. Let us leave for a moment these questions of how many major types of intellectual activity can be discerned—two, three or more—of what the qualitative characteristics of each type are, and of which criteria allow one to distinguish one given type from another. Let us limit ourselves to pointing out the profoundly qualitative distinctions between practical and theoretical (problematic) intellect, which have been established by a series of experimental studies. In particular, the brilliant experiments by Bogen on normal and mentally retarded (feebleminded) children without doubt revealed that the aptitude for rational, practical functioning represents a special and independent type of intellect; the differences in this area between normal and disabled children, established by the author, are very interesting (O. Lipmann and H. Bogen, 1923).

Studies on practical intellect have played and will long continue to play a revolutionizing role in the theory and practice of defectology. They raise the question of a qualitative study of mental retardation and its compensation, and of the qualitative determination of intellectual development in general. For example, by comparison with a blind child, a deaf-mute, whether mentally retarded or normal, turns out to be different in terms not of degree, but of

---

[*] *Es gibt ein Schwachsinn des Erkennens und einen Schwachsinn des Handelns.*

type, of intellect. Lipmann speaks about the essential difference in origin and type of intellect and when one type prevails in one individual and another in another (O. Lipmann, 1924). Finally, even the idea of intellectual development has changed. Intellectual development is no longer characterized by merely quantitative growth, by a gradual strengthening and heightening of mental activity; rather, it boils down to the notion of transition from one qualitative type to another, to a chain of metamorphoses. In this sense, Lipmann brings up the profoundly important problem of qualitative characteristics of age, by analogy with the phases of speech development established by Stern (1922): the stages of speech about objects, actions, relationships, and so forth. The problem of complexity and heterogeneity in the intellect demonstrates new possibilities for compensating within the intellect itself. The fact that aptitude for rational performance is present in profoundly retarded children reveals vast and absolutely new perspectives for the education of such a child.

6

The history of cultural development in an abnormal child constitutes the most profound and critical problem in modern defectology. It opens up a completely *new line of development* in scientific research.

A normal child's socialization is usually fused with the processes of his maturation. Both lines of development—natural and cultural—coincide and merge one into the other. Both series of changes converge, mutually penetrating each other to form, in essence, a single series of formative socio-biological influences on the personality. Insofar as physical development takes place in a social setting, it becomes a historically conditioned biological process. The development of speech in a child serves as a good example of the fusion of these two lines of development—the natural and the cultural.

This fusion is not observed in a handicapped child. Here the two lines of development usually diverge more or less sharply. The physical handicap causes this divergence. Human culture evolved in conditions of a certain stability and consistency in the human biological type. Therefore, its material tools and contrivances, its sociopsychological apparatuses and institutions are all intended for a normal psychophysiological constitution. The use of these tools and apparatuses presupposes, as necessary prerequisites, the presence of innate human intellect, organs, and functions. The creation of conformable functions and apparatuses conditions a child's socialization; at a certain stage, if his brain and speech apparatus develop normally, he masters language; at another, higher stage of intellectual development, the child masters the decimal system of counting and arithmetic operations. The gradual and sequential nature of the socialization process is conditioned by organic development.

A defect creates a deviation from the stable biological human type and provokes the separation of individual functions, deficiencies or damage to the organs. It thereby generates a more or less substantial reorganization of the entire development on new bases and according to a new type: in doing all this, it naturally disturbs the normal course of the child's acculturation. After all, culture has adapted to the normal typical human being and accommodates his constitution. Atypical development (conditioned by a defect) cannot be spontaneously and directly conditioned by culture, as in the case of a normal child.

From the point of view of the child's physical development and formation, deafness, as a physical handicap, appears not to be a particularly severe disability. For the most part, deafness remains more or less isolated and its direct influence on development as a whole is comparatively small. It does not usually create any particularly severe damage or delays in overall development. But the muteness which results from this defect, the absence of human speech, creates one of the most severe complications of all cultural development. The entire cultural development of a deaf child will proceed along a different channel from the normal one. Not only is the quantitative significance of the defect different for both lines of development, but, most importantly, the qualitative character of development in both lines will be significantly different. A defect creates certain difficulties for physical development and completely *different ones* for cultural development. Therefore, the two lines of development will diverge substantially from one another. The degree and character of the divergence will be determined and measured in each case by the different qualitative and quantitative effects of the defect on each of the two lines.

Frequently, unique, specially created cultural forms are necessary for cultural development in the handicapped child. Science is aware of a great number of artificial cultural systems of theoretical interest. Parallel to the visual alphabet used by all humanity is a specially created tactile alphabet for the blind—Braille. Dactylology, (i.e., the finger alphabet) and the gesticulated, mimed speech of the deaf-mute have been created alongside the phonetic alphabet of the rest of mankind. By comparison with the use of the usual cultural means, the process of acquiring and using these auxiliary cultural systems is distinguished by profoundly distinctive features. To read with the hand, as blind children do, and to read with the eye are different psychological processes, even if they fulfill one and the same cultural function in the child's behavior and have similar physiological mechanisms at their base.

To formulate the problem of cultural development in a handicapped child as a particular line of development, governed by special laws, with its own particular difficulties and means of overcoming them, represents a serious goal for modern defectology. The notion of primitivism in a child is basic here. At the moment, it seems as though singling out a special type of psychological development among children, namely, *the development pattern of the primitive child*, meets with no objections from any direction, although there is still some controversy about the content of this idea. The meaning of the concept of primitivism is defined by its opposite—acculturation. Just as being handicapped is the polar opposite of ability, so *primitiveness* is the polar opposite of *cultural development*.

A primitive child is a child who has not completed cultural development. The primitive mind is a healthy one. In certain conditions the primitive child completes normal cultural development, and achieves the intellectual level of a cultured person. In this respect, primitivism is distinct from mental retardation. The latter is a result of a physical handicap; the mentally retarded are limited in their natural intellectual development and *as a result of this* do not usually attain full cultural development. With respect to natural development, on the other hand, a "primitive child" does not deviate from the norm. His practical intellect may reach a very high level, but he still remains outside cultural development. A "primitive" is an example of pure, isolated *natural development*.

For a long time, primitivism in a child was considered to be a pathological form of childhood development and was confused with mental retardation. In fact, the outward appearances of these two phenomena are often extremely similar. Limited psychological activity, stunted intellectual development, deductive inaccuracy, conceptual absurdity, impressionability, and so forth, can be symptoms of either. Because of the research methods currently available (Binet and others), the primitive child may be portrayed in a way that is similar to the portrayal of the mentally retarded. Special research methods are necessary to discover the true cause of unhealthy symptoms and to distinguish between primitivism and mental retardation. In particular, the methods for analyzing practical, natural intellect (*natuerliche Intelligenz*) may easily reveal primitivism with a completely healthy mind. A. E. Petrova,[32] in giving us an excellent study of childhood primitivism and outlining its most important types, demonstrated that primitivism may equally combine with an exceptional, an average, and a pathological child's mind ("Children Are Primitives," in Gurevich (Ed), *Questions of Pedology and Childhood Psycho-neurology*. Moscow, 1925.

Instances in which primitivism combines with certain pathological forms of development are particularly interesting for the study of defects, since such instances occur most frequently in the histories of handicapped children's cultural development. For example, psychological primitivism and delays in cultural development may very often be combined with mental retardation. It would be more accurate to say that delays in the cultural development of a child occur as a result of mental retardation. But in such mixed forms, primitivism and mental retardation remain two *different* natural phenomena. It is in just such a way that congenital or early childhood deafness usually combines with a primitive type of childhood development. But primitivism may occur without a defect. It may even coexist with a highly gifted mind. Similarly, a defect does not necessarily lead to primitivism but may also coexist with a highly cultured type of mind. A defect and psychological primitivism are two different things, and when they are found together, they must be separated and distinguished from one another.

An issue of particular theoretical interest is alleged pathology in a primitive individual. When analyzing a primitive little girl who spoke Tatar and Russian simultaneously and who was acknowledged to be psychologically abnormal, Petrova demonstrated that the entire complex of symptoms, implying illness, stemmed in fact from primitivism, which, in turn, was conditioned by the lack of command of either language. "Our numerous observations prove," Petrova says, "that complete substitution of one poorly grasped language for another, equally lacking in fluency, does not occur without psychological repercussions. This *substitution of one form of thought for another diminishes mental activity particularly when it is already not abundant*" (ibid., p. 85). This conclusion permits us to establish *precisely* what constitutes cultural development from a psychological point of view and what, if missing, causes primitivism in a child. In the given example, primitivism is created by an imperfect command of language. But more generally, the process of cultural development basically depends on acquiring cultural psychological tools, which were created by mankind during its historical development and which are analogous to language from a psychological perspective. Primitiveness boils down to the inability to use such tools and to the natural forms in which psychological operations appear. Like all other higher psychological operations, all the higher forms of intellectual activity become possible only when given the use of similar kinds of cultural tools. "Language," says Stern, "becomes a tool of great power in the development of his [the child's—L.V.] life, his ideas, emotions and will; it alone ultimately makes possible any real thought, generalization and comparison, synthesis and comprehension" (W. Stern, 1923, p. 73).

These artificial devices, which by analogy with technology are sometimes called psychological tools, are directed toward mastering behavioral processes—someone else's or one's own—in the same way that technology attempts to control the processes of nature. In this sense, T. Ribot[33] (1892) has called reflex attention natural and conscious attention artificial, seeing in it a product of historical development. The use of psychological tools modifies the whole course and structure of psychological function, giving them a new form.

During childhood, the development of many natural psychological functions (memory, attention) either are not observable to any significant degree or take place in insignificant quantities. There is no way, therefore, that the development of these functions alone can account for the enormous difference in the corresponding activities of children and adults. In the process of development, a child is armed and rearmed with the most varied of tools. A child in the more advanced stages is as different from a child in the younger stages as an adult is from a child—not only in the greater development of functions, but also in the degree and character of cultural preparedness, in the tools at his disposal, that is, in the degree and means he has of controlling the activity of his psychological functions. Thus, older children are distinguished from the younger ones in the same way adults are distinguished from children, and normal children are distinguished from the handicapped ones. They are distinguished not only by a more developed memory, but also by the fact that they remember *differently*, in different manners, by different methods; they use memory to a different degree.

The inability to use natural psychological functions and to master psychological tools in the most basic sense determines the kind of cultural development a handicapped child will attain. Mastering a psychological tool and, by means of it, one's own natural psychological functions generates an *artificial development*, as it were; that is, it raises a given function to a higher level, increases and expands its activity. Binet explained experimentally the significance of making use of a psychological function with the help of a tool. In analyzing the memory of individuals with exceptional computational skills, he happened upon one individual with an average memory, but armed with a *skill in remembering* equal to and, in many respects, superior to that of those with exceptional computational skills. Binet called this phenomenon a simulated exceptional memory. "The majority of psychological operations can be simulated," he says, "that is, they can be replaced by others, which are similar to them in externals alone, but which are different in nature" (A. Binet, 1894, p. 155). In the given case a difference was discovered between natural memory and artificial or technical-mnemonic memory, that is, a difference between two ways of *using* memory. Each of them, in Binet's opinion, possesses its own kind of rudimentary and instinctive technical mnemonics. Technical mnemonics should be introduced in schools along with mental arithmetic and stenography—not in order to develop the intellect, but to make available a way of using memory (ibid., p. 164). It is easy to see in this example how natural development and the use of some functions as tools may not coincide.

There are three fundamental points which define the problem of cultural development for an abnormal child: *the degree of primitivism in the childhood mind; the nature of his adoption of cultural and psychological tools; and the means by which he makes use of his own psychological functions.* The primitive child is differentiated not by a lesser degree of accumulated experience, but by the different (natural) way in which it was accumulated. It is possible to combat primitivism by creating new cultural tools, whose use makes culture accessible to the child. Braille's script[34] and finger spelling (dactylology) are most powerful methods of overcoming primitivism. We know how often mentally retarded children are found to have not only a normal, but a highly developed, memory. Its use, however, almost always remains at the lowest level. Evidently, the degree of development of memory is one thing, and the degree of its use quite another.

The first experimental research into the use of psychological tools in handicapped children was recently carried out by followers of N. Ach.[35] Ach himself, having created a method for analyzing functional word use as a means, or as a tool, for elaborating conceptualization, pointed out the fundamental similarity between this process and the process by which the deaf acquire language (1932 [sic], but probably 1921). Bacher[36] (1925) applied this method to an investigation of learning disabled children (*debiles*) and showed that this is the best method for analyzing mental retardation qualitatively. The correlation between theoretical and practical intellect turned out to be insignificant, and mentally retarded children (to the extent of their debilitation) could apply their practical intellect much better than their theoretical intellect. The author sees in this a correspondence with similar results achieved by Ach in his experiments with brain-damaged individuals. Because the mentally retarded do not use words as tools for working out ideas, higher forms of intellectual activity based on the use of abstract concepts are impossible for them (ibid.). How the mastering of one's own psychological activity influences the execution of intellectual operations was discovered at the time of Bacher's research. But this is precisely the problem. Stern considers these two means of using language as different stages in speech development. He said: "...But subsequently a decisive turnabout in speech development occurs again, *a vague awareness of the meaning of language and the will to conquer it awakens*" (1922, p. 89). The child makes the most important discovery of his life, that "*everything has a name*" (ibid.); that *words are signs*—they are the means of naming and communicating. It is this *full*, conscious, voluntary use of speech that a mentally retarded child apparently does not attain. As a result, higher intellectual activity remains inaccessible to him. F. Rimat[37] was completely justified in selecting this method as a test for examining mental ability; the ability or inability to use words is a decisive criterion of intellectual development (F. Rimat, 1925). The fate of all cultural development depends on whether children themselves make the discovery about which Stern speaks. Do they master words as fundamental psychological tools?

Studies of primitive children reveal *literally the same thing*. "How do a tree and a log differ?" Petrova asks one such child. "I haven't seen a tree, I swear I haven't seen one" (There is a linden tree growing in front of the window). In response to the question (while pointing to the linden tree) "And what is this?" comes the answer: "It's a linden." This is a primitive answer, in the spirit of those primitive people whose language has no word for "tree;" it is too abstract for the concrete nature of the boy's mind. The boy was correct: none of us has seen a tree. We've seen birches, willows, pines and so forth, that is, specific species of trees (A.E. Petrova, in Gurevich (Ed.), 1925, p. 64). Or take another example. A girl "with two languages" was asked: "In one school some children write well, and some draw well. Do all the children in this school write and draw well?" "How should I know? *What I haven't seen with my own eyes, I cannot explain it* as if I had seen with my own eyes..." (a primitive visual response) (*ibid.*, p. 86). This nine-year old girl is absolutely normal, but she is primitive. She is totally unable to use words as a means of solving mental tasks, although she *talks*; she knows how to use words as a means of communication. She can explain only what she has seen with her own eyes. In the very same way, a "debile" draws conclusions from concrete object to concrete object. His inadequacy for higher forms of abstract thought is not a direct result of an intellectual defect; he is completely capable of other forms of logical thinking, of operations governed by common sense and so forth. He simply has not mastered the use of words as tools for abstract thinking. This incapacity is a result and a symptom of his primitivism, but not of his mental retardation.

Kruenegel (1926) is fully justified when he states that G. Kerschensteiner's[38] basic axiom does not apply to cultural development in a mentally retarded child. That axiom says that the congruence of one or another cultural form with the psychological structures of a child's personality lies at the base of cultural development: the emotional structure of cultural forms should be entirely or partially adequate to the emotional structure of individuality (G. Kerschensteiner, 1924). The fundamental problem in a handicapped child's cultural development is inadequacy, the incongruence between his psychological structure and the structure of cultural forms. What remains is the necessity of creating special cultural tools suitable to the psychological make-up of such a child, or of mastering common cultural forms with the help of special pedagogical methods, *because the most important and decisive condition of cultural development—precisely the ability to use psychological tools—is preserved in such children.* Their cultural development is, in principle, completely possible. In the use of artificial means (*Hilfer*) aimed at overcoming a defect, W. Eliasberg[39] justifiably perceived a symptom which is differential, which allows us to distinguish mental retardation (*demenz*) from aphasia (W. Eliasberg, 1925). The use of psychological tools is, indeed, the most essential aspect of a child's cultural behavior. It is totally lacking only in the mentally retarded.

7

We have taken a theoretical cross section of the most important problems of modern defectology noted above because a theoretical approach to the problem provides the most comprehensive, the most concise view, exposing the very essence, the nucleus, of the question. In fact, however, each of the issues merges with a series of practical-pedagogical, and concrete-methodological problems or, more precisely, boils down to a series of separate concrete questions. In order to tackle these issues, special considerations of each question would have been necessary. By limiting ourselves to the most general formulation of the problems, we will concisely indicate the presence of concrete, practical tasks in each problem. Thus, the problem of motor skills and motor deficiency is directly connected to the questions of physical training, and vocational and professional education for handicapped children. The problem of practical intellect is as closely connected with vocational training and with practical experience in acquiring daily living skills, the crux of all education for handicapped children. The problem of cultural development embraces all major questions of academic instruction. The problem of the analytical and artificial methods used in teaching speech to the deaf, which is particularly worrisome to defectologists, can be formulated with the following question: Should children be mechanically drilled in the simplest elements of speech skills, in the same fashion in which fine motor skills are cultivated? Or should children first and foremost be taught the ability to use speech, in other words, be taught the functional use of words as "intellectual tools?" as J. Dewey[40] put it. The problem of compensation in a handicapped child's development and the problem of social conditioning in this development includes all the issues involved in organizing communal living for children, in a children's social movement, in sociopolitical education, in personality formation, and so forth.

Our account of the basic problems of being handicapped would stop short of its most essential point if we did not attempt to project a base line in practical defectology, which inevitably derives from this formulation of theoretical problems. What we have designated in theory as the transition from a quantitative understanding of a disability corresponds completely with the primary feature of practical defectology; the formulation of positive tasks confronting special schools. In special schools we can no longer be satisfied with simply a limited version of the public school curriculum or with the use of modified and simplified methods. The special schools confront the task of positive activity, of creating forms of work which meet the special needs and character of its pupils. Among those who have written on this question, A. S. Griboedov has expressed this thought most concisely, as we have already observed. If we reject the idea that a handicapped child is a lesser likeness of a normal child, then, unavoidably, we must also reject the view that special schools are prolonged versions of public schools. Of course, it is extremely important to establish with the greatest possible accuracy the qualitative differences between handicapped and normal children, but we cannot stop here. For example, we learn from numerous contemporary observations of the mentally retarded that these children have smaller cranial circumferences, smaller stature, smaller chest size, less muscle strength, reduced motor ability, lowered resistance to negative influences, delayed associations, and decreased attention and memory span, and that they are more prone to fatigue and exhaustion, less able to exert their will, and so forth (A. S. Griboedov, 1926). But we still know nothing about positive characteristics, about the children's uniqueness: such is the research of the future. It is only half true to characterize such children as developmentally delayed in physical and psychological terms, weakened, and so forth; such negative characteristics in no way exhaust these children's positive and unique features. It is not the individual fault of one researcher or another that positive material is lacking. Rather, it is a calamity shared by all of defectology, which is just beginning to reorganize its principal bases and thus to give new direction to pedological research. In any case, Griboedov's basic conclusion formulates precisely this view: "In studying the pedology of retarded children, we can clearly see that the differences between them and normal children are not only quantitative, but also qualitative, and that consequently they *need not stay longer in school, nor attend smaller classes, nor even associate with those who have similar levels and tempo of psychological development. Rather, they need to attend special schools, with their own programs, with unique methodologies and special pedagogical personnel*" (1927, p. 19).

There is, however, a serious danger in formulating the question this way. It would be a theoretical mistake to make an absolute concept out of the developmental uniqueness of a child with one kind of defect or another, while forgetting that there are limits to this uniqueness prescribed by the social conditioning of the development. It is equally inaccurate to forget that the parameters of the special school's uniqueness are described by the common social goals and tasks confronting both public and special schools. Indeed, as has already been said, children with a defect do not constitute "a special breed of people," in K. Buerklen's phrase. Instead, we discover that all developmental uniqueness tends to approximate determined, normal, social types. And, the school must play a decisive role in this "approximation." The special school can set a general goal for itself; after all, its pupils will live and function not as "a special breed of people," but as workers, craftspeople, and so forth, that is, as specific social units. *The greatest difficulty and profoundest uniqueness of the special schools (and of all practical defectology) is precisely to achieve these common goals, while using unusual means to reach them*. Similarly, the most important feature for the handicapped child is the final point, one held in common with normal children, but attained through unique developmental processes. If special means (a special school) were used to attain special goals, this would not warrant being called a problem; the entire issue stems from the apparent contradiction of special means to achieve precisely the same goals, which the public schools also set themselves. This contradiction is really only an apparent one: it is *precisely in order that* handicapped children achieve the same things as normal children, that we must employ utterly different means.

"The goal of unified vocational schools is to create builders of a new life of communist principles," says Griboedov. "The goal of the auxiliary school cannot be the same since the mentally retarded, although they have been educated and molded to fit the society around them, and armed with the means of survival, cannot be builders, or creators of a new life; we demand from them only that they not keep others from building" (1926, p. 99). Such a formulation of the practical problems of therapeutic pedagogy seems to us unsound from a sociopedagogical and psychological point of view.

Can pedagogy, in fact, base its work on such a purely negative goal ("not hinder others from building")? Such problems are solved not through pedagogy, but by completely different means. An educational system without definite, positive societal goals is impossible; similarly, one cannot admit that a child, on completion of an auxiliary school, must limit his role in social life to staying out of the way! According to the data introduced by Griboedov himself (1926), more than 90 percent of the mentally retarded children who have received an education are capable of working and undertaking craft-related, industrial or agricultural labor. Can it be that a conscientious worker—in industry, agriculture or handicrafts—is not also a builder, or a creator of new life? After all, one must understand this "building" as a collective social effort, in which each worker participates according to his strengths. Data from German and American statistics about occupational distribution among the mentally retarded tells us that those who have completed an auxiliary school may be builders and are not all doomed to the role of "not hindering others as they build." From a psychological perspective, it is equally false to deny that there are creative processes present in mentally retarded children. Retarded children often register higher than normal children, not in productivity, but in the intensity with which these creative processes run their course. In order to accomplish the same things that a normal child does, the retarded child must display greater creativity. For example, to master the four arithmetic operations is a more creative process for the mentally retarded than for the normal school child. Griboedov sympathetically introduces Kruenegel's opinion of therapeutic pedagogy, which can be reduced primarily to (1) the exercise of residual psychological functions and (2) the development of compensatory operations (ibid.). But after all, this really means basing pedagogy on the principle of compensation, i.e., constructive development. This view suggests that illness (in general) should be reevaluated on the basis of our overall understanding of development in mentally retarded children. "The therapeutic factor must saturate and leave its imprint upon all the work in the school," Griboedov demands (ibid., p. 98), agreeing completely with the common view of a mentally retarded child as a *sick child*.

Still, P. Ia. Troshin[41] cautioned against the view which "sees in abnormal children only disease, forgetting that, in addition to illness, they have normal psychological lives" (1915, p. 2). Therefore, the principles embodied in the auxiliary school program of the People's Commissariat of Enlightenment* seems to us to be more correct: "The common goals and tasks, confronting any single vocational school also represent the goals and tasks of the auxiliary school" (*Programs of the Auxiliary School*, 1927, p. 7). Actual formation of programs on the same basis as the GUS** program for public schools is an expression of the school's fundamental goal: the closest possible approach of the retarded child to the norm.

---

* The People's Commisariat of Enlightenment (NARKOMPROS), the equivalent of a "ministry of education," was founded November 9, 1917. The first Commissar of Enlightenment was A. Lunacharskii. [Transl.]

** GUS stands for Gosudarstvennyi Uchennyi Soviet, or State Council of Scholars. This division of NARKOMPROS existed from 1919 to 1933. Its first chair, Pokrovskii, was Lunacharskii's second in command. [Transl.]

To construct a plan for an auxiliary school "independently of the plans for the common vocational schools," as Griboedov demands (1926, p. 99), means, in essence, to exclude the practice of therapeutic pedagogy from the sphere of social education. After all, even foreign schools are coming around to the idea of complexes[*] (combined programs), as Griboedov himself indicated (ibid.). R. Guertler's "Lesson with a Handkerchief" represents an incidental and primitive "complex," whereas what is basically proposed by the GUS "complex" is "a reflection of connections between fundamental, vital phenomena (nature, labor, society)" (*Programs of the Auxiliary School*, 1927, p. 8).

The mentally retarded child needs to have these links disclosed in the process of academic instruction *more than a normal child does*. Circumstances where this "complex" is more difficult than the "handkerchief" should be a positive strength in such programs, because raising surmountable obstacles also means carrying out the creative goals of education with respect to development. The statement of Eliasberg, who has worked so hard on problems of the psychology and pathology of abstraction and against the exclusive dominance of visual aids in auxiliary schools, we consider to be both sympathetic and profoundly just. Precisely because the retarded child is so dependent on his experience with visual, concrete impressions and develops abstract thinking to such a small degree when left to his own devices, the school must free itself from the abundant use of visual aids, which serve as an obstacle to the development of abstract thought. In other words, a school must not only adapt to the disabilities of such a child but also must fight these disabilities and overcome them. This constitutes the third fundamental characteristic of practical problems in defectology. There are, first, common goals, which confront both normal and special schools, and, second, the special features and uniqueness of means used in special schools. But apart from both of these, there exists the creative character of the entire school, which makes it a school of social compensation, of socialization, and not "a school for the weakminded," and which forces it not to conform to a defect, but to conquer it. That creative character emerges as the necessary feature in issues of practical defectology. These three points define the parameters of practical defectology.

As has been mentioned above, we have limited ourselves here to posing problems in their most general form. We have indicated that these are problems for which defectology is only beginning to approach solutions. They are aimed toward the future more than toward the past or the present of our discipline. We have tried to demonstrate that defectology studies development—a development which has its own laws, its own tempo, its own cycles, its own imbalances, its own metamorphoses, its own shifts from the center, its own structure— and that this is a special and relatively independent area of knowledge about a profoundly unique subject. In practical terms and in education, as we have attempted to show, defectology faces tasks the solution of which demands creative work and the introduction of special forms. To solve these and other problems of defectology it is necessary to find a solid foundation for both theory and practice. In order not to build on sand, to avoid the eclectic and superficial empiricism which characterized it in the past, in order to shift from a clinical-therapeutic approach to a positive, creative pedagogy, defectology must rest on the same philosophical dialectics and materialistic foundation and be guided by our pedagogy

[*] Vygotsky referred here to Soviet reforms which made broad curriculum changes. The reformed curriculum rejected the division of schoolwork into "subjects;" instead it taught pupils to work together under a single broad theme.

in general, that is, by the social foundation which determines our social education. These are the issues facing defectology as we know it today.

Chapter 1

DEFECT AND COMPENSATION[1]

1

In those systems of psychology, which place at their center an integral approach to personality, the idea of overcompensation plays a dominant role. "What does not destroy me, makes me stronger" is the idea formulated by W. Stern when he pointed out that strength arises from weakness and ability from deficiencies (W. Stern, 1923, p. 145). The psychological trend created by the school of Adler, the Austrian psychiatrist, is very widespread and influential in Europe and America. This so-called "individual psychology" (i.e. the psychology of personality) has developed the idea of overcompensation into a whole system, into a complete doctrine about the mind. Overcompensation is not some rare or exceptional phenomenon in the life of an organism. An endless number of examples can be given demonstrating this concept. Rather, it is to the highest degree, a common and extremely widespread feature of living matter. True, until now no one has worked out an inexhaustible and comprehensive biological theory of overcompensation. In a series of separate areas of organic life, these phenomena have been studied so thoroughly and their practical application is so extensive that we have substantial grounds for talking about overcompensation as a scientifically established, fundamental fact in the life of an organism.

We inoculate a healthy child with a vaccine. The child endures a mild case of the disease and upon recovering becomes immune to smallpox for many years. This organism acquires an immunity, i.e. it not only has recovered from a mild illness which was brought on by inoculation, but comes out of the disease healthier than before. This organism succeeded in producing an antidote which was considerably stronger than the vaccine administered. If we now compare our child with others who have not been vaccinated, then we shall see that with respect to this terrible illness he is overly healthy: he will not only not become ill now, like other healthy children will, but he will not even be able to become sick, he will remain healthy even when this poison again infiltrates the bloodstream.

While at first glance paradoxical, this organic process which transforms sickness into superior health, weakness into strength, and infection into immunity, bears the label of superior overdevelopment or "overcompensation," as some authors say. This means, essentially, that any injury to or negative influence on an organism evokes from it defensive reactions which are considerably more energetic and stronger than is necessary to render the immediate danger harmless. An organism represents a relatively closed, internally connected system of organs which possesses a large reserve of potential energy and concealed strengths. In a moment of danger it acts as a unified (integral) whole, which mobilizes its latent reserves of accumulated strengths and bombards the endangered location with much larger doses of the antidotes than the dose of bacteria threatening it. In this way, the organism not only compensates for the harm inflicted on it but always generates a surplus (of the antidote), gaining superiority over the danger and rendering the organism considerably more able to defend itself than before the onset of danger.

White blood cells rush to the infected area in greater quantity than is needed to combat the infection. This, too, is an example of overcompensation. If a tuberculosis patient is treated with an injection of tuberculin (i.e. tubercle bacillus) then the organism is being counted on to overcome it. The discrepancy between irritation and reaction, the inequality between the action and the counteraction within the organism, the surplus of the antidote, the cultivation of superior health through disease, and the ascendancy to a higher stage by overcoming danger are all important factors for medicine and pedagogy, treatment and education. Even in psychology this phenomenon was widely adopted when the mind began to be studied not in isolation from the organism —a soul dissected from the body— but within the organism's system, as its distinct, unique and higher function. Overcompensation was found to play no lesser role in the system of personality. It will suffice to look at modern psychotechnics where such an important personality forming function as physical exercise essentially amounts to the phenomenon of overcompensation. Adler turned his attention to defectively functioning organs which had been impeded or destroyed as a result of a handicap. Such organs out of necessity enter into combat and struggle with the external world to which they must adjust. This struggle is accompanied at times by increased illness and fatality but it also bears the seeds of increased possibilities for overcompensation (A. Adler, 1927). In the case of illness or removal of one of two organs (a kidney, a lung), the other organ takes over the full function of both and develops in a compensatory manner. Similarly, the central nervous system takes over the compensation of a single impaired organ, determining more precisely and perfecting the work of that organ. The psychological system superimposes on that organ a psychological superstructure which elevates and increases the efficiency of the remaining organ's operation.

"The sensation of having a defective organ constantly stimulates the individual's psychological development," Adler quotes O. Ruele[2] (1926, p. 10).

The feeling or consciousness of one's inferiority, caused by an individual's defect, reflects an evaluation of one's social position. This feeling becomes the primary driving force behind psychological development. "Significantly intensifying the phenomena of presentiment and foresight along with their operating factors such as memory, intuition, attention, sensitivity, interest, in a word, all the psychological features" (p. 111), overcompensation leads to the consciousness of superior health in a diseased organism, to the transformation of an inferiority complex into a superiority complex, a defect into giftedness and ability. Having struggled with a speech defect, Demosthenes went on to become one of Greece's greatest orators. It was said of him that he acquired his great art by increasing his natural handicap, by magnifying and multiplying the obstacles. He practiced his speech pronunciation, filling his mouth with stones and trying to overcome the roar of the ocean waves which muffled his voice. *"Se non vero, ben trovato"* (Even if it is not true, it is well thought up), goes the Italian proverb. The way to perfection is through the conquest of obstacles. The obstruction of a function stimulates a higher level of its operation. In similar ways, L. von Beethoven and A. S. Suvorov serve as examples of this. The stuttering K. Demulen was an outstanding orator; the blind, deaf-mute Helen Keller[3] a famous writer and prophet of optimism.

2

Two circumstances force us to take a special look at this doctrine. First of all, particularly in the circles of German social democracy, it is often linked with the teachings of K. Marx. Second, this doctrine is intrinsically tied to pedagogy in theory and in practice. We will put this question aside inasmuch as the doctrine of individual psychology is connected with Marxism; the solution of this question would demand a special investigation. We note only that there have already been attempts made to synthesize Marx and Adler and to study personality within the context of the philosophical and social system of dialectical materialism. We are attempting to understand the reasoning behind the rapprochement of these two lines of thought.

A new direction has already emerged, separating itself from the school of S. Freud[4] as a result of the differences in political and social views of the advocates of psychoanalysis. Apparently the political side played a significant role here inasmuch as F. Wittel (1925) tells how Adler and some of his supporters withdrew from the psychoanalytical circle. Adler and his nine friends were Social Democrats. Many of his followers like to stress this point. Ruele (1926, p. 5), who attempted to synthesize Marx and Adler in his work on the psychology of the proletarian child, states that "Sigmund Freud up until now has done everything to make his teachings available and useful only to the reigning social strata. As a counterbalance, A. Adler's individual psychology bears a revolutionary character and its conclusions fully coincide with the principles of Marxist revolutionary socialism."

As has already been mentioned, all this is debatable, but there are two aspects which make such a rapprochement psychologically possible and warrant attention.

The first is the dialectical character of the new doctrine; the second is the social basis of the psychology of personality. Adler thinks dialectically: personality develops by means of opposition. A defect, ineptitude, or inferiority is not simply a minus, a shortcoming, a negative attribute, but also a stimulus for overcompensation. Adler introduces "the basic psychological law of dialectical transformation: as a result of a subjective feeling of inferiority, an organic defect will be transformed into a psychological drive to compensate and overcompensate" (A. Adler, 1927, p. 57). From this position Adler allows us to include psychology in the context of a broad biological and social doctrine. Indeed, all true scientific thought is advanced by means of dialectics. Even Charles Darwin[5] taught that adaptation results from unfitness, from struggle, destruction, selection. Marx, too, taught that in contrast to utopian socialism, the development of capitalism will inevitably lead to communism through the demise of the capitalistic dictatorship of the proletariat and will not retreat to the sidelines somewhere, as might seem possible from a superficial glance. Adler's teachings also attempt to illustrate how an expedient and higher level arises from an inexpedient lower level.

As A. B. Zalkind correctly noted, the psychology of personality breaks away from the "biological stimulus approach to personality" and manifests itself "as a really revolutionary characterological movement" because, in contrast to the teachings of Freud, it puts the dynamic, formulating forces of history and social life in the place of biological fate (1926, p. 177). Adler's teachings stand in opposition not only to the reactionary biological schemes of E. Kretschmer,[6] for whom an innate constitution defines body structure, while character and "the entire subsequent development of human character is equated with a passive unfolding of that basic biological type inherent in man" (Zalkind, ibid. p. 174). Adler's teachings, however, are also in opposition to Freud's characterological system. Two ideas set Adler apart from Freud: the idea of the social basis for the development of personality and the idea of the ultimate direction of this process. Individual psychology negates the essential connection between the organic substrata and the overall psychological development of personality and character. The entire psychological life of an individual consists of a succession of combative objectives, directed at the resolution of a single task: to secure a definite position with respect to the immanent logic of human society, or to the demands of the social environment. In the last analysis, the fate of personality is decided not by the existence of a defect in itself but by its social consequences, by its socio-psychological realization. In connection with this, it becomes necessary for the psychologist to understand each psychological act not only with respect to the past but also in conjunction with the future direction of personality. We may call this the ultimate direction of our behavior. Simply put, understanding psychological phenomena from the perspective of both the future and the past essentially represents the dialectical need to perceive phenomena in eternal movement, and to bring to light their future oriented tendencies, determined by the present. Adler's teachings on the structure of personality and character introduce a new and profound future-oriented perspective, which is valuable for psychology. It frees us from the conservative, backward-looking teachings of Freud and Kretschmer.

Just as the life of each organism is directed by the biological need to adapt, so, too, the dynamics of personality are guided by daily social demands. "We are not in a position to think, feel, want, or act without some kind of goal before us," states Adler (1927, p. 2). Both a single act and the development of personality as a whole may be understood on the basis of their future-oriented tendencies. In other words, "The psychological life of a man, like a dramatic character created by a good playwright, strives for its final denouement of the fifth act" (ibid., pp. 2-3).

The future-oriented perspective, introduced by this interpretation of psychological processes, brings us to one of the two aspects of Adler's method which compels our attention: individual psychological pedagogy. In Wittel's opinion, pedagogy is the main area of application of Adler's psychology. At the same time, with respect to the psychological trend we have just described, pedagogy occupies the same place that medicine does for the biological sciences, engineering for physics, and chemistry and politics for the social sciences: namely, the highest category of truth, since man proves the truth of his thoughts only by application. From the outset, it is clear why precisely this psychological movement helps us understand child development and child rearing: in the unsocialized and unadapted state of childhood lie the very seeds of overcompensation, or the superior overdevelopment of functions. The more adapted some young animal species are, the smaller their potential for future development and rearing. A guarantee of superiority is given only in the presence of inferiority. Hence, ineptness and overcompensation represent the motive forces of childhood development. Such an understanding gives us the key to classical psychology and pedagogy. Just as the flow of a current is defined by its shores and its river beds, similarly, the main psychological line of a growing child's development is defined out of objective necessity by the social channel and social shorelines shaping personality.

3

The doctrine of overcompensation has an important significance and serves as a psychological basis for the theory and practice of educating a child with a loss of hearing, sight, and so forth. What horizons will open up to the pedagogue, when he recognizes that a defect is not only a minus, a deficit, or a weakness but also a plus, a source of strength and that it has some positive implications! In essence, psychologists learned this a long time ago; pedagogues have also known this. Only now, however, has this most fundamental law been formulated with scientific accuracy. A child will want to see everything if he is nearsighted, hear everything if he has a hearing loss; he will want to speak if he has a speech problem or a stutter. The desire to fly will appear in children who experience great difficulty even jumping (A. Adler, 1927, p. 57). The dynamic forces of any educational system spring precisely from this opposition between a given organic defect and desires, fantasies, and dreams, that is, the psychological drive to compensate for the defect or loss. In educational practice, this is confirmed at every step. If we hear that a boy limps and therefore runs better than anyone else, we understand that it is a question of this very law. If experimental research shows that, in comparison with the maximum reactions occurring under normal conditions, greatly accelerated and intensified reactions will occur in the face of obstacles, then again we have the same law.

The concept of exemplary human personality which includes an understanding of its organic unity must serve as the basis for educating an abnormal child.

In contrast with other psychologists, W. Stern examined the structure of personality in greater depth. He presumed the following, "We have no right to conclude that a person with an established abnormality has a propensity for abnormality. In the same light it is impossible to reduce a given abnormal personality to a specific isolated characteristic as the sole primary cause" (W. Stern, 1921, pp. 163-164).

We shall apply this law to somatics and psychology, to medicine and pedagogy. In medicine, there is a growing tendency to base the sole criterion for health or illness on the question of whether or not the entire organism functions expediently, while individual abnormalities are taken into account only inasmuch as they are normally or insufficiently compensated for by other functions of the organism (ibid., p. 164). Moreover, in psychology, microscopic analysis of abnormalities has led to reevaluation and an examination of these functions as an expression of an overall abnormality in the personality. If we are to apply Stern's ideas to education, then it will be necessary to reject both the concept and the term "defective (handicapped) children."

T. Lipps examined this question in the light of a general law for all psychological activity, which he called the law of damned up energy (*zakon zaprudy*).

"If any psychological event is interrupted or impeded in its natural course, or if, at some point, an alien element intrudes, then there occurs a flood of energy at the point of interruption, delay, or agitation in the course of the psychological event" (T. Lipps, 1907, p. 127). "Energy is concentrated at the given point; it is increased and can overcome the delay. It may continue to flow but in a roundabout way. Here, among other things, the high value placed on things lost or damaged is relevant" (ibid., p. 122). This constitutes the main idea of overcompensation. Lipps gave this law universal significance. In general, he viewed any drive as a manifestation of this phenomenon ("of flooding"). He explained not only comic and tragic experiences but also cognitive processes by the operation of this law: "When there appears some obstacle, any purposeful activity will necessarily be channeled through some previous aimless, automatic event." Present in the dammed up energy is the "tendency to move to one side. The goal, which is impossible to reach by a direct path, is attained thanks to an overflow of force channeled by one such detour" (ibid., p. 279).

The goal of any mental process can be attained only thanks to some difficulty, delay, or obstacle. The point of interruption of any automatic function becomes a goal for other functions; now directed at this point, they are transformed into purposeful (goal-oriented) activity. For this reason, a defect and the resultant disruption of the normal functioning of personality become the ultimate developmental goal for all individual mental powers. This is why Adler called a defect the basic motivating force in development and the final goal in life's plan. The formula "defect overcompensation" is the main line of development for a child with some functional or organic defect. Thus, the "goal" is defined beforehand, yet it only seems to be the goal, when in fact it is the primary cause of development.

The education and rearing of handicapped children should be based on the fact that along with a defect come combative psychological tendencies and the potential for overcoming the defect. Education of these children should take into account that precisely these tendencies emerge in the foreground of a child's development and must be included in the educational process as his motivating strength. Constructing the entire educational process on the basis of natural compensatory drives does not mean alleviating all difficulties that arise as a result of the defect. It means instead concentrating all strengths on the compensation of the defect, selecting, in the appropriate sequential order, those tasks which will bring about the gradual formation of the entire personality from a new standpoint.

What a liberating truth for the pedagogue! A blind child develops a psychological superstructure circumventing his impaired vision with only one goal in mind: to replace sight. Using every possible means available to him, a deaf child works out ways to overcome the isolation and seclusion caused by his deafness. Up to now we have neglected these psychological powers. We have not taken into account the desire with which such a child struggles to be healthy and fully accepted socially. A defect has been statically viewed as merely a defect, a minus.

Education has neglected the positive forces created by a defect. Psychologists and pedagogues have not been acquainted with Adler's law of the opposition between a physical handicap and the psychological drives to compensate. They have taken into account only the former, the defect. They didn't understand that a handicap is not just an impoverished psychological state but also a source of wealth, not just a weakness but a strength. They thought that the development of a blind child centers on his blindness. As it turns out, his development strives to transcend blindness. The psychology of blindness is essentially the psychology of victory over blindness.

An inaccurate understanding of the psychology of the handicapped has caused the failure of traditional education for blind and deaf children. The previous understanding of a defect only as a defect is similar to the view that the vaccination of a healthy child merely cultivates disease in him. In fact, it produces superior health. It is most important that education depend not only on the development of natural strengths but also on the ultimate goal toward which they must be oriented. Full social esteem is the ultimate aim of education inasmuch as all the processes of overcompensation are directed at achieving social status.

Compensation strives not for further deviation from the norm, even in a positive sense, but for a superior, if somewhat one-sided, twisted, hypertrophied development of personality, it nevertheless strives in the direction of the norm and toward an approximation of a certain normal social type. A definite social type always serves as the norm for overcompensation. We will find in a deaf-mute child, cut off from the world and excluded from all social contact, not a decreased desire to communicate but an intensified desire to be included in social life. Such a child's psychological capacity for speech is in reverse proportion to his physical ability to produce speech. Although it may seem paradoxical, a deaf child, even more than a normal child, wants to speak and vigorously (impetuously) gravitates toward speech. Our educational system has sidestepped this issue, and the deaf, without any instruction and in spite of it, have created their own language, arising from this desire to communicate. This is something for the psychologist to examine. Herein lies the reason why the deaf-mute have failed to develop oral speech. In exactly the same way, a blind child develops an increased ability to master space. In comparison with a seeing child, the blind child has a greater sensitivity toward that world which is accessible to us without the slightest difficulty, thanks to sight. A defect is not only a weakness but also a strength. In this psychological truth lie the alpha and omega of social education for children.

4

The ideas of T. Lipps, W. Stern, and A. Adler contain a wholesome nucleus for the psychology of the education of handicapped children. These ideas, however, are obscured by their vagueness, and in order to completely grasp their significance, we must explain more precisely how they relate to other psychological theories and views which are similar in form or spirit.

First of all, the unscientific optimism which spawned these ideas easily arouses our suspicions. If every defect gives reign to some compensatory strength, then it can be seen as a blessing. Is this really true? Overcompensation, in fact, is only one extreme of two opposite outcomes, one of two possible poles of development affected by a defect. The other extreme is the total failure to compensate, retreat into illness, neurosis, complete asociality from a psychological standpoint. Unsuccessful compensation transforms the child's energies into a defensive battle with illness, directed toward a false goal, heading life's entire course along a false path. Between these two extremes we find every possible degree of compensation from minimal to maximal.

Secondly, these ideas are easily confused with directly opposing views and can be mistaken for a return to the past, to a Christian mystical notion of weakness and suffering. Do we not find in the ideas indicated above a high value placed on the superiority of illness at the expense of health, on the recognition of the benefit of suffering, and, in general, on the cultivation of weak, wretched, and impotent forms of life to the detriment of the strong, the normal, and the powerful? No, the new doctrine places a high value not on suffering itself but on overcoming it; not on the humble acceptance of a defect but on mutiny against it; not on weakness alone, but on the impulses and sources of strength engendered in it. Thus, the new doctrine is diametrically opposed to the Christian understanding of the sick. At issue is not poverty but potential wealth of spirit; misery becomes the impulse for overcoming weakness and building up strength. There is a close affinity between Adler's ideal of strength or power and the philosophy of F. Nietzsche,[7] for whom the will to power was the primary motivating drive in man's psychological makeup. However, Adler's view that social significance is the ultimate goal of compensation just as clearly divorces psychology both from the Christian ideal of weakness and from the Nietzschean cult of individual strength.

Third, we must distinguish the doctrine of defect-overcompensation from the old, naive biological theory of organic compensation or, in any case, from the theory of the substitution of sensory organs [lit.:vicarious sensory organs]. Doubtless, this view already contained the first presentiment of that truth which states that the failure of one function serves as the impetus for the development of other compensatory functions. But this presentiment is expressed naively and is distorted. The relationship between sensory organs may be compared to the relationship between paired organs; touch and hearing directly compensate for the loss of sight in the same manner as one healthy kidney will take over the function of the other diseased one. In this case the impaired organ (the eye) automatically capitulates to the healthy organs and recedes into the background while the ear and skin, leaping over all sociopsychological instances, are stimulated to compensate. After all, loss of sight does not affect the vital and necessary functions. Science and practice have long since exposed the shortcomings of this theory. Factual research has shown that intensification of hearing and touch does not occur automatically as a result of impaired vision (K. Buerklen, 1924). On the contrary, in a blind child we are dealing not with the possibility of sight being automatically replaced but with the difficulties arising from its absence. These difficulties are resolved by the development of a psychological superstructure. Thus, we encounter the view that the blind possess a heightened memory, intensified attention, and enhanced verbal skills. A. Petzeld,[8] who has written the best work on the psychology of the blind (Petzeld, 1925), saw precisely the basic characteristic of overcompensation in this phenomenon. He proposes that what is the most distinctive feature in the personality of the blind is the power to internalize by means of speech the social experience of the seeing. H. Grisbach has shown that the teachings on the transference of one sense organ have not withstood criticism: a blind person is brought just as near to the seeing world as he is removed from it by this theory of transference (ibid., pp. 30–31).[*] There really is a kernel of truth in the theory that a defect is not limited to its isolated functional failure but also involves a radical reconstruction of the entire personality. A defect brings to life new psychological powers and gives them new direction. Only a naive understanding of the purely organic nature of compensation, a disregard of the sociopsychological aspect of this process, and an ignorance of the ultimate direction and overall nature of overcompensation distinguish the old doctrine from the new one.

Fourth, we must finally ascertain the true implications of Adler's doctrine judging by our recently formed therapeutic social pedagogy based on the data of reflex psychology. The distinction between these two circles of ideas can be summed up with the statement that our doctrine of conditional reflexes offers a new basis for constructing a mechanism for the educational process, the doctrine of overcompensation offers a new mechanism for understanding the very process of child development. Many authors, including this one, have analyzed the education of the blind and deaf from the point of view of conditional reflexes and have come to a more profound and important conclusion: There is no fundamental difference between the education of a seeing and a blind child. New conditional connections are formed identically from any input. The effect of organized external influences is a

---

[*] The reference seems to be to Petzeld who, apparently, cited Grisbach. No reference to Grisbach is supplied. [Ed.]

determining factor in education. The first school directed by I. A. Sokolianskii[9] worked out a new method for teaching deaf-blind children speech on the basis of this doctrine and with it achieved both amazing practical results and theoretical positions, which surpass the most progressive systems of European special eduction for the hearing impaired. We must not, however, stop here. It is impossible to think that theoretically all differences between the education of the blind, deaf, and normal children can be limited. This is impossible because, in fact, a difference exists and makes itself known. Historically, all past experiences with education for the deaf and the blind attest to this. It is still absolutely necessary to take into account the specific developmental characteristics of a child with a defect. The educator must become aware of those specific features and factors in children's development which respond to their uniqueness and which demand it. From a pedagogical point of view, a blind or deaf child may, in principle, be equated with a normal child, but the deaf or blind child achieves the goals of a normal child by different means and by a different path. It is also particularly important for the educator to know precisely the uniqueness of the path on which he must lead the child since it is impossible to state that blindness does not cause a profoundly unique main line of development.

Essentially, the ultimate character of all psychological acts—their future-oriented directedness— becomes apparent in the most elementary forms of behavior. Goal-oriented behavior had already been observed in the simplest forms of behavior which the Pavlovian school studied from the point of view of conditional reflex mechanisms. Among innate reflexes, Pavlov discovered a unique goal-oriented reflex. With this contradictory label he probably intended to point out two factors: (1) the fact that even here we are dealing with a reflex mechanism; and (2) the fact that this mechanism takes on the appearance of purposeful activity, that is, becomes intelligible only in relation to the future. "All life is the realization of one goal," says Pavlov, "the preservation of life." (1951, p. 308). Indeed, he called this reflex the reflex of life. "All of life's advancements, all its culture, are achieved by means of this goal-directed reflex and is achieved only by those people striving to attain a specific goal which they themselves have set" (ibid., p. 310). Pavlov straightforwardly formulated the significance of this reflex for education. His ideas coincide with the theory of compensation. "For a complete, true and fruitful manifestation of the goal reflex," he says, it must be placed under a specific amount of stress. An Anglo-Saxon, the highest embodiment of this reflex, knows this well, and therefore he will answer the question: 'What is the main condition for achieving a goal?' in a manner most unexpected and incredible to a Russian's eye and ear with the answer: 'The existence of obstacles.' It is as if he were saying: 'Let my goal-reflex exert itself in response to some obstacle and precisely then I will attain my goal, no matter how difficult it may be.' It is interesting that the possibility of failure is totally ignored with such an answer" (ibid., p. 311). Pavlov regretted that we do not have "any practical knowledge about such an important factor in life as the goal reflex; this knowledge is so essential in all areas of life, beginning with the most fundamental education" (ibid., pp. 311-312).[*]

C. Sherrington[10] has said the same about this reflex. In his opinion, a reflex reaction cannot really be understood by a physiologist without knowledge of its goal, and he can learn about this goal only by examining reaction in light of the whole organic complex of normal

---

[*] The Russian text does not provide for quotations within quotations. Thus Pavlov's ascriptions to a putative 'Anglo-Saxon' and Vygotsky's ascriptions to Pavlov are unclear in the Russian and were extrapolated in the translation. [Ed.]

functions. This position guarantees the right to synthesize both psychological theories. "The strategic position of the Adlerites," A. B. Zalkind states, "represents the very same dominant point, not only in general physiological terms but also in clinical and psychotherapeutic formulations" (quoted in *Advancements in Reflexology*, 1925, p. vi). The author sees the actual theoretical correspondence of these two theories as a confirmation of the "correctness of this basic path," along which both are headed (ibid.).

The experimental research, already cited, demonstrating that reaction may be strengthened and accelerated in the presence of opposing and obstructing stimulations, may be analyzed simultaneously with respect both to a manifestation of [an impulse for] dominance and a manifestation of overcompensation. L. L. Vasil'ev and I have described these phenomena under the label of dominant processes (Bekhterev,[11] and. Vasil'ev, 1926, L.S. Vygotsky, 1982). V.P. Protopopov[12] has shown that, judging by the greater persistency and intensity of concentration developing as reaction, "The physically handicapped surpass normal people" (1925, p. 26); he explained this by the characteristics of the dominant process. This means that the potential for overcompensation is greater in the handicapped.

It is impossible to analyze questions of education without a future perspective. Detailed examination will lead us to conclusions which attest to this fact. Thus, I. A. Sokolianskii came to the paradoxical conclusion that the education of the deaf-blind is easier than the education of the deaf-mute, the education of the deaf-mute easier than that of the blind, that of the blind easier than that of normal children while, in fact, this sequence is really established by the degree of complexity and difficulty of the pedagogical process. He saw in this the direct result of the application of reflexology to a reexamination of the views on abnormality. "This is not a paradox," asserts Sokolianskii, "but the natural deduction of the new views on the nature of man and the essence of speech" (in *The Ukrainian Herald of Reflexology...*, 1926). Protopopov came to a similar conclusion in his experimental research, namely that for the blind-deaf "the opportunity for social communication can be established with extreme ease (1925, p. 10).

How do such psychological presuppositions benefit pedagogy? It is absolutely clear that it is beneficial to compare the education of blind-deaf children with that of normal children on the basis of the degree of difficulty and complexity only when we have in mind equal pedagogical goals under various conditions (normal, hearing children). Only a common task and a single level of pedagogical achievements can serve as the overall measure of difficulty of education in both cases. It would be foolish to ask which is more difficult: to teach a gifted eight-year-old child the multiplication table or a retarded child advanced math. Here the ease in the first case is conditioned not by specific traits but by the easiness of the task. It is easier to teach a blind-deaf child because the level of his development, the aspiration for his development, and the educational goals to be met are minimal. If we wish to teach the normal child only the minimum, hardly anyone will argue that this would demand more work. On the contrary, if we were to assign the teacher of the deaf the same large-scale tasks facing the educator of a normal child, hardly anyone would undertake the task, let alone seek to do it with less effort. Who can more easily be developed into a specific social unit such as a worker, a shop-assistant or a journalist; a normal child or one who is blind and deaf? One can only answer this question in more than one way. As Protopopov states, for the deaf-mute the opportunities for social communication are easily established, however, in minimal proportions. A club for the deaf or a boarding school (*internat*) will never become the center of social life. Or let it first be proven that it is easier to teach a blind-deaf child to read a newspaper or to enter into social discourse, than it is a normal child. Such conclusions inevitably arise if we examine only the mechanics of education without taking into consideration the course of development of the child himself and his perspectives.

The operation of overcompensation is determined by two features: by the range and extent of a child's disability, the degree of divergence in his behavior, and the social demands made for his education, on the one hand, and by the compensatory reserve and the wealth and diversity of functions on the other hand. This reserve is meager in a blind-deaf child; his ineptness is huge. Therefore, it is not easier but immeasurably more difficult to educate blind-deaf children than normal children, if the same results are desired. As a result of all these constraints, what remains and has a deciding significance for education is the possibility that a child with defects may achieve full, even superior social standing. This is achieved exceedingly seldom. However, the possibility itself for successful overcompensation stands out like a blazing torch, like a lighthouse guiding the path of education.

To think that every defect will inevitably have a fortunate outcome is just as naive as it is to think that every illness will certainly be ultimately cured. Above all, we need a temperate view and realistic evaluations. We know that the problems in overcompensating such defects as blindness and deafness are enormous: the compensatory reserve is poor and insufficient and the developmental path exceedingly difficult.

Therefore it is even more important to know the correct direction. In fact, even Sokolianskii took this into account, and to it he owes the large success of his system. It is not this theoretical paradox which is so important for his method, but an excellent, practical, conditional setting for education. According to his method mimicry (sign language) not only becomes absolutely pointless but the children themselves do not use it even on their own initiative. On the contrary, oral speech becomes an insurmountable physiological need for them (in *The Ukrainian Herald of Reflexology*..., 1926). This is something about which not a single method in the world can boast and which serves as the clue for the education of the deaf-mute. If oral speech becomes a necessity and supplants mimicry for the children, then it means that instruction is directed along a line of natural overcompensation of deafness; its direction is in line with and not in conflict with the children's interests.

Traditional instruction in oral speech, like a worn cogwheel, did not mesh with the whole mechanism of a child's natural strengths and drives. It did not stimulate inner compensatory activity and was therefore ineffectual. Beaten into children with classical cruelty, oral speech became the official language of the deaf. The task of education, however, must be summed up as a mastery of a child's inner developmental strengths. If Sokolianskii's chain method has achieved this, then it is because the method in fact incorporated and mastered the forces of overcompensation. These initial successes are not a reliable indicator of the merits of the method; this is a question of techniques and their perfection. Finally, it is a question of practical success. Only the physiological need for speech ensures success and is of primary importance here. If the secret for creating this need (i.e., establishing the goal) has been discovered, it is speech itself.

The position established by Petzeld has the same meaning and value for the education of the blind: the possibility of knowledge for a blind person means the possibility of acquiring full knowledge of everything; a blind person's potential for understanding means basically the possibility of understanding everything completely (A. Petzeld, 1925). As the author sees it, two characterological features categorize the entire psychological makeup and structure of personality in a blind person: an unusual spatial limitation and a total mastery of speech. A blind person's personality grows out of the struggle between these two factors. To what extent Petzeld's principle will be realized in a blind person's life, what measures and what time frame will be needed for its implementation, are questions for the practical development of education. After all, even normal children, more often than not, fail to realize their full potential in the course of their education. Does the proletarian child really achieve that degree of development for which he has the potential? The same can be said of blind children. However, in order to correctly design even a modest educational plan, it is extremely important to discard the constraints limiting our mental outlook, that is, those constraints which supposedly, by their very nature, frame the special development of such a child. It is important that education aim to realize social potential fully and consider this to be a real and definite target. Education should not nurture the thought that a blind child is doomed to social inferiority.

Summing up, let us dwell on one example. Although in recent times scientific analysis has worked to deemphasize the legend of H. Keller, nevertheless her fate best illustrates the entire course of our thoughts developed here. One psychologist noted absolutely correctly that if Keller had not been blind and deaf, she would never have achieved the development, influence, and fame, which came her way. How is one to understand this? First of all, it means that her serious handicaps evoked enormous compensatory powers. But this is still not all: you see, her reserve of compensations was excessively meager. Secondly, this means that if it had not been for an exceptionally fortunate concurrence of circumstances, which transformed her handicap into social pluses, she would have remained an underdeveloped, plain inhabitant of provincial America. But Helen Keller became a sensation; she became the center of social attention; she turned into a celebrity, a national hero, into a miracle for many millions of American citizens. She became the pride of the people, a fetish. Her handicap became socially useful to her; it did not create an inferiority complex. She was surrounded by luxury and fame; special steamboats were even made available for her educational excursions. Her education became the concern of the entire country. Immense social demands were made of her: there were those who wanted to see her become a doctor, a writer, a preacher! And she became all of these. Now it is almost impossible to tell what really belonged to her and what was done for her by citizen demand. This fact best illustrates the role played by the social demand for her education. Keller herself wrote that if she had been born into a different setting, she would have sat in eternal darkness and her life would have been a wasteland, cut off from any communication with the outside world (1910). In her biography everyone recognized living proof of independence, strength and spiritual life, entrapped in the body's prison. Even given "ideal external influences on Helen Keller," one author writes,[13] "we would not have seen her rare book, if her dynamic, powerful, albeit caged-in spirit had not burst forth irrepressibly to meet this influence from the outside"* (H. Keller, 1910, p. 8). Understanding that the condition of being deaf-blind is not only the sum of two components and that "the essence of the concept of deafness and blindness goes much deeper" (ibid., p. 6), the author seeks this essence in a traditional religious, spiritual interpretation; yet the life of Helen Keller did not contain anything mysterious. Her life graphically demonstrates that the process of overcompensation can be defined entirely by two factors: by the popular social demand for her development and education, and by her reserve of psychological forces. This widespread social demand for Helen Keller's development and for a successful social victory over her handicaps determined her fate. Her defect not only did not become a brake but was transformed into a drive which insured her

---

* This translation is from Vygotsky's text, not from the quoted author. Also see endnote 13 for this chapter. [Transl.]

development. This is why Adler is right when he advises us to examine and act in connection with the integral life plan and its ultimate goal (A. Adler, 1927). Even Kant thought, according to A. Neyer, that we will understand an organism, if we analyze it as a rationally constructed machine; Adler advises us to examine the individual as a personified tendency toward development.

*   *   *

There is not a grain of stoicism in the traditional education of children with mental defects. This education has been weakened by a tendency toward pity and philanthropy; it has been poisoned by morbidness and sickliness. Our education is insipid; it nips the pupil in the bud; there is no salt to this education. We need tempered and courageous ideas. Our ideal is not to cover over a sore place with cotton wadding and protect it by various methods from further bruises but to clear a wide path for overcoming the defect, for overcompensation. For this we need to assimilate these socially oriented processes. However, in our psychological grounding for education, we are beginning to lose the distinction between the upbringing of animal offspring and the upbringing of children, between training and true education. Voltaire joked that, having read J. J. Rousseau,[14] he felt like walking on all fours. This is precisely the feeling which almost all our new science about the child evokes: it often examines a child as if he were on all fours. This notably, is what P. P. Blonskii recognized. "I like very much to put a toothless child in the pose of a four legged animal: it always tells me a lot personally" (1927, p. 27). Strictly speaking, science has studied the child only in this position. A. B. Zalkind calls this the zoological approach to childhood (1926). There can be no argument: this approach to the study of a human being as one of the animal species, as a higher mammal form, is very important. But this is not all and not even the main thing for the theory and practice of education. S. L. Frank,[15] continuing Voltaire's symbolic joke, says that, in contrast to Rousseau, nature for Goethe "does not negate, but straightforwardly demands the vertical position for man; it does not call man back to a simplified prehistoric primitivity, but forward toward the development and a greater complexity of human nature" (1910, p. 358). Of these two poles, the ideas expressed here are closer to those of Goethe than to those of Rousseau. If the doctrine on conditional reflexes traces man's horizontal course then, the theory of overcompensation gives him a vertical line.

Chapter 2

PRINCIPLES OF EDUCATION FOR PHYSICALLY

HANDICAPPED CHILDREN[1]

1

The Revolution, which redesigned our schools from top to bottom, barely affected the special schools for handicapped children. In schools for blind, deaf-mute and mentally retarded children, everything stands now precisely as it did before the Revolution, if one does not take into account a few unessential mechanical changes. Thus, work remains even now unrelated in theory and in practice to general principles of social education and to our Republic's system of public education. The problem is that in order to connect abnormal child education (education for the deaf, the blind, the mentally retarded, and so forth) with the general principles and methods of social education, we must find a system which would successfully coordinate special education with normal education. Before us stands the enormous creative task of rebuilding our schools on new principles. We must project basic policies for such an undertaking, in other words, start from the beginning.

Given all of its merits, our special school is noted for one basic shortcoming: be they blind, deaf-mute, or mentally retarded children, the special school locks its pupils into the narrow circle of the school collective; it creates a small, separated, and secluded world; everything is adjusted and adapted to the child's defect. Everything focuses attention on the physical handicap of the child and does not introduce the child to real life. Instead of helping children escape from their isolated worlds, our special school usually develops in them tendencies which direct them toward greater and greater isolation and which enhance their separatism. Because of these shortcomings, not only does the overall upbringing of the child become paralyzed but even special education sometimes amounts to almost naught. Take, for example, the speech of a deaf-mute child. In spite of excellent instruction in oral speech, the speech of a deaf child remains in embryo because the secluded world in which he lives does not create a need for it.

Such a secluded system of education for the blind, deaf-mute, and mentally retarded came to us from Germany, where it flourished and was developed to its logical limits.

Therefore, at first glance, it served as a tempting example. If you read the description of German special schools, you will see that they represent far from-ordinary-schools. They grew into a series of very complex institutions, which have as their final goal the expansion and advancement of certain special devices for blind and deaf-mute children, to which they have become accustomed in school and which they cannot do without. The number of institutions often exceeds several dozen. If you pursue this, you will learn that some well endowed schools even own small banks in order to open up credit for the blind and deaf-mute for the purpose of trading and trade activity in their future lives. All such institutions serve the same goal: social charity. In this way, a certain type of fortress is created, solidly conquering for itself a corner of the outside world, and nevertheless bequeathing a certain position on the defective child, even after leaving school. In Germany, even a university education for the blind has until now worn a certain distinction for its special system. The well-known Marburg University includes courses for the blind, which hospitably invite blind citizens from the USSR to come to receive a higher education. It is assumed that those blind persons who wish to specialize in an area of higher education should be separated from the general mass of the student population and placed under special conditions. Precisely because of this, on the one hand, Germany claims to have only an insignificant number of defective children, and, on the other, thanks to the fact that Germany has established maximum isolation of these institutions, many share an opinion about the strength and merit of the German system.

This system differs radically from our pedagogical practice. In our country, instruction and education of the blind and other handicapped children must be seen as a problem of social education; both psychologically and educationally this is a question of social education. In fact, it is exceedingly easy to notice that each physical handicap (be it blindness, deafness or mental retardation) causes, as it were, a social aberration. As soon as his defect is noted, a blind child, from the first days of his birth, acquires some special position even in his own family. His relations with the surrounding world begin to take a different course from that of a normal child. One can say that blindness and deafness mean not only a breach of the child's activity with respect to the physical world but, most importantly, a rupture of all systems which determine all functions of the child's social behavior. That this is actually so will become absolutely clear, it seems, if we fully explain this point of view. It is self-explanatory that blindness and deafness are biological factors, and in no way social. The fact of the matter is that education must cope not *so much with these biological factors as with their social consequences.*

When we have before us a blind child as a subject for education, then we have to deal not so much with blindness by itself as with those conflicts which face the blind child on his entrance into the world. At that time, all the systems which determine the child's social behavior are disrupted. And therefore, it seems to me from a pedagogical point of view, the education of such a child amounts to rectifying completely these social ruptures. It is as if we have before us a physically disjointed hand. We have to set the affected organ. The main goal is to correct the break in social interaction by using some other path.

I shall not go into a scientific analysis of the psychological conception of deaf-muteness or blindness. I permit myself to dwell only on those generally accepted notions which can usually be found in literature. *Blindness or deafness as psychological factors do not exist for the blind or deaf person himself.* We are wrong to imagine that a blind person is submerged in darkness, that he feels as though he has fallen into a dark pit. Corroborated both by objective analysis and the subjective impressions of the deaf themselves, sufficiently authoritative research has testified to the fact that such a conception is absolutely false. The blind do not directly sense their blindness, just as the deaf do not feel that they live in an oppressive silence. I would like to point out only that for the educator, as for any person dealing with a blind child in hopes of educating him, blindness exists not so much as a direct physiological factor but as a result of the social consequences of blindness with which he must cope.

In scientific literature and in public opinion, a false conception has taken firm hold about the nature of the biological compensation for a defect. It is believed that nature, in depriving us of one of the senses, seems to compensate by an extraordinary development of the remaining sense, that is, that the blind have an extremely acute sense of touch and that the deaf stand out for their strongly developed sight. Blindness and deafness have been understood in narrowly organic terms. The pedagogical approach to such children has also been from the point of view of biological compensation (for example, if we take out one kidney, then the other takes over the former's function). In other words, the question of defects has always been posed in crude physical terms. Our whole system of special education [has been], from this perspective, therapeutic or medicinal pedagogy. Moreover, it is clear to every educator that a blind or deaf-mute child is first of all a child and, on a second level, as the German psychologists say, a special child, a blind child or a deaf-mute child.

If, in good conscience, you accept the recently conducted psychological analysis of experiences connected with blindness and deafness (I refer to the most fundamental work in the area of the psychology of the blind, the work published by Buerklen this year), you will be able to see how the psychological makeup of a blind person arises not *primarily* from the physical handicap itself, but *secondarily* as a result of those social consequences caused by the defect. Our task consists of seeing to it that medicinal-therapeutical pedagogy does not deprive a child of normal nourishment, because the doctor is wrong who, when prescribing medicine for an ill person, forgets that the sick must also eat normally and that it is impossible to live by medicine alone. Such pedagogy produces an education which from the outset focuses on disability as a principle; as a result, we have something radically different from the fundamentals of social education.

The place of special education in the general educational system is extremely easy and simple to determine if we proceed from its position in relation to education as a whole. In the final analysis, any educational process may, as the physiologists now put it, be reduced to the creation of certain new forms of behavior; to the formation of conditional reactions or conditional reflexes. However, from a physiological point of view (a position more dangerous for us in this respect), the education of a defective child does not differ in principle from the education of a normal child. Blindness and deafness physiologically mean simply the absence of one of the sensory organs, as we used to say, or one of the analyzers, as the physiologists now say. This means that under the condition in which one of the paths of contact with the outside world is absent, it may, to a large measure, be compensated for by other paths.

The view of external, experimental physiology [sic],[*] which is a very important view for pedagogy, holds that conditional forms of behavior are in principle connected by the

---

[*] Vygotsky seems to be referring to what is, in English, regularly called "physiological psychology;" that branch of psychology descending from what Boring called the "psychological physiologists" of the late 19th century. [Ed]

same path with the various sensory organs, or various analyzers. A conditional reflex may be induced from the eye just as well as from the ear, from the ear just as from the skin, and consequently, when in the educational process, we exchange one analyzer for another, one channel for another, we have embarked on the path of social compensation for a given defect.

After all, it is not important that the blind should see letters. It is important that they should know how to read and to read in the same way that you and I read, and that they learn to do this just as normal children do. It is important that a blind person write, and not just move his pen around the paper. If he learns to write by perforating paper with a pen, we again have the same principle and practically an identical phenomenon. Therefore, the formula by Kurtman, who agrees that it is impossible to measure the blind, the deaf-mute and the mentally retarded by the same standard as the normal child must be reversed.

One should and must approach a blind and a deaf-mute child, psychologically and pedagogically, with the same standard used for a normal child.

Essentially there is no difference either in the educational approach to a handicapped child and to a normal one, or in the psychological organization of their personalities. P. Ia. Troshin's book (1915), now famous in our country, includes this extremely important idea. It is an error to see only illness in abnormality. In an abnormal child, we perceive only the defect, and therefore, our teachings about these children and our approaches to them are limited to ascertaining the percentages of their blindness, deafness or distortion of taste. We dwell on the "nuggets" of illness and not on the "mountains" of health. We notice only defects which are minuscule in comparison with the colossal areas of wealth which handicapped children possess. These absurd truisms, which, it would seem, are difficult to dispute, radically conflict with what we have to say in theory and practice about special education.

I have in my hand a booklet published in Switzerland this year.[2] In it we read some notions which to our educators sound like a great and important discovery: It is necessary to relate to a blind child just as one would to a seeing child, that is, to teach him to walk at the same time as a seeing child learns to walk, and to give him as much opportunity as possible to play with all children. In Switzerland, these notions are considered absurdities while in our country we believe the opposite to be true. It seems to me that there are two directions in special education implied here: orientation toward illness; orientation toward health. Both the statistics of our practical experience and the data from our scientific theory force us to recognize the first as a false direction for our special education. I could cite some data in this field but will limit myself to a reference to the accounts of the last congress in Stuttgart,[3] which took place this year, on questions of the education and well-being of the blind. Here, the German and the American systems came into conflict. The educational system of the former is oriented towards the shortcomings of a blind child, the other toward the child's remaining reserve of health. Although the collision of the two systems occurred in Germany, it turned out to be a shattering experience for the Germans. The German position proved to have no justification in life.

I allow myself to illustrate one point of special education upon which I am advancing as the main thesis. It can be formulated as follows: any question of special education is at the same time a question of special education in its entirety. For the deaf, only the organ for hearing is affected; all remaining organs are healthy. Because of his hearing impairment, the deaf child cannot learn human speech. It is possible to teach the deaf child oral speech by means of lipreading, by connecting the different representations of lip movement which accompany speech; in other words, it is possible to teach a child "to hear with his eyes." In this way, we can successfully teach the deaf to speak not only one specific language, but several languages with the help of kinesthetic (motor) sensations evoked during articulation.

This method of instruction (the German method) has all the advantages over other methods, such as the methods of mimicry (the French method), or the method of manual alphabet (dactylology, writing in the air), because such speech makes communication possible between the deaf and the hearing and serves as a tool for developing thought and consciousness. For us, there was no doubt about the fact that it is precisely oral speech, the oral method, which must be placed at the head of the agenda in education for the deaf-mute. However, as soon as you turn to practice, you will immediately see that this particular question is a question of social education as a whole. In practice, it turns out that instruction in oral speech has produced exceedingly deplorable results. This instruction takes up so much time, and it usually does not teach one to build phrases logically but produces pronunciation in place of speech; it limits vocabulary.

Thus, this approach causes an extremely difficult and confused situation, which theoretically is favorably resolved by one method, but in practice produces the opposite results. In German schools, where this method of teaching the deaf-mute oral speech is used, the greatest distortions of scientific pedagogy can be observed. Because of the exceptional cruelty and coercion applied to the child, he successfully learns oral speech, but his personal interest is lost along the way. Mimicry is forbidden in these schools and is cause for punishment. Nevertheless, educators have not found the means to eliminate mimicry. The famous school for the deaf, named after J. Vatter,[4] is renowned for its outstanding successes in this respect, but the lessons in oral speech are conducted with enormous cruelty. When forcing a pupil to master a difficult sound, the teacher could knock out his tooth and, having wiped the blood from his hand, he would proceed to the next sound.

This practical side of life is at odds with the method itself. The pedagogues assert that oral speech is unnatural for the deaf-mute; that this method is unnatural, since it contradicts the child's nature. In this case, we are convinced that neither the French, the German, the Italian, nor a combined method can offer a way out of this dilemma, that only the socialization of education can offer the solution. If a child has a need for oral speech, if the need for mimicry is eliminated, only then can we be assured that oral speech will develop. I am forced to address the specialists, and they find that the oral method is better verified by life. Within a few years after completion of school, when the students gather together, it turns out that, if oral speech was the condition for the children's existence, then they mastered this speech completely; if they had no need for oral speech, then they returned to the muteness with which they first entered school.

In our schools for the deaf-mute, everything conflicts with the children's real interests. All their instincts and drives become not our allies in the cause of education, but our enemies. We have produced a special method, which in advance is at odds with the child; before beginning, we want to break the child in order to engraft speech onto his muteness. And in practice this forced method turns out to be unacceptable, by its very nature it dooms speech to atrophy. From this I will not draw the conclusion that oral speech is unsuitable for our schools. I want only to say that not a single issue of special education can be addressed solely within the narrow framework of special education. The question of instruction in oral speech is not a question of methods of articulation. We must approach it from a different, unexpected angle.

If we [seek to] teach the deaf-mute to work [but] if he learns to make Negro rag dolls to sell and to make "surprises" and carry them around to restaurants, offering them to the guests, this is not vocational education but training to be beggars who find it more convenient to beg for alms with something in their hands. In such a situation, it might be more advantageous for a deaf person than for a speaking person because people will buy more readily from the former. If, however, life demanded oral speech[*] as an inescapable necessity, and if in general the question of vocational training were posed in normal terms, then one could be assured that the acquisition of oral speech in the schools for the deaf-mute would not pose such a problem. Any method may be carried to an absurdity. This has happened with the oral method in our schools. This question can be correctly resolved only if we pose it in all its breadth, as a question of social education as a whole. This is why it seems to me that all our work should be reexamined from beginning to end.

The question of vocational education for the blind compels us to come to the same conclusions. Labor is presented to children in an artificially prepared form, while the organization and collective components of labor have been excluded; these components are taken on by the seeing for themselves, and the blind person is left to work in isolation. What results can be expected when the pupil is only a laborer, on whose behalf someone else carries out the organizational work and who, not being accustomed to cooperation with others at work, turns into an invalid upon graduation from school? If our school introduced the blind child to industrial and professional labor which included the social and organizational elements, the most valuable educational elements resulting from vocational training for the blind might be totally different. Therefore, it seems to me that maximum orientation toward normal child activity must serve as the point of departure for our reexamination of special education. The entire problem is extremely simple and clear. No one would think of denying the need for special education. It is impossible to say that no special skills are needed by the blind, by the deaf and the mentally retarded. But these special skills and training must be subordinated to general education, to general training. Special education must merge with the overall child activity.

3

Let us turn to mentally retarded children. Even here, the basic problem is the same: the fusion of special and general education. Here, it seems the air is a bit fresher, and new ideas from the public school have already penetrated this area. But even here, the basic problem has remained unsolved up until now, and in this case, the puny calves of special education push out the fatted calves of mainstream education. In order to illustrate, I will dwell on how A. N. Graborov[5] resolved this question in his book *The Auxiliary School* (1925), the best book we have at our disposal in this area. I will say in advance that here this question has been decided basically in the old way—to the advantage of the fat calves. The author is completely right when he says that methods developed from practical experiences of educating mentally retarded children have significance not only for the auxiliary school, but also for the regular public school. It is so much more important to be able to clearly and distinctly define the fundamental positions of auxiliary education. It is even more important for special education to understand definitively certain fundamental laws of general education. Unfortunately, neither foreign nor Russian literature clearly defines either. Scientific

---

[*] "Oral speech" is not a pleonasm for Vygotsky. He writes also about "written speech." The term *speech* must be taken to mean approximately "linguistic communication." See *Volume 1: Problems of General Psychology* of *The Collected Works*. [Ed.]

thought has still not penetrated the barrier between the theory of normal child development and the theory of abnormal development. Until this is accomplished, until accounts have been completely squared off between abnormal pedagogy and general pedagogy, both will remain incomplete, and defectology will inevitably be without principles. This could not have been more clearly stated in Graborov's book. The book is a breath of fresh air without any doubt, and the author wants to keep abreast of the new approach to education—he wants to but he is not able to.

These are only a few minor points, which when carefully reviewed turn out to be not simply details, but indications of the groundlessness which we have just mentioned. In actual studies of abnormal development and its various forms, physical abnormality has been distinguished from psychological abnormality. In the second category, we find mentally retarded children (but are they *physically* healthy?) as well as children "with partial failure in only the emotional, volitional sphere." "In this case you almost always find deficient development of the intellect" (A. N. Graborov, 1925, p. 6). Here you have a model of the vague manner in which the question of moral deficiency has been conceptualized. Precisely in these few lines, mentioned in passing, we find pedagogical negligence, carelessness, inconsistency, and weakness. We also find the weak psychological hypothesis that insufficient mental development causes problems in the emotional-volitional sphere: "In any discussion or effort to arrive at a decision, the struggle among motives is usually insignificant; motives of a moralistic or lawful nature are usually ignored by the subject, and egotistical tendencies tend to prevail" (ibid.).

How simple it all is! The trouble is not that the author expresses himself at times with vagueness and confusion; the trouble is, rather, that we have no clear-cut conception of child defectology, and it is impossible to build any pedagogical theory on such fogginess. Whenever there is a "prevalence" of egotistical motives, any approach to child education becomes impossible. After this, we are not surprised by the author's following assertion: "A defective child in the classroom means the breeding ground for contagion within the school" (ibid., p. 20). It comes as no surprise that the German system is partial to an isolated educational system, in which the "auxiliary school makes no attempt to return to the normal [mainstream] school within a certain time period the children entrusted to them" (ibid., p. 29). The fundamental understanding of child defectology, as it is practiced according to English law and American juridical practice, with all types of organic idiosyncrasies, is suddenly transformed into a new pedagogical theory. The pedagogical side of the matter is therefore overflowing with judgmental errors. No, the judgments, taken separately are *approximately* true, (that is to say they are sometimes true but at the same time not true) because the theory as a whole is full of that fundamental groundlessness which has characterized psychological theory. *Third*, the author says that during schooling "we must implant in him {the child—L.V.} firmly established habits of social behavior" (ibid., p. 59). And finally, *fourth*, "it is necessary to adequately orient the child to his surrounding world" (ibid.).

The above named necessities come third and fourth. Well, what comes first and second? Enculturation of the senses and psychological medical support. Here again we have not details but the cornerstone. If enculturation of the senses and psychological support are of primary importance, and social habits and orientation to the surrounding world are *third* and *fourth*, we have not traveled a single step from the "classical" system of therapeutic pedagogy with its nursing home atmosphere, with its zealous attention to microscopic illnesses, with its naive confidence that the psychological makeup may be developed, cured, "*brought into harmony"* and so forth, by *therapeutic* measures without regard for the general development of "habits of social behavior."

Inasmuch as our system resolves the main issue of any educational program in defectology,—namely the interaction between general and special education—it is reflected in a basic view of the problem. Must we medically treat the defect "in a handicapped child," concentrating three-fourths of his education on the correction of this defect, or must we develop the enormous deposits and deep layers of psychological health within the child? "All work is of a compensatory, corrective nature," says the author (ibid., p. 60); and with that statement the core of his system is revealed. Other approaches, such as the biogenetic point of view, "the discipline of the natural causes" (ibid., pp. 64, 72), concur totally with this statement. And the same could be said of the vague phraseology which accompanies attempts to define the "final" goal for "vocational education" as "harmonious development," and so forth (ibid., p. 77). One asks oneself: Are these details which the editor inadvertently left in, or are they essential elements of a theory doomed to scientific and pedagogical groundlessness inasmuch as they represent a system of education without a precise point of departure? For a resolution one turns, of course, not to comments made in passing, but to those chapters which elaborate on the question, where there is to be found a system of "exercises in psychological orthopedy" (a psychological support system) (ibid., Chapter 14) with its classic "lessons in silence" and, along the same lines, *Egyptian labor** for children, senseless, burdensome, synthetic and futile. I have selected a few items as examples:

> Exercise #1...On the count of one, two, three, complete silence is to be established. The end of the exercise is signaled by the teacher's rap on the table. Repeat 3 or 4 times, hold to the count of 10, then 15, 20, 30 seconds. The pupil who does not hold out (who turns around, begins to talk, etc.), has to continue on an individual basis or in groups of 2–3 people. The class follows...

> Exercise #2. On command silence is established. The teacher gives one of the pupils a task which must be executed as quietly as possible. After each exercise is completed, a 20–30 second rest follows, then discussion. The number of exercises equals the number of pupils in the class...Examples: 1) Misha, going up to the board, takes chalk and puts it on the table. Then, he is to take his seat quietly, and so forth. Quiet.

And so on and so on. In another exercise: "hold the position you have assumed as long as possible" (ibid., pp. 158–159).

> Give each child a thin book with a hard cover or a small board of an appropriate size, which must be held horizontally. On this plane he must hold a piece of chalk, or even better, a small stick whittled out of wood about 10-12 cm. in length and about 1–1.5 cm. in diameter. The slightest movement will topple this stick over. In the first position, a child stands, with his heels together, toes apart, and holds the small board in both hands; another pupil sets the stick on it {they should take a photograph!— L.V.}...

> Exercise #4: the same exercises ... only without spreading the feet: toes together" (ibid., p. 159).

---

* Slave labor. The reference is, apparently, Biblical; to *Exodus*. The italics are Vygotsky's. [Transl., Ed.]

One can say without a vestige of polemical fervor or exaggeration that the senselessness of these exercises is striking and by far exceeds the nonsense of the old German book of translations, although they are both in the same category: "Do you play the violin?" "No, my little friend, but this man's aunt is going abroad." The exact same senselessness.

Moreover, all the exercises in psychological support and the cultivation of the senses constitute similar nonsense: one must learn to finish as quickly as possible the tasks of carrying a dish full of water, threading beads, throwing rings, unstringing beads, tracing letters, comparing tables, striking an expressive pose, studying smells, comparing the strength of smells. Who can be reared from all of this? Does this not sooner transform a normal child into a mentally retarded child rather than develop in the retarded child those *mechanisms of behavior, psychology, and personality which have not yet meshed with the sharp teeth of life's intricate gears*? How does this all differ from "the sharp teeth of the little mice of our neighbor" in the French primer? If you bear in mind that "each exercise is repeated frequently in the course of a series of lessons" (ibid., p. 157), and that precisely these exercises constitute "the first and second place" among the school's priorities (ibid., p. 59), then it becomes clear that until we dispense with pre-scientific pedagogy and turn the auxiliary school 180 degrees on its axis, we will develop *nothing* with our conical stick (of 10–12 cm. length and 1–1.5 cm. in diameter) on a thin board and will achieve nothing in our attempt to educate the retarded child, but instead only force him into greater retardation.

This is not the place for a full development of all the positive possibilities for exercises in psychological support and sensorimotor control at play, at work activity, and in a child's social conduct. However, one cannot help but mention that these same lessons in silence, if conducted without commands and with meaning, regulated by real need, and by the mechanism of play, would suddenly lose the character of Egyptian torture and would serve as an excellent educational means. The argument is not whether or not to teach a child to observe silence, but which means to employ to this end. Do we need lessons in obedience upon command or lessons in purposeful, meaningful silence? This frequently cited example illustrates the overall description of the difference between the two different systems: the old, therapeutic system and the new social pedagogy. And what does segregation of the sexes mean in the education of mentally retarded children other than a harsh retreat into the recesses of the old theory and digression into its isolated positions (A. N. Graborov, 1925)? It is embarrassing to repeat these absurd truths about the pointless separation of the sexes and about the direct benefit of acquainting boys and girls with each other, as if these truths applied tenfold to a retarded child. Where, if not in school, will a retarded boy have real human contact with girls? What will seclusion in his already *extremely barren and meager life* do for him besides intensify his instinctual drives? And all the wise reasoning about the "appropriate exercise of satisfaction" will not save the theory at its most vulnerable point. "You cannot give a child candy and then use it as an incentive to do something right. The reverse should be true ... Suffering precedes pleasure" (ibid., p. 100). As a result the candy comes afterward, and that's all there is to it.

No, it is impossible to construct a theory and system of education on good intentions alone, just as it is impossible to build a house on sand. If we begin to say as well that the "goal of education is to create a harmonious education," and by harmony we mean "the manifestation of a creative individuality," etc., we will create *nothing*. The new pedagogy for the handicapped child demands, first of all, a courageous and decisive rejection of the outdated as-old-as-Adam systems, with lessons in silence, beads, orthopedy and cultivation of the senses, and second of all, a disciplined, sober, and conscientious assessment of the real goals of social education for such a child. These are the necessary and unavoidable prerequisites for the long-overdue and slow-in-coming revolutionary reform of [the education for] handicapped children. For all their freshness, such books as that by A. N. Graborov have come only halfway. From these examples, it is clearly seen that the special problems—such as teaching speech to deaf-mute children, training blind children in vocations, establishing sensorimotor control among the mentally retarded, and, indeed all questions of special education—can be answered only on the basis of social education as a whole. It is impossible to decide them in isolation.

4

It appears to me that the development of our school represents an extremely outdated form of education in comparison with the practice of the West Europeans and the Americans. We are a good ten years behind in comparison with the techniques and devices of the West European schools, and it would seem to us that it is necessary to be on an equal footing with them. But, there are two answers to the question of what constitutes success in Europe and America. On the one hand, this success includes features which we need to cultivate in our schools, and on the other hand, these steps were taken in precisely a direction which we must categorically reject. For example, the achievements by the Germans in the area of work with the blind have caused quite a sensation around the world. (I dwell on this aspect, because it is elucidated in S. S. Golovin's book.[6]) The work is connected with the name of P. Perls,[7] and the results can be formulated in one phrase: the introduction of the blind into heavy industry on the basis of real, very successful experience.

For the first time in the history of mankind, the blind have begun to work with complex machinery, and this experiment has proved very fruitful. The Berlin Commission on the Investigation of Professions Suitable for the Blind recognized 122 professions beyond of that narrow circle of professions set aside for the blind (blind musicians, choristers, craftsmen and the helpless), the greater part of which are connected with jobs in heavy industry.

In other words, the highest form of labor (polytechnical skills and social, organizational experience) turned out to be absolutely suitable for the blind. Nothing needs to be said about the colossal value such a statement has for pedagogy. It is tantamount to the notion that it is possible to overcome this handicap by granting the blind full entry into the labor force.

One must take into consideration that this experiment involved those who became blind during the war and that we make expect to encounter some difficulties when we turn to those who were born blind. Yet there is no doubt that theoretically and practically, this experience, on the whole, can be applied to those born blind. Let us note two important principles which serve as the basis of assumption for this work. The first is that the blind will work side by side with the seeing. In no job will the blind work by themselves, alone in isolation. They will definitely work together in cooperation with the seeing. Such a system of cooperation has been worked out so that it is easier to apply it to the blind. The second principle is that the blind are not to specialize in one machine or job alone. For pedagogical reasons, they are to transfer from one division of machinery to another; they are to switch from one machine to another because general polytechnical fundamentals are needed for participation in production as a conscientious worker. I will not begin to cite passages. I suggest, however, reading those sections from Golovin's work where he lists the machines on which the blind are to work: presses, punching presses, cutting machines, threading machines, drills, electric lathes, and so forth. Hence, the labor of the blind turns out to be fully suitable for heavy industry.

This is the healthy and positive side of European and American special pedagogy to which I have already referred. This aspect we must adopt for our special schools. But I must say that in all countries up until now, these accomplishments have been directed along a course which is at its very core profoundly alien to us. You know how sharply our social education differs from that of the Americans and the Germans. According to our general direction, the use of new pedagogical technology must proceed along a completely different path; it should be swung around 180 degrees. I shall not begin now to comment concretely about how this path will be realized, because I would have to repeat the truisms of overall social pedagogy, on the basis of which our system of social education is constructed and contained. I allow myself simply to make the following points: There is only one essential guiding principle for overcoming and compensating for the various defects—pedagogy must orient itself to a lesser degree toward deficiency and illness and to a greater degree toward the norm and the child's overall health.

What constitutes our radical divergence from the West with respect to this question? Only the fact that there it is a question of *social welfare*, whereas for us it is a question of *social education*. There it is a question of charity for invalids and social insurance against crime and begging. It is extremely difficult to get rid of the philanthropic, invalid-oriented point of view. We often hear assertions that biogenetic cases are of interest not as much for special education as for social disdain. The way the question was posed amounts to a *radical untruth*. The question of educating handicapped children has until now been kept in the background mainly because more pressing questions demanded our attention during the first years of the Revolution. Now the time has come to bring the question before wide public attention.

Chapter 3

THE PSYCHOLOGY AND PEDAGOGY

OF CHILDREN'S HANDICAPS[1]

1

Any physical handicap, be it deafness, blindness or inherent mental retardation, not only changes a person's attitude toward the world, but first and foremost affects his relationship with people. Any physical defect, or flaw, is conceived as a behavioral abnormality. Even within his or her family, a deaf or blind child is first of all a special child, toward whom one develops an exclusive, unusual attitude, which is different from that toward other children. To begin with, the child's misfortune changes his social position within the family. And this occurs not only in those families where such a child is seen as a heavy burden and an infliction, but also in those families where the blind child is surrounded by redoubled love, by care and tenderness increased tenfold. Precisely in these families the increased dosage of attention and pity is a heavy burden on the child and serves as a fence separating him from the rest of the children. V.G. Korolenko[2] in a short novel about a blind musician, faithfully illustrates how a blind child became the center of the family and its unconscious despot, and how the entire house conformed to his slightest whim.

Later on, the physical handicap gives rise to a completely unique social setting unlike that in which a normal person lives. Any breach of human "associative activity" (to use an expression of V. M. Bekhterev) results in the actual disruption of the entire system of social relations. All contacts with people, all aspects defining a person's "geometric" place in his social milieu, his role and fate as a participant in life, all the functions of daily life are realigned from a new standpoint. A physical defect somehow causes a social dislocation, absolutely analogous to a physical dislocation, when, for example, an injured limb—a hand or foot—slips out of joint, when correct nourishment is disrupted, when an organ's normal function, connections and joints are abruptly disconnected, when the organ's operation is accompanied by pain and inflammation. Both the thoughtful testimonies by the blind themselves and the simplest everyday observations of a handicapped child's life, in conjunction with the statistics gathered from psychological scientific analysis, attest to this fact.

76

Unfortunately according to scientific pedagogical literature and the common view, questions regarding handicapped children have up until now been posed and decided as mainly a biological problem. Each physical handicap has been studied predominantly from the viewpoint of those changes which it introduces into the biological formation of the personality in its relationship to the natural, physical world. In this respect, pedagogues always talk about compensation which, when accompanied by training, can make up for one of the organ's impaired functions. Thus, the question has been posed within the narrow limitations of a given organ, which can be trained to develop certain skills in order supposedly to compensate for a deficiency in much the same way that a second kidney may take over the operation of an impaired kidney.

More simply speaking, from both the psychological and the pedagogical points of view the question has commonly been posed in crude physical and medical terms. A physical handicap has been analyzed and compensated for as just that, a handicap. Blindness has been defined as simply the absence of sight, deafness the absence of hearing, as if we were dealing with a blind dog or a deaf jackal. In addition to that, we have lost sight of the fact that, in contrast with the case of animals, a physical handicap in a human being can never affect the personality directly because the eye and ear of a human being are not only physical organs but also social organs, because between the world and a human being stands his social environment, which refracts and guides everything proceeding from man to the world and from the world to man. Human beings do not have simple, asocial, direct communication with the world. A loss of vision or hearing means, therefore, first and foremost the failure of serious social functions, the degeneration of societal ties, and the disruption of all behavioral systems. In psychology and pedagogy, the problem of a child's handicap must be posed and comprehended as a social problem, because the social aspect, which formerly went unnoticed and was usually considered secondary, in fact, turns out to be paramount and central. This must be placed at the head of our list. We must boldly look at this social problem as such, straight on. If, psychologically speaking, a physical handicap means a social dislocation, then the pedagogical training of such a child means putting him back on life's course just as one resets a sprained or aching organ. A few of the simplest considerations are called for to affirm this thought.

First and foremost, it is necessary to part with long outdated scientific theory, still flourishing in public opinion because of the existing legend about the biological compensation for a physical handicap. The opinion seems to exist that nature, when depriving a man of one sensory organ (an eye or an ear), endows the other organs with greater receptivity, as if compensating for the fundamental handicap. Thus, miraculous half-truths exist about unusual sensations of touch in the blind and of sight in the deaf. We find the basis for these tales in the true observation that with the failure of one perceptory organ, others seem to replace it and begin to carry out functions which they normally do not perform. A blind person learns more about things with the help of his hands than does a seeing man. A deaf person deciphers human speech according to lip movements, which no hearing person normally does. According to research data, however, neither the sense of touch of a blind person nor the sight of a deaf person exhibit any thing unique in comparison with the normal development of those senses in the hearing and seeing.

Apropos of this, A. V. Birilev[3] says: "In all these cases, the sense of touch, as experienced by the blind on the basis of elementary, rudimentary tactile sensations, does not differ significantly from this sense in normal people" (1901, p. 5). The difference in the subtlety of tactile sensations in the sighted and the blind has still to be established by precise research. If, in isolated cases, a difference in the sense of touch may actually be ascertained, then it occurs in such an insignificant degree that it in no way explains to us that enormous difference between the sense of touch in the blind and the same sense in the sighted, a difference which anyone can easily observe.

Sight allows a deaf-mute to see differently many things which we do not notice; his visual perception is, however, often inferior to that of a normal person, and in any case, not superior. N. M. Logovskii[4] asserts that in rare cases "the [eye] of the deaf-mute is developed to such a degree that ordinary sight is surpassed [no ref]."

An exceptional sense of touch in the blind or an extraordinary sense of sight in the deaf can be fully explained by the special conditions in which the organs are placed. In other words, the reasons for this are not constitutional or organic, resulting from some peculiarity in the organ's structure or in the nervous system, but are functional, appearing as a result of prolonged use of a given organ for different purposes than is the case in normal people.

If a blind person knows how to read with his hand and can easily decipher that chaos of raised dots—or so a printed page of Braille seems to every seeing person—then this happens only because, for a blind person, each combination of dots constituting a separate letter is repeatedly accompanied by a corresponding sound. The sound signifies this letter and is associated with it just as closely as the visual inscription of the letter is linked to sound for us. Consequently, on the basis of a blind person's previous tactile experience (different from that of a seeing person), each combination of Braille dots, when touched by the blind persons, will stimulate a reaction corresponding to the sound. The sounds make up words, and the chaos of dots is structured into an intelligible text. This process is completely analogous to a visual text for normal people, and from a psychological point of view there is no fundamental difference. For an illiterate person the average page of a book will seem like an incoherent conglomeration of unintelligible signs, just as Braille seems to our fingers. At issue here is not a superior or inferior sense of touch, but literacy, that is to say, previous experience in deciphering, perceiving, and interpreting, be it by means of our letters or by Braille dots. A seeing person may learn to read Braille script with his fingers as easily as a blind person. Completely analogous is the process of lip-reading speech by visually following lip movements which produce this or that sound. Thus in the same way, a deaf person learns to "listen with his eyes." Here again this skill is not based on a particular development of sight, but on the unique aspect of his literacy; on the associations between certain movements and the appearance of a given object, and so forth.

All these processes may be quite correctly represented as processes which cultivate conditional responses to certain conditional signs or signals (stimuli) and which may fully comply with all the mechanisms of training conditional reflexes, mechanisms established by I. P. Pavlov (1951) and by V. M. Bekhterev (1928). The frequent coincidence in time of two stimulations (a specific sound in conjunction with a given combination of dots) results in the fact that a new stimulation (the dots) may by itself provoke the same reaction as the sound which coincides with it at the same moment. The new tactile stimulus seems to become the substitute for the former, acoustic one. The laws which govern the delay of and differentiation of conditional reflexes fully account for the process of rapidly deciphering Braille letters.

Based on this objective analysis of higher mental activity in animals and in human beings, one may draw the fundamentally important conclusion that a conditional reflex may be trained to react to *any* external stimulation, no matter whether it comes from the eye, the ear, the skin and so forth. A dog learns to salivate in an identical way in response to a blue light, to the beat of a metronome or to a scratch behind its ear. It is only of importance that a new conditional stimulus coincides a few times with a fundamental, innate, unconditional stimulus. Any element of the environment, any component of the world, any phenomenon may act as a conditional stimulation. The processes of training a conditional reflex will be the same in all cases. Precisely this law is the most important, fundamental position for the pedagogy of handicapped children—namely, the law that the training of conditional reactions in the blind or in the deaf (touching dots to read or reading lips to hear) is essentially the identical process. Consequently, the educational process for the handicapped remains essentially the same as for normal children. The only difference is that, while in individual cases (blindness or deafness) one organ of perception (analyzer) is replaced by another, the qualitative content of the reaction itself remains the same as for the entire mechanism of training. In other words, psychologically the behavior of the blind and the deaf-mute may be fully equated to normal behavior. In principle, the education of the blind and the deaf is in no way different from the education of a normal child.

One must adopt the idea that blindness and deafness do not mean anything other than the absence of one of the means of forming conditional ties with the environment. The eye and the ear—called receptors in physiology and organs of perception or external senses in psychology—have a biological purpose: they alert the organism to distant changes in the environment. These senses, according to the interpretation of G. Decker (1923), serve as outposts of our organism in its struggle for survival. Their immediate task is to perceive and analyze external environmental elements and to break down the world into the separate components with which our purposive reactions must deal, in order to adapt our behavior as closely as possible to the environment. By itself, as a whole complex of reactions, human behavior remains, strictly speaking, undisturbed. A blind or deaf person is capable of the entire scope of human behavior, that is, of an active life. The uniqueness of the child's education can be summed up as the substitution of one way of forming conditional links for another. We repeat once again: The theory and psychological mechanism of education in this case are the same as for a normal child. If we explain the extraordinary sense of touch in the blind and sight in the deaf in the same way, then it follows that these sensory peculiarities owe their origin to the functional abundance of conditional associations transferred to these organs from other, no longer functioning ones.

Neither a blind person's sense of touch nor a deaf person's sight play the same role in their behavioral systems as they do in the behavioral systems of normal seeing and hearing persons. The duties and functions of touch and behavior are different with respect to the organism: they must make a huge number of connections with the environment, connections which for normal people occur in other ways. The produced functional wealth of these senses is acquired through experience and is often mistaken for something inherent, structural and organic.

By rejecting the myth of biological compensation and by correctly understanding the psycho-physiological nature of training compensatory reactions, we may approach in earnest the key issue with respect to pedagogical theories about the handicapped, namely, the role and significance of special pedagogy (education for the blind and the mute) within the overall educational system, and its relationship to general educational principles. Before resolving this question, let us sum up our conclusions. We can say that our psychological survey has in principle not turned up any particular, outstanding individual pedagogy for the handicapped child. The education of a defective child constitutes the topic of only one chapter in the general theory of pedagogy. Hence, it directly follows that all questions of this difficult chapter must be reexamined in the light of general principles of pedagogy.

2

The fundamental position of traditional special education for handicapped children was formed by Kurtman [no ref]. He considered it inappropriate to apply the measurements for normal children to blind, deaf or mentally deficient children. In theory and in practice, this position is the widely accepted alpha and omega of special education in both Europe and in our country. We, however, hold precisely the reverse psychological and pedagogical position: One can and must measure the blind, the deaf-mute and the mentally retarded by the same measures which are applied to a normal child. "Essentially there is no difference between a normal and abnormal child," says P. Ia. Troshin, "both are human beings; both are children; for both development follows certain laws. The difference lies only in the means of education" (1915, p. xiii). This assertion comes from a researcher who stands closer to a biological rather than a social viewpoint on questions of psychology and pedagogy. Nevertheless, he cannot help but note that "a child's abnormality constitutes the product of abnormal social conditions in the vast majority of cases" (ibid., p. xv). The greatest mistake occurs when "one sees in abnormal children only disease, forgetting that in addition to illness, they still have a normal psychological life which—on the strength of particular conditions—takes on such a primitive, simple and understandable form, which we will not find in normal children." (ibid., p. 2).

The greatest mistake—the view of a child's abnormality as only an illness—has made our theory and practice subject to a most dangerous delusion. No matter what the affliction may be, whether it be blindness, deafness, catarrhs of the Eustachian tube, or perversion of taste, we meticulously analyze every corpuscle of the defect, every little speck of disease found in abnormal children, while we never notice the gold mines of health inherent in each child's organism, no matter what the affliction may be.

It is beyond understanding why this last, simple notion has not become a scientific, practical truism, and why until now special education has been spent 90 percent of its time on the children's illness and not on their health. "First, a human being and only then, second, an exceptional human being, that is, a blind person." Here is the slogan for a scientific psychology of the blind, which first and foremost incorporates the general psychology of a normal person and only "on a secondary level," considers the special psychology of the blind (F. Gerhardt, 1924, J. Buerklen, 1924). It is necessary to state outright that blindness (or deafness) in no way exists as a psychological factor for the blind person (or the deaf person) himself. A seeing person's notion that blindness means living in constant darkness (or that deafness means complete submersion in silence and muteness) is an incorrect, naive opinion, representing a false attempt on the part of normal seeing people to delve into the psychology of the blind. We want to imagine how a blind person experiences his blindness, and to this end, we come up with some preconceived notions based on our own daily, normal personal experience from which we subtract light and visual perception of the world. A. M. Shcherbina (1916), a blind person himself, has demonstrated rather convincingly and graphically that this typical notion is incorrect and, especially from a psychological point of view, that this is a completely inaccurate picture of the inner life of the blind child which V. Korolenko painted.

A blind person does not directly sense the dark and *in no way* feels submerged in blackness; "he makes no effort to free himself from the curtain of darkness," and, generally speaking, in no way senses his blindness. "Unbounded darkness" is never directly felt by a blind man, and his psychological condition in no way suffers pain as a result of his lack of vision. Darkness not only appears to the blind person as immediate reality but is even consecrated by him "with a certain intensity of thought," according to the evidence presented by Shcherbina (1916, p. 5). As a psychological phenomenon, blindness in no way means unhappiness. Blindness becomes a tragedy only as a social phenomenon. A blind person's failure to see light does not correspond with the sensation that a seeing person has when wearing a blindfold. Rather, a "blind person" fails to see light with his eyes in the same way a seeing person fails to see it with his hand, to use the wonderful analogy of A. B. Birilev (1924, p. 81). Therefore, whoever agrees with Korolenko's view that an instinctive, organic attraction to light constitutes the basis of a blind person's psychology errs grossly. Of course, the blind person wants to see, but this appears to him not as an unfulfillable organic need, but as "a practical and pragmatic" need. As a rule, Shcherbina asserts, the blind person's unique psychological mind-set forms and evolves "as if by second nature: in this situation," he testifies, "I was not able to directly sense my own physical shortcoming" (1916, p. 10).

This constitutes our essential point. Blindness is not a disease but the normal condition for a blind child; he senses his uniqueness only indirectly and secondarily as a result of his social experience.

How, then, does a blind person experience blindness? In various ways, depending on the conditions in which his defect is realized. In any case, that stone in his heart, that intense sadness, that inexpressible grief which forces us to pity a blind person and think with horror about his life—all this originates as a result of secondary social factors, not biological ones. A blind person's conception of the world is not devoid of objective reality. The world is not revealed to a blind person as if through a haze or a curtain. We have completely failed to take into account how the blind organically and naturally develop almost miraculous powers of touch. The thought that the blind are not only not poorer but in fact richer than the seeing borders on scientific truth. The famous blind deaf-mute Helen Keller wrote that the sense of touch gives a blind person certain delightful truths, which a seeing person must do without, since this sense for him has not been perfected.

Thus the so-called sixth (thermal) sense allows the blind to detect objects at a distance, and the seventh sense (perception of vibrations) allows the deaf to catch movement, music, and so forth. Neither sense represents, of course, anything specifically new for the normal mind. In fact, they are merely those senses which normal children possess, but in the blind, they are developed to perfection. Yet, we cannot imagine what significance these senses can have for the processes of learning about the world. Obviously, to us it will seem pathetic when a deaf person, upon listening to a piece played on the piano, exclaims: "Oh, how beautiful! I feel it with my feet" (Decker, 1923, p. 91), but this fact is very important in itself. Music, thunder, the roar of the sea exist for the deaf, as H. Keller has testified, just as night and day, distant objects, size and form, and so on exist for the blind (A. A. Krogius,[5] 1907).

The unfortunate lot of the blind is not brought about by the physical condition of blindness, which by itself is not a tragedy. Blindness serves only as the ground for the onset of a series of tragedies. "Lamentations and sighs," Shcherbina asserts, "accompany a blind person throughout his entire life; thus, slowly, but surely an enormously destructive process sets in" (1916, p. 39). He describes an incident in a school for the blind when "the attendant had to feed an eight-year old boy with a spoon simply because his family never permitted him the opportunity of learning to eat by himself" (ibid., p. 40). Here is why pedagogical hygiene quite correctly recommends treating a blind child just as one would a sighted child; he must start school at the same time as all other children and must learn to help himself; he must be forced to play with seeing children (*lasst es soviel wie moeglich mit sehenden Kindern spielen*); never allow him to feel pity for himself because of his blindness and so forth. As a result, blindness will be experienced by the blind as a "series of minor inconveniences," in the words of Shcherbina (ibid., p. 39). And many blind persons subscribe to his opinion: "Along with all this, life for me has had its own singular charm, which I would not give up for anything no matter what the personal pleasure" (ibid.). In answer to the particular and highly instructive question about whether or not a blind person knows light, A. V. Birilev, himself blind, has shown which fundamentally important pedagogical deductions should be made from the psychological assertion that one must know light. This is necessary not for the reason that a blind person instinctively yearns for light; when acquiring knowledge of light, it is not necessary to translate the world of colors into the language of sounds and so forth. "Light represents the conditions of activity for all others; those practical conditions, the influence of which one must assess accurately in order to understand both another's and one's own modes and rules of behavior stemming from these conditions" (A. V. Birilev, 1924, p. 93). A blind person must know that he is not seen from the street if he is standing behind a window curtain; that when a light is burning in his room and the windows have no curtains, everyone will see him, and so forth. He must possess the most essential knowledge accessible to the average person through the eyes. Humanity conceives of the world mainly as a visual phenomenon, and we must prepare the blind child for a life in this world. Subsequently, he must know what light is. With respect to the most critical question of educating the blind, the only correct, realistic point of view suggests this solution.

In the process of educating the blind, even the problem of light is resolved not as a biological problem but as a social one. In this particular case, it seems to us that the basic way of thinking about light develops its own extreme form of expression.

Thus, from a psychological point of view, a physical defect causes a disruption of normal social forms of behavior. If the behavior of a living organism equals its interaction with the world (and it is a system of adaptive reactions to the environment), then changes in this system above all cause a degeneration and disruption of the social relations and conditions under which normal behavioral processes occur. Certainly all psychological characteristics of a handicapped child have as their basis a social, not a biological core.

In various social circumstances, blindness exhibits different psychological traits. For the daughter of an American farmer, for the son of a Ukrainian landowner, for a German duchess, and for a Russian peasant or a Swedish proletarian, blindness represents absolutely different psychological factors. Psychologically, blindness does not restrict the scope of mental activity. When educating a handicapped child, be he blind or deaf, precisely the same process is required to develop new forms of behavior and to establish conditional reactions as is necessary when educating a normal child. Consequently, questions of education for handicapped children can be decided only as a problem of social pedagogy. Based on methods for socially compensating the natural defect, the social education of handicapped children is the only scientifically sound and ideologically correct path. Special education must be subordinated to and coordinated with social education. Moreover, special education must organically merge with social education and become its major component. Any special medicinal diet prescribed for a handicapped child must not undermine his overall normal diet. Only an incompetent doctor would deprive his patient of normal food, prescribing just medicine and pills. Precisely this path was taken by our special schools: where *Heilpaedo-gogik* (therapeutic pedagogy) has consumed the normal school, special education has overrun social education. We do not deny the necessity of special instruction and training for handicapped children. On the contrary, we assert that teaching the blind to read and the deaf to develop oral speech requires special pedagogical techniques, devices and methods. Only a scientific knowledge of these techniques can create a real pedagogue in this area. On the other hand, we must not forget that, above all, it is necessary to educate a child *not as a blind child but as a child.* Otherwise, to educate a child as a blind or a deaf child means to nurture blindness and deafness; it means that the pedagogy of children with defects will become a defective pedagogy.

Our special schools have, for example, sacrificed the child to blindness and deafness. The school has lost sight of what is healthy and normal in a child. This tradition was inherited from the European special school, which by its social roots and pedagogical orientation is totally bourgeois, philanthropic, and religious to the core.

If you read accounts of the conditions in German schools for the blind and the deaf, you will be astonished by the sophistication of pedagogical techniques, the hygienic conditions, and so forth. But an unbearable savor of the almshouse, a musty atmosphere of some kind of crypt, and an unhealthy pious air wafts from every page. According to N. Hoppe [no ref.] what is most important in the upbringing and education of blind-deaf-mute children in Germany is that they should bear with faith and patience the cross laid upon them by the Lord and should learn in their darkness to hope for eternal light.

What is important is not that blindness is simply a fact for the blind person himself, but that for all ages and countries a certain system of educating the blind and a certain attitude toward them has become socially unavoidable. Liberate the special school from its slavery—that is, from the physical handicap to which it has become enslaved,—which only nurtures but does not cure. Liberate the special school from any trace of philanthropic and religious orientation. Rebuild it on healthy pedagogical ground. Free the child from the unbearable and senseless burden of special schooling. These are the tasks which have been set for our schools both by a scientific understanding of the problem and by the demands of reality.

Achieving the religious miracle of mankind's eternal dream—giving sight to the blind and speech to the deaf—is the task of social education as it emerges in the greatest era of the final reconstruction of mankind.

In all probability, mankind will sooner or later conquer blindness, deafness, and mental retardation. But it will achieve this goal much sooner in a social, pedagogical setting than in a medical, biological system. It is possible that the time is not far away when pedagogy will be ashamed of the very notion of a "handicapped child," which signifies some unalterable defect in the child's nature. A deaf person who speaks and a blind person who works are both participants in life in the full sense of the word. They will not consider themselves abnormal and will not give others grounds to think so. It is our responsibility to see to it that a deaf, blind, or mentally retarded person is not handicapped. Only then will this notion, which, in itself, is a true sign of our own inadequacy, disappear. Thanks to eugenic measures, thanks to an altered social structure, mankind will arrive at different, healthier conditions of life. The number of blind and deaf will shrink incredibly. It may be that deafness and blindness will disappear altogether. But long before that happens, they will be conquered socially. Physically, blindness and deafness will still exist on earth a long time. A blind person will remain blind and a deaf person deaf, but they will cease to be handicapped because a handicapped condition is only a social concept; a defective condition is an abnormal extension of blindness, deafness, or muteness. Blindness by itself does not make a child handicapped; it is not a defective condition, an inadequacy, abnormality, or illness. Blindness becomes these things only under certain social conditions of a blind person's existence. This is a sign of the difference between his behavior and the behavior of others.

Social education will conquer physical handicaps. When this occurs, probably no one will understand us if we say that a blind child is defective; instead, they will say that a blind person is blind and a deaf person is deaf and *nothing more.*

3

Blindness means the failure of one of the sensory organs (analyzers). Certain pedagogues are mistaken when they assume that the essence of education for the blind consists in the development of their remaining, intact sensory organs (analyzers) for hearing, touch, and so forth. Scientific literature has repeatedly proved false the widely accepted opinion that the blind all seem to possess exceptional musical abilities because of a particularly keen sense of hearing. Every blind person is by birth a blind musician, or so everyone usually thinks. Yet, until now, the blind have not produced one great musician; not even an average musician has advanced from their ranks. Musical education of the blind has produced only a large number of church singers, street musicians, pianists and orchestra players for low-class variety shows. Ideologically, this notion is related to the legend about biological compensation for a physical handicap and must be discarded along with the latter. When observing sensations in handicapped children, Ia. P. Troshin noted that the common pedagogical view greatly over exaggerates the primary, fundamental significance of the sensory organs. Preservation of the sensory systems and their development in no way guarantee a higher, complex formation of the personality.

At issue here is apparently not the development of the sensory organs as the first task of deaf and blind education, but the development of certain more complicated, integral, active and effective forms of child experience. He who assumes that the ill effects of blindness can be compensated for by training the visual and auditory senses is mistaken and holds a totally outdated point of view which disregards the sphere of social pedagogy.

The creation of a social pedagogy for the blind in order to replace the old therapeutic philanthropic approach is a task of the greatest scientific importance and of immense practical value. Now there only remains to explore certain select points. This chapter is devoted to this task. In place of biological compensation, the idea of social compensation must be advanced. The mind, particularly reason, is the function of social life. Naked physical stimulus from light does not render a full picture of reality. The interpretation given it by means of social reality and thought will, according to J. Dewey (1907), ascribe an entire wealth of meaning. In this way, blindness, deprivation of only the "naked physical stimulus," does not hermetically seal the windows onto the world; it does not deprive one of "full reality." It only forces the social *interpretation* associated with these physical stimuli to be carried over to and associated with other stimuli. What is important is to learn to read, not simply to see letters. It is important to get to know people and understand their psychological makeup, not simply to stare them in the eye. The eyes take on the subordinate role of an instrument for some other activity and may be substituted for by the activity of another organ. A. V. Birilev is justified in thinking that a blind person can use another person's eyes or another person's experience as a vehicle of sight. In this case, the other person's eyes assume the role of an instrument or vehicle, not unlike a microscope or a telescope. When we are told that for a blind person the study of optical phenomena "is possible in the circumstance where another person is used as the vehicle of experience, that is, for acquiring knowledge about the phenomenon under investigation" (A. V. Birilev, 1924, p. 90), then this affirms a greater and more important truth, if only just as a methodological rule on how to deal with one of the chapters in physics in schools for the blind. In this context, an important thought is established independently of the most immediate practical deductions. This notion proposes that what seem to be absolutely unsolvable, absurd questions in the area of a blind child's education turn out to be solvable as soon as *another person* is drawn into the picture.

In education for the blind, or in any branch of special education, the leap that heals (*salto vitale*) goes beyond the limits of individual pedagogy, beyond that "duet" between the teacher and the pupil, which has been the basis of traditional education. As soon as a new element—in this case the use of another's eyes, that is, collaboration with a hearing person—is drawn into the process of educating the blind, then we immediately find ourselves, in principle, on new ground: The blind person acquires his microscope and telescope, which infinitely widens his experience and closely intertwines him in the general weave of the world.

Psychologically, the task of educating the blind child boils down to combining all the special symbol and signal systems linked with the other sensory analyzers: skin nerves, auditory nerves, and so forth. Only in this way does the education of the blind differ from the education of everyone else. A portion of the conditional associations is redirected to the skin or to any other part of the nervous system. A blind person reads, feeling the perforated dots with his fingers. What is important is that he reads *in precisely the same way as we do*; that he does this using different means, his fingers, not his eyes, cannot have any major significance. Does it make any real difference if you read a German text in Latin or Gothic script? Meaning is what is important, not the signs in themselves. We may change the signs but the meaning will be preserved.

From this, of course, it follows that the special education of blind children must occur in a special school which builds up the skills in this particular symbol system. The basic principle of pedagogy for the blind child will mean, then, the use of *a different symbolic system which maintains the same content as any other instructional or educational process.*

However, the special school systematically breaks off contact with the normal world; it isolates the blind child and puts him in a narrow, closed off, small world, where everything is calculated for and adapted to the defect, where everything reminds him of it. This artificial milieu has nothing in common with that normal world where the blind adult will ultimately have to live. In the special school, a close, hospital-like atmosphere and regime are soon created. The blind child moves in the narrow circle of the blind. This environment nurtures the defect and fixes the child's attention on his blindness, "traumatizing" him. Blindness is not overcome in such a school but is intensified. In such a school, not only is there no development of those strengths which could help the blind child enter the normal world; instead these strengths become systematically atrophied. Mental health and the normal formation of the psyche become disorganized and disintegrate; blindness turns into psychic trauma. But what is most important, according to Shcherbina, is that the special school reinforces the "psychology of separatism," which, even without the special school, is already strongly felt by a blind person.

The special school by its very nature is antisocial and encourages antisocialism. We have to think not about isolating the blind person from life as soon as possible, but about introducing him into life as early and as extensively as possible. A blind person will have to live a normal life in the seeing world; he must, therefore, learn in a general [hereafter, "public"] school. Therefore, certain elements of his special education and upbringing must be taken beyond the special school and introduced into the public school. In principle, Shcherbina's proposed system of combining special and public education should be created. In order to overcome the antisocial nature of the special school, scientifically based experiments must be conducted to integrate the education of the blind with that of the sighted, an experiment which possesses an enormous future. At this point the cycle of development evolves dialectically. First, as thesis we had a common education for abnormal and normal children, then as antithesis, special education. Our task today is to create a synthesis, which will combine in a certain higher unity the healthy elements of the thesis and the antithesis.

Another measure would be to tear down the walls of our special schools. Closer contact with the sighted will deepen the roots of life, and broaden interaction with the world based not on passive study, but on active, effective participation. It will bring the blind child out of the narrow circle imposed on him by his defect into participation in the Young Pioneers and the youth movement[*]: all these components constitute the key factors of social education and can set enormous educational forces into motion.

Until now, we learn from all accounts of schools that the "Komsomol[**] shunned" the blind child. Thus, the task is not so much the education of blind children as it is the reeducation of the sighted. The latter must change their attitude toward blindness and toward the blind. The reeducation of the sighted poses a social pedagogical task of enormous importance.

We must radically reorganize even labor in schools for the blind. Until now, work has been organized on the basis of individuality and philanthropy. Blind children have been taught by those auxiliary means which lead to begging. What should constitute the future base of their life has not been taken into account in music instruction, in knick-knack weaving, and other vocational skills. Normally, vocational training in schools for the blind has been presented in an artificial, experimental form. All duties of a social, organizational origin, usually taught to the seeing, are eliminated from the programs for the blind. The blind remain those who carry out the orders of others. This is why this "vocational training" produces invalids. Such training not only does not develop organizational work skills and the ability to apply these skills in life but deliberately atrophies this ability. Meanwhile, it is precisely the social and practical aspects of labor which have the greatest pedagogical significance for the blind. Under no conditions does work mean only making brushes or weaving baskets, but something immeasurably greater.

From an educational point of view, work and training usually have meant individual handicrafts and amateur tinkering. Such work has almost no adequate general, vocational, polytechnical foundation and no industrial, professional significance. Finally, such work does not give training in collaborative work activity. This means that only a very narrow circle of crafts and work opportunities become available to the blind. Collaboration with the sighted must become the basis for vocational training. This basis creates true interaction with the seeing, and work turns out to be that narrow door through which the blind enter life. Create healthy work and all the rest will come of its own.

---

[*] Vygotsky refers here to organized youth groups attached to the Soviet Communist Party. [Transl.]

[**] The Komsomol is the Communist Youth League. [Transl.]

Vocational training in schools for the blind still has one extremely important problem: Nowhere has sheer verbiage become so deep-rooted as in pedagogy for the blind. A blind person receives everything in chewed-over form; he is retold everything. On this account, he is threatened by a particular danger above and beyond those longstanding general problems of the verbal method. Words are particularly imprecise for a blind person inasmuch as his experience unfolds differently (let us recall, how in the ancient and wise fable, the seeing guide explains what milk is like to a blind man). A word for a blind person is an "empty sound." When everything has been presented in chewed-over form, we can only conclude that the blind person himself has forgotten how to chew. A seeing child will learn where to develop his inquisitive skills. We condemn the blind person, however, to an eternal need for a guide. Of course, methods for independent individual development are more difficult to devise for a blind person than for a seeing person, but they exist and must be discovered. We must always remember that blindness is a permanent, normal condition for the organism under discussion. Psychologically speaking, this does not mean anything different than merely a certain change in the general course of social adaptation. This special training is essentially so easy that it cannot create a very serious deviation from the normal course of development. Still, it does lead the child away from the average path. Therefore, it must be compensated for with a tenfold curve back to life. Education of the blind must be oriented toward the world of the seeing. This is the permanent "north" of our pedagogical compass. Until now, we have proceeded in precisely the reverse direction: we have fixed our attention on blindness, forgetting that only a seeing person can introduce a blind person to life; if the blind lead the blind, will not both fall into the pit?

4

The task of educating deaf-mute children, in all probability, constitutes the most interesting and difficult chapter in pedagogy. A deaf-mute person is physically more capable of knowing the world and of actively participating in life than is a blind person. With the exception of a few, usually not very significant, disorders which are related to the [proprioreceptive] sense which conveys information about certain changes of the body's position in space and its balance (N. A. Popov,[6] 1920), the deaf mute retains almost all the possible physical responses of a normal person. Of greatest importance is the fact that deaf-mute children retain sight and, thanks to this, can control and develop their own movements with absolutely normal precision. As a human machine, and an instrument of work, the body of a deaf-mute person differs very little from the body of a normal person; consequently, deaf-mute children retain the full range of physical possibilities, bodily development, and acquisition of habits and work skills. In this sense, deaf-mute adults are not deprived of their share and are, therefore, immeasurably more fortunate than blind people. All sorts of occupations are accessible to deaf-mute adults, with the exception of a very few areas directly connected with sound such as the tuning of musical instruments. If, in spite of this, deaf education has up to now taken advantage primarily of an unusually narrow circle of useless trades, the fault lies in nearsightedness and a philanthropic, invalid-oriented approach to deaf education.

The right approach to this very problem opens enumerable doors to life, to the opportunity for work integrated with hearing people, and to the possibility of the highest forms of collaboration. Avoiding the dangers of parasitism, collaboration addresses the social aspects of a deaf child's well-being and becomes the basis for all his education. However, more about this below. At this point let us finish our discussion of work. The production and sale of knick-knacks, work with arts and crafts,—all this represents isolated and segregated work, which fails to take into consideration the future and is in no way justified from a scientific point of view. The loss of sound represents a less severe defect than the loss of sight. The world is presented to the human consciousness primarily as a visual phenomenon. Sounds play an immeasurably smaller role in human nature. The deaf person ultimately does not lose a single essential element of the world. It would *seem* that deafness, then, must constitute an immeasurably smaller handicap than blindness. From a biological point of view this is really the case; a deaf animal seems far less helpless than a blind animal. It is not the same, however, for a human being. Deafness in human beings turns out to be an immeasurably greater misfortune than blindness because it isolates them from communication with people. When a human being is deprived of speech, muteness cuts him off from social experiences and excludes him from common ties with others. Deaf-muteness is primarily a social handicap. It disrupts the social bonding of personality much more directly than does blindness.

Thus, the first task of education for the deaf is to return speech to them. This is possible. The fact of the matter is that deafness affects only the auditory and not the vocal nerves and centers. The speech organs and the connecting nerve paths and centers remain intact. Thus, deafness is never an organic affliction but simply means underdevelopment. As a result, a deaf person does not hear words and cannot learn speech. Therefore, teaching a deaf child oral speech involves more than the substitution of one sensory system for another—the eye for the ear. When a deaf person learns to read the speaker's lips and seemingly hears with his eyes, this also involves yet another important psychological mechanism, a key component of speech, namely the mechanism which sends back to the speaker his own vocal vibrations and allows him to control and regulate the course of speech (L. S. Vygotsky, in the collection *Psychology and Marxism*, 1925). In the case at hand, this mechanism is replaced by kinesthetic sensations, occurring during articulatory movements. These sensations are extremely weak, and transmission of all sounds by means of lip movement alone is far from accurate. Articulation during speech demands invisible movements inside a closed mouth; therefore for a deaf-mute child, instruction in oral speech turns into a gruelling, miserable ordeal.

In addition to teaching oral speech (the so-called German method), two other languages exist for deaf people: 1) a natural language: mimicry and the language of gestures; and, 2) a systematic language of signs: a conventional alphabet which consists of various movements of the hand and fingers, called dactylology, or "writing in the air." Both of these languages are immeasurably easier for a deaf person; the language of gestures constitutes a deaf person's natural language, while oral speech is unnatural for the deaf-mute (N. M. Lagovskii, 1911). However, of these three possible languages, we must, without doubt, give preference to the most difficult and most unnatural one: oral speech. For a deaf person, oral speech comes not with ease but with enormous difficulty, yet it produces far greater results. In fact, although mimicry constitutes the initial language for a deaf-mute child and is the basis of the French method (N. M. Lagovskii, 1910), nevertheless it must be discarded, since mimicry is an inadequate and limited language. It closes the deaf child off in a very narrow and confining world with only those who know this primitive language. Mimicry very quickly degenerates into jargon, comprehensible only within one or another school and permits communication only with a small number of people. Mimicry allows one to convey only the crudest, tangible and concrete meanings. It never reaches a level of abstract concepts and ideas. In contrast, speech is not only an instrument for communication but also an instrument of thought; consciousness develops chiefly with the help of speech and arises out of social experience. Hence, it is clear that mimicry dooms a deaf person to total underdevelopment.

Many researchers have asserted that the consciousness of deaf-mute adults deprived of speech only slightly exceeds that of anthropoid apes. One can dispute this statement but may agree in any case with the opinion of Tsekh (quoted by N. M. Lagovskii, 1911, p. 116), who said that "thought in deaf-mutes, who are limited to their own observations and experiences, resembles human cognition only in form and not in substance . Natorp is right when he says that 'a human being becomes a human being only thanks to the human community . . . An isolated human being is, strictly speaking, only an abstraction, similar to an atom in physics'" (1911, pp. 76-77). Even human perception would not develop in a person cut off from human community. Precisely, speech is the foundation and vehicle of such social experience; even when thinking in isolation, we maintain the function of communication. In other words, without speech, there is no consciousness, no self-consciousness. One can easily be persuaded that consciousness arises out of social experience by the example of the deaf-mute. Whether this is true or not, in any case teaching a deaf-mute child speech means giving him not only the possibility of communicating with other people, but also of developing consciousness, thought, and selfconsciousness. It returns him to a human condition.

Hence, mimicry has been condemned from a scientific and social point of view. Dactylology (writing in the air, a systematic language of signs, a manual alphabet) turns out also to be insufficient in and of itself for the instruction of deaf-mute children. It still remains a language incomprehensible to those surrounding the mute child. Consequently, mimicry places a barrier between the child and the world: it requires a mediating link in the form of another human being, who understands this form of communication and who can serve as a translator from dactylology into the dominant language.

It has been proposed that the manual alphabet and mimicry be introduced as auxiliary devices for teaching speech. W. Stern and others hold such theoretical positions, and such has been the practice of certain American schools. Experience has shown that, without a doubt, mimicry (gestured language) is incompatible with oral speech, that, according to psychophysiological laws, mimicry (gestured language) supplants oral speech. J. Heidzig,[7] formerly an avid proponent of sign language (mimicry) later labeled the use of sign language in schools for deaf children "a fox in a chicken coop," and called schools which combined methods "neither fish nor fowl" (quoted by F. Werner,[8] 1909, p. 48), because there is no one method contained in them. F. Werner (1909) quite convincingly illustrated that the means of thinking and the means of communication must be one and the same. Abbot Charles de l'Epie[9] said, "Our language is not their language" (quoted in F. Werner, 1909). The task of the purely oral method consists of imparting our language to the deaf. Hence, the purely oral method remains the only one which can return a deaf-mute child to human-kind. However, this method is infinitely difficult for children. Only because of exceptional cruelty has it been successfully sustained and developed in German schools. Exceptional and unheard of cruelty is the unavoidable companion of the purely oral method, because its proponents themselves recognize the fact that, *"Of all instructional methods, the oral method is most antithetical to a deaf person's nature. However not one of these methods can return a deaf mute child to human society with the same success that the oral method has"* (F. Werner, 1909, p. 55).

Education of the deaf-mute stands in opposition to the child's very nature. It is necessary to break the child's nature in order to teach him to speak. This is the truly tragic problem of deaf education. Heidzig was thoroughly correct in saying that "the police should close all deaf schools, in which gestured language (mimicry) has been completely eliminated" (quoted by F. Werner, 1909, p. 48). And in fact, it is impossible to ban gesticulated language (mimicry): it is the natural language of the child. It may be forbidden, and its users punished, but this does not mean that it is defeated.

We have purposely selected this difficult question in order to show that this central but unique question of deaf education is at the same time a general question of social education and that only as such is it possible to solve this problem. If we want to impart oral speech to the deaf child, we must pose the question in broader terms than a mere superficial discussion of the special characteristics and virtues of the method. This method is miraculous, but it forces the student to pull out his hair; it results in the mastery of a few words, with which the student cannot usually construct a logical phrase; mimicry is therefore used on the sly, and this forces teachers to act as policemen in order to catch the pupils who have lapsed into gesticulated language and so forth.

What is the solution? Of course, the only way out is to go beyond the narrow confines of articulation and pose the question as a whole. A knife by itself is neither good nor bad—everything depends on whether it is used by a surgeon or a criminal. Oral speech by itself is neither good nor bad; only in the overall system of education is it justified or condemned. In the old system, the oral method was murderous; in a new system, it can become beneficial. Of course, we must perfect both the method and the instructional techniques. We must struggle against the analytical method of teaching isolated sounds; we must fight for the whole phrase and search for ways to subordinate mimicry to oral speech.

In this respect G. Forchhammer's[10] manual-oral system is scarcely the most interesting; it advanced written speech as the most important means of teaching speech. The combination of mouth and hand coupled with a mute person's enunciation is important in that, first of all, it puts the hand movements in a subordinate position with respect to the oral speech, introducing these movements to signify the otherwise-unseen elements of sounds. Psychologically, this system promises much because it facilitates the acquisition of oral speech, and permits one to advance to pure speech, and so forth.

But neither this system nor any other in and of itself resolves the situation. We must organize the child's life so that speech will be necessary and interesting to him, and sign language uninteresting and unnecessary. Instruction must follow the child's line of interests and not counteract it. A child's instincts must be made his allies and not his enemies. A need for the language common to all mankind must be created and then speech will appear. Experience speaks for itself. When students who have finished school arrive at this point five or six years later, then, as it usually turns out, life completes the work of the school. If the deaf are frequently placed in circumstances where speech becomes necessary to them, they will develop it and conquer it completely. If, however, they remain in the background in life as spongers, they will return to muteness. Our special school is unable not only "to submerge a child in speech," according to Stern, but everything about it is organized in such a way that it stifles the need for oral speech. Speech springs up from the need for communication and thought. Thinking and communication come as a result of adaptation to complicated living conditions. A. Gutsman is justified in saying that the majority of deaf students graduating from school do not have sufficient skills for coping with the phenomena and demands of social life (1910, p. 6) [no ref.]. This occurs, of course, because the school itself isolates children from the world. In summing up the arguments of the opponents of the purely oral speech method F. Werner said: *"Everything should remain in general as it was before."* We say that *everything must be restructured* in order that the oral method bear fruit.

Mainstreaming [lit. coeducation] with normal children has been proposed many times. Now unfortunately it can no longer remain just a question of future priority; Grazer's slogan (quoted in Werner, 1909, p. 35) is our slogan: "We must proceed until every elementary teacher can teach even the deaf child and, subsequently, until each elementary school becomes simultaneously a school for the deaf." Until we reach this stage, we must bridge the gap between education and life in every way possible and bring the school closer to normal life.[*] We must return to the position of M. Hill[11] which is that speech must be developed in a deaf-mute child since life creates it in a normal child. The solution here is not to be found in the German or French or Italian system but only in an approximation of life. G. Wende,[12] when surveying the development of deaf education in Germany, correctly noted three eras: (1) *Am Anfang was das Wort* (in the beginning was the word); (2) *Am Anfang was die Sache* (in the beginning was the matter); and, (3) *Am Anfang steht die Tat, das Ereignis* (in the beginning stands the action, the event) (G. Wende, 1915) [no ref.].

Neither speech by itself nor visual, concrete instruction of speech can satisfy us. Articulation is not a goal in itself. Speech always exists plus something else; speech is a part of our overall behavior, of an act, action, or experience. All other specific and general observations about education are secondary with respect to this central point and to the demand for an early start (at the age of two) in teaching deaf children speech and verbal associations with various objects, and so forth. Active and productive participation in life must begin in school; everything must be based on this principle. If school children learn to make Negro ragdolls and to sell them on the street, they will never learn oral speech because nothing is easier for a deaf-mute person than begging for alms. Through active organization of his life at school, the pupil will acquire the ability to enter life. We must part with the German school as our ideal—with its nepotism and its unending, small-minded, patronizing custody of pupils (deaf children in some schools are not left alone a minute without supervision), and with its mechanical instruction of articulation.

Thus, the question of teaching deaf-mute children oral speech turns out to be not only a particular question of method but also a central question with respect to the fundamentals of deaf education. Once having mastered the central point, one may then draw the circumference and connect the radii with this center point. This all-encompassing central point means the *social education of a deaf-mute child in the complete sense of the word.*

5

The concept of mental retardation is the most vague and difficult concept in special education. Until now we have had no scientific criteria for establishing the true character

---

[*] At the last congress of the social welfare for the blind at Stuttgart in August 1924 (see *Life of the Blind*, 1924, no. 5.) the German system of separate education for the blind was subjected to shattering criticism. The American practice of closely communicating and cooperating with sighted people stood in opposition to it. Undoubtedly the same will for the deaf-mute. {L. V.}

and degree of retardation, and in this area. we have not gone beyond the limits of crude empiricism and approximation. For us, there exists one thing beyond all questioning: mental retardation is a conception which encompasses a mixed group of children. Here we find pathologically retarded children, physically defective children who are as a result retarded. In this general group, we meet other various forms and phenomena as well. Thus, along with pathological retardation, we will also find children who are normal in the physical sense of the word but who are retarded and underdeveloped because of difficult, adverse conditions in their lives and at school. These are socially delayed children.

Therefore, retardation is far from always a fact, conditioned by a lengthy series of hereditary mutations; it very often occurs as the result of an unfortunate childhood. From a pedagogical point of view, we may assume in both situations quite similar phenomena, which may be characterized by complete or partial underdevelopment of an entire organism. In the case of child mental retardation, with the exception of illness, we are dealing with underdevelopment and nothing more.

For such children, the basic processes of life can occur absolutely normally; hence, they may serve as the source of our knowledge about the nature of children in general. Troshin was absolutely correct when he expressed the thought that basic processes occur in children in their purest, normal, transparent, and simple form and that the study of a child must begin with these purest and simplest forms.

A very frequent formula in pedagogical practice and literature defines the task of educating profoundly retarded children as follows: Make them into "socially neutral personalities." The point is that, in the given situation, social education can seemingly pursue totally negative goals. It would be a very grave error to close one's eyes to the positive goals which face pedagogy, to say nothing about the fact that "socially neutral personalities" do not exist in general. Life is infinitely complex and differentiated; there is always a place for the active not the passive or neutral child, even for the less gifted child. The child himself possesses everything needed to become an active participant in social life. The myth of an inferior social instinct or about "a certain reduction of social impulses" in a retarded child (A. N. Graborov, 1925) must be discarded. It is a fact that the social personality of a retarded child is impaired and underdeveloped. Nowhere is the social nature of a handicapped condition so apparent as in this case. A retarded child is self-ostracized from peer ranks. Once branded a fool or handicapped, the child is placed in absolutely new social circumstances and his or her entire development proceeds in a completely new direction.

A defect is strengthened, nourished, and reinforced by its social consequences. With respect to this problem, there is not a single instance where the biological can be separated from the social. Nowhere is this more obviously clear than in the question of sex education. Many authors (for example, A. N. Graborov, 1925) have supported segregated sex education in auxiliary schools. But the sexual drive is more apt to be reduced rather than sharpened or increased in segregated children. Any abnormality which occurs in their sexual behavior is of a secondary nature. Therefore, the correct social organization in auxiliary schools definitely assumes coeducation for boys and girls. A central pedagogical problem even in these schools is the connection between special education and the general principle of social education. "Psychological support systems" and "enculturation of the senses," touched upon in certain didactic materials, must be thoroughly integrated into play, into classes, and into work. When presented as mere lessons, classical lessons in silence are senseless and oppressive. However, games involving silence or moments of meaningful silence when children understand why silence is necessary are a wonderful educational technique. "Special" education must lose its "special" character, and then it will become a part of the general educational system. It must proceed in conjunction with a child's interests. The auxiliary school, created only to assist the regular school, must *never in any way* sever ties with the latter. The special school will often have to take in retarded children temporarily but then must return them again. Reestablishing the norm, and completely discarding everything that drags the child down, the defect and retardation—this is the aim of the school. It should not be embarrassing to go to school, and "Whoever enters, leave all hope behind," should not be written on the school door.

Let us imagine that,in some country, thanks to particular circumstances, handicapped children are seen as something exceptional and some special mission or social role is bestowed on them. It is difficult to imagine this, but it is completely possible; after all sometimes a blind person seems to be a born judge, wise man, or prophet. Imagine that blindness were what was needed to be socially useful. It is clear then that blindness would then mean a totally different social lot for man; blindness would turn from a defect into a virtue. Inasmuch as it is true that, subjectively speaking, blindness does not constitute a defect for the blind person himself or herself, we must accept then the notion that in such a country blindness (or deafness) never could be a defect or a blind child handicapped. Consequently, the term "defective"* is already a social appraisal of blindness or deafness. The time for such imagined countries in any scientific discourse is long since past, and such examples have lost all their demonstrative effect. There is, of course, no such country anywhere; it is a purely logical construct. But we have considered it possible to make use of such reasoning in our conclusion to this article because our task is not merely to introduce and praise a new concept, but to explain in depth the basic idea that blindness and deafness cannot be seen as handicapped conditions. If we create such a country, where a blind or deaf person will find a place in life, where blindness will not mean abnormality, then blindness will not be seen as a handicap there. Social pedagogy is summoned forth to implement this fundamental principle of the psychology of defectology. The fundamental idea is to over-come the very notion of a handicap. By the example introduced here, we wished to show that this assertion is not a paradox, but a perfectly obvious idea, clear from beginning to end.

---

* *Handicapped*, in modern terminology. [Transl.]

PART II

SPECIAL PROBLEMS OF DEFECTOLOGY

THE BLIND CHILD[1]

They {the blind—L.V.} develop capacities which we cannot expect in the seeing, and we must as-
sume that a special breed of people would arise if blind people, without integration with the seeing,
were to communicate exclusively with each other. (K. Buerklen, 1924, p.3)

1

If we put aside particulars and disregard details, it is possible to illustrate how scientific views on the psychology of the blind have developed along one path from antiquity to the present day, at times disappearing in a fog of false ideas, then reappearing again with each new scientific gain. Just as a magnetic arrow points to the north, so, too, does this path point to the truth and permits us to evaluate every historical delusion by the degree of its deviation from this path, by the angle of distortion of this main line.

Inasmuch as knowledge about the blind has sought the truth, it can essentially be summed up by one central, evolving idea—an idea which mankind has tried to master for centuries because it represents an understanding not only of the blind, but also of man's psychological nature in general. In psychology of the blind, as in any branch of knowledge, it is possible to be deceived in various ways but there is only one road to truth. This truth can be stated as follows: Blindness is not merely the absence of sight (the failure of one isolated organ); blindness causes a total restructuring of all the strengths of both the organism and the personality.

Blindness, in creating a new, unique cast of personality, brings to life new forces; it changes a function's normal tendencies; it creatively and organically remakes and forms a person's mind. Consequently, blindness is not merely a defect, a minus, a weakness, but in some sense is also the source of manifestations of abilities, a plus, a strength (however strange or paradoxical this may seem!).

This idea has evolved in certain main stages, the comparison of which illuminates clearly the direction or tendency of its development. The first epoch may be designated as a mystical period, the second as a naive, biological period, and the third, the modern period, as a scientific or social-psychological stage.

2

The first epoch encompasses antiquity, the Middle Ages and a very significant part of modern history. Up to now, the vestiges of this period have been visible in popular folk views of the blind, in legends, folktales, and proverbs. Blindness was viewed first and foremost as a great misfortune, to which people reacted with superstition, fear and respect. Along with the treatment of the blind as helpless, defenseless, and abandoned creatures, there arose the general conviction that the blind possess higher mystical powers of the soul, that in place of their lost physical vision, they gain spiritual knowledge. Even today, there are still many who say that a blind person is predisposed toward spiritual light. Obviously, we find a particle of truth in all this; yet, it is twisted by the fear and ignorance of the religious-minded person. According to legend, the blind were often the preservers of folk wisdom, as well as singers and prophets of the future. Homer was a blind man. They say about Democritus that he blinded himself in order to completely devote himself to philosophy. If this is not really true, the fact that such a legend was possible and did not seem absurd to anyone, bears witness, in any case, to a view which held that a philosophical gift may be strengthened by the loss of vision. It is curious that the Talmud, which confers the status of the dead on lepers, the deaf, and the childless, uses a euphemistic expression in reference to the blind: "a man with an abundance of light." German folk sayings and proverbs of traditional wisdom preserve traces of this view: "Solomon found wisdom in the blind, because they do not take a step without first having firm ground to stand on." In his research on the blind in sagas, fairy tales and legends, O. Wanecek[2] showed that inherent in folk culture is the view of a blind person as a person with an awakened inner vision, as a person endowed with spiritual knowledge unknown to other people.

Christianity, which brought with it a reappraisal of values, basically changed only the moral content of this idea, and left its essence unchanged. "Those who are last here," which, of course, includes the blind, have been promised to be "first there." In the Middle Ages, a most important dogma in the philosophy of blindness gave blindness a certain spiritual value as it did any deprivation or suffering; the church porch was given over as personal property to the blind. This signified simultaneously both their beggarliness in earthly life and their nearness to God. It was said at that time, that in a sickly body lives an exalted spirit. Again, some mystical second nature was discovered, some spiritual value, some positive sense. One must call the second stage in the development of the psychology of blind "mystical" not only because it was colored by religious overtones and beliefs, and not only because the blind were associated with God in every possible way: According to the Jewish wise men, those seen, but unseeing are brought near to Him who sees but is invisible.

At the heart of the matter are the capabilities ascribed to the blind, such as supersensitive powers of the soul, which in their connection with blindness, seemed enigmatic, miraculous, and incomprehensible. These views arose not from experience itself, not from testimony of the blind about themselves, not from a scientific study of the blind and their social role, but from the doctrine of the spirit, the body, and faith in an intangible spirit. And *still*, although history has utterly destroyed this philosophy and science has thoroughly unmasked its unfoundedness, a particle of truth is concealed at its deepest roots.

3

It was only the Renaissance (the eighteenth century) which brought forth a new era of understanding blindness. In place of mysticism, science has taken hold; in place of prejudices, experience and knowledge. This epoch's greatest historical significance for the problem under examination is found in the fact that, as a direct result, the new understanding of psychology created instructors and educators of the blind, bringing social life within their reach and making culture available to them.

On the theoretical level, this new understanding was expressed in the doctrine of the "vicarious" (substitution) of the sensory organs. According to this view, failure of one of the sensory functions is compensated for by an increase in the functioning and development of other organs. Just as in the absence or disease of one of the paired organs—for example, the kidneys or lungs—the other healthy organ develops in a compensatory manner; the latter's functioning is augmented and takes over for the diseased one, assuming part of its function. Similarly, a visual impairment causes a more keenly developed sense of hearing. Entire legends have been created around the superior visual capabilities of the deaf. These legends speak about a wise, benevolent nature (which cares for its creations), which with one hand takes away and with the other gives back all that was taken. It was believed, that thanks to this very fact, every blind person is a blind musician, that is, a person who is gifted with a heightened, exceptional sense of hearing. A unique sixth sense, unimaginable in the seeing, was discovered in the blind. Actual observations and facts from life are at the basis of all these legends, but they have been falsely interpreted and therefore distorted beyond recognition. K. Buerklen has compiled all the opinions of various authors (H. A. Friche, L. Bachko, Stukey, H. W. Rotermund, I. W. Klein and others), who have developed this idea in different forms (K. Buerklen, 1924). Research investigations very quickly, however, brought to light the groundlessness of such a theory. They pointed out the indisputably established fact that the blind do not develop an above-average sense of touch or hearing, and that, on the contrary, these senses are very frequently developed to a lesser degree than in the sighted. Finally, whenever we encounter increased tactile sensitivity then, in comparison with the normal function, this phenomenon turns out to be of a secondary, dependent, derivative nature, a result of development rather than its cause. This indicated phenomenon does not arise out of direct physiological compensation for loss of sight (as an enlargement of a kidney does) but proceeds along a very complicated and roundabout route of overall sociopsychological compensation, without substituting for or replacing the failing organ.

Consequently, there can be no discussion of any substitution of the sensory organs. Lusardi [no ref.], correctly noted that the fingers will never teach a blind person to actually see. E. Binder [no ref.], following in the footsteps of Appia [no ref.], illustrated that the functions of sensory organs are not transferable from one organ to another and that the expression *vicarious senses*, i.e., the substitution of sensory organs, is not correctly used in physiology. The research studies of Fischbach [no ref.], published in the physiological archive of E. Pflueger [no ref.] have played a decisive role in refuting this dogma and has demonstrated its lack of substance. Experimental psychology has resolved this dispute. It has cleared the way for an accurate understanding of the underlying facts of this theory.

E. Meumann[3] called into question Fischbach's view which states that all the senses are adversely affected in the presence of one defective sense. He asserted that in fact substitution of sensory functions does occur in its own fashion (E. Meumann, 1911). W. Wundt[4] came to the conclusion that substitution in the area of physiological functions is a particular case of exercise and adaptation. Consequently, substitution must be understood not in the sense that other organs take on the physiological functions of the eyes, for example, but as a complex restructuring of all psychological activity, caused by the disruption of one of the main functions and redirected with the help of association, memory, and attention to the creation and formation of a new kind of organic equilibrium in place of the one destroyed.

If, however, such a naive biological conception turns out to be false and must be replaced by some other theory, it has, all the same, made an enormous step forward on the road toward the attainment of some scientific truth about blindness. This dogma was the first to hoist the banner of scientific observation and empirical criteria and to come to the conclusion that blindness not only is a defect, a deficit, but that it also activates new strengths, new functions and performs creative, unique work. This theory, however, could not indicate the precise nature of this activity. The enormous practical significance which such a step toward truth possesses can be demonstrated by the fact that this epoch created child care and education for the blind. One dot of Braille has done more for the blind than thousands of do-gooders; the opportunity to read and to write has turned out to be more important than the "sixth sense" and the refinement of touch and hearing. In memory of V. Hauey,[5] founder of education for the blind, the following words were written as an address to a blind child: "You will find light in education and labor." In knowledge and labor, Hauey found a solution to the tragedy of blindness and pointed out the path along which we are now traveling. Hauey's era gave education to the blind; our era must give them work.

4

Science, in modern times, has come closer to grasping the truth about the psychology of a blind person. The school of the Viennese psychiatrist, A. Adler, which worked out a method of individual psychology (that is to say, a social psychology of personality) has pointed out the significance and the psychological role played by a physical defect in the process of development and formation of personality. If, because of a morphological and functional abnormality, some organ falls short of normal operation, then the central nervous system and mental apparatus take on the task of compensating for the organ's impaired function. They create a psychological superstructure over the malfunctioning organ, and this superstructure strives to shore up the organism at its weakened and threatened point.

Contact with the external environment provokes a conflict, caused by the disparity between the deficient organ (or function) and its tasks; this leads to an increased chance of illness and fatality. This conflict also creates increased possibilities of and the stimulus for overcompensation. In this way, the defect becomes the stimulus for and the main motivating force behind the psychological development of the personality. If the struggle ends in victory for the organism, then it not only copes with the difficulties caused by the defect, but it itself rises to a higher level of development, turning deficiency into competence, a handicap into ability, weakness into strength, inferiority into superiority. Thus, blind from birth, N. Saunderson[6] compiled a geometry textbook (A. Adler, 1927). What an enormous exercise in psychological energy and compensatory drive it must have taken for him not only to cope with the spatial limitations facing a blind person, but also to grasp the concept of space in its higher forms, accessible to mankind only in scientific thought, that is, in the constructions of geometry. Even here, where we possess many more levels of this process, the fundamental law remains the same. It is curious that in art schools (for painting), Adler found 70 percent of the students to have some abnormality of vision and as many students with speech defects in schools of drama (A. Adler in *Heilen and Bilder*, 1914, p. 21 [sic, unidentified]). A vocation and talent in painting evolved from impaired vision while an acting ability sprang from surmounted speech defects.

A positive outcome is not the only, nor even the most frequent, result of this struggle to overcome a defect. It would be naive to think that every illness always ends favorably, that each defect turns happily into ability. Each confrontation has two possible outcomes. The second outcome means a hasty retreat into illness and neurosis. It may consist of a failure to compensate, complete submission to the feeling of weakness, asocial behaviour, the creation of a defensive position out of weakness, the transformation of weakness into a weapon, a fictitious goal for existence, in essence madness and the impossibility of a normal psychological life for the personality. Between these two poles, there appears a huge, inexhaustible variety of different degrees of success and failure, competence and neurosis, minimum and maximum success. The existence of extremes marks the boundaries of this phenomenon and offers a radical expression of its essence and nature.

Blindness creates hardships when the blind child enters life. Conflicts flare up on the path. To all intents and purposes, the defect is conceived of as a social disorder. Blindness puts its bearer in a definite and difficult social position. An inferiority complex, uncertainty, and weakness arise as a result of the blind person's assessment of his own position. Tendencies to overcompensate develop as a psychological reaction. These tendencies are directed toward the formation of a socially accepted personality, toward the achievement of a position in the social world. These tendencies strive to overcome the conflict, and, subsequently, do not develop the senses of touch, sound, and so forth, but encompass the entire personality, beginning with its innermost core. They strive not to replace sight but to overcome and overcompensate for the social conflict, the psychological instability resulting from the existence of the physical defect. This, in essence, is the new view.

Formerly, it was thought that the entire life and development of a blind child would proceed along the path of blindness. He who wishes to understand the blind solely on the basis of blindness will understand blindness just as inaccurately as he who sees only disease in inoculation. It is true that vaccination means an injection of disease. In essence, however, vaccination instills superior health. In the light of this law, all individual observations about the blind can be explained according to this main course of development, according to a single scheme of life, according to a final goal, a "fifth act," as Adler maintained. All individual psychological phenomena and processes must be understood not in connection with the past but with an orientation toward the future. In order to fully understand all the abilities of a blind, person we must bring to light tendencies rooted in his psychology, embryos of the future. Essentially, this meets the general requirements of scientific dialectical thought; for a complete interpretation of a given phenomenon, one must analyze it in connection with its past and its future. Adler introduced a future-oriented perspective into psychology.

5

Psychologists long ago noted the fact that a blind man in no way experiences his own blindness in spite of the common opinion that says a blind man feels submerged in darkness. According to the excellent words of a highly educated blind man, A.V. Birilev, a blind person fails to see light not in the same way a blindfolded sighted person fails to see it. A blind person sees it through his hand, i.e., he does not directly sense or feel that he is deprived of vision. "I could not sense my own physical deficiency directly," A.M. Shcherbina testifies (1916, p. 10). The basis of a blind person's psychological make-up does not consist of "an instinctive organic attraction to light" or a drive to "free himself from a dark curtain," as V. G. Korolenko states in his well-known novella, *A Blind Musician*. For a blind person, the ability to see light has a practical and pragmatic meaning, not an instinctive, organic one. A blind person only indirectly, in a reflected manner and only in social circumstances, senses his defect. It would be a naive mistake on the part of a seeing person to assume that we will find in the mind of a blind man blindness or its psychological shadow, its projection or reflection. In his mind there is nothing but the drive to overcome blindness (tendencies toward over-compensation) and the desire to achieve social standing.

All scientific investigators agree, for example, that we generally find a more highly developed memory in a blind person than in the seeing. E. Kretschmer's last comparative research investigation (1928) illustrated that the blind possess a better verbal, mechanical, and rational memory. A. Petzeld introduced that fact and established a series of investigative studies (A. Petzeld, 1925). Buerklen collected the opinions of many authors, who all agreed on one point: they all affirmed the existence of a unique strength in the blind, that is, a highly developed memory which usually surpasses memory in the sighted (K. Buerklen, 1924). Adler would have asked the following: What causes a strongly developed memory in the blind; what conditions this overdevelopment, which behavioral functions of personality does it fulfill, and what need does it meet?

It would seem more correct to say that a more highly developed memory tends to occur in the blind, regardless of whether this in fact depends on many complicated, very high-level conditions. This tendency, which is unquestionably established in the mind of a blind person, can be completely explained in terms of compensation. In order to achieve a position in society, a blind person is forced to develop all his compensatory functions. A blind person's memory develops under the pressure of drives to compensate for the inferiority caused by his blindness. One can see this in light of the fact that his memory develops in an absolutely specific way, determined by the ultimate goal of this process.

Attention in a blind person exhibits varied and contradictory basic qualities. Some authors (K. Stumpf[7] and others) are inclined to see increased activity in the area of attention. Others (Schroeder and F. Tsekh), mainly teachers of the blind who have observed the behavior of blind pupils in class, assert that their attention is less developed than that of the sighted. Yet, it is erroneous to regard the comparative development of mental functions in the blind and the seeing as a quantitative problem. One must question not only the quantitative but also the qualitative functional difference of the same activity in the blind and in the sighted. In what direction does attention develop? What is the issue to be addressed? Even here, when establishing qualitative abilities, there is a general correspondence. Just as memory in the blind tends to develop in a specific way, so, too, attention in the blind tends to proceed along a specific line of development. Or more accurately put, the overall tendency to compensate for blindness takes over both mental processes (memory and attention), giving both the same direction. The unique character of attention in a blind person is a special power of concentration on acoustic and tactile sensations, which enter his field of consciousness consecutively, in contrast to visual sensations, which enter the field of vision simultaneously, causing a rapid change and dispersion of attention as a result of the competition of numerous synchronic stimuli. Whenever we wish to concentrate our attention, in the words of K. Stumpf, we shade our eyes and artificially become blind (1913). In connection with this, we note the opposite, equalizing, and limiting tendency in the attention of a blind person. Total concentration on one object, complete oblivion to the surrounding world, and total preoccupation with that object (all characteristic traits which we observe in the sighted) cannot occur in the blind. Given the circumstances, a blind person is forced to maintain certain contact with the external world by means of his ear; therefore, to a certain degree, he must always disperse his auditory attention to the detriment of his concentration (ibid.).

In each chapter of the psychology of the blind, it would be possible to show the same thing that we have just noted in the case of memory and attention. Emotions, feelings, fantasy, and other psychological processes in the blind are all subordinated to the overall tendency to compensate for blindness. This unity of all life's purposive orientation is what Adler calls the "major lifeline," or main line—life's sole plan, which is unconsciously realized in external fragmentary episodes and periods. It permeates them like a common thread serving as the basis for the biography of personality. "Insofar as during the course of time, all spiritual processes flow in a selected direction and find their own typical expression, a number of tactical devices, aspirations and abilities take shape, overlaying and outlining the already defined course of life. This is what we call 'character'" (O. Ruele, 1926, p. 12). Contrary to Kretschmer's theory, according to which character development is only a passive unfolding of that basic biological type congenitally inherent in man, Adler's teachings explain and derive the structure of character and personality not from a passive unfolding of the past alone but also from an active adaptation to the future. This serves as the basis for the fundamental law of the psychology of the blind: The whole is deduced and understood not from the parts; rather the parts may be perceived from the whole. The psychology of the blind may not be constructed from the sum of isolated abilities, individual signs of this or that function. Rather, these abilities and deviations themselves become understood only when we proceed from a united, integral life plan,—from the guiding course of a blind person's life—will we determine a place and meaning for each ability and separate sign with respect to the whole and in connection with it, that is, in connection with all the remaining signs.

Up to now, science has made few attempts to analyze the personality of the blind people in its entirety and to unravel the guiding course (*Leitlinie*) of its development. Researchers have approached the question, for the most part, by compiling and studying the particulars. To this series of synthetic experiments belongs the most successful work mentioned above by A. Petzeld. His basic position is the following: The blind are most affected by their limitation of free movement, that is, their helplessness with respect to space, which, in contrast to the social position of the deaf, makes for their immediate identification as blind people. In return, a blind person's remaining strengths and abilities can function normally to an extent that we do not find in the deaf-mute. The most salient characteristic of the personality of a blind person is the disparity between his relative helplessness with respect to space and his potential, via speech, for adequate and complete communication and reciprocal understanding with the seeing (A. Petzeld, 1925). That characteristic fits fully within the psychological scheme of defect and compensation. This is but one isolated example of the opposition between a given organic abnormality and psychological drives, yet it establishes the fundamental dialectical law of psychology. In the case of blindness, the source of compensation is not the development of touch or the refinement of hearing but speech—the use of social experience, and communication with the sighted. Petzeld mockingly cites the opinion of the eye doctor, M. Duefur, who holds that we must make the blind helmsmen of ships so that, with the help of a refined ear, they are to catch the sound of any danger in the fog. For Petzeld (1925) it is impossible to seriously seek compensation for blindness in the development of hearing or other individual functions. On the basis of his psychological analysis of the spatial notions of the blind and the nature of our sight, Petzeld concludes that the basic motivating force compensating blindness—the drive to acquire access to the social experience of the seeing by means of speech—does not encounter any natural developmental limitations within the essence of blindness itself. He asks whether there is anything a blind person cannot know on account of his blindness. And he comes to the conclusion which has enormous fundamental significance for all psychology and pedagogy for the blind: The blind person's ability to acquire knowledge is an ability to know everything; a blind person's understanding is basically an ability to understand everything (ibid). This implies the potential of the blind to acquire complete social worth.

It is very instructive to compare the psychology and the potential for development in the blind and in the deaf. From a purely organic point of view, deafness is a less serious defect than blindness. A blind animal, in all probability, is more helpless than a deaf animal. The world of nature enters to a greater degree through the eyes than through the ears. Our world is organized more as a visual phenomenon than as an acoustic one. There are almost no biologically important functions which would be affected negatively by deafness; in the case of blindness, however, there is a loss of spatial orientation and freedom of movement which is the most important function for an animal.

Thus, from a biological point of view, a blind person has lost more than a deaf person. However, with regard to human beings, for whom artificial, social, and technical functions are the most vital, deafness means a much greater deficiency than blindness. Because deafness causes muteness and deprives a person of speech it isolates a human being and excludes him from the social contact upon which speech depends. Both as an organism and as physical body, a deaf person has greater possibilities for development than does a blind person. However, a blind person, both as a personality and as a social individual, finds himself in an immeasurably more favorable position. He has speech and, together with it, the possibility of complete social status as a full-fledged member of society. In this way, the major line of psychological development for a blind person is aimed at overcoming his defect by means of social compensation, by acclimating himself to the experience of the seeing world with the help of speech. The word conquers blindness.

6

Now we can turn to the basic question indicated in the epigraph: Does a blind person represent a special species of people in the eyes of science? If not, then what are the parameters, dimensions, and values of his personality traits? In what capacity does a blind person take part in social and cultural life? In principle, we have already answered this question with everything said above. In essence, the answer has already been given within the limiting conditions of the epigraph itself: If the compensatory processes were not guided by communication with the seeing and by the need to accommodate oneself to social life—if the blind were to live alone among themselves—then only in these circumstances would a blind man develop into a special type of human being.

There is no principal difference between a seeing and a blind child either in relation to the ultimate goal toward which a blind person's development is directed, or in regard to the very mechanism which activates the forces of his development. This is the most important position in the psychology and pedagogy of the blind. Every child is endowed with a relative organic inferiority with respect to the adult society in which he grows up (A. Adler, 1927). This permits us to examine any childhood as an age of uncertainty and inferiority, and any development as something directed at overcoming this condition by means of compensation. Thus, the ultimate developmental goal—the achievement of social status—and the entire process of development are identical for a blind and a seeing child. Both psychology and physiology equally recognize the dialectic character of psychological acts and responses. This is the overall character of higher nervous and mental activity. The necessity to struggle and to overcome an obstacle provokes an increase of energy and strength. Let us imagine an absolutely adjusted being whose vital functions confront no obstacles whatsoever. Out of necessity, such a being will be incapable of any development, of advancement to a higher level of functioning, or of any forward movement, because what is there to incite him to advance? Therefore, precisely in this unadapted state of childhood lies the source of enormous developmental possibilities. These phenomena belong to a number of similar elementary factors common to all forms of behavior from the lowest to the highest; it is therefore, impossible to consider them as some kind of exceptional features in the psychological makeup of the blind person's own peculiar nature. The reverse is true: a heightened development of these processes in the behavior of a blind person is an individual case of a general law. Already, in instincts (i.e., in the simplest forms of behavior) we meet both characteristics which we have described above as the basic features of the psychology of the blind: the singlemindedness of all psychological acts and their intensification in the presence of obstacles. Therefore, an orientation toward the future does not constitute an exceptional property in the psyche of the blind but is a universal form of behavior.

I. P. Pavlov, when analyzing the most elementary conditional links, stumbled across this fact in his investigative work and described it by calling it a goal-directed reflex. With this seemingly paradoxical expression, he wanted to illustrate two points: (1) the fact that these processes occur as a type of reflex action; and (2) the fact that they are directed toward the future in light of which they can be understood.

It remains to add that not only are the final goal and all developmental paths leading to it the same for a blind and for a seeing person, but also the main source from which this development draws its contents is the same for both—language. We have already introduced Petzeld's opinion that language (i.e., the use of speech) is precisely the tool for overcoming the consequences of blindness. He established, therefore, that the process of using speech is, in principle, identical for both the blind and the seeing. On this basis, he explained the theory of surrogate representations by F. Gitschmann [no ref. see Petzeld, 1925?]: "What is red for a blind person," he states, "has the same relationship of meaning as it has for a seeing person, although for the former it can be an object only of meaning and not of perception. Black and white in his understanding are the same opposites as for the seeing, and significance in relationship to objects is no less meaningful. The language of the blind, if one yields to fantasy, would be completely different only in a world of blind people. Duefur is right when he says, that a language created by the blind would hardly be similar to ours. But we cannot agree with him when he says, "I have seen that, in essence, the blind think in one language and speak in another" (A. Petzeld, 1925).

Thus, the main source from which compensation draws its strengths turns out to be the same for both the blind and the seeing. In analyzing the process of educating a blind child from the point of view of the doctrine of conditional responses, we arrived, in time, at the following conclusion: In a physiological sense, there is no fundamental difference between the education of a blind and of a seeing child. Such a concurrence should not surprise us, as we should have expected in advance that the physiological basis of behavior reveals the same structure as does the psychological superstructure. Thus from two different points we arrive at the same end.

The concurrence of physiological and psychological data should convince us even more of the accuracy of our basic conclusion. We may formulate it in the following way: Blindness, as an organic abnormality, gives impetus to the compensatory processes, leading to the formation of a series of peculiarities in the psychology of the blind and reorganizing all separate, individual functions from the standpoint of life's basic goal. Each individual function in a blind person's psychological makeup presents its own characteristics, which are often very significant in comparison with the sighted. In the event of an exclusively blind world, this biological process taken by itself, as it forms and accumulates features deviating from the norm, would inevitably lead to the creation of a special breed of people. Under the pressure of social demands from the seeing world (i.e. demands for overcompensation and for use of speech)—demands which are identical for both the blind and the sighted—the entire development of these features takes shape in such a way that the structure of a blind person's personality, when taken as a whole, tends to achieve a certain normal social type. Even in the presence of individual deviations, we can still have an overall normal type of personality. The credit for establishing this fact belongs to W. Stern (1921). He accepted the doctrine of compensation and explained how from weakness comes strength; from deficiencies, merits. In a blind person, the ability to distinguish by touch is refined in a compensatory manner, not by an actual increase of nervous stimulation, but by repeated practice in observing, evaluating and understanding differences. Similarly, in the realm of psychology, failure of one property can be partially or fully replaced by the fortified development of another. A weak memory, for example, may be counterbalanced by the cultivation of comprehension, which serves to promote keenness of observation and memory. Lack of will or initiative may be compensated by suggestibility and the tendency to imitate, and so forth. An analogous view is reinforced in the field of medicine: The single criterion for health and illness is whether the entire organism functions purposively or ineffectually; a partial deviation is assessed only inasmuch as it is or is not compensated for by the organism's other functions. In contrast to a "microscopically refined analysis of abnormalities," Stern advances the following position: Individual functions may embody a significant deviation from the norm and still the personality or the organism as a whole may be absolutely normal. A child with a defect is not necessarily a defective child. The severity of his abnormality or his degree of normality depends on the results of compensation, that is, on the ultimate formation of his personality as a whole.

K. Buerklen notes two basic types of blind people: one strives as hard as possible to reduce and totally eliminate the gap separating a blind person from a sighted person; the other, on the contrary, underscores his difference and demands recognition of that special form of personality which concurs with a blind person's experience. Stern proposes that this contrast is also of a psychological nature; the blind men probably represent two different types (K. Buerklen, 1924). In our understanding, the types designate two extreme results of compensation: the success and failure of this basic process. We have already stated that, by itself, this process, regardless of unsuccessful results, does not encompass anything exceptional, inherent only in the psychological makeup of a blind person. Let us add only that such an elementary operation as practice (exercise), which is basic to all forms of activity and development, is considered by modern psychology to be an individual example of compensation. Therefore, it is just as erroneous to regard a blind person as a "special type of person" on the basis of the presence and domination of the process in his psyche, as it is to close one's eyes to certain profoundly different features which characterize this general process in the blind. W. Steinberg (cited in K. Buerklen, 1924, p. 8) justifiably derides the current slogan: "We are not blind, we only cannot see."

All functions and all properties are reorganized under the particular developmental conditions of a blind person's life; it is impossible to reduce all differences to one factor. At the same time, however, a blind person and a cited person can have the same overall personality type. It is correct to say that the blind understand more about the world of the sighted than the sighted understand about the world of the blind. Such an understanding would be impossible if a blind person's development did not approximate that of a normal person. Certain questions arise: How is the existence of two types of blind people to be explained? Is this due to organic or psychological causes? Does this not refute the positions advanced above, or at least, does it not introduce substantial limitations and amendments to these positions? In some blind people, as Shcherbina has well described, the defect is organically compensated for: "a second type of nature seems to have been created" (1916, p. 10), and even with all the difficulties associated with blindness, they find in life a particular charm which they would not agree to give up for any personal gains. This means that a blind person's psychological superstructure compensates for his deficiency in such a harmonious way that it becomes the basis of his personality; to deny it would mean to deny himself. These incidents fully confirm the doctrine of compensation. In the case of failure to compensate, the psychological problem becomes a social problem: Is it indeed really true that the healthy children of mankind's great majority achieve everything they could or should, given their psychophysiological makeup?

7

Our survey is complete; we are now ashore. It was not within our scope to fully illuminate the psychology of the blind; we wished only to note the central issue of the problem, that knot into which all the threads of the blind person's psychological makeup has been tied. We found the basis of this to be the non-scientific concept of compensation. What, then, distinguishes a scientific conception of this problem from a non-scientific one? If the ancient world and Christianity envisioned a solution to the problem of blindness in the mystical powers of the soul, if naive biological theory envisioned it as an automatic organic compensation, then the scientific formulation of this idea is that blindness is a social and psychological problem. From a superficial glance, it may easily seem that the idea of compensation has set us back in time to the Christian medieval view of the positive role of suffering, of the infirmity of the flesh. In fact, it is impossible to imagine two more opposed theories. The new doctrine places positive value not on blindness in and of itself, not on the deficit, but on the strengths, on the resources for overcoming the deficit, and on the stimuli for development which are inherent within it. Not simply weakness, but weakness as a source of strength stands out as the positive pole. Ideas, like people, are better known for their acts. Scientific theories must be judged according to the practical results to which they lead.

What, then, is the practical side of all the theories touched on above? According to Petzeld's accurate observation, theoretically a reassessment of blindness found Homer, Tiresias, Oedipus to be real living proof of the boundlessness and unending possibilities of a blind person's development. The ancient world created the idea and produced real examples of great blind men. The Middle Ages, on the contrary, embraced the idea of underestimating blindness, in practice despising the blind. According to a true German saying, "*Verehrt: ernaehrt.*"* Antiquity venerated the blind, while the Middle Ages treated them like fodder. Both ideas are an expression of the inadequacy of prescientific thought and its inability to rise above a one-sided conception of educating the blind: Blindness was recognized either as a strength or as a weakness. The thought, however, that blindness is both,—that is that blindness is weakness which leads to strength—was inconceivable for that epoch.

The beginning of the scientific approach to the problem of blindness was, in effect, marked by the attempt to create a systematic education for every blind person. This was a great era in the history of the blind. Petzeld correctly stated, however, "The fact itself that one may approach the functioning capability of a blind person's remaining senses quantitatively and analyze them experimentally indicates that state of affairs which characterized antiquity and the Middle Ages has remained the same." (A. Petzeld, 1925, p. 3). In his era Duefur advised making helmsmen out of the blind. This epoch tried to rise above the one-sidedness of antiquity and the Middle Ages and for the first time to combine both ideas about blindness. This was the origin of necessity-out-of-weakness and possibility-out-of-strength, the new outlook on education of the blind. However, at that time, no one knew how to unite these two opposites dialectically so that the relationship between strength and weakness was presented in a purely mechanical manner.

Finally, our epoch understands blindness as a socio-psychological problem and has at its disposal three types of weapons to struggle with blindness and its consequences. It is true even in our time that thoughts frequently surface about the possibility of a direct conquest over blindness. People simply do not want to part with that ancient promise that the blind will recover their sight. Until quite recently we were still witnessing revived illusory hopes that somehow science will return sight to the blind. In such outbreaks of unrealized hopes, the threadbare vestiges of distant antiquity and a longing for miracles have essentially resurfaced. Such hopes are not the basis of our new epoch, which as it has been said, has at its disposal three types of weapons: social prophylaxis (preventive inspection), social education, and social labor of the blind. We have three practical whales on which the modern scientific approach to blindness rides. Science must finalize all three forms of the struggle and carry through to the end the progress made by previous epochs in this direction. The notion of prophylaxis (preventive inspection) of blindness must be imparted to the vast popular masses. It is necessary to liquidate the isolated, invalid-oriented education of the blind and to erase the demarcation between the special and the normal school. The education of a blind child must in actuality be organized on the same terms as education of any child capable of normal development. Education must, in fact, make a blind child become a normal, socially accepted adult and must eliminate the label and the notion *defectiveness* which has been affixed to the blind. And finally, modern science must give the blind the

---

* "He who is honored is fed." [Transl.]

right to social labor, not in degrading, philanthropic, invalid-oriented forms (as has been the standard practice up to now) but in forms which correspond to the true essence of labor. This alone will create an indispensable social position for any individual. Is it really not clear that all three of these tasks posed by blindness are by nature essentially social problems and that only a new society can solve these problems once and for all? A new society will create new types of blind people. Today, in the USSR, the first stones of this new society are being laid and this means that the first features of this new type are being formed.

PRINCIPLES OF SOCIAL EDUCATION

FOR THE DEAF-MUTE CHILD[1]

1

The system of social education for deaf-mute children, which I will describe below, exists not only as a theoretical construct but has, in fact, been put into pedagogical practice before our very eyes in the USSR, particularly in the RSFSR (the Russian Soviet Federal Socialist Republic). Admittedly, both the theoretical and the practical elaboration of this system is far from perfected and I am not in a position to discuss results and final conclusions. I can, nevertheless, share experiments from the first steps taken along this path, that is, the first efforts by scientific pedagogues to create social education for the deaf. The fundamental principles of this system, however, can now be formulated with such completeness and clarity that we may count on a certain degree of success in our endeavors to bring to light the fundamentals of the new direction which we support. Our task is dictated not only by a desire to add our experience to the general world picture, but also, in my opinion, by two telling considerations.

The first of these stems from the fact that we still do not have a scientifically developed, authoritative system. Such a system exists neither as a pedagogical theory of the education of a deaf child, nor as a psychological theory of the chronological development and physiological characteristics linked to his hearing loss and to the social limitations caused by the absence of aural speech. In both theory and practice, all the brilliant successes in the education of the deaf remain to date more or less isolated incidents which need to be incorporated into an orderly scientific system. It seems to me, therefore, that any attempt to approach the problem at hand from the point of view of those fundamental principles which permit us to establish a system of deaf education must be in full accord with a modern scientific approach to the question.

The second consideration stems from the fact that, in working out a new system, we ran up against the necessity for a radical reexamination of a number of individual methods, techniques, propositions, and laws of deaf education, including the most crucial question:

instruction in oral speech. On the basis of the principles we have proposed, we are forced in many respects not only to criticize traditional techniques for teaching the deaf but also to enter into direct and sharp disagreement with these techniques on a series of counts. The most notable accomplishment of our work seems to me to be the agreement, which we discovered time and time again between the inferences made on the basis of our prerequisites on the one hand and, the positions taken, on the other hand, by scientific research and leading pedagogical thought in all countries. This concurrence convinces us once again of the correctness of our positions and allows us to summarize and introduce into the system all that is progressive and viable from worldwide experience in this area.

Before stating the principles needed for the social education of deaf children, we must take into consideration some of the primary scientific prerequisites of a new system. The prerequisites concern the psychophysiological character of a deaf child and the process of his education. Any physical handicap—be it blindness or deafness—not only alters the child's relationship with the world, but above all affects his or her interaction with other people. Any organic defect appears as a social abnormality in behavior. It goes without saying, of course, that blindness and deafness, in and of themselves, are biological factors; in no way, are they social factors. However, the educator must deal not so much with these factors alone as with their social consequences. When we have a blind boy before us as the object of education, then we must deal not so much with blindness itself as with the conflicts which arise for a blind child when he enters life. After all, from the very beginning, he interacts with the environment differently than do normal people.

For a blind or deaf child, blindness or deafness represent normality, not a condition of illness. He senses the handicap in question only indirectly or secondarily, as a result of his social experiences. What then does a hearing loss mean, in and of itself? It must be accepted that blindness and deafness indicate nothing other than the mere absence of one means of forming conditional links with the environment. The eye and the ear —organs which are called *receptors* or "*analyzers*" in physiology and *sensory organs* or *organs of external of perception* in psychology—are organs which receive and analyze external elements of the environment; they break down the world into its separate parts, into the external stimuli which are linked to our appropriate reactions. All this helps the organism to adapt more precisely and delicately to its environment.

On the basis of experiments with dogs, the Russian physiological school of I. P. Pavlov came to the conclusion that any innate hereditary reflex, if matched with a neutral external stimulant, can become associated with that stimulus. Subsequently, this reflex can be excited by a new influence without the help of the primary stimulus. Pavlov's school called the new reflex the *conditional reflex* in contrast to the former, the *unconditional reflex*. In dealing with the behavior of animals as a whole and even the behavior of human beings, this school was inclined to view all behavior as consisting of both unconditional, hereditary reflexes and conditional reflexes acquired through individual experience. The latter will also be conditional reactions in the strict sense of the word, because they depend exclusively on the conditions in which the organism (both the dog and the human being) are found. In making this distinction between hereditary and conditional reflexes, the American psychological school of behaviorism[2] agrees entirely with the Russian school.

Undoubtedly, the key to the physiological nature of any educational process lies in the study of conditional reflexes. From a physiological perspective any educational process may be seen as a process of developing conditional reflexes to certain conditional signs and signals (stimuli, submitted to all the mechanisms for educating and training conditional reflexes brought to light in Pavlov's experiments).

From this research we may draw two immensely important conclusions with respect to the topics of interest to us. The first of these most essential conclusions drawn from this objective study of higher mental activity of animals and humans establishes the following: A conditional reflex may be evoked to respond to any external stimulus coming from the eye, ear, skin and so forth. Any external element, any part of the world, any phenomenon, any sign can perform the role of a conditional stimulus. The processes of training a conditional reflex will be the same in all cases. This means that the physiological substrata of the educational process (i.e., those physiological changes which educational influences cause in the child's organism) will in essence and in nature be absolutely identical in all cases. Consequently, both light and sound can play a completely analogous physiological role. The most important fundamental position held by the pedagogical specialists on childhood handicaps is contained in precisely this law: The psychophysiological character of training conditional reflexes in a blind child reading Braille and in a deaf child reading lips is absolutely the same as for a normal child. Hence, the very nature of educating handicapped children in essentially is the same as it is for educating normal children.

The entire difference lies in the fact that in individual cases (in the case of blindness or deafness) one organ of perception (sensory system) may substitute for another. The qualitative content of the reaction, however, remains the same as the entire mechanism of its training. In other words, from the psychological and pedagogical points of view, the behavior of a blind child and of a deaf-mute child may be fully realized on the same level as normal behavior. In principle, the education of a blind child and a deaf child does not differ from the education of a normal child. In this process, human behavior, the behavior of a human being as an aggregate of reactions, remains undisturbed. Blind and deaf children are capable of achieving full human development, that is, an active life. The entire uniqueness of this type of education boils down to the substitution of one path of conditioning for another. Again I repeat: *The principles and the psychological mechanism of education are the same here as for a normal child.*

The second conclusion, practically no less important for special education of the deaf, may be stated as follows: Any new conditional reaction may be cultivated only on the basis of an already existing, sufficiently stable reflex, whether it be inherent or developed by former experience. Strictly speaking, education cannot impart to the organism any single, completely new movement; it can only modify, reshape, and combine reactions which the organism already has at its command. According to the accurate statement of G. Lessing,[3] "Education cannot grant a person anything he cannot already do for himself; it gives him that which he can give himself but only faster and more easily" (cited by F. Werner, 1909, p. 18). For pedagogy this means, that in the presence of any educational influence, it is necessary to take as a starting point and a basis the natural tendencies of the child. And inversely, a child's drives or natural instincts cannot simply be prohibited and changed by a pedagogue. Apropos of this, E. Thorndike says that it is impossible to turn Niagara back toward Lake Erie, and hold it there but it is possible, having built side canals, to harness its power to turn the wheels of factories and plants.

In psychology and in pedagogy the problem of a child's handicap must be posed and comprehended as a social problem, because the social aspect formerly diagnosed as secondary and derivative, in fact, turns out to be primary and major. One must boldly look at this problem as a social problem. If, psychologically speaking, a physical handicap means social derailment, then, pedagogically speaking, to educate this child means to set him back on the right course in life in the same way a dislocated or injured organ is reset. Thus having formulated our demand that the pedagogue be guided by the natural inclinations of those forms of behavior to be cultivated, we approach the starting point of any social education system for deaf-mute children, namely, preschool education, the importance of which has, as far as I know, been underestimated both in theory and in practice in a number of countries.

2

The groundwork for all future educational work is laid in preschool education, in the children's home, and, in particular, in the teaching of speech. Precisely on the basis of this central question, I will try to illustrate the main significance of preschool education, which we hold as the cornerstone for the entire system. Instruction in speech begins with its natural foundations: a child's babble, natural mimicry, and gestures form the basis for developing verbal skills. Speech is viewed as part of the overall social life of a child. Usually, under the traditional conditions for teaching speech to a deaf-mute child, these natural instincts died out very soon. They weakened and disappeared under the influence of unfavorable external conditions. Next, there followed a period of nonverbal development when a child's speech and consciousness took different paths of development. And the [deaf] child did not began to receive special instruction in speech and phonetics until the beginning of school age. By that time the development of the child has usually advanced so far in a different direction that the slow instruction of speech becomes a painfully arduous task without any practical application. This is on the one hand. On the other hand, the mimed gesticulated skills have already been strengthened to such a degree that oral speech is too weak to struggle against them. Any active interest in speech has been killed, and only with the help of artificial measures and exceptional severity, sometimes even cruelty applied to the child's consciousness, does he succeed in learning speech. But we all know equally well how hopeless it is in educational practice to rely only on the conscious efforts of a child when they run counter to his principal interests and habits.

In a preschool children's home, real-life conversation with a child begins at the age of two with a synthetic lip-reading of whole words, phrases, names, directions, and an unconscious imitation of oral speech. These are the two fundamental methods for teaching speech at this early age. In this way the habit of expressing one's desires and thoughts orally is established. Speech is used immediately in all the practical, social contexts of its functions. In play, work, and daily life, a child unwittingly and unself-consciously learns to use speech, to understand it, to fix his attention on speech, and to organize his life and behavior so that, without speech, these things turn out to be impossible. At the youngest stage, for children of two to five years of age, there is no formal training of the reproduction of sounds and their separate elements. Practice consists of babbling which provides preparation for each new word in lip-reading. It occurs along the natural course in which a child exercises his breathing, his voice and speech organs. We do not fear mispronunciation, mis-articulation or confusion of separate sounds and the like. We know that even a normal child travels this path before mastering correct speech. However, his speech develops immediately and organically from babble; immediately it is intelligible and suitable for communication. Yet, if we were to wait until a child has learned to utter each sound correctly and to teach him only after this to put sounds together into syllables, and syllables into words—if we were to proceed from the elements of speech to its synthesis—we would never hear live authentic speech from the child. The reverse path seems natural: mastering integral forms of speech before its individual elements and their combination. In both phylogenetic and ontogenetic development, a phrase precedes a word, a word a syllable, a syllable a sound. Even a separate phrase is almost an abstraction; speech arises sooner in greater wholes than in sentences. Therefore, speech comes to children immediately as something meaningful, necessary and vital; as logical speech and not as articulation.

The role of reflex imitation and automatism during the initial stages of speech instruction is emphasized in the system of K. Malisch[4]: "The more automatic the process of teaching pronunciation," he states, "the greater the results will be, because a conscious effort on the part of the child will slow down his progress. Practical experience will convince one of this. If a mother placed a child on his feet during his first attempts to walk and directed his attention to his feet, she would, by doing this, only delay the natural process of learning. Consequently, at the first stages of learning, no conscious effort should be directed to the act." (quoted in G. I. Kuelpe, 1926, p. 82). The path of imitation is the most natural one. In learning to walk, the child must unavoidably go through the stage of stumbling to acquire sureness of foot. The process of mastering speech is similar to the process of walking. The child must go through a stage of his own particular, incorrect infantile language and master the sounds in the process of speaking. Speech must precede sounds. Therefore, we strive to encourage, develop, and reinforce speech in a child as soon as possible, not fearing, but even welcoming, the child's original features, forms, and irregularities in speech. We do not fear imitations of sounds in a deaf child, just as we do not fear them in a normal, hearing child. If each cow is a "moo" for him, and each dog a "bow-wow," this moves him ahead and is a plus. Inasmuch as the percentages of the absolutely deaf is not great, the development of acoustic attention must accompany speech instruction. In this way, the residual hearing is used and developed at the same time that voice and breathing are practiced.

At a later stage, speech is perfected and reinforced, acquired sounds are polished, new ones are composed into words and phrases, and literacy is acquired. But we still maintain the prerequisite of natural speech, not that produced by lessons of artificial articulation, but that nurtured by the child's entire environment. This is the same demand, expressed by M. Mill in a more general form: "It is necessary to develop speech in a deaf child in the same way that life creates it for a normal child" (quoted in F. Werner, 1909, p. 38). Our aim is to put this rule into practice.

"The sequence in speech development in the deaf-mute child," states N. A. Rau[5], the founder of the first kindergarten for the deaf in Russia, "must be a replica of the speech development of a normal child. The stages of speech development should be the same as for a normal child; the difference lies only in the means, the methods, and the amount of time—a deaf-mute child will be able to say at 3 or 4 what a normal child already says in the first year of life" (1926, p. 59).

At this level, the basis of future speech is already laid. Speech not only fulfills the function of communication between children but also appears as an instrument of thought. "Synthetic reading from the lips," Rau says, "is the beginning of cognition by means of the spoken word. When reading from the lips, the child notices the picture of the mouth and movements of the speech organs and already closely unites this picture with comprehension and comprehension with the movement of the mouth and tongue. For example, the expression 'come here' is already familiar to him, and when he himself has to come to another person or mentally summon one, he sees within himself, as it were, the utterance of this phrase. The child's individual muscles of the speech organs move completely involuntarily when pronouncing this phrase. Gradually, depending on the frequency of reading certain words, phrases, and directives on the lips, a child's comprehension is fortified just as is his inner pronunciation. Still not able to pronounce orally, he already speaks mentally. We have arrived at the most valuable aspect of our work with preschoolers: The habit of understanding, thinking, and expressing one's thought by means of the spoken word" (ibid. p. 63). In this way, natural speech occurs immediately in all the diversity of its functions. It organically takes root in the child's life and it begins to shape both the life and the behavior of the child pivoting around social experiences, the most important organ of which is speech. This is why, when summing up what kindergarten gives a child, N. A. Rau correctly states, "Experience has proved that preschool education of the deaf-mute child must be solidly grounded in live oral speech, which is the only means available to him for communicating with the hearing world: Only through preschool instruction in respect to the live spoken word, only through the spoken word in the milieu of the hearing" (ibid. p. 67).

3

Subsequent instruction in oral speech for the deaf-mute of school age continues to develop the same principles and aspects which have already been noted in kindergarten. Even here, the basic underlying principles remain the struggle against the analytical, artificial, lifeless, phonetic method, a struggle for the whole word, for an intelligent (meaningful) phrase, for logical living speech. I will dwell briefly on only two of the new and original methods which are in practice in our schools and which correspond to this principle. The original method elaborated by I. Golosov,[6] the teacher at the institute for the deaf-mute in Moscow, represents the first attempt to teach oral speech by means of entire words. The author's basic intention is to teach the deaf-mute speech in the same way our small children acquire speech. A preliminary elaboration of the method was begun in 1910 and was put into practice in Warsaw in 1913. However, only during the revolutionary years in Moscow was the elaboration of theory and practice of this method fully worked out. The main point is that children immediately perceive words [in their entireties], and not parts of words. The word bolsters interest in speech and instills in children the confidence needed to begin to learn to speak. In the process of learning entire words and phrases, the formulation of sounds occurs. Experiments have produced favorable results. Thus, from October to May in the 1923-1924 academic year, the first group of children learning by this method mastered twenty-two sounds. Lip-reading is given primary importance over the analytical method, on which the techniques of pronunciation are based. Lip-reading is connected to reading of the printed letters and writing. Sounds are not presented separately but are worked on as parts of a whole, at first one-syllable words and then in whole phrases and even stories.

It is necessary to say that in its the essential features, Golosov's method corresponds with Malisch's method for using entire words, although the two sprang up absolutely independently of each other. This concurrence tells us that we are heading in the right direction. Malisch's method demands, first of all, "living" speech. Communication begins straight away with the instruction of logical (meaningful) speech: "Children are taught only what has logical meaning, what school-children can understand and can immediately use for communication in their surrounding milieu" (quoted in G. I. Kuelpe, 1926, p. 81). All four aspects of speech instruction—lip-reading, writing, articulation, and reading written language—are closely fused. However, lip-reading, even here, remains at the head of the list. "Satisfactory pronunciation is achieved solely by means of the reflex method" (ibid.); the basis of the analytical method is rooted precisely in the conscious separation of each sound and each kinetic sensation connected with it.

Judging by the last German Congress on the Education of the Deaf-Mute in Heidelberg in June 1925, this method originated in Germany, the birth place of the classical analytical phonetic method, but has not been substantially developed there. In his report, G. Leman[7] stated that neither now nor probably at any time in the future will it be possible to call a single primary method for teaching spoken speech the only correct one. Leman recognized, however, that Malisch's method has proved the possibility of teaching speech to the deaf in whole phrases and that the child's overall development and his verbal development advance faster by this method than by phonetic instruction. Furthermore, Leman also permits the use of mimicry[*] at the first stages of instruction. The gains from the new method are enormous! But neither the author nor his critics have finalized their conclusions and they have only half formulated their requirements. "Select instructional material according to the degree of difficulty in pronunciation! Then, as far as possible, take into account the child's needs for speech. At the same time, teach children to lip-read, write and read words and phrases!" (K. Malisch, 1926, p. 87). These stipulations decrease the principal significance of the method; it loses its revolutionizing effect and is reduced to a simple reform of techniques. If the child's needs for speech are taken into account only incidentally and "at one's convenience," while the difficulty of the pronunciation remains the basic principle for selecting material, (that is, the thread running throughout all speech instruction) and if articulation remains the fulcrum, while lip-reading together with writing serve only as auxiliary means, then we have taken many steps backward. We have regressed to a purely phonetic method or, more accurately, to its pedagogical premises. Leman, Malisch's critic, directly and openly expresses misgivings as to the intelligibility and distinctness of articulation [achieved] with this method and recognizes that "complete agreement between speech instruction and the cognitive development of deaf-mute children is impossible at the first stage of education" (1926, p. 88). Here again, speech is severed from the general development of the child. Thus, Malisch's method takes us only halfway.

But we cannot be satisfied with only a technical reform and a partial improvement. Our principles compel us to fully reexamine the entire system. We must have the courage to proceed to the end of the road without stopping halfway. I. A. Sokolianskii's method [Sokolianskii, 1926?] makes such an attempt. This method leads us to the use of lip-reading as a primary means of speech instruction. Here, the attempt was made to employ as the primary vehicle of thought not those extremely unclear verbal sensations, but the more sharply defined, and for the deaf-mute child, more accessible images of words on the speaker's lips together with words written on the board and with motor sensations received from the movement of the hand in the process of writing. The deaf-mute is given a complete phrase which retains all three aspects; meaningful, intelligent, and completely logical elements and not the selective, phonetic elements of the words. Our task consists of submerging the deaf-mute in an environment of our speech. He becomes accustomed to meaningful speech completely mechanically, without even noticing it, and he does not have to endure monstrous efforts to go from presentations of graphic speech to logical speech.

---

[*] This is the commonly accepted Russian term for sign language. [Transl.]

This mechanical and reflexive nature is the most important distinction in Sokolianskii's method.

At first, phrases are given exclusively in the imperative and are necessarily associated with action:

> Conditional reflexes are nurtured. A phrase is given according to a prescribed order first by means of lip-reading accompanied by direct instructions, that is, by a natural mimed gesture: 'Children, get up!' The teacher indicates with his hand what it is necessary to do. This is repeated two or three times. Then this phrase is read only from the lips without the gesture—as we say, with conditional instruction—and the children perform the necessary action. Seven or eight repetitions with conditional instructions are enough to establish a reflex. The phrase is firmly fixed in the mind. In the course of time, when the children have accumulated an adequate number of phrases in the imperative form, this same material will be reworked in the present and past indicative forms (M. N. Kotel'nikov, 1926, p. 74).

But the most remarkable feature of this method is that it goes much further. During the same lesson, not only is the phrase given in its entirety, but in the course of twelve minutes, a series of signs and phrases is mastered—on the average a whole chain with seven to ten links. For example, "Children, get up! Children, come here! Children, raise your hands! Children, go to your places! Children, sit down!" After this chain is mastered by lip-reading, the same chain is given in written form; control is verified by means of reading the elements and establishing the fact that the children are correctly responding to each sign. The chain either is written on the board or is hung up beforehand on a prepared poster. Mastering the chain in written form requires 3 or 4 repetitions (ibid. pp. 74–75). Mastering the chain by reading from the lips takes, on the average, twelve minutes; reading from posters, six to seven minutes! "A month and a half elapses and the children begin to decipher separate words in the links, and then, on the basis of these words, they begin to guess how to respond to a new sign in new links. Subsequent chains are composed on the basis of previous ones by repeating, exposing, extensively drilling, reinforcing, and assessing the material included in them" (ibid., p. 75).

The mastery of writing proceeds very rapidly by means of this method. Technically, pronunciation is developed along a special path, at special lessons, but it is always subordinated to the basic task of teaching speech by means of lip-reading two hours daily. It is impossible to establish precisely when speech and lip-reading merge in the child and we will not forget that normal hearing children also have a stage at which they understand more than they can pronounce. With the same method of instruction, deaf children find themselves in this period of speech development for a long time.

If the methods described by us still need many years for perfection and verification by experiment, then, in any case, one thing is already beyond a doubt: This is the direction in which education for the deaf must proceed.

4

We are still a long way from regarding any of the above mentioned methods, or in general any one method, as the final, saving remedy. On the contrary, we maintain the opinion that no one method in itself, no matter how it meets the child's psychophysiological characteristics, can solve the problem of oral speech development for a deaf-mute child. It is impossible to decide this question outside the general system of education. Malisch's method is the best example of this. Because it is part of the traditional system, it loses all significance. Speech instruction depends on the solution of more general pedagogical questions. If we say that the phonetic German method is condemned to failure, then it is not because it is a failure in and of itself. By itself, it is an ingenious method. But it requires exceptional cruelty for its implementation; it upholds mechanical pressure and prohibition of mimicry. It is suitable for the instruction of pronunciation and articulation, but not for teaching speech because it results in dead, artificially produced, and totally useless speech. F. Werner, one of the strongest and most honest advocates of this method, says, "Of all the methods of instruction, the oral method more than any other is unnatural for the deaf mute" (1909, p. 55). Instruction by this method contradicts the deaf child's nature. It is even necessary to break the child's nature in order to teach him speech. Here is truly the tragic problem of special education for the deaf.

We have dwelled on the most difficult issue in order to show the following: the central, but specific problem of teaching the deaf is at the same time a concern of overall social education, and only as such can it be resolved. If we want to present oral speech to the deaf child, we should address this question on a wider scale than a discussion of a method's specific traits. A method may be miraculous but if it forces us to treat the pupil cruelly, if it does not produce meaningful speech, we must give this method up. Where is our way out? Of course, the only solution is to extend the question beyond the narrow framework of articulation lessons and to pose it as a question of education as a whole. A knife by itself is neither bad nor good; it all depends on the use to which it is put in the hands of a doctor or a criminal. No one method by itself is good or bad. Each method finds its justification or its censure only within the general system of education.

The oral method of the old system was murderous; in the new system, it may become a rescuer. The child's life must be organized so that speech is necessary and interesting to him, and so that mimicry is uninteresting and unnecessary. Education must be directed along the lines of the child's interests, and not contrary to them. It is necessary to make a child's instincts his allies, not his enemies. The need for a universal language must be created, and then speech will appear. Experience tells us this. Life tells us this. According to W. Stern, not only is the traditional school unable to immerse the child in speech, but everything about the school is organized so that it kills the need for oral speech at school. Speech is born of the need for communication and for thought. Thought and communication appear as a result of adaptation to life's complex conditions. A. Gutsman [no ref], in evaluating the German experiment, is justified in saying that the majority of deaf graduates from school do not have sufficient skills to cope with the occurrences and demands of societal life. Of course, this is a consequence of the fact that school itself isolates them from life.

The most important weakness of the traditional school is that it systematically tears a deaf child away from the normal milieu, isolating and placing him in a narrow, closed-off world, where everything conforms to his handicap, where everything is calculated with regard to his defect; everything reminds him of it. This artificial environment is, in many ways, divorced from the normal world in which the deaf will have to live. In the special school, a closed, hospital-like regime is soon created. The deaf person moves in the narrow circle of the deaf. Everything in this environment accentuates his handicap; everything fixes his attention on his deafness and traumatizes him precisely for this reason. Here not only is there no development, but those forces in the child which would subsequently have helped him enter life become systematically atrophied. His mental health and psychological condition become disordered and deteriorate; deafness turns into a trauma. The special school increases psychological separatism; by its nature, such a school is antisocial and nurtures an antisocial disposition. The only solution is a radical reform of the entire educational program.

This solution for deaf education in the RSFSR has been prompted by the entire revolutionary experiment with schools for normal children. Above, I have attempted to defend the thesis that, in principle and from a scientific point of view, there is no difference between the education of a normal and of a deaf child. Therefore, the school for the deaf is guided by the principles of public education and is based on the general concept of the revolutionary work-oriented school. Beginning with preschool institutions, work for the deaf-mute child is built on a broad basis of social education. The central idea is that education is viewed as part of social life and as preparation for the child's participation in this life. According to one theoretician's definition of a vocational school, the basic goals of social education are training and education in society, through society and for society. The social environment and its structure are the final and deciding factors in any educational system. Concurrently, physiologists tell us that the social system and its structure and environmental conditions are the determining factors for shaping conditional forms of behavior. Therefore, the school also must recognize its role as a vehicle for social education, as the place for and means of organizing children in their surroundings. This is the basis of education for the deaf-mute inasmuch as it is just as impossible to learn speech away from societal life, as it is to swim standing on the shore.

Labor is that fundamental pivot around which the life of society is structured and erected. Man's social life and his study of nature are linked to the activity of labor. Labor, society, and nature are the three fundamental channels which guide educational and formative work in school. I shall not begin to review here the various well-known concepts of the labor-oriented school but I must point out that, when applied to a deaf child, vocational training offers the solution to all impasses. The most important thing is that work-oriented education offers the best path for entrance into life; it guarantees an active participation in life from the first years. Therefore, in the case of a deaf-mute child, it guarantees everything connected with it: communication, speech, consciousness.

Physically, a deaf-mute is more able to know the world and participate in it actively than a blind person. With the exception of a few, usually not very significant, cases of imbalance, the deaf-mute retains almost all the possible physical reactions which normal children possess. As a working apparatus, as a human machine, the body of a deaf-mute varies very little from that of a normal person. Consequently, a deaf person maintains the full range of possibilities for physical development and the acquisition of skills and vocational aptitudes. With the exception of a very few areas, directly connected with sound, all forms of work activity are accessible to him. And if, in spite of this, the education of the deaf until now has, for the most part, made use of only a narrow circle of useless trades, then this shortsightedness and philanthropic, invalid-oriented approach to education of the deaf is to blame. With the correct approach to this question, an enormous variety of opportunities can open up, offering the opportunity to work side by side with a normal person, and to escape the dangers of separation. This should be the foundation for the education of the deaf.

N. K. Krupskaia[8] characterized the overall character of educational programs based on labor in the following manner: "Orientation toward work activity and an investigation from this perspective of the interrelationships between people and nature, the individual and society, economics, politics, culture, the present and the past, will impart a general educational, polytechnical character to the content of instruction" (1970, p. 214).

A professional education is built on the basis of a polytechnical, labor-oriented program. This allows for complete mastery of some form of work and guarantees entrance into the mainstream of life and participation in it. The organization and development of the children's collective are based on labor-oriented education. The tasks of such an organization are not limited to an attempt to normalize the child's life; they extend much further. The organization of the children's collective turns into an educational process, which helps instill in children an awareness of themselves as an organic part of adult society. Perhaps almost for the first time in the world, our schools are developing an experiment in the self-organization of deaf children. The children create a student self-government, composed of sanitary, economic and cultural commissions, etc., which totally envelop the children's life. Living skills, social behavior, initiative, leadership qualities, collective responsibility grow and strengthen in this system. Lastly this social educational system for the deaf is crowned by a children's communist movement, i.e. participation in the Young Pioneers, which involves children in the life of the working class and acquaints them with the experiences and struggles of adults. The heartbeat of the world is felt in the Pioneer Movement; a child learns to see himself as a participant in life on a world scale. In this child's play, the sprouts of those serious thoughts and actions ripen which will play a decisive role in this life. What is new in all of this, is that for the first time the child enters the mainstream of present day life. Moreover life is directed toward the future whereas it usually had been based on past historical human experience.

At the top level the children's Pioneer Movement turns into the Young Communist Movement, a sweeping, wide-scale, social and political education whereby the deaf-mute child lives and breathes with his whole country. His pulse, his efforts, his thoughts beat in unison with the masses.

*   *   *

This system of social education is in itself new and represents the Revolution's main contribution to the education of the deaf. It is only necessary to introduce the enormous and inexhaustible possibilities which such an educational program can have for the development of speech, consciousness and thought in order to comprehend the significance of this system. In place of philanthropic charity, education of the deaf in the USSR has been established as a function of the State, to be directed and organized by public educational agencies. While we are still poor we cannot contribute a full measure of the means and forces required by this cause. The deaf-mute children grew poor along with the rest of the country in the years of the blockades, war and famine.* Today along with the rest of the Soviet Union, institutions for the deaf are experiencing a period of advancement, strengthening and rebirth. The number of educational institutions for the deaf rose sharply in the first year of the Revolution; it rose

---

* Vygotsky alludes not only to the economic hardship experienced during World War I, before the revolution, but also to the years of Civil War, 1918–1921. The Civil War divided the country and subjected much of the countryside to peremptory demands to support the various armies involved. After the Bolshevik government unilaterally withdrew from World War I in March 1918, Russia's former allies blockaded the new state, forbidding shipments of food and medicine as well as military supplies, meanwhile offering support to anti-Bolshevik groups. For these and other reasons of internal policy, famine was a considerable problem during the Civil War years, at its worst in 1921–1922.

in the period of fundamental demands by the masses, in a period of severe need which constituted the pressure for opening an increasing number of new institutions.

We are far from the thought that we have achieved some final point of development in this matter. On the contrary, we think that we are only at the beginning of our journey. But we believe that we have chosen the correct path, that we are headed in the appropriate direction and that the future belongs to the social education of deaf children.

COMPENSATORY PROCESSES IN THE DEVELOPMENT OF

THE RETARDED CHILD[1]

1

We are indebted to medical clinics for their diagnostic descriptions of mentally retarded children, yet such clinics took little interest in the development of the child afflicted by retardation. Because of the character of the practical problems facing a medical clinic, such institutions could not probe deeply into the problem of child development inasmuch as child retardation relates to a number of clinical forms which are readily ameliorated and in general are not responsive to therapeutic treatment. These forms of underdevelopment did not become the topic of serious investigation in clinics because there has never been any practical incentive toward this end nor have efforts been made in any other direction of clinical thought. Clinics were mainly interested in the possibility of determining those symptoms which can facilitate our recognition of mental retardation and distinguish this form from other similar handicaps—but it could do no more. With these goals in mind, clinics raised the problem of the development of the oligophrenic child. They established that an oligo-phrenic child does develop—not regress—just as the mentally ill child does. This fact is reiterated by a series of other indicators. With the help of these indicators, a child's mental debilitation is discerned and distinguished from other forms externally resembling it.

In conjunction with the clinical approach to the problem, mental retardation was taken "as a thing" and was not examined as a process. Interest was expressed in signs of stability and constancy while the dynamics and laws of development of the mentally retarded child and their correspondence with the laws of normal child development were left unexamined. Because this was essentially beyond the clinic's realm of vision, it was inevitably put aside.

Rehabilitational pedagogy, or education in special schools, obtained its primary infor-mation about the nature of mental retardation from clinics. The practicum was designed on the basis of the picture drawn as a result of clinical study. Initially, when the bourgeois school confronted the problem and the fact of mental retardation, this was sufficient since it set for itself the negative goals of barring passage into the school for normal children and, with the

122

assistance of this barrier, sought to weed out those children not capable of learning there or who were unwilling to. These were the problems even A. Binet posed in his approach to the diagnosis of mental retardation.

Anyone will understand the hopelessness of making a selection according to negative indicators. If we undertake such a weeding out, then we risk isolating and consolidating into one general group those children whose positive attributes have little in common. If we begin to separate out non-black colors based solely on this distinctive feature, then we will end up with a motley mixture. We will have red, yellow, and blue together only because they are not black. Common pedagogical practice on a broad scale (European and American) has shown that determining negative signs has led to precisely the same end as if one had decided to select colors according to a negative sign; the group of children thus selected will appear highly heterogeneous in composition, structural dynamics, and capabilities as well as in the causes which led to this condition. Even for the bourgeois school, these signs are insufficient because, when the question was posed as to how to educate and train mentally retarded children in order to bring them up at least to the minimal level of the demands they face, it turned out to be impossible to explain mental retardation on the basis of a purely negative definition. It is impossible to be guided only by what a given child lacks, by what he is not. On the contrary, it is necessary to have some conception, even if the most vague understanding, of what his capabilities are and what he represents. In this vein the bourgeois school accomplished exceedingly little.

At the moment, our school is facing enormous tasks of historical importance and is undergoing a decisive turnabout in the whole theory and practice of educating and training both the normal and the retarded child. Our auxiliary school senses the inadequacy of its main theoretical aims and its scientific foundation, which may seem to stem from the aforementioned sources. The first issue before us is the new practical goal and task confronting the study of mentally retarded children. It is not a study for the sake of a study, but a study for the purpose of finding the best form for practical actions, and of solving the historic task of actual conquest over mental retardation, a task facing great social calamity, a remnant of a class structured society. This task subordinates such a study to the needs of practical education now before us. These needs demand a positive differential approach to the study of mentally retarded children, that is, a study from the viewpoint of a child's positive characteristics and of a breakdown of the general mass of mentally retarded children.

At present, the best bourgeois research scientists also recognize that saying a that child is "mentally retarded" is the same as saying that a man is ill without stating the type of illness. One may establish the fact of retardation, but it is difficult to define its essence, derivation, and developmental fate for the child. Thus, the main task facing investigators of mental retardation is to conduct a research study into the development of the mentally retarded child and into the laws which guide this development.

In light of the foregoing, it seems to me that today I must dwell on three questions which make up the contents of my report.

The first question: What is there in the development of a mentally retarded child that works not against us but in our favor? What processes arise in the course of development itself which result in a struggle to overcome retardation and in the child's ascendance to a higher stage? The second question: What kind of structure and dynamics characterize mental retardation as a whole? Indeed, the picture of mental retardation has not thoroughly revealed those processes which work in our favor. In order to understand the significance and place of those favorable processes, we must understand their place and significance in the general structure of mental retardation. The third question is contained in the maximal pedagogical deductions drawn from the disclosure of the first and second questions. Therefore, I will briefly shed light on all three basic questions.

The general premise which serves as my point of departure and which, it seems to me, should be prescribed as the basis for the scientific study of the development of mentally retarded children, is the notion of the unity of laws governing development in both normal and abnormal children. Of course, this position by no means negates the fact that the laws governing a mentally retarded child's development acquire a qualitatively unique, specific expression and that the task is not limited to maintaining this unity. The task consists of showing how child development laws, united in essence and principle, find a concrete, special expression in the case of a retarded child. This is the first and central prerequisite which must be addressed from the very outset.

The question of methodology may be expressed as follows: Up to now, the conception which has been adopted in the West and which speaks of two forms of child upbringing—that based on biological factors and that governed by social factors—has dominated the scene. It has been assumed that in the presence of biological defects, children develop "along biological tracks" and that in their case we may dismiss the laws determining the social development and formation of a normal child. This mechanistic notion is unfounded methodologically speaking. From the very outset we must settle on a position without the conception of which everything else would remain theoretically groundless. This is the general position about the alliance of social and biological regularities in child development. The difficulty in understanding the development of a mentally retarded child arises from the fact that retardation is taken as a thing and not as a process. The issue of such a child's development is hidden from view. Hence came the notion that the primary disturbance in the case of oligophrenia is beyond question that which is primary—namely, the fundamental and leading factor governing the child's entire development. Nevertheless, from the view-point, of dialectics there couldn't be a more erroneous and inaccurate conception than this. Precisely in the process of development, the primary loss, which appears in the early stage of development, is repeatedly "diminished in importance" by newly occurring formations.

Allow me to say a few words with respect to the concept known as the *sublation* of biological laws. The Russian word for this term, *sniatie,*** is sometimes misunderstood. It was taken from the German *aufheben* but the German conveys a double meaning. When the word *sublation* is used in relation to some organic feature, this does not mean that this feature is eliminated. Instead, the feature is sublimated and preserved, embedded somewhere within; it recedes into the background, yielding to those regular features which arose at later stages. Therefore, it is understandable that those biological laws which appear as primary factors, determining the very first stage of development in a mentally retarded child, appear to be "interred but not destroyed"—they are "sublated" in the course of his development,"[2]

Because of their utmost importance, we must analyze the laws of this second type; they represent the fundamental premises for the subsequent thoughts which I wish to develop.

Allow me to return to the first part of our discussion, to the question of those processes which are relevant to us with respect to the development of retarded children. In the development of any child burdened by a given handicap, there occur certain processes which stem from the reaction of both the child's organism and his personality to those difficulties encountered. Both the child's organism and his personality react to a particular deficiency

---

* The Russian term means "to take away," "to take off," "reaping," or "relieving." [Transl.]

precisely when in the process of developing. During active adaptation to the environment, the organism and the personality work out a series of functions, with the help of which they compensate, equalize, and sublate the deficits. In my opinion, this issue represents such a clear, general biological concept that it hardly requires further detailed discussion. In order to educate a mentally retarded child, it is important to know how he develops. What is important is not the deficiency, the abnormality, the defect or handicap by itself, but the ensuing reaction, that is, how the child's personality develops in response to the encountered difficulties stemming from the handicap. The mentally retarded child does not consist of gaps and defects alone; his organism as a whole is restructured. The personality as a whole is balanced out and compensated for by the child's developmental processes.

It is important to learn not what type of illness a person has, but also what type of person is afflicted with the given illness. The same holds true with respect to deficiencies and defects. For us it is important to know not only what kind of defect has been diagnosed in a given child and how the assessed child has been affected, but also what kind of child possesses the given defect, that is, what role this defect plays in the child's individual makeup, what kind of restructuring occurs, and how a child copes with his handicap. The processes of illness could not be exposed unless it first be understood how the organism itself struggles with the illness, and that there are two kinds of symptoms: on the one hand, symptoms indicating a failure of certain functions and, on the other, symptoms indicating a struggle with these losses.

Precisely the same thing may occur in the area of abnormal child development: as long as one approaches such a study from the point of view of failure to develop, then a complete, correct, and adequate understanding of the child will not be achieved.

In order to dwell concretely on those mechanisms and laws which govern the emergence and development of compensatory processes, I must say a few words briefly about the theoretical meaning and interpretation of the compensation principle. In its application, this principle has hardly been extended to the development of a mentally retarded child, especially from a theoretical viewpoint. At first, it seemed to me and other investigators that the greatest conquest in understanding the compensatory processes in a mentally retarded child was his classification into a distinct factual category and the application of the compensatory principle to this factual basis. The concept of compensation has been far from sufficiently worked out, even in the area of those sciences which operate with this concept and which are more developed than the studies of mentally retarded children. Some fundamental positions which must project the correct methodological view for our understanding of the compensation principle and in the light of which we must examine our material are, however, clear, and we may speak about them in schematic form.

The first and basic position conflicting with our understanding of the problem of compensation in a retarded child is the interpretation of the very nature of this phenomenon, which, as we shall see, may be twofold. Some believe that the single and exclusive basis of compensatory processes is the actual subjective reaction of the child's personality to that situation which was created as a result of the defect. This theory assumes that the necessary and sole stimulus for developmental compensatory processes is the child's awareness of his deficiency and the emergence of an inferiority complex. From this feeling, from the consciousness of one's own inadequacy, comes a reflex action: the struggle to overcome the awareness of one's own inadequacy and to raise oneself to a higher level.

On precisely this basis, the Adlerian school in Austria and the Belgian school deny the mentally retarded child the possibility of the intensive development of compensatory processes. The train of arguments by these defectologists is as follows: In order for compensation to occur, it is necessary that the child become aware of and deeply feel his deficiency. For the mentally retarded child, however, the difficulty lies in the fact that he in no way sees himself in the critical light needed in order to recognize his own inadequacy, to come to an effective conclusion, and to overcome his retardation. In this respect, the published empirical research by DeGreef[3] on the development of a mentally retarded child is of interest. He established those signs which are currently called *E. DeGreef symptoms* and which constitute the increased self-esteem observed in children with mental retardation. If the child is asked to give a comparative appraisal of himself, his comrades, and his teacher, then it will turn out that the test subject will tend to consider himself the most intelligent. He will not recognize his retardedness because of an increased sense of self-esteem. The development of compensatory processes is made difficult, if not reduced to nil, because the mentally retarded child is satisfied with himself; he does not notice his deficiency and consequently is deprived of that tormenting experience of feeling inferior which, for other children lies at the basis of the formation of the compensatory processes.

As I perceive it, compensation may be understood in another way more closely corresponding to reality and in connection with the fact that compensatory phenomena in the area of consciousness were later analyzed in other areas. The task consists of explaining how these compensatory developmental processes arise in instances where they are not linked to awareness, where the defective functions cannot give rise to a feeling of inferiority and inadequacy and to an awareness of the defect. I do not want to say that compensation in the area of consciousness ranks with those compensatory occurrences in which, for example, the human body develops an impulse reaction to an injection of a certain amount of poison into its organism.

A theory that seeks to give a real explanation to occurrences of compensation must explain these phenomena in their entirety and must take into consideration the fact that, even at the lowest level of development, compensatory processes are connected with consciousness. Those authors who are obliged to answer this question answer it in the spirit of vitalism, believing that any element of a biological process has in it a psychological component, that certain vital mind-forming forces set the compensatory processes in motion, and that this psychological component is present in organic, compensatory processes in an undetectable form. This theory rests on an idealistic point of view, inasmuch as it attempts to produce a subjective understanding of compensation.

Meanwhile, the study of simpler organic processes of compensation and their juxtaposition to other processes results in the following factually based assertion: The source, or initial stimuli, for the emergence of compensatory processes are those objective difficulties with which a child struggles in the process of development. He struggles to get around these difficulties or to overcome them with the help of a whole series of such formations not initially found in his development. We have observed the fact that, when coping with difficulties, the child is forced to proceed along a roundabout path in order to overcome them. We have observed that the process of a child's interaction with his environment gives rise to a situation in which the child is propelled along a path of compensation. The following serves as a most important argument for this: The outcome of compensatory and developmental processes as a whole depends not only on the nature and severity of the defect, but also on the social reality of the defect, that is, on those difficulties which the defect causes from the viewpoint of the child's social position. For children with handicaps, compensation occurs in totally different circumstances depending on what the situation is, in what kind of environment the child is reared, and what difficulties arise for him as a result of his handicapped condition.

The cause of compensatory development is connected with the question of compensatory reserves. Where does this strength come from? What is the driving force behind compensatory development. According to one theory, the source is the inner goal-directed nature of life's developmental process itself and an inner integrity of personality. Despite its straightforwardness, this theory turns into a teleological position, which holds that each child is endowed with a certain purposefulness, a dynamic impulse or inner drive that draws the child in some indefinable way toward development, toward full self-assertion; some instinctive life force pushes the child ahead and guarantees his development, no matter what.

That compensatory developmental processes have at their disposal a certain objective purposefulness and that they set in motion certain healthy functions in a child's development can hardly be doubted. Even Charles Darwin was faced with a materialistic interpretation of these processes, and with their causal explanation, in other words, with showing the source of this objective purposefulness. In contrast with teleology, we do not begin our discussion of compensation with an examination of some inner burst of forces; we see that the reserve of compensatory forces is, to a large degree, to be found in the social-collective life of the child. Collective behavior is where he finds the material to build the inner functions which are realized during the process of compensatory development. It goes without saying that the wealth or poverty of a child's inner reserves (for example, the degree of mental retardation) is the essential and primary factor in determining to what degree a child will be capable of using this material. Furthermore, we need not mention, that the fate of a "debile" (a feebleminded child) and of an idiot differs substantially because their inner reserves differ so drastically. This again, however, is not the determining factor at higher stages, and in many cases this discrepancy is eliminated in the process of the child's development.

The last aspect which must be made clear in a fundamental understanding of compensatory processes is as follows: Clinics succeeded in bringing to light a series of new psychological conditions and in showing that the compensatory process can give rise to certain unhealthy symptoms. In actuality, compensation may lead the child along the path of a real or a fictitious and false equalization of his deficits. A central issue of interest to investigators in their assessment of compensation is the distinction between development based on real compensation and that based on fictitious compensation. No one questions the fact that compensation may serve as the main source of additional, beneficial developmental features. However, it is also true that compensatory features may also have an unhealthy character. It is methodologically important to single out those additional symptoms which arise in the course of compensation and which normalize, smooth over and promote the deficiency, further developing symptoms of fictitious compensation at a higher stage.

After a brief discussion of these aspects allow us to proceed to a few basic, concrete theses, which characterize the compensatory development of a retarded child.

First is the widely known substitution of extremely important functions, which both normal and abnormal children have in common. We are speaking about the fact that psychological operations may in their external appearance resemble each other closely and may even yield identical results but with respect to structure in a person's inner nature, or in what a person does in his head (as they say), by way of causal connections, these may have nothing to do with each other. This is the case primarily because the majority of psychological functions may be "simulated," to use a figurative expression of Binet, who first established this principle, naming it the "simulation of psychological functions": for example, the simulation of an excellent memory. As is well known, Binet analyzed people with outstanding memories, distinguishing between those who possessed an outstanding memory and those with an average memory. They later were able to retain in their memory a long series of digits or words, in many cases surpassing what the average person is able to remember. A person with an average memory would substitute the process of association and reflection for the process of recall. Presented with a long series of digits, the test subject would replace them with letters, images, words, and a graphic account; this constituted the key which helped him reconstruct the digits and therefore achieve the same results as those who possessed a really outstanding memory. The test subject, however, achieved this result by substitution. Such a phenomenon Binet called the "simulation of an outstanding memory."

I would not have begun speaking about this topic if it did not have bearing on exceptional cases and it were not a general principle of child development, if I did not know that, when it comes to the successful development of memory, each of us, in reality, is by no means indebted only to the fact that memory develops just as it is, but to the fact that each acquires a series of techniques and devices to substitute for memory. There are psychological processes and operations which expand the memory and bring it to a high level of development. Before us is not the exception but the general rule.

Substitution of certain psychological operations for others has been studied in the area of almost all intellectual mental processes. Only relatively recently have substitution processes been evaluated clinically and pedagogically from the viewpoint of their significance in the development of the retarded child. Research has shown that usually not one of the psychological functions (neither memory, nor attention) is performed in a single mode. On the contrary, each is performed by diverse means. Subsequently, wherever we face an obstacle, a deficiency, a limitation, or simply a task which exceeds our powers of natural ability in any given function, the function, it turns out, is not mechanically canceled; it is realized, brought to life, and performed with the help of that which it does not possess; for example, the essence of direct recall becomes a process of combination, imagination, thinking, and so forth.

I introduce here the general thesis which allows us to assess in its entirety the principle of substitution of psychological function and the diversity of these operations, by means of which functions may be realized. You know that in the development of memory a substantial change occurs approximately on the boundary of the transitional age: a change occurs in the corelation between the process of recall or memory, and the thought processes. For a young child, to think means to remember, that is, to reproduce former situations. This tendency in the memory process is revealed particularly clearly when we pose the task of defining an abstract concept. You can see then that in place of a logical definition, the child reproduces a concrete situation from previous experience. For an adolescent, to remember means to think. The process of remembering recedes into the background and is substituted for by cognitive manipulation.

This general position, as you see, defines the developmental stage of individual functions. At the same time, it presents the most simple form of the phenomenon with which we are dealing in the development of an abnormal child in general and of a mentally retarded child in particular. If we bear in mind how a blind child reads or a deaf-mute child begins to speak, then we will see that at the basis of these functions lies the substitution principle which allows, for example, a deaf child to speak not only with the help of one mechanism (the one we use) but also with the help of another mechanism. It turns out that the usual way of performing speech functions is not the only one, and that the absence of one means may be substituted for by other means of functioning.

A deciding role in the substitution processes throughout a child's entire social development is played by auxiliary means (speech, words, and other signs), with the help of which a child begins to stimulate himself. The role of auxiliary means that enriching the child's development leads as well to the second fundamental principle characterizing compensatory processes, that is, the hypothesis of the collective as a factor in the development of a normal and an abnormal child.

Allow us to begin our discussion of this second principle by stating a general psychological law which is contained in the fact that a series of higher psychological functions proceed along the most varied paths. This is easier to understand when one judges by the example of how thought develops its highest form in connection with speech. You know that speech initially develops as a means of communication and mutual understanding, as a communicative, social function. Inner speech, (i.e., speech by means of which a human being thinks) emerges later and is the basis for assuming that its formation process occurs only at school age. The path which transforms speech into a means of communication, into a function of collective social behavior, the path which transforms speech into a means of thinking, into an individual psychological function, gives us some idea of the law governing the development of higher psychological functions. This law may be expressed in the following manner: Any psychological function occurs twice in the process of a child's development, first as a function of collective behavior, as an organization of the child's collaboration with his social environment, and then as an individual behavioral operation, as an internalization of psychological activity in the narrow and precise sense of the word. In precisely the same way, speech is transformed from a means of communication into a means of thinking, which characteristically searches for methods to substantiate a judgment; it occurs in a child of preschool age no earlier than the first arguments within the child's collective, no sooner than the necessity arises, stimulating the child's own assertion. As one researcher put it, not only children but also grown-ups willingly take their own words to be true; little proof is demanded. The necessity of logical reflection about an assertion depends on collective operations, such as arguing.

Research has shown that one of the most characteristic voluntary processes, namely, the process of subordination, also develops in the child within a collective. On the basis of play, Western researchers in particular first demonstrated that a child at play develops techniques for submitting his behavior to the rules of collective behavior; subsequently, this emerged organization turns into inner behavior and becomes individual psychological behavior.

Thus, we see that a child's collective behavior not only activates and trains his own psychological functions but also serves as an impetus for that completely new form of behavior which arose in the historical period of in the development of humanity and which appears in the structure of the personality in the form of higher psychological functions. The collective becomes the source of development for these functions, and all the more so in a mentally retarded child.

The general developmental path of child speech may be charted in its collective form. If we say that the child has mastered speech and that he begins to better submit his own psychological processes to his own control, then speech turns into a means of thinking as well. Experimental research has revealed the difference between the coefficient of development of psychological processes and their real role in a child's life. One may have a good memory but make poor use of it, and alternately, one may perfect it so that it will produce a greater practical effect, so that it is greater than a highly developed but poorly used memory. For the normal child, there will be movement upward if at an older age, development is achieved not as a result of the direct (nonmediated) growth of a function but as a result of its use, its subordination. It is essential that the series of higher psychological functions proceed from external to internal [activity—Transl.] Just as speech serves as the basis for development, so, too, does the external form of collective collaboration precede the development of a whole series of inner functions. Here, we run into trouble on one essential point: The source of and nurturing environment for the development of higher psychological functions is the child collective but it is distinguished by varying optimal intellectual levels of the children in the collective. In his research, E. DeGreef points out a distinctive feature of a mentally retarded child: He understands other mentally retarded children better and has a higher estimation of them than does a normal child, because he is dealing with a difference within his own level of understanding.

In the history of child development (and our own psychological development), passive functioning significantly surpasses the active performance of any psychological function. A child begins to understand speech earlier than he begins to speak. We are capable of understanding a book written by a genius but are often not able to convey its contents; the extent of our verbal comprehension is greater than our capacity for the active production of speech.

A one-sided collective, composed entirely of mentally retarded children who are absolutely identical in level of development, is a false pedagogical ideal. It contradicts the basic law of development of higher psychological processes and conflicts with the general notion of the diversity and dynamics of psychological functions in any child, and particularly in a retarded child. Earlier investigators have proposed that the intellect is a single, simple, uniform, homogeneous function, and, that if we have before us a debile (a feebleminded child), then all his functions are uniformly reduced. More comprehensive research has shown that the intellect, emerging in the process of complex development, cannot by nature be uniform, structurally simple or undifferentiated. On the contrary, what is called the intellect represents a diversity of functions in a complex whole. But this unity does not mean uniformity; it does not mean homogeneity. Analysis of this complicated structure's dynamics has led researchers to the conclusion that it is impossible to maintain the position that in the case of retardation all the functions of the intellect prove to be identically affected because, in representing a distinct quality, each function thereby uniquely affects the process underlying mental retardation.

I shall introduce an example. You know that only in the last ten years a relationship between motor control and mental development has been taken into consideration. It was believed that diverse forms may combine but that they do not necessarily go hand in hand, figuratively speaking. Subsequent research has shown that the development of motor operations may occur and may indeed appear as one of the central areas of compensation for mental retardation. Inversely, in children with motor delays intellectual development may be reinforced. Isolating and understanding the qualitative uniqueness of intellectual, verbal, linguistic, and motor development show that retardation never affects all intellectual functions identically. The relative independence of functions within their unity results in the compensatory development of one function and its effect on another.

Two aspects of this issue remain to be discussed.

Observation of normal children has shown that the development of psychological functions depends on more than the growth and change of functions. Consider, for example, memory, attention and so forth. Because functions never operate in isolation but in certain combinations, psychological development at an older age occurs as a result of changes in the systematic relationship between functions, that is, because of the so-called *interfunctional connections*. What is meant by the accepted term *logical* memory is a certain relationship between memory and thinking. In the early period of childhood development, functional relationships are different than at a later stage.

Investigative study of the mentally retarded child has revealed that in such a child, interfunctional relationships take shape distinctively and differently in comparison with those that come to light in the development of a normal child. This sphere of psychological development, the change in interfunctional connections and relationships, the change in the internal structure of the psychological system, is the most important area for the operation of compensatory processes in forming personality. The functions themselves do not determine the motor connections and interfunctional relationships as much as does the way in which these functions are brought into unity.

And finally, we have the roundabout paths of development, that is, the achievement or realization of some new point of development, of some new formation on a roundabout path of development. Here, the cause which provokes the child to overcome difficulties has enormous significance. If these difficulties do not cause the child to lose his zeal or do not force him to flee from them, but activate him, then they will lead to a roundabout path of development.

What is most significant is the creative character of a retarded child's development; the old pedagogical theory assumed that external causes automatically influenced the character of a mentally retarded child's development. It might seem improper to apply this high-flown word *creative* to the comparatively small achievements of the retarded child. But for a "debile" mastery of the four operations of arithmetic implies the occurrence of far greater creative processes than it does for a normal child. What comes to a normal child almost "as an (unrealized) native endowment" presents the mentally retarded child with great difficulty and becomes a task which requires the surmounting of obstacles. Thus, such achievement [for the mentally retarded child] manifests a creative character. I think that this is the most essential point in the literature on the development of mentally retarded children.

In the first section, I have attempted briefly to outline those processes in a mentally retarded child's development which work in our favor, by which we must be guided in our attempts to overcome his retardation.

It would be erroneous, however, to think that these aspects close the gap in the developmental process, that a wise Mother Nature leads the child along the path of conquest, gives him the strength to eliminate his retardation. How wrong it would be to think that the organism's struggle with illness always leads to a happy ending, that each organism under any conditions copes with illness in an identical way.

It is necessary to say a few words about the fact that developmental laws for an abnormal and a normal child unfold before us according to essentially one and the same law. Adverse environments and influences, occurring during the course of the child's development, more frequently and more sharply lead a mentally retarded child to those negative additional features which not only do not help him surmount his retardation but, on the contrary, aggravate his primary deficiency and encumber him further. One may ask: Why speak about these processes, about environmental influences on the mentally retarded child, if we recognize from the outset, that for the most part, under negative influences the child's retardation is not only not eliminated during development but new peculiarities are added? One must speak of these processes only because the problem is really clarified by the aggregate of that which is bright and that which is dark. As I will try to show, however, in the case of retardation, primary complications in a child's development are considered which arise in the course of his social formation and which may be overcome only if we are able to study the root of their causes. But more about this later.

The essence of the thought which conveys the entire two or three decades of collaborative scientific work in this direction can be summed up as follows: Mental retardation is not the simple, homogeneous whole that it was pictured to be by former research investigators. For example, I analyze a mentally retarded child, I establish a series of indications which reveal his retardation. One asks: Are all the symptoms of equal value? Do they have an identical relationship to the primary cause? Are they all primary symptoms? Do they all arise at the same time by means of the same mechanism? Are there among them primary and secondary symptoms, some arising earlier and others later? On the basis of the earlier symptoms, which are more prominent forms or latent features of psychopathology?

Development shows that the pedagogical and psychological picture of mental retardation which unfolds before us is not a homogeneous whole, that those symptoms which indicate retardation cannot be lined up in one row, that mental retardation has a complex structure. In order to gain an understanding of this structure, it is necessary to turn to the development of the mentally retarded child and not to the nature of those pathological processes which lie at the basis of retardation, because the complexity of the structure arises in the process of development. The central and simpler model for analysis is the separation of the primary features constituting the very nucleus of the child's feeblemindedness—features directly caused by the child's biological deficiency, the basis of his retardation—from those symptoms of a secondary, third, fourth, fifth and sixth nature and so forth, which, as the result of a specific environment, cause the child to meet additional difficulties and accumulate additional complications. The development of later features on top of the initial formations leads to the necessity for a differential analysis of mental retardation.

With respect to clinics, one must say that they see oligophrenia as a combined group. The study of personality structure in an oligophrenic child has been advanced for the first time in the study of child development. Here, for the first time, the central thought of our work has matured: It is insufficient just to say about this child that he is "mentally retarded" (this is the same as saying he is "sick," and not curing him). This means only to pose the problem but not to solve it. In other words, it is necessary to explain the nature of the cultural retardation which confronts us; what kind of structure does it have, what are the mechanisms and the significance of the processes forming this structure, what is the dynamic cohesion of its individual symptoms, what is the complex whole from which we take our picture of a child's mental retardation, and how do we distinguish the types of mentally retarded children.

Children are chosen to attend the contemporary auxiliary school according to the principle of negative selection (A. Binet). Our auxiliary school must work with raw material, with mental retardation in general; this constitutes the main difficulty of this approach in differentiating mental retardation. Differentiation must become the fundamental rule of all our new practical work.

The study of mentally retarded children shows that the picture we have of a child of eight can in no way be related to the core of his debility, i.e., his primary inner deficiency. Allow me to take the concrete example with which I began. Clinical observations show that, in some mentally retarded children, there occurs an extreme divergence and discrepancy between the underdevelopment of elementary functions and the development of higher psychological functions. Underdevelopment occurs in two forms: Either we observe the poorly developed elementary functions along with a radical development of higher psychological functions, which mask the retardation of the child, or there is a disproportionately weak development of higher psychological functions in comparison with the development of organic functions. We meet this latter case more frequently. Before me is a ten-year-old mildly retarded child—a debile. According to the evaluation of test results, his mental retardation was equated with a three-year delay, i.e., he lagged behind a normal child by three years. This means that the conclusive data on the child must show a picture resembling that of a normal seven-year-old child. It turns out that such a numerical approach is inaccurate. If the higher psychological functions of a mildly retarded [lit. debile] child are much more underdeveloped than those of a seven-year-old child, then we have to draw the important pedagogical conclusion that, in contrast to the development of his elementary needs, the underdevelopment of his higher psychological functions could surrender to good pedagogical influence.

Attentive investigators have posed the question: Whence do the unequal underdevelopment of lower/organic, and of higher/psychological functions originate? If retardation in the area of higher and lower development occurred identically as a direct result of a primary cause, the question would not arise. This irregularity has led for the first time to an empirical formulation of the question: Is the underdevelopment of higher functions in a mildly retarded child caused directly by the primary cause or is this a secondary complication? Experimental data and clinical research could not give the answer. The underdevelopment of higher functions in a mentally retarded child is connected with cultural underdevelopment because he is excluded from the cultural environment and from the "nurturing support" of his milieu. Because of his deficiency, he is not influenced by the environment. As a result his retardation increases and negative features are accumulated along with additional complications in the form of social underdevelopment and of pedagogical neglect. All this surfaces in the form of secondary complications and means an absence of good upbringing. In the setting in which he grew up, he took less than he could have; no one tried to unite him with his environment, and, if the child has few and meager connections with the child collective, then we may see a case of secondary complications.

I could name a series of symptomatic complexes which represent secondary and tertiary formations scaffolded on top of the core problem. I could illustrate the causal mechanism of their emergence, but I will now limit myself only to this statement: All the negative aspects characterizing a mentally retarded child may simply mean a developmental passivity instilled in him from the very outset. Positive and negative factors continually influence the child. Thus, we have an accumulation of a series of secondary formations which can just as well proceed along a line of equalization and can cause additional complications in the initial picture of mental retardation.

I have no choice but to draw a pedagogical conclusion. It is necessary right now, today, to turn our attention to the second line of development, to the influence of the environment on a mentally retarded child's development; for this, it is necessary to examine additional, accumulated complications resulting from mental retardation. This problem has an enormous pedagogical significance and is closely connected with a practical problem facing the school. Indeed, all other conditions being equal, the formations which emerge much later and that are less connected with the primary derivative factor are easier to eliminate in resolving the problem of mental retardation.

As soon as it has been proved scientifically that a given complex of symptoms is not of primary but of secondary, tertiary, fourth, or fifth etc., significance, then you have illustrated the creation of a nucleus which submits to formative pedagogical influences. That is to say, when all other conditions are equal, they may be the more easily eliminated or distanced from the initial cause.

If we are going to talk about a group of mentally retarded children, whose retardation is based on some pathological deficiency or brain damage, then we must note that the nucleus of the "debility" itself and all the phenomena connected with this deficiency submit with greater difficulty to pedagogical influences, yielding only to indirect, constant influence and training. However, since one is powerless to remove the effect of the cause, then one will also not be able to remove the phenomena related to the core. Precisely the reverse is often true, when we talk about complications of a secondary, third, or fourth nature. Superimposed on top of the primary difficulty, such complications are first to be suspended; and as one contemporary author has stated, the elimination of secondary complications in a mentally retarded child changes the entire clinical picture of mental retardation to such a degree that the modern clinic would refuse to recognize retardation if the educational process were carried to its logical end.

Speaking in general about the mentally retarded child and reducing mental retardation to all that we observe in the child, we reconstruct today's clinical picture: The clinic will fulfill its own official purpose but without an analysis of what belongs to the core of retardation, and of what the child has picked up, what he has acquired. The picture will seem unclear; accordingly, that which is secondary will be attributed to such a degree to that which is primary that this will significantly reduce the parameters of possible influence. The empirical picture will in no way agree with the real picture of debility, particularly in those instances where secondary features have, to a certain degree, been eliminated. S. Lewenstein[4] proved experimentally that additional complications significantly yield to psychotherapeutic influence. E. Kretschmer clinically affirmed the law established by Lewenstein: Secondary complications are most easily liquidated in the process of the afflicted child's development.

I tie all this together with the last of the theses which forms our summary and which radically distinguishes modern pedagogy for mentally retarded children from traditional pedagogy. This thought is paradoxical: Everything forces us to suppose that the higher functions turn out to be more educable than the elementary functions. The old pedagogy limited the mentally retarded child in his development. Then the method of sensorimotor training was initiated so that training of the eye and the ear or learning to distinguish colors took up half the therapeutic work until recently. The results of training sensorimotor skills have been inconsequential. Theoretical and experimental research has shown that the sense of smell, for example, showed insignificant and extremely weak development; the higher functions, the higher processes, turned out to be more responsive to training. Allow us to introduce two theoretical proofs which are at the core of this phenomenon and the paradox will seem clear.

Experimental research on twins is one of the contemporary methods used to distinguish between hereditary attributes and those attributes conditioned by the social environment. Science uses an experimental approach which most closely affords us the opportunity to solve these questions. As is well known, twins can be from one or two eggs. The uterine period of their development takes place in an identical environment. If we compare two pairs of twins—one-egg and two-egg twins—and determine to what degree the psychological functions of both sets are similar, then it turns out that the "A" functions (the higher psychological functions) of both sets of twins brought up in the same environment render an approximate coefficient of similarity. This means that these functions depend very little on heredity and, consequently, depend on certain circumstances, on their social milieu. The coefficient of similarity for "B" functions (primary psychological functions) in the same sets of twins is different: These functions turn out to be more conditioned by hereditary factors than is true of the higher psychological functions.

Experimental research studies on motor functions have led to a common thesis: The more elementary the motor processes are, the greater the difference there is in the coefficient of similarity (the one-egg pair showed a greater similarity than the two-egg set). The higher the motor functions, then, all conditions being equal, the greater the co-efficient of similarity in both pairs of twins. The highest motor functions are the more trainable, because they are not phylogenetic but acquired during ontogenesis. The results of experimental research show that the higher psychological processes are more educable because the source of their structural development is the collective education of the child.

One of L. Terman's[5] students, Quade, conducted experimental work in America and demonstrated that the dynamics of development of elementary functions and higher psychological functions are not one and the same. The same can also be observed in mentally retarded children. Thus, the development of higher processes curbs mental retardation.

I want to finish by pointing out that the conclusions, no matter how general and inconsequential, are nevertheless closely tied to two fundamental tasks which face us and which must provide a certain turnabout in our auxiliary school. These tasks involve general compulsory polytechnical education. The old auxiliary school avoided these tasks with a tendency to strive for minimalization. On the one hand, the reduction of an elementary education and, in the best cases, an approximation of a simplified program of five years meant a minimum development and put to the question the possibility of a child's subsequent education and adaptation. On the other hand, this school was based on a nondifferentiated approach to mental retardation. It did not make a distinction between individual complexes of symptoms and mental retardation itself in any given child. Therefore, pedagogy treated children psychologically as one single, homogeneous whole without distinguishing between the more estranged and weaker links, which could, in the first place, be torn off and eliminated.

The actual development of the problem of general and polytechnical education with respect to mentally retarded children should constitute a topic of special research. I consider it possible and necessary to limit myself to pointing out the fact that those generally formed conclusions which theoretically restructure the traditional pedagogical approach to mentally retarded children are the ones most closely tied to the actual concrete task facing our schools today. However, this connection is a task for special research and is beyond my power.

And we ask, therefore: Is the principle of compensation the sole principle which determines the uniqueness and basic features of a mentally retarded child's development? No, it is not the sole one, but one of the many principles. It goes without saying that a total and thorough evaluation of this principle is possible only within the framework and system of all aspects which characterize development as a whole. We have asked whether compensation is the determining factor? This depends on what we have in mind. If we have in mind the specific viewpoint which I addressed in my introduction—changing the approach of research investigators from a vitalistic one to a positivistic one—then the compensatory method has a decisive significance. In this respect, the principle of compensation needs to be isolated from subjective psychological factors, which we have already mentioned and about which it will be necessary to speak further as we work out other related problems.

Is this [compensatory] principle the main organizing principle at work? Of course not. It is the moment, or force, which indexes the character of development,—the category of processes through which the retarded child passes—which has its has unique lawfulness, development and fate. Does this mean that the immediate task of pedagogy is an analysis of compensatory processes? I have already said that by themselves these processes may serve both as a basis for equalization and as a source of new pathological symptoms. And therefore, I think that this principle in its general form, is an empty form. When we speak about pedagogy and processes of labor in polytechnical education, compensation becomes the main and fundamental principle of all of education. But may one assert that the development of a mentally retarded child is defined by compensatory processes alone? It is impossible to pose the question in this manner. It is important to explain that it serves as the fulcrum of support for all-around development of the child. It seems to me it is absolutely clear that our definite task is to detect, discover, and analyze those processes which serve as the fulcrum of support, precisely in child development, and on which one must build when dealing with retarded children in a polytechnical school.

In describing how some functions take the place of others, I have indicated that we are dealing with inescapable general forms of the maximum use of all possibilities. If this inescapable path of development assists mentally retarded children in a broad sense, then it means that this developmental path is necessary and that the questions about whether a polytechnical education is possible for a mentally retarded child and whether he has the capabilities that make this education realistic are questions of a utopian nature.

In stating that the former focus of therapeutic pedagogy, with its heavy emphasis on the training of elementary functions, must be replaced with the mental development of higher functions on the strength of their maximal educability, I have in mind those rigorous demands made by a polytechnical education.

If apprehension arises as to whether one should emphasize and count on the development of elementary functions, then one may ask: What results did the school achieve when it proceeded exclusively along the line of training elementary processes, assuming that the child is capable of development only in this area? It is worth mentioning the dogma of visual methods which has been advanced because the mentally retarded child has little aptitude for the development of abstract thought, and therefore gravitates toward graphics and concrete thought. Should we follow the former example of the traditional school and educate only by visual methods and proceed along the line of least resistance because the mentally retarded child achieves few successes in the area of abstract learning? We must direct all attention to uncovering and overcoming the deficiency at the point where it turns out to be the most vulnerable.

The research results of the last ten years in the use of M. Montessori's sensorimotor system have shown that even where training of elementary functions in the normal and the mentally retarded child is introduced, development occurs because of higher functions; when, as a result of training, a child's sensitivity to smells increases, then he also exhibits a more attentive attitude and keener sense of analysis.

2

The new academic year (1927) is, in a certain sense, a turning point in the history of our auxiliary school for mentally retarded children. The Main Social Educational Agency (*Glavsotsvos*) published the auxiliary school's programs, drawn up on the basis of the last edition of the plan by GUS [the State Academic Council]* for the first stage of city schools. Many years of work have gone into bringing the public and the special school closer together; general principles of social education have been introduced into the special schools and special schools have been redesigned along those principles. This task is of great fundamental and practical importance and was proposed by programs which draw the auxiliary school into the current of overall pedagogical creativity. "The general goals and problems facing an integrated vocational school, are at the same time the goals and the tasks of the auxiliary school" ("Programs of the Auxiliary School," 1927, p. 7). This publication answers the question about the character of the auxiliary school with absolute clarity. The general principles used to design a program in the auxiliary school are the same as for the programs of schools for normal children; the immediate goal of the auxiliary school coincides with the immediate goal of the school for normal children at Stage 1 inasmuch as it strives to produce collectivists, that is, "to supply the knowledge and skills which are most essential for vocational activity and cultural life and to arouse in the children an active interest in their surrounding world" (ibid.). The programs merit a separate, detailed discussion.

First of all, a few words about the rapprochement of the auxiliary and the normal school. In many countries, this tendency toward combining the two has been distinctly reported. Let the mentally retarded children study longer, let them learn less than normal children; let them finally be taught differently with the help of special methods and techniques adapted to the unique abilities of their condition, but let them learn the same thing as all the children; let them receive the same preparation for future life in order that they may later participate in it to the same degree and on equal footing with all others. Thus, this tendency may be expressed most simply. The most important argument for giving the auxiliary schools the same goals facing the normal school is the established and verified fact of the work capabilities of the enormous majority of graduates (90 percent) from the auxiliary school. They are able to enter society's work force, and not just at its lowest levels along with severely retarded children (imbeciles), but also in the industrial, agricultural, the vocational work force. What kind of a different education may be given to these future builders and workers besides the general social education which the rest of the children in the country receive? It is true that pupils of the auxiliary school must be introduced to these general goals by different paths; this justifies the existence of the special school, and constitutes its uniqueness.

This trend found expression in 1926 in Germany, when the possible change in the name of the auxiliary school (*Hilfsschule*) was put to question. Children and parents found something offensive in the old name; a transfer to this school branded the child's reputation. No one wants to go to "a school for fools;" the very fact of the child's attendance at this school meant a degradation in his social position. Adler's followers say that this school develops a feeling of inferiority (*Minderwertigkeitsgefuehl*), which is expressed in an unhealthy way in the child. The shadow of inferiority even falls on the teacher at this school.

---

* *Gosudaarstvennyi uchenyi sovet*, Narkompros (that is, the People's Commissariat of Enlightenment (Education)), RSFSR (1913–1933). [Transl.]

New names were suggested: "rehabilitational pedagogical school," "special school," "medical-pedagogical school." Meanwhile, an appropriate name has not been found, probably because the problem lies not in the name alone, but in the entire social and pedagogical setting of the auxiliary school, in the fact that it should not be a "school for fools," and that the education provided there should be—and not in name alone—the same nationwide general social education. It is our intention to reflect the connections among life's fundamental phenomena (nature, labor, society), to develop a scientific world view in a retarded child, and to build in him at school a conscientious attitude toward his future.

The traditional auxiliary school operates along a line of least resistance. It accommodates and adapts itself to the child's retardation: a retarded child masters abstract thinking with the greatest difficulty because the school excludes from its material anything which demands any attempt at abstract thinking, and it bases its instruction on concreteness and visual methods. The principle of the absolute sovereignty of visual aids is at present undergoing a serious crisis, analogous to the crisis with respect to the same principle in the general school. In fact, should the school proceed along the line of least resistance and only adapt itself to the child's retardation? Should it not, on the contrary, struggle with retardation and direct its efforts along a line of greatest resistance; at overcoming those difficulties in the child's development which are created by the defect? W. Eliasberg, who has studied the psychology and pathology of abstract thought, justifiably cautions against the absolute dominance of visual aids in the auxiliary schools. Operating on exclusively concrete and visual representations, we hold back and impede the development of abstract thinking, the functioning of which cannot be replaced in the child's behavior by any visual techniques. Precisely because the retarded child has difficulty with abstract thinking, the school must develop this ability using all possible means. In the final analysis, the school's job is not to adapt itself to the defect, but to overcome it. A retarded child, even more than a normal child, requires that the school develop in him the rudiments of thinking, because, when left to himself, he will not master this operation. In this sense, the aim of our programs is to give the mentally retarded child a scientific outlook, to open him up to connections of a nonconcrete order, to develop while he is still in school a conscientious attitude toward his entire future: for therapeutic pedagogy this is a test of historical significance.

It is well known what difficulties sensorimotor training and technical psychological support present to the special school. Exercising a child's sensory and motor organs in the traditional school has turned into a system of artificial, isolated activities which are uninteresting and therefore painful for the children, like the lessons in silence, the study of smells, the distinction of noises and so forth. Both our school and the schools abroad have found the solution in an integration of all these exercises into play, labor, and other children's activities. For example, a fruit and vegetable garden presents an unlimited realm of opportunities for children's exercises, for emotional development, for advancement. Meteorological observations, the construction of barometers and thermometers, an acquaintance with elementary physics, the study of plant and animal life, elements of natural science, patterning the various plant and animal forms, simple implementation of vocational tools and so forth—all this can be brought together and centered around work in the garden. Once they are made an integral part of some attractive work activity, sensorimotor exercises will lose their artificial oppressive character in the eyes of children.

THE DIFFICULT CHILD[1]

The psychology of a difficult child* presents a most crucial problem for investigation from various angles, because the notions of "difficult child" and "hard-to-raise child" are very broad. Here, in fact, we confront categories of children who differ greatly from one another, who are united by one negative attribute: they all present difficulties in terms of upbringing. Therefore, the terms "difficult child" or "hard to raise child" are not scientific terms and do not represent any definite psychological or pedagogical content. It is a general label for huge groups of children who differ from one another; it is a prefatory term, advanced out of practical convenience.

The scientific study of these forms of childhood development has still not reached the point of enabling us to have more definitions at our disposal. It has been justifiably pointed out, particularly in recent times, that the problem of the difficult-to-raise category should not be limited only to the age of childhood. In fact we often confront in the behavior of adults forms which represent a direct analogy with childhood difficulties, and if one cannot call adults hard-to-bring-up because we do not bring them up, then in any case these people are difficult to handle. In past attempts to shed light on this concept, cases were cited where adults in a family have turned out to be the difficult family members or problem workers in a production line or in a social activity. It has been successfully shown in concrete terms that from a psychological point of view these adults exhibit precisely the same displays of difficult character and other symptoms as do children. In other words, what was at issue were those forms of character or degree of personal capabilities which led to a series of difficulties and deficits in social adaptation, activity, and behavior. The problem is becoming more and more widespread, and the most authoritative American psychologists working in this area propose isolating the problem in a special branch of psychological knowledge which they preliminarily call "psychology of border-line phenomena." With this label, they had in mind not only the impairment of nervous processes, which assumes neuropathological or psychological forms, but activity which, while remaining within the boundaries of the norm,

---

* The term is a strict translation of the Russian *trudnye*. Perhaps a more idiomatic, if somewhat outdated English expression, would be "problem child." It seemed advisable to retain a strict translation leaving the interpretation of the term to the reader. [Ed.]

nevertheless presents very serious problems, interrupting the correct course of a person's upbringing, social and work activities, and personal, and family life.

In view of the unusual complexity and breadth of this theme, allow me to dwell only on two basic points which have pivotal meaning: the problem of the formation of a child's character and the problem of his natural talents. An enormous number of difficult children present problems primarily in these two areas. We usually have before us either a child who is difficult to educate because of few or very low natural capabilities or a child who is difficult to manage because of those tendencies in his behavior and character which make him difficult to live with. It is difficult to handle him, he does not submit to school discipline, and so forth. Let us turn to the problem of a difficult character and the problem of a child's character formation.

1

In psychology, the problem of character has recently undergone revision and reexamination. It is not my task to describe the full scope of this problem: I am interested only in the aspect connected with the problem of a difficult-to-raise child.

In modern doctrines on character research, investigators have been conducting work in two opposite directions. Some psychologists are investigating the biological basis of what we call human character or, more accurately, the humanizing temperament [or "human-guiding" temperament]. They study the interrelationships of organic systems which correlate with one or another behavior pattern. E. Kretschmer's well-known doctrine may serve as the most striking example of research based on knowledge of the human body. Other investigators study not merely the biological character but also how it develops in various conditions of the social environment in which the child must build his character. In other words, these researchers are dealing with character in the full sense of the word, and not with temperament. They have in mind those tendencies in a person's behavior which are not so much inherent at birth, as cultivated on the basis of qualities acquired during the process of upbringing, of development, of adaptation to one or another environment. Research of the second order presents the greatest interest because, as I will try to show, it more closely approaches the problem of the formation of deviations in a child's character or a difficult character.

I permit myself to begin with a concrete example which will clarify how modern psychologists are inclined to picture the formation of certain character traits, or a certain behavioral tendency. Let us say that we have before us a child who is afflicted with a hearing loss as a result of one or another cause. It is easy to imagine that this child will experience a series of difficulties in adapting to his surroundings. During play, other children will leave him in the background; he will lag behind on walks; he will be eliminated from active participation in children's festivities and conversations. In a word, a child with a hearing impairment will be placed, because of his simple organic deficiency, in a lower social position than other children. We want to say, that in the process of adapting to the social milieu, this child will run up against more obstacles than will a normal child. How will this circumstance affect the formation of the child's character?

I think that the development of a child's character will proceed along the following fundamental lines: As a result of poor hearing, he will confront difficulties; therefore, a heightened sensitivity, attentiveness, curiosity, distrustfulness with respect to his environment will develop. Perhaps he will cultivate still another series of particular psychological traits, the appearance of which is understandable if we take into account that these character traits are the child's response to the difficulties encountered on his path. The child who, as a result of his deficiency, becomes the object of derision among his comrades will develop increased suspicion, curiosity, and caution, and an entire complex psychological superstructure. We understand this complex system of attitudes and behavioral modes to be a reaction, or response to the difficulties the child encounters in the process of adapting to his social environment.

We are able to note three basic types of such forms of reaction in the child. One of these is well known in psychiatry; in medicine, it is called the delirium of the hard of hearing. This group is so different from others that psychiatrists long ago singled it out. Those forms of response mentioned above begin to occur in the hard of hearing. Suspicion, distrust, overanxiety, and caution develop in the person who is beginning to lose his hearing. Each word from those surrounding him gives him cause for strong anxiety; it seems to him that people are thinking something bad about him. He loses sleep and begins to feel that he will be killed. He is ready to accuse others of conspiring against him. Each new face arouses suspicions in him. In the final analysis, he develops a persecution mania.

Are these character traits the same, according to my psychological nature, as those with which I was born? I propose that a given formation appears in response to difficulties arising in the course of adaptation to the environment. If a hearing defect did not cut this person off from his surrounding environment, and normal relations with other people continued, then there would not be anything particular about his behavior. Although we have the right to say that this is simply a case of a response formation, suspicion, and caution, it is, however, a well-known behavioral way of relating to the environment, a mode cultivated in response to those difficulties which a person confronts. But this is a fictitious condition does not stem from reality, inasmuch as close friends and relations do not wish him evil. Further, those means of behavior cultivated by a sick person in response to difficulties do not really overcome them. The difficulties themselves arise on the basis of ideas which are divorced from reality and on the basis of the unreal means used by the afflicted person in his struggle with these phantoms. Modern psychologists suggest that such a system of character formation be called fictitious compensation. They say that this attitude of caution, suspicion and overanxiety arises as a form of compensation when a person tries to defend himself in some way in the face of difficulties. If we turn to the example with which I began, then we see that the two opposing lines of character development are also possible in the case of a hard-of-hearing child. The first (which we can call real compensation) occurs in response to more or less realistically accountable difficulties. Thus, if a hard of hearing child develops a heightened sensitivity, keenness of observation, curiosity, attentiveness, and sharpness and learns to recognize by vague signs that which other children learn by means of auditory perception, he does so because he has a healthy regard for his difficulties. He will not leave his watch post lest he miss something. This is called real compensation. We have already discussed fictitious compensation.

Finally, the last type of compensation. It may assume the most diverse forms. Here, we do not encounter the two types of compensation already identified (hallucinatory and real compensation). The third type—the most difficult to define—is so multifarious, so far removed from external unity, that it is difficult to define with one word. Here, however, is a rough explanation. Imagine that a child experiences a certain weakness. Under certain conditions, this weakness can become a strength. The child may cover up his weakness. He is weak and hears poorly. This lowers his responsiveness to other children and elicits a greater solicitude on the part of others. And he begins to cultivate an illness within himself in order to obtain the right to have more attention. He seems in devious ways to reward himself for the difficulties he experiences. Adults know what kind of advantages can be made of illness: when responsiveness on the child's part is lowered, he can place himself in an exceptional position. A child takes particular advantage of this position within the family where, because of his illness, he suddenly becomes the center of the attention of all surrounding him. This example of withdrawal into illness for the sake of camouflaging one's weakness represents the third type of compensation. It is difficult to determine whether or not it is real. It is real in the sense that the child achieves certain advantages; it is fictitious because not only does he not rid himself of his difficulties but, on the contrary, he accentuates them even more. We have in mind the child who makes his deficit into a burden. When exposed to sound, he is apt to make his loss appear far greater than it is in reality because it is more-or-less advantageous for him to do so.

A reaction of a different nature can, however, occur. A child may compensate for his difficulties by exhibiting responsive, aggressive actions with respect to his social environment (his peers, his parents, the school). In other words, a child may take compensatory action of yet another kind. Allow us to illustrate with the concrete example of this deaf child. He may exhibit an increased irritability, stubbornness, and aggressiveness toward other children; he will attempt to eradicate by practical means the deprivation caused by his defect. Holding last place in any game, this child will, as a consequence of his hearing loss, try to play a greater role. He will always gravitate toward younger children. Such a course of compensation is very distinctive. Here we find the cultivation of certain character traits, which we conventionally would call love of power, a tendency toward "autocracy", stubbornness, that is, the tendency to insist without fail on one's own way, although what was suggested in no way runs counter to the child's desires. What links this last case of a child's character development with the previous example of a child who withdraws into illness and cultivates his defect? To a certain degree, this third type of compensation is real because the child achieves by other means what his defect has denied him, and at the same time, of course, it is also fictitious compensation because although he gets what he wants in a collective of younger children by stubbornness, he does not really overcome the difficulties confronting him.

On the basis of these examples, we are able to say that a child's character development is based on the mechanism of compensatory reaction; the child responds by trying to overcome the difficulties confronting him. This reaction can occur in three different forms: the real, the fictitious or the average type of compensation, already mentioned by us. From the examples introduced, it is absolutely clear that we have entered the area of the psychology of a hard-to-raise child because, even in the case of real compensation, we will encounter difficulties in cultivating the child's character. In an attempt to surmount the unhappiness caused by the degradation of his real position, the child who develops quick-wittedness and other positive qualities will also develop certain deficits caused by those aspects which cannot be compensated for. This will be an undesirable process and, to a significant degree, harmful. We cannot call it an unhealthy process because it leads to health. Still one cannot call it healthy because it occurs in an unhealthy fashion.

When the child encounters difficulties inherent in the environment itself, he collides with uncontrollable phenomena which affect the formation of his character. As a result, the child forms a conflicting character, wherein the emotional qualities are intermixed and you can never assuredly say what is going on inside the child. Instead, you say, "I do not even know what to say; he was thoroughly out of hand, and now you can't praise him enough," or on the contrary, "He was well behaved and now is unmanageable."

If you take other cases of compensation, then you will have before you a difficult child in the complete sense of the word. You will have before you character traits with which pedagogues must carry on a long struggle and which interfere with the normal development necessary for special situations.

2

I shall allow myself to devote a few words to a discussion of some of the effective means which such a psychological understanding of childhood personality problems suggests. Nowhere has this new system for educating a difficult child been formulated into a developed program (nor has it had its last say) although attempts are being made in various countries including ours. I should only like to illustrate for you the psychological principle which one should use as the basis for educating such a child. The Viennese pedagogue, A. Friedmann,[*] calls this principle "methodological dialectics." It is an approach in which we find it necessary to use the opposite of the direct goal in order to achieve the necessary result. Friedmann tells us about a nervous, excitable child, who, with his nervous fits, could hold everyone around in fear and submission. During a lesson he runs up to the window with his knapsack and shouts, "I will throw it out the window." The teacher says, "As you wish," and the child stops in bewilderment because, as the teacher explains, she outwardly yields to the child in order to gain the upper hand over him, in order to be on the offensive. The teacher understands that the boy wants to fling the knapsack out the window because he want to frighten her and not because he is fed up with the lesson. With her answer, as if yielding to the child, the teacher immediately nips this reaction at the root, thereby putting the boy in a difficult position. And each such example of upbringing, each such move, made with an understanding of the psychological roots of one or another of the boy's reaction or condition, is calculated to adjust externally to his defect while taking the upper hand over him. In other words, to yield to him in order to advance. This is what Friedman calls the principle of "methodological dialectics." We use this principle in a situation where we refuse by direct intervention to suppress certain reactions in the child.

If we begin to understand the causes which provoked various difficulties, and if those difficulties, leading to negative character traits, had been eradicated in the beginning, and not upon their manifestation, then we would be able to use the defect to transform those character traits into positive ones. This combination of actions will be called the *principle of methodological dialectics*. For example, within any group of children, there is always one disorganizer, a child who disrupts other children at work, who violates group discipline. We will try to influence this child in the following way: We offer him the role of class organizer; we make him the leader of the group, and then relative harmony will prevail within the group. Relative harmony, because such a course of action is very dangerous, if we do not get the upper hand over this leader in time. Otherwise, as Friedman says, the best you're doing is posting a thief to guard your amber jewelry. But if you don't put in this role the child who is striving to attain a certain position within the group and who expresses this desire by

---

[*] Designated as a German pedagogue in a note above.

disrupting classes in this role, then his desire will find another outlet. If, however, you curb his autocratic obstinacy, he will proceed along the channel which is advantageous for you. In this case you will gain a transformation in the child's attitudes and a conversion of his weakness and negative traits into pluses, into strengths, and into what may lead to the development of positive character traits.

As a conclusion to our discussion of the first problem, I would like to point out what a critical psychological problem the difficult child poses, what minuses and pluses are interlaced, how in this case one contradiction supersedes another and how those same difficulties which trip up a child may further develop both positive and negative character traits.

An old observation tells us that a hard-to-handle child is frequently gifted, although in this instance one has to confront childish illusions, stubbornness, and the like. It is hard to admit that all this psychological energy, this entire direction of behavior could not be deflected from certain paths of development and redirected along others. I cannot say that this problem is easily solved or that solving it theoretically will suffice to change everything in practice and provide some means whereby suddenly all of what the child has already developed will swing from left to right and vice versa. In fact, this problem is infinitely difficult because, if development has proceeded along the wrong path, then an entire series of organic and external forces and circumstances, including incidental occurrences, promote development precisely in this direction. It is far more complicated and difficult to purpose-fully guide development. In this case, an all-encompassing and captivating influence is needed. More-or-less external means often turn out to be very effective when we speak about a child who does not display great resistance. However, all these means, as wonderful as they may be in and of themselves, may turn out to be ineffective when you confront fierce resistance on the part of the child. Such resistance really represents enormous strength because the child resists not because he wants to be obstinate but because certain causes determining his character development have, from the outset cultivated this stubbornness. We are beginning to find only the most general techniques for our very time-consuming and complicated task of remolding the child.

3

Allow me to dwell on another psychological problem, very closely connected to unmanageability, namely, the problem of giftedness. There are those gifted children who present difficulty with respect to upbringing as a result of certain character defects and there is also another large group of children with learning problems related to one or another defect of giftedness; that is to say, there is a lag in the general reserve of their psychological development which interferes with learning in school and with the acquisition of the knowledge which other children acquire. It goes without saying that I have chosen questions concerning only the crudest traits and am omitting overlapping cases where a difficult-to-educate child may also be difficult to handle. I am omitting border-line cases and those which do not come under the already indicated headings. The problem of giftedness is also being reexamined much more intensely than the problem of character development. If in theories on character we see the continuation of two fundamental lines well known since the times of ancient psychology—the theories linking character either with physical features or with the social circumstances of one's upbringing—then in regard to the problem of giftedness, modern psychology is making a complete turn around (in the full sense of the word).

It is very difficult to lay out the problem of giftedness systematically. As with the question of character, I again permit myself to touch on only one side of the problem. The question of unity in plurality has direct bearing on the question of the education and development of a difficult-to-educate child. This question can be phrased as follows: Does giftedness represent a single, homogeneous, integrated factor or function of a specific nature, or are many forms concealed behind this one general label? The question has passed through many stages, and in the history of the doctrine of giftedness few chapters as extensive as this one are to be found.

Allow me to dwell on the aspect of giftedness as it is directly connected with the problem of a difficult child. All psychological investigations address the fact that, rather than constituting a single function, giftedness comprises a series of various functions which are united in one whole. In conjunction with this, we conceive of giftedness as a shaped function. In particular, the definition for "a debilitated childhood" indicates that our conception of giftedness is not precise enough. We call a child with negative qualities a *debile*. Any child who accepts disciplinary instruction in school with great difficulty is seen in our country as a hard-to-educate child. When a certain function is measured, attention, for example, and it turns out to be lower in a mentally retarded child than in a normal child then what has been pointed out is what the mentally retarded child lacks but not what he possesses.

It turns out that children with similarly impaired functions possess different additional capabilities which normal children do not have. Therefore O. Lipmann is absolutely correct when he says that no psychologist should resolve to define a feebleminded child solely as feebleminded. A psychologist must not do this precisely for the same reason that a modern doctor cannot diagnose a patient only by the degree of his illness. When a child is taken to a doctor, the doctor determines not only the negative but also the positive aspects of his health that compensate for his physical state. In precisely the same way, a psychologist must differentiate a child's delay and analyze its essence.

I shall point out basic combined forms of retardation and development in children who have been studied by modern psychologists. I must add the reservation that the question will not be totally exhausted by the forms mentioned below. Still, these forms should show the complex state which the psychology of a mentally retarded child has reached and the difficulty posed by a solution which indicates only a retarded child's deficiencies.

In initiating a discussion of this problem, it is necessary to say at the outset that the identification of motor deficiency is very important. Various authors have begun to observe this particular form of childhood delay, which was labeled in various ways: *motor debility*, *motor idiocy*, and so forth. Yet, however we label it, we are essentially dealing with one and the same thing. We have before us a child who does not have an obvious, severe impairment of his motor apparatus; nevertheless the child exhibits a delay in the character of his movements. This may be analyzed in two different ways: First, either by using an elaborated scale which notes the type of movements delayed at six, seven, eight, nine, and ten years of age and to determine the delay over a two- to three-year period or, second, by putting together with the help of R. I. Rossolimo's scale, the components of mental retardation and by pointing out the fact that the child does not have sufficient coordination between the left and the right hand so that the child proves to have difficulty in combining the movements of his hands, and so forth. The former distinction between mental and motor retardation has broken down. More often than not, they go hand in hand, but sometimes, and frequently enough, a motor delay is not accompanied by an intellectual delay, and vice versa, an intellectual delay does not necessarily accompany a motor delay.

Kruedelen's[2] latest research in Germany has shown that the vast majority of debiles have motor capabilities which are lower than their age levels. This fact has enormous fundamental meaning both for the theory of childhood retardation and for practical work with children: If the two links of development can flow independently of each other, then it is clear that the very word *retardation* is in need of further elaboration. This is my first point. Second, as research has already shown, one developmental link may serve in relation to the other as the central link of compensation; that is, it is possible to augment what the child already possesses. Independently of his circumstances a child will develop either his motor abilities intensely or, vice versa, his cognitive abilities, and the intellectual side of his development will be strengthened. This fact has enormous significance for the psychological theory of giftedness. Tested on the basis of broad material, it would support the view that a tendency toward heightened development in some areas assumes the possibility of a developmental deficiency in other areas where the child comes up against difficulty. This fact has been corroborated statistically. But even if we were not dealing here with definite mathematical values, the psychological significance of the indicated fact is in no way diminished; it is important that such a correlation is possible and that motor development in delayed children leads to positive results. Precisely on this basis we can explain why 90 percent of the children who are not able to learn in public schools are able to perform complicated forms of work above the level of those elementary tasks prescribed for imbeciles.

Mental retardation is in itself diverse. Thus, one may speak of a mild mental retardation. In this case, retardation and compensation may occur independently of one another and even proceed to an antithesis in as much as one link serves as compensation for the other damaged link. This will be called *practical intellect.*

Contemporary psychologists conventionally call the ability of an animal or a child to act rationally *practical intellect.* W. Koehler's research on apes has shown that the ability to act purposefully is not necessarily connected with the ability to make rational arguments. His observations tell us that the child who, in a theoretical aspect seems severely retarded, turns out to be significantly advanced with respect to practical intellect and practical activity. The child has advanced the area of his practical, purposeful activity much further than his theoretical development. Lipmann used Koehler's method to study imbeciles and found that in the case of extensive intellectual retardation practical sense proved to be considerably higher than intellectual reasoning. A whole group of these children proved to be capable of rational activity. Lipmann set up an extremely interesting experiment: He asked his test subjects to solve one and the same problem, first by action, and then theoretically. The task consisted of grabbing an object from a swinging pedestal. When the test subject approached the object and attempted to get it, we have one result; when he began reasoning, the nature of his reasoning yielded quite another result. The test subject could not solve the puzzle theoretically whereas practically he did a good job solving it. Long ago study of the intellect in mentally retarded children already showed that very often the child is much more resourceful in practice than in theory; that he knows how to act purposefully and "thinks" much better with his hands than with his head. Several investigations have shown that practical and theoretical intellect may exist in reverse ratio to each other and that, precisely because of a weakness in abstract thinking, the development of a child's practical thinking is intensified and vice versa.

I permit myself to explain this in relation to cultural development. Both cultural development and practical development are connected with the use of cultural means of thinking, in particular verbal thinking. In recent times, psychologists have discerned a form of child thought which sheds light on the problem of cultural development; this is *child primitiveness*, where the degree of cultural development is minimal. Allow me to introduce an example of child primitiveness, which we have borrowed from A. E. Petrova, who analyzed this phenomenon in the clinic of M. O. Gurevich. A child severely delayed in her adaptive reactions was analyzed. The child had lived in many institutions and was then sent to the psychiatric hospital because of suspected mental illness. In the hospital, no mental illness was discovered and the child ended up in Gurevich's experimental clinic. The child—a Tatar girl—who in early childhood exchanged one not yet firmly established language for another, learned to understand those who spoke in that language but was absolutely untrained to think in it. The girl had not become accustomed to the fact that, on the basis of words alone, one could draw a conclusion. The psychologist gave her a series of intellectual tasks requiring practical activity in some and words in others. When faced with practical activity, the test subject produced positive results. She reacted to the verbal tasks with incomprehension and inability to think. For example, the girl is told, "My aunt is taller than me, and my uncle is still taller than my aunt. Is my uncle taller than me?" The little girl responded, "I don't know. How can I tell you whether your uncle is taller, if I have never seen him?" She answered responded to all question in the same manner: If she had not seen with her own eyes, then she could not tell you anything. She could not imagine that on the basis of two verbal sentences she could use words to come up with a third sentence. This was impossible for her. The child was delayed in her cultural development, in the development of verbal thinking, but she was not a *debile*, she was not feebleminded, although on the surface she was similar to a debile: Her reasoning was weak, she gave nonsensical answers, and she refused to complete the simplest reflective operation. But we have made a gross error if we think that the girl did not know how to draw a conclusion on the basis of practical data.

Allow me to sum up: There is now under way an extensive reexamination of old conceptions in the area of understanding child giftedness and the negative aspects linked with it such as learning problems and abnormal behavior.

The old conception of giftedness as a single function has given way and in its place there has arisen a position based on the functional complexity of its individual forms. Therefore, I think that it is most appropriate to finish this discussion by pointing out which form of psychological investigation one should select when studying learning problems. A child is brought for consulting because the suspicions of the pedagogues indicate that he appears to be mentally retarded. Previously, they would usually be convinced that the child is not performing as he should, that he does not orient himself in the simplest surroundings, and the result would already have been predetermined. The first demand that modern psychology has placed before us is never to identify with only the child's negative characteristics because this still says decisively little about the child's positive traits. The child, let's say, does not possess certain knowledge; he does not, for example, have any conception of the calendar, but we do not know definitely what he can do and does know. The present research study can be summed up with the statement that the characteristics of a retarded child must necessarily be twofold. Similarly, modern medicine gives a twofold classification of tuberculosis: On the one hand, it characterizes the stage of the disease's development, and on the other it indicates the degree of the compensating process. Indications 1, 2, and 3 show the gravity of the illness, while A, B, and C show compensation for the disease. Only the combined data give a complete picture of the person's illness because, although one patient may have been much more deeply infected with the disease than another, his process of compensation may be greater. A person may be in the third stage of tuberculosis, but his compensation may be such that he finds himself completely able to work, while another, suffering from a far milder infection, may also exhibit less compensation so that the development of the disease plays a more destructive role.

In an analysis of an abnormal child, the defect alone tells the psychologist nothing unless he determines the degree of compensation for the defect, until he shows what lines of counterbalancing behavior will form and what attempt the child will make to compensate for those difficulties which he encounters. In practice, this dual character has become a typical phenomenon almost everywhere. In fact, we may even have defect and compensation of a triple character. Those who have had the occasion to study children closely, know how frequently one or another function in a retarded child—let's say, memory—may prove in and of itself to be rather highly developed. The trouble, however, lies in the fact that the child's ability to control it may be weak. Precisely the same was true of the primitive girl about whom we have already spoken in this discussion. The girl reasons well. In her reasoning there is contained a complete syllogism, but her inability to include it in a verbal chain of reasoning leads to her apparent severely retarded appearance.

We often encounter types in whom the levels of the organic basis for memory is in and of itself very high, or significantly departs from the average level, or surpasses it, yet the ability to remember and to use this ability for the performance of higher cultural processes proves to be minimal. I will introduce a case of a severely retarded child whose visual memory was developed to such a degree that he, not being able to read, proved able to execute the following tests: Before him were arranged notes with names and a rather large number of faces pictured on cards. A note lay before each image. Subsequently, the notes were reshuffled and the child, according to the inscription, again laid them out as they should be. And still, in spite of a colossal visual memory, this child could not learn to read, because the task of remembering, and mastering letters and connecting them with sounds, and so forth, turned out to be beyond his power. His capacity for acquisition was minimal.

A new idea has arisen in current research—to give double, even triple characteristics: the characteristics of practical intellect, practical knowledge, and its practical use. In a word, in place of the general definition of feeblemindedness or a learning disability, there is an attempt, first of all, to determine how it is expressed; secondly, to examine how the child himself attempts to cope with this phenomenon; and third, to learn which path the school must take in order to overcome the defects afflicting the given child.

What kind of pedagogical inferences dictate a new approach to research? Allow me to demonstrate this with a concrete example. We well know that mildly retarded children are distinguished by insufficient development of abstract thinking, and therefore, their education is based on visual aids. Visual education, however, develops in the child only visual thinking and cultivates his weaknesses. Not one contemporary pedagogue will dispute the fact that the visual method of education can occupy a central place in the auxiliary school, but when taking into account the child's mental weakness, it is necessary to form in him a certain basis for abstract thought, using visual material as auxiliary means. In other words, it is necessary to advance the mentally retarded child's overall line of development. In modern pedagogy (even in those countries less inclined toward a revolutionary pedagogy), a certain principle has begun to make headway: It is necessary to develop thinking in children in the auxiliary school and to cultivate in them social concepts, and the use of visual material is the basis for doing this.

Thus, if we summarize our practical deductions from all that has been reported here, then it is possible to say the following: The entire difference between the new and the old practice is that the new negates old suppositions but goes further. If we earlier understood a child's unmanageability only as a complex of deficits, then modern psychology tries to show what is concealed behind the minuses. If the old upbringing was inclined to yield to the defect, to follow along behind it, then today's training takes into account the deficit and yields in order to take the upper hand over it and to overcome the defect that has made the child hard-to-handle or difficult to educate.

MORAL INSANITY[1][*]

The pedagogical reform taking hold in a majority of European countries and in America is nurtured to a significant degree by certain psychological conceptions and theories. Pedagogy faces still another pressing problem, namely, the problem of "moral insanity." This problem is now being reexamined theoretically and practically both in Western Europe and in America on the basis of a common psychological premise. The English term for moral deficiency expresses the most extreme view of this condition as an organic illness (literally; *moral insanity*, or madness). All children who have exhibited amoral behavior and who have violated generally accepted moral norms have come under the conception of moral *insanity*. This includes juvenile prostitutes, delinquents, homeless and neglected children, and so on. Over a period of time, the insubstantiality of this conception of moral madness and ethical deficiency (its milder stage) has been sufficiently exposed from all sociological, psychological, psychopathological and pedagogical angles.

The work of P. P. Blonskii, A. B. Zalkind, and others has shown that a morally defective child is not a child with an innate organic defect, but rather a child who has been derailed socially. The reasons for moral deficiency should be sought not in the child, but externally, in the socioeconomic, cultural, and pedagogical conditions in which the child grew up and developed. In different conditions that are more auspicious for child development, in a different environment, a difficult child very quickly loses the traits of moral deficiency and starts down a new path. The problem of "moral insanity" is posed and solved in our country as a problem of environment. Normalizing the environment has become the basic educative practice in this area. In recent years, European scientific and pedagogical thought has arrived at a similar understanding of this problem. At the first German congress on therapeutic pedagogy (1922), the report "Psychopathy and Neglect,"[**] based on significant child research, concluded that, psychopathological factors play an insignificant role among the factors and reasons causing childhood homelessness, delinquency, and the like. For the

---

[*] The term is written precisely as shown, in Roman characters, in the Russian text. [Ed.]

[**] Various types of children are included in this group: juvenile delinquents, as well as difficult and neglected children. In general, the composition of this group rather completely embraces the category of so-called morally deficient children. {L.V.}

children under investigation, no single group of characteristics was found that would destine or doom a child to delinquency solely as a result of psychopathy. Cautious reservations have been expressed only with respect to a negligible number of children.

At the very same congress, a purely theoretical report, "On the Defects of Will from the Point of View of Normal Psychology," decisively repudiated for the first time the notion of *moral insanity* as mental illness. The speaker asserted that whenever there is a question of lapse of will expressed by a loss of one set or another of values and standards, (such as motives of behavior), the cause should be sought not in innate defects of will nor in the perversion of separate functions, but in the environment and upbringing, which failed to establish appropriate values. The speaker noted that *moral insanity* should be understood not as a disturbed emotional state but rather more simply as a gap in the individual's moral upbringing. In the speaker's opinion, these phenomenon would never be attributed to mental illness if one listed all the cases where "value motives" are lacking in normal people. One person may be insensitive to aesthetic values, another to social values and so on. Each individual has his own *moral insanity*. Recently in 1927, M. Wertheimer, one of the founders of the current popular trend in psychology —structural psychology*— defended this way of understanding moral deficiency. This psychological trend originates from a holistic understanding of psychological life and mental development. According to this view, a psychological phenomenon always represents not the simple sum of its separate parts or component elements, but an integral whole which has its own laws and characteristics, and which cannot be derived from the laws and properties of the parts. The whole defines its own parts, and not the inverse. The formation of this whole defines the mental process and could be called image or structure (*Gestalt*). Therefore, for research, it is necessary to start from the whole and not from the parts.

The theory of an integral approach to the study of psychology led its supporters to the need to understand a child in relationship to his environment. Let us remember that as a result of this holistic principle we also found it necessary to study children within the environment in which they grew and developed. In part, this approach to the morally defective child is upheld by Professor. S. S. Molozhavyi[2] and others. A child belonging to a specific psychopathic type, Molozhavyi states, exhibits crudity, delinquency, egoism, obsession with the gratification of elementary needs, a primitive intellect, little vivacity, a decreased sensitivity to painful irritations, and so forth. Here we see the characteristics of ethical deficiency, or *moral insanity*, which dooms the child from birth to asocial behavior. And this will be the picture if we look at a child's actions in isolation, reducing them to certain "features," and then composing the child's character from these features. Experiments in moving such children into a different, better environment have demonstrated that in the new composite, the individual traits frequently acquired a completely new appearance: the children become mild-mannered, courteous, alert, and lively. It often turns out that we were dealing with children who possessed a heightened sensitivity. The observed sensitivity had been nothing more than a defensive reaction, a self-defense, a biological defensive armor against the diseased influences of the environment.

Soviet psychologists and pedagogues note, with a feeling of satisfaction, the increased interest abroad in reexamining the doctrine of moral deficiency; they interpret this as yet another proof of the correctness of the path which our pedagogy has taken in this respect, a path noted in the resolutions of the Second Congress on the Social and Legal Defense of

---

* That is, Gestalt psychology. [Transl.]

Minors (1924). The division of children —as described by these resolutions— into normal, ethically deficient, ethically retarded, and so on was considered inadmissible by the Congress. We must pause at this crossroads in Soviet and foreign pedagogy not only to obtain new scientific corroboration of a resolution which we accepted and long ago put into practice but also to compare our experience with that of those abroad in order to verify our own example. This is absolutely necessary in order to consolidate revolutionary reforms and to formulate our own scientific work.

THE DYNAMICS OF CHILD CHARACTER[1]

1

Because of the very way in which the question was formulated, room has not been left in psychological theory and pedagogical practice for the study of child character nor for the examination of its development and formation. The question has been approached statistically, so that character has been viewed as a steady and constant entity, always internally consistent, present, and seen as a given. Character has been understood as a status, not as a process; as a condition, and not as a formation. The classical formula of this traditional view was given by T. Ribot, who set forth two necessary and sufficient conditions for establishing an understanding of character: unity and stability. With this formula he implied a unity across time. The true sign of character, according to Ribot, is that which appears in early childhood and remains constant throughout the course of life; genuine character is innate.

Recently, the statistical view of character found complete and total expression in the theory of E. Kretschmer, for whom character is connected with the structure of the body; a psychological mental construction side by side with a somatic construction. In his opinion, both the former and the latter—body structure and character structure—are defined in the final analysis by the innate endocrine system. Kretschmer makes a distinction between two large, complex biotypes, the schizothymic and the cyclothymic. From these two types, a great many normal shades of temperament are formed in a widely varying mixture. These extreme biological types are connected with two basic forms of mental illness: schizophrenia and manic-depressive psychosis (cyclical). This doctrine, as A. B. Zalkind justly points out, has strongly affected child psychology (1926).

We find that P. P. Blonskii has extended and developed, or rather, transformed Kretschmer's viewpoint into a science about the child. "One of the merits of Kretschmer," Blonskii states, "is the establishment of the connection between the structures of body and of character. I go further and assert that different temperaments distinguish not only different individuals, but also different ages. In particular, a cyclothymic temperament is characteristic of the baby-tooth stage of childhood" (1925, p. 182). Adolescence replaces the cyclothymic temperament with the schizoid temperament (ibid., p. 227). The only change that the static

153

conception of character has undergone with reference to the child is that it replaces a unified type of character, predetermined and fatally conditioned by the endocrine system, with a sequence of changes as one type follows another. The very principle of stability which Ribot enunciated remains inviolable here. Character type, it turns out, takes hold only at a certain age, and not according to an established constitution. The chain of stable types through which the child consecutively passes is still a static, not a dynamic, series. This is the fundamental distinction of both doctrines, resembling, in this respect, the majority of characterological theories. As we have noted, A. B. Zalkind justifiably calls this trend an absolute, *biological, static* approach to character (1926). According to his assessment of it, "The development of human character is merely a passive unfolding of that biological type which is inherent in the person." (ibid., p. 174).

Kretschmer's scheme does not work for the division of characterological traits by age. None of this, however, prohibits us from attempting to elucidate the prevailing predominant specific content of each stage in development. This specific content, not now taken into consideration by any of the existing characterological systems, undergoes extraordinary changes under environmental influences. This is why it is dangerous to attach rigid "labels" to any systems *in the given state of science.* The incompleteness of this viewpoint, like all static, non-dynamic views, lies in the fact that it is powerless to solve questions of origin, development, and growth. Such a view is necessarily limited, therefore, to a theoretical statement and generalizations and to the collection, correlation and classification of empirical data without insight into the true [underlying] nature of the studied phenomena. "If the outward forms of things coincided directly with their essence, then every science would be superfluous," wrote K. Marx (K. Marx, F. Engels, *Collected Works*, vol. 25, Part II, p. 384). Thus, this viewpoint, which is satisfied with the form of the "appearance of things"—that is, with bare empirical data, without an analysis of their "essence"—is an unscientific point of view. Such a theory starts in a fatal manner from the conclusion. This is why characterology, from Hippocrates[2] to Kretschmer, has struggled in vain with classification as the fundamental problem of character. Classification can be scientifically substantial and productive only when it is based on an essential indication of phenomena dispersed among various classes, that is, when it presupposes an earlier knowledge of the essence of things. Otherwise, classification will necessarily be a scholastic division of empirical data. And such will be almost all classifications of character. The essence of things, however, is a dialectic and is revealed in the dynamics of a process in motion, change, formation, and distinction, that is, in the study of genesis and development.

Characterology—historical and contemporary—recalls the condition of the biological sciences before C. Darwin. Scientific thought tried to take into consideration, to regulate, and to introduce a system and sense into the great diversity of vegetable and animal forms. But it did not possess the key to understanding this diversity of forms, accepting it as fact, as data, and as immutable evidence of the creation of all being. The key to biology was found in evolution, in the idea of the natural development of living forms. Just as biology began with *the origin of forms*, so, too, psychology should begin from *the origin of individuals*; the key to the origin óf individuals is the conditional reflex. If Darwin gave us the biology of forms, then Pavlov gives the biology of individuals, the biology of personality. The mechanism of the conditional reflex reveals the dynamics of personality; it shows that personality arises on the basis of the organism like a complex superstructure, created by the external *conditions* of an individual life. It is namely this doctrine that ultimately resolves the ancient argument between nativism and empiricism. It shows that *everything* in personalities is built on an inherited, innate basis and, at the same time, that everything in them is superorganic, conditioned, that is, *social.*

The doctrine of conditional reflexes does not simply render what is God's to God and what is Caesar's to Caesar. It shows us that, precisely in those conditions which restructure inherited experience, there is a fundamental motive force which pushes development ahead and causes change. The innate reaction is only the material: Its fate depends on the formative conditions in which it is destined to emerge. An unending number and great variety of things can be created on this innate foundation. One can hardly find a better illustration for proof of what is almost an absolute—the reeducability of human nature—than the conditioned salivary response to the debilitating painful irritation caused by a strong electrical current. Placed under appropriate conditions, (i.e., being fed at the time of painful shock) a dog begins to respond to induced burns and pains with a positive reaction, which in the language of subjective psychology is called *joyful anticipation*, and in the language of objective psychology *a digestive reflex.* The dog not only does not guard itself from pain but actually is drawn to it. On viewing the experiment, C. Sherrington, as J. Bon [no ref.] reports, exclaimed: "Now I understand the joy of the martyrs as they climbed onto the pyres" (cited in Iu. P. Frolov, 1925, p. 155). Thus, the biological, by means of social factors, melds into the social; the biological and organic into the personal; the "natural," "absolute," and unconditioned into the conditioned. This is the true material of psychology.

C. Sherrington recognized an enormous psychological future in this experiment with the dog; he saw the key to the solution of the origin of higher forms of human psychology. In essence, he stated what can be translated and interpreted for our purposes as the following: In order to understand the character of the martyr who climbs joyfully onto the fire, we must ask from what are the *conditions* from which this character will necessarily arise. What causes the martyr to enjoy this? What is the history, that is to say, the dynamics and conditioning (or conditionality), of this joy. Character is conditioned (or conditional); such is its dynamic formula. Static character is equal to a sum of certain basic signs of personality and behavior. It is a diametric cross-section of personality, in its unchanging status, and its ready condition. To understand character *dynamically,* however, means to translate it into the language of a fundamental whole within its entire social environment, to understand it in its struggle to overcome obstacles, *in the necessity of its emergence and unfolding*, in the internal logic of its development.

2

The logic of character development is the same as the logic of any development. All that develops, develops by necessity. Nothing is perfected or goes forward from the internal "vital impulse" which H. Bergson[3] proposes in his philosophy. It would be a miracle if character developed when not under the pressure of necessity which commands and pushes it toward development. What is the necessity in which the motive forces of character development are embedded? To this question, there is only one answer: the fundamental and definitive necessity of all human life—the necessity to live in a historical, social environment and to reconstruct all organic functions in agreement with the demands set forth by this environment. Only in the capacity of a defined social unit can the human organism exist and function.

This position serves as the point of departure for A. Adler's system of individual psychology (the social psychology of personality). We set aside here the question of the relationship between this doctrine and Marxist philosophy. This is a complex question, which can be debated and, above all, demands particular and special research. Adler's basic philosophical positions are distorted by metaphysical elements. The characterological interest is limited to Adler's practice. With good reason, Adler calls this doctrine "positional psychology" in the profoundest sense of the word and in contrast to dispositional psychology. For the former, psychological development proceeds from the social position which the personality has attained; for the latter—from the organic disposition, that is, predisposition. Here the original meaning is returned to the concept of character. *Character* means an *engraving* in Greek.

Character is the social imprint on personality. It is the hardened, crystallized, typical behavior of personality; it is the struggle for social position. It is a secession from the primary line, the leading line of development, the unconscious plan of life, from the integral course of development of all psychological acts and functions. In connection with this, it becomes absolutely necessary for the psychologist to understand each psychological act and the person's character as a whole, not only with respect to the person's past but also with respect to his future. This can be called the ultimate direction of behavior. Just as in a film, a frame-sequence representing one moment of motion remains incomprehensible without the subsequent moments, outside the motion as a whole, similarly the trajectory of a bullet is defined by the final point or gun sight. In precisely the same way, every act and every feature of character raises the following questions: Toward what is it striving? What is its goal? Into what is it transformed? Toward what does it gravitate? In essence, this understanding of psychological phenomena—not only from the past, but also from the future—does not designate anything other than the dialectical necessity of accepting phenomena in unending motion, of disclosing the future-oriented tendency of phenomena, determined by the present. As, in the historical sphere, we shall never understand fully the essence of the capitalist system if we look at it statically, outside the tendencies of its development, outside its necessary connection with the future system maturing in its womb, so, too, in the sphere of psychology, we shall never understand fully the human personality if we are to look at it statically as a sum of phenomena, of acts, and the like, without an integral biographical plan of personality, without a main line of development which transforms the history of a man's life from a row of disconnected and separate episodes into a connected, integral, life-long process.

3

No one instinctive action of an animal can be understood and interpreted by us if we do not know its final "goal," the point at which it is aimed. Imagine the behavior of an animal before sexual unification. It may be understood only if taken as a whole, only if seen from the final act, the last link at which all the preceding links on this chain are directed. The motions of a tiger, lying in wait for its prey, will be completely meaningless if we do not have in mind the final act of this drama, when the tiger devours its prey. We could go down the evolutionary ladder to the very lowest organic functions, and everywhere we would find the very same trait: the final character, the ultimate direction of the biological reaction. If the teeth of an animal masticate and grind food, this can be understood only in connection with (the fact) that the food will be digested and assimilated by the organism, that is, in connection with the whole process of digestion and nourishment. A general biological formulation of the very same idea is, essentially, what is usually conditionally called the immanent teleology of the organism, or that methodological principle according to which we view parts of the animal body as organs, and their activity as organic functions acquiring meaning and sense only in relation to the organism as a whole.

Thus, the final character of psychological acts, or their future-oriented tendency, appears already in the most elementary forms of behavior. As we have seen, not one instinctive action can be understood fully if not examined from a future perspective. I. P. Pavlov confirmed this fundamental fact in the brilliant term *goal reflex*. Studying the simplest and most basic forms of innate activity of the nervous system, Pavlov came to the conclusion that a unique unconditional reflex should be formulated—the goal reflex. By using a paradoxical term, Pavlov from the first glance underlines the uniqueness of this reflex: It is directed at the attainment of a *goal*, and may be understood only from the viewpoint of the future. At the same time, this form of activity is not a particular exception, but rather the most normal reflex. Precisely because of this, Pavlov replaces here the term *instinct* with the preferred term *reflex*. "This term clarifies the idea of determinism; the connection between stimulus and effect, cause and result becomes more self-evident" (1951, p. 306).

It is curious that Adler, when expounding on this notion of the future-oriented tendency of behavior, calls to mind Pavlov's experiments in training a conditional, signal reflex (A. Adler, 1927). And it is all the more curious that Pavlov's explanation of a goal-reflex mechanism is similar to the doctrine of compensation. He saw in this reflex "life's most important factor," which is particularly indispensable for a most crucial area: education. The mechanism for training a goal reflex by means of the presence of obstacles was established in both Pavlovian and Adlerian psychology. T. Lipps called it the law of *damming up* and saw in it a common law of psychological activity, concluding that energy, when concentrated at a given point, is increased and may overcome the restraint, and even flow in a *roundabout* way. This already contains the idea of compensation. In general, Lipps explains any drive as a result of this law; he thought that all purposeful activity was achieved precisely at the time when an obstacle arises in the path of preceding aimless or automatic events. Only thanks to the dam, the restraint, the obstacle, does a "goal" become possible for any mental process. The point of interruption or disruption of any automatically operating functions becomes the "goal" for other functions, which aim at this point and, therefore, have the appearance of purposeful activity. Thus, the "goal" is a given beforehand; in essence, it only appears to be a goal but, in fact, constitutes the primary cause of all development.[*]

---

[*] There has been extensive comment on the notion that behavior could be accounted for because motive forces or psychic energy were conserved and re-directed. Despite disputes among advocates who explored the notion from a variety of philosophical vantages, Vygotsky's Marxist treatment of the theme here reveals its prevalence in the *Zeitgeist* of the early 20th century. The list of Freudian mechanisms (*displacement, suppression, repression, sublimation,* and so on) may be read as a detailed elaboration of the ways in which Lipp's *Stauungen* are re-directed. A relatedness between the Freudian and Pavlovian approach has later been noted among students of instinct (see, for example, Lorenz, K., *On Aggression.* New York: Harcourt Brace Jovanovich, 1966.) Interestingly, Vygotsky does not acknowledge the degree to which Adler's formulations are derivative from Freud's. Instead they are presented in a context which would make them appear to be essentially related to the Pavlovian view although he asks whether Adler's views are thoroughly Marxist (Section 2 of this chapter) and concludes that they are and they are not (see the Concluding Section of this chapter). In the passage here, Vygotsky provides a remarkable clarification of the degree to which the Pavlovian system and its kindred systems are teleological in their formulation although he associates teleology with idealism, which he eschews. Later in the chapter, overlooking Freud's therapeutic ambitions, he denies that this teleology may be available

The dynamic theory cannot be limited to a statement about the factual existence of a goal-oriented reflex, that is, of a fatalistic psychology. This theory strives to learn how this goal reflex arises, that is, what constitutes the causal conditionality and determination of these forms of future-oriented behavior. The answer to this question lies in Pavlov's formula for the existence of obstacles. The existence of obstacles (as psychology showed even before Pavlov) is not only the main condition for the *attainment of a goal* but also the indispensable condition for the very *emergence* and *existence of the goal*.

The two basic psychological assumptions on which the dynamic theory of character rests—clarification of the future-oriented mind set and the principle of compensation in psychological development—are therefore, inwardly connected. One is essentially the dynamic continuation of the other. The existence of obstacles creates a "goal" for mental acts, that is, it introduces into development a future-directed mentality. The presence of this "goal" creates a stimulus for compensatory tendencies. These are two moments of one and the same psychodynamic process. We note in passing that, in order to completely understand the internal logic of the views presented here, one must bear in mind a third basic assumption: the principle of social conditionality in developmental processes. This principle is intrinsically connected with the first two assumptions for the reason that it forms, in causal sequence, the first, all-defining principle and that in inverse causality or goal-directed order it contains the ultimate, or final, moment of the very same integral process: *development out of necessity*.

The social conditions in which a child should take root comprise, on the one hand, the entire scope of a child's unadapted state and serve as the genesis of his developmental creative forces; the obstacles which thrust a child forward developmentally are rooted in those conditions of the social milieu in which he *is supposed* to grow. On the other hand, the child's whole development is oriented toward achieving a necessary social level. Here, we have the start and the finish, the alpha and omega of his development. Chronologically, the three moments in this process can be explained as follows: (1) a child's unsocialized, unacculturated nature places powerful obstacles in the path of psychological growth (the principle of social conditionality for development); (2) these obstacles serve as stimuli for compensatory development and become the final goal, determining the whole process (the principle of future-oriented psychology); and (3) the presence of obstacles augments the operation of certain functions and forces their perfection. This results in triumph over these obstacles and hence in adaptability or assimilation (the principle of compensation). The fact that personal interaction with the environment stands at the beginning (1) and at the end (3) of the process, gives the process a closed, circular form and allow us to examine the process in its direct (casual) and inverted (goal-oriented) aspect.

4

If we understand, however, how strength arises from weakness and how capabilities arise from defects, then we hold in our hands the key to a child's "giftedness." The dynamic theory of giftedness is, of course, still a matter for future discussion; until now, and even now, this problem has been resolved purely statically. Researchers have approached child

in the Freudian system. Throughout, Vygotsky, the optimistic Marxist and educator, favors the theory which provides the latitude for environmental manipulations and the greatest possibilities for the amelioration of defects. [Ed.]

giftedness as a fact, as a given, and have asked only one question: "What is the numerical score?" They are interested only in the numerical points and not the actual components of aptitude. In the dynamic theory of child character, prerequisites are given for the creation of a new, dialectic doctrine about the plus and minus of a child's aptitude, i.e., about the child's talents and handicaps. The former atomistic and quantitative point of view immediately reveals complete theoretical bankruptcy. Let us imagine a man with a poor memory. Suppose that he knows about his shortcoming, and examination has shown a poor recall of meaningless syllables. According to established *use* in psychology—which we should more appropriately call *abuse*—we should conclude that this man's inadequate memory is due to hereditary causes, or illness. Strictly speaking, in this manner of research the conclusion usually contains what has already been expressed in different words in the premise. For example, in the given case, if someone has a poor memory or somebody remembers few words, then he supposedly has little capacity for retention. The question should be put differently: "To what purpose is a memory weak? What necessitates it?" We can establish this purpose only from an intimate knowledge of the individual as a whole; our understanding of this component arises from an understanding of the whole.

The dynamic point of view allows us to see giftedness and deficiency as two different results of one and the same process of compensation. Only scientifically unwarranted optimism would assume that the mere presence of a defect or handicap is sufficient to cause compensation and to transform the defect into a strength. Overcompensation would be a magical process, and not a biological one, if it transformed all types of shortcomings into merits, irrespective of the internal-biological and external conditions in which the process occurs. We could not make a more implausible and absurd caricature of this idea than if we were to go to extremes by saying that any defect facilitates higher development. It would be very easy to live if this were really the case. But in fact, compensation is a battle, and every battle can result in two completely opposite outcomes: victory or defeat. Like all battles, the result depends on the relative strength of the fighting sides. In the given case, it depends on the severity of the defect and on the strength of the compensating reserves. If compensation successfully overcomes a defect, then we have a picture of a fully developed child with superior abilities. If compensation is not successful, we have primitive, incomplete, delayed, and malformed development. One pole of this process borders on genius, the other—on neurosis.

Neurosis, a retreat into illness, and the totally asocial nature of this psychological position, all testify to a *fictitious* goal which directs the lifelong course along a false path, distorting the mainline of development and the child's character. Thwarted compensation turns into a defensive battle, with the help of illness; the conqueror defends himself by building on his weakness. Between these two poles, these two extreme cases, falls an entire gradation of compensation—from minimal to maximal. This is the definition of child giftedness (aptitude), to which we are accustomed—the definition most often stated and encountered by us in practice. The uniqueness of the dynamic approach does not lie in a change in the quantitative analysis of aptitude and its special forms, but in the refusal to attribute to this appraisal a self-contained significance. By itself, the defect says nothing about development as a whole. A child with a particular defect is still not a defective child. Along with a defect come stimuli for overcoming it. The development of giftedness, similar to the development of character, is dialectical and evolves by contradiction.

5

An internal contradiction guides character development along a path of "psychophysical contrast," as Adler literally named the antithesis between organic deficiency and psychological compensation.

S. Freud advanced a well-known thesis on a characterological triad (accuracy, stinginess, and obstinacy) and on its connection with anal eroticism. Or consider yet another Freudian thesis: "Subjects suffering from enuresis are noted for their excessive, ardent ambition" (S. Freud, 1923, p. 23). "The internal necessity of similarly connected phenomena" (ibid., p. 20) is far from completely clear and comprehensible even to the author of this theory himself. We are justified in asking what significance for future life these character traits can have. What is the connection between this triad and anal eroticism? Why is *life-long* behavior defined by this trait? What keeps it from atrophy? What nourishes it? On the contrary, if, as in the case of a child's impaired hearing ability, we are shown how *greater* sensitivity, suspiciousness, anxiety, curiosity, and other similar functions strive to compensate for a hearing impairment by means of reaction formations and compensations, and in order to construct a defensive psychological superstructure over the defect, and if we are shown how these develop, then the logic of character, its social and psychological conformity to laws becomes intelligible and understandable.

For Freud, "initial inclinations which persist unfailingly" come to light in character traits. Character is rooted in the *distant past*. For Adler character is the side of personality which is future-oriented. Freud, in his dream interpretations, proceeds from remnants of the past and remote childhood experiences, while Adler views a dream as a military reconnaissance, a sounding out of the future, and a preparation for future activity. This latter approach may be taken toward the doctrine of personality structure and character. This new doctrine introduces a future-oriented perspective, a highly valuable perspective for the psychologist. This perspective frees us from the inertia of conservative and backward theories. Indeed, for Freud, a man is chained to his past, like a convict to his wheelbarrow; all of life is determined in early childhood from elementary combinations and, without exception, boils down to living out childhood conflicts. It remains incomprehensible how all subsequent conflicts, traumas, and experiences could constitute only outer layers encrusted on remote infantile experiences, which constitute the trunk and core of one's entire life. In the new doctrine, the revolutionary future-oriented perspective allows us to understand the development and life of a personality as an integral process which *struggles forward* with objective necessity toward an ultimate goal, toward a finale, projected by the demands of social existence.

The psychological perspective of the future offers theoretical possibilities for education. By nature, a child always appears inferior or "unfinished" in a society of adults; from the beginning, his very position gives grounds for the development of feelings of inferiority, insecurity, and embarrassment. For years on end, a child remains unfit for independent existence, and in his inadequacy and childhood awkwardness lie the seeds of his development. Childhood is a period of social ineptness, "inferiority," as well as a time for compensation by taking advantage of one's strength; a time for the conquest of position in relation to the social whole. In the process of this conquest, a human being as a specific biotype is transformed into a human being as a sociotype; an animal organism becomes a human personality. *The societal mastery of this natural process is called education.* It would be impossible, if a future-oriented perspective, defined by the demands of social existence, were not impregnated in the most natural processes of child development and formation.

The very possibility of an integral plan in education and its future-oriented attitude testifies to the presence of such a plan in the developmental process which strives to master education. Essentially, this means only one thing: *Child development and character formulation are socially oriented processes*. O. Ruele says the following about this lifelong line of development: "It is his {the child's—L.V.} thread of Ariadne, which leads him to the goal. Insofar as all mental functions proceed in time in a selected direction and all mental processes acquire their own typical expression there will result an aggregate of forms of tactical devices, aspirations, and capabilities overlaying and outlining life's determined plan. This is what we call character" (1926, p. 12).

Many important scientific discoveries about the child have been made along these lines. Thus, despite S. Hall[4] and his biogenetic theory, the excellent classic investigations of K. Groos[5] have shown us that play, as a fundamental form of natural training for young animals and small children, can be understood and explained not by its connection with the past, but by its future-oriented tendencies. For the child, play arises as a result of the insufficiency of his natural abilities to cope with life's difficult tasks resulting from his impracticality. Childhood is a biological time for the "acquisition of skills, required by life, but not developed directly from natural abilities" (1916, p.71). It is a time for compensating for underdevelopment. Play is the natural means of a child's self-education, an exercise oriented toward the future. Recently, a new point of view in regard to the psychological nature of exercising has been advanced and strengthened. It is, essentially, a further development of Groos's idea. In accordance with this view exercise which is, generally speaking, most important in the developmental process of education is a compensatory process in the process of cultivating the functions of personality.

Only in the light of Groos's theory of play and the new theory of exercise can one really understand and appraise the significance of a child's movement and its educational sense. A child's movement (in certain components) must be analyzed as an experience in the rationalization and organization of group play among children on an international scale. That is, play in a revolutionary era, which, like any game, prepares the child for the future, implants the fundamental lines of his future behavior. The very idea and practical application of such play would be impossible if the development of personality were a passive unfolding of innate primary abilities. The idea of consciously stretching out all human life from childhood on and directing it along one continuous straight line, demarcated by history, may be well substantiated but only on the condition that character is not born, but created. The correct name for the process of emergence of character is not *unfolding*, but *enculturation*. Precisely this viewpoint gives us the key to understanding personality in its social aspect, the key to understanding its class-oriented character, not in a literal-metaphorical sense, but in the real, concrete sense of an imprint made by social class on the biological structure of personality. A.B. Zalkind points out that the basic failing of static theories of character is an inherent contradiction: these theories are based on the fundamental fact that every human being is not only a biological, but also a historical unit, whose character bears historical traits.

"Can class position (the position of the exploiter or the exploited), or a historical epoch (revolution, reaction) instigate one character type or another?" (A. B. Zalkind, 1926, p. 188). With this question, the difference between these two ways of interpreting character is brought into sharp focus. One approach adheres to the biological determination of character; the other approaches character as a historical form of personality. The first view was explicated in the famous thesis of G. Kompeire who examined character as a completed totality of signs, fixed from the moment of birth. "Without lapsing into paradox," he states, "one might say that a child who subsequently will be industrious will exhibit this inclination by the manner in which he seizes and holds the feeding bottle" (in *Mental Life of the Child*, 1916, p. 261) [Ref not provided but see Kompeire, 1910, 1912]. In other words, character is born with the human being and is already present in the manner in which the newborn seizes and holds the bottle. In contrast to this view, Groos sees the enormous biological significance of play as a natural means of formatting features which lead us away from inherent nature to a new, "acquired" human nature, or, "using (an old expression) here, in a certain sense from the old Adam toward a new Adam" (K. Groos, 1916, p. 72). But character is the new Adam, the new second nature of man.

*   *   *

In recent years Adler's doctrine, particularly his applied and practical pedagogical views, have exerted a great influence on the theory and practice of social education in Germany and Austria. Pedagogy is the most important area of this psychological doctrine. In the words of O. F. Kanitz, this doctrine already has, therefore, great significance for the socialist workers' movement, which puts primary importance on the influence of environment and education: "This gives a psychological foundation to the words of Marx; our social being determines our consciousness" (O. F. Kanitz, 1926, p. 165). In particular, Kanitz insists that the practical yield from Adler's work, the application of this theory to education, is at variance with a capitalistic system and its cultural environment. "*In a word, once individual psychology is put into practice it shatters the framework of the capitalist social order* and in this way a bourgeois psychologist of this particular bent will sometime and somewhere experience his Damascus" (ibid., p. 164). In 1925, at the Congress on Individual Psychology in Berlin, Kanitz put forward the following thesis: "Individual psychology will penetrate the masses only when it is guided by the world view of the masses" (ibid.).

As has already been said, we will leave aside the complex question of the interrelationship of individual psychology and Marxism. We do consider it necessary, however, to point out the presence of two opposite tendencies intrinsic in this doctrine in order to shed light on the factual status of this question.

A. Adler's doctrine is supported by a mixed, complex basis. On the one hand, it affirms that the ideas of K. Marx, more than anyone else's, can have significance for individual psychology. On the other hand, he avidly absorbs the ideas of H. Bergson, W. Stern, and other idealists and notes the concurrence of many of his ideas with the basic points of their philosophy. With complete justification, Adler states that the intention of establishing a relationship between individual psychology and philosophy entered neither his thoughts nor his work. Adler, who tries to give a gnoseological basis to this theory, was right when he says that separate elements of this doctrine have associations, which were found by purely empirical means, that is, this theory does not have its own philosophically consistent methodology.

Precisely because of this, it absorbs philosophical elements of the most irreconcilable nature. All of contemporary psychology is undergoing a crisis, in the sense that there exists not one but two psychologies. Until now, both have been developing side by side as a materialistic psychology based on the natural sciences and an idealistic, teleological psychology. This idea has been expressed in the works of modern psychologists such as F.

Brentano, H. Muensterberg, W. Dilthey, E. Husserl, P. Nathorp and many others. Adler's psychology, like all other forms of modern psychology, contains in undeciphered form the principles of these two completely incompatible, directly opposing scientific systems. Hence arises the methodological struggle within this direction of psychology, accompanied by attempts to formulate this trend methodologically with the help of one or the other system.[*]

---

[*] The Russian text ends this chapter with an ellipsis. In this passage Vygotsky seems to re-iterate thoughts which appeared in his *Questions of Theory and the History of Psychology: Historical Significance of the Crisis in Psychology.* (Voprosy teorii i istorii psikhologii: Istoricheskii smysl psikhologicheskogo krizisa) in [Rus.] Volume 1 of the *Collected Works.*

DEFECTOLOGY AND THE STUDY OF THE DEVELOPMENT

AND EDUCATION OF ABNORMAL CHILDREN

The question at hand today is how to break out of biology's hold on psychology and to move into the area of historical human psychology. In reference to our subject, the word *social* has great significance. First of all, it marks as social everything cultural, in the broadest sense of the word. Culture is the product of man's social life and his public activity; therefore, the very formulation of the question of cultural development takes us directly into the social plane of development. Furthermore, it would be possible to illustrate that a sign, a tool, located outside the organism, is separate from personality and is essentially a social organ, a social means. Even further, we could say that all higher functions are based not in biology nor in the history of pure phylogenesis; the mechanism at the very basis of higher mental functions is a social mold. We could say that the final goal toward which the history of a child's development leads is the social genesis of higher forms of behavior.

The structure of the child's complex forms of behavior is the structure of roundabout paths; it supersedes when a psychological operation proves to be impossible on a direct path. However, inasmuch as these roundabout paths have been acquired by mankind in the course of his cultural and historical development, and inasmuch as the social environment offers the child a series of roundabout paths from the very beginning, quite frequently we do not recognize that development occurs in this way.

A simple example. Let us imagine that we must compare two groups of objects to determine which has more. If you break down a certain group of objects into a certain number of parts (distribute the toys or checkers among those present), the most simple operation would be the following: The objects will be divided by eye in the manner of young children or primitive people. We, as cultured people, as well as children of older school age, will act in an indirect way, and in this way the main goal of dividing will recede into the background. Cultured people first count the number of objects, and then the participants present, and then execute an arithmetic operation; let's say, they divide sixty-four objects among four participants. The number they come up with indicates how many objects each should have. Only after this will they set about the distribution. In other words, the basic goal undoubtedly is not reached directly and immediately upon setting the task. Similarly, for a young child the goal is also set aside and placed at the end while the in between stage is filled up with a series of operations which assume the appearance of roundabout way of solving the task.

Similarly, a child begins to count on his fingers when not in a position to give a direct answer to the teacher's questions about how much 6 and 2 is; he counts off on his fingers 6 and then 2 and says, "8." Here again, we have the structure of a roundabout way of performing an operation, in this case, calculation. Not having a ready, automatic answer, a child uses his hands, which, earlier, were for him only part of the background. In the given case, the hands, having no direct bearing on the question, take on significance as tools, once the child's direct attempt to complete a task is cut off. On the basis of these hypotheses, we could determine the functions themselves and the very purpose of this cultural operation in the child's life. The indirect-path structure forms only when some obstacle occurs on the direct path, when some reaction to a direct path is interrupted; in other words, when the situation demands more than a primitive reaction. As a general rule, we may regard this behavior as complex cultural operations in a child. The child begins to find recourse in a roundabout way, when reaction along a direct path is made difficult, in other words, when the child is faced with demands for adjustment which exceed his capabilities, when he cannot cope with the task by means of a natural reaction.

As an example, we introduce our experiment, which represents a modification of an experiment by J. Piaget[1] in the area of child egocentric speech. We observe egocentric speech in a child in approximately the same situation as does Piaget, but we have assigned ourselves the task of tracking which factors determine egocentric speech. In contrast to Piaget's experiment, we make it difficult for the child. We observe him at the moment he is drawing freely but we organize the procedure in such a way that the child will be missing a colored pencil. When he becomes involved in his drawing, we imperceptibly remove the model from which the child is drawing. If he traces the drawing onto tracing paper,[*] we imperceptibly remove the drawing pin so that the paper rips. In a word, we organize a child's performance in such a way that he encounters a series of difficulties. We ascertained in these cases that egocentric speech immediately increased to 96 percent at the time when its normal coefficient is about 47 percent, illustrating the fact that egocentric speech is activated when the child is confronted with difficulties. Let's imagine that a child is drawing; he needs a red pencil. If the pencil lies in front of him, will egocentric speech arise? No. A child needs a pencil, he takes it and draws. Now let's imagine that a child needs a red pencil and there isn't one in front of him. The child looks around—no pencil. Here is where egocentric speech arises—in reasoning. "The red pencil has gone, I have to have a red pencil!" or "The rabbit will be without ears!" or "I'll have to draw with a grey one" or "If I soak the blue one in water, it will be red," and the child does this. In other words, where it is impossible by action to manage a situation, reasoning happens onto the scene in order to gauge how to plan one's performance or how to obtain the missing object. Sometimes, the child tries to be aware of what is going on. This roundabout way occurs when the direct route is cut off.

The experiment confirms that a child's egocentric speech is an important function of inner speech, in that it plans one's performance. We know the extent to which it arises in a person's head, influences what he does, conditions his action and his attitude toward the surrounding world and to what extent it characterizes a person's behavior. We find the origins of this planning in the egocentric speech of a child.

---

[*] Literally, *cigarette paper*, thin, translucent slips of paper commonly used to roll one's own cigarettes.

E. Claparéde,[2] a Swiss researcher, points to laws governing the structure of detour operations; these laws he calls the laws of difficulty and awareness. Claparéde investigated how a child reacts to what is similar and to what is different, and he came upon the following facts: Reaction to things that are similar occurs earlier than reaction to things that are different, yet the verbal determination of difference occurs earlier than the verbal definition of sameness. Claparéde explains this in the following way: With respect to similarity, a child has no difficulty; he responds directly without need to resort to roundabout ways. With respect to differences, he makes many more mistakes, undertaking one and then another action, and in this way, he discovers how a roundabout operation works. Claparéde formulated this law as follows: We interpret in words and translate our operation from a plan of action into a verbal plan in accordance with the extent to which we have learned to adapt, and in accordance with the extent to which our performance is obstructed.

Furthermore, not only investigators of egocentric speech but also those examining more complex operations show that the structure of roundabout paths arises when an operation occurring along a direct path is blocked. In other words, the basic function, the basic task of higher forms of adaptation, is realized when adaptation by direct routes is difficult for the child.

There exists still another extremely important position, and it may be formulated as follows: Development of higher forms of behavior is achieved under the influence of necessity; if a child has no need to think, then he will never think. If difficulties created by us force the child to correct his behavior, to think before acting, and to become aware in words, as Claparéde says, then a corresponding supposition will arise. If we organize the experiment so that the child does not encounter difficulties, then the percentage of his egocentric speech will immediately fall from 97 percent to 47 percent, i.e., it will decrease by half.

Previously, psychologists studied the process of a child's cultural development and the process of his education in a one-sided manner. Thus, everyone asked which natural factors in a child's psychology provide for cultural development and to which natural functions should the pedagogue turn in order to lead the child into this or that cultural sphere. They studied, for example, how speech development or learning arithmetic hinges on a child's natural functions, how it evolves in the process of a child's natural growth, but they did not study the reverse: How language acquisition or arithmetic reshapes the school child's natural functions, tearing away from and crowding out old lines and tendencies in his development.

Now, educators are beginning to understand that on entering a culture a child not only gets something from culture, assimilating it, inculcating something from the outside, but that culture itself reworks all the child's natural behavior and carves anew his entire course of development.

The distinction between the two paths of development (natural and cultural) becomes the fulcrum for a new theory of education.

The second point is even more important. First and foremost it leads to introducing a dialectic approach to the education of the child. If earlier, no distinction was made between the two developmental lines—between the natural and the cultural—and one could naively picture a child's cultural development as a direct extension and result of his natural development, it is now no longer possible to entertain such an understanding. Past researchers did not see a serious conflict in the transition, for example, from babble to the first words, or from the perception of numerical figures to the perception of the decimal system. They considered one to be more or less a continuation of the other. Recent investigators have shown, and this constitutes an invaluable service, that, where we formerly envisioned a smooth path, there exists, in fact, a rupture. Where there seemed to be a blissful movement along a smooth surface, in fact there occur leaps. More simply speaking, new research material has observed turning points in development where previous research presumed movement along a straight line. This new discovery has shed light on those main points in child development that are most important for education. However, it is natural that with the emergence of this new position the old conception about the character of education itself is dying out. Where the old theory could speak about assistance, the new one speaks about struggle. In the first instance, theory taught a child to walk slowly and calmly, while the new one teaches him to jump. This radical change in the educational point of view arises as a result of our reexamination of the basic problems of a child's cultural development. It may be illustrated apropos of each methodical problem, apropos of each chapter of our investigation.

The task of each scientific theory entails an examination of the relationships existing between the environment and the organism, as well as an examination of the most important types of these relationships. This new position, however, expresses the factually true thought that child development in each cultural epoch more or less coincides at certain points with its line of cultural development. Thus, if you examine a phenomenon phenotypically, then, at first glance, it actually seems as if, at a certain stage of the brain's development and accumulation of experience, the child acquires human speech; at a higher stage, he masters numerical notation and still later, under favorable circumstances, he enters the world of algebra. Here, a full concurrence or coordination of the developmental lines seems to occur. But this is a deceptive point of view. It conceals the real absence of convergence and a complex conflict which arises at each junction with a new developmental stage, because, in fact, the line of a child's natural development, when left to its own devices, never shifts over to the cultural line of development.

The transition of natural material into historic form is always a process called forth not by a simple organic change, but by a complex change in the developmental type itself. Thus, we may draw the following fundamental conclusion from the history of a child's cultural development in education: Education must make an uphill climb precisely where it previously saw clear sailing; it must make a leap where before it seemed possible to limit itself to a step. The primary merit of this new research consists precisely in the fact that what was considered a simple picture has now been revealed as a complex one. This point of view represents a real revolution in educational principles when one applies this approach to the question of an abnormal child.

However, this question is principally a different matter than in the case of a normal child's education. The entire apparatus of human culture (the outer form of behavior) has been adapted to a human being's normal psychophysiological organization. Our entire culture is intended for a man who possesses certain organs—a hand, an eye and ear—as well as certain functions of the brain. All our instruments, our technology, all our signs and symbols are intended for a normal human being. Hence, there arises an illusion of convergence, of natural transition from natural forms to cultural forms. Such a natural transition, by the very nature of things, cannot occur and we have just attempted to reveal its true essence.

As soon as we have before us a child deviating from the norm—a child afflicted by some psychophysiological deficit—then even a naive observer will see that convergence immediately gives way to a strong divergence, to discrepancy and disparity between the natural and the cultural lines of child development. Left to himself and to his own natural development, a deaf-mute child will never learn speech, and a blind person will never master writing. In this case education comes to the rescue, creating artificial, cultural techniques, that is, a special system of cultural signs and symbols which are adapted to the specific psychophysiological characteristics of an abnormal child.

Consequently, in the case of the blind, tactile print replaces visible print. The raised dots of Braille permit the blind to compose an entire alphabet, to read by touching these dots on a page, and to write by perforating the paper and poking out raised dots. In a similar way, dactylology (or finger spelling) allows the deaf-mute to substitute visual signs and various hand positions for the various signs of our alphabet and to compose a special way of writing in the air which a deaf child reads with his eyes.

Education has proceeded even further and teaches the deaf-mute child oral speech, inasmuch as his verbal apparatus is not usually damaged. A child is deaf from birth becomes mute as a result of the fact that he is deprived of auditory perceptions. Education teaches a deaf child to understand oral speech by reading the lips of a speaking person, that is, by replacing the sounds of speech with visual images, movements of the mouth and lips. A deaf-mute learns to speak by using touch, by using signs to imitate, and by using kinetic sensations.

These specially devised roundabout paths of cultural development for the blind or the deaf-mute, this written and oral speech created especially for them, is extremely important in the history of cultural development from two perspectives. The blind and the deaf are seemingly nature's true experiment for revealing to us that the cultural development of behavior is not necessarily connected with this or that organic function. Speech is not necessarily tied to the sound apparatus; it may be embodied in another sign system, just as the written language may be transferred from the path of vision to the path of touch.

Cases of abnormal development allow us to observe with the greatest clarity the divergence between cultural and natural development. This divergence essentially occurs in a normal child as well, but in the case of the deaf or blind child it appears with far greater distinctness precisely because a striking disparity is noted between those cultural forms of behavior intended for the normal human psychophysiological make-up, and those behavioral forms available to the handicapped child. Most important, however, the cultural forms of behavior serve as the only path of education for an abnormal child. This path means the creation of roundabout ways of development at that point where it proves to be impossible to proceed by direct paths. Braille for the blind and writing in the air for the deaf-mute are just such roundabout psychological means of cultural development.

We have grown accustomed to the thought that a human being reads with his eyes and speaks with his mouth, and only a great cultural experiment demonstrating that it is possible to read with the fingers and speak with the hand can bring to light the entire complexity and dynamics of behavior. Psychologically, these forms of behavior succeed in overcoming that which is most important: They succeed in cultivating speech and writing in a blind or deaf child in the proper sense of these words.

It is important that a blind child be able to read just as we read, but this cultural function is performed by an absolutely different apparatus than is normally the case. Similarly, from the point of view of cultural development, what is most important for a deaf child is that universal human speech is made available to him by a completely different psychological apparatus.

And thus, these examples first teach us that cultural forms of behavior do not depend upon a specific psychophysiological apparatus. Second, it is clearly apparent from the example of deaf-mute children that the development of cultural forms of behavior occurs spontaneously. Deaf-mute children, when left to themselves, develop a complex language of mimicry, a unique means of speech. This particular form of speech is not created for the deaf-mute but composed by the deaf-mute themselves. A unique language is created and it differs from all modern human languages more than these languages differ from each other because this unique means of speech dates back to the most ancient proto-language of mankind, the language of gesture or even only of the hand.

Left to himself, deprived of any education, a child sets off on the path of cultural development; in other words, in a child's natural psychological development and in his surrounding milieu, in his need to communicate with this environment, we find all the ingredients necessary for cultural development, which occurs, as it were, like combustion. A spontaneous transition occurs in the child from natural to cultural development.

Both above-mentioned points, taken together, bring us to a radical reevaluation of the present-day view of the education of an abnormal child. The traditional view proceeds from the position that a defect means a minus, a flaw, a deficit, which limits and constricts the development of the child who is characterized first and foremost from the standpoint of the failure of one or another function. The entire psychology of the abnormal child was founded upon methods intended for the functions which lapsed from the psychology of normal children.

In place of this conception, we find another, more dynamic, examination of a handicapped child's development; it takes as its point of departure the basic premise that a defect has a twofold influence on a child's development. On the one hand, it is a deficit and operates directly as such, creating a flaw, an impediment, and difficulties in the child's adaptation. On the other hand, precisely because the defect creates obstacles and impasses to development, disrupting the normal equilibrium, it serves as a stimulus for the development of roundabout paths of adjustment, of substitute functions which build a superstructure and which strive to compensate for the deficit and bring the entire system of the disturbed equilibrium into a new order.

Thus, the new point of view prescribes taking into account not only the child's negative characteristics, not only his minuses, but also a positive contour of his personality. This view presents a picture of complex developmental paths. The development of higher psychological functions is possible only along paths of cultural development, whether or not this development proceeds along lines which master external cultural means (speech, writing, arithmetic), or along the line of an internal perfection of psychological functions (the development of voluntary attention, logical memory, abstract thought, concept formations, volition, and so forth). Investigations have shown that an abnormal child is usually delayed precisely in this respect. Cultural development, then, does not depend upon the organic deficit.

Thus, the history of child cultural development permits us to advance the following thesis: Cultural development is the main area for compensation of deficiency when further organic development is impossible; in this respect, the path of cultural development is unlimited.

When speaking about giftedness, we especially wish to emphasize that culture equalizes differences in aptitude and that cultural development obliterates the natural domination of organic underdevelopment or, more accurately, makes it historical.

It remains only to add that, when it comes to the cultural development of inner behavioral means (voluntary attention and abstract thinking), certain techniques must be created for roundabout paths which exist for the development of both external and inner means of cultural behavior. In order to develop the two higher functions—attention and thought—we must create for the mentally retarded child something comparable to Braille for the blind or dactylology for the deaf, that is, a system of roundabout paths of cultural development must be proposed at that point where the defect has cut off direct routes.

PART III

QUESTIONS AT THE FOREFRONT
OF DEFECTOLOGY

THE STUDY OF THE DEVELOPMENT

OF THE DIFFICULT CHILD[1]

Definition and Classification

1. The group of children whose behavior deviates from the norm and who therefore stand out from the general mass of children with respect to education,—that is, *problem children in the broad sense of the word*—must be divided into two basic types: (a) the type of child whose behavior deviates from the norm as a result of some organic defect (physically handicapped children including blind, deaf, blind-deaf, and crippled children along with mentally retarded or feebleminded children who suffer from some organic defect); and (b) the type of child whose behavior deviates from the norm as a result of some functional disorder (difficult children in the narrow and strict sense of the word, such as delinquents, children with character disorders, and psychopaths).

A third group of children who stand out with respect to education consists of exceptionally "gifted" children. Their selection from the general mass of children poses a serious problem which was but recently recognized. Between the so-called normal, average child and the difficult child, we find marginal cases with combined or borderline forms of unmanageability and learning problems.

2. *Selection* of difficult and mentally retarded children should, as a rule, be made in the very process of education. We must not confine our selection to absolutely blatant examples of severe physical handicaps (blindness, idiocy, extreme forms of imbecility and so forth) which keep children from attending the general, public school. During the course of the pedagogical process, we must also weed out from the general student population those individuals in need of special instruction. It is possible, even necessary, to use traditional, systematic techniques (the scales of Binet-Simon and others) as orientational means, yet it would be dangerous to make pedagogical diagnoses on the basis of such investigations alone. These techniques merely select children for *special instruction*; the instructional methods will be discussed below.

3. *Assessment* of children weeded out from the general mass must occur on the basis of the distinction between organic and functional forms. Given the present state of advancement in respect to this problem we may correctly differentiate among three categories of mentally retardation: debility [learning disorders or feeblemindedness], imbecility and idiocy [by degree of severity]. The principle for differentiating the selected children must be established in accordance with their type of development and behavior as well as in accordance with the overall integral signs of each child's personality—not in accordance with isolated symptoms and defects.

Mentally Retarded Children

4. The basic principle for studying a mentally retarded child is the position that each defect creates compensatory stimuli. Therefore, a dynamic study of a retarded child cannot be limited to an assessment of the degree and severity of the deficit but, without fail, must take into account the child's developmental and behavioral processes of compensation (substitution, restructuring, and equalization). It might be useful to accept the *threefold manifestations* of compensation certain authors have proposed—that is, the three possible reactions of organisms to defects, as follows: (1) a compensated defect, (2) a subcompensated defect, and (3) a decompensated defect (compare classification *tbc.*). This definition of a child's defect still tells the pedologist nothing (cf. Weinmann [no ref], K. Birnbaum [no ref], L. Lindworsky [1919], W. Stern [1921], W. Eliasberg [1925], Peirce [no ref], Feisen [no ref], and many others).

5. It is of exceptional importance to study a mentally retarded child from the viewpoint of his *motor activity*. Motor delay, motor debility, and motor infantilism (T. Heller [no ref], Dupré [no ref], A. Homburger [1926]), along with motor idiocy, may accompany, in varying degrees, all forms of mental retardation and may give unique shape to the child's development and behavior. These motor deficiencies may be absent in cases of mental retardation and, on the contrary, may occur in the absence of mental deficiency. The principle of psychogenetic unity (F. Schultz [no ref]) in child development and behavior necessarily demands *dual* characterization (intelligence and motor ability) in any study of a mentally retarded child. By itself motor retardation to a large degree allows for compensation of a deficiency (A.Homburger, Nadoleczny [no ref], T. Heller), and everything stated in proposition 4 [above] wholly applies here. Working on its own, relatively independent of higher intellectual functions, and easily trainable, exceptional motor ability often represents the main area of compensation for an intellectual defect and of equalization of behavior. In investigative and practical work, Dr. N. I. Ozeretskii's [no ref] metrical scale may be taken as the point of departure for the study of exceptional motor capability.

6. Practical intellect—the ability to act rationally and purposefully, that is, practical, natural intelligence (*praktische natuerliche Intelligenz*)—seems to border on exceptional motor ability. Judging by its psychological nature, however, practical intelligence must be placed in a special category of research on mentally retarded children. This research must take as its starting point the work of O. Lipmann or W. Stern and, without fail, must also be based on the principle advanced by W. Koehler and Lipmann. Representing a particular qualitative type of activity, practical intellect can be combined to a varying degree with other forms, each time creating a unique picture of development and behavior. Practical intellect can serve as the fulcrum for compensation, as the means of neutralizing other intellectual

defects. Without consideration of this fact, the entire picture of development will be incomplete and often inaccurate.

7. The higher types of mental activity (usually affected in cases of feeblemindedness), which are sometimes called theoretical, gnostic[*] activity, and so forth, are based on the use of logical forms of thought, on concepts which arise on the basis of language and which comprise and accretion from a later historical period of human culture and are a product of social psychology. Such thought is peculiar to an acculturated human being; it boils down to the use of certain cultural signs as tools and may be analyzed by the instrumental method. The method created by N. Ach to analyze experimentally concept formulation and used by Bacher in his study of mentally retarded children can serve as our starting point. This method alone allows us to determine the level a child reaches in the course of his conceptual development.

8. The study of a mentally retarded child must be based mainly on qualitative tests, *and not on a quantitative determination of the defect.* The goal of studying such a child is to determine *the type of behavioral development,* and not the quantitative level which individual functions achieve. By itself, the intellect does not represent some single whole but is generally conceived of as various qualitative types of behavior and forms of activity; a defect in the area of one form may be concealed by the development of another (O. Lipmann and H. Bogen [1923], L. Lindworsky).

9. All of the above-named ways of examining a mentally retarded child, just like other methods, are usually formulated in the context of research. They are undeniably significant and beneficial but may be scientifically applicable only in a *prolonged study of the child in the process of his education.* In the last analysis, we must study not the defect, but the child who is affected by a given defect. Therefore, an integral study of a child's personality in its interaction with the surrounding environment must be made the basis of all investigative research. The data of all pedagogical observation can be augmented by a systematic observation according to a determined scheme (that of S. S. Molozhavyi [no ref], for example), and by the data of a natural or pedagogical experiment. Only with cognizance of the child's emotional and volitional behavior together with other aspects of the child juxtaposed with his general type of social behavior (i.e., the main line—*Leitlinie*—of his development) will we be able to correctly assess his mental defect.

10. Any organic defect results in behavior of the child which degrades his social position. The secondary, psychological formation (the inferiority complex and so forth) must be taken into account in the study of a mentally retarded child. The dynamics of the defect's compensation, the functional trainability, and the ability to change, are determined precisely by social psychological complications (the coefficient of his educability).

Difficult Children

11. Functional cases of behavioral deviation from normal development must be regarded as problem children in the strict sense of the word. The nature of such cases consists for the most part of a *psychological conflict* between the child and his environment or between

---

[*] The currently used term *cognitive* is probably meant. Certainly no connotations of mystical Gnosticism are intended though *gnostic* is precisely the term appearing in the Russian. [Ed]

individual aspects and layers of the child's personality. Therefore, the study of hard-to-educate children must always begin with an investigation of the fundamental conflicts.

12. Initially, when working out the methods for studying a difficult childhood, one may take as a point of departure the division scheme which was proposed by W. Gruelle [no ref], who distinguished among: (1) cases of unmanageability, conditioned by traumatizing environmental influences (*Milieu* - M); (2) cases conditioned by inner psychological factors in the child's development (*Anlage* - A); and (3) mixed cases (MA), which in turn fall into two classes depending upon the dominating role of either factor (Ma or Am). According to Gruelle, inner psychological factors (A) by no means indicate the certainty of pathological implications.

13. The classifications of difficult-to-educate children proposed by Gruelle, Folgtlender [no ref] and others may be used as an empirical scheme in an analysis of a difficult child.

14. Inasmuch as each conflict that leads to the occurrence of unmanageability is rooted in particular, personal, and unique conditions in the history of the child's development, one must apply an individual psychological method and perspective to the study of the difficult child. The conflict is usually caused by processes deep within the layers if the child's mind and is often rooted in the unconscious. Therefore, in any study of a difficult-to-educate child, it is necessary to employ methods which penetrate deeply and take into account the intimate side of the child's mind. However, in its classical form, the method known as psychoanalysis is not applicable to the study of a difficult child.

15. The scheme for studying a difficult child, elaborated by the doctrine of "individual psychology," may be used initially as a means of investigating the conflict lying at the heart of the unmanageability. One should make any changes, expand this scheme and apply it to the specific features of our population of hard-to-educate children. One should also work out a modification of S. S. Molozhavyi's scheme for studying the problem child. One aspect of this scheme, valuable for this task, is the method of correlating behavior with environment. We must create a variant of this scheme for the special problem of studying a difficult child. Tests for analyzing volition, emotions, fantasy, character, and so forth, may be used as supplementary and approximate means (H. Rorschach, Bueran, Donney).

16. The study of a difficult child, more than of any other category of children, must be based on extensive, prolonged observation during the educational process of a pedagogical experiment, so that the products of the child's creativity, his play, and of all aspects of his behavior are assessed.

Gifted Children

17. The identification of gifted children is dictated by pedagogical considerations, namely by the brisk tempo of their development and particularly of their academic learning. We must attempt to make such an identification by scientific means in the form of an experiment. Theoretically, we should address the particular type of gifted development in question with respect to special education (musical and so forth).

Mixed and Borderline Cases

18. The presence of borderline and combined forms of disability should be given special attention, since borderline cases make it possible in large measure to avert the deterioration or obstruction of the child's development, whereas mixed forms (a hard-to-educate mentally retarded child, and so forth) demand especially complex investigative and analytical techniques. The method of an integral approach to the child guarantees accuracy in studying these forms. This method takes into account not only the isolated defects and shortcomings in his behavior, but the entire main line of his development, the compensation for physical defects, secondary psychological complications, sociopsychological conflicts caused by the defect, and the dynamics of developmental ability to change. For borderline forms of mental retardation, it is most appropriate to use a pedagogical experiment in which these children are separated into specific groups within the school.

Organizational Questions

19. Any study of difficult and retarded children undertaken for the purposes of selecting them as candidates for a special school and for assigning them to various specific types of auxiliary institutions, as well as for the purpose of directing their education, must be conducted by a *specialist*, who is knowledgeable in psychopathology, defectology and therapeutic (rehabilitational) pedagogy. Only the cooperation of the pedologist, the pedagogue, and the doctor can guarantee success.

20. The organization of *pedagogical consulting offices* (Heilpaedagog, Beratungsstelle), which in Germany, Austria and other countries serve as a brilliant justification of their name, should be extremely important for an accurate assessment of difficult and retarded children as well as for the supervision of practical work on the part of the individual schools and pedagogues. These consulting offices should be centers for studying mentally retarded and difficult children.

21. It is absolutely essential to organize and correctly guide scientific research on these questions and practical investigative work of this nature. The Europeans have been successful in their study of the education of difficult and mentally retarded children only because of a very close association of both forms of work (theoretical and practical). The fundamental task of our scientific research is to establish principles and methods for the standardization and diagnosis of retarded children.

BASES FOR WORKING WITH MENTALLY RETARDED AND PHYSICALLY HANDICAPPED CHILDREN[1]

1. *Defect and Compensation.* Any defect or physical handicap whatsoever challenges an organism to overcome that defect, to make up for the deficiency and to compensate for the loss which it represents. Thus, the result of a defect is invariably twofold and contradictory. On one hand, it weakens the organism, undermines its activity, and acts as a negative force. On the other, precisely because it makes the organism's activity difficult and disturbs it, the defect acts as an incentive to heightened development in the organism's other functions; it nudges, awakens the organism to redoubled activity, activity which might compensate for the deficit and overcome the difficulty. This is a general law, equally applicable to the biology and to the psychology of an organism: The negative character of a defect acts as a stimulus to heightened development and activity. Two basic types of compensation can be distinguished: direct and organic, and indirect or psychological. The first usually takes place when one of a pair of organs is impaired or destroyed. For example, when a kidney or lung fails, the remaining organ in the pair develops compensatorily, taking over the function of the ailing organ. Whenever direct compensation is not possible, then the central nervous system and psychological apparatus bear the burden of creating a protective superstructure over the ailing or deficit organ. This superstructure is composed of higher functions which fulfill the tasks of the defective organ. According to A. Adler, awareness of an *organ defect* serves as a perpetual stimulus to psychological development.

Educating a child with one or another defect usually depends on indirect, psychological compensation, inasmuch as organic compensation for blindness, deafness, and other such defects is impossible.

2. *The Three Basic Types of Defects.* It is appropriate to investigate every defect from the perspective of its relationship to a child's central nervous system and psychological apparatus. Three separate apparatuses, each fulfilling a separate functions, can be identified in the activity of the nervous system: the perceptive apparatus (linked to the sensory organs), the responsive or motor apparatus (linked to the working organs of the body, the musculature, and the glands), and the central nervous system. A defect in any of these three will influence

178

the development and education of a child in a different way. Accordingly, the basic types of defect may be usefully identified as follows: (a) impairment or defect in the receptive organs (blindness, deafness, deafmutism); (b) impairment or defect in a part of the responsive apparatus or motor organs (crippling); and (c) defect or impairment of the central nervous system (feeblemindedness). Not only the type of the defect but also the type of compensation (it evokes) will differ in each of the three cases.

3. *The Psychophysiological Bases for Educating a Child with a Defect.* "Essentially, there is no difference between a normal and an abnormal child," says P. Ia. Troshin, "Both are human beings, both are children, and the development of each follows the same laws. The difference is only in the method of their development" (1915, p. XIII). Any training, in the last analysis, leads to the establishment of some new norms of behavior, to achieving conditional responses or conditional reflexes. In psychological terms, there is no difference in principle between training a child with a defect and training a normal child. One of the postulates of contemporary experimental physiology which is most important for pedagogy states that conditional forms of behavior (conditional reflexes) are in principle linked equipotentially* with each of the various sensory organs. Conditional reflexes can be elicited by way of the eye, as by way of the ear; by way of the ear, as by way of the skin. What is important is not that a blind person should see letters; what is important is that he should be able to read. It is important that a blind person should read in exactly way we read, and that he learn to do this in the same way that a normal child does. Thus, Kurtman's formula [no ref], which states that the blind, the deaf, and the feebleminded [mentally retarded] cannot be measured by the same standards as normal people, should be replaced by its exact opposite. From a pedagogical and a psychological point of view, the same standards can and should be applied to blind, deaf-mute, and similar children as are applied to normal children. However, the methods for the training and development of a child with a defect are, in their essence, different from those for a normal child. Thus, although the psychological nature of the instruction process is, in principle, absolutely identical, the techniques for instructing a child with a defect must always differ deeply and distinctively from those used to train a normal child. In principle, to read with the eye and to read with the fingers are exactly the same thing, but technically, they are profoundly different from one another. This demonstrates the necessity for creating a special system to train and teach children with defects (that is, special education for the blind, the deaf, and so on). This is the fundamental principle of special education: different symbols, methods, techniques, and formal skills, coupled with content that is absolutely identical with normal schools in all the training and learning processes.

4. *The Sociopsychological Bases for Training the Child with a Defect.* Any bodily deficiency not only alters a person's relationship to the physical world but also affects his relationship to other people. Above all, a child with a defect is a special child; the relationships that form around him are exceptional, unusual, and unlike those around other children. First, his misfortune alters his social position, and his positioning in his environment alters the environment. All ties with other people, all those situations which define a person's place in his social milieu, and his role and fate as a participant in life—all these functions of social existence are refashioned; a physical defect, as it were, generates social dislocation. The defect itself is not the tragedy. "Sighs and lamentations," says A. M.

---
* Although the term in the text is literally "identical," the Lashley/Luria equipotentiality principle seems to be its referent. [Transl.]

Shcherbina, "accompany a blind person throughout the course of his life; in this fashion, slowly but surely, an enormous and destructive result is achieved" (1916, p. 39).

In and of itself, an organic defect (blindness, deafness, etc.) is a biological fact. But an educator should not deal with this fact, in and of itself, so much as with its social consequences. When a blind child is the object of education, it is not with blindness alone that we must deal so much as with the conflicts which emerge for such a child as he encounters life. Therefore, rearing a child with a defect should be a social education. In an exactly similar fashion, the processes of compensation, which are generated in children under the impact of a defect, do not fundamentally direct themselves toward making up for the defect organically (which is impossible). Rather, they are directed toward psychologically overcoming, substituting for, and equalizing the deficit, and toward striving for social worth or something close to it. A defect, as stated above, is not only negative, not only a deficiency, but also a plus, a source of strength and ability, a stimulus to compensation. A deficit occurs alongside psychological tendencies in the opposite direction, with the strengths needed to overcome that deficit. Science points out the path for educating a handicapped child; the entire child-rearing process must be built around the natural tendency to compensate for a defect.

5. *The Psychological Foundations for Training and Teaching the Blind Child.* The basic features of a blind child's inner (mental) and outer (physical) development arise as a result of the stressful restriction of his spatial perception and performance, the limitations of his freedom of movement, and his helplessness with respect to spatial relationships. All the remaining strengths and abilities can function fully. In the view of A. Petzeld [1925], the most characteristic feature of a blind child's personality is the contradiction between relative helplessness in spatial relationships and the ability to maintain complete and entirely adequate relations and mutual understanding with the sighted through speech. It is precisely speech and relations with the sighted which are based upon speech, that act as the basic methods of compensation for a blind child. Left to his devices, locked into the limits of his own experience, and excluded from social experience, the blind child would develop into a thoroughly peculiar being, profoundly different from the normal individual and altogether unprepared for life in the seeing world. "They develop features," says K. Buerklen about the blind, "the like of which we do not perceive among the seeing. One is therefore forced to hypothesize that if the blind had to deal only with the blind and had nothing to do with the seeing, an entirely different kind of person might develop" [no ref., probably 1925 or 1926].

Words defeat blindness. It is therefore neither the development nor the enhanced strengthening and sharpening of the other senses (hearing, awareness, etc.)—that is, not direct organic compensation for absent sight by the remaining senses, as is postulated in the theory of vicarious sensation—that constitute the fundamental challenge in training a blind child. The challenge consists instead in using speech to accustom a blind child to the social experience of the seeing, in adapting the child to work and social life among those with sight, in compensating through knowledge and understanding for the spatial experience and first-hand visual impressions that are unattainable by him. Also of importance is the physical training of a blind child: the development of movement and the use of hearing and awareness.

6. *The Psychological Bases of Training and Teaching the Deaf-Mute Child.* A deaf-mute child is physically much better adapted than a blind child. The world is represented in human understanding primarily as a visual phenomenon. Sound plays a lesser role in the natural system. In biological terms, the deaf-mute person has an immeasurably smaller deficit for which to compensate than does a blind person. In reality, a deaf animal is surely

less helpless than a blind one. But this is not true of humans. Deprived of his powers of speech, the deaf person is more powerfully excluded from human social life than is a blind person. R. Lindner [no ref], after carrying out detailed psychological research on deaf-mute children, reaffirmed an older opinion: When he is deprived of speech, a deaf-mute child's psychological development reaches barely above that of an ape.

Teaching speech to a deaf-mute child begins with lip-reading, that is, with the child's ability to grasp and understand a visual picture of speech. Just as, to us, speech is composed of various sound combinations, so to the deaf, speech is composed of the various images and speech movements which form words and phrases. A deaf child can be taught to speak, as muteness is not based on deficits in the speaking apparatus, nor in the brain centers for speech, nor in the connecting nerve paths. Instead, his muteness derives from a lack of speech development, which in turn results from the absence of hearing and from the impossibility of absorbing spoken language from his surroundings. By copying the lip movements of speaking people, a deaf child can grasp and develop spoken language which is very close to normal speech; so close that pedagogues and psychologists in England, for example, propose to call children who have learned such spoken language not deaf-mute (since their muteness has practically been overcome) but rather deaf. Side by side with spoken language, there is a so-called "hand alphabet," in which each letter is represented by a particular conventional sign. There are a variety of possibilities for development in a deaf-mute child.

7. *Educating the Blind Deaf-Mute Child.* Educating a blind deaf-mute child raises more difficulties and presents more obstacles than educating either a blind or a deaf child. Still, such a child has limitless possibilities for development and education, as long as the central circuitry of the nervous system and the mental apparatus are undamaged in a blind, deaf-mute. The names of Helen Keller and Laura Bridgeman are universally recognized as two blind, deaf-mutes who attained very high levels of mental development thanks to their education and teaching. Helen Keller succeeded in becoming a famous writer and proponent of optimism. The data about Laura Bridgeman are more modest, but also more trustworthy and scientifically accurate: she had a command of language, reading, writing, elementary arithmetic, geography, and natural history.

The basis for training a blind deaf-mute child lies in teaching him speech. Only with the ability to speak can he become a social entity, that is, a human in the real sense of the word. Such a child establishes contact with his surroundings through touch. Through his sense of touch, he receives the signs of the deaf-mute "finger alphabet" (dactylology) as well as the raised points of the Braille alphabet for the blind. In this way the child learns to understand speech and to read. Such a child can learn to speak with the aid of the "hand alphabet" or using natural speech, learned through imitation. True, such learning is very complicated by comparison with the teaching of a deaf child, since a blind deaf-mute cannot see the articulating lip movements of the person with whom he is speaking and his imitation can be guided only by his sense of touch.

8. *Cripples.* Crippled children* are usually much closer to the normal type of child than either the blind or the deaf and require much less special training than they do. The difficulties connected with educating a cripple are largely external in character (the inability to walk to school, to write, to work and so forth). An intrinsic danger rests in the possibility that emotional equilibrium will be lost because of the difficulties and special sociopsychological

---

* The term *physically handicapped*, currently in use in the United States and elsewhere, was not in the Russian vocabulary of the 1920's and 1930's. [Transl.]

situation created by the crippled child's position in his environment. Thus the task of education is to avert the occurrence of feelings such as inferiority, despair, and the like.

9. *Children with Serious Illness.* Very frequently, a child's handicapped conditions stems from an illness. Examples are child epileptics, psychopaths, etc. Here, training must be linked with treatment, and it must be a function of curative pedagogy. Doctor and pedagogue together can cope with the task. It is often impossible to draw a hard-and-fast line between curative measures and education. More and more frequently, contemporary psychiatry is beginning to link psychotherapy (that is, treatment by psychological methods) with education, even in the treatment of adults. Psychiatry makes use of a variety of psychological methods, the essence of which is the development of the personality of the sick individual. Treatment brings the ill child's personality to full bloom through education.

10. *Mentally Retarded Children.* The general rubric of *mentally deficient* usually includes the entire group of children who, because their development remains at a below-average level, display an inability to proceed in step with the rest of the children in their school studies. In fact, taken as a group, retarded children form a unit that is complex in structure, since the nature reasons for the deficiency can vary widely. In any case, it is worthwhile to distinguish two types of deficient children: those who are deficient as a result of illness and those who are retarded because of organic defects. The first group are not necessarily "defective" children, but children who are ill. Their retardation [backwardness] stems from illness (usually nervous or psychological) and may become negligible with treatment. Only the second group—those whose permanent organic defects appear as feeblemindedness [retardation]—are distinctive. Children of this kind are divided into three different groups: idiots, whose development does not exceed that of a two-year-old child, who are incapable of using tools and instruments, and almost incapable of learning to speak; imbeciles, who do not surpass the development of children between the ages of two and seven but are capable of learning the simplest forms of labor, though not of undertaking any independent work; and finally, debiles or morons who have the least degree of deficiency and who are capable of a relatively full education and assimilation of material but demonstrate less activity in the higher functions and a slower tempo of development. They maintain traits of a child's intellect (twelve-year old) throughout life, and need special training in auxiliary schools.

Educating these children presents greater problems than training blind or deaf children. With mentally retarded children, the central apparatus is damaged, their compensatory abilities are poor, and the possibilities of development are often limited by comparison with normal children. If original symbolic systems and unusual methods of learning characterize the education of deaf and blind children, then in order to educate a mentally retarded child, it is absolutely necessary to change qualitatively the very content of educational work.

Still, compensatory processes as a rule always play a role in the development of even this type of child. Once in a while, they lead to the formation of special talents (in the areas of memory, observation, and so forth); most frequently, these processes are demonstrated by the development of practical intellect; that is, the capacity for conducting themselves reasonably, motor talents, etc.

11. *Children with Defects and Normal Children.* The process of compensation called forth by a defect can have a variety of outcomes which depend on the severity of the defect itself, on the compensatory ability (that is, the strengths of other organs and functions of the organism that are drawn into compensating for the defect) and finally on education (that is, on the training brought to bear on this process in one or another conscious direction). Where

compensation is unsuccessful, we have before us a deeply ill, sharply abnormal, and gravely handicapped child. If compensation succeeds, it can lead to the working out of compensatory functions, to the manifestation of talents. Most frequently, we observe compensation in the intermediate range, more or less approximating a specific social personality type. In this case, we have before us a normal child who is socially valuable and capable of work.

FUNDAMENTAL PRINCIPLES IN A PLAN FOR PEDOLOGICAL

RESEARCH IN THE FIELD OF "DIFFICULT CHILDREN"[1]

Although the plan for pedological[2] research work* has not been finally formulated or approved, its most important bases and even its contents can, in large part, be considered adequately clarified. This past summer, a planning conference of research institutes reviewed and confirmed the basic outlines of the project which had already been worked out; the conference responsively expanded it and introduced certain changes.

Despite the lack of a finalized research program, with all points and details worked out, the fundamental characteristics of the plan can be viewed as already elaborated and resolved in its current form; the basic paths of research work in pedology have been outlined. We believe, therefore, that it is necessary, precisely now before the plan is finally confirmed, to assess the principal positions which guided the commission in the plan's development so as to validate and elucidate its basic direction.

Our first point of departure in structuring the plan was the recognition that an indivisible link exists between the pedology of "difficult childhood" and all other pedological work. In our field of science, the primary struggle in earlier development has been to establish this very close tie —and to include "difficult childhood" as an organic part of the general system of Soviet pedology. Consequently, this recognition is also the cornerstone for the construction of all further work. The pedology of "difficult childhood" is viewed not as a specialized domain to be found outside the general laws of child development and outside the general goals and tasks of its training nor as if it were an outcast scientific community torn away from its metropolis, living an independent life and directed by its own laws. Rather, it is viewed as part of general pedology, applied, however, specifically to those particulars of child materials which are generally concerned with difficulties.

The tie between the pedology of "difficult childhood" and general pedology entails two separate features. First, the pedology of difficult childhood works with specific child material

---

* Project plan under development by a commission consisting of D. I. Azbukin, L. S. Vygotsky, M. O. Gurevich, L. V. Zankov, and E. V. Livshits {L. S. V.}

184

on problems which are of first-order significance for general pedology as well. Just as, in the famous phrase, pathology gave birth to the science of physiology, so the fundamental laws of childhood development and training appear with even greater distinctness when they are studied in forms which diverge from the normal path. The study of a damaged mechanism, one which is disturbed in process, acts as the equivalent of an artificial experiment and appears as a kind of natural experiment, permitting deeper penetration into the structure of a given mechanism and into the laws which direct the flow of a given process.

The problems of plasticity and of variability in a child's organism, of his educability, the problem of social conditioning in personality development as a whole or in its various aspects—these are general problems of pedology. They, as well as more parochial problems (the problem of mental development and giftedness, character formation, and speech development) receive experimental study only when we address the experiments set for us by nature, by studying the development and training of mentally deficient, deaf-mute, or psychopathic children. We believe that the pedology of difficult childhood should acquire information for pedology in general, just as knowledge was gathered through pathology about the anatomy and physiology of the human organism.

No one denies recognition to the internal links between general pedology and the pedology of difficult childhood, it seems. Without fear of exaggeration, one might say that resolving basic problems in general pedology would often be made more difficult, if not impossible, if it were not guided by the pedology of difficult childhood.

The second, more essential, feature is that the pedology of difficult childhood becomes a scientifically viable and practical field of knowledge only when it is built upon the same methodological basis as general pedology. Then we will not have pedological anarchy, that which calls itself, in B. Schmidt's [no ref.] words, contemporary curative pedology, when in fact it is often an eclectic conglomeration of purely empirical knowledge. Instead, it will become the scientific study of development in difficult children manifesting a truly scientific recognition of a problem.

Still, with its close but two-fold connections to general pedology, the field which interests us possesses a series of specific peculiarities; it therefore stands in a different relationship to the general science than other sub-disciplines. This unique relationship of our sub-discipline creates new and added difficulties in planning. These consist in the fact that the pedology of difficult childhood should include all ages from the cradle to adolescence, as well as an enormous variety in types of difficult children. We may, therefore, expect from early on that the task of planning for this sub-discipline might be less well executed than for others.

The plan's second point of departure—apart from its links with general pedology—arises from its continuity with all pedological work which has been carried out in this subdiscipline to date. If the fundamental purpose of the whole plan were to be expressed in the broadest way and, consequently describe all the work in the pedology of difficult childhood for the next five years, it might be said that the basic goal of such work would have to consist of the following: (a) consolidating those examinations of the problem of difficult childhood which occurred during the Revolutionary years; (b) reinforcing the essential methodological and theoretical framework of the new pedology of difficult childhood; (c) and the development and extension of those very lines of research which provide the only possible ways of creating results from many years of collective efforts in a new pedology of difficult childhood based on a Marxist framework.

The foundations of the current plan were laid at the first pedological conference. On one hand, the conference completed and systematically formulated the essential methodological premises which lie at the base of instruction and training of difficult children. In this fashion, it established and noted the departure points of our plan. On the other hand, the conference frankly elaborated upon the most important part of the plan for scientific research work in this area and identified it in its resolutions. Thus, the work of the planning commission essentially consisted of continuing and validating those tasks which had been identified at the conference. Thanks to this, continuity was maintained with the early work about which we have spoken. The introduction to the conference of appropriate resolutions speaks to all the features that link our plan with the results of the work done at the conference. Taken together, they represent the first step along a path leading to the creation of a Marxist pedology of difficult childhood and of therapeutic pedology. They offer a rather rich resource for determining the perspective and directions of future lines of research in a sub-discipline of the pedology of difficult children which will be closely tied to general pedological issues.

We will not detain ourselves here over the concluding work accomplished by the conference nor over the basic platform worked out by the conference. As we have already mentioned these were the basis for the construction of our plan. One can familiarize oneself with these through the resolutions of the First Pedological Conference. We only consider it necessary to mention the continuing linkage with preceding work, without which it is impossible to understand the whole plan correctly. Correspondingly, four fundamental criteria were judged basic to the plan in working out the contents of the next five years' research work; they contain the leading directions of the plan, its goals and its purposes, and they guide the selection of themes.

The first criterion is the theoretical formulation of the pedology of difficult childhood and defectology (therapeutic pedology) on a Marxist basis. The second is the study of the social conditions of development in a difficult child (the social as well as the biogenic circumstances). The third is the discovery of developmental dynamics in a difficult child as the first approach to the dialectical study of problems in pathological pedology. (These include the dynamics of conflict, of defects, of anomalies in character and, generally, all the mechanisms which create educational difficulties and are involved in their persistence.) The fourth is the elucidation of the pedological bases for pedological practice as they relate to concrete plans for the construction of Soviet schools and training institutions for difficult children.

The four criteria should also define the order of priorities for work on scientific themes. The themes which lie outside these basic directions were altogether eliminated from the next Five Year Plan as not urgent enough, although completely justifiable. Once the fulfillment of the plan is entirely assured, they might, therefore be pursued outside of it.

In compiling the plan, we took the view that, at the current level of pedological development, any further movement forward or even any consolidation of what we have already gained is entirely impossible without a philosophical and methodological formulation of our area of knowledge. Until now, as we have already pointed out, the area has been governed by unadorned empiricism and pure eclecticism, which together have led to pedagogical anarchy. Consequently, the following most accurately characterize the status of contemporary pedology of difficult children in Europe and America: There is a search for a philosophical base; there are attempts to establish and validate a methodological basis for making anomalies the object of study as well as the formulation of techniques and methods for their study; there is a tendency to formulate theoretical bases in this area; and there are, on one hand, demands for the establishment of boundaries for the discipline and on the other, characteristically, demands to define its true relationship to other broad sciences. This thirst for philosophical formulations at once reveals the level of maturity pedology has achieved and the related crisis which it is currently experiencing.

We do not perceive any aims for the pedology of difficult children other than those indicated by its link with pedology and pedagogy, in general. The broad aims and tasks in training and teaching laid out by pedagogy are, at the same time, the aims and tasks of special training for the difficult child. The general laws of development and training of the child as an organism are also the laws of development and training for the difficult child. What is distinctive is that these general tasks of development are resolved by special means; the broad aims of development are attained in special ways.

The fundamental task of research work in the area specified here is precisely to study those particular paths of development for a difficult child and to elaborate the special means of attaining the general goals of education. But in order that this task be resolvable, it is necessary that we realize, methodologically speaking, what it is that we seek, through what epistemological means we order the propositions that interest us, and what in a general sense is the methodological character of this field of pedology.

A second point is closely linked to the immediate execution of the tasks we have named, and that is the clarification of the influence exercised by environmental factors on the development of a difficult child. As we know, what has served as a basis for reexamining the problems of difficult childhood was (1) the study of social factors surrounding children who are difficult to educate and (2) an understanding that all phenomena are primarily socially conditioned phenomena. A natural outcome of this reexamination was the demand for social education for the difficult child. One might say that no chapter of our pedology is so closely, so organically, linked to pedagogy as the chapter on the difficult child. This applies first of all to the child whose difficulties are of social origin. But the child who is afflicted with a physical defect who develops in a given kind of social environment also, in fact, experiences serious influence from this factor on all paths and in all directions of his development.

A third point is closely connected with this; that is the discovery of developmental dynamics in a difficult child. The best that European clinics and laboratories have to offer us about the study of the difficult child is along the lines of a dynamic understanding of a defective and difficult childhood. More and more, such an understanding is changing the old statistical and purely quantitative approach to these problems. The new understanding lays bare before us complex paths leading to the creation of educational difficulties and projects ways to change and overcome them. The dynamic understanding of educational difficulties consists of a spontaneous dialectic; such a dialectic is a part of any truly scientific knowledge. For us, its mastery must be the first step along the path of conscious dialectical elaboration of these complex problems of human development.

Finally, there is praxis—that most powerful revolutionizing factor in the training and education of a difficult child. It demands the introduction of a series of themes which are of first importance from a practical point of view.

Our entire plan was based on the statements of the appropriate institutions, with those of the GlavSotsVos* in first rank, the available production plans of various institutes,

---

* The Main Social Educational Agency. [Transl.]

statements of research themes, and finally, from among the themes which were naturally derived from the four criteria noted above and were introduced by the committee. In elaborating the plan, we proceeded from a general position; that is, we recognized the legitimacy of two kinds of themes.

A. B. Zalkind's thesis for the general plan holds that fundamental research attention in the next pedological Five-Year Plan, must be devoted to immediate attention to the pedagogical process. Still, at the same time, fundamental research must continue and become more profound: research into the psychophysiology of the developing human, resolving those problems most immediate to the building of socialism. In constructing the plan, we also proceed from the assumption that both these lines of research work must be present in the study of all groups of difficult children [lit.: difficult childhood]. We believed that the best organizational form for implementing the plan is one in which our institute stands at the center of research in each field and others support the same line of research with auxiliary work.

We selected the following varieties and types of difficult childhood as the foundation for the research: troubled children in mass schools; children difficult to train in the proper sense of the word (homeless, delinquent, or pedagogically neglected) psycho- and neuropathic children, mentally retarded, blind, deaf-mute, logopathics, and the mentally and physically ill. We believed that each of these areas must be assured of deep somatopedological and psychologoreflexological research, as well as the practical research work which is usually referred to as investigation.

Comparing these requirements with a real picture of contemporary pedological work in the field of difficult childhood, we might note that the organizational principle we have put forward is, on the one hand, justified and realized in life itself—in the specializations being formulated or planned at most institutes. But on the other hand, there is a serious disparity between the plan and the true disposition of things. We believe that the imbalances in research on the pedology of difficult childhood, which appear as spontaneous resolutions of unresolved research areas, must be overcome by a concentration on and creation of new research in areas that are insufficiently studied, as well as by the rational reassessment of work in progress.

For example, the problem of development in a child who is difficult to educate in the proper sense of that word (neglected, delinquent, pedagogically disregarded, and generally sociogenetically difficult) is, in practice, barely studied at all. The problem of development of the difficult-to-educate child has cardinal significance for the plan as a whole and has stood at the center of reexaminations of this question since the revolution, but it has not been studied in a direction that would require any revision of our knowledge about difficult childhood and, with a few individual exceptions (unconnected researchers working in that area), it is hardly studied. Random research into this problem, conducted, incidentally, in unconnected research institutions, is first of all, frequently not in the hands of those who can genuinely devote themselves to the problem. Secondly, such work in no way replaces the deep and fundamental revision of the problem and the research into all the mechanisms of education during troubled childhood which the problem deserves.

It is impossible to fool oneself into believing that someone will do this work for us. One must bear in mind that the problems we have designated remain as yet unresolved, and that all pedagogical work in the area is, in practice, supported only by those general principles, perspectives and understandings which have been advanced at another time.

The plan presupposes the creation of an institute or special department for the study of difficult childhood, similar to the major institutes which work in the areas of research about mental retardation, and neuro- and psychopathy. If one examines the three sections of pedological research work, it is immediately obvious that there is an enormous disparity represented by an immeasurably greater elaboration of the last two issues, in comparison with the almost complete lack of such elaboration of the first. One must take into account that, both in worldwide science as here in the USSR, there are still two pedological approaches to this subject. What has been accomplished to date has in no sense resolved all debates. Meanwhile, the approach taken by all our special conferences and our practical work is scientifically unsupported at present.

The plan assumes the concentration of all problems linked to this area in the Institute of Methods for School Work;[3] this institute must be the center. Two considerations support this assumption: (1) The institute would take a most active role in posing the question, and in the principal reconsiderations of all studies on difficult childhood, the institute would provide the basic methodological research on this question; (2) given its ideological and scientific aims, this institute could, in the best of ways, support the elaboration of this study of the environment for children who are difficult to educate. Finally, it is to be expected that research and study on the environment of the hard-to-educate child, as a special approach in pedological work, along with laboratory and clinical methods, would be directly linked to general pedological and pedagogical research on environment.

Problems of neuro- and psychopathic children are now researched in the Institutes for the Preservation of Healthy Children,[4] with basic centers in Moscow and Leningrad. These institutes, whose structure includes clinics (e.g., the Narkomzdrava Psychoneurological School-Sanitarium in Moscow),[5] can more fully support the elaboration of the problems in therapeutic pedagogy in the proper sense of that word, as well as broad biological and psychoneurological research on child psychopathology and neuropathology. Still, even in these institutes (or for supporting work, in others), it might be important to strengthen practical investigative work. Such investigation would serve the population just as pedological laboratories fulfill this work with respect to feebleminded [retarded] children (in their selection in schools).

Further, it would be desirable to begin research on the social conditionality of development and on the reeducation of a given child into a different social sphere. The supplemental psychological-pedagogical elaboration of these problems can be entrusted to the Second MGU[*6], if a proposed department of neuropedagogy is organized there. Its tasks would be to ground pedagogical practice in this field and to train personnel for psychoneurological school-sanitaria. Further work on problems of development for ill and physically abnormal children (tubercular, syphilitic, crippled children, etc.) must be concentrated in Institutes for the Preservation of Children's Health.

The study of early, especially constitutionally induced, manifestations of difficulties in education must constitute a new chapter in learning about difficult children; this new chapter has only in the most recent past begun to include preschool and nursery ages. The study of difficult children of nursery-school age must be turned over to the Institutes for the Preservation of Motherhood and Infancy in Moscow and Leningrad, while research into

---

[*] The Second Moscow State University was also known as the "Red University." [Transl.]

difficult-to-educate pre-schoolers should be given over to the Medico-Pedagogical Stations[7] in the Institute of Scientific Pedagogy at the Second MGU.

Finally, neurologically and mentally ill children can be studied only at a children's clinic. Even here, we believe, the children's division of existing medical clinics should be widely "pedologized and they should not only solve problems of an exclusively medical or therapeutic nature, but also deal with those which are pedological in origin. Thus, the introduction of a pedologist-worker onto clinic staff was advanced at the planning conference as a highly desirable measure.

We cite the article of E. K. Sepp[8] in the first issue of our journal.* It seems to us that this article shows clearly enough how much a neurological clinic and a psychiatric clinic can work out the really fundamental and deep problems of development in an abnormal child (severe retardation and its relation to mild retardation, aphasia and its relation to other speech disorders, psychosis and its relation to mild character disorder).

Further, the field of physical handicaps is entirely an undefended sector. Here, it is vital to create new research cadres and research bases. We would consider the Institute of Scientific Pedagogy to be the central institute in this field. The basis of its work should serve to tie both pedagogical clinics and experienced research institutions more closely to the Institute.

The problems of mental retardation must be studied further along two basic lines. On one hand, they should be looked at largely from the biological and reflexological perspective in Leningrad in the Children's Research Institute[9] with the cooperation of the Institute on the Brain, and on the other hand, at the Medico-Pedagogical Station at the Second MGU in Moscow from the psychopedagogical side.

Reflexological research into difficult childhood and the working out of psychological problems should be concentrated in the Institute on the Brain, while investigative work on mental retardation and psychopathic children should be concentrated in the Children's Research Institute in Leningrad.

Realizing the research tasks which confront the pedology of difficult childhood depends upon the correctness of basic aims as well as upon the organization of research work.

---

* *Questions of Defectology.* [Transl.]

THE COLLECTIVE AS A FACTOR IN THE DEVELOPMENT
OF THE ABNORMAL CHILD[1]

1

Contemporary scientific research, occupied with the problem of comparative research into the development of normal and abnormal children, proceeds from the general assumption that the laws governing the development of normal and abnormal children alike are basically the same. In the same way, the laws governing vital activity remain fundamentally the same, whether for normal or ill-functioning conditions in an organ or organism of the body. The task of comparative psychology is precisely to find the general laws which characterize the normal and abnormal development of a child and which wholly encompass all areas of child development.

Recognizing the general applicability of the laws of development to the normal and pathological spheres is the cornerstone of the comparative study of children. But these broad regularities find their own concrete manifestations in one situation or another. When dealing with normal development, these regularities are realized in one complex of conditions. Where something atypical unfolds before us, something which deviates from the norms of development, those same regularities, now appearing in an entirely different complex of conditions, take on a qualitatively individual, specific appearance, one which is not an absolute copy or photographic replica of childhood development. Thus, comparative research must always maintain dual tasks in its field of vision: (1) establishment of general laws and (2) uncovering their specific manifestations in the different variants of child development. Thus, we must start out from the general laws of child development and then study their peculiarities as they apply to abnormal children. This should be the path of our research even now, in examining the problem which interests us, the problem of the collective[2] as a factor in the development of an abnormal child.

Obviously, we will limit ourselves to only summary and abstract statements of those positions in the light of which we are intending to investigate the development of the abnormal child. The basic proposition which interests us can be formulated in the following manner: Research on the development of higher psychological functions persuades us that both their phylogenesis and ontogenesis have social origins.

As far as phylogenesis goes, this proposition has hardly ever met with serious opposition because it is entirely clear that the higher psychological functions (that is, thinking in concepts, reasoning, speech logical memory, voluntary attention and so on) coalesced in the historical period of human and anthropoid development. These functions arose not in the biological evolution of a human bio-type, but through the historical development as a social creature. Only collective social life developed and elaborated all those higher forms of intellectual activity, which are characteristic of humans.

As for ontogenesis, only recently have the results of a series of studies on child development made it possible to establish that the building and formation of higher forms of psychological activity are completed in the process of a child's social development, in the process of a child's relationships, and in his cooperation with the surrounding social sphere. On the basis of some of our own work and work of our collaborators, we have elsewhere formulated this proposition in the following way: Observation of the development of the higher functions shows that the construction of each of them is clearly subsumed under one or another lawful regularity. Specifically, every higher psychological function occurs twice during the process of behavioral development: first, as a function of collective behavior, as a form of cooperation or cooperative activity, as a means of social accommodation (i.e., on an interpsychological plane) and, again, a second time, as a means of a child's individual behavior, as a means of individual adaptation, as an inner process; that is, on an intrapsychological plane.

In order to follow the transition from the collective form of "working together" to the individual form of a child's behavior, we must understand the principle for building the higher mental functions in the making.

In order that this overly general and abstract proposition about the collective origins of the higher psychological functions not remain simply an unclear verbal formulation, in order to fill it with concrete contents, we must clarify by using practical examples to show, in the words of P. Janet [1930?], how this important basic law of psychology works in the psychological development of a child. By the way, examples can help us significantly in studying the results of the application of these laws to abnormal child development. The examples serve as a bridge, tying together concrete facts, linking the laws of normal development and abnormal development.

We could take the process of speech development as the first and simplest example illustrating the general law. It is sufficient to compare the beginning and final moments in speech development; then, one can see to what extent the formulation we have just addressed is justified. In fact, in the beginning, speech appears in a child in the role of communication, that is, as a means of communicating, of influencing the surroundings, of linking up with it, as a form of working with other children or adults, as a process of working with others and of cooperation. But it is worth comparing the beginning moment of speech development with more than just its final stage, namely, the speech function in an adult. It is also worth comparing the first moment with one of the following stages of development—for example, with the fate of the function of speech at school age or at an interim stage—to see how speech at that point becomes one of the most important means of thought, one of the most important and leading inner psychological processes of a child.

This first stage of speech in the process of thought formation led many researchers to reach an entirely false conclusion. They concluded that thinking is nothing other than soundless, mute, inner speech; thinking is speech without sound. This extreme perspective equated the processes of thought with inner speech. No matter how false this equation may be, it is deeply significant: The mistake, which led to this inaccurate identification, would not have arisen if the speech processes were not indeed so close to the thought process and so deeply and intimately intertwined with it that only special and subtle analysis can reveal the inaccuracy which lies at the basis of that understanding.

If we glance at the entire cycle of speech development, seeing it as a psychological function from its beginning to its final moments, then it is easy to understand that the cycle wholly conforms to that very important fundamental rule in psychology mentioned above. This rule shows how the path from outer speech to inner speech goes through a whole series of changes during a child's development, how the most important form of collective behavior—social cooperation with others—becomes an inner form of psychological activity for the personality itself. Let us briefly take note of the most significant moments in the process of transformation from outer to inner speech.

The first turning point and a decisive stage in the subsequent development of child thought is that form of speech which contemporary psychology often calls *egocentric speech*. When studying child speech from the functional perspective at the early, preschool age, we can easily establish that speech activity takes two basic forms. On one hand, there is socialized speech. The child asks questions and answers questions put to him, voices objections, makes requests, informs or tells something. In a word, he uses speech as a form of working with the people around him. On the other hand, there is egocentric speech; the child speaks, as it were, to himself aloud, and for himself. For example, while busy at some activity such as drawing, playing with a toy, or manipulating subjects, he carries on a dialogue, as it were, with himself; he does not enter into cooperative speech with those around him. This form of speech may be called *egocentric*, since it performs an entirely different function from verbal communication. Still, since egocentric speech was first studied, a correct psychological understanding of it has run into a number of difficulties.

J. Piaget was first among contemporary researchers to study, describe, and measure in sufficient detail the phenomenon of egocentric speech in children of various ages. He was inclined to attribute no very real meaning to this form of speech as far as the subsequent fate of a child's thought was concerned. For Piaget, the fact that a child accompanies his own activity with spoken utterances is just an expression of that general law of child activity according to which a child still does not distinguish some forms of activity from others. That is to say, a child becomes involved in the process of activity with his whole being. That general, discerning, undifferentiated activity appears not only in a child's motor functions but in his egocentric speech. Thus, egocentric speech appears to be something like an extra, peripheral function, which accompanies the child's basic activity like the accompaniment of any basic melody. But this accompanying activity, this egocentric speech, fulfills no independent psychological function; it has no reason to be there. Nothing essential would be changed in a child's behavior if that accompaniment disappeared.

Indeed, according to Piaget's observations and very careful measurements, egocentric speech does not develop; rather, it is curtailed with the child's progressive development. Its most luxurious flowering occurs at an early age. As early as mid and pre-school years, it takes a turn which is not a sharp nor abrupt but still decisive. It experiences a breaking point after which its development begins constantly, though slowly, to decline. At the beginning of the school years, according to Piaget's research, the coefficient of egocentric speech (a numerical indicator of diffusion and frequency in the behavior of a child of a given age) falls to zero. Thus, the functional and genetic evaluation of egocentric speech speaks to the fact that it is a product of insufficiently developed child behavior, stemming from the idiosyncratic set of the early childhood years and disappearing as the child's behavior reaches a higher level of development. In other words, egocentric speech, in Piaget's opinion, is an incidental product of child activity, an epiphenomenon, some kind of free supplement to other kinds of activity, an expression of the incomplete nature of a child's behavior. Functionally, it is not necessary to anything, and nothing essentially changes in the behavior of the child; genetically, it makes no contribution to development; rather it is fated to slow disappearance and curtailment.

In light of new and more profound research, we feel it must, however, be recognized that this evaluation of egocentric speech does not correspond to reality from either a functional or a genetic perspective. With special research devoted to studying the functional role of egocentric speech,[*] we have been able to establish that it begins to play a unique and altogether specific function in a child's behavior, even early on—and that it cannot be regarded as a by-product of childish activity. Egocentric speech, as our research showed, is not included in the process of a child's behavior as an accompaniment, going along with the basic melody of one activity or another. Speech is not simply added to basic activity, more-or-less indistinguishably in step; rather, it becomes involved in the flow of that activity, and actively restructures it, changing the appearance of its structure, composition, and manner of functioning. Thus, by measuring the coefficient of egocentric speech in a child, we have been able to establish that this coefficient almost doubles in situations which are linked with troubling conditions.

Analysis of that same fact led us inescapably to a reevaluation of the functional role of egocentric speech. This means that a child reacts by using egocentric speech above all when his basic activity runs into an obstacle, a difficulty, which diverts the activity from its usual flow. From the psychology of thought, however, we know that it is precisely in circumstances linked with such difficulties that intellectual reaction occurs. The psychological function of the intellect arises precisely in the process of adapting to new circumstances and different conditions—thinking means overcoming difficulties.

Thus, the link between egocentric speech and problems in and of itself leads to the notion that egocentric speech in a child's behavior begins very early to fulfill intellectual functions—that is, it begins to serve as a means of thought. But decisive confirmation does not come from the mere fact of more frequent egocentric speech in the face of difficulties. Rather it comes from an analysis of the forms of egocentric speech which appear in a child's behavior in response to obstacles. Analysis shows that a greater part of a child's egocentric speech under such circumstances acquires an intellectual character. Speech does not just reflect the confusion arising from some activity; the child, as it were, asks himself questions, formulates his problem in words, as he gropes about for solutions.

Let us give the simplest of examples from our own experiments, showing clearly what we have in mind when we speak about the intellectual function of egocentric speech. The child is drawing a tram car. When outlining the last wheel, he presses down hard on the pencil so that the lead breaks, bouncing off to the side, and the wheel is left unfinished. The child first tries to complete the circle he has begun with a broken pencil, but nothing is left on the paper except impressed outlines. The child stops, looks at the paper, and pronounces

---

[*] See "Thought and Speech," *Collected Works* Vol. 2, Russsian Edition. [Engl. Ed.: Vol 1]

"broken"—and then goes on to a different part of the picture, exchanging the pencil for paints. From this, it is clear that the word "broken," uttered by the child to himself, without reference to anyone present, was indeed a decisive moment in his activity. At first, it seemed that the word referred to the pencil and simply stated the fact that it was broken. Further observation revealed that this was not so. We can imagine the detailed sequence of the child's behavior more or less in the following manner: The child tried to finish drawing the last wheel; he didn't succeed and found a way out of the difficulty by changing the theme of the picture. The unfinished wheel came to represent a broken wheel, and the entire picture began to unfold further, not according to the earlier model of an already finished drawing, but in a completely different direction. In the final version, the picture depicted a broken tram car, which had been in an accident, and which had been removed for repairs onto a side track.

One might ask: Can such an egocentric utterance in a child, concentrated in one word, be defined as simply accompaniment, going along with the basic activity—the drawing— and can one see in that one word only a by-product of the child's activity? On the contrary. It is clear that this word and its communication represent a key moment, a turning point, in the child's activity. Like a plan, that word contains within it, in condensed form, the entire further behavior of the child; it signifies a resolution discovered for a difficult situation, an expressed purpose, a sketch for future action. That word is the key to the entire future behavior of the child. In particular, the word became the solution of the problem which confronted the child at that moment when the pencil broke. That which was formulated in the word was then carried out in action. These new, complete relations between a child's words and actions (which we observed, admittedly, in the most primitive form) already fully merit being called an intellectual function of egocentric speech. A child resolves a problem in words; with the help of egocentric speech, he identifies the path of his actions; consequently, he is thinking in words, even if in a very primitive and extremely elementary form. An analysis of similar facts is also in accord, showing that egocentric speech fulfills an intellectual function and becomes a primitive method of children's thinking out loud in a difficult situation.

We will not discuss further the changes in composition, structure, and method of children's actions which take place in connection with the appearance of primitive verbal thought in the shape of egocentric speech. We will only say that these changes are, in the highest degree, serious and significant. This is understandable; if speech is included in a child's behavior as more than a second, parallel-moving kind of reaction, then attaching words does not represent merely an accompaniment with respect to the fate of basic activities. Rather, it represents the molding of the most basic melody of children's activities. Thus, we can conclude from this that egocentric speech fulfills an important function in children's behavior; it acts as the child's first, most initial verbal thought.

But, if this is the case, then one must anticipate in advance that the genetic fate of egocentric speech, and its role and function in the developmental process have been falsely evaluated in earlier research. In fact, if egocentric speech changes nothing in behavior—if it is merely a by-product and does not fulfill any function—it is completely natural that, with age and with the development of the child, it should disappear, vanish from behavior. But if it is by nature nothing other than the first stage in the development of children's thought, then it would be difficult to anticipate anything other than its being a close, internally inseparable link to the next stage in the development of a child's verbal thought processes. And, in fact, a variety of research allows us to conclude these things: We have, in egocentric speech, one of the most important moments in the transition from outer to inner speech; it is only the first step in the formation of inner speech and, consequently, in the verbal thought process of a child.

Egocentric speech (according to results we have formulated elsewhere) is still, physiologically speaking, outer speech. It still can be heard; the word occurs outside; the child is thinking out loud; his thoughts are not far from conversation. Outer speech still displays all the characteristics of an ordinary monologue, a conversation out loud with oneself. However, psychologically, inner speech is already there; that is, we have before us speech which basically, fundamentally, and decisively changes its function, transforming itself into a way of thinking, into an internal way of behaving, into a specific form of activity in a child's intellect.

We will not now discuss in detail all the factors that are said to be useful in recognizing egocentric speech as a first step in the development of inner speech in a child. Let us say only that the disappearance of egocentric speech by school age is further accompanied by other factors which show that the formation and development of inner speech occurs specifically during early school age. But, on the basis of this and many other facts, we have developed the hypothesis which states: Egocentric speech does not disappear entirely from a child's behavior; instead it changes its character and transforms itself into inner speech. This transformation is prepared for fully by the development of egocentric speech and is completed on the borderline between pre-school and school years. We have followed one of the most important transformations from outer to inner speech, and we could say that, in essence, the function of verbal thought develops in the following way: The child absorbs social forms of behavior, which he begins to apply to himself just as others earlier applied this method to him or as he himself applied them to other people.

Thus, to the question "Where do the higher processes of child thought come from? How are they built up, and through what means do they develop?" we should answer: "They arise during the process of a child's social development by means of the transferral to himself of those forms of cooperation which the child absorbs in the process of interaction with the surrounding social environment." We see that collective forms of cooperative work precede individual forms of behavior, grow out of their foundation, and act as the direct roots and sources of their appearance. It is in this basic sense that we formulated the law about the dual appearance of the higher psychological functions in the history of a child's development. Thus, the higher functions of intellectual activity arise out of collective behavior, out of cooperation with the surrounding people, and from social experience.

We can offer a few more examples which demonstrate the interdependence between the development of collective forms, on the one hand, and individual methods of behavior with respect to the higher psychological functions, on the other. First of all, let us mention argument. In their time, J. Baldwin [1904?, 1911?] and E. Rignano [no ref.] expressed the idea, that true thought is nothing other than discussion or argument carried on within an individual. Piaget was able to substantiate this idea genetically and to show that a conflict of opinions, an argument, should arise early in a children's collective, so that thought might later develop among children of that collective as a special process in inner activity which would be unknown to a child of an earlier age. The development of reflection is begun in argument, in the conflict of ideas; such is the fundamental conclusion of this research.

And, in fact, as Piaget has very wisely expressed it, we readily take ourselves at our own word. In the process of individual thought, the very task of checking, demonstrating, disproving a known position, and motivating confirmation cannot take place. Demonstrating the accuracy of one's thoughts, raising objections, presenting reasons—all of this occurs through a task of adaptation and can arise only in the process of children arguing with each other. "This is my spot," said a child whom Piaget observed. "You must give it to me, because I always sit there." "No, it's mine," objected the other, "because I got here first and took it."

The seeds of future reflection—an understanding of justifications, proof, and so on—are already contained in the most primitive of children's quarrels.

In the history of a child's reflection, itself closely linked to argument, we can observe the genetic interdependence between collective forms of cooperation and individual methods of behavior with respect to the development of intellect. If so, then, based on the example of a game with rules, we can also observe (as a number of researchers have shown) the same genetic dependence in connection with the development of a child's volition. The ability to direct one's own behavior, to restrain and even replace spontaneous, impulsive actions with those that do not stem from the spontaneous influence of an external situation but which arise instead in the attempt to subordinate one's behavior to the rules and tasks of a specific game—the ability to coordinate one's actions with those of one's companions (in a word, all of the elements of the earliest stage of self-direction which merit the name of *voluntary processes*)—first emerges and appears in some collective form of activity. A game with rules here again serves as an example of this. Later, these forms of cooperation, which led to the subordination of behavior to a given game's rules, become internalized forms of a child's activity, voluntary processes.

A game with rules, consequently, occupies the same place in the history of a child's will as arguments and discussions occupy in the history of the development of reflection.

If the theme of this work permitted us to examine in detail each of the higher psychological functions, we would be able to demonstrate that the rules we formulated above equally include such functions as attention, memory, the practical intellect of a child, his education, and so forth. The development of a child's personality is seen in all cases as a result of the development of his collective behavior; everywhere we can observe one and the same law of shifting social forms of behavior into the sphere of individual adaptation.

We have already said that this law has special meaning for an accurate understanding of the development and underdevelopment of the higher mental functions of an abnormal child. Defects and lack of development of the higher psychological functions are related to one another in a different way than defects and lack of development are related in the elementary functions. This distinction must be mastered in order to unlock the whole enigma of the psychologically abnormal child. Although underdevelopment of the elementary functions is often the direct result of one defect or another (for example, motor underdevelopment due to blindness, underdevelopment in speech because of deafness, underdevelopment of thought due to feeblemindedness, and so forth), underdevelopment of higher functions in an abnormal child usually arises as a result of additional, secondary phenomena, which compound with his primary characteristics.

All contemporary psychological research on abnormal children is permeated with the basic idea that the image of mental retardation and other forms of abnormal development in a child represents a structure that is in the highest degree complex. It is a mistake to think that from the defect itself all the criterial symptoms and a complete characterizing picture can be derived immediately and decisively as though it were the fundamental nucleus. In fact, it turns out that those particularities which constitute the picture have a very complex structure. They display extremely intricate structural and functional interconnections and, along with the primary characteristics of the child stemming directly from the defect, they show also secondary, tertiary, and other complications which derive not from the defect itself but from the defect's primary symptoms. Thus, additional syndromes arise in an abnormal child, like a complex superimposition upon the basic picture of development. The ability to distinguish between what is basic and supplementary—what is primary and secondary in an abnormal child's development—is a requisite condition not only for an accurate theoretical understanding of the problems which interest us, but also for practical actions.

However paradoxical it may seem, all the scientific tendencies of contemporary defectology (if one takes its practical conclusions) orient us in a direction that is most unexpected from the point of view of traditional praxis. These tendencies teach us that the greatest possibilities for the development of the abnormal child most likely lie in the higher, rather than the lower, functions. For a long time, the laws of T. Ribot, H. Jackson,[*] and others have been tacitly recognized as the basic premises in defectology. These laws say that the order of pathological destruction is opposite of the order of the construction of the functions. That which appears latest in the developmental process suffers first in the process of destruction. The processes of development and destruction are linked but in an inverse relationship.

From this perspective, it seems natural that, when a series of pathological processes are present, disintegration begins with the higher, most recent, most complex functions, leaving the primary ones alone and not touching the lowest functions. The application of this law to underdevelopment might be understood as follows: The sphere of higher psychological functions has always been considered to be close and beyond the ability of the abnormal child. Thus all pedagogical efforts have been directed at the advancement and perfection of the lower, more elementary processes. More clearly, the doctrine affected sensorimotor education in both theory and practice, inasmuch as in training and education that doctrine dealt with distinct sensations, different movements, separate elementary processes. The mentally retarded child was not taught to think, but to distinguish among smells, among nuances of color, among sounds, and so on. And it was not only sensorimotor training but the entire rearing process of the abnormal child that was oriented toward alignment of the elementary and the lower functions.

Current scientific research demonstrates that this perspective is mistaken. Precisely because of the theoretical bankruptcy of this pedagogical system, the approach described above has turned out to be of so little value and of such little practical usefulness that it has developed into the deep and serious crisis which has, at the moment, overtaken the whole field of education for abnormal children. In truth, as research shows the lower, elementary processes are, on the one hand, the least susceptible to training, the least dependent on external events, on the social development of the child. On the other hand, since they become the first symptoms, flowing directly from the very nucleus of the defect, they are closely tied to that nucleus that they cannot be defeated until the defect itself has been eliminated. And, since the elimination of the defect is impossible, it is natural that the struggle with the primary symptoms has been doomed beforehand to futility and failure. Both these instances taken together have meant that the development and training of the elementary lower functions have confronted almost insurmountable obstacles at every step.

Moreover, the dialectic of development in an abnormal child and his training is such, that his development and training must be completed not by direct but by indirect means. As we have already stated, the mental functions arose during humanity's historical development and depend in their structure on the collective behavior of the child; they represent

---

[*] Jackson, John Hughlings (1834-1911) wrote extensively on aphasia and speech disorders. [Ed]

an area which, in greater measure than the others, allows for leveling and a smoothing over of the effects of a defect and offers greater possibilities for the influence of education. Still, it would be erroneous to think that an abnormal child's higher processes are better developed than his elementary processes. With the exception of a small number of cases (such as, for example, the underdeveloped elementary motor processes of the blind or the deaf), the higher processes usually suffer more than the elementary ones. This should not discourage us. It is true that the underdevelopment of the higher processes is not primarily, but secondarily conditioned by the defect. And, consequently, they represent the weakest link in an abnormal child's chain of symptoms. Therefore, this is where all educational efforts should be directed, in order to break the chain at its weakest point.

Why do the higher functions fail to develop in an abnormal child? Not because the defect directly impedes them or makes their appearance impossible. On the contrary, experimental research has now demonstrated without a doubt that it is theoretically possible to develop those modes of activity which lie at the base of the higher functions. Thus, the underdevelopment of the higher functions is a secondary structure on top of the defect. Underdevelopment springs from what we might call the isolation of an abnormal child from his collective. This process proceeds in approximately the following manner. Any given defect in a child produces a series of characteristics which impedes the normal development of his collective relations, cooperation, and interaction with others. Isolation from the collective or difficulty in social development, in its turn, conditions underdevelopment of higher mental functions which would, otherwise arise naturally, in the course of normal affairs, linked to the development of the child's collective activities.

Below, we will clarify this with a simple example. For the moment, let us simply say that the difficulties which an abnormal child experiences in collective activity become the reasons for underdevelopment of his higher functions. This is the fundamental conclusion to which our reexamination of the question has brought us. But unlike the defect itself, which is a factor in the failure of the elementary function's development, the collective, as a factor in the development of the higher psychological functions, is something which we can control. As hopeless as it is in practical terms to battle with the defect and its natural consequences, it is valid, fruitful, and promising to struggle with difficulties in collective activities.

In other words, when elementary functions fail to develop, we often are powerless to eliminate the cause leading to their underdevelopment. Consequently, we struggle with the symptoms rather than with the causes of retardation. With the development of higher mental functions we can affect not only the manifestations but the very cause; we struggle not just against the symptoms but with the illness itself. In the same way that medicine employs as its basic method causal therapy—rather than symptom therapy—in order to eliminate the reason for disease—and not only its particular burdensome effects—so, too, must curative pedagogy strictly distinguish between causal and symptomatic educational activity.

Precisely this possibility of eliminating even the most proximate reason for the underdevelopment of the higher psychological functions puts the problem of the abnormal child's collective activity at the forefront and opens up absolutely invaluable opportunities for the pedagogy of abnormal children.

Before us remains the task of briefly reviewing the concrete expression of these general propositions as they are applied to the feebleminded [retarded], the blind, and the deaf-mute child.

2

Research on collectives of feeblemended [retarded] children has begun relatively recently. It has led to the establishment of extraordinarily interesting regularities about the formation of collectives. We have, for example, the published observations of V. S. Krasusskii [no ref.], which show that very feeblemended [retarded] children enter into the formation of a collective with a variety of levels of mental development. This is one of the basic conditions for the existence of a collective. Yet in the majority of cases, the persistent and long-lasting collectives are made up of children who are at different levels of mental retardation.

One of the traditional methods of our pedagogical practice is the method of recruiting or selecting school-groups on the basis of equal levels of mental development. This assumes that children at the same level of mental retardation make up the best collectives. Research shows that feeblemended [retarded] children, when left to themselves, never group according to this principle. More exactly, they always violate this law.

Analysis of the [available] data, says our author, permits us to arrive at only one conclusion. The most desirable social combinations to which children are attracted are idiots and imbeciles and imbeciles and debiles. What happens in terms of social relations is a kind of mutual catering to one another. The intellectually more gifted have the opportunity to demonstrate social activeness with respect to the less gifted and less active. The latter, in their turn, get what they lack from social interaction with more active children; not infrequently, this becomes an unrecognized ideal to which the intellectually deficient child aspires. The most frequent age difference in unhampered social groupings of children is from three to four years. It is as though these data repeat the principles which apply variability in the intellectual development in normal children.

Let us not dwell on the details of that observation. Let us say only that there are other features which are characteristic of the life of collectives and which demonstrate that the same mixing of intellectual levels in a collective is the most dynamic.

Let us look at the following material as an example. When imbeciles are put with imbeciles, the number of people per group averages 2.6, and the average length of time that the collective lasts is 6–7 minutes. Similarly, when debiles are put with other debiles, their numbers averaged 2.0 people with an average duration of 9.2 minutes. On the other hand, when imbeciles and debiles were put together, their collectives averaged 5.2 members and the duration was 12.8 minutes. Unfortunately, most research on the problem of collectives among mentally retarded children studies the external, formal features, such as numbers, the collective's duration in existence, and so on but not the inner structure of each child's behavior nor the structural changes in the collective. Thus there seems to be a formal bias toward limiting observation to activities in which there is movement, to points of cessation of activities, to redistributions, and the like. If we moved from these formal features to the more profound changes which the personality of the feeblemended [retarded] child undergoes and which are hidden beneath this formal features, we would see that each of the children who made up the collective acquired a new quality and specialness by assimilating himself into some kind of [larger] entity. The study of unimpeded social life among severely retarded children will uncover a whole new side to the biological incompleteness of an idiot's or imbecile's personality; it will offer the opportunity to approach the problem of mental retardation from the perspective of social accommodation for the child. This area must be made the focus of attention in pedagogical work with severely retarded children. It will, of course, also place in our hands the key to the complex problem of recruitment into groups of severely retarded children.

The formulation offered by V. S. Krasusskii seems to us to be entirely justified. He says we must have an exhaustive and well-rounded understanding of the unencumbered social life of the children we are studying. Only then can the question of social compensation for a defect be discovered and detailed for each concrete circumstance.

Let us finish with these data. Although in itself true, it seems to us that it would be inappropriate to say simply that new sides to the personality of a severely mentally retarded child are revealed in open children's collectives; it would be more correct to speak of the fact that, in these collectives, the personality of the severely retarded child truly finds a dynamic source of development, and that, in the process of collective activity and coopera- tion, he is lifted to a higher level.

It is now clear how profoundly antipedagogical is the rule of using sameness as the basis for choosing collectives for retarded children. In doing this, we not only go against the natural tendency in the development of children; what is more important, we aggravate rather than ameliorate the most immediate cause of increased underdevelopment of higher functions when we deprive the mentally retarded child of collective cooperation and relations with others who stand higher than he does. Left to himself, the severely retarded child is drawn to the less retarded one—the idiot to the imbecile, the imbecile to the debile. This difference in intellectual level is an important condition of collective activity. The idiot who finds himself among other idiots, or the imbecile among other imbeciles, is deprived of this dynamic source of development. P. P. Blonskii, although he may have given an excessively paradoxical form to his ideas, nonetheless noticed that an idiot deprived of the right education suffers more from this than a normal child. And this is indeed the case.

It is therefore not difficult to imagine that the effects of the wrong education retard real possibilities much more in the case of a feeblemended [retarded] child than they do for a normal one. And everyone well knows to what degree a normal child who is deprived of the appropriate educational conditions shows the effects of pedagogical neglect and that these effects are almost indistinguishable from actual feeblemindedness. If one bears in mind that we are talking about severely retarded children, who are generally more narrow and limited in development than mildly retarded children, then the degree to which everything said above applies to even the mildly retarded child becomes clear. E. DeGreef approached the problem which interests us from the internal, qualitative side, and he demonstrated the following simple fact.

If one asks a feeblemended [retarded] child to evaluate his own mind and that of his comrade and of an adult educator (as that researcher did in his experiments), the mentally retarded child will habitually rank himself first, then his friend (also a retarded child), and in third place, the normal adult. The complex question of the exaggerated self-image of the mentally retarded child does not interest us for the moment and we leave it aside. That problem is, in itself, in the highest degree important, but peculiar. Let us focus on something else. Let us ask ourselves why, in the eyes of the mentally retarded child, the other feebleminded child is wiser than the normal adult. Because, DeGreef answers, the mentally retarded child understands his comrade better, because between them there is the possibility of cooperation, relations, and coactivity. On the other hand, an understanding the complex intellectual life of an adult is unattainable by the mentally retarded child. This is why, in paradoxical form, Blonskii, like DeGreef, formulates this absolutely accurate idea: Genius, from an imbecile's perspective, lies within the limits of psychological debility.

We should stop here and draw some conclusions. We see that the pedagogy of the collective is of the first order of importance in the whole structure of education for a feeblemended [retarded] child. We can see what value general collectives of normal and retarded children have, what importance the selection of the group and the distribution of intellectual levels has. In these conditions, we find a basic pedagogical norm, which is all but a general law for the education of all abnormal children.

When we compare the pedagogy of the collective for retarded children with that for normal children and ask ourselves what they have in common and what differences exist, we get the same answer we always get when we talk about a comparison of the different pedagogical measures used for normal and abnormal children: We see the same pedagogical aims with distinctive ways of attaining those goals, goals which are unattainable by abnormal children using the direct path. Thus, the general formula for comparing the pedagogy of normal and abnormal children is entirely appropriate for the problem at hand: the pedagogy of the child collective.

3

For a blind child, the same problem of underdevelopment of the higher functions occurs with respect to collective activity; this problem takes concrete form in an entirely different field of behavior and thought. However, if one investigates this problem accurately, its roots reveal a resemblance to those basics which we have already examined with respect to mentally retarded children. For ease and simplicity's sake, let us begin with a pedagogical statement of the problem. A blind child is immediately deprived of visual perceptions of visual forms. A question arises from that situation: How can this deficient activity be replaced for him?

Until now, this has been the key question in the pedagogy of the blind. Thus far, people in this area of pedagogy have come up against the same difficulties that have been encountered in the pedagogy of the feeblemended [retarded] child. Pedagogy has attempted to attack the question head on. Traditional psychology answers the question of how to struggle against the effects of blindness and psychological underdevelopment by cultivating sensorimotor activity, training the senses of touching and hearing, and using the so-called sixth sense of the blind (or the methods which blind people somehow detect large objects in a space directly in front of them using a method or sense which is unknown to seeing people). Traditional pedagogy also insists on the importance of visual aids in teaching the blind, on the necessity of filling up the meager reserve of impressions about external activities from other sources. It is just possible that if this problem were soluble, then such efforts might be crowned with complete success. That is to say, if we were to find some equivalent or some surrogate for the spatial and visual impressions of a seeing person, then, as W. Steinberg says, with the aid of that surrogate, we could compensate to a known degree for those omissions in a child's experience which result from blindness. But as far as concrete ideas and perceptions go, this task is insoluble. The whole difficulty consists precisely in the fact that no training of the sense of touch, no sixth sense, no extremely refined development of one or several of the usual methods of perception, and no auditory impressions—none of these things can act as a true equivalent or prove to be a substitute of equal value—to those visual images which are missing.

The pedagogue therefore embarks on an effort to replace visual images through other senses without understanding that the very nature of perception conditions the immediate character of activity. It also causes the impossibility of concretely replacing visual images. Thus, as far as the elementary processes go, we can never create a real possibility of concrete substitution for insufficient spatial images in the spheres of perception and performance.

Nevertheless, it is perhaps not useless to attempt to transmit perceptions of a visual form, or even the aesthetics of architectural perceptions, by using pictures made up of raised dots. Still, whenever the attempt to create surrogates for the visual perceptions of the sighted is made (this is especially the case for raised-dot pictures), it reminds one of a famous tale about a blind man which A. A. Potebnia [1922?] uses to show that a single generalization is far from knowledge. A blind man asks his guide: "Where have you been?"—"I wanted a drink of milk." —"What is milk like?"—"It is white."—"What is white?"—"Like a goose."—"And what is a goose like?"—"It is like my elbow." The blind man felt the guide's elbow and said, "Now I know what milk is like!"

Meanwhile, psychological research on the personality of a blind child demonstrates more and more clearly that perception and representation are not the natural sphere of compensation for the effects of blindness; compensation occurs not in the realm of elementary processes, but in the realm of concepts, that is, in the higher functions.

A. Petzeld, in his famous proposition, formulated this theoretical possibility of unlimited knowledge for a blind person. In his research, he showed that, although a blind person's impressions are extremely limited, he is in no way limited in abstract knowledge. The basic conclusion of his work—and it is a conclusion of profound practical and theoretical substance—is that a blind person has the possibility, in principle, of knowing everything even though he may lack identifiable impressions.

An analogous question has often been put with respect to humanity as a whole. It is asked, in a critique of the sensualists: If a person possessed not five, but four, senses, how could his mental and cognitive development take place? From the sensualist perspective, one might expect that the absence of one of the five senses would lead to the construction of an entirely different picture of reality and would bring about an entirely different direction in human psychological development, from the one which is realized on the basis of five senses. Still, we must answer the question in a slightly unexpected way.

We propose that, with only four senses, nothing essential would change in human cognition, and thought (that is, the method of reworking given experiences) would remain exactly the same in principle. However, our image of the realities surrounding us would be composed not only on the basis of immediate impressions, but also on the basis of experience, and rational reevaluation. Consequently, both the blind man and the seeing man, in principle, know much more than they imagine; they know much more than they can absorb with the help of their five senses. If we really knew as much as we could absorb directly through our five senses, then not a single science (in the true sense of that word) would be possible. For the links, dependencies, and relationships among things which are the content of our scientific knowledge are not the visually perceivable qualities of things; rather, they come to light through thought. This is also the way it works for a blind child. Thought is the basic area in which he compensates for the inadequacy of his visual perceptions.[*]

---

[*] Vygotsky's proposition stated here in 1931 has since been extensively elaborated upon both in psychology and the philosophy of science beginning perhaps with the 1930's and continuing to the present. Vygotsky's rather clear statement, albeit simple and preliminary, seems to have gone unnoticed.

The developmental limitations in higher knowledge go beyond the sensorimotor train-ing which is possible in the elementary processes. *Thought is the highest form of compen-sation for the insufficiencies of visual perceptions.*

Overcompensation in thought leads to two dangers which we would like briefly to mention. The first and basic danger is verbalism, and it is widespread among blind children. Verbalism is the use of words for which no meaning can be found, the content of which remains empty. The blind person, using the same speech as the sighted, intersperses it with a series of words whose meanings are inaccessible to him. When the blind man says "I saw him yesterday," or "Today is a bright day," he is using words in each of these cases the direct meaning of which is inaccessible to him. Using empty words with no content is the basis of verbalism.

Such verbalism becomes a false, fictive compensation for the inadequacy of perceptions.

Nevertheless, if the word in question corresponds to some meaning based in the experience of the blind person, even though the direct visual meaning of that word is a subject inaccessible to him, what we have is not verbalism, not fictive, but true compensation—the working out of an understanding relative to a subject, which is otherwise unattainable through perception and representation. As Petzeld correctly formulated his position, a black table is as black for a blind person as for a sighted one. Proof of this lies in a daily fact from the lives of the blind, something they themselves carefully recount. For example, N. Saunderson, blind from birth, wrote a famous geometry text, and the blind A. M. Shcherbina, according to his own testimony, explained optics to her seeing comrades as they studied it in a high school physics class. The fact that the blind can work out entirely concrete comprehensions, on a par with the sighted, about subjects which they cannot absorb through sight is a factor of first-rate importance in the psychology and pedagogy of the blind.

The danger of verbalism brings us to the second danger—the danger of false under-standing. Formal logic and the history of psychology have explained the process of forming understanding thus: First the child acquires a series of concrete perceptions and images; from mixing and superimposing separate representations one over the other, gradually general outlines are composed from a series of different impressions; the outlines from various sources are erased or suppressed, and a general understanding dawns, very like F. Galton's collective photographs.[3]

If this path corresponded to reality, then the law Petzeld formulated about the possibility of unlimited knowledge for the blind would be impossible. If the path to the formation of a concept lay only through perceptions, then a blind person would be unable to arrive at an understanding of the color black which is adequate for our comprehension. The under-standing held by the blind would necessarily be a false understanding and would represent, in the sphere of thought, something analogous to what we call verbalism, that is, the use of empty words.

Here is the difference between formal and dialectical logic in studying a concept. For formal logic, a concept is nothing other than a general representation. It arises as a result of a series of many broad indications. The fundamental law, to which the movement of a concept belongs, is formed in logic as a law of inverse proportionality between the extent and the content of a concept. The broader the extent of any concept (that is, the more general an understanding and the broader the group of examples to which it applies), the weaker its content, (that is the number of indications of the concept which we hold in our minds). The path to generalization is thus a path which leads away from the riches of concrete reality toward the world of concepts, the kingdom of empty abstractions, far from living life and from living knowledge.

In dialectical logic, it is quite the opposite: A concept seems richer in content than does a presentation. Thus the path to generalization is not a path formally divided into separate indications. Rather, it is an uncovering of the links of the relationship of a given matter with another. If the subject becomes truly intelligible, not through immediate experience, but in all the many links and relationships which define its place in the world and its connection to the rest of reality, then one's understanding is a deeper, more real, truer, and more complete reflection than the envisaged one.

But, and this is the most important thing that we have said so far, understanding, like all the higher psychological processes, develops in no other way than in the process of collective actions by the child. Only cooperation brings a child's logic to fruition; only socialization of a child's thought, as Piaget formulated it, leads to the formations of concepts.

This is why the pedagogy of the blind must participate here in studying the issue of cooperation with the sighted, as a basic pedagogical and methodological problem in teaching the blind. Collective thinking is the fundamental source of compensation for the effects of blindness. In developing collective thinking, we are eliminating the secondary effect of blindness; we are breaking through at the weakest point in the chain created around the defect; and *we are eliminating the very reason for the underdevelopment of psychological functions in a blind child*, opening up before him uncharted and unlimited possibilities.

4

Nowhere does the role of the collective as a factor in the abnormal child's development appear in the foreground with such clarity as in the development of a deaf child. Here, it is entirely clear that all the difficulties and limitations created by the defect are encompassed, not in the handicap itself, but in the effects, the secondary complications, called forth by that handicap. In itself, deafness might not be such a burdensome obstacle to intellectual development in a deaf-mute child, but for the absence of speech, called forth by his muteness, which becomes an enormous obstacle along that same path. Thus, all the individual problems in a deaf-mute child's development are united, focused, on the problem of speech.

This is the problem of problems for all pedagogues for the deaf.

Above, we have discussed the development of higher forms of thought and logic in a child with respect to the socialization of those functions. In that context, it should be absolutely clear that the absence of speech in a deaf-mute child complicates his full participation in the collective, tears him out of the collective, and becomes one of the fundamental obstacles to the development of his higher mental functions. Experimental research demonstrates this at every step: whatever we take away from a deaf-mute child in social relations, he later lacks in thought. A vicious circle has developed around this question; practical pedagogy has not yet found an exit.

On one hand, the fight against artificial speech, against phraseology, and the attempt to teach live, active speech, which offers the opportunity of social relations rather than just intelligible pronunciation of sounds—all this requires a reexamination of the role played by speech in the traditional education of deaf-mute children. If, in the traditional education, speech totally consumes all other aspects of education and becomes an end in itself, then it loses its vitality for that very reason. The deaf-mute child is taught to pronounce words, but he is not taught to speak, that is, to use speech as a means of communicating and thinking. Therefore, along with artificially inculcated speech, he more willingly uses his own language of mimicry, which fulfills for him the dynamic function of speech. The struggle between oral speech and mimicry (sign language), in spite of the good intentions on the part of the pedagogues, ends, as a rule, in the victory of sign language, not because mimicry is a psychologically natural speech for the deaf-mute, but because it is authentic speech with all the riches of functional meaning. The artificial addition of pronouncing words out loud lacks life's richness and is only a dead imitation of living speech.

Thus, the task that now stands before pedagogy is that of returning the life to spoken speech; making that speech necessary, understandable, and natural for a child; and restructuring the whole system for educating him. The following proposition is of primary focus: The deaf-mute child is a child first of all—and only afterwards deaf and mute. This means that the child must first of all grow, develop, and be educated, following the general interests, inclinations, and rules of the child's age; during the process of development he should master speech. The problems of education in general—the problems of socio-political education—are now arising as the foci in educating deaf-mute children. It seems entirely justifiable that, by inculcating collectivism, social behavior, and cooperative work habits in deaf children, we are creating the only real foundation on which speech can grow. And, indeed, pedagogy has attained striking successes by following this path, a path which one can say without exaggeration is radically changing the character of our schools.

It quickly becomes clear that this is only one side of the question. The other side lies precisely in the inadequate speech development of these children and serves as a colossal obstacle in their sociopolitical education. If, at first, it seemed that social education was a prerequisite for the natural development of live speech, then later, it appeared that socio-political education itself is absolutely necessary as one of the basic psychological requirements in the development of speech.

As a result, pedagogues had to turn to mimicry as the only language through which deaf-mute children could absorb a series of thoughts, positions, and information without which the content of their sociopolitical education would be absolutely dead and lifeless. Thus, simply because our school has begun a radical reexamination of the question of the relationship between speech training and other aspects of education for deaf-mutes, and because it has answered that question in a diametrically opposite fashion from the way it was resolved in traditional education, the problem of speech now looms before us with more pungency than in any European or American country.

Everything depends on which demands are placed on the education of a deaf-mute child and which goals are expected of that upbringing. If we require only external mastery of speech and an elementary adaptation to independent life, then the question of speech training will be resolved relatively easily and satisfactorily. If, however, the demand is for a limitless broadening of goals, as they are extended here—if the goal of the deaf-mute child is to approach the fullest possible self-worth in all ways except in hearing, if we strive to bring a deaf-mute school as near as possible to a normal school—then this will create an agonizing discrepancy between speech development and overall development for the deaf-mute child.

The vicious circle is closed permanently, when we arrive at the third and final consideration, namely the exclusion of the deaf-mute child from the general collective, the limitation of deaf-mute children to their own society, and likewise the rupture in relations and cooperation with the hearing. Thus, the whole circle consists of three intertwined factors. Social education is based on the underdevelopment of speech; the underdevelopment of speech leads to exclusion from the collective; and exclusion from the collective stalls both social education and speech development.

We have been unable here to indicate a radical solution to this question. Most important of all, we think, is the fact that contemporary pedagogy and the contemporary state of science about speech education for deaf-mute children, in both theoretical and practical guises, will unfortunately not allow us to break down this resistance with a single blow. The path toward overcoming these difficulties is much more tortuous and roundabout than one might hope. This path, in our opinion, will prompt development in deaf-mute children and in part in normal children as well; this path consists of polyglossia, that is multiple paths for the development of speech in deaf-mute children.

In connection with this, it becomes necessary to reevaluate traditional and practical attitudes toward the various forms of speech for the deaf-mute, and, first of all, of mimicry and written speech.

Psychological research, both experimental and clinical, agree in their demonstrations that polyglossia (that is, the mastery of several forms of speech) is an unavoidable and fruitful method of speech development and education for the deaf-mute child, given the current state of pedagogy for the deaf. In connection with this, radical changes should be made in the traditional view about the competition among a variety of forms of speech and about their mutually restrictive nature on the development of the deaf-mute child. We must also pose the theoretical and practical question concerning their coordination and structural composition at various stages of learning.

This latter question, in turn, demands a complex, differentiated approach to speech development and to the education of a deaf-mute child. The experience of the most advanced European and American pedagogues, especially the Scandinavians and Americans, testifies to the presence of a complex structure for combining different forms of speech, as well as a differentiated approach to speech education for the deaf-mute child. Rather than being simply acceptable, all this suggests in turn a whole series of problems and questions for the theoretical and practical pedagogy of the deaf. These might jointly be resolved, not at the level of methods, but at the level of the methodology of speech education. Their resolution absolutely demands an elaboration of the psychology of the deaf-mute child.

Only a serious investigation of the laws of speech development and a radical reform in the method of speech education can bring our schools to a real, rather than a minimal, victory over muteness in deaf children. This means that, in practice, we must make use of all possibilities for speech activity for a deaf-mute child. We must not approach mimicry with condescension and scorn, treating it as an enemy. Rather we must understand that different forms of speech do not only compete with one another or disrupt one another's development, but that they can also serve as steps on which the deaf-mute child climbs to the mastery of speech.

In any case, pedagogy cannot close its eyes to the fact that expelling mimicry from the domain of speech communication permitted to deaf-mute children also eliminates a major part of their collective life and activity, and consolidates, exaggerates, and expands the fundamental obstacle to their development—their difficulties in forming collective activity. Therefore, research on the collective of deaf-mute children, on the possibility of collective cooperation with hearing children, and on the maximal use of all kinds of speech that are accessible to the deaf-mute child—all these are necessary conditions for a radical improvement in the education of deaf-mute children.

Traditional pedagogy for deaf children is based on individual lip-reading in front of a mirror. But conversation with a mirror is bad conversation, and therefore, instead of speech, one gets a lifeless, mechanical imitation of it. Speech that is severed from collective activity with other children, becomes dead speech. At first, our pedagogy moved the center of gravity to the social collective education of a deaf-mute child. But, then it severed speech from that education in the collective and so very soon it felt the painful gap between social demands and speech potentials in the deaf-mute child. Only by linking the two together, only by introducing the collective as the basic factor in speech development, only *speech in the collective* can decisively break out of this vicious circle.

*   *   *

With our discussion of deaf-mute children, we have finished our exposition of the basic features which make up the themes of this chapter.

In conclusion, we should like to indicate that our aim has by no means been some sort of exhaustive and final resolution of the questions we have posed. Rather, this is simply an introduction to boundless areas of research—and only that. The basic principal and fulcrum for all our pedagogy for the abnormal child requires us now to be able to understand anew, in the light of real, natural phenomena, the links between cooperation [collective activity] and the development of higher mental functions; between the development of the collective and the abnormal child's personality.

—Communist pedagogy is the pedagogy of the collective.—

INTRODUCTION TO Ia. K. TSVEIFEL'S BOOK:

ESSAY ON THE BEHAVIORAL CHARACTERISTICS AND EDUCATION OF THE DEAF-MUTE[1]

The problem of development and education for deaf-mute children is one of the most complex theoretical problems in scientific pedagogy. The system for educating deaf-mute children and teaching them speech is restructuring itself before our eyes. It requires a profound and thorough penetration into the laws of development among deaf-mute children, and into the structure and dynamics of their personalities. Still, until recently, scientific research on deaf-mute children very notably avoided those questions posed by the education of deaf-mute children and by the problems of teaching them speech. The obstacle to scientific research was often the absence of speech in such children, their muteness. This became a barrier between the speaking teachers and their mute pupils, between the researcher and the object of his study. It is only relatively recently that a series of examples and methods have been worked out to eliminate this barrier successfully and that we have established certain fundamental regularities which govern the development of the deaf-mute child.

Ia. K. Tsveifel', in the book introduced here, has attempted to lay out systematically the basic results of pedagogical and psychological research on deaf-mute children in a popularly understandable way. The author everywhere draws on his own rich experience and on the contemporary status of one or another scientific issue. He recounts all the basic methods for teaching deaf-mute children live speech and distinguishes the positive and negative aspects of those methods. He broaches the major problems of the sociopolitical, polytechical, physical, and artistic education of deaf-mute children. Tsveifel' even touches on the psychological characteristics of such education recounting the generally acceptable methods for determining the intellectual development and level of talent in deaf-mute children.

One fundamental idea permeates the entire opus: Only through labor and speech, only through social education in the truest and deepest sense of the word, can a deaf-mute child really overcome the obstacles which stand in the way of his development. Then, he will participate in social life as a fully valued member.

Until now, most researchers have been following a false path in evaluating deaf-mute children and their aptitudes. We could cite the example of a basic conclusion drawn by R. Lindner, who is the author of the most complete and systematic research on the intellectual development of deaf-mute and hearing children. The author [sic] proceeds from the fact that, with few limitations, the deaf-mute show us a human genotype which develops with exclusively natural influences. According to Lindner, the deaf-mute is a prototype of the natural man.

The author [sic] maintains that the exclusion of speech severely limits the influence of other people on a deaf-mute; the development of his genetic talents depends on the objects which he sees and feels. This condition in the deaf-mute is similar to the condition of a man who has no traditions, who never learned, and whom we usually call a "primitive" person.

It is true that a deaf-mute child is surrounded by a multitude of objects that are entirely different from those surrounding a primitive man, and moreover a deaf-mute is surrounded not only by natural objects, but by cultural objects also. However, the cultural objects speak to him in the same language as natural objects. That is, cultural examples without clarification effect him as natural examples might.

Thus, Lindner views deaf-mute children as beings who stand at the first stage of human development, on the edge of human existence, on the very threshold of history, as beings who lack all cultural development because of their shortcomings in speech.

As he draws conclusions from his research, the author [sic] corroborates the old opinions of philosophers, which they derived purely through speculation—such as the views of J. G. Herder, F. Kant, A Schopenhauer and others who held that children lacking speech (that is, deaf-mute children) should be seen as humanoid animals, incapable of mental activity, unable to attain anything more than orangutans or elephants can, who have minds only potentially but not in actuality.

Lindner compares the intellectual development of deaf-mute children with the intellectual reactions of humanoid apes (the famous research of W. Koehler,[*] and he comes to the conclusion that his work allows him to present the old position of the philosophers in a new light, saying that the uneducated deaf-mute child is condemned to remain on the level of animal existence.

As is known, Koehler distinguishes two features in which he sees real differences between the intellect of anthropoid apes and primitive humans; first, the existence of speech and, second, a very limited life span.

In the words of Lindner, the speechlessness of the deaf-mute child is shared by the anthropoid ape. It is true, that the child has mimicry, but, according to the observations of the author that language in fourteen and fifteen-year old children attains only the level of development comparable with the live speech of a child of two-and-a-half. The second feature noted by Koehler—the limitations of life-span—also fails to divide deaf-mute children from anthropoids. In Lindner's view the deaf-mute is entirely a genuine being.

Only on one point did Lindner see a significant difference: in the area of the motor agility of the hand and its form-generating capacities. With the exception of that instance, the comparison of deaf-mute children with the hearing and with anthropoids shows, in the author's works, that inherited tendencies are inadequate alone to form a human being.

---

[*] For more elaborate discussions of Koehler's research on apes, see, for example, L. S. Vygotsky and A. R. Luria, *Essays on the History of Behavior: Ape, Primitive Man, and Child*, Moscow, 1930, or *Language and Speech* in Volume 1 of the English version of the *Collected Works*.

The old position of the philosophers appears before us in a new light, and above all not in the fashion in which it was usually understood. The deaf-mute is not an animal; it is, rather a natural human being, locked into his innate tendencies. But those tendencies are not enough in their own right to lift him essentially, even a little bit, above the level of an animal. As long as deaf-mute children lacked instruction in live speech, their gifts could not develop, and even now they seldom reach full development.

The mistake underlying all the mentioned judgments is that the question was posed without taking into account either the deaf child's social development or his education. Still, the whole question about the human nature of deaf-mute children is essentially a question of social experience in his upbringing. Instead of metaphysical constructs or empirical studies which are based on the superficial resemblances of observed features, the criterion of pedagogical practice is advanced here: The only proper way to pose the problem of development in deaf-mute children is as a *historical* problem.

The most profound problems of thought and speech, the structure and dynamics of the social development of an individual and his highest psychological functions, the formation of character, and many other questions are directly related to the problem of deaf-muteness. These issues are deliberately not examined in this book, and that decision entirely corresponds to the book's tasks and character. Before us is not theoretical research, but practical guidance for educating deaf-mute children.

However, based on the elimination of the division between physical and mental work, this system of education and speech instruction *within the general Soviet educational system* not only opens up historically unprecedented perspectives for a deaf child's development and his inclusion in social life as fully-valued being; it not only contains a *guarantee of actually overcoming the muteness of deaf children*; this methodology also represents a scientific *magnum opus* of inexhaustible theoretical significance for understanding man and *his development*.

INTRODUCTION TO E. K. GRACHEVA'S BOOK:

THE EDUCATION AND INSTRUCTION OF SEVERELY

RETARDED CHILDREN[1]

The present book, presented in literary form, represents the results of thirty five years of experience in educational work with profoundly retarded children—idiots and imbeciles. In itself, the experience of pedagogical work is not only of practical, but also of scientific interest, since all education for severely retarded children—and particularly idiots—in its purely practical goals becomes a psychological and pedagogical experiment independent of its author's intentions. A history of the education for severely retarded children, therefore, adds a large and valued contribution to general knowledge about child development and about many psychological problems.

Phenomena which we observe among severely retarded children continue to retained first-order significance for the resolution of numerous [general] psychological questions. One of the most authoritative contemporary researchers in child psychology says, therefore, with good reason, that the basic lines of development in the human psyche can be best followed in creches for the newborn and in shelters for idiots. As K. Buehler [1924?, 1927?, 1930?][*] suggests, nurseries, asylums, and maternity wards are places where one can find out most about the make-up of the human soul and about the broad lines of its development.

Still, until lately, the rapprochement of theory and practice in the education of abnormal children with general psychological learning has been somewhat one-sided. Psychology has made wide use of materials accumulated through practice. However, theory itself and the practice of educating such children has borrowed little (if anything) from general psychology and pedagogy. This circumstance has led to detrimental results for one, as well as the other field of knowledge.

---

[*] Buehler wrote in German on developmental psychology, language acquisition, and Gestalt perception. He is cited extensively by Vygotsky in other works. [Ed.]

Thus, the theory and practice of educating severely retarded children has, for a long time, remained doomed to extremely slow development inasmuch as it has been isolated from the main routes along which developments in general psychology and pedagogy ran and has had to stay on its own side of the street. It is hardly surprising that the contemporary position in this matter has, in many respects and instances, progressed relatively little since the initial, classical period, when the possibility, in principle, of educating and teaching severely retarded children was first demonstrated, and when the first fundamentals in the practical application of principles of education were laid out.

Under such stagnant conditions, educational practice progressed little, and those psychological and pedagogical experiments which (as we have already said) are part of all education for severely retarded children have been kept one-sided. General pedagogy and psychology have contributed little to the theory or the practice of education for profound oligophrenics. They themselves have received less and less from these most valuable scientific and practical experiences.

Thus, both sides have lost—both general, and special pedagogy.

Currently gaining recognition is the idea that the basis of the one-sided rapprochement of the two parts of pedagogy and psychology rests on a false premise. That premise assumes that the principles of education and instruction on which general pedagogy is based and which are used in the education of normal children cannot be carried over into the field of education of retarded children. However, enormous practice in educating mildly retarded children, so-called debiles, shows that this assumption is based only on preconceptions and that, actually, normal and abnormal children are linked by numerous transitions and general pedagogical principles. These principles receive qualitatively unique and concrete expression in various circumstances and can actually be formulated with greater completeness when they include normal as well as abnormal children. The experience reflected in the present book by E. K. Gracheva occupies a *transitional position* between an earlier and later period in the development of pedagogy in this area. The first, its roots belong to the period of the classics. It goes back to the system of E. Segen [1903] and others who laid out basic positions about the education of severely retarded children. On the other hand, this experience has carried over into our period and represents part of the general work of educating retarded children in the Soviet Union; it is realized as an attempt to restructure the whole theory and practice of educating abnormal children on the basis of the same fundamental principles as those used for general Soviet pedagogy.

Such duality could not but be reflected in the book, and it must be understood as the historical product of two epochs with a different character, during which this experience grew and accumulated. The basic question which confronts us when we speak about educating severely retarded children is as follows: Is it worth expending colossal efforts on the instruction and education of severely retarded children, and particularly of idiots, if the results attained in comparison with those attained by the normal child are so insignificant? The disproportion between the efforts and the results of work has more that once filled with pessimism the many researchers who approach this problem from the practical side.

Under the influence of pessimistic views about severely retarded children, a lowering of demands usually takes place—we have an infamous narrowing of the boundaries which the educators of these children set for themselves. Under the influence of such views and self-constraining tendencies the educational tasks placed before these children are very limited only to what is most necessary.

This view, in both theory and practice, is incorrect, and we see the central significance of E. K. Gracheva's book in her refutation of this pessimistic minimalist theory. She promotes the notion of pedagogical optimism in regard to severely retarded children with the magnificent language of facts, facts carefully selected over almost a half century. What is more, this is authentic optimism, verified by practice, and supported by scientific criticism.

P. P. Blonskii, in a somewhat paradoxical form, essentially expressed the profoundly true and fundamental position shared by all contemporary educators of retarded children. He said that an idiot without education looses his potential to advance and suffers not less, but more, than a normal child. If we tried to express positively what has been said here negatively, then we could conclude that an idiot, exposed to a correspondingly special, organized, and rational education will realize his capabilities not *less, but more, than a normal child*. Education is more necessary for a handicapped child than for a normal one—that is the fundamental idea of all contemporary pedagogy.

The naive view according to which a child needs education less, the less he himself has, is profoundly incorrect. If *one measures retarded children with measures appropriate for them*, then, with the help of a specially designed education, their progress in fact renders more significant and tangible results than the education of normal children.

Thus, the disproportion between the effort expended and the result achieved in educating severely retarded children seems illusory. Actually, great educational efforts expended on severely retarded children reap enormous results, if, we repeat, one uses the correct measures as a basis. Instead of the false, seemingly inversely proportional ratio between the degree of retardation and the degree of need for education, contemporary science puts forward a position of the direct proportionality of the two quantities.

At one point, severely retarded children were deprived of all education. Retardation and education were viewed as incompatible concepts. Then, it was shown both theoretically and practically that retarded children could be educated despite their deficiency. This was the great classical period in the development of special education.

Contemporary conditions in this area could be most correctly described with a different formula. That is, retarded children, *despite their deficiencies—in fact, because of their deficiencies*—should and must be educated.

We must not forget one decisive factor with which we are dealing when we speak of education for severely retarded children. We are referring not to quantitative, but to qualitative meanings and values for those improvements in their development which have taken place under the influence of specially designed education. This qualitative evaluation decides the whole question. In fact, it has now become a truism that children's development is not completed gradually and evenly, so that every year a child will have moved forward and up at an identical tempo. The pace of development reminds one, least of all, of the movement of a clockwork mechanism in good working order.

The basic rule of child development consists in the fact that the tempo of development is maximal at the very beginning. Very complex mutual relationships exist between development and duration, as contemporary research shows. An array of biologists, who have studied the developmental process and its relationship to time, have come to the conclusion that, even in the earliest stages, a significant delay in growth takes place, as this process moves forward. Using Mainot's measure to determine the tempo of fetal growth with extrauterine development, embryos weighing 0.006 gm., by comparison, weigh 3,200 gm. as neonates. The growth percentage comes out an enormous number (about 530,000 percent),[*] particularly by comparison with weight-gain in the following years in the life of a man. Taking the weight of a twenty-year old man as 60 kgs, Mainot's weight-gain for the twenty years of extra-uterine life returns a modest ratio: 1:19. Even during the first year of life, a rapid diminution in the rate of growth takes place. In the first month of life the rate of weight-gain is 23 percent but the rate drops to 2.8 percent in the first twelve months.

Thus, we see that the complex, dialectical character of the developmental process is reflected, as Mainot formulated it, by the level of development depending upon the stage in aging. However, the tempos of growth and aging, at the same time, attain their maximum rate at very early stages and the rapidity of aging diminishes with growth.

A. Gesell,[2] a famous contemporary American researcher, says that these laws serve as an example of what is called the paradoxical aspect of development. In fact, a child never develops as intensively as in his earliest stages. But at the same time, he never ages as intensively as in those same early stages. With the progress of the developmental process, the tempo of development slows, but the tempo of aging also diminishes. Thus, in the economics of mental development, as A. Gesell would have it, the value of a month is determined by its position in the life cycle.

This proposition alone allows us to see that education, which advances the development of the severely retarded child by several years or even a few months, bears a connection with the segment of that process which in a normal child falls in the earliest years and which, consequently, becomes the richest and most saturated, the densest and most valuable period of development as a whole. If the value of a month in the economics of mental development is determined by its place in the general life cycle, then the value of those months of mental development, which advance the severely retarded child with the help of an educator, must be relatively speaking, equivalent to many years of advancement and development for the mildly retarded child and especially for the normal child.

The qualitative aspect is even more important in comparison with the evaluation of the initial, basic, and primary stages in the development of a child. Contemporary child psychology has undoubtedly revealed the fundamental, paramount, and central meaning of the first stage in the development of a child. The most necessary functions develop first. The first to appear is basic not only in the sense that, without this base, nothing further can be built above it but also in the sense that the decisive marks which distinguish man from an animal are established and develop precisely in this early period. It is enough to mention erect posture and speech, which have long since and correctly been considered the distinguishing marks of humans.

In comparison with what children acquire in the first year or two of their lives, all other acquisitions are insignificant. To J. P. Richter belongs a thought also shared by L. N. Tolstoy: A greater distance divides a speaking child from a newborn infant than Newton from a schoolboy. The paramount significance of the first stages in the development of a child were well defined, from the dynamic side, by K. Buehler, when he called all processes of development at the earliest ages *processes of becoming human (Menschwerdung).** The period of becoming human is really more specific and important than the following period in the development of a man. Precisely this period decides the basic choice between animal and human existence.

** Actually 533,333 percent. [Ed.]

* The literal sense of the German word is intended here. The word also means *incarnation*.[Ed.]

We always talk about normal children, about the qualitative and quantitative meaning of the first two years in their development, in order to demonstrate graphically the psychological meaning of those same steps in the development of severely retarded children. Such children make these steps with the help of specially organized education, and they would never be able to make them without such help. The relationship between the first and the following steps in the development of a normal child provides an entirely truthful scale, a very precise reflection of the relative value of those steps made by a severely retarded child as well as by less retarded or normal children under the influence of special education.

Under the influence of education, the severely retarded children advance precisely along that same segment of the path which normal children cover during the first, fundamentally important years of life. Thus, the acquisitions made by severely retarded children under the influence of education are, from the developmental perspective, *the basic values which a human child can acquire, and without which he would have to remain at a stage of half-animal existence. Education makes idiots into men. With the help of education, a severely retarded child goes through the process of becoming human.*

In saying this, we have described all that is of value in principle and practice for the education of a severely retarded child. This cannot become a reliable formula, which reveals to us the goal and meaning of every separate area of education for severely deficient children, no matter how narrow and insignificant the character of successes in that area.

To teach severely retarded children is not only to teach them to feel, to embrace, to hear, and to see, *it is rather to teach them to make use of one's five senses*, to govern them, wisely to employ them according to one's own ends. It means informing them of the smallest elements, and also the *very bases* of human perception of reality.

The same can be said about the remaining areas in the education of severely retarded children, which are elucidated with ample clarity in this book.

In the area of education for severely retarded children, there still remains a debated question, which must be taken up here, about the nature of that educational process. Those minimalist and pessimistic pedagogical theories to which we referred above attempt in practice to link the education of severely retarded children with dressage;[*] that is, they try to shift from the processes for becoming human to the training of a half-animal. Obedience is the first demand made of such children. The automatic performance of useful habits becomes the ideal of all education.

In our time, the idea of dressage for the severely retarded child is usually grounded in the theory of education based on the teaching of conditional reflexes; that is, specifically only in that part of the educational process which is identical in its physiological basis for men and animals. The ideal of such education is the precise standardization and correct gradation of all external stimuli which operate on the child and their elicitation from the child of automatic reflex responses. Of course the significance of the purely reflexive and automatic features in general education and in the education of the severely retarded in particular cannot be underestimated. Moreover, the role of these features in the education of severely retarded children is, undoubtedly, profoundly significant and in many ways exceeds the role played by those features in the education of a normal child. However, the effort to limit the entire education of severely retarded children to the training of automatic, reflexive habits of movement is as much a false and mistaken idea as is the attempt to limit education

---

[*] A system for training animals.

in the first and decisive three years of life to the formation of conditional reflexes. As has already been said, such an education is in scandalous negation of the content of the beginning stages of development revealed by K. Buehler's formulation, that is, with the process of becoming human. When contemporary advocates of reflex-oriented education for severely retarded children try to base all education on automatization, they are committing the same error that reflex theory perpetrated in the education of children at early ages. Severely retarded children who have mastered the rudiments of thought and of human speech and primitive forms of work should be and are able to get something more from education, qualitatively, than simply a reserve of automatic habits.

We will not deal critically or in depth with those foundations on which is built the experience that this book lays out. We have already indicated its historically caused dual nature. It is thus not surprising that we encounter in the book, alongside the authentically contemporary, much that is passé, that belongs to a different historical epoch. In particular, this is in greatest measure applicable to those chapters in which the problem of sensorimotor education is discussed as the more-or-less artificial training of various organs.

We will point out only one fundamental instance, which might provide a necessary clarification of the experience described in the book and which might act as a principle addendum. The subject is the social nature of education and the role of the collective in the education of severely retarded children.

New research has shown that free collectives of severely retarded children form themselves [into collectives] according to an extremely interesting principle. Thus, according to V. S. Krasusskii's observations, these children have a tendency to create and enter into collectives consisting of individuals of varying intellectual levels. The author shows that there are several regularities in the selection of the objects of social relationships. The most frequently occurring the social relationships consist of idiots with imbeciles, of imbeciles with severe debiles and so on.

Analyzing the collected data, Krasusskii reaches a conclusion: The idiot and the imbecile, or the imbecile and the profound debile* are the most desirable social combinations, those to which children resort the most frequently. In social relationships, the same mutual service takes place. The intellectually more gifted have an opportunity to demonstrate great social activity with respect to the less gifted and active. The latter, in their turn, draw from their social relations with the more gifted and active that which is unobtainable to them and that which often acts as an unconscious ideal, toward which the intellectually inadequate child strives.

It is obvious that an enormous educational factor is represented by the presence of children of various intellectual levels in collectives, as well as by the cooperation of the children who make up the given collective. In free collectives, in Krasusskii's opinion, where the participants do not see themselves as the simple sum of the peculiarities which characterize the individual children, and where each of the members acquires new peculiarities and qualities, as it were re-creating themselves into something whole—in such free collectives, the personality of severely retarded children is represented in an entirely new light. The study of free social life among severely retarded children uncovers from an entirely new side the biological sense of inadequacy in the personality of the idiot and the imbecile and points to the possibilities for development. The study of the social life of severely deficient children

---

* Here again, "idiot" is a severely retarded child, "imbecile" a moderately retarded child, while "debile" implies a child with mild retardation or mild learning disabilities. [Transl.]

allows an approach to the problem of intellectual deficiency from the perspective of the social adaptability to these children to life around them. Krasusskii suggests that the question recently posed by L. S. Vygotsky about social compensation for a defect can be illuminated and elaborated on only in the presence of an exhaustive and multi-faceted understanding of free social life among those children being studied.

In this sense, the contemporary theory and practice of education for severely retarded children is appropriate to the practical resolution of those problems which the founders of thought on this matter already vaguely sensed. None other than Segen, almost one hundred years ago, said to an educator about severely retarded children: "If he always lies down, make him sit; if he sits, make him stand; if he doesn't eat by himself, hold his fingers; if he doesn't look and doesn't see, talk to him and look at him. Feed him like a man who works and make him work, work with him. *Be for him his will, his mind, his activities*" (1903, pp. 74-75).

The developmental path for a severely retarded child lies through collaborative activity, the social help of another human being, who from the first is his mind, his will, his activities. This proposition also corresponds entirely with the normal path of development for a child. *The developmental path for a severely retarded child lies through relationships and collaborative activity, with other humans.* For precisely this reason, the social education of severely retarded children reveals to us possibilities which might seem outright Utopian from the viewpoint of purely biologically based physiological education (as Segen called his system).

The term *idiot*, if we recall another remark of E. Segen, literally means *solitarius*, a lone man: He is really alone with his sensations, without any intellectual or moral will. "Physically—he cannot; mentally—he knows not; psychologically—he wills not. He would be able, he would know, if only he wanted! But the whole misfortune lies in the fact that, first of all, he does not want!"(1903, pp. XXXVII-XXXVIII).

Not one of the intellectual capabilities, Segen said, can be counted as entirely lacking in an idiot, but he has no ability to apply those capabilities freely to the development of a moral and attractive character. In him, that freedom from which moral will is born is inadequate.

Contemporary scientific research is wholeheartedly proving this profound intuition of Segen's to be correct; namely, that the source of idiocy is solitude. Social education is precisely the path to the development for severely retarded children, the path based on the elimination of solitude, which is the very essence of idiocy. In this respect, Segen correctly compared the education of severely retarded children with the learning of speech by deaf-mutes. He cites J. Pereira, who at the beginning of the eighteenth century advanced the idea of studying the speech of deaf-mute children. Segen said: "Pereira had the same perspective as I do. He found that some functions can be reconstructed where they are lacking; in this respect he was an inventor in the full sense of the word. The possibility of educating idiots is without doubt based on an analogous, if less bold, assumption" (ibid., p. 23). Currently we might say: Analogous but all the more bold!

In this respect, as we have already said, it is the social education of severely retarded children which becomes the sole sustainable and scientific path toward their education. In addition, it alone is capable of recreating the absent functions where they are not, because of a biological sense of inadequacy in the child. Only social education can lead severely retarded children through the process of becoming human by eliminating the solitude of idiocy and severe retardation. L. Feuerbach's[*] wonderful phrase, might be taken as the motto to the study of development in abnormal children: "That which is impossible for one, is possible for two." Let us add: That which is impossible on the level of individual development becomes possible on the level of social development.

THE PROBLEM OF MENTAL RETARDATION[1]

Until recently, within the problem of mental retardation it has been the intellectual deficiency of a child, his feeble-mindedness, that has occupied the foreground as the basic feature. This is locked into the very definition of such children, who are habitually called *mentally retarded* or *mentally deficient*. All other sides of such a child's personality are regarded as arising secondarily and as depending upon that basic intellectual defect. Many are inclined not even to see real distinctions between the affective and volitional spheres of these children and of normal children.

True, this intellectualistic direction (which reduces the whole problem of mental retardation to feeblemindedness) has long encountered opposition from many researchers. Thus, E. Segen indicated that, of all the deficiencies these children have, the most important, to him, is the lack of motivation. A disorder in the sphere of motivation, in his words, is more important than all other physiological and psychological disorders taken together. Volition is the key factor in all activity, all abilities, and it is absent in the mentally retarded child. The keystone in the dome of the building is missing. The whole building will collapse if, while taking pleasure only in the external trimmings and decorations, you forget to add the cementing substance to your work, that is, if you do not bind together the new possibilities, which you have developed your pupils, with an organic link: free will.

But in speaking of a disorder of motivation as the major deficiency in these children, E. Segen does not have in mind only that highest stage in volitional development, which he calls the keystone in the dome of the whole building. He also suggests that the very foundations, the primary, elementary volitional impulse in these children is destroyed in a most profound manner; that this aptitude must be lacking in them, and it is, indeed, lacking in them. These children are not only entirely without motivation—especially moral and intellectual motivation,—but they also lack that primary volition which is not so much the keystone but the foundation of the whole building. Not a single intellectual aptitude can be viewed as altogether absent in these children. However, they are unable to apply their abilities freely to phenomena of a moral and abstract character. They lack that freedom from which moral will is born. "Physically—he cannot; mentally—he knows not; psychologically—he does not wish to. He would be capable, and he would know, if only he wished to; but the whole misfortune lies above all in his not wishing to" (1903, pp. XXXVII-XXXVIII).

Thus, the initial and the final link in the whole chain of development, from the first and lowest to the highest function of the will, are severely underdeveloped in these children.

Still, this viewpoint, though expressed long ago, has not essentially influenced the development of scientific ideas about the nature of mental retardation. As has already been said, the such views emerged from a narrowly intellectual orientation and have continued to perceive feeblemindedness as the basic cause of mental retardation.

In recent times we have been seeing a new theory emerging, as it were, to replace the intellectualistic approach to the problem; this theory attempts to place primary importance on the disorder of motivation in retarded children. This approach seems to derive from two sources.

On one hand, the problem of mental retardation, which is for the most part not innate but acquired, has in the last decade undergone radical reexamination in contemporary psychopathology. The earlier understanding of mental retardation was limited and confined to a purely intellectual deficiency; now, after more profound study of various forms of retardation, this understanding has proved inadequate. Observation of the retarded in conditions of schizophrenia and epidemic encephalitis have brought us to the necessity of introducing such ideas as affective dementia, motivational dementia, and so on. The fate of paralytics, cured of malaria and restored to partial or complete intellectual capacity, has also posed questions about the reversibility of retardation and about the role of non-intellectual factors in the origins of dementia. All this, taken together, forced researchers to emerge from the limiting confines of the intellectual sphere and search for explanations about the nature of retardation in the broader links and dependencies of psychic life, where the conditions which most closely determine even intellectual activities are evidently based.

On the other hand, having encountered a clinical point of view to the problem of retardation, contemporary experimental psychology has brought the problem of affective and volitional life to our attention in an entirely new fashion. Research into affect and activity, which for the first time has the possibility of broad systematic experiment, can establish a series of laws which govern that side of our mind and can show its primary significance for all psychological life, in general and in particular in the intellectual functions. This could not fail to lead to the elimination of the intellectualistic perspective in the study of retardation nor to require investigators to hunt for an explanation of children's retardation in the broader links of psychological life, which reach far beyond the limits of personal intellect. As W. Koehler says, nowhere is the intellectualist attitude as bankrupt as in the study of intelligence.

Thus, the need arose to subject retarded children to broader psychological research and to clarify the dependence of their mental deficiencies on the overall handicapped state of their psychological life, and above all, on a disorder in the sphere of motivation.

We find in the recently published work of K. Lewin,[*] where he first tried systematically to work out a dynamic theory of children's retardation, the fullest expression of both

---

[*] Lewin, Kurt (1890-1947), an important figure in Gestalt psychology (sometimes referred to as *dynamic psychology* or *structural psychology* in this text), is also discussed by Vygotsky in some of his other works. Yet there is no *direct* reference to any of Lewin's works in any of the six volumes in Russian and so there may be reason to believe that Vygotsky's knowledge of Lewin was obtained through secondary sources. Further, the specific supportive experiments which are cited seem to be Soviet replications involving retarded popula-

tendencies, emerging from both the clinical psychiatric side and from the experimental psychological side. As always in such cases, the new directions which arise as reactions to the previously reigning views accurately evaluate the limitations and shortcomings of the old views and an effort is made to carry out research in broader areas of mental life, and to emphasize correctly the fact that retardation absorbs the personality as a whole and is not an isolated illness. But there is also an over-extension in the opposite direction when almost all the meaning offered by explanations of the nature of retardation are rejected because of their intellectualist defects.

Although it is entirely correct in reproaching the former theory for its fruitless construction, for the absence of positive characteristics in identifying the special personality of a mentally retarded child, the new theory itself is inclined to characterize the intellect of such a child primarily in a negative way.

The new theory, born of German structural psychology, derives from an understanding of the nature of the intellectual act, which was developed by Koehler in his famous research on the intellect of anthropoid apes. According to Koehler, the essence of the intellectual act consists in restructuring the field of vision. Images, which had previously been perceived as isolated wholes, form a single closed structure as a result of this act. Parts of certain wholes, which did not stand in isolation previously, become independent or linked to new structures together with other parts of other wholes. Briefly, structures in the field of vision change abruptly and a new grouping of individual wholes takes place within these structures.

Having, in this fashion, reduced the intellectual act to an alteration in structures, the new theory concludes that the intellectual act in a mentally retarded child, in and of itself, displays the same nature in all of its basic characteristics as that act in a normal child. One could not say that a mentally retarded person fails to take in those structures nor could one say that they are less clearly delineated structures for him. One could not even say that his intellectual processes are less intensive. Sometimes they even give the impression of being more intensive than in a normal child. Exactly as for a normal child, or for an anthropoid, the intellectual act for a mentally retarded child consists in the changing of structural relationships in the [perceptual] field.

The new theory is willing to recognize only two characteristics which distinguish the intellect of the retarded child from the intellect of a normal one. The first (and purely extrinsic) difference consists in the following: for the typical changes in intellectual structures to occur in retarded children conditions cannot be the same as for normal children of the same age but must consist of simpler and more primitive tasks. The second qualitative difference consists in the fact that a retarded child thinks more concretely and graphically than a normal one. Thus, we see that, instead of an intellectualistic theory of retardation, a new theory is coming to the fore, one which not only sees as its goal the rejection of intellectualism, but which also tries to minimize the significance of intellectual defects, as such, by its explanation of the nature of retardation in children.

The difference in the intellect of a retarded and a normal child appears insignificant; the nature of the intellectual process appears identical for both; consequently, it is not in the

---

tions rather than the well-known studies which members of the Gestalt school conducted in Germany, Austria and the United States. The reader may be interested in the ensuing passage more as *a rendering of the understanding* of Lewin among Russian students of psychology at the date of this essay (1935) than as a systematic and accurate account of Lewin's positions. A note on Lewin by the Russian editors appears with the following chapter on "Diagnostics." [Ed.]

realm of the intellect where one should search for reasons explaining the characteristics of mentally retarded children in comparison with normal children. On the contrary, those unimportant distinctions in the area of mental processes themselves should be explained on the basis of a restructuring of motivation. The position (which results) is the opposite of that which held sway during the domination of the intellectualistic theory about retardation in children. The latter was inclined to see the central focus of the problem of retardation in the intellectual defect, and it regarded other characteristics of personality in retarded children, including affective disorders, as secondary and deriving from the primary defect of the mind. By contrast, the new theory is trying to push the affective disorder toward the center of the problem, not only removing intellectual inadequacy to the periphery, but even trying to excise it from the central disorders of affect and volition. In brief outline, this is the contemporary position on questions about the nature of mental retardation.

Every researcher in this area encounters two views, which are polar opposites; one view tries to separate mental retardation from intellectual defects, and the other tries to separate it from disorders in the affective sphere. Each direction poses the question as an alternative, "either-or." Thus, any systematic research, and especially any attempt to realize and to summarize theoretically the scientific data in this area, must direct its attention to the cardinal point about the whole problem, the one which divides contemporary theory about children's retardation into two camps. However, simply confronting intellect and motivation in retarded children is not enough to solve the problems of mental retardation. It is necessary to understand what is most important and basic, namely, the relationship or interdependency between affective and intellectual defects in mentally retarded children.

The question of the relationship between affect and intellect in retarded children must therefore stand at the center of our research. The task of that research must be the development and construction of a working hypothesis about the nature of mental retardation in children. To accomplish this task with what we have at our disposal, the only path must be critical and theoretical research on those clinical and experimental data which contemporary science has to offer.

Since the intellectualistic theory on mental retardation is widely known, we need not lay it out in detail, but we will briefly describe the factual outlines of the anti-intellectualist tendency in the dynamic theory of retardation in children, which was developed by Lewin. As we have said, this theory tries to answer the question about the nature of mental retardation, not by directly studying the intellect in retarded children, but by conducting experimental research on their volition and needs. Such research, which focuses on a study of the most deep-seated foundations of personality, may uncover the true reasons for intellectual disorders in children. In factual terms, the new theory is based upon experimental research on the processes of psychological saturation and on the influence of unfulfilled desires (the return to an interrupted activity), as well as on the processes for substituting other activities for unsatisfied needs.[*] To what, from the factual side, does this research lead?

The first study showed that no essential differences in the speed of saturation can be observed during the process of psychological saturation for mentally retarded children at the age of eight to twelve years and for normal children. Experiments negate the established

---

[*] The reference here is generally to *the need to find closure*, the construct which Gestalt theory used to account for motivation and describe its nature. It provided the basis for many well-known experiments. *Saturation* is the phenomenon we experience when a word or object looses its meaningfulness if we concentrate on it for any length of time to the exclusion of its relationships to its context. [Ed.]

view, which holds that mentally retarded children have less aptitude for work than normal children. Nevertheless, mentally retarded children display a typical difference during the process of saturation itself; among such children, pauses and accessory activities appear more often as a result of conflict between the desire to continue work and the onset of saturation. Either the child is occupied with his task or he entirely interrupts his work with a pause or with some other occupation.

A normal child responds to conflict much less dramatically, with greater elasticity, with more gradual and connected transitions. He finds a way to resolve conflict with a compromise, which allows him not to interrupt abruptly the work he has begun. The behavior of retarded children in this situation displays a much more uneven character and follows an "either-or" rule. Functional passivity, constraint, and a sluggish dynamics of psychological material are some of the fundamental distinctive features which characterize retarded children.

The second study, on interrupted activity, arrived at similar conclusions. As is known from experiments on normal children, all activity assumes the presence of affective stimulation, which finds its release upon completion of the interrupted operation. If a child is interrupted and is not given the opportunity to conclude work he has begun, if he is sidetracked with some another activity, then an impulse to return to the interrupted activity will arise. This shows that an unsatisfied need continues to affect the child and impels him to finish the interrupted activity. Experiments have shown that the tendencies to return to interrupted activity are more sharply pronounced in retarded children than they are in normal children. If this tendency appeared among normal chidden 80 percent of the time in M. Ovsiankina's [no ref.] experiments, it appeared 100 percent of the time among retarded children. Consequently, here also, retarded children not only failed to demonstrate weakness by comparison with normal children, but in a certain sense they displayed a stronger expression of the tendency which, among normal children, was observed to be less pronounced.

Finally, a third study was devoted to the question of substitute activities in retarded children. It is clear from experiments with normal children that if, following the interrupted uncompleted activity, a child is assigned another task which is connected in one or another way to the activity involved in the first task, then the new activity easily replaces the first; that is, it leads to the satisfaction of the need which was not met by the interrupted activity. This is expressed in the following way: After the substitute activity, the child no longer displays a tendency to return to the interrupted activity.

A comparison of feebleminded children with normal ones in this respect showed: (1) under conditions in which an activity acted as a substitute for normal children, their return to the interrupted activity fell from 80 percent to 23 percent while for retarded children the return to interrupted activity fell from 100 to only 94 percent; (2) the possibility of substituting one activity with another thus turned out to be close to zero among retarded children. Substitution is possible among these children only when the original and the substitute activity are almost identical: for example, if, instead of the task of drawing an animal, the task of drawing the same animal again is assigned as a substitute; or if, instead of building a bridge of stones, the task is to build another bridge of stone. Even given such extreme similarity between the original and the substitute activity, the tendency to return to the interrupted activity fell insignificantly (to 86 percent) among retarded children.

Thus, the possibility of substitution in the area of affective motivation appears much more limited and less pronounced for retarded than for normal children.

If we compare the experimental data we have just mentioned with observation of the daily behavior of mentally retarded children, then it turns out that these observations, in part, concur with the results of experiments and, in part,sharply contradict them. The inclination of a retarded child to stick to an undertaken goal, his inertia, his sluggish dynamics which are often expressed as pedanticism—all seem to confirm that which has been discovered experimentally. But, at the same time, the retarded child, according to observation, is easily distracted from the matter at hand. He does not finish it and is easily satisfied by incomplete and unfinished solutions to the task. K. Gottschaldt showed that these children are easily satisfied by simpler activities if the first task is difficult for them. Thus, it seems that a retarded child displays, at the same time, a peculiar inertness and fixity, which eliminate for him the possibility of substitute activities. However, at the same time, he maintains a clearly expressed tendency to substitute easier activities, or more primitive variations of the activity, for more difficult ones.

Such are the factual data which lie at the basis of the general theory of personality for mentally retarded children. That theory emerges from a study of the individual differences which characterize one personality or another, as well as from the factual basis indicated above.

K. Lewin distinguishes among three kinds of individual characteristics of human beings. He gives first place to the differences in personality structure. People may be distinguished from each other, first of all, on the degree of differentiation of their personality structure. Thus the difference between a child and an adult is demonstrated first by a considerably smaller degree of differentiation in the separate spheres of psychological life and the separate psychological systems. Where the personality of an adult displays relatively high differentiation in various spheres of activity and interest, such as family, profession and the like as well as different layers of structural construction, the personality of a child displays much less differentiation, and a dynamically stronger* and more syncretic structure.

The second difference involves not degrees of differentiation, but the nature of the construction of the structure itself. The overall structure may be more or less harmonious. Various spheres of personality may be united with one another and delineated from one another in different ways. For the structure of personality, it is not a matter of indifference how the delineation of separate areas of psychological life takes place, or in which parts development is stronger and in which weaker. The example of personality disintegration may serve as a model for the altogether original construction involved in building personality structure.

Lewin puts in second place the differences in psychological material and the conditions of psychological systems. Psychological material itself, which undergoes structural differentiation, can be distinguished in individual people by the different stages of softness, elasticity, hardness, or fluidity. An infant, for example, is distinguished from an adult not only by the lesser degree of differentiation in the separate spheres of psychological life, but also by certain characteristics of psychological materials—above all by extreme pliability and fluidity. Thus the features of psychological tension in any system may define the characteristics of the psychological material as such. Tension may build up more slowly or more quickly.

---

*L. S. Vygotsky, in following the terminology of K. Lewin, undoubtedly had in mind the more stable, less alterable and less plastic structures in the dynamic plan. {Editor of the Russian version.}

In addition to the differences which exist in this respect for one situation or another in everyone, and in addition to the known characteristics of psychological material generally inherent to it in one personality or another, the characteristics of psychological material will appear dissimilar in various systems. For example, in the area of irreality, a great fluidity and dynamics of systems is revealed, just as it is among the earlier and later spheres of psychological life in the personality. Thus, in comparing characteristics of psychological material it is necessary to take the homologous parts of a child's personality.

Finally, Lewin puts into third place differences in the content and the meaning of systems. Given identical structures of personality and identical characteristics in materials, the meaning and content of the corresponding psychological systems can be different in a Chinese child and in a Russian one. The content of goals and ideals, the meaning of different areas of life, are likewise different in different children. These individual characteristics, in much greater degree than in the first two groups studied, constitute dependence on specific historical conditions.

If one tries to explain the nature of mental retardation from the perspective laid out above, from factual results to experimental research, and from the theoretical considerations just described, it becomes necessary to clarify what radical specifics in the personality structure differentiate a mentally retarded child from a normal one. It seems that the retarded child displays much less differentiation of psychological life than a normal child of corresponding age. Not only is his mental age lower than that of a normal child of the same years, but as a whole the mentally retarded child is more primitive, infantile. Based on the degree of lack of differentiation, he reminds one of a child of a much younger age. All that is indicated by the term *infantilism* is connected, above all, in Lewin's opinion, with inadequate differentiation in psychological life.

Further, a retarded child seems, by comparison with a normal one, much more mature in the sense of having a less dynamic quality, less mobility in his psychological systems, having greater hardness and brittleness. If he reminds one of a younger child in the degree of differentiation, he reminds one more of an older child in the characteristics of his psychological material.[2] From these two basic characteristics of a retarded child, Lewin infers almost all essential, characteristic traits of children of this type. Their pedantic qualities and fixation on given goals derives from the lower mobility of their psychological material. This also explains the paradoxical relationship of a retarded child to substitute activities. Any activity can acquire a substitute function with respect to another action, if they correspond with each other as dynamic systems. "A" and "B" represent, as it were, dependent parts of a single dynamic whole.

If one accepts this, then it becomes clear that the emergence of substitute functions for any activity acquires, for a retarded child, a decisive meaning; it acquires the characteristics of a transition from one activity to another. If a second activity is given to a child as an entirely novel experience, then, in otherwise equivalent conditions, the substitute functions of that child will appear to be much lower than they would in circumstances where the second activity developed out of the first. In this second situation, what develops is the unified dynamic system which is necessary in order that one activity act as a substitute for another. With normal children, a certain degree of similarity between the two tasks is adequate to ensure that the two dynamic systems will form links between themselves. This is not the case among retarded children. For them, the second task is something altogether new and is not linked to the preceding task. Only in the event that the second task develops naturally, both situationally and spontaneously, from the first can the second task take on the meaning of a substitute function, because then it is dynamically linked to motivations developing from the first task.

Given the more sluggish dynamics of the psychological systems in retarded children, substitute functions can develop among them in certain situations, not more weakly, but more strongly than among normal children. If, by some means or other, a second task can be offered in dynamic linkage with a first, then the substitute meaning of the second activity will appear particularly clearly in a retarded child.

The material of psychological systems and its characteristics in retarded children are directly linked to the emergence of structures and their characteristics. To a much greater degree than a normal child, a retarded child demonstrates a tendency toward what K. Lewin called the "law of either-or." Given the rigidity and inertness of his psychological make-up, such a child will exhibit tendencies toward strong dynamic structures, structures which are both syncretic and undifferentiated. Therefore, his psychological systems turn out to be either entirely differentiated or entirely fused to one another. A retarded child does not display those graded, linked but gradual transitions, as it were, between absolute differentiation and absolute fusion of his psychological systems —those elastic and mobile relations among psychological systems which are observable in a normal child. This, Lewin believes, is one of the fundamental features of mentally retarded children, one which explains the so frequently encountered contradictions in their behavior.

The inclination toward structures linked according to the "law of either-or" also determines the relationship of retarded children to the surrounding world. A retarded child—in much greater degree than a normal child—can find himself in either one situation or in an entirely different one. Individual situations appear to him to be much more separate and exclusive entities than they do normally. He is therefore helpless when a task requires that he link separate situations or that he simultaneously participate in two situations. Because of this, a retarded child displays great tenacity and energy in the pursuit of a definite goal, great strength and concentration of attention in one field, more than would a normal child. But if thanks to external influences, the situation changes, then by virtue of the same "law of either-or," he will move more easily than a normal child to the new situation and entirely abandon the old. Thus, a mentally retarded child is particularly sensitive to external forces, which can easily, most easily, destroy an immediate situation and create a new one. Finally, Lewin also derives certain important distinctions in a retarded child's intellect from these characteristics in his affective dynamics: intellectual inadequacy or deficiency, specificity, little intellectual fluidity, and overall infantilism with preserved ability of perception.

The characteristics in the affective sphere of a mentally retarded child which Lewin found, he believes, can be explained by the characteristics in the intellectual processes of such a child. As we have seen, the essence of the intellectual act lies in the fact that two elements, which are separate from one another, become dependent parts of a single whole, or an initially single entity splinters into relatively independent areas. As a result of this, changes take place in the structure the whole field. Obviously, inadequate general dynamism in psychological systems must make an intellectual act of this nature more difficult, since dynamism determines changes in structural entities in a field.

Experimental data speak to the fact that mentally retarded children appear less independent when faced with tasks that require dynamism, variability, and the regrouping of structural relationships. Such tasks come up against the firmness and rigidity of structures that have already emerged, on the one hand, and against the slower dynamism of their psychological systems, on the other. A mentally retarded child reveals a structure that is much more durable, more inert, and more reserved than does a normal child. This very sluggish dynamism in the psychological systems must lead to the fact that the formation of weak, changeable structures will take place only with difficulty.

We have seen that inadequate differentiation in the personality of a mentally retarded child equates him with a normal child of much younger years. As is known, concreteness and primitiveness of thought are also distinguishing characteristics of the early years. However, the difficulties in abstract thought which a mentally retarded child displays remain even at an age when a normal child will have already left behind concreteness and primitiveness of thought. The concrete character of thought in a mentally retarded child indicates that, for him, every thing and every event acquires its own meaning that is, its own particular situation. He is unable to separate them as independent parts, distinct from their situations. Thus, the process of abstraction (that is, the creation of groups, and the interrelating of those groups on the basis of certain essential relationships amongst subjects) proceeds only with difficulty in such a child. In its essence, abstraction requires some distancing from a situation, a situation which is bound up as a whole for a mentally retarded child. Especially difficult for him are those generalizations which require the most abstraction from a situation, and which are arrived at in connection with fantasy, understanding, and unreality.

Lewin believes the most essential characteristic of these children is the absence of fantasy. This does not mean that they lack ideas. The children often have an excellent memory for concrete facts. But at the same time, their thoughts lack imagination, because they lack the dynamism which is required as a precondition for any activity of imagining. Research into the fantasies of mentally retarded children, with the help of G. Rorschach's tests, fully confirms their poverty. Abstract thought, as well as imagination, requires a particular fluidity and mobility of psychological systems. Naturally, therefore, both these areas are especially undeveloped in mentally retarded children.

Let us examine one more question which directly relates to the central problem of our research, and that is the problem of perception in the mentally retarded child. Inadequate differentiation in the psychological systems of a mentally retarded child, along with the concreteness and primitiveness of his thoughts, leads also to inadequate differentiation in the perceived and experienced world. The breaking down and differentiation of psychological life are served by a wealth of methods for perceiving reality which are at the disposal of the personality. Given the inadequacies of differentiation in the personality, a mentally retarded child's perceived and experienced world appears at once more monotonous, more stagnant, and more set than that of a normal child of the same age. In a specific sense, a functional equivalence exists between the greater degree of differentiation in the personality and its greater fluidity in given situations and tasks. In other words, the way in which reality is perceived defines the character of activities with respect to that perceived reality.

A normal child is able to alter his perceptual field at will. This is linked to an ability to concentrate his attention at will on separate facets and factors of a situation. Inadequate differentiation in the personality of a mentally retarded child leads to the underdevelopment of arbitrary attention. In this respect, the lack of differentiation in the personality plays a larger role than the relation to the psychological material. This is confirmed by the fact that a mentally retarded child acquires greater mobility with age. This is because the degree of differentiation in his personality grows, like a normal child's (although not within the same scope nor at the same pace), while at the same time the characteristics of the psychological material do not essentially change for such a child over time.

We can limit our exposition of Lewin's dynamic theory to what we have already said, and move on to a critical examination of the facts and theoretical principles which underlie that theory.

The dynamic theory of mental retardation is, of course, a matter of enormous interest. It advances all study on mental retardation. It brings up the question of mental retardation not only within the narrow limits of intellectualistic theory, but also within the broader framework of psychological life overall. By this very fact, the dynamic theory, without being conscious of that fact, and regardless of its errors, is laying one of the foundation stones upon which all contemporary study of childhood mental retardation should be based. This cornerstone is the notion of the unity of intellect and affect in the development of normal and of mentally retarded children. The new theory contains this very idea in an occluded, undeveloped form which flows out of logical necessity from the theory's entire structure and experimental bases. Nonetheless, it remains unrealized, at least, in its true meaning.

This represents, at once, all that is negative and all that is positive in the theory we are examining. Everything that is positive is linked to the basic cornerstone of the idea; the negative lies in the fact that the idea remains incompletely explored and incompletely realized. The inadequacies of the dynamic theory lie, above all, in the fact that problems of intellect and of affect are approached in an antidialectic, metaphysical fashion, independently of the idea of development. This is most clearly visible in that part of the theory devoted to the problem of the intellect.

In determining the nature of the intellect, Lewin is content with that vision of the understanding which can be introduced on the basis of Koehler's well-known research on the intellect of anthropoid apes. Thus, the intellect is examined not in its highest and most developed forms, but at its initial, primitive, and elementary forms. That which characterizes the nature of the intellect at that lowest stage is accepted and passes for the essence of thought. The entirety of a child's rich and varied intellectual development remains outside the researcher's attention. The nature of the intellectual act is assumed to be metaphysically unchangeable. That, which makes up the nature of the intellectual act in its lowest form, at the beginning of its development, in the prehistorical period of its existence, during the zoological form of its manifestation, is taken to represent the invariable essence of the intellect, which will always be the same, identical throughout the entirety of its development. It seems as though nothing can change in the nature of the intellectual act, nothing new can be contributed to that nature during the whole historical development of human thought from the first words pronounced by men to the highest forms of conceptual thought. Indeed, the definition which Lewin gives us for the intellect has been applied equally to chimpanzees, to children, and to adults. Naturally, if one cites as intellect only the general and only that which exists at all stages of development, we can doubtless add one more link—namely, the mentally retarded child—to Lewin's series of examples which already include the chimpanzee, the child, and the adult.

One could hardly dispute the fact that, by its nature, the intellect of the mentally retarded child does not stand lower than the intellect in a chimpanzee, nor could one dispute that it displays those same essential characteristics of the intellect found in apes. But Lewin's method of reasoning altogether robs his conclusions of their value. Of what value, in fact, is his conclusion that the intellectual act in a mentally retarded child is not by nature different from that act in a normal child if, in defining the nature of that act, the psychological standard, the unit of measurement employed is the intellectual operation in apes? Basically, Lewin's words do not mean what he meant them to say. Least of all does he prove that the intellect of a mentally retarded child is in no essential part of its nature different from the intellect of a normal child. He only shows that the intellect of the mentally retarded child is in its nature no different from the intellect of a chimpanzee. If one further takes into account that, for Lewin, the intellectual act remains in its nature unchanged throughout the child's development, then it becomes clear that the equivalence of a mentally retarded and a normal child's intellect is an idea empty and barren of content. By posing the problem independently of the notion of development, by looking at the intellect as a metaphysically unchanging essence, which in its earliest stages of development already has all those traits in full which are characteristic of its nature, these things inevitably lead to the equivalence of the examples of intellects described above. This becomes particularly clear if one follows the process by which Lewin poses the problem of intellect and affect. Both problems do not appear in his work in identical conditions. However, as we shall see below, he also poses the problem of affect in the same anti-dialectical and metaphysical fashion in which he poses the problem of the intellect. Nonetheless, there is a basic difference between his approach to one problem and his approach to the other.

When Lewin studies affect he distinguishes among in its component parts. He distinguishes among the characteristics inherent in the materials of the dynamic systems, the structure of those systems, the meaning of those systems, and separates, further, the traits of affect into more concrete and individual varieties. He deals with the intellect, however, in sum, as a single entity, a single-faceted, homogeneous, and indivisible whole, as something preformed, something that not only is immutable during development, but that also contains no internal components which result from the complexity of its construction and from the functioning of intellectual activity. Thus, that undoubted dependence which exists between the intellectual and the affective processes and which has been discovered in even the most elementary forms of the intellect—observed and studied by Koehler in apes—that dependence escapes Lewin. Koehler himself, more than once, remarks on the enormous impact of the affective tendencies on the intellectual operations of chimpanzees. This dependence of intellectual operations on the actual affect is seen by Koehler correctly as one of the essential traits of this primitive stage in the development of the intellect.

K. Koffka,[*] analyzing Koehler's experiments, also points out that ape's reasoned activities cannot be called intentional actions. By their dynamic nature, they remain exclusively on the plane of instinctive consciousness. Is there any purpose to referring to the actions of chimpanzees as intentional acts? Koffka shows that chimpanzees' reasoned activities are at the opposite pole from intentional activities. Evidently, these primitive forms of intellectual activity are linked to affect and to the will, by some means different from the linkage of the rational actions of men. In part, underestimating this side of the matter led Koehler to falsely identify chimpanzees' actions with man's use of tools. Obviously, not only do the intellectual functions change and improve during development, but so does the relationship between the intellect and the affect.

This is the crux of the issue, and we will return to it below. Now we would like to show that, although Lewin examines the problem of affect in a much more analytical way, by breaking it into its component parts, than he does with the problem of the intellect, he nonetheless preserves his metaphysical and anti-dialectal approach. Lewin examines the affective processes which arise from both true and unreal needs[**] and from the stimulating

---

[*] Another important Gestalt psychologist cited by Vygotsky elsewhere. See Koffka, 1924, 1925, 1926, 1932, 1943. [Ed.]

dynamic tendencies linked to them, as something primordial and independent of psychological life as a whole. He recognizes only one-sided dependence. Everything in psychological life depends on its dynamic bases. But Lewin does not see the second side of that dependence, that is, that the dynamic basis itself alters during the development of the psychological life and, in its turn, displays its dependence on those changes which the whole consciousness experiences.

He does not know the dialectical rules which state: During development, the cause and the effect change places; having arisen on the basis of given dynamic prerequisites, the higher psychological formations acquire an inverted influence on the processes that created them; in development the lower is replaced by the higher; in development, not only do the strictly physiological functions change, but, in the first instance, so do the interfunctional links and the relationships among separate processes change especially the relationship between the intellect and the affect. Lewin examines affect independently of development and independently of the rest of psychological life. He assumes that the place of affect in psychological life is unchanging and constant throughout the duration of development and, consequently, that the relationship between intellect and affect is of constant magnitude. In fact, Lewin considers only a partial case from among all the diverse developmental relationships between intellect and affect which have actually been observed —a part of the case concerned with regularities specifically at the lowest and most primitive stages of development. Then, he elevates this special case into a general law.

It is true that, at the very beginning of the development of the intellect, there is a moment at which the general laws proposed by Lewin, in fact, apply. In the initial developmental stages, the intellect can indeed be found to be more or less directly dependent on affect. But, it is equally true that it is completely improper to define the nature of intellect according to the initial, elementary, forms selected by Lewin. It is therefore impossible to accept the view that the relationship which exists between intellect and affect at the early stages of development is something unchanging and constant, something typical and regular for the whole process of development. As we have already remarked, W. Koehler correctly noted that nowhere does intellectualism appear so bankrupt as is in the theory of the intellect. Until recently, the bankruptcy of intellectualism has been discovered mainly during the attempt to adapt the intellectualist perspective in the explanation of the nature of affect and volition. But it is not without basis that Koehler affirms that this perspective is even more discredited when the attempt is made to adapt it to the analysis of the intellect itself and, by this means, to infer the nature of the intellect and its development from within itself. Lewin does not deserve this reproach, since he attempted to derive the intellect and its nature from the characteristics of affective life. Nonetheless, he falls into two other, no less serious, methodological errors.

Like most representatives of structural psychology, Lewin is inclined to deny, without recognizing it, the presence of all specific regularities inherent in thought. It is true that the intellect cannot be entirely explained from within itself, that it is formed and acts not according to the laws of thought (since it is not a formation artificially generated by human thought) but represents, rather, a naturally developing function of the human brain, a function of human consciousness. But it is also true that, in studying the intellect and its characteristics, it is impossible to ignore the particular regularities of thought and to accept them

---

** In K. Lewin's terms, "quasi-needs." {Rus. Ed.}

as simple mirror reflections of those regularities which govern the affective sphere, or as a shadow cast by affect.

It is true, and most important, that Lewin, having avoided the dangers of intellectualism, falls into another danger entirely opposite to the first. In studying volition, he falls into "voluntarism." In the meantime, we might accurately apply to voluntarism that which Koehler said about intellectualism and assert that voluntarism is nowhere more apt to demonstrate its failings as in the study of volition. It is also true that, as it is impossible to infer the nature of thought from within itself, ignoring the whole history of thought, the system of linkages, dependencies, and relationships necessary for thought to arise, so is it also impossible to infer the nature of the will from within itself, ignoring consciousness in general and all those most complex linkages and dependencies which in fact are the only context in which human will arises and develops.

Essentially, the methodological flaws of intellectualism and of voluntarism are one and the same; that is, the metaphysical quality of both studies is equally inherent in both of them. The basic flaw of intellectualism is that it looks at the intellect as a primordial, unchanging, and original essence outside of the real history of its development and outside the real conditions in which it functions. The fundamental flaw of voluntarism is the same. It examines volition, that primary and dynamic basis of psychological life, in the same fashion, that is, as a primordial, original, and autonomous essence, isolated from the real conditions of its existence and experiencing no alterations during development.

Thus, a critical analysis of the dynamic theory of mental retardation in children requires that we conclude that the general failure of the theory of the intellect and the theory of volition (as they are represented in contemporary structural psychology) means that Lewin's particular theory is also a failure. But as we have already indicated, Lewin's theory and especially its experimental basis contain a very valuable nucleus. We must reveal that nucleus in order to find a more correct structure for our working hypothesis on the nature of children's mental retardation. As we have already said, that kernel is the idea of unity between the affective and intellectual processes. Anywhere where the dynamic theory of mental retardation leads more-or-less automatically to the idea of unity, it advances scholarly knowledge; anywhere where the theory undermines that idea, it will drag us back to abandoned scholarly ideas which have only historical significance.

In order to uncover the correct kernel in the dynamic theory and discard the husk which surrounds it, we must first distinguish quite clearly and distinctly those hidden theses about the unity of affect and intellect contained in the theory which are not acknowledged by its author. For this purpose, we must, first of all, introduce one essential change in the theoretical conclusions which Lewin makes on the basis of his experimental data. We will attempt here to clarify our own thoughts on one particular issue.

K. Lewin considers the concreteness of thought as one of the essential characteristics of a mentally retarded child's intellect. However, he attempts to derive the concreteness of thought from those characteristics which he established experimentally in relation to affective processes. He says that, in comparison with the normal child, the dynamic systems of a mentally retarded child are distinguished by less fluidity and more solidity. The direct tendency in thought toward concreteness can be associated with this slower dynamics and inertness. The observations which Lewin makes in support of this proposition seem to us, of course, to be convincing. But what is present here is a dual dependence, where Lewin dwells only on the single-sided dependence of thought on affect.

It is true that the concreteness of thought and the sluggish pace of the dynamic systems are internally connected and that they represent a unit, a single entity, and not a double entity which is accidentally combined in mentally retarded children. Concreteness of thought and action in mentally retarded children signifies that every thing and every event acquire for them their own meaning depending on the situation, that those things and events are inseparable from the specific situation. Therefore, any abstraction will be difficult. Anything linked to understanding, to imagination, and to the unreal will be in the highest degree difficult for such children.

It would be too simple to look at this situational dependence and difficulty in abstraction and concept formation to be only a derivative of the sluggishness in the affective systems. To the same degree, the opposite is also true. Even Lewin himself acknowledges that affective systems and tensions arise at the point of intersection between some situation and some need or requirement, that is, during the child's encounter with reality. The traits which the affective system will muster in the encounter with the given situation will also finally depend on how the child recognizes the situation, how far he can interpret it and to what degree he errs. If one looks at all those sections of Lewin's theory which elaborate on the dependence of the child's intellectual characteristics upon his affective disorder, the same can be seen everywhere.

Only the fact of linkage really emerges from the experimental data Lewin offers; the fact of the internal unity of intellectual and dynamic characteristics, no more and no less. This is indisputable, inarguable. But there is no justifying (except on the preconceived voluntaristic basis) the assertion that the affective side of this entity should be seen as independent, while the intellectual second side should be seen as dependent. On the contrary, both theoretical analysis and experimental research which we will discuss below, requires us to accept intellect and affect as having their internal regularity, a regularity which characterizes them as a single entity. But as long as we have, until now, preserved that entity, we have preserved its features. As soon as we divide that entity into its elements, we immediately lose those traits which belong to the whole and all possibility of being able to explain them.

Always accepting affect as the cause which calls forth one or another trait is as baseless as accepting oxygen as the cause of whatever characteristics are displayed by hydrogen when the subject under discussion is the explanation of some trait inherent in water. If, for example, we want to explain why water extinguishes fire, we would separate water into its component elements in vain, and would discover, to our surprise, that hydrogen itself burns, while oxygen supports burning. Only if we replaced this analysis (which divides the entity into elements) with another analysis which separates complex entities into their component simple entities, and which further does not lay out and represent that unity inherent in the whole in the most simplified of forms, can we then hope to find that our analysis will lead to a satisfactory solution to the problem.

Thus, the closest condition for the solution of our problem is to find an indissoluble unit of intellect and affect. This we can do if we introduce a single theoretical correction into Lewin's reasoning. According to his theory, the issue stands as follows. There are two kinds of dynamic processes: On the one hand, a free, flowing, mobile, and changing process; on the other, an inert, constrained rigid dynamics. These two types exist, just as two types of activity exist—thinking, on one hand, and real action in an actual situation, on the other.

Both types of dynamic processes exist entirely independently of the intellect, just as the two kinds of activity exist entirely independently of the dynamics. Further, both types of dynamics can combine in various ways with both sorts of activity. Then, we might encounter a variety of combinations of dynamic and intellectual traits depending on which dynamics and which functional elements entered into the composition of the entity under investigation. In fact, this is not so.

Lewin himself was forced to come to the conclusion that thinking, by its very nature dynamic, is more fluid and free than the dynamics of real situational activity. This proposition, of course, has not an absolute significance, but a relative one. It shows that regardless of the absolute degree of dynamism, the relative degree of dynamism is always greater in the area of thought than in the area of activity. For example, a mentally retarded child has, in general, a dynamic pace that is at best only sluggish. However, this sluggishness is less manifest in thought than in action. Drawing upon the enormous quantities of facts which Lewin cites, as well as those which we have established in our own experiments, discussed below, one is forced to admit that matters stand somewhat differently than Lewin indicates.

There are not two kinds of dynamics existing independently of the nature of those functions inactivated by the dynamic processes, nor are there two kinds of activities which are independent of the dynamic systems at their base. However, there do exist two unities of dynamic functions—thinking and real activity. Each of these has its own dynamic aspect. This means that inherent in thought, as a particular kind of activity, is a dynamics of a special kind and character. Similarly, inherent in real action is its own system, which is also of a specific character and kind among the (various) dynamic systems. Two kinds of dynamics do not exist outside a given particular type of concrete activity. In the interest of theoretical study, we could, in the abstract, separate the two kinds of dynamics from the kinds of activities that are linked to them. However, one would have always to bear in mind that once we move away from the real state of affairs the dynamics do not, in reality, exist outside of the function which it sets in motion.

But we also know that neither of these types of activity—thought and real action—represents fields that are separated from one another by an impassable chasm. In fact, in living activities, we constantly observe the transition of thought into action, and action into thought. Consequently, neither dynamic system—though more mobile when linked with thought, and less mobile when linked to action—is isolated from the other. What should be, and in fact is, observed at every turn is the transition of the fluid dynamics of thought into the hard, rigidifying dynamics of action and back again, that is, the transition likewise from the sluggish and constrained dynamics of action into the fluid dynamics of thought. Let us note several important points which will help us to develop this fundamental idea.

There is, first, that regularity which is displayed as a result of the dependence of thought on the affective and dynamic processes which Lewin took to be a general law but which, in fact, applies only to the particular case. The broad dynamics in the psychological field (that which make us think and act) always lie at the beginning of the intellectual processes. Our actions do not arise without cause; they are motivated by known dynamic processes which are spurred by needs and by motivation. Similarly, our thoughts are always motivated, always psychologically conditional; they always flow from some affective motivation or other, which they set in motion and direct. Thoughts which are not motivated dynamically are as impossible as actions without a reason. It is in this sense that Spinoza had already defined affect as that which increases or decreases our body's ability to act, and as that which forces thought to move in a specific direction.

Thus, dynamic conditionality is inherent in thought and action alike. But as Lewin himself acknowledges, the dynamic motivations in thought are distinguished (from those in action) by greater fluidity. Great fluidity and freedom in the course of the dynamic processes are inherent in thoughts; this fluidity and freedom appear in associations, substitutions, communications in general, and in all linkages in general which might arise between separate affective motivations. The degree to which reality is represented or reflected somehow or other in thoughts is the same degree to which thoughts preserve the positive and negative motivating factors which derive from things. E. Minkovskii [no ref.], for example, showed that there are some things about which we are, in practice, unable to think, and other things which we are unable to carry out in any specific fashion because each contradicts the basic affect which they call forth in us. As Minkovskii showed, for example, we are unable to think systematically about our own death, just as we are unable to do other things which call forth strongly negative affective attitudes in us. It stands to reason that affective reactions, when connected with things, enter into thought only in an extremely weakened fashion. Sticks cannot burn in a mental fire, nor does an imagined dog bite. Even a child can, in his thoughts, move in a direction which is entirely impossible in any real situation.

As F. Schiller[*] says, thoughts easily accommodate one another, but in space (real air) they collide brutally. Therefore, when a child begins thinking in one or another real situation, not only does it mean a change of situation as far as his perceptions go nor only an alteration in his field of thought but also, above all, it represents a change in his dynamics. The dynamics of a real situation, as they change into the fluid dynamics of thought, start to reveal new properties, new possibilities for action, for amalgamation, and for communication amongst separate systems. However, this direct movement of dynamics, from an actual situation to thought, would be useless if there was not return movement, a reverse transformation of the fluid dynamics of thought into the rigid and durable dynamic system of real action. The difficulty in fulfilling a series of intentions is linked precisely to the fact that the dynamics of thought, which are fluid and free, must be converted into the dynamics of real action.

As experiment shows, one can detect three basic phases in this transition from the dynamics of thought to the dynamics of action and back again. These three phases correspond to three fundamental problems in affective dynamics: (1) the transformation of the dynamics of a psychological field or of a situation into the dynamics of thought; (2) the development and unfolding of the dynamic process of thought itself; and (3) its return transformation into the dynamics of action.[**] An action reflected through the prism of thought has already been transformed into a different action, one that is meaningful, conscious, and consequently free and voluntary; that is, it stands in a different general relationship to the situation from action which is directly conditioned by the situation and which has not gone through the direct and reverse transformation of dynamics.

A radical methodological error of Lewin's theory is the fact that he separates the problem of dynamics from the problem of intellect and that he sees no links between them. This mistake is evident not only in his dynamic theory of mental retardation but, above all, and principally, in his general theory of affect and will. Thus, Lewin finds it remarkable that human beings should experience freedom in organizing any, even meaningless, intentions and those dynamic requirements which correspond to these intentions. This freedom is characteristic of a cultured person. In children and primitive human beings, it is present in

---

[*] ? Schiller, Friedrich (1759-1805) The German dramatist and poet? No reference supplied. [Ed.]

[**] The text, as it has been made available, omits the (3), indicating the third phase. We have added it. [Transl.]

an immeasurably smaller degree; this distinction differentiates men from their nearest relatives in the animal world even more essentially than man's higher intellect.

In fact, these new possibilities for free and rational action evidently represent the characteristic trait which separates humans from animals. This is what Engels means when he says that no animal has been able to leave the stamp of its will on nature; only man has been able to accomplish that. (K. Marx and F. Engels, *Collected Works*, vol. 20).

It is possible that man's higher intellect (by comparison with that of animals) might in itself have had no real meaning in the life and history of humanity if it had not been tied to entirely new possibilities for action. Even man's intellect could not have developed outside the conditions of specifically human activity, in particular, outside of labor. Lewin's greatest mistake was in setting up an opposition between the freedom of human action and human thought. We know that volitional freedom is nothing other than a recognized necessity, such as domination over nature.

In our research into the higher psychological functions, we have always seen that meaningful, active remembering and attention are the same thing, approached from different angles: One can as accurately speak of voluntary attention and logical memory, as one can speak of logical attention and voluntary memory; at the same time and in altogether equal measure the higher psychological functions are the essence of intellectualized and volitional functions; awareness and possession go hand in hand. In all of this (which is one of the most central propositions of our theory, indeed in the study of the higher psychological functions), the unity of the dynamic reasoning systems is wholly included. The realization of function gains other possibilities for action. In large part to realize means to dominate. Among the higher psychological functions there are present in some measure functions of an affective nature and functions of an intellectual nature. The whole point is that thought and affect are parts of the same, single whole, and that whole is human consciousness.

Things do not change because we think them but the affect and the functions linked to them do change to the extent that they are recognized. They then stand in a different relationship to the consciousness and to the other affect; this, consequently, alters their relationship to the whole and to its unity. Therefore, if we return to the example we cited about the unity of concreteness in thought, on the one hand, and, on the other hand, to the sluggishness of the dynamic systems, then, we might say that any stage in the development of thought has a corresponding stage in the development of the affect. In other words, every stage of psychological development is characterized by particular traits in the dynamic, reasoning systems which are specific to it as an integral and indissoluble whole. The inertia and relative passivity of the dynamic systems unavoidably exclude the possibility of abstraction and conceptualization because they unavoidably lead to complete association with a situation, and to concreteness and to graphic thought. They lead in this direction to the same degree that concreteness of thought and the absence of abstraction and comprehension themselves lead to stagnation and passivity in the dynamic systems.

If in the activity of real situations we observe dynamic mobility and fluidity, it is always characterized by the tendency of thought to participate in the process of our external activity. One might say, that the participation of thought in activities occurs in the same degree as the degree to which the dynamics of our activity demonstrate the properties of fluidity and mobility. And, the opposite: the presence of possible action in thought, the concreteness and graphic qualities of thought are displayed in the same degree, as the degree to which the intellect displays traits of sluggishness and slower dynamics.

The dynamics of thought are not mirror images reflecting the relationship prevalent in real actions. If thought in no way changed dynamic activity, then it would be completely unnecessary. Naturally, life determines consciousness. Consciousness arises out of life and forms only one of its features. But once awakened, thought itself defines life. Or more accurately, a thinking life defines itself through consciousness. As soon as we separate thought from life, from dynamics, and from necessities, we have deprived it of all reality; we have put off all paths to the clarification and explanation of the traits and chief purposes of thought: to define lifestyle and behavior, to change our actions, to direct them, and to free them from the power of concrete circumstance.

Special research has shown that the degree of development is the degree of conversion from the affective dynamics—the dynamics of real action—to the dynamics of thought. The path from contemplation to abstract thought, and from there to practical action, is the way leading to the transformation of the stagnant and relatively fixed dynamics of a situation into the changing and fluid dynamics of thought, and to the transition of the latter back into the rational, free, and purposeful dynamics of practical action.

We should have liked to illustrate in depth, using experimental examples from our comparative research on normal and on mentally retarded children, this proposition about the unified dynamics of reasoning systems and about the transition from the dynamics of thought to the dynamics of action, and back. We will limit ourselves to three series of experiments which correspond analogously to Lewin's research described above. The difference between our experiments and Lewin's lies in the fact that we attempted to study both the intellectual and the affective sides in solving corresponding tasks.

In the first series of experiments, we studied, as Lewin did, the processes of saturation in activities for both normal and retarded children. But we made the meaning of the situation itself into the variable quantity in our experiment. We allowed the child to get his fill of some activity and then waited until that activity ceased. During this process, we did not limit ourselves to measuring the time passed up to a point of complete saturation with the given activity, and we did not halt the experiment at the point after saturation occurred. It was only then that we began the experiment. When the child ceased to work and showed clear signs of complete saturation with negative affective motivation resulting from that work, we tried to learn by what means it would be possible force him to continue the activity. For mentally retarded children, it proved necessary to change the situation itself, to make it more attractive, to recreate it so that its negative character might be replaced by a positive one. Thus, in order to get the mentally retarded child to continue the activity after saturation, we had to replace the black pencil with a red-blue one and replace that with a selection of colored pencils. Then the selection was replaced by a brush and paints and those were replaced by chalk and a blackboard. Ordinary chalk was replaced by colored chalk.

For the normal child, it was sufficient to change the meaning of the situation, without changing anything in it, in order to call forth a no less energetic continuation of the activity which the child had already tired of. Thus, a fair number of children who had quit work complaining of a pain in their hands or of their complete inability to draw more faces or doodles would ask to work on a little longer in order to show another child how it should be done. The sense of the situation changed for the child when he stood in the position of the experimenter or filled the role of teacher or instructor. He continued the same work, but the situation had acquired an entirely new meaning for him. Then it became possible, as our experiments revealed, to take sequentially away from the child the blackboard and the blue chalk, leaving white chalk; to exchange the white for paints; to remove the paints and replace them with colored pencils; to remove the colored pencils, replacing them with a red-blue pencil; to take that away, replacing it with an ordinary black pencil; and, finally, even to remove this last, leaving behind some poor stub of a pencil. The meaning of the situation was defined for the child by all the power of affective incentive, regardless of the fact that the situation gradually lost all of its attractive traits, traits which derived from things and from direct activity with them. This possibility of influencing the affect from above, changing the meaning of a situation, was something we were unable to achieve with mentally retarded children of the corresponding age.

Thus, we were able to show, in the first series of experiments, not only that certain possibilities of thought come up against limitations stemming from inertness in dynamic systems, but also that the fluidity of the dynamic systems themselves can be directly dependent on thought.

In the second series of experiments, we studied, as did Lewin, the tendency to return to an interrupted activity given unrelieved affective inducement. As he did, we established that this tendency appears in no less a degree among mentally retarded children than among normal ones, with this difference: For the mentally retarded child, this tendency appears, as a rule, only in a visual situation, that is, when the materials of the interrupted task lie before him. At the same time, the normal child will demonstrate the tendency regardless of the appearance of the situation and regardless of whether the materials are immediately visible.

Thus, the very possibility of remembering, imagining, thinking about the interrupted action created the possibility of saving those processes and the affective incentives linked with them. A mentally retarded child, who is directly tied to the concrete situation, appears in this experiment (in Koehler's expression) a slave to the realm of the senses. He returned to the interrupted action only when the situation impelled him, pushed him toward it, when the unfinished thing required the completion of the interrupted action from him.

Finally, in the third series of experiments, we tried to study, in both normal and mentally retarded children, the character of the substitutions in affective tendencies which occurred in response to interruptions of activities. We put the experiment together in the following fashion: As an initial activity, the children were given the task of modelling a dog out of plasticine. Then this activity was interrupted, under one circumstance, by the substitution of another task which was similar to it in meaning (i.e., drawing a dog through glass). Under another circumstance, the substituting task was linked to the initial action through the character of the activity (i.e., making rails out of plasticine for the car standing here on the table.)

The study showed an essential difference between mentally retarded and normal children in these experimental situations. For the majority of normal children, the task which was analogous by meaning (drawing the dog) appeared as a substitute action much more frequently than did the task which was analogous in the character of activity (modeling rails). Among mentally retarded children, exactly the opposite relationship appeared. The task which was analogous in meaning had practically no value as a substitute, while the task which was analogous in terms of the character of the activity, in almost all cases, revealed unity of real and substitute action.

It seems to us that all these facts, taken together, indicate that the dependence of the intellect on the affect, which Lewin determined, is only one side of the matter. Given the corresponding choice of experimental situations, the reverse dependence, that of the affect on the intellect, stands out equally sharply. As we see it, this permits us to conclude that the unity of the dynamic reasoning systems, the unity of affect and intellect, is the basic proposition on which, as on a cornerstone, study about the nature of congenital mental retardation during childhood years should be built.

The most important change to be made in Lewin's dynamic theory of mental retardation and which should be included in our hypothesis (if we want it to agree with the basic data of contemporary psychology), is to take note of the proposition cited above about the mutability of the relationship between affect and intellect. We have already spoken more than once about the fact than the affective and intellectual processes together represent a unity, but that it is not an immobile and permanent unity. It changes. And the changing relationship between affect and intellect is the very essence of the entire psychological development of a child.

As research shows, we will never be able to understand the true character of children's thought development and of children's affect if we do not pay attention to the following circumstance: During development, it is not so much the traits and structure of intellect and affect that change, as it is the relationship between them. Further, changes in intellect and affect are directly dependent on changes in their interfunctional links and relationships, and on the place they occupy in the consciousness at various stages of development.

Comparative investigations of mentally retarded and normal children show that it is worth seeing the differences between them, in the first place, not so much in the light of particularities in the intellect itself, or in the affect itself. Rather, it is worth seeing them in terms of the unique relationship which exists between these spheres of psychological life and the path of development; a relationship which shapes the relationship of the affective and intellectual processes. Thought can be a slave to the passions, their servant, but it can also be their master. As is known, those cerebral systems which are linked directly to the affective functions are arranged in an entirely unique way. They turn the brain on and off; they are at once the lowest, the earliest, and the most primary of the brain's systems and the highest, latest, and specifically human of its formations. Studying the development of a child's affective life—from its most primitive to its most complex forms—demonstrates that the transition from the lowest to the highest affective formations is directly tied to changes in the relationship between affect and intellect.

No less than the new psychology, the old psychology recognized that there was a unity of consciousness and that there were connections among all its functions. It recognized that memory was always tied to attention and to perception. And that perception, in turn, was tied to recognition and to comprehension. But the old psychology posited a single tie among the functions; the unity of consciousness, and the pre-eminence of the structure of consciousness (as a whole) over the structures of its separate functions. It posited that this tie was a constant quantity which nothing could change during the development of the individual functions and which might therefore be set apart, as a kind of general psychological multiplier, without doing any harm. It was not enlisted in those operations which investigators conducted on the remaining individual functions. This was a postulate of the old psychology in order to separate consciousness from its function and to look at functions as isolated and independent elements of the consciousness. This postulate is wholly and completely refuted by contemporary psychology, which has shown that the mutability of interfunctional ties and relationships; that the restructuring of the systems of the consciousness occurs with respect to the appearance of new interrelationships among functions; that these compose the principal content of all psychological development in both normal and abnormal children.

This is wholly relevant to the question which interests us about the relationship between affect and intellect. The change in their relationship during development is a particular case of the mutability in interfunctional ties and relationships in the system of the consciousness. Changes in that relationship are the basic and decisive fact in the whole history of a child's intellect and affect. Whoever misses that fact also misses the main, central point in the whole problem. To understand the specific nature of a mentally retarded child means first of all that we must not simply shift the center of gravity away from the intellectual deficiency to the defects in the affective sphere. We must also rise above the isolated, metaphysical study of intellect and affect as self-contained entities; we must recognize their internal linkage and unity, and free ourselves from the view that the tie between intellect and affect is the one-sided dependence of thought on feeling.

To tell the truth, to recognize that thought depends on affect is not to recognize very much: it is but to turn inside out the study of J. F. Herbart [1906?]* who inferred the nature of feeling from the laws of thought. To go further, one must do that which has always been an unchanging condition of the transition from the metaphysical to the historical study of a phenomenon: one must examine the relationship of intellect and affect, a relationship which forms the focus for all the problems which interest us, and we must examine that relationship not as an object, but as a process.

---

* The reference is assuredly to Herbart, Johann Friedrich (1776-1841), the German philosopher and psychologist known as the father of scientific pedagogy. [Ed.]

THE DIAGNOSTICS OF DEVELOPMENT AND THE

PEDOLOGICAL CLINIC FOR DIFFICULT CHILDREN[1]

1

Pedological research on unmanageable children finds itself in a peculiar situation indeed. Researchers have quickly learned how to use an overall methodology, as it has taken shape recently in our theory and practice. And they have begun to apply this methodology, not without success. As a result they have been capable of dealing successfully with a series of relatively simple, but practically important, problems which life's conditions require of pedology. This methodology quickly exhausted its possibilities, however, revealing the relatively narrow limits of its applicability. The investigators themselves unexpectedly discovered that they were drinking from a much shallower glass than they had imagined. The boundless possibilities which they had foreseen for this pedological methodology were, in practice, quickly exhausted; the methodology easily overcame the first and easiest obstacles in its path but proved powerless when confronted by more serious tasks, such as those arising from the very process of research. Thus, methodology is currently in a state of deep crisis, and its resolution should determine the next and most immediate steps in the development of pedological research into problem childhood.

If this crisis goes unresolved, then radical developments in the field of pedological research will encounter the greatest obstacle of all, that is, its practical insignificance, the limited utility of its results. But if a way out of the crisis is to be found, then the methodology of pedological research into difficult childhood must confront the enormous, historical meaning of its tasks, which is the only proper way for the methodology to correct itself. Thus, whether our methodology develops or deteriorates as it evolves on its tortuous path, depends on the resolution of the current crisis. Therefore, a correct analysis of that crisis is absolutely necessary, to clarify all the issues involved in the continued existence and development of the pedology of difficult childhood.

We will try to demonstrate, through a brief analysis, that within the crisis of our methodology itself lies the key to the possibility of resolving and responding to that crisis, as well as to the possibility of lifting pedological methodology to a higher plane and transforming it into a true means for attaining scientific knowledge about the nature and development of problem children. The essence of the crisis is as follows: The pedology of difficult childhood has reached that decisive and historical moment which occurs in the development of any science; it has reached a point where, by making an enormous leap, it can cease to be a simple, apparently scholarly, empirical field and become a truly scientific way of thinking and comprehending. The pedology of difficult childhood is now confronted with making itself into a science in the true and subtle meaning of that word. The crisis was created by the fact that, during the process of its development, this field of knowledge has confronted tasks which can be resolved only through real scientific research. Thus, resolution of this crisis means transforming the pedology of difficult childhood into a science in the literal and subtle senses of the word.

If we ask ourselves what our methodology lacks to become a real means of scholarly research, if we are willing to dig to the hidden roots of the current crisis, then we will see that those roots extend in two distinct directions. On one hand, those roots lie in the theoretical side of the pedology of difficult childhood, which is closely linked to its methodology. On the other, they also lie in the general methodology of research on normal children, which is likewise a basis for the specific methodology of difficult childhood. Let us take a look in each of these directions.

Let us begin with a brief recollection. Taken independently, it has no serious significance, but it was nonetheless the point of departure for developing the thoughts expressed in this article and can therefore serve as a concrete illustration of the issue which is central to the problem of interest to us here. A few years ago, while doing practical work, I happened to hold a pedological consultation on difficult childhood with an experienced clinical psychiatrist. The object of the consultation was an unmanageable boy of eight, just starting school. Those peculiarities of his behavior, which had already been noticed at home, became even more marked at school. According to his mother, the child had strong and unmotivated fits of temper, passion, wrath, and anger. In such a state, he could be dangerous to those around him; he might throw a stone at another child or attack someone with a knife. We questioned the mother, then let her go while we consulted with one another, and finally recalled her to convey to her the results of our consultation. "Your child," said the psychiatrist, "is epileptoid." The boy's mother became attentive and started to listen closely. "What does that mean?" she asked. "It means," the psychiatrist told her, "that the boy is irritable, wrathful, and temperamental; it means that when he is angry, he forgets himself and he can be dangerous to those around him; he might throw a stone at another child, and so forth." Disillusioned, the mother exclaimed, "But I have just told you all this myself."

To me, this was a memorable event. It forced me for the first time to think seriously about how parents and pedagogues benefit from taking a child for consultation, for a diagnosis, what they learn from the answers of specialists. One should say outright—they benefit very little, sometimes almost not at all. More often than not, the consultation restates the parents' story and observations, adding only scientific terminology, as in this case of the epileptoid child. Unless the parents or pedagogues are under the spell of scientific terms they cannot help but notice that they have, essentially, been deceived. What information they have offered has been returned to them, embellished with clever and more often than not foreign, incomprehensible terms.

Naturally, one should not fall prey to oversimplification and vulgarization because of this. Doubtless, the meaning of the term *epileptoid*, which the scholar-clinician used to describe the child, is infinitely more succinct and richer than the limited, first-hand observations and knowledge that the mother had of her child. However unsophisticated the concept may seem to us, the term *epileptoid* subsumes briefly and in generative form, many consistent traits, which in turn lead to those occurrences which the term describes. Nevertheless, the problem is not that the scientific concept was inaccessible to the mother, nor that she was inadequately prepared and knowledgeable. The problem is that the concept itself cannot solve the practical problems which the mother of an unmanageable child confronts, and which have lead her to undertake a consultation.

Dissatisfaction with a definition, presumably, can be explained. Contemporary study on psychopathological constitutions is insufficiently extensive; therefore, we must, willy-nilly, make our peace with whatever level of sophistication exists for a given problem and patiently wait until science makes significant gains in that area. One might argue that the reason for dissatisfaction lies in the fact that even that scientific content which contemporary clinicians do include in that particular concept did not reach the mother. Then, the root of the matter lies not in the concept itself, but in the inability or impossibility of transmitting that understanding to a person who is professionally unprepared. But both of these explanations, it seems to us, might be equally untrue. It seems to us that, even if the person before us had been fully and completely able to understand the entire scientific content of the given diagnosis, and even if studies about epileptoids were highly sophisticated, even then, the mother in the example I have just given would still have been basically correct. It could be that both the sophistication of a concept and the degree to which that concept is understood are essential in determining the practical successes of a given diagnosis, but that is not the end of the matter. The fact is that the researchers' ideas were not directed toward the goal; these ideas did not provide an answer to the central question, the question inherent in the situation itself, and they were unable to contribute anything beyond that which was already clear before the scientific diagnosis. Nor were they capable of providing even a grain of practical assistance to the person they were intended to help. The mother did not think of her child as ill; the psychiatrist likewise did not say that the child was ill. What the mother sought was not a medical, but a pedological diagnosis, despite the fact that she understood the word *pedology* no better than she had understood *epileptoid*. She did not know how to react to the child's explosions, how to act with him, how to get rid of those explosions, and how to make it possible for him to attend school. The diagnosis did not offer answers to any of these questions.

If we move from this specific case to the great majority of our consultations and analyze the majority of diagnoses made during those consultations, we will see that these, too, miss the point, that they make the same mistake the psychiatrist made with his diagnosis in the example. The difficulty is that the very concept of pedological diagnosis is still unclear. We expend an extraordinary amount of work on the theoretical development of pedology's problems. Many people are also working on pedology's practical contributions toward life's tasks. But nowhere, surely, is the separation of theory and practice within the same field so great as in pedology. Pedologues conduct research about children, measure their characteristics, make diagnoses and prognoses, offer prescriptions; but, it is still true that no one has attempted to define what a pedological diagnosis is, how one should be given, or even to describe what a pedological prognosis is. And instead pedology has taken the worst of directions; it has borrowed directly from other sciences, replacing a medical diagnosis with a "pedological" one. Alternatively, it has reacted purely empirically, reproducing the content of parents' complaints, in different words, as part of a diagnosis, or, at best, offering parents and pedagogues the dry data of individual, technical research methodologies (such as A. Binet's scale of mental age, etc.).

Inadequate preparation in the general field of pedology is responsible for this helplessness. In P. P. Blonskii's biting words, general pedology is still like a salad of different bits of information and knowledge; in the strictest sense of the word, it is an inadequately formulated science (Blonskii, 1925).

Blonskii's own *Pedology* (1925) has doubtless played a historical role in the development of our field. Blonskii himself claims that it helps formulate pedology as a science. Yet, he ends the work as follows, with an example of how pedology offers practical results in life: "It seems to me," he says in the conclusion, "that there is no more appropriate way to finish this book than by recounting what happened the day I finished it." He then tells how a teacher selected the three most difficult children from a beginning class in its first stages for the purposes of pedological research. "We chose these children for research and today received the first results," Blonskii tells us.

> Volodia tested out at a mental age of 5.2 years. It is hardly then surprising that our "five-year-old" cannot absorb writing or school procedures. Mitia's mother is an epileptic and he himself suffers fits. It is natural to suggest that his mirror writing is rooted in a cortical defect in the corresponding nerve centers or in those nerve paths which lead through areas affected by epilepsy. Shura's father is a hard-drinking alcoholic, that is a cyclothymic....The child has a heavy discharge from one ear and has become almost completely deaf....Thus, even the most superficial of research gave us an understanding of the children and, as a result, knowledge about their education. The pedological prescription: Volodia's intellectual education should incorporate Montessori's preschool methods, and then strenuous efforts should be made to place him in an institution with preschool-level procedures. Mitia's physical health should be improved, while avoiding those things that make him nervous, and he should be encouraged in direct writing tasks, without reprimanding him for his mirror-writing. For Shura, we hope his ear will heal and that schizoid age will lead to a mollifying his cycloid qualities and create greater equanimity; in the case of serious excitation, we prescribe calming drugs (ibid., pp. 317–318).

True, Blonskii himself notes that these are just general pedological prescriptions and that more detailed analysis will yield more detailed pedological prescriptions. But it is not the degree of detail which interests us here; rather it is the direction in which this analysis is moving. What are its components, in this instance? A mental age derived, arithmetically, through testing; facts ascertained about Shura—that his father is a hard-drinking alcoholic and cyclothymic, while his mother is an incredibly talkative, active, and vacuous woman, that is, a hypomaniacal cycloid; that the child has a chronic discharge from one ear and is almost deaf; in other words, what we have is a partially deaf hypomaniacal cycloid. It seems to us that the three diagnoses and the pedological prescriptions based upon them adequately reveal that they are, in reduced form quite like the diagnosis of the experienced psychiatrist we have described.

Thus, the first problem in identifying the crisis currently experienced by the methodology of research on difficult childhood is the lack of clarity in those basic concepts which link it to pedological research (diagnosis, prognosis, prescription, etc.). Pedology has not yet established accurately what it should study, how it should be defined, what it should be able to predict, and what advice it should be able to offer. Without clarifying these questions, which are common to all pedological research, it is impossible to transcend that pathetic and meager empiricism in which our practical methodology now wallows. But pedology will be able to answer these questions if its basic theoretical positions are carefully and consistently framed and the correct practical conclusions drawn from them.

The second problem which identifies the crisis lies, as we have said, not so much in pedological research's general methodology, as in the pedology of difficult childhood itself. The current situation in the pedology of difficult childhood recalls the state of the psychiatric discipline before E. Kraepelin—that is, before a scientific system had been established for psychiatric clinics. This historical parallel seems most instructive to us: It not only permits us to console ourselves with the knowledge that other sciences have survived situations similar to our own; it also directly indicates a solution to that situation, or, more accurately, it shows how other sciences, in their time, surmounted analogous crises; it therefore also delineates exactly the task which now faces the field of pedology.

It is a known fact that, before E. Kraepelin, psychiatry was based on external descriptions of the various manifestations of mental illness. With reference to this period in psychiatry's development, O. Bumke[2] says that psychoses were then classified strictly according to their various symptoms and external manifestations, a process analogous to using symptoms such as a cough or jaundice for the study of internal ailments. Clearly, the character of various internal disorders and their internal links could not be discovered this way. Similarly, it was useless to seek cures or prophylactics for these ailments on this basis. Kraepelin was the first to create a taxonomy of mental ailments taking into account the manifestations or symptoms of those ailments (that is to say, at least the signs and indications of those ailments behind which the real pathological process was hidden) as well as their origins, courses of development, clinical outcomes, attendant anatomical features, and other factors, which together defined the pathological processes and provided true portraits of the ailments. Thus, Bumke says that Kraepelin's classification of mental illness, after first being ridiculed and then recognized, was quickly accepted worldwide. Hardly surprisingly, this fundamental change in psychiatry's basic perspective, the move to examining the essence of diseases rather than their manifestations, coincided with establishing the very bases of scientific psychiatry. Bumke adds that we orient ourselves by Kraepelin, even when the opinion we are expressing is very different from his.

It seems worthwhile to delve deeper into this analogy. One has only to imagine psychiatry during the epoch Bumke discusses to see how closely it resembles pedology in its current state. Psychiatric diagnosis was then based on individual symptoms, and psychiatrists characterized mental illnesses under rubrics such as *hallucinations* and *deliria*, in the same way that medicine categorized disease in the pre-scientific era in terms such as *cough, headache, rheumatism*. If we imagine ourselves to be in the place of a doctor of that period, we can see that he was forced to make diagnoses similar to those a pedologue now makes. If a sick man came, complaining of a cough, the learned doctor probably gave the cough a Latin name and, with that diagnosis, let the patient go. If the patient naively asked what this learned name meant, the answer most likely repeated the same things that he had told the doctor not long before. Similarly, if a patient or his relatives told a psychiatrist that the patient heard things no one else heard or saw remarkable things in empty space, where no normal person saw anything, then the doctor characterized the illness as *hallucinations*. If asked what hallucinations meant, he probably responded: "It means the sick man hears voices, sees non-existent things."

This analogy has not only a superficial, but a much more profound, basis and unless we discover it, we will not be able to find the correct methodological solution to the questions of interest to us. We will not understand how medicine and psychiatry ceased making such diagnoses; we will not understand what we must add to contemporary pedology before it can cease making these diagnoses and begin making true ones. The essence lies, as a contemporary psychiatrist described it, in the difference between phenotypical and causal-dynamic perspectives on phenomena. According to this author, old-style botany divided plants into groups based on the shape of their leaves, flowers, and so on, in accordance with their phenotypical forms. Nevertheless, the same plants might differ widely in appearance depending on whether they grow in a mountainous area or on a plain. Yet it is frequently observed that very large differences occur in living things with identical phenotypes, based on their gender, the stage of their development, and the specific environment in which they are currently developing or in which they developed. Such observed differences have led biology to revise certain phenomenological concepts and make what might be called conditionally-genetic concepts.

Each phenomenon cannot be defined on the basis of its appearance at a given moment. Instead, it is characterized by an established group of possibilities as to its nature. Evidently, a particular phenotype arises only given a specific complex of conditions, or, one might also say, in a specific situation. Furthermore, experience has long since taught biology that two formations or processes which are phenotypically identical can be dissimilar in causal-dynamic terms (that is, in their reasons and their actions). In fact, physics and, more recently, biology have demonstrated that, on one hand, phenotypical similarities can be combined with deep causal and dynamic differences, while, on the other, strong phenotypical differences can coexist with close causal and dynamic similarities between two phenomena or processes.

Thus, we would be correct in concluding that it is not only developmental problems which push science toward the transition from phenotypical to genotypical concepts. In fact, research into causality and into real relationships of all kinds will always require movement toward the formation of corresponding concepts in biology, physics, math, history and economics. This situation is no less significant for psychology as we attempt to solve questions about what becomes apparent and what disappears, about causes, conditions, and other real relationships, mental complexes and events which seem to be inadequately differentiated on the basis of their phenomenological peculiarities. It is possible that, here, too, formations which have developed in entirely different conditions and according to entirely different rules might be closely related to one another. K. Lewin,[3] who has recently expressed this idea, offers a series of psychological examples to support it.

As long as a science has not begun to walk up this path, as long as it is immersed exclusively in research on the external manifestations of things, it will remain on the level of empirical knowledge; it cannot be a science in the real meaning of the word. Medicine suffered from this when it defined diseases by their symptoms, telling a coughing man that he had a cough and someone complaining of a headache that his head hurt. The explanation which repeated the content of the question in different words was like Moliere's doctor who explained opium's power to lull one to sleep by saying it was a soporific. We can thus see the deep methodological nature of the question introduced by our recollections above. It was not fortuitous that it was an ordinary woman who pinpointed the basic methodological flaw of an entire science, when she pointed out to her listeners that a designation does not make the external observation of some phenomenon more profound, nor can it in any way enrich or add to the knowledge of any naive observer who is watching those external manifestations closely.

The worst is that, given such a state of affairs, our knowledge not only fails to lift us to the level of a true science; it leads us, instead, directly toward false conclusions and deductions. This is because the essence of things does not directly coincide with their appearance. He who judges things only from incidental appearances judges them falsely. He will inevitably make false suppositions about the realities he studies and will give false practical instructions for influencing those realities. He who groups together all coughs or all headaches will have grouped together phenomena which have nothing in common. Such a person will have also created for himself a false notion of reality, and he will never figure out how to cure a cough. The whole point is that science studies the links, dependencies, and relationships which exist among things, and which are the basis of reality.

Let us take a simple example. Before Charles Darwin, when the phenotypical perspective held sway in biology, the whale was associated with fish rather than with other mammals—because of its external structure and because it spends its whole life in the water; that is, in terms of phenotypes, it has much more in common with a shark or a pike than with a deer or a rabbit. Nonetheless, genotypically (that is, from the point of view of its development and those real relationships which determine its lifetime's activities), the whale is a mammal, not a fish. He who perceived a fish when he looked at a whale had a basis for that conviction in observation. And while the observation was in itself correct, the observer was unable to interpret it.

When Darwin created his remarkable evolutionary theory, he created the possibility for moving from a phenotypical to a conditional-genetic perspective. What happened to biology at this point is something which every science has gone through or ought to go through. Pedology should now do the same.

We have apparently arrived at an uncomfortable conclusion—that pedology lacks a Darwin; that we must wait for our own genius before we can emerge from this crisis. Anyone who believes this is again basing his judgments on the external appearances of things; he is not looking for the profound internal foundations in analyzing the analogy we have offered above; he is sliding across the surface, and he will be as short-sighted a prophet as was W. James[4] when he pessimistically evaluated the psychology of his own time, saying that it was still waiting for a Galileo that would turn it into a science.

It is evident to the ordinary contemporary research psychologist that the essence of those things psychology studies does not correspond exactly to their phenomenological aspect. But pedology has not yet given much recognition to these ideas. To this day, pedology can often be defined as a science of symptoms.

"Apparently," says Blonskii, for example, "the qualitative growth of materials in an organism requires a series of changes in that organism, in its constitution, and in its behavior. I have called the sum of these changes an *age-related symptom-complex*. As we know, childhood can be subdivided into a number of different phases and stages. Each of these various epochs, phases, or stages is basically a particular age-related symptom-complex. Pedology studies the symptom-complexes for the various epochs, phases, and stages during childhood with attention to their chronological order and their dependance on a variety of conditions" (1925, pp. 8–9).

In these remarks, we can see a theoretical attempt being made to bolster pedological research by making symptom-complexes, grouped according to external indications, its primary object. As we have shown above, this principally phenomenological orientation will inevitably lead us to establish false relationships, to distort reality, and to orient ourselves incorrectly for action inasmuch as it identifies and judges reality and the relationships underlying reality on the basis of symptoms.

We are not prepared to say that there is no science anywhere for which symptoms are the object of the research. The object of scientific research is always that which expresses itself through symptoms. However, science itself is concerned with basically theoretical answers to questions about the real nature of objects which it studies only on the basis of their external manifestations. Nothing is clearer from the above analogy with scientific psychiatry than the fact that this, and only this, is required, and that pedology can thus become such a science before it has its own Darwin. From the historical experience of psychiatry, one can clearly see how a science can undergo the transition from empirical knowledge to real scientific knowledge without resolving the basic issues of that science at the same time—that is, without understanding the essence of the phenomena studied by that science. Whatever genius E. Kraepelin[5] had, he was not a Darwin. His contributions to psychiatry cannot be equated with evolutionary theory. He said nothing about the essence of mental illnesses, but he made this concept into an unknown, an X, while making it possible to undertake the search for this X scientifically and to begin understanding it through scientific methods. By studying Kraepelin's activities in the discipline of psychiatry, we can establish the immediate and altogether realistic program for action necessary for transforming pedological research from the empirical observation of symptoms into a scientific method for understanding reality.

The successful shift of psychiatric knowledge and thought from a phenotypical to a conditional-genetic perspective is the basis and the essence of the changes in scientific work Kraepelin introduced in psychiatry, and this shift took place without his having resolved questions about the nature of those processes which he undertook to study. Kraepelin did not attain an understanding of mental illness equivalent to conception of evolutionary theory in contemporary biology. Nevertheless, he created an entirely scientific clinical biology of mental illness. In this way, he demonstrated that, in practice, it is the method of truly scientific conceptualization itself which is essential to resolving questions about the essence and nature of those processes which the clinic examines from the vantage of evolutionary theory. It is not evolutionary theory itself, but, on the contrary, the mastery of a scientific method of conceptualization that is key to solving such questions. Thus, Kraepelin was, after all, the Darwin of contemporary psychiatry, but without contributing an "evolutionary theory."

In place of a theory which could have substituted for evolutionary theory in psychiatry, he put an X. What he did what had already been done several times in the history of scientific thought and turned out to be fundamental to solving basic methodological problems in very different areas of knowledge. To use J. W. Goethe's felicitous phrase, he [Kraepelin] turned the problem into a postulate. If, in his area, the fundamental issue of scientific research was to discover the nature, the essence, of mental illness, then Kraepelin postulated the following: The real basis of the picture that we observe clinically—a picture composed of the symptom-complex, the process and outcome of a particular illness—is precisely the essence of mental illness. Since he was unable to define the nature of that illness more precisely, he assigned it a hypothetical value. In doing this, he was doing what we do in algebra when we indicate a series of quantities by the letters X, Y, and Z Identifying these unknown quantities by letters does not hinder us from undertaking the mathematical activities (of adding, multiplying, dividing, raising them to a power, or taking a root) which is the only way to discover the value of X.

E. Kraepelin drew up a series of such equations for psychiatry. In solving those equations, clinical psychiatry in fact embarked upon a scientific path. Rather than studying symptoms, which are the external signs of phenomena, it shifted to studying the essentials of mental illness. In the process, a strict and lasting system for understanding mental illness was created which abandoned forever the classification and diagnosis of mental illness based on symptoms. Psychiatry then identified such classic forms as schizophrenia, manic depressive psychosis, and so on without yet knowing which essential processes underlay these illnesses. Nevertheless, as we have already said, it shifted to a truly scientific system of thought. It made the transition from the study of symptoms to the study of that which underlies the symptoms—in other words, from those external appearances to the study of their internal nature.

Contemporary pedology must do the same thing, if it intends to master the scientific method of thought. It must abandon the study of symptom-complexes for the study of the developmental complexes which are expressed in those symptoms. There is no reason not to suppose that the developmental processes of normal and abnormal children, or educational methods for dealing with problem children, cannot be identified in the same ways that clinicians are able to identify mental illnesses. Indeed, there is good reason to believe that children's development and their educational problems actually take a reasonably limited number of basic and significant types of forms and mechanisms. Creating pedological clinics for research on difficult children means precisely that causal-dynamic links must be distinguished empirically and theoretically, that the richness of those links must be described so as to fully convey their dependence on conditioned-genetic circumstances, on basic types, and on the forms and mechanisms of development in both normal and abnormal children.

To accomplish what Kraepelin did, in the field of pedology for difficult childhood, we must radically reexamine one of the central problems which concerns pedology—the problem of typology. We have habitually used a deductive approach in solving this problem. One takes all the forms of abnormality and educational problems, and then, one divides these into various kinds and classes using a simple scheme. For example, we learn from such typologies of problem childhood that there are normal, socially neglected, and defective children and that these last can be subdivided into children with general instability of reactions, child-cerebropaths [sic], children with inadequate sense organs and crippled children. Within these groups, the usual typology is organized purely deductively and must be based on those combinations which define the possible types of abnormal children. The usual typology can serve as an example of an acceptable classificatory scheme.

It is easy to see that the reasoning underlying such a system is extremely simple. There are good and bad environments, as well as good and bad genes; therefore, there are as many types of problem children, as there are arithmetic combinations of pairs to be derived from these four elements: good environment and poor genes, good genes and good environment, bad environment and good genes, and bad genes and bad environment. What is important is the formal emptiness, abstraction, and lack of content inherent in such a scheme. The very method used to formulate it is anti-scientific, pedantic, and in principle opposed to the methods used in creating scientific classification systems in biology and psychiatry. The scientific classification system in biology was created experimentally, not speculatively, and it was based on the evolution of types. In exactly the same way, psychiatry and, indeed, all branches of clinical medicine have never created nosological classifications based exclusively on combining all possible selections of disease-causing factors.

We must follow a new path: We must study actual realities, identify and describe different mechanisms, forms, and types of underdevelopment among children and the educational problems of such children; we must accumulate these facts, check them, and draw general theoretical conclusions; and finally, we must accustom ourselves to the fact that *retarded* as an expression means as little in contemporary pedology as *sick* means in contemporary medicine. Each of these expressions has a purely negative meaning, indicating that the individual who stands before us is developing unsatisfactorily, in one case, and, in the other, does not command perfect health.

But the task of scientific knowledge is to determine the nature of that retardation or of that illness. Just as indications of a good or bad environment fail to explain anything definite to a pedagogue in the midst of research about the real process of child development, so indications of a contaminated environment will tell a doctor nothing about the nature of an illness.

Thus, the task facing contemporary pedology is the creation of a replacement for the static, abstract structure of its typology; the creation of a dynamic typology of problem children, a typology which is based on the study of the real forms and mechanisms in child development, forms and mechanisms which are expressed as various symptom complexes. If we examine the practices of current developmental diagnostics, we can see that it in no way responds to these demands. Let us use, as an example, K. Schneider's interesting work *Collective Diagnosis*, [ref. not supplied] one of the few works dedicated to the theoretical elaboration of practical pedology's basic ideas. This author argues that "diagnosis" should be understood in a somewhat different, even a bit broader, sense in pedology than in medicine. A pediatrician or a psychoneurologist, for example, in making a diagnosis, will ascertain that there is a defect, or some kind of illness. In doing this, he usually uses the symptoms and etiological features linked to that particular illness. A pedagogue arrives at a diagnosis differently. He attempts to establish the particularities of a child's development at a specific moment. He is not interested in individual symptoms, or complexes of symptoms (syndromes); he is interested in their mutual limitations and relationships within a child's developmental mechanism as well as in the conditions determining this last. In Blonskii's phrase, he must offer the whole picture of symptom-complexes, as well as an etiological analysis.

Unquestionably, the basic task as defined by Schneider is correct. Still, if we look at the way in which pedological diagnoses are formulated in this same article, we see that we are still far from meeting the demands we ourselves are making. In working through a pedological problem, the author believes, a diagnosis represents one of the most important elements in the accumulation of scientific research material; still, he would find it possible to formulate diagnoses using the entire staff of an outpatient clinic, all of those who participated in the investigation and in the collection of final data. Schneider even refers to the resulting diagnosis as a "collective" one. In practice, at least five people participated in making Schneider's collective diagnoses: a pedagogue-pedologue, a psychoneurologist, an anthropologist, a pediatrician, and a technical secretary. In reality, at least one more person close to the child (parent, the school doctor or school pedologue) was added to the group and not infrequently, other workers from the institution, such as the pedologues studying the children, the doctors or the specialists, were also included.

But if we look at this collective diagnosis from a scientific standpoint, we see that it is not at all what we described when formulating our requirements theoretically.

Let us not discuss the first part of the analysis, called *pedological analysis*, during which the necessary materials for diagnosis are collected. Let us rather cite what the author considers to be the specific diagnosis. Schneider refers to this as "pedological synthesis". He believes that problems in intellectual-functional activity (weak attention, delayed association) are apparently found in connection with heightened nervous stimulation, on one hand, and on the other, imperfect means of analysis (weak vision, adenoids). A diminished capacity for prolonged mental effort results in weak scholastic productivity. And being raised at home (with corporal punishment, parental arguments, and abuse) impedes, rather than helps, the development of this capacity.

We have only to analyze such a diagnosis in order to see that it briefly repeats the same data which had been cited prior to factual investigation; it adds nothing new to that data, other than a problematic relationship ("evidently") and a connection between an unhelpful assertion—diminished capacity for prolonged mental effort results in weak academic productivity—and factual events. This is a diagnosis by Moliere's doctor all over again, a diagnosis which restates in different words the very phenomenon for which an explanation was requested. That kind of diagnosis is not a pedological synthesis at all, but simply a summary of pedological analysis; that is, it is simply a summary of the assembled factual material.

Thus, it is clear that the advice contained in the third part of the research contains absolutely nothing that cannot be ascertained even without pedological diagnosis. The prophylactic and therapeutic advice comes to the following: first, cure the nose (get rid of the adenoids); second, select a pair of glasses for permanent wear; third, register with a dispensary; and fourth, take a twenty-minute walk daily before bed. The sociopedological advice comes down to two recommendations: first, do not overload the patient with homework, and second, initiate individual teaching at school to develop the patient's attention and accelerate his processes of association.

And what is most remarkable about this diagnosis and its practical recommendations? There is no reference to development; there is a total absence of any theory stating the basic requirements of a pedological diagnosis. Why, all of this could as successfully be applied to an adult! There is nothing here specific to child, to any particular stage of a child's development, or consequently to pedology as a science. Apropos, A. Gesell[6] noted that developmental diagnostics is an absolutely independent scientific problem, and one which must be met by using scientific means. Gesell forces the question: On what should such developmental diagnostics focus? In his opinion, both the control and development of such diagnostics should be concentrated in the field of children's psychoneurology. And it is true that developmental diagnostics should include all the methods and principles which both normative and clinical perspectives have brought to the evaluation of developmental conditions.

As A. Gesell sees it, one of the advantages of the term *development* is that it requires us not to make any particularly sharp distinctions between the body and the mind. He correctly says that developmental diagnostics should not limit itself only to the mental side of development; it should encompass all developmental phenomena, for an ideal psychological diagnosis could never be made independently, without any relationship to supporting and supplemental data. The term *development* makes no superfluous distinctions among vegetative [autonomic], sensorimotor, and psychological development; it leads toward scientific and practical accord among all the given developmental criteria. Ideally, a full developmental diagnosis encompasses all phenomena, both psychological and social, in relation to the anatomical and physiological symptoms of that development. "It follows from this," says Gesell, "that, in the limited sense of the word, the scientific foundations of developmental diagnostics have both medical and psychological properties" (1930, p. 365).

Since psychiatry is one of the universally recognized, fundamental medical specialties, one might ask: Could one not imagine psychiatry to be defined to include the tasks and practice of developmental diagnostics? Much can be said in favor of this. "There are many reasons," Gesell continues, "for thinking that the whole area of developmental diagnostics should be closely linked with pediatrics. These reasons are not only logical, but practical, in nature" (*ibid.*, p. 366). As he acknowledges, the principal role of pediatrics, historically, has been the diagnostics and cure of illness, but the thrust of contemporary pediatrics is moving the control and prevention of illness into prominence. This new purpose is so important that it has involved not only sick, but also weak and even normal children. Indeed, this purpose is so important that it has occasionally encompassed the psychological and functional sides of development. Supervising the correct feeding of a child thus becomes the natural basis for much broader and equally prolonged control over his development.

The logical contradictions in Gesell's last statement are self-evident. He understands that the tasks of developmental diagnostics are much broader than those of pediatrics. Yet, beginning from the logical proposition that developmental diagnostics should be attached to an area of specialization already in existence, he chooses pediatrics. In doing so, he forgets that, if pediatrics becomes an organic part of a broader field, then that whole field should develop independently and scientifically—and that is what is now happening in pedology. Pediatrics should evolve as one of the pedological disciplines, disciplines which formulate diagnostics and cure illnesses, diagnose illness, and guard children's health through the general study of the laws and dynamics of their development. In this connection, Gesell exhibits a tendency which is characteristic of many researchers—the natural tendency to overstep the limits of his competence and not permit himself to acknowledge the methodological necessity of creating a new scientific discipline, namely, pedology. Like another of Moliere's characters, such authors speak in pedological prose without themselves recognizing that fact. The fact remains that a complete solution to the problems of developmental diagnostics can be attained only by means of sequential and all-encompassing solutions to its basic questions, and those are questions about the nature of and the laws governing child developmental processes.

2

What remains is for us to move on to the second major issue in this article: To provide a summary of our various research attempts which were all pervaded by the single general idea of transforming the methodology for studying development and its diagnostics from a phenotypical to a causal-dynamic perspective. The basic proposition from which we begin here is the correct interpretation of the purpose of pedological research. In our view, this purpose is to discover the internal consistencies, the internal logic, the internal links and dependencies which define the course and the structure of children's developmental processes. Until recently, as researchers, we paid much more attention to the question of the dynamics of the course and process of development than to the question of its structure. In reality, however, these are but two sides of a total entity. And not only can there be no independent solution of each, there cannot even be a proper formulation of the issues if one is considered without the other.

Gesell formulates a basic principle of developmental research absolutely correctly when he says:

> One of the highest genetic laws is as follows—all current growth is based upon that growth which took place in the past. Development is not simply a function which can be determined entirely by X units of heredity and Y units of environment. It is an historical complex, which at any stage reflects its past content. In other words, the artificial separation of heredity and environment points us in a fallacious direction; it obscures the fact that development is an uninterrupted process which feeds upon itself; that it is not a puppet which can be controlled by jerking two strings (1932, p. 218).

Elsewhere, Gesell says that the developmental stages in normal and in abnormal children flow continuously and organically from one another, as the action does in a well-ordered drama. If we want to understand the outcome, we have to sit through all the acts.

Thus, the fundamental methodological issue in pedological research is to discover the internal logic in the drama of child development, to discover the dynamic links among its various crises and events.

We will not pause for long here, on the first and fundamental stages in our refinements of a pedological methodology. We refer the reader to a series of reports and other works in which these various stages are described at appropriate points. In order that the continuity and internal logic of all these stages be intelligible, we will cite here only those principal propositions which derive from those earliest stages. Our first inferences led us to conclude that traditional research methods (such as the Binet scale, Rossolimo's profile, and others) are based on a vision of children's development that is purely quantitative. In reality, they are basically limited to characterizing a child in an exclusively negative fashion. Child development, as this method envisions it, is considered to be a purely quantitative growth process equating qualitatively homogeneous and heterogenous entities with each other and essentially confounding them at any stage of development. One year's development is always one year's development, whether one is referring to a child's movement between the sixth and seventh years or from the twelfth to the thirteenth. To Binet, this was a fundamental concept; he invariably measured a year's development using five indicators, each of which counted as an equally important quantity in determining a child's mental age, regardless of whether that age happened to occur in the twelfth or the third year of the child's life.

This represents a fundamental failure to understand the issues of development and the new qualitative forms which appear during the developmental process, and it led, above all, to mistaken approaches, even in the quantitative aspects of development. The issue of development and its chronological organization are shown here in a distorted light, because no account has been taken of that basic law, which says that the value of a month in mental development is determined by its place in the life cycle. Indeed, the opposite principle is at work here; the value of a month in mental development is determined independently of its place in the life cycle.

The assumptions are different in calculating Rossolimo profiles. In this case, a unit of memory is equated with a unit of attention, despite a qualitative uniqueness in the psychological functions. What generally results is a calculation of development whereby units of attention are added to units of memory as though they were equivalent, just as kilograms and kilometers merge into a single general sum in the head of a naive schoolchild.

Both of these conceptualizations (that is, an exclusively quantitative vision of a child's development and the negative characterization of a child) represent practical reactions to the job of purely denying and excluding children from general schools which were deemed inappropriate for them. These conceptualizations are unable to offer positive charac-terizations of certain types of children, and such methods are unable to capture the qualitative uniqueness of these children at any given stage in their development. These methods not only directly contradict contemporary scientific views on the process of child development, but they are also contradictory to the demands for the special education of abnormal children.

Contemporary scientific notions of child development are improving in two ways which seem on the surface to be self-contradictory but are, in essence, actually interdependent. On one hand, some thinking is oriented toward examining the psychological functions, clarify-ing their qualitative individuality, and establishing their relative developmental indepen-dence (such as studies of motor abilities, practical intelligence, and the like). The second trend is directed toward studying the dynamic integration of these functions, discovering the wholeness of a child's personality, and clarifying the complex structural and functional links among developments in various aspects of the personality. Child development is a single but not uniform whole; it is not a homogeneous process. The complex make-up of the developmental process does not exclude but rather envisages the primary significance of a dynamic and structural union of all sides and processes of development into a single whole.

A system for studying children which derives from these propositions, which has positive characterization as its goal, and which could serve as the basis for an educational plan should rest on three principles: First, it should separate the collection from the interpretation of facts; Second, it should specialize research methods for the various functions as much as possible (excluding only those methods of summarization which try to encompass everything); And finally, for diagnostic purposes, it should interpret the facts gathered through research both typologically and dynamically. In this respect, the contem-porary psychology of disturbed childhood can contribute not only its methodological principles, but also some important ideas about the nature of those very processes in child development which we are studying.

Let us use the problem of studying mentally retarded children as a concrete example. Here, we can cite a vast wealth of concrete data about the dynamic links and about the evolution of individual functions to which we referred above. In a report to a pedological conference, we have ourselves formulated the basic principles for a dynamic characterization of mentally retarded children. These ideas are presented in detail in our "The Fundamental Problems of Contemporary Defectology."* The complexity and lack of homogeneity attend-ing not only dynamic unification, but also substitution and the separation of primary and secondary factors—in a word, the complexity of the structures attending mental retarda-tion—have already been discussed there. Our research on deaf-mute, mentally retarded, and hysterical children (the results of which we had the opportunity to present at a psy-choneurological conference) pursued the same ideas further. We will briefly repeat the

---

* The title and the summary of the contents correspond to the introductory article of Part 1 of the present volume although Vygotsky's description here of the location of the original publication does not precisely correspond with the location supplied for the Introduction to Part 1 in the notes to the Russian Edition. [Ed.]

content of that research here. We pause for a discussion of that research, since it was the starting point for further developments on the issues which interest us here.

The fundamental proposition, which might be of methodological interest, is the following factual statement: In studying unmanageable and anomalous children, one must observe a strict distinction between developmental delays, on the one hand, and primary and secondary deviations, on the other. A fundamental result of our research was the following conclusion: For unmanageable and anomalous children, deviations and delays in intellectual and in character development are, as a rule, always linked to secondary complications; these may be complications in any one of the personality's facets or in the personality as a whole. Correctly formulating the question about the relationship between delays, on the one hand, and primary and secondary deviations, on the other, is key to both research methodologies and special educational methodologies for such children.

Our study of secondary complications in the development of anomalous and difficult children has convinced us of the existence of concrete symptom-complexes which are theoretically and practically most important; they are by nature more plastic and more dynamic, and, as a result, they can act as the basic sphere for applying therapeutic pedological measures. This research has shown that, in the presence of oligophrenia, deaf-muteness, and hysteria, developmental delays in the higher intellectual functions and in the higher character layers of the personality are secondary complications which respond to the correct therapeutic and pedological measures.

Basically, this encompasses the problem in its entirety. Obviously, no single item is the direct and definitive source of all the manifestations we encounter or of all the symptoms we identify. The relationship of symptoms to their underlying causes is an immeasurably complex one. While we might have begun by suggesting that a single defect (such as deafness or mental retardation) could lead directly to the creation of the whole known picture which characterizes a particular child's development, now we know that each symptom bears a different, very complex, relationship to its underlying cause. Symptoms cannot be deduced, without connection, from defects the way a coin can be pulled out of a change purse which contains them. All symptoms cannot be drawn up into a single line, each segment of which will bear precisely and exactly the same relationship to the cause underlying them all. To insist on such a conclusion would be to ignore the developmental process, and the picture presented by a mentally retarded child is, after all, the product of development. Therefore, that is a picture with a complex content and structure.

By way of an example, let us examine the personality structures of mentally retarded children who, according to our observations, are typical of a variety of impairments. Let us first stipulate that this example is in no way the developmental path which every mentally retarded child necessarily follows. The whole point is that linkage among the various symptoms is dynamic and that their genetic, functional, and structural ties are not formed in stereotypical ways generated by matrices. The center or basis of the entire picture should be the picture of retardation, a phenomenon still inadequately studied—the nucleus of retardation, as one might call it—in order to distinguish it from the second and third layers of complication which have overlaid it.

The first and most frequent complication to arise as a secondary symptom in cases of mental retardation is underdevelopment in the higher psychological functions (the higher forms of memory, thought, and character which are formed and arise during a child's social development). Amazingly, in this context, however, underdevelopment of the higher mental functions is not in and of itself, necessarily connected to mental retardation. But the two often occur together, because what connects them is not a mechanical, but a genetic, structural-functional link, the discovery of which would not be particularly difficult if a series of special studies were devoted to this purpose.

As research has shown, collaborative work* is one of the central factors in children's cultural development. The collective, according to new studies, emerges as the primary factor in the development of the higher psychological functions. A retarded child's intellectual level is so different from other children's that he is excluded from children's collectives. Either he develops outside a collective, or (more commonly) his developmental progress in the collective and the social side of his developmental progress are abruptly curbed, slowed down asymmetrically since progress is blocked specifically by his mental retardation. We have observed numerous retarded children who have occupied one and the same position in a certain children's collective for years on end, not participating actively in the life of the collective, and moving further away from it at every step. These conditions also govern lower forms of collaboration with other children; consequently, they impose underdevelopment in the social sides of behavior as well as underdevelopment in the higher psychological functions, which are formed as social behavior develops.

This is how underdevelopment in the higher psychological functions occurs. It is of interest because such underdevelopment is indirectly, rather than directly, linked to retardation. Thus, underdevelopment of the higher psychological functions is not a clear and direct corollary to mental retardation in a child; it is a secondary complication, the mechanism for whose development we have only schematically described here. Another remarkable fact: Where both of those factors, which we described above as fundamental to the creation of primitivism in a child, have been paralyzed from the outset by the conditions surrounding a mentally retarded person's development, secondary complications may not accompany retardation.

Even more remarkable, we have observed cases where increased cultural development in a mentally retarded child (development which clearly does not correspond to development in his primary psychological functions) has become the chief compensatory sphere, as it were, for such a child. We are inclined to believe that something of a similar nature, though asymmetrical in form, lies at the base of what is called *salon retardation*. The essential conclusion from what we have just described is this: In principle, a retarded person is capable of cultural development; in principle, he is capable of creating higher psychological functions within himself; but in practice, he is often culturally underdeveloped and lacking in those higher functions because of his unusual developmental history.

Here, anticipating our argument, we might already point out that fact which, we believe, is of central significance for the whole group of phenomena we are citing: The distinction between primary and secondary developmental delays is not only of theoretical interest. It has deep practical interest because secondary complications and delays are the more responsive to therapeutic pedagogical activity where mental retardation and the symptoms deriving from it are the direct cause and, consequently, cannot be eliminated. Incidentally, we will elsewhere discuss specifically the dialectic of influences at work in the development of abnormal children with respect to their complex personality structures. Let us now move on to examine the other syndromes which we encounter in a mentally retarded child's developmental history.

---

* An important key to Vygotsky's notion of zone of proximal development, a notion now widely discussed and reinterpreted in Western circles of psychologists and educators. [Tranl.]

Closely linked to the syndrome of underdevelopment in the higher psychological functions is an unusual group of symptoms; in the discipline of child psychology, E. Kretschmer referred to them as *primitive reactions*, and contrasted them with personality reactions. A primitive reaction is a spontaneous, affective category, one which is not mediated by a complex personality structure. In Kretschmer's terms, a primitive reaction is a reaction in which stimuli, after they are experienced, are not altogether assimilated through a fully developed personality, but are directly and reactively expressed by impulsive, instantaneous actions, or by deep psychological mechanisms, such as those of a hypobulic or hyponoetic* type. Both impulsive reactions and reactions in the hypobulic-hyponoetic layers are reactions Kretschmer found largely in primitive peoples, in children, and in animals. This is why he united them all under the label, "primitive reaction."

In educated, culturally developed adults, such primitive reactions can arise because a traumatizing influence attacks and paralyzes the higher layers of the personality. As a result of this paralysis, deeper psychogenenic layers of the mind are the ones which experience the isolated stimuli and, as if taking the place of the higher mechanisms, appear on the surface. Primitive reactions, in Kretschmer's terms, can take place under other circumstances—in infantile personalities or in retarded, weak-nerved, and weak-willed psychopaths who are suffering from alcoholic shock, cranial trauma, or hidden schizophrenia. In such people, even mild annoyances call forth primitive reactions. It is Kretschmer's opinion that a tendency to outbursts, fits of passion, sudden actions, and hysterical tension can become almost characterological stigmata for such individuals, since life's normal irritations can often provoke primitive reactions from them.

There are two remarkable factors in this description of primitive reactions. One is directly related to pedology: Primitive reactions, as we have already said, are often normal occurrences of childhood. Puberty, with its mental disequilibrium, its particularly tense affective state, is a stage especially disposed to abrupt actions. Thus, our current understanding of "primitive reaction" only makes sense if we reexamine it, bearing in mind what is normal in a child's development. The second remarkable factor is that these primitive reactions are equally frequently encountered in the development of both normal and of pathological personalities. According to Kretschmer's terms (which he also adapts to a different form of behavior, specifically to the hypobulic syndrome, which we will discuss below), this phenomenon is not something that derives from an illness, like some kind of strange swelling, nor is it something entirely unfamiliar. On the contrary, this mechanism exists within the normal organization of behavior, and illness only creates the conditions under which it becomes visible and apparent. "Thus, what we view as a kind of diseased, foreign body, as a devil or a twin to the purposeful will in hysterics," says Kretschmer, "is also to be found in the higher animals and in small children. For them, it represents their whole will. At their stage of development, it is a normal and more-or-less natural manifestation of wanting. The hypobulic type of will represents, both ontogenetically and phylogenetically, a lower stage in the will's organization. This is precisely why we refer to it as hypobulic" (1928, pp. 125–126).

In discussing the origins of the catatonic symptom complex of the hypobulic type, Kretschmer says:

---

* Hypobulia = lowered ability to act. From Gr. hypo- = under + boule = will. But see discussion which follows and Kretschmer. Hyponoetic - no definition found, but see Kretschmer. From Gr. hypo- + noesis = experience, perception. [Ed.]

In the same way, the catatonic syndrome is not a newly generated product of the disease of schizophrenia; it bears no similarity to an unusual form of swelling which appears on some part of the body where there was nothing before and where, organically speaking, nothing should be. Catatonia does not create a hypobulic complex of symptoms, it merely brings it to the surface. It takes that which is a normal and important part of the expressive psychophysical apparatus in higher living beings; detaches it from its normal ties; isolates it; confuses it; and tyrannically forces it to function with too much force and too little purpose. Since such a variety of diseases as wartime neuroses and endogenous catatonia have the same hypobulic roots, it follows that hypobulia is more than an important transitional stage in the developmental history of higher living beings, which then disappears or is replaced by the arrangement of the will. Indeed, we see that hypobulia is probably a vestige organ, the stamp of which remains, to a greater or lesser degree, even in the mental life of an adult human (ibid., pp. 126–127).

Thus we see that a genetically earlier mechanism can appear in the widest possible variety of illnesses, and that the mechanism is a normal one at certain stages of development and cannot, therefore, be understood except in the light of development. We can further see that this same mechanism, this same complex of symptoms, may consequently be a characterological stigma of a problematic or improper development. This returns us once more to the basic requirement of our methodology: To understand how a single regularity can be indicative of both the normal and the pathological state, and to conclude that development is the key to understanding disintegration, and that disintegration is, in turn, the key to understanding development. We will almost immediately return to this problem in order to complete our description of the "primitive reaction" syndrome. Let us say that it is entirely correct to understand this primitive reaction as a simple, uninhibited manifestation of a chain of powerful affective reactions (called *explosive reactions*) which respond directly through action like short circuits, when affective impulses avoid the entity of the personality. The difference here is that this chain of responses does not express itself in the form of an elementary motor response, but through more complex activity—suicide, murder, arson, and so on.

It is worth noting that, through short circuiting within these actions, part of the reaction proceeds without strong emotional pressure. Following instantaneous, undifferentiated motivation, an action is completed which cannot be explained by the personality of the actor nor by the pressures of a coercive situation. What appears in this case is nothing less than lack of inhibition of fleeting instantaneous impulses; that is, a serious isolated infraction which deviates from the traditions of the integrated personality. This kind of affectively weak, unexpected action always leads us to suspect a serious process of disintegration or disruption in the personality. Thus, we can correctly see "primitive reactions" as a symptom of inadequate development or incipient disintegration of the personality.

It is particularly easy to understand what we mean by *primitive reactions*, if we compare them with reactions of the personality. They arise under circumstances in which the personality is not fully developed or when the meet a side of the personality which is not in complete agreement with them. Such reactions are nonspecific to the personality; they can be found in any type of personality although they do distinctly characterize one specific type of personality—namely, the primitive personality.

We found similar complexes of primitive reactions especially often in mentally retarded persons, but not only in the so-called primitive, or unmanageably retarded. This syndrome can also be observed, in more or less the same degree, even among mentally retarded children who are better off in characterological terms. One can see from what we have just said that this type of reaction is not a direct consequence of retardation itself; it is one of its secondary syndromes, or perhaps it is connected at even a greater distance from first-cause syndromes. A primitive reaction is one which avoids the personality; consequently, an underdeveloped personality appears in this kind of reaction. Thus, we are correct to examine primitive reactions from a diagnostic perspective; we are there confronted with one of the distant consequences of retardation—the underdeveloped personality—and it is a consequence that has a whole series of other expressions, which are as characteristic of a retarded person. We will list some of them in order to demonstrate graphically how a particular approach can indicate links between phenomena which do not at first appear to have any direct relationship, but which, with appropriate analysis, turn out indeed to be phenomena of one and the same order.

DeGreef recently reported some extremely interesting experiments on self-evaluation by the mentally retarded. In this remarkable research, he establishes that the retarded display a particularly characteristic symptom of heightened self-esteem, which we suggest should be called the *DeGreef symptom*. The experimenter draws three circles for a retarded child. He explains that the first circle represents him (the subject in the experiment), the second his friend, and the third his teacher, and finally asks him to draw straight lines from each circle so that the longest line indicates who is the most intelligent, the second longest the second in intelligence, and so on. As a rule, the retarded child will draw the longest line for himself. This absence of a critical relationship to himself, this heightened self-esteem, is a most curious phenomenon in the developmental and structural history of a retarded individual's personality. DeGreef correctly links this phenomenon with a retarded child's underdeveloped social understanding. The researcher most wisely remarks that everything that passes the understanding of a retarded person seems to be foolishness to him. This is why he is so egocentric in evaluating his own intellect. DeGreef suggests that for someone who is severely retarded [imbecilic], genius lies within the psychological limits of retardation.

We have also often observed the existence of this symptom in the mildly mentally retarded [debiles] and particularly in the severely retarded [imbeciles]; however, we added these observations to those from a series of analogous experiments with normal children and established that the phenomenon indicated was also not the product of oligophrenia, or like some unknown "swelling." Instead, it is the simplest symptom of underdevelopment and by nature belongs to the same group of phenomena as primitive reactions do. The observed occurrence indicates the early stages in personality development, when the personality is not yet formed. This is when a child not only rates himself overly highly but also, in the comparative evaluation of others (where he is not directly involved), he exhibits egocentric and affective strivings to construct that evaluation on the basis of emotional inclinations or attitudes toward himself. We were able to show that a child values most highly those he loves, those who are closest to him, or those who please him; he cannot distinguish affective from intellectual evaluations.

Thus, the occurrence which DeGreef observed evidently has its roots in the affective character of children's evaluation and self-evaluation. Still another mechanism of symptom formation is possible in this case: There might be fictive compensation, in the shape of heightened self-esteem, as a reactive characterological formation in response to the difficulties which a child encounters in his environment, and in response to the low esteem his environment has for him. Everyone thinks him a fool; he believes himself to be smartest of all. In this respect, it seems to us that DeGreef is profoundly incorrect when he suggests, after examining the occurrences we discovered, that the presence of the given symptoms eliminates the possibility that compensatory mechanisms could work in mentally retarded children. DeGreef asserts that a retarded person is self-willed and he believes himself to be the smartest of all; consequently, he cannot feel his own diminished worth and the tendency toward compensation which arises out of it. His conclusion seems hasty to us. It is precisely on the basis of weakness, on the basis of his feelings of diminished worth, that the DeGreef symptom arises. It arises as a result of compensation, but it is the result of fictive, incorrect, and subjective compensation.

Thus, we would say that primitive reactions and the DeGreef symptom are part of the same syndrome of underdeveloped personality, but they are characteristic of it in different ways: From the negative side, primitive reactions, from the perspective of the lack of formation in the personality; from the positive side, the DeGreef syndrome, from the perspective of compensatory development in the personality.

A third syndrome also lies close to the primitive reaction syndrome, but does not merge with it. This is the syndrome of the underdeveloped will, which was beautifully described in Kretschmer's analysis of hysteria. We will call it *hypobulic* as he did, to indicate that, in its early developmental stages, it is a normal genetic stage in the formation of the will. The most remarkable thing about this early stage in volitional development is that the will and the affect are identical in primitive psychological life. Every affect is also a tendency; every tendency takes on traits of the affect. The purposeful will opposes the hypobulic mechanism, which is acknowledged in qualitatively characteristic types of the will. Thus, hysterics especially, but in general all people evincing hypobulia (Kretschmer correctly notes that hypobulia is not, pathologically speaking, a new phenomenon of hysteria, nor is it generally specific to hysteria alone) are not weak-willed, as Kretschmer himself correctly says; they are, rather, lacking in purpose. The essence of the given occurrence is lack of the higher purposeful will rather than lack of the will as a whole:

> The question has often been asked: Are hysterics weak-willed? But no answer can be reached when the question is formulated this way. The doctor says to his patient, an abasia sufferer, who is unable to stand on his feet, that he has volitional weakness. Of course, it is volitional weakness, because he could stand on his feet, if he would only force himself to. Still, isn't there strength of will hidden in this lack of desire, a stubborn and unwavering strength which many healthy, strong-willed people have never demonstrated during their whole lives? Thus, in short, such people are not weak-willed, but lacking in purpose. Weakness of purpose is the psychological essence of the condition which we call *hypobulic*. Only by separating these two volitional instances from one another can we understand what is at issue: man, unable to direct himself but not altogether without aim, uses enormous volitional strength in order to paint a picture of most pitiful lack of volition (E. Kretschmer, 1928, pp. 135–136).

Mentally retarded children very frequently display traits of a hysterical kind; they are predisposed to this by the very delays in their development. We will not discuss this in detail here. Let us only say that we have often observed hypobulic mechanisms in the behavior of the retarded, who do not carry any of the stigmata of hysteria, and this behavior shows no signs at all of hysterical fits, although it is very close to those forms of primitive volitional types displayed by normal children in early stages of development. Related to this are the appearances of negativism, stubbornness, and other hypobulic mechanisms which, as we have said, are nothing other than symptoms of children's development: rhythmic movements, storms of movement, negativism and suggestibility, and, finally, the last and most important factor, Kretschmer calls "weakening" or "disengaging" and which helps us understand the problem which interests us. The fact of this disengagement is that the different layers or functions which usually operate together begin to act in isolation, or even against one another. This occurrence has particular importance in understanding the lives of the mentally healthy or unhealthy. Although they also constitute the basis for schizophrenic disorder, these functions are also the basis in the normal human being of such activities as abstraction, concept formation, and so on. It has been established from experimental research with healthy and ill schizothymics* that there is a typological relationship between the capacity for disengagement and schizothymic-type [schizoid and schizothymic] personalities. The concepts of analysis and abstraction—fragments of concepts in the broader domain of mental phenomena—are disengagements.

Thus, we see again that the capacity for disengagement is a characteristic of the normal as well as of the unhealthy mind. In this connection, Kretschmer's idea is significant: whenever treating schizophrenia and related conditions, nature itself indicates the path for psychotherapy to us. Kretschmer suggests making use of whatever disengagements the patient has so that he internally distances those things [fantasies, daydreams] as much as possible, crystallizing them and separating them from the sphere of other activities, and begins gradually to relate to them as we do. In other words, we should reinforce disengagements psychotherapeutically, but in the particular way required to separate day-dreams from reality.

We can often again observe all these hypobulic syndromes in mentally retarded children in the form of more-or-less independent syndromes. These syndromes are to be found in a dynamic relationship with the basic defect. They appear at various stages in the development of mentally retarded children; however, as observations show, they are usually tertiary or even later complications of the basic defect.

Two remarks might bring final clarity to this question. One of these remarks particularly concerns mentally retarded children with clear signs of hysteria; what is characteristic is not a pure type of hypobulic process, but something different—a sharp break, a sharp conflict between the hypobulic and the conscious will, on one hand, and a pathological form of hypobulic reaction, on the other. In its purest form, this syndrome appears even in children who are not hysterics. The second remark deals with the fact that this syndrome, as well as the syndromes of cultural underdevelopment and delayed personality development mentioned above, are often encountered during a retarded child's development, but they are not a necessary accompaniment to that development. They might appear, or not; although they are typical of that development, they nonetheless are almost never encountered at the exact same place in the developmental process. This indicates that the character of their links to the first cause, their relative weight, their relative significance, and their role in the developmental process are never absolutely identical.

---

* Since *schizothymia* is defined as a tendency "not to be considered even potentially morbid" in *current* psychiatric usage (see English, H. and English A. V., *Comprehensive Dictionary of Psychological and Psychoanalytical Terms*, 1958, or Chaplin, J. P., *Dictionary of Psychology*, 1976), a "healthy schizothymic" is really redundant. The accuracy of the translation would have been violated but not the intended meaning had the phrase been rendered as: "...research on schizothymics and schizoids..." [Ed.]

The essence of hypobulic reactions, as we have already said, lies in volitional underdevelopment, in the immediate power of the affect on behavior, and in the fact that the volitional processes are managed not under the influence of motivation, but under the influence of irritation. Hence, the successes of primitive and essentially inappropriate educational means which (as Kretschmer correctly describes them) consist of partially physical and partially psychological stimuli. They effect, however, only the hypobulic. A method, through which we act on the will under the strained conditions of hysteria, Kretschmer suggests, can be understood rather as animal training [lit. *dressage*]. Only gradually, when the whole will begins to develop and predominate over the hypobulic will, can we move away from dressage and from physical influences to the direction of the will through motivation, to what we call education (E. Kretschmer, 1928, p. 125). Often, despairing of the possibility of convincing such a child, we try simply to coerce him; we simply want to calm him down. Kretschmer concludes that the whole will derives from motivation and the hypobulic [will] reacts to stimulation.

The difficulty in discovering this syndrome in mentally retarded children lies in the fact that the syndrome does not appear in open conflict, antagonistically to the personality, nor does it act as an entity foreign to the whole personality—like a devil or a double (which happens in hysterics). Nevertheless the essence of underdevelopment, in the will and in the earlier mechanisms which take the place of the will, remains the same.

Finally, in last place among the most frequently encountered secondary complications in the development of retarded children, we must list all the superimposed neurotic structures, for which the retarded person represents a most fertile ground. We will not now enter into a detailed analysis of these superimposed neurotic structures, since they are among the most clearly understood and studied of these related cases and symptoms. Let us only say that, in observing these superimposed neurotic structures, we are not watching the typical child neuroses or psychoneuroses in their clinical forms. We have in mind those borderline neurotic tendencies, formations, mechanisms, and dislocations which still fall within the normal range and which occur almost without fail as a result of conflicts during the development of a retarded child. First, let us note the extremely low evaluation given the child by his environment, and the objective difficulties which are unavoidable for him. And let us note that the child comes to recognize this low evaluation objectively and subjectively and that he reacts to it by developing a series of tendencies, ways of behaving, and by establishing character traits which are clearly neurotic. In addition to this, the very fact of underdevelopment is a stimulus to develop internal conflicts which are at the basis of superimposed neurotic structures. Superimposed neurotic structures also often act as a stimulus in amassing, organizing, using, and directing other syndromes in the underdevelopment of the child. They all act, as it were, in the service of neurotic tendencies which are driven by them.

Briefly, such is the structure of the personality of a retarded child. We shall not at this point introduce conclusions from our analysis. Let us say only that our research shows without a doubt how complex the structure of mental retardation is and how necessary clinical study is.

3

For greater clarity, we should also like to indicate that analogous changes are currently taking place in psychiatry, and particularly in the psychopathology of the childhood years. Here, we see the attempt to move from clinical classification, from static construction to a dynamic one, to examining the formation of a pathological character during the developmental process. As an example, we cite G. E. Sukhareva's[7] research, "On the problem of the structure and dynamics of constitutional psychopathy in children (schizoid forms)" (1930), which was presented at a conference on human behavior.[8] The structural-analytic orientation occupies a visible place within the contemporary currents in psychiatry. The problem of delineating diagnostics with multiple measures, of differentiating primary, secondary, and other levels within diagnostics—all this is a specific step in the development of psychiatric thought. The new directions in psychiatry have also influenced teaching about psychopathy . A number of authors, with a variety of perspectives, have voiced questions about the need to replace the clinical-descriptive method of studying psychopathy with a structural-analytic one, the final goal of which would be to analyze profound links and relationships between the separate components of the psyche (the construction of the architectonics of personality, according to K. Birnbaum) [no ref.].

Sukhareva makes an attempt in her research to approach the study of child psychopathy methodologically in a way that differs from past procedures at the clinic (of which the present author is a member). "If, in a series of works on child material," Sukhareva says, "we have previously made it our goal to delineate a nosology of separate and relatively distinct forms of child psychopathy, to describe the somatic syndromes which characterize them, and thus to approach the question of their biological underpinnings, we are undertaking a different task in our present work. Now, on the basis of our clinical material, we seek to analyze the dynamics of various forms of children's constitutional psychopathy and to follow how the unfolding psychopathological picture changes in relation to a child's age and the sociocultural and life-situational factors of his surroundings" (1930, pp. 64–65).

A dynamic approach to the study of psychopathy inevitably opens up another side to these problems, namely the structure of the individual psychopathic forms. And here, there is a direct similarity with our experiences on the pedological side, namely, the complexity of the structures which interest us. This complexity is a direct result of that which psychopathy itself is examining as a dynamic whole, namely development. Sukhareva says:

> Above all, the complexity of these structures drew our attention. In analyzing the development of the psychopathological picture in each individual psychopathic case, we could not fail to notice how uneven our knowledge is of the pathogenesis and original mechanisms of individual symptoms. In addition to those symptoms which were specific, and basic to a given form of psychopathy and direct expressions of biological shortcomings, we noticed a series of additional symptoms. Formed secondarily and reactively, these symptoms must be looked at as an adaptation of the whole remaining personality to a given inadequacy; they are the result of actions by various compensatory mechanisms which adapt the personality in question to a particular shortcoming in a given life situation. Only the general direction of development in these compensatory mechanisms, only the path which reactions must follow, depends on the personal predisposition of a particular subject. The content and form of the reaction are significantly limited by external factors: the environment, education, the level of development, the given life situation, and so on. From this constant combining

of endogenous and exogenous, of constitution and constellation, from the combination of basic primary symptoms with secondary reactive layers, we get the very
complex structure of a psychopathological picture for each separate case. To separate
the primary basic symptoms from the additional secondary and reactive formations
is the basic task of all structural analysis (ibid., p. 65).

The amazing coincidence which we have been able to demonstrate between the results
of our research, as cited above, and the directions in which contemporary analysis in
psychopathy are moving have not come about by chance. They have been conditioned by
two factors: First, the same findings about psychopathy, especially about childhood psychopathy, is appearing in pedology—that is, pedology is beginning to examine the problem of
character, dynamically, in development. The second factor is that psychopathy, in and of
itself, is evidently very close to what we call *defects* from a developmental perspective. The
basis of a psychopathy lies not in an unhealthy process, but in a somewhat limited condition,
an anomalous variant of personality, or, more correctly, in some inadequacy, some shortfall
in the characterological substrata of the personality. It is therefore not surprising that the
developmental dynamics of a child with such an inadequacy coincides in some basic fashion
with the developmental dynamics of a child burdened with a defect. We see this coincidence
as one of the most powerful indicators that our research is generally methodologically
correct.

To return to Sukhareva's work, it should be said that the earliest symptom of schizoid
psychopathy is psychomotor disorder. Other disorders appear later. Still later there appear
peculiarities in the area of inclinations and emotional reactions, which are characteristic of
schizoids. Less common, but still encountered in pre-school years, are portions of psychasthenic behavioral elements and weak capacity to express emotional experiences. Remark-
ably, the characteristic peculiarity for this childhood period—asking questions—is often
taken as a kind of obsession in schizoid children. This is because this normal symptom of
development is so emphasized by the general course along which a child's psychopathic
personality unfolds.

Sukhareva notes that the:

> The school years, the beginning of study, and life in the collective, are all intense
> stimuli [irritations] for the schizoid, leading to the further unfolding of the clinical
> picture with all its additional layers. Here the peculiarities in a schizoid's social
> position begin to appear. In preschoolers, autism is not yet sharply defined. If there
> are elements of quarrelsomeness or lack of sociability, one still need not refer to real
> secretiveness or reserve. The development of these traits must be seen as further
> changes in the schizoid personality, as reactions to inadequate adaptation to the social
> environment (ibid., p. 67).

Traumatization stemming from contact with children's collectives, with ridicule, and
with comrades' jokes result in greater reserve and withdrawal from the collective. The
following symptoms appear at school in this connection: hebephrenic behavior, affectation,
grimacing, and an inclination for silliness and absurd games.

> "The appearance of such traits in school," says Sukhareva, "can be examined not only
> as a particular age-related phase in the appearance of schizoid features, but also as a
> specific reaction in adapting to a school environment, where the schizoid is not

acknowledged and where the most convenient position—that of buffoon—is allotted to him. A series of new symptoms appear in the school years which are the product of constant interaction between the constitutional peculiarities and the specific environment and its irritations. Let us pause only to discuss those two which appear most frequently in our material: the psychasthenic and the paranoid. The psychasthenic syndrome is most frequently encountered in reaction to poor adaptation to the demands of a surrounding school environment and in one particular kind of schizoid—one who is mild, pliable, and has diminished vitality. Reserved treatment by collective and continual ridicule create a feeling of inferiority, fear before one's stronger comrades, timidity, indecisiveness, an asthenic position with respect to the surroundings. As proof of the reactive nature of this syndrome, we cite our cases in which the syndrome becomes discontinuous and disappears with a change in situation. The role of reaction is even clearer in the formation of the paranoid syndrome. The most fertile soil for its appearance is when the schizoid—emotionally cold, asthenic, with a heightened evaluation of himself and heightened egotism—encounters conditions that wound his self-love. A consistent desire to shine, to be better than others, given his awareness of his own unworthiness, creates a disturbing emotional backdrop, suspicion, and an insecure attitude to his surroundings. This paranoid syndrome is, at an earlier age, less noticeable and becomes more prominent with the parallel growth of the personality.

New changes in the personality development of a child of this type are linked to the onset of puberty" (ibid., pp. 68–69).

We will not repeat here the complications linked to the period of sexual maturation in children of this type. Let us simply say that these complications bear traits of developmental symptoms and that, as the material shows, after puberty many of the psychopathic peculiarities abate. Adolescents are quieter and have more equanimity. In other words, we could say, that the catamnestic [or historical follow-up] material we have gathered allows us to offer a satisfying prognosis (for our cases of schizoid psychopathy), not only with respect to the influence which rehabilitative-pedagogical actions have on them, but also with respect to their future chances. Those symptoms which are closest of all to the biological roots are the primary basis of unhealthy predispositions and these are related to the number of early symptoms. The older the child, the more differentiated his psyche, the more complex and richer the symptomatology of his schizoid psychopathy, and the more room is occupied in his clinical picture by secondary, reactive, and compensatory formations. An analysis of schizoid psychopathy has permitted us to separate the primary basic symptoms from the complex picture. It can be reduced to three types of symptoms: psychomotor perturbation, perturbation of inclinations and emotional reactions, and peculiarities in associative work and thought. These basic symptoms are the direct expressions of the biological insufficiencies of a schizoid. The roots of inadequacy, its biological underpinnings, should be sought in the innate shortcomings of specific (extrapyramidal) cerebral systems and in some kind of anomaly in the endocrine apparatus.

It is worth noting the amazing coincidence between development in the doctrines concerning psychopathy and doctrines about the abnormal child in general. Evidently, questions in psychopathy are decided in the process of studying the development of children with innate shortcomings in specific cerebral systems, with unique inadequacies, and these are part of the overall teaching on abnormal child development, the overall teaching on borderline conditions and transitional forms between illness and normality. It is therefore not surprising that basically the same regularities of movement and personality structure for children can be observed in oligophrenia and as well as in psychopathy. It remains for us to turn our attention to the second side of the problem, namely to the link which exists between additional reactive formations and the basic symptoms of underdevelopment.

Let us return to Sukhareva's research. The question raised is whether there is some kind of connection between reactions and the constitutional background against which they arise, and whether it is possible to identify some kind of lawful regularity in the various complex characterological structures. "On the basis of our data," says the author, " we can answer in the affirmative" (1930, p. 71). The conclusion from this research is of particular interest. It seems that the schizoid mind is more vulnerable to specific perturbations:

> The factors which belong to this group are connected with wounding the patient's self-esteem. His "id" also leads him somehow to conflicting experiences as does a strict education with its continual constraints and grievances or any difficult life situations which can wound the self-esteem and generate a feeling of his own insufficient worth. We have not infrequently noted the traumatizing role of family quarrels in the personal history of our patients: parental discord, quarrels because of the child, enforced separation from one of them, jealousy toward another family member. (It is interesting to note that such factors as material insufficiencies, weak supervision, and ties to the street play a much less significant role, since in a group of schizoids the psychopathy of that factor plays the primary role in the development of reactive conditions.) (ibid., pp. 72–73).

The selectivity of a schizoid's mind is expressed not only by the choice of stimulants, but also by its particular response to dangerous external factors.

> The most common form of reaction in our material was various neurotic conditions (we observed them in one-third of all of our cases). One might think that the frequency of this reaction in schizoids was hardly accidental, since the schizoid mind (with its personal traits and inclinations, its absence of any unity of experience and weak reactions) offers a series of pre-prepared mechanisms for their creation. (ibid., p. 73).

These neurotic conditions are extremely varied and include a series of symptoms ranging from the mildest (such as excitability, dream disturbances and nightmares) to hysterical reactions and the most severe symptoms of the conditions discussed above.

> Another frequent form of schizoid reaction to external dangers is a variety of characterological dislocations, prolonged psychogenic character changes. In studying these characterological dislocations, the following fact drew our attention: There is no sharp distinction here between psychopathic reactions and psychopathic conditions, because to the strongest stimuli the schizoid mind responds with the strongest reactions, which in many cases are already irreversible. As a consequence, the whole structural plan of the personality is changed and, unlike other acute and reversible conditions, the resulting picture can be characterized as a pathological personality development. In our cases, this pathological personality development followed two directions: First, it sharpened of the basic traits of the schizoid mind; second, it manifested new symptoms which are not specific to any constitutional type.[*]

---

[*] Because of some possible typographical errors in the Russian text, it is not clear whether the quotation from Sukhareva ends here or at the end of the section. [Ed.]

Vulgarity, bitterness, brutality, and mistrust are some of these symptoms... It is not difficult to explain the mechanism which creates these changes. Grave external conditions set the schizoid at odds with his surroundings; he becomes mistrustful and bitter; without the possibility of confirming his "id" in a corresponding fashion, he often acts paralogically, enhancing all of his negative traits, often intentionally acting rude and vulgar. Schizoid psychopaths who have spent several years in children's homes are in poor shape and offer a characteristic image of such a pathological personality development. They are more brutal, vulgar, and negative. The general emotional background is more gloomy; one observes paranoid syndromes more frequently among them, than among other schizoids....

One can conclude from the above structural analysis of schizoid psychopathy that external factors can modify the development of a schizoid's character. The clinical picture of schizoid psychopathy is not a stable one and, during a subject's life, a series of oscillations can occur, influenced, from side or another, by his environment and his experiences. The basic directions of these swings, that is, the direction of his reactions, are to be found in the limits of the particular constitution.

Conclusions

1. Schizoid psychopathic development should not be regarded as the passive unfolding of a genetically created inadequacy. It is a dynamic occurrence, a process of adaptation between the given personality and its surroundings.
2. The basic symptoms of schizoid psychopathy appear even in early childhood. Its symptomatological development is often uneven and undergoes many jolts and dislocations as a result of exogenous factors.
3. Two series of symptoms should be distinguished in the picture of schizoid psychopathy: (a) the basic and primary symptoms, which are direct psychological manifestations of biological inadequacies; and (b) secondary symptoms in the shape of various reactive conditions and characterological dislocations which are the result of complex interaction between exogenous and endogenous factors (ibid., pp. 73–74).

Enough emerges from this research to show that its basic results coincide with those we described previously. Their essence can be said to illustrate the complexity of the structures of mental retardation or children's psychopathy. The heterogeneity of its various factors and of its developmental dynamics gives us the key to understanding these structures. It is true that it is often quite difficult to resolve questions about the origins of one or another syndrome. But in the world of contemporary research there can be no doubt that the development of a child-psychopath or a mentally retarded child is not merely the passive unfolding of specific traits which have been there from the beginning; it is a development in the real sense of the word—that is, it includes a series of new formations.

4

We need only to indicate the practical meaning of such analysis. It might seem a dangerous enterprise, this desire on the part of researchers to separate primary syndromes from secondary ones, to find the ties that link them, to discover the mechanisms of symptom-formation. What difference does it make to which complex a symptom belongs to? Of what importance is it whether a complex is of secondary or tertiary formation? In fact, all of this is far from unimportant in pedagogical and therapeutic practice. The lamentably poor state of contemporary curative pedagogy can in large part be explained by the fact that pedology did not undertake scientific evaluation of the very occurrences which it was called upon to change and to correct. In this respect, it seems to us that a new chapter in the study of abnormal children's development might open up new practical horizons.

Let us begin with the simplest of observations. Clearly enough, the actual defects and developmental delays underlying oligophrenia are insurmountable, given our current abilities. It is also true that fatalistic views, which argue that this task will never be resolved, cannot withstand criticism, and, above all, not factual criticism. Even now, we know that new ideas are being put forward about a whole group of oligophrenics, the so-called *archicapillary* forms of retardation; a new constitutional-causal therapeutic practice is taking shape, which is capable of removing the cause of developmental delays and which can radically alter a condition. The enormous significance of research by E. R. Jaensch* and the scholars around him lies not only in the kind of practical use it offers. It also lies in what was accomplished at the same time, a change in principle which pointed to the possibilities of constitutional-causal treatment in cases of children's underdevelopment. In practice, however, hardly anything has been changed at all by this research. Until now, the handicap and the symptoms which stem directly from it have been the most resistant, the least pliant, and the least susceptible to educational and therapeutic influences.

The further a symptom is from the primary cause, the more responsive it is to educational and therapeutic influences. At first, this conclusion appears paradoxical: Underdevelopment in the higher psychological functions and in the higher characterological formations is a secondary complication in oligophrenics and psychopaths. In fact, it is less resistant, and more susceptible to influences and more easily eliminated than underdevelopment in the lower, or elementary, processes which are caused directly by the handicap itself. In principle, something arising as a secondary formation during a child's development can be foreseen and counteracted, or can be eliminated curatively and pedagogically.

Thus, the higher [functions] are the more easily influenced. By the way, there is certainly nothing surprising in this superficially paradoxical situation. In fact, it repeats in a new form something that has been known for a long time: The more elementary and, consequently, the more directly, biologically, limited a function is, the more it eludes the educational influences intended to direct it. An example to clarify this notion: We could refer to all the zealous research which has recently been undertaken on identical and fraternal twins. Let us cite S. Lewenstein's [no ref.] research. A basic conclusion can be drawn from this research: The more independent a psychophysical reaction is from volitional influence and the more that reaction acts on the sympathetic and parasympathetic systems, the more similar that reaction in identical twins and the less susceptible it is to educational influence. The opposite is also true: The more our psychomotor reactions remain outside those systems and the less they depend on heredity, the more responsive an object they are for therapeutic and pedagogical influences.

Applied to normal pedagogy, this means that, although identifiable basic motor characteristics are inherited, the degree of motor control depends on education. In particular, research into the educability of abnormal children allows the author to reach a conclusion about the effect of training on hysterical reactions: Hysterical reactions are rewarding objects

---

* E. R. Jaensch (1883-1940), a German psychologist known best for his work on perception. [Ed.]

for rehabilitation; further, the earlier retraining begins, the less frequently those reactions will be forced into a particular pattern by the laws of psychophysical habit.

The overall results of other research on twins demonstrate the following: The further down the path of development a particular function or formation stands, the more receptive it is to education and retraining. In particular, Lewenstein has contributed a great deal to experimental analysis of the educability for various symptoms and sides of an abnormal child's development. He was able to show that, here, too, the law of relative maximal educability (of the higher functions as compared to the lower ones) is fully applicable to abnormal children. Lewenstein correctly cites G. Revesz's [no ref.][*] who, at the Third Congress on Therapeutic Pedagogy, indicated that, thanks to Kretschmer's work on biological types, pedagogy was not only launched in a new direction but it had also recognized the limits of its influence, and that as long as we are forced to acknowledge the limits subsumed within a type, we are protected from baseless pessimism, as well as from excessive optimism.

S. Lewenstein shows that questions about the boundaries of educability cannot be solved in a continuous, mass, homogeneous fashion for all functions or for all sides of the personality; he shows that the problem must be differentiated for the various aspects of personality and that biological types do not contain omnidirectional metaphysical boundaries with respect to development and educability. Therefore, rehabilitational pedagogical work, as it exists within traditional pedagogy, is being radically changed and restructured in the light of new work about abnormal children's development. The old pedagogy's basic dogma in educating abnormal children was education of the lowest biological functions: training the eyes, ears, and nose to distinguish smells, sounds, and colors, and developing sensorimotor skills. Each child continued in this training for about a decade. Not surprisingly, the results were always pathetic since the training followed the avenue least likely to succeed. The focus of all educational work lay on the least educable function. Where those functions did respond to pedagogical activity, contemporary research shows that this was happening despite the intentions and interpretations of the pedagogues themselves, since development in the elementary functions takes place at the expense of development of the higher psychological functions. A child learns to distinguish colors, sounds, and smells better not because his hearing and sense of smell are refined, but because of development in his thought, purposeful attention, and other higher psychological functions. Thus, the standard orientation of the whole special section of traditional therapeutic pedagogy had to be turned 180 degrees; its center of gravity had to be moved from educating the lowest to educating the highest psychological functions.

Discovering these general indications did not terminate research. We must go further and ask ourselves: If personality structure in an abnormal child is so heterogeneous and so complex, where are the weakest and most pliable points in that structure, the points which education should attack first? If the chain of mental retardation is made up of links which are heterogeneous in terms of development and resistance, then where is the weakest link in this chain at which it can be broken? The answer to this question brings us once again to the fundamental problem in psychotherapy and in therapeutic pedagogy. Secondary formations are the weakest links in the chain, and they respond first to intervention.

As a general rule, one could say that the further a syndrome stands (in terms of its formation and the place it occupies in the structure) from the primary cause, from the

---

[*] Revsz, G. A psychologist best known for his contributions to the theory of language functioning. See his *Ursprung und Vorgeschichte der Sprache.* Bern: A. Francke, 1946. [Ed]

handicap itself, the easier it will be to eliminate it by psychotherapeutic and curative-educational means, all other things being equal. Let us give some examples. Until recently, it was believed that psychotherapeutic influences acted only on psychogenic illnesses. This is indeed true if one defines treatment in terms of causal therapy alone; that is, therapy that eliminates the cause of the illness. In this case, it is clear that causal psychotherapy (that is, treatment which eliminates the cause of the illness) is possible only where the reason for the illness is a psychological formation. Then, a psychoneurosis or a psychogenic reactive condition can be cured only psychotherapeutically, but delirium in a typhoid patient or disordered thinking in aphasia cannot, of course, be cured by psychotherapeutic methods.

At the basis of this outlook lies the mistaken idea that all therapy must necessarily be causal therapy, and that other forms of treatment (such as symptomatic treatment or treatments which arouse and strengthen the organism itself to combat disease) must be altogether abandoned. In fact, this is not the case in the theory and practice of contemporary medicine; still less is it the case in education. Here, in the problem of development, the dynamic coupling of causes acquires greatest significance; cause is so far distant from its after-effects and so different from them that applying this idea of rehabilitation therapy to therapeutic pedagogy deprives it of at least nine tenths of the areas in which it can be successfully applied.

Recently, Kretschmer wrote an outstanding article devoted to the problem of therapy for schizophrenia and borderline conditions. Parenthetically, the modernity of this remarkable psychopathologist is clearly visible in the two different courses his work takes. One direction consists of statistical and constitutional research and the other is concerned with developmental dynamics for understanding and studying psychopathological conditions. We think that we, too, should quickly make use of these two directions in Kretschmer's work. Of particular interest to us is the methodological basis of the psychotherapeutic system which Kretschmer selects for schizophrenia. Such psychotherapy must develop from the following fact: One of the basic causes of this group of illnesses lies in hereditary pre-dispositions. The course of the illness entails bodily changes, and can lead to death. In severe cases it leads to prolonged handicaps which do not respond even to the strongest efforts of psychotherapy. To deny this is to be sacrificed to uncritical psychotherapeutic optimism. The broad basis of schizophrenia can only be overcome by therapy which is applied to the constitution of the patient. In principle, this is entirely possible, since the constitution is not a given, but a biological power struggle in which one can participate if one knows its internal dynamic. Even its endogenous character is not a given, but anti-biological fatalism has paralyzed psychotherapeutic thought for many years. This prevented anyone's exhausting the possibilities of psychotherapy and forced them to perceive organic handicaps where there were psychogenic arabesques, which had grown up in the soil of scant process.

The contributions of E. Bleuler[9] and K. G. Jung[10] lie in their recognition of this complex psychological reactive structure built on top of the organic symptoms of schizophrenia. But does it follow from the recognition of schizophrenia's organic causes that psychotherapeutic influences can have no significance for this illness? That is how we used to think, but it is an altogether false and scientifically unsupported opinion. We should not idly stand by, feeling sorry for schizophrenics. Rather, we must change our approach sharply and, on the basis of the given condition, immediately construct something new, because what interests us most in practice is not endogenous damage, but social manifestation of the disease. Even while involved with the problem of therapy for people with schizoid tendencies, Kretschmer notes that typical developmental delays were to be observed during sexual maturation. Delays took place here during the normal protest phase, which everyone experiences.

We will not dwell here on the wealth of factors which unfold in the context of this problem. Let us note only a single factor which is particularly interesting to us. While evaluating the possibility that schizophrenia is psychogenic, Kretschmer points out that, during the war, when hordes of hysterics descended on hospitals, there were no schizophrenics among them. In Kretschmer's opinion, this statistical observation shows which psychological stimuli provoke the schizophrenic process. Many life-threatening situations and vital emotions (fright, fear of one's life, hunger, cold, thirst, pain) do not in this respect appear particularly dangerous. Schizophrenics are surprisingly unreceptive to this whole scale of feelings. During the war, a number of authors observed the stony calm under gunfire of those in the first stages of schizophrenia. If life's basic emotions played any kind of significant role in schizophrenia, the statistical result mentioned above would be impossible. Different groups of affects—erotic and religious in nature—play a larger role in the structure and content of this disease. Here, there is room from the mutual interplay of endogenous and psychogenic factors; here again, we come up against the question and problems of a multi-variable diagnostic. Such a multi-variable diagnostic lead us to reaffirm the multi-layered and heterogeneous, rather than homogeneous, nature of personality development, despite health, illness, or current condition.

S. Lewenstein demonstrated the following propositions experimentally. In his opinion, there were schizophrenics who were receptive to treatment, and those who were not. Those who were susceptible manifested additional characteristics, in psychological experiments, which were similar to hysteria. On the basis of his own [clinical] experience, E. Kretschmer confirms the first half of this thesis; when schizophrenia is accompanied by a neurosis-resembling superstructure, it has much broader therapeutic chances. We should note that G. E. Sukhareva's material says that the construction of neuroses in schizoids is often a lengthy process, manifesting a tendency to become fixed and to respond poorly to therapeutic influences. It seems to us that we must understand this in relative terms: that is, in comparison with the formation of neuroses in normal, or at least non-psychopathic, personalities. If one compares these formations with pure cases of schizophrenia, one can quickly be convinced of a paradoxical fact—patients with additional manifestations are more susceptible to therapeutic influences. It is interesting that schizophrenics do not see sick persons as an exception to the general rule; they relate identically to an ill and to a healthy child. "It should be said," Sukhareva notes, "that among the severe forms of schizoid psychopathy with low productivity and with many neurotic superstructures, there are cases which, given the current state of our knowledge, cannot be differentiated from mild, slowly progressing schizophrenia." (1930, p. 70). Here, what interests us is not the evaluation of our knowledge of this issue, but something much more profound, namely, the recognition that we should reject, in principle, any difference between the development of healthy, psychopathic, and ill children.

But what is most significant follows. Lewenstein is correct only in the first half of his thesis that patients with additional hysterical superstructures are more receptive to treatment. Although, as Kretschmer says, even endogenous schizophrenia is often receptive to therapeutic activity, organic process in the nervous system resists psychotherapy as long as it retains remnants of functions. This is confirmed by experience with work therapy in hospitals. Let us imagine, by analogy, that, during an earthquake, the underground tremors disturb some kind of complex building. In such a case, disintegration will follow the lines of the building's construction, its internal design, even though the process of destruction itself was initiated by an external cause which had nothing to do with the building's design. The same is true of the personality. Even if schizophrenia is induced by organic causes, in-so-far as the personality and the mind disintegrate in its presence, such disintegration should be studied according to psychological laws, in-as-much as both the personality and the mind were formed according to those laws. And because the organic process creates the possibilities of development and functioning in the psychological processes, they underlie psychotherapeutic and curative-pedagogical influences and directions.

One might ask: Exactly what should we expose to this influence? Besides psychomotor orthopedics, personality construction, encapsulating the formation of individual delusions, regulating experiences, and disengaging autistic and realistic tendencies, we should concern ourselves, as Kretschmer indicates, with treating the residue of pathological experiences and formation of delusions, as well as with teaching speech and social behavior. Incontestably, this is the direction which a psychotherapist's work should take. This consists not in eliminating causes, but in struggling with results. The ability to find the weak link, the one which is receptive to influence, is the main basis of all psychotherapy and all therapeutic pedagogy. In the same way as symptomatic, reenforcing, and compensating treatment are possible, all possible kinds of therapeutic education are possible. One can struggle with personality disintegration not only by eliminating the reasons for it, but by actively building the personality, establishing its unity, aiding its struggle against disintegration, stimulating its development, and so on.

E. Kretschmer concludes by asking himself a question: To what purpose do we treat schizophrenics? What are the possibilities that lead us in this direction? The question as to whether something positive can be created from the ruins is answered by the researcher in two ways.

> One of the basic goals of contemporary psychotherapy is clear: It can create a useful, working, machine from all this chaos and from the disruption of negativism, auto-matism, and capricious ideas. With a psychotherapy that gives brilliant results, we can make use of the tendencies toward psychomotor automatization that are found in schizophrenia, and through carefully considered education, we can create useful stereotypes, working stereotypes[*] from the useless ones. This decision is a logical, consistent, and clear idea. Anyone who has personally arrived at it in a big hospital might say that there is something gratifying in this strict march of schizophrenic labor battalions. It has style. Also, work therapy is, in simple situations, an irreplaceable means of reviving whatever health remains—and this applies to hysterics as well as to all kinds of neurotics. Without the positive strength of purposeful work, their personality loses its solid basis. Furthermore, embedded in a schizophrenic's logic is not only the inclination of a stereotypical working machine, but its exact opposite— the vision of an autism which understands everything, for which there can be no judgments by others; the contemplative vision of an Indian mystic, far from bustle and labor. And inasmuch as contemporary life minimizes all that is original—and all schizophrenics certainly hold that standard high—what appears before us is another view of psychopathic schizophrenia. If we make useful working machines from the mass of average schizophrenics, then from the few, the best of them, we will create originals, true mystics. The task of re-creating a personality in post-schizophrenics— not by blandly copying normal people, but by creating a specifically schizophrenic

---

[*] Perhaps the term is intended to mean "string of automated behavior." One meaning of the French *stéréotypie* is "motor tic." [Ed]

personality with all the spiritual nuances of that type—is an extremely difficult one. It repays the doctor's lost capital only in the best of cases, but then it repays him fully, since among schizophrenics, as among other people, the wise are a tiny minority [E. Kretschmer, 1928? 1932?]

It is not Kretschmer's separation of the two visions—the spiritual personality and the working machine—which is remarkable here, but the general methodological suggestion that nature has included, even in the sickest and most pathological personalities, a basis, a type, which will guide their further development and education. In this sense, to move from the pathological to the normal is not to cross an impenetrable boundary.

To conclude the theoretical side of the question at hand, we must finally discuss that point for which the whole course of the preceding exposition has been a preparation. In everything we have considered above the following is the most important and essential: The investigator must not only penetrate the dead structure of the various syndromes but above all, he must understand the dynamics of their linkages, their ties, and their interdependence, their relationships. Only those who master the internal dynamics of the process can hold the key to resolving the issue of education for abnormal children in a practical fashion. To decipher the ties and the dynamic, dependent, relationships which underlie the complex structure of an abnormal child's personality is to understand the internal logic of that structure.

Kretschmer's comments on schizophrenia are remarkable in this respect. K. Jaspers,[11] Gruhle,* and others, he says, erred in designating the absence of affect as the principal criterion of a schizophrenic's psychological life. The behavior of schizophrenics seems as senseless as Egyptian hieroglyphics, until it is deciphered. Together with Blueler, one must master the jargon and translate it into German.** Then, one can discover intelligible links and complex influences (which are often not very different from the corresponding formations in neurotics). And this can be applied wholly to any development in an abnormal child. There, the ability to intervene, to decipher hieroglyphics, is a basic requirement; with it, a researcher can uncover an intelligible picture of the child's personality and behavior. Without it, access to research about such children and the influences on them is forever closed.

In C. S. Lashley's[12] wonderful phrase, one of the basic proofs of the non-mechanical and non-atomistic activities of our nervous system is the observance of intelligibility, linkages, and structure in personality behavior even in the pathological breach. In the cerebral system, in his opinion, the unity of activities evidently lies even deeper than structured organization. In working with animals and with sick people, he was more and more surprised by the absence of chaotic behavior, which might have been expected given the size and form of the lesions. Major attacks on sensory and motor abilities, amnesia, emotional defects, and dementia were all observed, and under all these conditions, the remaining behaviors were produced in an orderly fashion. The resulting behavior might be fantastic, or it might be a caricature, but it was not altogether disorganized. Even dementia was not altogether senseless: It was characterized by a lower level of understanding and complexity in those corelationships that could be understood. But that which a sick person can perform, he does in an orderly and intelligible fashion.

---

* Most likely, Hans Gruhle, a psychopathologist active among the Gestalt theorists in the 1920's. [Ed]

** A flippant allusion to Bleuler's work in unravelling the associations and speech of schizophrenics. [Ed]

Thus, even something evidently senseless obviously makes sense. "There is method to his madness," Polonius says in *Hamlet*. Lashley graphically asserts that if one imagined experimentally created chaos in behavior, no real chaos would result. The nervous system, he says, has the capacity of self-regulation, which gives a coherent, logical character to its functioning regardless of what violations may exist in its component anatomical parts. Let us imagine that we could cut the cerebral cortex, turn it inside out, and replace it back to front, linking the fibers haphazardly. What effect would such an operation have on behavior? According to traditional theory, we should expect total chaos. According to the perspective established by C. S. Lashley, one would expect very insignificant disruptions in behavior. The subject under investigation would perhaps need some re-education—and even this might not be needed since we still know neither the [neurological] localization nor the character of the habit. Furthermore, during re-education, the subject might display normal capacities for understanding relationships and for rational action in his own experiential world.

Thus, questions of deciphering, interpreting, and discovering intelligible and reasonable links, dependencies, and relationships are the principal and basic tasks of a researcher in our field. It seems to us that, in this respect, the task of the researcher extends broadly beyond the simple study of techniques and methodologies for various experiments. The question is to a much greater degree that of cultivating both thinking and the ability to discover connections, than a question of mastering techniques well. Kretschmer indicates that verbal description of the constitution is basic to the methodology he used. This preceded any measurement and should always be achieved independently of it because, he says, the eye should not in advance encounter any obstacles in those measurements. Everything depends on the possibility of complete, creative training of our eyes. Individual measurements through a template, without ideas and intuitions about the general structure, will hardly move us from our point of departure. In Kretschmer's opinion, a measuring stick sees nothing and, of itself, will never bring us to understand biological types, which is our goal. But once we have learned to see, we will quickly notice that a compass gives us precise and neat validations; it gives us numbers and formulae, and sometimes provides important amend-ments to what our eyes have detected. As a result, we need to reevaluate the role of the measuring stick and the eyes in enabling us to measure and to see. This reevaluation should take place not only in the research methodologies dealing with the body's composition, but also in any pedological researcher's methodology. The task of methodology is not only to learn to measure, but also to learn to see, think, and associate. This means that our excessive fear of so-called subjective factors in interpretation and our attempts to attain research results through purely mechanical and arithmetic methods—as happens in Binet's system—are unfounded. Without subjective reevaluation (that is, without thought and interpretation), the deciphering of results and evaluation of the data is not scientific research.

5

What remains is for us to produce a scheme for pedological research as we understand it. We think that one of contemporary pedology's basic mistakes lies in the inadequate attention paid to practical work and the cultivation of developmental diagnostics.[*] Basically,

---

[*] When Vygotsky speaks of "the cultivation of a developmental diagnostics," he means not simply the procedure of mathematical assessments but the cultivation of and ability to discover and decipher connections between measurements and the real facts and essentials in a child's development. [Transl.]

no one teaches this art to the pedologue, and the vast majority of our pedologues fail entirely to cultivate this side of matters. In this respect, pedology is in much poorer shape than pediatrics and other parallel disciplines. A pediatrician often knows not more, but less, about children's pathology than a pedologue knows about children's development. But a pediatrician has mastered what he knows, and he can turn his knowledge into practice.

Not long ago, in the press, an agronomist described a colleague who ended up in America and set about looking for work there. This scholar-agronomist unfurled his diploma and began describing his education, his length of service, and his research, but what he was asked, above all, was what he could do. Actually, it also would be worth asking this question of contemporary pedology. It must consider what it is capable of doing, and it must learn to apply the inactive fund of its knowledge to life. We think that it is only through developmental diagnostic work, through clinical pedological work, that pedology can finally take shape as a science, but this cannot be attained by pursuing an exclusively theoretical approach.

We suggest that an outline for pedological research (with application to difficult and abnormal children) should be founded on several basic elements, which we will introduce in the order of their importance. First place should be occupied by the carefully collected complaints of parents, the children themselves, and their educational institutions. One should begin with precisely this, but it would be worth collecting these complaints altogether differently from the way it is usually done. (They are given in generalized form; instead of facts, we heard opinions, prepared conclusions, often tendentiously abbreviated). In parents' complaints, for example, one often reads that the children are malicious, retarded. The researcher is interested in facts, facts which a mother or father should point out to him.

In this respect, the basic principles of character research acquire a large methodological significance. Clearly, one should avoid not only subjective evaluations, but, let us add, all generalizations which have to be taken on faith and are not proved during the course of research. The fact that the father considers his child malicious should be taken into account by the researcher, but it should be taken into account properly, that is, as the father's opinion. This opinion must be tested during research but to do this, one must uncover the facts which are the basis for forming that opinion. These are facts which the researcher must interpret for himself. "If we ask a simple peasant woman," says Kretschmer, "whether her brother is timid, peace-loving, and energetic, we will often get unclear and uncertain responses. If we ask, on the contrary, whether he acted like a child when he should have gone off alone to a dark hayloft, or how he behaved when there was a fight in the tavern, the same woman will give us clear and distinctive information, which because of its lively freshness bears the stamp of truth. One must be well acquainted with the life of the common man, peasant and worker alike, and become wholly part of it; in questioning a patient, it is worth pausing not so much on an outline of character traits as on his life in school, in church, in the tavern, and in his daily activities, all of which is based on concrete examples. I therefore attach special importance to expanding the examination as much as possible in this concrete way" (1930, p. 138) [sic] [Kretschmer, 1928? 1932?].

It is essential to take even the subjective testimony of the child itself into account. But even here we may have testimony which is known to be unreliable taken as evidence of certain known facts. A child might pass himself off as other than he really is; he might simply lie, but that in itself remains a fact and of the highest value to a researcher. The researcher must take into account and explain the fact of self-evaluation and the fact of lying.

We have been told of a famous neuropathologist who, because he rejected all significance in subjective evidence, tried to protect himself from any influences stemming from the patient's complaints and always began with objective research. For this purpose, the doctor came up with a simple procedure: when he embarked on the study of a patient, he always asked him to breathe through his mouth, to prevent the patient from voicing his complaint and pain. When the patient, naturally astonished by the fact that the doctor was not examining what hurt him, tried to explain his complaint, the researcher interrupted the visitor and reminded him again to breathe through his mouth. This exemplifies, in extreme and exaggerated fashion, the altogether misleading tendency to ignore subjective data. We have already indicated elsewhere that the value of subjective evidence is analogous to the value of evidence from the accused and the victim in a court of law. Any judge might act entirely without grounds if he attempted to decide the case exclusively on the basis of complaints from the defendant or the victim. But it is equally groundless to try to avoid altogether the evidence of both interested parties (who therefore distort reality). The judge weighs and compares facts, checks them, rearranges them, criticizes them, and then comes to some conclusion.

This is how a researcher also acts. In practical pedological research, one must begin by absorbing a simple methodological truth: Often, a scientific researcher's primary task is to establish some fact which cannot be found directly in reality. The path of research leads from symptoms to that which lies behind them, from the constitution of symptoms to developmental diagnostics. Therefore, the belief that scientific truth can be established directly is false. All of traditional psychology is based on the false belief that psychological occurrences could be studied only by direct observation with the aid of introspection. Incidentally, as V. N. Ivanovskii correctly points out in *Methodological Introduction to Science and Philosophy* (1923), this notion is based on a false premise.

A final clarification of this question is linked to the introduction of the concept of the *unconscious*, to the discipline of psychology. Formerly, psychology, particularly British psychology, often rejected altogether the possibility of studying any psychological condition of an unconscious nature, on the grounds that we are not aware of these conditions and therefore we do not know anything about them. This judgment derives from the premise (unquestioningly accepted as a given) that we can study and, in general, know only things of which we are immediately conscious. But this premise is not a necessary one, since we know and study many things of which we are not immediately conscious; things that we learn about through analogy, construction, hypotheses, deductive reasoning, and so on; things we know, in general, through indirect means. All images of our past, for example, are created this way, put together from a variety of structures and plans, and based on materials which often bear absolutely no resemblance to the final images. When a zoologist determines the dimensions of an extinct animal from its bones, as well as its external appearance, and its life style, and can tell us what it fed on, and so on, all of this is not found directly by the zoologist, nor directly experienced by him. He draws conclusions on the basis of various directly knowable indications from the bones, and so on.

The unconscious can be studied in exactly the same way, that is, by using its known traces, its echoes, and its manifest effects on those things which are directly knowable. The human personality is a hierarchy of activities, and far from all those activities are linked to consciousness. Therefore, the psychological sphere is of much broader scope than the conscious sphere (in terms of direct knowability). And everything we say here about the unconscious is equally applicable to the conscious side of the personality, taking into account, also, that far from everything is absolutely accurately reflected even in consciousness, nor are all things reflected in ways which necessarily correspond to reality. In studying the conscious processes, a researcher should move from the indications, manifestations, and symptoms, to the essentials which lie behind them. This applies even more significantly the non-psychological developmental phenomena. It is easy to see that this whole question is fundamentally linked to the matter we discussed in the first part of this article, when we wrote about the transition from a phenomenological perspective (studying only manifestations and classifying things by their external appearance) to a conditional-genetic one (which studies the essence of things as they unfold during development).

A researcher should remember, as he embarks on studying indications, data, and symptoms, that he should be studying and determining the peculiarities and the nature of a developmental process which will not appear directly before him but which are basic to all those indications which he can observe. Thus, a researcher's task, in extensive pedological research as well as in developmental diagnostics, is not only to establish the known symptoms and to list and systematize them—nor is his task only to group events according to similar external characteristics—rather, it lies exclusively in penetrating to the deeper essentials of the developmental processes by thoughtfully analyzing these external data.

Contemporary pedological research often tries to prepare final conclusions about developmental levels, based on the mechanical and arithmetic analysis of external symptoms; this is what both the Binet and Rossolimo methods do. This research does neither more nor less than try to economize on the most important part of any scientific work—that is, on thought and reflection. A pedologue who works with the Binet or Rossolino methods establishes certain facts; then, he analyzes them using purely arithmetic methods.[*] The result, reached in an entirely mechanical fashion, is altogether lacking in reflective analysis. The result is a travesty, especially if compared with scientific diagnostics in other fields. A doctor measures the temperature and pulse, acquaints himself with the results of chemical analyses, studies the X-rays, and then he reflects, and linking all this to the side of the picture he already knows, he penetrates to the internal pathological process which has produced all the symptoms. And it would be absurd to suggest that a mechanical summary of the symptoms could, by itself, produce a scientific diagnosis. With this, we can finish our discussion of the first point in our outline.

Our second point[**] is the child's developmental history, which should be the basic source of all further evidence and the fundamental background for all further research. The factors which contribute to a given child's developmental history are well known. [Third], it is relevant to introduce an explanation of any inherited peculiarities, the milieu, and the main characteristics of a child's development in, and out of, the womb. There is a fourth factor, one which is usually omitted but which, from our point of view, is absolutely necessary, and that is a personal history of the child's education [upbringing]. This most

---

[*] Although Vygotsky's criticism of the state of Soviet pedology (i.e., its concentration on measuring I.Q. and a child's differences) agreed with early Stalinist criticism, Vygotsky was subsequently attacked as "a pedologist." This baseless criticism of Vygotsky illustrates the contradictory extremes to which Stalinism went in establishing state control over academic disciplines, in the 1930's. For example, it seized upon Alexander Pushkin's formula "it is impossible to verify harmony [of the soul] by algebra" and applied it to all branches of the sciences and arts. It became a high Stalinist formula for attacking semioticians, formalists, and "pedologues" alike, despite the fact that Soviet Marxist–Leninist researchers in these fields depended heavily on quantification. This tendency was beautifully foreseen and satirized in E. Zamiatin's 1925 anti-utopian novel, *We*. [Transl.]

[**] The first point is the introduction of the symptoms of trouble or illness. [Transl.]

important influence from the environment, at least in developmental term—it directly forms a child's personality—is usually skipped altogether in a developmental history, while, at the same time, such things as the cubic footage of living space, the laundry routine, and other secondary details are transcribed in detail.

General and fundamental to compiling a scientific history of a child's development is the requirement that this educational and developmental history be a causal description of the child's life. Unlike a simple chronicle or a simple listing of individual events (such-and-such happened in such-and-such a year, something else in another year), a causal description lays out events in such a way that it puts them in cause and result sequence, uncovers their relationships, and examines a given period of that history as a single, intertwined, and changing entity; it tries to discover the laws, links, and changes according to which that entity was built and which it follows. Usually, the pedological history of a child's development is composed of a list of separate events, not internally linked amongst themselves, connected only as in a questionnaire, and organized chronologically. Lacking, however, is a developmental history; that is, the interconnected, dynamic, unified whole. The usual descriptions remind one more of chronicles than of a true historical representation of events and their changes.

Here, Anton Chekhov's[*] rule about the internal construction of a literary tale is entirely applicable. It discusses the need to link all parts of a story by an internal tie; for example, if the author, on the first page of the story, in describing the decor of a room, mentions that a gun hangs on the wall, then that gun must shoot on the last page of the story—or else there was no reason to have mentioned it in describing the room's decor. In a child's developmental history, every fact included must similarly serve the purpose of the whole. The gun mentioned at the beginning must, absolutely, shoot before the end. No fact at all should be included simply for its own sake. Every fact must be so interconnected with the whole that it would be impossible to discard it without destroying the whole structure.

The ideal developmental history should unfold with the same strictly logical regularity as a geometry theorem. We feel that, in the early stages of pedology, as we strive to learn and master the art of scientific developmental diagnostics, it would not be bad to borrow some logical rigor of geometry theorems, even if we were to lean a bit on the support of geometry. One should, at any rate, remember that what one wants to demonstrate at the end of a developmental history should be succinctly formulated (at least in the mind of the researcher) at the beginning; at the end, the position which was to have been proven should be clearly enunciated. This should be true not only of the developmental history as a whole, but also of the separate factors which compose that history.

From this, it should be clear that the center of gravity in a child's developmental history must be moved from external events, which any nanny could collect as well as a pedologue could (when the child was able to sit up, speak, and so on), to the study and establishing of internal links through which the developmental process is revealed. Once more, we see the path from the superficial to the profound, from that which is obvious to that which must be sought, from a phenomenological analysis of occurrences to a determination of their deeper causes. E. K. Sepp, a clinician of neurological disorders, believes that all sciences at first go through a period of primarily describing phenomena in a predominantly statistical fashion. Systematization, the similarity of phenomena, and frequently encountered combinations

---

[*] Chekhov, Anton P. (1860-194). The Russian dramatist and short story writer. [Ed]

which form natural complexes are recognized as the proportion of collected material accumulates. This entire period might be referred to as *descriptive* or *phenomenological*. The next stage in the development of any science is the establishment of the internal connections among phenomena and the determination of their causal dependencies. The route to this consists of decomposing the complicated complexes of phenomena into their component elements and then re-creating all possible combinations from those elements. The distinguishing characteristic of this stage is that it studies and analyzes the dynamics of the various processes and factors which yielded the phenomena that were earlier explored statistically and phenomenologically. One is forced to add that pedology, unlike medicine, even in its purely descriptive domain, is at a very low level. (In medicine, description found clearer expression through the differential diagnosis of illness.) Pedology must, at one and the same time, assimilate the methods of analysis and the dynamics of processes, as well as lift description to a higher level.

With reference to heredity and environment, it is worth saying that typically both these factors are included in children's developmental histories without reference to cause—that is, without being integrated into the task and goal of that history. Meanwhile, the purpose of pedological research is to present heredity as a factor in a child's development; therefore, the study of heredity by pedologists should proceed along an entirely different path than in medicine, genetics, and other areas. A child specialist is usually interested in heredity exclusively in relation to pathogenic etiological factors. For this reason, what we observe is a series of curiosities, which have unfortunately become cliches in practical pedological thought. In a history of heredity, there may be noted, for example, that the father and grandfather of the child being examined suffered from alcoholism. The pedologue uses this fact to explain the strange behavior of a child who is the subject of complaint—that in class, for no visible reason, he throws himself on the floor, plays the fool, and disrupts class. The child specialist reasons simply that the child's father and grandfather drank and that this must have some kind of effect on the child's behavior.

The example just given of the use of teachings about heredity in the field of pedology is not an exception. Rather, it is typical of how developmental histories in this field are put together; it clearly shows the futility, fruitlessness, and falsity of this path. Let us assume that in a given case the researcher was actually correct, and that the father and grandfather's alcoholism should have been used to explain their son and grandson's odd behavior. But what innumerable links, intermediate connections, and transitions connect cause and effect! How incompletely the researcher carried out his task! What a gap in the developmental history if it ties together only the first and last links in this long chain, simply and directly, and skips over everything in between! What a frightening simplification of reality, what a vulgarization of the scientific method!

So, our first task consists in following the influence of heredity on child development through all its intermediate links, so that any developmental occurrences and any inherited factors are placed in genetically clear interrelationships. A second requirement is that the analysis of heredity in pedology should be infinitely more encompassing than in pathology. We should undertake this analysis in order to clarify the inheritance of traits, which form part of the constitution and which appear during a child's development. This should be one of the primary sources for our knowledge about the make-up of children. Thus, a pedologue not only must concern himself with the pathological factors of inheritance but must also clarify generally all the inheritable constitutional possibilities for a particular family.

Another required factor in pedological research should be what Kretschmer calls "characterological research into family." Even with respect to an individual patient, one should not confine oneself to the personality of the patient alone.

> The same thing takes place in characterology as in body structure. Classic characteristics of a constitutional kind are more clearly represented in close relatives than in the patient himself. Further, where there are several constitutional types intermixed in a single patient, we can, in such cases, see the various components clearly isolated and disassociated in other family members. In short, where we want to know the construction of a constitution, we should devote attention to heredity. Therefore, for many years, I have included in my most important case reports everything that could be discovered about the character, illnesses, and body structure of blood relatives. The structure of a patient's constitution emerges especially clearly, if we introduce this most important item into the outline in concise terms (E. Kretschmer, 1930, p. 139) [sic].

E. Kretschmer offers an example of characterological research into the environment:

> In this family, we find pure versions of those character traits which we will later call schizothymic. Beginning with healthy schizothymic characters...and ending with clearly psychopathic ones, and including those which perch life-long on the verge of psychopathy, from the mother's abortive pre-senile psychosis to the son's serious schizophrenia. Among these few family members, we can observe all the nuances and transitions from illness to health (ibid., pp. 139–140).

Thus, the usual inquiries into heredity which a pedologue makes of the parents, and which he limits to indicating the presence of mental illness, alcoholism, and so on, are altogether inadequate for research into the real complexities of the occurrences and happenings which lie at the base of such an inheritance.

Even the study of a sick person cannot be limited to the study of only those individuals who are themselves ill. A researcher is following a false method if he investigates only the members of the family who are ill. "In this case," says Kretschmer about his example,"the researcher should say that he can observe a polymorphic inheritance of a psychosis, since the son is descended from an epileptoid father. Biologically, this is not a particularly surprising way of thinking. Actually, the path of inheritance here is altogether different. Selected indications of illness, by themselves, never give us a complete picture of heredity" (ibid., p. 145).

Contemporary genetic research—which deals with both constitutional problems and with research on twins—offers a researcher an enormous amount of material for the deepest constitutional analysis of a child's personality with respect to heredity. Studies on twins indicate the developmental dynamics of inherited traits. Studies of psychopathic constitutions in terms of heredity indicate how complex are the laws of construction, disintegration, intersection, and combination for the transmission of even the most basic character syndromes. Research shows, for example, that, where epilepsy has a large number of genes in one group, they can combine or disassociate, resulting in a variety of clinical forms. The researcher must remember that the facts of heredity and its dynamics appear as the whole only through character research into a whole family, and certainly not through the study of only selected members of that family. The study of heredity, in the way it has been carried out until now, is exactly analogous to our studying human physical development or conditions without looking at the whole organism and only examining the condition of one or two organs. Similarly, individual family members whom we study are only segments of the dynamic genetic entity which is represented by the whole family.

This kind of complex character study of a family ought to underlie the constitutional analysis of a child's personality. Nor does the task end here. This hereditary data must be observed within the history of the child's further development, their fate must be traced, and basic laws must be established linking particular inherited inclinations and the child's further line of development. What has been said here applies not only to character, but to a child's physical development, particularly his stature. Let us use L. S. Geshelina's [no ref.] work as an example: It examines the impact of hereditary and environmental factors on children's growth. An accurate constitutional study of a child's growth—that simplest of phenomena—requires studying both hereditary and environmental influences. This latter, however, is possible only by studying the whole family.

The next factor to which attention should be devoted is the study of hereditary influences as part of a single entity, of which environmental factors are also a part. The various factors and indicators in the environment, then, cannot be presented just as an unordered list; the researcher should present them as a structured entity, structured, that is, in terms of the child's development. We will never be able to conduct a full and final study of the environment in a child's developmental history if we fail to take into account those same things we discussed with respect to heredity.

Just as the grandfather's alcoholism sometimes directly explains the grandson's behavior, so some conditions of family and daily life (close living quarters, bad parental relationships, the presence of other examples, etc.) are directly related to complaints about a child's behavior. Here again, it is often believed that an adequate scientific explanation has been found if an obvious environmental factor is pointed out. The researcher discovers that there are difficult economic, moral, or living conditions in a patient's family. The analysis is finished. But any neighbor is capable of offering that kind of analysis; in such situations, the neighbor might say, "But just look at how those people live!"

But a pedologue is not limited to constructing such narrow-minded links between difficult living conditions and an unmanageable child. A scientific approach differs from an empirical secular one precisely in that the former tries to discover the deep-seated internal dependencies and mechanisms which create one environmental influence or another. The task of scientific analysis is certainly not completed until this is done; until it is shown how, through which intermediate links, by what psychological mechanisms, acting on which aspects of the developmental process, the environmental conditions in question led to these particular phenomena of unmanageability.

In dealing with the complex structure of personality development in psychopathic children, we used the example of the influence of the environment on schizoid-type psychopathic children. We saw that such factors as inadequate material provision, hunger, need, vital emotions, street ties, fear, fright, and poor supervision play a relatively small role in the accumulation of additional syndromes of unmanageability for this particular group of children. But in groups of cycloid psychopaths, these factors play a leading role in developing reactive states. While, on the contrary, for schizoid-type children, any factors linked to the frustration of the patient's personality and which leads to conflictual experiences (a severe upbringing with constant demands and humiliations, a disorderly family life, parental discord, arguments over the child, separation from one of the parents, difficult living conditions, wounded self-esteem) are traumatic factors.

It is remarkable that, not only is there selectivity among the various environmental influences, but there are also various kinds of reactions within children's development to various environmental conditions. In one third of her cases, Sukhareva noted that the most common reaction to the particular environmental conditions was a variety of neurotic states. "One might think," she says, "that the frequency of a particular reaction in schizoids is not accidental, since the schizoid mind has a series of pre-set mechanisms (such as the peculiarities of their lives, their inclinations, their lack of any unity of experience, and the weakness of their reactions) which would lead to their occurrence" (Sukhareva, 1930, p. 72). But evidently, in the other two thirds of the cases, the same or analogous condition generated altogether different reactions. The pedologue's task is not the formulation of one or another danger-inducing factor; it is rather to establish what dynamic link exists between some environmental factor and the lines of development in a single child. The discovery of developmental links and mechanisms remains the principal, basic task; without resolving it, pedological research cannot be called scientific research.

This gives rise to the problem of education. As we have already said, this side of the question is usually passed over silently in a child's developmental history. And it is all but the most important factor in the material that a researcher has at his disposal. Usually, the characterization of a child's education includes only such exceptional events on the order of corporal punishment, and even such an event may be reported only in the most general of terms. Yet it is education, broadly understood, that should comprise the basic pivot around which the child's personality development is to turn. A particular line of development should be seen as a necessary and logical result of a particular line of education. Thus, without the scientific examination of a child's education, a pedologue will never be able to construct a scientific image of a child's development. It should be understood that, by education, we mean not only teaching, but all educational measures consciously undertaken by the parents in relation to the child. We are referring, then, to education in the fullest meaning of the word, as it is understood in contemporary pedology.

We have already cited A. Gesell's position, which characterized all higher genetic laws as follows: All development in the present is based on past development. Development is not a simple function which can be wholly determined by adding X units of heredity to Y units of environment. It is a historical complex which, at every stage, reveals the past which is a part of it. In other words, the artificial duality of environment and heredity can misdirect us, for it leads us away from the fact that development is a continuous and self-conditioning process, rather than a puppet which can be managed by jerking two strings. We bring this point up a second time since it seems to us to be central to the meaning of practical pedology. Unfortunately, in common practice, a child's developmental history is usually set out in terms of precisely that misleading dualism of environment and heredity. Practical pedology is rarely able to envision both as one entity, and the child is usually represented exactly like a puppet which can be manipulated by jerking on two strings; his development unfolds like a drama manipulated by two powerful influences.

The ability to envision environment and heredity as a single entity can be attained only by the practical application of what Gesell calls pedology's basic law to the concrete study of child development. This law shows that development is a self-limiting process in which the influences of environment and heredity are synthesized. This means that a pedologue should portray any new stage in a child's development as necessarily and logically flowing from the preceding stage. The logic of self-advancement during development, the unity and struggle of the opposites intertwined in the same process, should be clarified. One should not see each new stage in a child's development as the fresh product of the mutual crossing of X units of heredity with Y units of environment. To discover the self-advancing process of development means understanding the internal logic, the mutual limitation, the linkage, and the interlocking of various factors within a single entity, as well as the struggles of opposites included in the developmental process. Development, according to a well-known definition, is precisely the struggle of opposites. This view alone can support truly dialectical research on the process of children's development.

The next section in our outline is the symptomatology of development. The purpose of this section is to present pedological status, as it were, as the determination of the level and character of development which a child has attained at a given time. Here, all other evidence which can characterize a child's condition and his developmental level can be introduced as auxiliary material, but this material should be included only from a pedological perspective. As an example of such material, one could cite medical diagnoses, pedological evidence concerning a child's success, the preparation and education of the child, and so on. But central to the whole section is the problem of symptomatology, that is, of scientifically establishing, describing, and determining the symptoms of development.

In this respect, our practical work lags unacceptably far behind the ideal. It should be enough to point out that, in its ability to establish known facts and to test them pedologically, our research lags very far behind the corresponding clinical research. We could cite as examples a number of factors which are frequently encountered in practice. For example, for a particular child it may be established that shyness forms part of his character. Without further analysis, a mental conclusion is reached, or an assumption is made, about the schizoid cast of his personality. Meanwhile, a further thorough analysis of the same facts, which had at first led to the conclusion that the child was reserved, shows that the degree of shyness expressed does not even fall within the transitional range, between the pathological shyness associated with the corresponding psychosis and an altogether normal reserve, which might be encountered in a normal person undergoing specific experiences. That is, the very character of this reserve does not permit it to be identified with the kind of reserve which could be taken as symptomatic of a pathological condition, or one which lies on the borderline between psychological illness and psychological health. It further turns out that this reserve is not the same reserve which is so characteristic of a psychopathological personality structure, but that it can be justified, explained, and differentiated in relation to various experiential complexes in the child's developmental history.

Thus, a critical examination of the facts shows that pedology's failure to describe, distinguish, and qualify diverse phenomena leads to designating them with the same name given to other events which superficially resemble them. Thus, the general label is enough to generate, simply, by an altogether mechanical association, memories of psychopathy; it replaces the processes of thought and rational analysis of facts, which should be primary in research, with the processes of reflection and associative tendencies. This example alone shows us how important it is to be able to establish the facts themselves and to describe them. It shows what high standards are needed for this purpose, and how one needs to know in advance exactly how a fact should be noted and described. In the example just cited, the collector of facts overlooked what is most important: the degree to which something is present, and the character of its relations to the other symptoms, and its motivation, that is, the place of that particular syndrome within the whole syndrome.

But it is still more important to devote some attention to a second factor connected to the symptomatology of development, and that is the pedological qualification of observed phenomena and facts that have been observed. Too often, in our practice, what are called developmental symptoms are in fact observations from life, indicated by causal labels, which have entered the terms of pedological research directly from the lexicon of the casual observer. As a result, one encounters such terms and labels as *stubbornness* and *spite*, which are used without any knowledge of the character of the facts which lie at the base of these designations, or of their interpretation in pedology. However, the simplest of observations will demonstrate that the same fact not only has infinite manifestations of degree but can also have entirely different significance, depending on the context in which it is found and the factors of which it is composed. In short, what is taken under a single label to be one and the same phenomenon, in fact, when examined carefully, turns out to be two different phenomena which are mixed or confused because of the unscientific approach applied to them. If we take phenomena which are, in practice, very common with difficult children, such as children's onanism, enuresis, or capriciousness, we see that a researcher often tries in vain to extract the grain of fact from the enveloping layers of labels, designations, and generalizations.

In this respect, as we have already said, clinical medicine has moved far ahead of pedology. No doctor would be satisfied by simply indicating that a patient has a rash, or that he is subject to seizures. The kind of rash, or the kind and nature of seizures must be described in careful, scientific detail, so that the seizures can be examined as symptoms of epilepsy or hysteria, or so that the rash can be viewed as a symptom of syphilis or scarlet fever.

Above all, what is lacking in contemporary pedological research is precisely this scientific determination of symptoms and the pedological examination of observed events. We have already mentioned the mechanical, arithmetic, and cursory nature of the methods by which contemporary psychometrics ascertains symptoms. Of course, we could not do other than see the coefficients of mental retardation as one of many symptoms, but it is the method by which the symptom is measured that characterizes contemporary pedology. As the reader will remember, this symptom is arrived at on the basis of an automatic summarization, a simple calculation from a series of facts of very differing origins (as though measuring and adding kilograms and kilometers), which are then treated as equivalent and equally important units. This is related, not only to the problem of measurement in pedological symptomatology, but equally to the whole qualitative and descriptive determination of various developmental symptoms. Some pedologues refer especially to symptomatological diagnosis, by which they convey one of a sequence of steps through which the development of a diagnostic methodology in pedology proceeds, as in medical diagnostics, whose experience is heavily used by pedologues. But, one must add, that whether in empirical or symptomatological diagnostics, the scientific determination of developmental symptoms remains altogether poorly elaborated. The questions of evaluating various indicators of development, or deducing indices, and of comparing a child's condition to some permanent standard magnitude, are connected to this problem of developmental symptomatology. Since scientific research into development has begun only relatively recently, these questions also remain particularly underexplored.

In contemporary pedological practice, two basic research directions can be distinguished: Gesell called them normative and clinical psychology. The task of normative psychology is, in our view, purely auxiliary. This is one of the problems in the symptomatology of development. The point of studying symptoms scientifically is not only to describe them, but to distinguish them in terms of their divergence from permanent magnitudes. What is thus included in the tasks of the symptomatology of development is not only the raw data of height, weight, chest size, and other anthropometric measurements, but also deduced indices, indicators, and other relevant measurements and the evaluation of deviations from standard magnitudes in terms of sigmas and other indicators.

We are altogether in agreement with Gesell, who points out that there is a big difference between psychological measurements and psychological diagnosis. Let us clarify this: Psychological measurements pertain to the domain of establishing the symptoms; diagnosis belongs to the final judgement of an occurrence as a whole, an occurrence which manifests itself in these symptoms, which is not susceptible to direct perception and which must be evaluated on the basis of study, comparison, and interpretation of the given symptoms.

There are few diagnostic methods which act automatically. There are, for example, blood tests and cardiograms, which offer rapid and accurate determinations of disease but, in medical diagnostics, all clinical data must, as a rule, be weighed and interpreted in aggregate. If this is true of somatic diagnoses, it should also be correct for psychological diagnostics, and it should be doubly so, given the current state of psychometric techniques. In this respect, Gesell strictly differentiates psychometrics from clinical research in the diagnostics of mental developments. But psychometric research is only one of the factors in establishing the symptoms without which the diagnosis itself could not be made correctly. "Clinical psychology is a kind of applied psychology which, through measurements, analysis, and observation, tries to determine correctly the mental structure of the subject. Its goal is to interpret human behavior and determine its boundaries and possibilities" (A. Gesell, 1930, pp. 297–298).

As soon as an element of responsible diagnostics appears in psychological treatment, psychological measurements, as such, resume secondary importance. Psychometrics offers only a point of departure for analysis, or provides the background for composing the picture. Clinical or diagnostic methods require not only accurate measurement, but creative interpretation. This is why a competent clinical psychologist must accumulate first hand a large quantity of material from experience, about average, as well as exceptional, subjects. He must construct working ideas from this experience, ideas which he can manipulate in their every part and in every circumstance. Psychological diagnostics needs a comparative normative method. The term *normative* here means a kind of psychology which systematically works out objective standards and descriptive formulae for the purpose of comparatively evaluating mental abilities and possibilities. Clinical psychology can be defined as using psychological norms to study particular cases of development or behavior. Establishing norms is a characteristic which distinguishes psychology and psychiatry. This term also sets off the difference between purely psychometric procedures and comparative differential diagnostics.

Although Gesell continually spoke of the problem of mental development, methodologically all of this could also be extended to the diagnostics of development as a whole. Gesell's aim was also to establish a diagnosis of the developmental path. He collected in sequential order ten patterns of development, each of which on average contained thirty-five indicators. On the basis of the well-worked-out symptomatology of mental development at an early age, one could diagnose the progress of development. Gesell himself emphasizes that the concept of development is a central one, since it applies equally to physical and mental development.

Gesell describes in detail various aspects of clinical research, which we will not examine here in depth. He begins with the approach to the child, follows the whole course of the research, and finishes with questions which, at first glance, appear to have purely technical significance, but which in fact crown the whole symptomatological problem in pedology. In touching on the question of the mother-child relationship during an experiment, in examining this relationship, Gesell indicates that the very fact that a child's behavior changes in the mother's presence should become an issue in clinical research. The close link between the diagnosis of development and parental guidance is a basis for using the relationship between mother and child as a component in any clinical task.

6

In truth, everything we have said above was in preparation for the next point in our formulation, that of pedological diagnosis. This is the central and focal point in the name of which all the preceding has been developed, and upon which all that follows will build. As in a magic trick, all the problems of clinical pedology focus on the problem of pedological diagnosis. This is the fundamental guiding concept; we must therefore examine it carefully. What we have so far said was intended to provide limits to the problems of symptomatology and diagnostics, which are usually defined during practical work; it was also intended to place each in correct relationship to the other, to show that establishing symptoms never automatically leads to diagnosis, and to demonstrate that the researcher should never permit economy at the expense of reflection or of creative interpretation of symptoms.

If we turn to diagnostics, in the proper sense of the word, we see that contemporary practice identifies several kinds of developmental diagnostics. Gesell refers to both differential and descriptive diagnostics. At the base of descriptive diagnostics lies the conviction that a descriptive method permits one to avoid many of the mistakes involved in absolute psychometric definition and to take advantage of comparative methods. "If our method," says the author, "at first glance can be faulted for its lack of specificity, it is for that very reason distinguished by clinical clarity and concreteness, characteristics which exist in descriptive and comparative formulations. We hope that the method of comparative evaluation will advance well-grounded clinical conclusions, rather than encourage automatic results and computations. The comparative method requires the researcher to use all of his previous experience in resolving a given problem. It also helps him to systematize his experience as it accumulates. The methodology has a single, overall virtue for any subjects— be they normal, subnormal, above average, young people or adults; it is comparative in character" (1930, p. 340). The final evaluation of a developmental condition is based on a careful examination of the number and character of positive or negative results, a comparison of the child's development with some outline or other of development according to age. But the final evaluation must not be reached by the mechanical assembling and classifying of indicators in verbal form; it must be reached by judging and evaluating the whole behavioral picture, as well as being based on rules of normative behavior for a given developmental level which the investigator has worked out for himself.

One of the real dangers threatening pedological diagnostics is the overwhelmingly general nature, the indefiniteness, of the clinical conclusions which it makes. In order to avoid this, Gesell recommends separate conclusions in four major areas of behavior: namely the motoric domain, speech, adaptive behavior, and social behavior. As we have already mentioned, we at one time ourselves advocated even more differentiated research into individual functions in children. In order not to digress into a discussion of which points should be noted in this differentiated kind of research, let us only say that, in and of itself, maximal specialization of research in the various functions is of the greatest importance.

The second kind of diagnostics, so-called differential diagnostics, is built on the same comparative method of research. "In our clinical work," Gesell says, "we try to maintain the rule of conducting as many comparisons as time and place allow; we try not to reach decisive conclusions until we have enough data for a comparative evaluation. One must recognize that a variety of situations are possible when, even following such comparisons, we do not come to definite conclusions and can formulate only a temporary descriptive diagnosis. In such cases, the child should be entered into the record for further investigation" (ibid., pp. 344–345).

Here, he broaches an aspect of pedological diagnostics that is in the highest degree important. That most important aspect is that, unlike medical diagnostics, pedological diagnostics cannot and should not be based on research on ambulatory patients—that is, outpatient research should not be the basic form of pedological study of a child. A repeated series of slices from a child's development, a series of symptoms taken from the living developmental process are, as a rule, necessary to formulate and confirm a diagnosis. As a rule, the pedological diagnosis should not be offered conjecturally. Given one comparative evaluation, we must compare different perspectives or given behaviors among ourselves. Then, we will acquire the ability to develop analytical evaluations.

> A diagnosis of development should not be determined exclusively on the basis data acquired of a series of data from tests and measurements. Diagnostics is not a process of numerical determination. A cautious inference does not lose by being expressed with descriptive clarifications and comparative formulations. Data from tests and measurements form the objective basis of a comparative evaluation. Schema of development offer standards for development. But, diagnosis in the true sense of the word should be based on critical and careful interpretation of data derived from a variety of sources (ibid. p. 347).

As we have already said, even if we are referring only to the diagnostics of children's mental development, nonetheless, diagnosing development

> is conceivably not limited to measuring the intellect. It is based on all the manifesta-tions and indicators of maturation. A synthesized, dynamic picture of those manifes-tations which in their totality we call *personality* also enters into the investigative framework. We cannot, of course, measure character traits precisely. We can, with difficulty, succeed in specifying what it is that we call personality. However, from the perspective of development diagnostics, we need to find out how the personality is formed and how it matures (ibid., p. 347–348).
>
> The term *development* does not make false distinctions among the autonomic, affective-motor, and psychological developments. It leads to a scientific and practical concurrence of all accessible criteria of development. Ideally, a complete develop-mental diagnosis encompasses all phenomena of a psychological and neurological order in connection with anatomic and physiological developmental symptoms... Future developments in anthropology, physiology, and biochemistry will doubtlessly provide us with norms enabling greater accuracy in evaluating levels of development (ibid., p. 365).

As stated earlier, other differences in developmental diagnostics are linked to differentiating the successive stages in the development of a diagnosis. A. A. Nevskii [no ref.] distinguishes a "symptomatic" (or empirical) type of diagnosis, which is limited to ascertaining particular characteristics or symptoms, and which reaches immediate practical conclusions on that basis. He mentions, as an example, recruitment for special schools, where the sole criterion for the selection of children is a low psychological profile, or a low indicator of abilities on one of all existing testing methods in use. Unless the reasons for retardation of a given child can be established, diagnoses of mental retardation (oligophrenia, retardation) in clinical psychiatry still remain essentially only symptomatic diagnoses, even though they are based on more-or-less multifaceted research conducted by a physician.

In our view, a symptomatic or empirical diagnosis is, strictly speaking, not a scientific diagnosis. Their fault does not lie in their failure to establish cause, but in some other considerations. After all, the fact remains that many truly scientific clinical diagnoses also fail to establish causation. Illnesses whose causes are unknown to us (cancer and schizophrenia, for example) may be scientifically diagnosed.

In this sense, a psychiatric diagnosis of oligophrenia is a scientific diagnosis, even should it fail immediately to establish the cause which called it forth, and even if it fails to specify whether it is an illness of the endocrine apparatus, or related to damage sustained by the fetus in utero, or appeared as a result of alcoholic degeneration.

The crux of the matter does not lie in causation. A scientific diagnosis can be established even when the reasons for the process identified in the diagnosis remain unknown to us. The truth of the matter is that, if we have a scientific diagnosis on the basis of established symptoms, we can, proceeding from that diagnosis, perceive that there is some kind of process which lies at the base of those symptoms. Thus, when E. Kraepelin formulated a definition of oligophrenia, he pointed out the most important part of the process, which underlies all the symptoms which oligophrenia manifests. The researcher identified it as an overall delaying of mental development, and this was the basis for his truly scientific diagnosis. It is a mistake to try to see a diagnosis in the simple determination of certain symptoms or of factual data. The practical shortcomings of such diagnostics are so clear, and so limited by errors in the way they formulate the basic questions, that it is not worth identifying them in detail. Nevskii, very accurately, compares such developmental diagnoses with the diagnoses made in primitive empirical medicine, which saw a patient with a cough or with thin blood and then took those symptoms as the illnesses themselves.

A second stage in developmental diagnostics involves etiological or causal diagnostics. Nevskii here identifies specifics: Such diagnoses are built by taking stock of basic factors and discovering causality. This is done on the basis of calculable indices, not only from the presence of specific symptoms, but also on the basis of those causes bringing them forth. Taking into consideration the unusually complex interweaving among the various factors and the complex character of their activities, pedological characterizations and pedological diagnoses should not simply represent some statistical condition. They should also uncover the specific dynamic process.

Again, we see an inadequate distinction being made among those processes which are appropriate to discovering a diagnosis. We have already mentioned that statistical conditions are a problem in symptomatology and not in developmental diagnostics. However, even an understanding of the dynamic process of alteration among symptoms does not constitute a developmental diagnosis in the proper sense. Only a determination of the developmental process, or a discovery of characteristic symptoms, can be a true basis for pedological diagnosis. Errors in etiological diagnosis usually come from two sources: First, as we have already indicated, very often etiological analysis is understood in an overly simplified manner and they are produced with the most remote reasons, or the most general and least substantive formulae, such as predominating biological and social factors, etc. A second source of error is the lack of knowledge about the order of causes, which are the most proximate causes determining an event and which are the more remote causes, which only determine an event in the long run but are not an immediate reason for it. Because of the extraordinary difficulty of analyzing causes, we believe that such analysis should be specifically indicated in this outline at a given point, and we shall return to this below. Meanwhile, let us say that some authors' attempts to link the symptomatological picture directly to etiological analysis, bypassing diagnosis, inevitably leads to the disappearance of a central principle, and a determining point in pedological research.

Nevskii calls the third stage in development diagnostics "typological diagnostics." With the aim of trying to predict the path which development will take in the future, we should try to identify the various types of development, the various paths that development might follow. The development process always follows one plane or another. It always holds to some type or another. In other words, the many and varied individual situations which exist can be reduced to a certain number of typical situations; thus, our diagnostics should consist in identifying the type of a child's personality, in the dynamic sense of that concept.

Here, we are pointing out a very important matter, which can be better appreciated by referring to it as a *typological problem*. Usually, this issue arises as a constitutional problem, or else as a differential pedological one. In this case, we prefer to speak of the clinical pedology of children's development, in general, and of difficult children, in particular, as the scientific basis of a pedological diagnosis. We have made it clear above that this means that, when we refer to the task currently confronting pedological research (similar to Kraepelin's task in psychiatry), we refer not only to the deductive identification of a certain number of typical forms in children's development and the establishment of typological diagnoses; we also refer to the clinical separation and description of the basic ways in which the process of children's development takes place, and of the formation of educational difficulties in children. Only by using this as a base can pedological diagnoses be formed.

In order to diagnose epilepsy or schizophrenia, one must have a concept of epilepsy or schizophrenia; the absence of such concepts creates a major obstacle to pedological diagnosis. This was Kraepelin's problem in psychiatry. Creating clinics on children's development and children's educational difficulties means creating a conceptual system which expresses the real and objective processes in the development of children and in their educational difficulties. Only on the basis of such a conceptual system can a scientific pedological diagnosis be formed, since the uniqueness of the scientific analytical research methods we use consists in the fact that we study a particular concrete event from the perspective of identifying the clinical image of development to which it conforms.

Thus, not all research can be viewed as diagnostic research. Diagnostic research presupposes an already established conceptual system, which can be used in reaching a diagnosis and which can subsume a particular individual event under the broader concept of epilepsy, schizophrenia, and so on. It would be incorrect to say that contemporary pedology has any such conceptual system. On the contrary, the system lacks elaboration, a fact which derives from the neglect, until recently, of practical diagnostic questions in pedology. For this reason, a chasm, an enormous separation, has developed between what pedology knows and what it is able to do. If pedology were truly able to mobilize everything it knows about children's development and apply it to the problems of practical diagnostics, it would already have some kind of conceptual system, which would have to exist as the basis of scientific diagnosis—even if the system were a poorly developed one. Let the first pedological diagnoses be descriptive, not fully established, with inadequately defined propositions with changing contours that are not altogether precise; but at the same time, let them be correctly directed in terms of method and methodology from the beginning—that is, let them be diagnoses in the true sense of the word.

The next point in our outline of pedological research is the discovery of causes—not only the determination of the data appearing as ultimate causes, but also the specification of the form of more immediate causes. We spoke in detail above of the mistakes usually made on this point. Therefore, there is no need to dwell further on this point. It is enough to say that the central problem in etiological analysis is discovering the mechanisms for symptom formation: how they evolve, what mechanisms help them arise and establish themselves, and what are causal conditions for particular symptoms. The research process described here is a circle, which begins by establishing symptoms, then moves from the symptoms to the process which is basic and central to them, and leads to the diagnosis; it should finally take us from diagnosis back to symptoms, this time uncovering the causal motivation and source of those symptoms. If the diagnosis is correct, it should demonstrate its accuracy by uncovering the symptom-generating mechanisms; it should make us understand the external view of those events, which are the manifestations of a particular developmental process. Further, if the diagnosis always takes account of a personality's complex structure (which we also discussed above) and defines its structure and dynamics, then etiological analysis should uncover the mechanism of the intertwining of the syndromes in which that complex personality structure and dynamics is expressed.

Above, in our discussion of heredity and environment, we indicated how far removed a simple discussion of the various activity factors is from a true analysis of environmental and hereditary causes. We also said that etiological analysis must always show (1) how a given developmental stage is conditioned by the self-advancement of the whole, the internal logic of the development process itself, and (2) how one stage necessarily developed from the preceding stage of development, rather than being the mechanical sum of environmental and hereditary factors which are new to each stage. Lifting the etiological analysis of development to truly scientific heights means, above all, searching for the causes of the events which interest us in the developmental process itself, and uncovering its internal logic and its self-advancement.

We need pause only briefly on the next two points in our outline, since the preceding has prepared the reader to understand them. The fifth point is prognosis, the ability to predict the path and character of children's development on the basis of all the research stages previously completed. We have to indicate here again that establishing a prognosis, in pedological research is usually poorly carried out. What usually distinguishes such a prognosis is its limited content, a reduction to general formulae, the use of two or three abstract stereotypes. In fact, the content of a prognosis should reveal the whole unity of the developmental process, including all the complexities of a child's personality structure and dynamics detected by the diagnosis. The content of a prognosis is the same as that of a diagnosis, but the former is built on so understanding the internal logic of the autonomous developmental process which marks the route of the child's development and which can be natural and genuinely projected onto any other conditions which retain the form of previous ones. A particularly crucial part of a prognosis lies in its division into periods. A pedologue should be able to predict what will happen in the developmental process in a year, how the next stage of growth will unfold (for example, at school age for a pre-school child, or at sexual maturation for a schoolchild), what the final outcome of the development process will be, and what the mature personality will be like, as far as the present allows us to judge.

The sixth, and final, point is the pedagogical (or therapeutic pedagogical) recommendation, for the sake of all pedological research is conducted. These are the prescriptions which often turn out to be excessively lacking in content, abstract, or, as indicated above, frequently only return to the pedagogue that which it received from him. Thus, such stereotypical formulae for pedagogical recommendations such as "an individual approach" or "involvement in a collective" tell the pedagogue decidedly nothing. Either, first of all, they do not demonstrate how the recommendation is to be accomplished, nor, secondly, do they say anything about the nature of the individual approach or the involvement in a collective. If pedagogical recommendations are to be derived from scientific research and be the most important practical result of that research, they must be concrete, have content, and offer complete, specific, detailed, and clear indications as to the measures to be applied to the child and as to the phenomena or symptoms that are to be eliminated by application of those methods. (Only this way can the pedagogical prescriptions demonstrate the entire validity of the diagnostic research).

As we have shown, the poverty of our therapeutic pedagogy—and particularly in general practical pedagogy as it is to be applied to anomalous children—is, in part, attributable to the fact that no special methods or means of pedagogical activity have been cultivated at the center of pedological research; these could have been built only on the scientific understanding of a child. Prescription represents a practical criterion for all pedagogical research. It is the final goal of research and it gives meaning to that enterprise. We are convinced that real cultivation of pedological prescription, derived from a rich, scientific and substantive clinical study of children, will lead to a hitherto unseen flowering of all curative pedagogy, and to the whole system of individual pedagogical measures. On receiving a recommendation, a pedagogue should be able to know what it is he has to struggle with in a child's development, what means are appropriate to that purpose, and what effect they should have. Only knowing this can he evaluate the results of his activity. Otherwise, pedagogical recommendations will long rival pedagogical prognoses in their imprecision.

FROM ADDRESSES, REPORTS, ETC.

**[The Notes from the Russian Edition Are Entered
with Article in This Section.]**

Experimental Verification of New Methods for Teaching Speech to Deaf-Mute Children

These theses were compiled by Vygotsky for an address to the Pedological Soviet of the Gosudarstvennyi Nauchnyi Soviet (State Scholarly Commission) on questions of educating blind, deaf-mute, and mentally retarded children on May 25, 1925. They are printed here for the first time.

1. Speech instruction for deaf-mute children is a field now undergoing a certain crisis throughout the world. In various countries, strenuous efforts are being made to find the best method. No single system, which is in any way solidly grounded in science and recognized by all, currently exists. The unsatisfactory nature of former methods, especially of the German analytical methods, is becoming more apparent. Everyone is searching for a new system. In such circumstances, we must experiment.

2. In Russian schools, the situation is worse than in foreign schools. With the exception of two or three schools in the capital, there are almost no schools where a single system is being applied throughout. More strenuous efforts are being made by local talent. Every thoughtful teacher inevitably becomes a reformer. In addition to the general administrative and pedagogical weakness of our schools, the lack of adequately prepared cadres of specialists who might introduce these changes hampers the decisive undertaking of reforms. There are no cadres at the highest level (established scholars and theoreticians), nor at the middle level (methodologists, teachers at institutions of higher learning, and school directors), nor even at the lower level (teachers in public schools). This is our situation.

3. What is pushing us toward experimentation? Why is it so vitally necessary, so urgent? Why not permit ourselves to direct our energies, first of all, to the improvement of the overall

conditions of our schools, making special issues secondary and leaving them for more leisurely working out? There is one cardinal reason. The issue of speech instruction is, for the deaf-mute, the central, fundamental problem in their social education. Without some decision on this issue, we cannot, practically speaking, move toward the restructuring of the entire school on the basis of new principles. The tenor of the new schools and a new system for speech instruction must take shape in tandem, developing organically from the same ideas. The present method makes social education impossible, because social education cannot be accomplished without language. Furthermore, the language which is now offered children at school, be it verbal or mimed, is in essence an asocial language. Therefore, we must begin with speech.

4. What are the shortcomings of the former system? The pupil had to slave to complete the full course of speech instruction. Speech lagged behind development. He acquired not speech, but pronunciation; he developed not language, but articulation. Inevitably, he created his own language—mimed speech. In fact, all deaf-mutes speak with the aid of mimicry; speech is alien to them. In practical terms, speech contributes nothing as far as they are concerned. It rarely promotes their development and formation; it fails to act as a tool for accumulating social experience and for participating in social life. Besides, oral speech contradicts basic propositions in the psychology of language. It tries to construct words from sounds, and phrases from words. Thus, it is psychologically and pedologically bankrupt, socially fruitless; in practice as in life, it is almost useless.

5. What is the essence of reform? On closer examination, the faults of the former system are not based on any particular errors by its creators, who were brilliant psychologists and good pedagogues in their own right. For its time, and given its underlying educational theory, it was a faultless system. It inculcated in the student a sense of obedience; it instilled in him a religious and moral sense of his own shortcomings; and it gave him the speech to understand the sermon in church, the official language of the state, and the invalid-oriented, philanthropic sphere of relations in which he was placed. This is what was required of oral speech instruction, since it was believed that a child would correctly understand his position in society if he understood the language of the church, if he learned what the law was, and if he learned to respect society for its benevolence.

No single special system is intelligible unless it is seen against the general backdrop of socio-pedological ideas then current, the attitudes of the time, and the connections among these factors. The school determines the nature of the special system, not the reverse. It follows that the general school system predetermines the nature of reform, and reform cannot be limited simply to a single change in a special method. The problem of speech for deaf-mute children will be resolved not by special methods, but by the overall restructuring of our schools on the principles of social education. Speech will emerge in a deaf-mute child when the need for it arises, when it facilitates a school child's life and experiences. In order for that to take place, a reorganization of his whole life is needed, not just methodological change. Overall social education is fundamental to resolving the question of speech.

6. What, then, is the role of special methods? The perspective developed here does not, by any means, reject the importance and the significance of special methods in speech instruction. On the contrary, it is only through a careful formulation of the question that speech instruction can acquire a meaning that is not exclusively technical but has a meaning in principle. The schools' new structure must not only work out a technique for speech instruction. Evaluation of that technique must invariably be based on principles, both pedological principles and principles in social methodology. Here, one is impossible without

the other. Without a social basis to education, no technique can impart speech to a deaf child; without techniques of speech instruction, it is impossible to give children a social education.

7. Given the motives indicated above, and in view of the difficult circumstances in which we are beginning our experiment, we will not be able to carry it out over a broad area. We must limit it to a few schools, or even to individual classes. The entire experiment has a single purpose: To test the merits of various systems and to determine the degree to which they are valuable and correspond to the overall plan of our education. We cannot wait for the results of West European or American experiments and make use of recommendations that have already been completed; those experiments will be based on different principles and will take place in different schools. What do we hope to gain from our own experiment? We want an indication of which teaching technique will allow us most expediently and easily to introduce a child to speech and to its mastery. It is a fight for the complete sentence and the word against an acoustic concoction of speech; a struggle for the unity of oral speech against the jargon of mime (sign language); a fight for naturally stimulated speech development in live situations against the lifeless acquisition of speech through classes.

8. The content of experiments: The most interesting of today's synthetic systems for speech instruction must be experimentally evaluated. In the next three years, we must proceed with the experimental evaluation of methods from the work of K. Malisch, G. Forchhammer, and I. A. Sokolianskii.

9. Procedure for conducting the experiment: First of all, the experiment must pass through laboratory preparation. That preparation must be given over to a single individual, as his responsibility. Preparations should consist of (a) the precise adaptation of the system to the Russian language; (b) the development of a three-year plan of instruction; (c) the formulation of methods and techniques of teaching; and (d) the organization of auxiliary aids, materials, and texts.

10. Experiments should be conducted with six groups; two groups per method.[*] Those six groups should contain children up to and through kindergarten who are at the babbling and early language stages. In any case, the groups must not include children already studying at school. It would be preferable if a single school were converted into an experimental school for three years; within it a kindergarten and six sections of the first year could be opened. If an experimental school should prove impossible, then regional schools might be chosen for the experiment. It would be highly desirable to isolate these children from those who use mime.

11. Experimental controls: Simultaneously, in other schools, control groups must be organized to consist of children who are approximately similar in age, preparation, and health. These children should complete a traditionally taught course in speech instruction, with teachers who are identical in knowledge and abilities.

12. Annual evaluations of the experiment is called for. A commission on method should be placed in each school to keep a continuous and close account of the experiment. It is desirable to keep an accurate diary of the school's work. Overall evaluation should proceed on the basis of (a) material evidence of the children's speech development; (b) the social role of language in their lives; and (c) the time and effort expended in instruction.

13. Once the plan is introduced, it will be necessary to (a) organize a library around the issue of speech in the deaf-mute; (b) link up with creators of methods in Ukraine, Denmark,

---

[*] The three methods implied are presumably those, mentioned in Paragraph 8, above, of Malisch, Forchhammer and Sokolianskii respectively. [Ed]

Germany, and other countries; (c) supply the material means for carrying out the experiments.

14. The experiment cannot be carried out in the conditions usual in our former schools. The whole educational system must be adapted to this experiment.

15. The crucial question in the experiment, as in general with matters dealing with the deaf in the Russian Soviet Federated Socialist Republic, is the question of preparing cadres of specialists for organization of scientific work in defectology. If possible, the most appropriate procedure would be to organize the experimental schools in connection with existing institutions of higher education which already have defectology divisions. The current state of rarely pursued scientific research work and the instruction by the allied academic departments is in no way satisfactory. Only the creation of a scientific center for work with deaf-mute children, only reforms of the departments of pedagogy for the mute and the organization of research can serve as a fertile ground for the experiments we are undertaking. Otherwise they will inevitably degenerate into amateurism and will be condemned to complete futility.

Methods for Studying Mentally Retarded Children: Thesis of an Address

Thesis for an address to the First All-Russian Conference on Special Schools which met in 1928. It appears in print here for the first time.

1. Traditional methods of research, such as A. Binet's scale, G. I. Rossolimo's profile and others, are based on purely *quantitative* conception of childhood development and, in essence, limit themselves to the *negative* characteristics of the child. Both these tendencies speak to the purely negativistic task of weeding out of general schools the children who are inappropriate to them. These methods are unable to present the *positive* characteristics in a particular kind of child nor perceive his qualitative uniqueness. Thus, these methods directly contradict not only contemporary scientific norms on the process of child development, but also the need of abnormal child for special education.

2. Modern scientific concepts of child development reach out into two apparently contradictory directions that are, in reality, interdependent. One direction is concerned with the *differentiation* of psychological functions from each other, the clarification of their respective qualitative features, and their *relationship* to independent developments (e.g., studies of motor skills, practical aptitudes, and so on). The other direction is concerned with the dynamic interconnections among these functions, the discovery of the unity of the personality of the child, and the clarification of the complex structural and functional links among developments in various aspects of the personality.[*]

3. A system of research founded on these propositions and charged with the *positive* characterization of the child provide the basis for an educational plan dedicated to three main principles: (1) the principle of *distinguishing the acquisition* of facts from their *interpretation*; (2) the principle of *maximal specialization of methods for investigating individual*

---

[*] The differentiation of psychological functions in handicapped children is the key to contemporary research and practice in the areas of diagnostics and education at the Scientific Research Institute of Defectology in Moscow today. [Transl]

functions; (3) the principle of *dynamic* and *typological* interpretation of data gained through investigation for diagnostic purposes.

Anomalies in the Cultural Development of the Child

Precis of an address to a meeting of the Defectology Section of the Institute of Scientific Pedology at Moscow State University II on April 28, 1928. It was published in Voprosy defektologii (Questions of Defectology), 1929 (cover date, 1930), Vol 2 (8).

In the process of cultural development, a child absorbs not only the content of a cultural experience, but also the methods and manners of cultural behavior and thought. He masters those special cultural means, such as, language, arithmetical symbols, etc., created by mankind during its cultural development A child learns to use certain signs functionally as a means to fulfilling some psychological operation or other. Thus, elementary and primitive forms of behavior become mediated cultural acts and processes.

On the basis of contemporary research, it can be established that the cultural development of higher psychological functions occurs in four basic stages. The first of these is the *natural-primitive stage*, or the most primitive of the forms of cultural behavior, in which the child or savage completes arithmetic operations through direct perception of quantities. The second stage is the so-called *stage of naive psychology*, when a child accumulates certain experience about the means of cultural behavior, but cannot make use of those means. In the third stage of *externally mediated acts* the children already make proper use of external signs to carry out one or another operations (counting on fingers, and so on). Finally, at the fourth stage external signs are replaced by internal ones and the activity is internally mediated (for example, in doing mental calculations). In the anomalous cultural development of the mentally retarded or physically defective child, the child is arrested or constrained at one of the stages of cultural development enumerated here for a longer than the normal child is.

From the Article "Conference Results"

This article was written to summarize the First Pedological Conference, which took place in Moscow between December 27, 1927 and January 4, 1928. It was published in the journal, Narodnaoe Prosveshchenie (People's Education) 1928, Vol. 2.

The problem of defective children and with children who are difficult to educate occupied a major part of the conference. On the basis of the materials presented, the conference established that the new perspective on the nature and origins of children who are difficult to educate was shown to be correct and fruitful on the basis of the pedagogical work with children who are difficult to educate, as it has unfolded over the past decade, and the pedagogical study of children. This consistent Marxist perspective considers childhood neglect and educational difficulties to be first and foremost the result of social and economic factors with the exception of a certain percentage of cases in which biological deficiencies and mixed forms turn out to be the causes of pedagogical "difficulties" among children. A number of studies of the socio-economic factors among difficult children have shown that precisely these factors are the fundamental cause of problems of childhood in a significant number of cases and that if the primary cause is dealt with, the difficulties will be resolved. Research has uncovered broad possibilities for reeducation and for bringing pedagogical influence to bear on children who are difficult to educate and established it as the basis for all educational practice. In its turn, biological research has yielded valuable material for the battle with those forms of childhood educational difficulties which have biological bases.

Because of objective conditions, the psychology of a difficult childhood has not yet accumulated and worked on enough of its own material collected from this new perspective, and pedology has had to operate from the positions and methods of general psychology. Further advancement in this area, organizing serious scientific research work, creating an extensive methodology for research on difficult children and the social roots of their "difficulties"; these are the immediate tasks laid down by the conference. The conference noted a series of concrete problems which need scientific investigation: The problems of working with children who are difficult to educate within the framework of the general schools; the issue of labor, and the organization of collectives in institutions for the educationally difficult; and the problem of a methodology for the study of difficult children.

Broad scientific and practical work has occurred in the last decade in the psychology of mental retardation and physical defectiveness. A major reexamination of basic problems in this area has replaced the former, narrowly biological, treatment of defects with a new socio-biological approach to conditioning of all development in mentally retarded and physically deficient children.

Thanks to much effort, our special schools have succeeded, according to the general opinion of specialists in the area, in raising themselves to a level they had not attained before the Revolution. The results of the revision of the psychological problems of mental retardation and physical defectiveness from the new perspective have provided the basis for a radical reexamination of pedological practice in special schools. Some old practices of the pre-revolutionary special school—such as the isolation of children from life surrounding them and the orientation of all pedological work toward the defect—have been repudiated. Special schools have been incorporated into the mainstream of Soviet pedagogy and reconstructed on the basis of general principles for special education. These schools rely upon special work of the Young Pioneers in labor preparation.

Here, as in all other areas, the attention of the conference and center of gravity of its resolutions fell not on results but on perspectives; more on the future than on the past; on that which is yet to come, rather than on that which has already been. A condensed list of future tasks for psychology enumerated by the conference included: preventative issues in educational difficulty or forecasting problems and improving the pedagogical health of all educational work, its conditions, and the daily life surrounding the children; questions of a dispensary system for mentally retarded and physically defective children; establishing principles and methods for the standardization and diagnostics of difficult childhood; attracting psychologist-specialists to work in institutions which are strongest in the education of difficult childhood; introducing a psychological base for the pedagogical and curative-pedological practice for educating difficult children. By comparison with the vastness of these tasks, what we have already accomplished seems a small part of the path, the longest piece of which lies in the future. But the conference judged in this as in all of our psychological work, the past is significant only as an approach to the vastness of the future.

On the Length of Childhood for Mentally Retarded Children

Brief contents of an address to a session of the Defectology Section of the Institute of Scientific Pedology at Moscow State University II, on December 18, 1928. Published in the journal Voprosy defektologii (Questions of Defectology) 1929 (cover date, 1930) Vol. 2(8).

The question of the structure and functions of childhood for normal and abnormal children is linked to the question of the length of childhood and its various stages. The duration of childhood basically depends on the complexity of an organism, its conduct, and the complexity and variability in its surroundings. The fundamental symptoms of childhood are development and plasticity. There are scientific bases for the supposition, made by G. V. Murashev [no ref.] on the basis of his own research, that a mentally retarded child's childhood is shortened, rather than prolonged beyond that of a normal child. The pedagogical inferences to be drawn from this assumption, should it be validated, would be expressed primarily as a struggle for a more prolonged childhood for mentally retarded children and as a reevaluation of the traditional principle of considering such children to be at lower ages in the course of their growth. Theoretically, it would lead to an altered understanding of mental retardation. A mentally retarded child would be considered not only to be retarded but as developing in an accelerated way within the limits of his own particular type of retardation.

On the Question of Speech Development and Educational Training for Deaf-Mute Children: Theses of an Address

Theses of an address to the Second Conference of School-Workers Who Work with Deaf-Mute Children and Teenagers. The conference took place in 1930. Published here for the first time.

1. The revolutionary restructuring of schools for deaf-mute children has required a theoretical and practical reexamination of the problems of speech development and instruction for deaf-mute children. Practice has justified the basic principles which lay at the base of this reexamination.

2. Further developments in education for the deaf and its closer approach to general schools will lead to the necessity of further revisions of the existing problem in its practical and theoretical aspects, since present demands for speech instruction are not being fulfilled.

3. Regardless of the theoretical and practical success of education of the mute, further reexamination will require us to recognize that the problem of speech instruction for the deaf-mute child can for the most part not be considered as solved with respect to the relationship between speech instruction and general education for the deaf-mute child.

4. In this respect, the need arises to reexamine the traditional theoretical and practical relationship among various kinds of speech in deaf-mute children and particularly required is a reexamination of the relationship between *mimicry and written language.*

5. Experimental and clinical research in psychology concurrently demonstrate that polyglossia (the mastery of a variety of forms of speech) is unavoidable; given current

conditions in pedagogy for the mute. It is the most fruitful path for speech instruction and speech education for deaf-mute children.

6. Therefore, there should be a radical change of the traditional view which holds that various forms of language compete with each other and mutually interfere with the development of the deaf-mute child and we should set forth the theoretical and practical question about cooperation among them and the evolution of complexity in structure at various levels of instruction.

Cultural Development of Anomalous and Difficult to Educate Children: Theses of a Lecture

Theses of the lecture delivered at the First Conference on the Study of Human Behavior, which took place in Moscow in February 1930. It was published in the book: Psycho-neurological Science in the USSR (Moscow/Leningrad, 1930).

1. The cultural development of a child includes not only the process of forming the higher psychological functions but also the development of higher manifestations of character.

2. As a rule, deviations and delays in the development of intellect and character in anomalous and difficult children are connected with the cultural underdevelopment of each side of the personality, or of the personality as a whole (primitivism in oligophrenia and hypobilic mechanism in hysteria).

3. The correct methodological approach to the question of the relations between primary and secondary deviations and delays in the development of an anomalous or difficult child offer a key to the methods of research and the methods of social education for such a child.

4. The study of secondary complications in the development of an anomalous or difficult child (cultural underdevelopment) opens up some concrete symptom complexes that are most important in both a theoretical and a practical connection. These symptom complexes are more plastic and more dynamic in their psychological nature, and they therefore are the fundamental sphere for the application of curative-pedological activity.

5. Clinical psychological and experimental psychological research into cultural underdevelopment in deaf-mutes, oligophrenia, and hysteria has shown that delays in the development of the higher functions and the higher characterological layers of the personality are secondary complications, which respond to therapeutic-pedagogical influence.

Comments on Lectures by P. D. Mernenko, P. O. Efrussi, and A. M. Scherbina

The three following comments by Vygotsky on lectures by P. D. Mernenko, P. O. Efrussi, and A. M. Shcherbina were printed in the journal Voprosy defektologii (Questions of Defectology) in 1929 (cover date, 1930) Vol. 2 (8). Lectures on various questions concerning "auxiliary schools" were systematically conducted by the Defectology Section of the Institute of Scientific Pedology at Moscow State University I in 1928-1929.

Discussion of a Lecture by P. D. Mernenko

Mernenko, Pelageia Dmitrievna, Director, Children's Diagnostic Section of the Experimental Defectology Institute until 1932. Vygotsky's remarks were directed at the lecture entitled, "Development of the Sense of Touch and Its Role in Child Development," delivered on June 19, 1928.

The positive side of the lecture is its theory on the sense of touch. Indeed, the sense of touch has great significance for spatial representation (this is of special salience for the blind, among whom this sense is especially clearly observed). Still, it is necessary to develop the analyzers [the senses] from a functional perspective, to develop not the analyzer [a given sense] but the ability to use it. We are forced to respond negatively to the question whether one should develop the accuracy of analyzers [the senses]. Human progress does not at all consist of increased accuracy in the work of the analyzers [the senses].

The work of P.D. Mernenko is valuable; her observations must be collected and elaborated upon.

Discussion of a Lecture by P. O. Efrussi

These are Vygotsky's remarks on P. O. Efrussi's lecture entitled "The Composition of Participants and the Programs of Special Schools," delivered on May 15, 1928.

The question of pedagogical neglect and mental retardation conjoin in the question of the cultural development of a child—the higher mental functions can develop only on the basis of some cultural development. The root of inadequate differentiation lies in the fact that the methodology adopted for the study uncovers only negative properties. Nevertheless, in recent years, there have been significant gains which permit further progress. The lecture is extremely valuable in that it poses a question about the analysis of the established definition of *mental retardation* and the extension of its distinctions.

Discussion of a Lecture by A. M. Shcherbina

Vygotsky's statement on A. M. Shcherbina's lecture "On the Question of the Expediency of Developing a System to Produce Mathematical Activity in Blind Individuals." November 27, 1928.

Any single regulated and fixed system has negative as well as positive features. There is the danger that fixed systems will not only fail to encourage exploration, but retard it. We do not have a single generally accepted and established method even for the most important parts of the pedagogical process in schools for normal children, (for example, for the teaching of reading). And this is altogether understandable for no single method has a sufficient scientific basis for acceptance as the single most expedient system. Research on systems of mathematical symbols for the blind should be initiated; it has enormous practical and theoretical significance. But, we must still decline at the moment to consolidate a monopoly for any single system.

AFTERWORD

E. S. Bein, T. A. Vlasova,[*] R. E. Levina, N. G. Morozova, Zh. I. Shif

The productive life of the outstanding Soviet psychologist Lev Semenovich Vygotsky serves as an ideal example in the theoretical struggle for the creation of truly scientific disciplines in psychology and defectology and for the creation of the dialectical-materialist study of normal and troubled children. On one hand, the examination of anomalous children in the light of broad psychological laws played a large role in the discovery of various developmental anomalies. On the other hand, psychological problems were illuminated by new theoretical and factual explanations and discoveries in the light of data from defectology. Problems in defectology always occupied an important place in Vygotsky's theoretical and experimental research. Vygotsky made a most important contribution to the creation of a scientific basis for Soviet defectology. His experimental and theoretical research in the field of abnormal childhood remains fundamental to productive work on defectological problems. Vygotsky's work helped to restructure practices in the field of special instruction.

Vygotsky's interest in the personality of mentally retarded and physically impaired children developed early in his scientifically active career. He first became interested in the problems of studying mental retardation in Gomel while working in teachers' seminars. For the duration of his creative life, Vygotsky critically examined theories on the psychological development of normal and abnormal children and analyzed various kinds of anomalous development. His analysis was directed toward uncovering the internal nature of the pathology—from the genesis of the primary handicap to the appearance of secondary, tertiary, and lower-order symptoms in the development process; from accounting for the interfunctional links and ties that were formed, to understanding the peculiarities of an anomalous child's entire personality. A far from complete list of his contributions to psychology in general as well as defectology includes: his theory of the unity of learning and development (where learning plays a leading role in a child's psychological develop-ment), his work on the zone of proximal development (which even now remains part of defectology and of general psychology and pedagogy), and the concept of the unity of intellect and affect in the mind.

---

[*] Member of the Soviet Collegium of Editors.

Vygotsky's first published work on defectology appeared in 1924, in research he undertook at the Institute of Psychology together with work at NarKomPros [People's Commissariat of Enlightenment] in the subsection on the education of handicapped children. Defectological research was naturally part of his scientific activity. In 1925–1926, Vygotsky organized a laboratory on the psychology of abnormal children in Moscow at 8, Pogodinskaia St., where the Medical-Pedagogical Station of NarKomPros for the RSFSR was situated at the time. This proved to be the predecessor to the Experimental-Defectological Institute of NarKomPros, formed in 1929 and now the Scientific Research Institute of Defectology, attached to the Academy of Pedological Sciences of the USSR). During his last years, Vygotsky was the scientific director of this Institute.

The theory of psychological development, formulated by Vygotsky in studying abnormal children, lay at the base of his research into anomalous childhood. His scholarship demonstrated that the general laws of children's development are also followed in the development of abnormal children.

Demonstrating the similarity of psychological regularities between normal children and children with developmental deviations allowed Vygotsky to substantiate the broad notion of development in the anomalous child's personality. The researcher showed that in addition to the development of the separate sides of the personality and consciousness there was also a development in the relationships among them. In anomalous children all these relationships are altogether unique. They develop in the course of different developmental periods, at different tempi, and with different qualities, and are accompanied at each stage of development with the formation of specific structures that are characteristic of the anomaly. In analyzing the different variants of handicap structures, Vygotsky disclosed the unique relationship of affect and intellect, of the higher and lower psychological functions.

These productive thoughts do not exhaust the results of Vygotsky's work on problems of development in normal and abnormal children. In the 1930's, the last years of his life, Vygotsky's approach to the problems of psychological and defectological research broadened. In the forefront of the plan were placed the issues of generalizing ideas about specifics of the developmental processes in normal and anomalous children. By examining this process in childhood years and demonstrating the cardinal fact of changes in inter-functional ties, Vygotsky posed a most important methodological question about the changing structure of psychological processes and of consciousness in normal and anomalous children at various ages and stages.

All of Vygotsky's work was consistently imbued with the idea that the specifically human characteristics of the mind are socially conditioned and led to the demonstration of that idea. He showed that social activity, and pedagogical influences in particular, are an inexhaustible source of formations of the higher mental processes both in normalcy and pathology. Vygotsky's conception foresaw not only general, but also specific regularities of psychological development which could appear in pathologies. As opposed to the "philanthropic-invalid" and "social-charitable" views, Vygotsky brought forward questions of social education and instruction of anomalous children.

His idea about the possibility of mental development (and not merely the absorption of knowledge and skills) during education played a decisive role in the restructuring of special pedagogy.

Vygotsky placed his defectological research in opposition to biologizing concepts; these latter affirm that there are special laws of development for anomalous children. He emphasized that the fundamental issue (deriving from the fact that the same general laws condition both normal and abnormal children's development) was that the social conditioning of development was a basic and general law for both kinds of children. Vygotsky also believed that the process of personality development was conditioned by a unity of social and biological factors; he indicated that this unity could not be expressed as a mechanical, statistical combination of hereditary and environmental factors, but was instead a complex, differentiated, and dynamic entity, which changed in relation to individual mental functions as well as in relation to various growth stages. Therefore, it is important to determine the role and significance of each of these factors in order to correctly understand the process of a child's mental development.

Any psychological process carries within itself both hereditary predispositions and environmental influences. But the relative weight of each of these influences is different for different aspects of the mind, at different ages. Vygotsky further emphasized that the development of complex mental processes (purposeful attention, active remembering, reflective activity) as well as those of character and behavior, all of which undergo lengthy development (during pre-school, school, adolescent, and young adult ages), and are immeasurably more dependent on the surrounding environment (on educational and teaching conditions, surrounding culture and daily-life, the character of associations, the form and methods of activities, and so on) than on heredity. Thus, according to Vygotsky, all this is not only a condition but also a source of a child's development. From the first days of his existence, a child finds himself acted upon by his surrounding social environment and interacts with it. This action and interaction determines his development and, as it were, leads it along. Still, the hereditary component, no matter how small it may be, also participates in the formation of the higher mental functions.

One of the basic ideas which Vygotsky defended with sharp polemics was the idea that a difficult child's characteristics should be examined, not statically, not as the sum of his defects and his shortcomings, but dynamically. Unusual qualities in this area cannot be understood through the traditional quantitative approach, which views the handicapped child under examination primarily from the negative side. Thus, a distinction between abnormal and normal children was seen in the fact that a handicapped child's attention was weaker, the grasp of his memory and the duration of his remembering shorter than a normal child's, and so on. Such examination led to a more parsimonious understanding of the mental characteristics of mentally retarded and physically impaired children. The notion of development, which Vygotsky advanced in the process of working out a general psychological theory on higher mental functions and which was introduced into defectology, played an important part in eliminating this "arithmetical concept of handicap."

In discovering the underlying dynamic at the base of development in mentally retarded, physically impaired, and learning-disabled children, Vygotsky succeeded in demonstrating the positive side of these children's personality. This optimistic purpose—searching for the positive capacities for development in anomalous children—is the most important of Vygotsky's defectological work, especially in his work on developmental diagnostics. Vygotsky fixed his attention—and this is the originality of his approach—on those capacities still remaining in such children and which could act as the basis for the evolution of their potential abilities. What interested Vygotsky was a child's potential, not his handicap.

L. S. Vygotsky insisted on a new approach to the anomalous child. While rejecting the study of the external manifestations of individual functions, given some anomaly or other, he advocated a genetic examination of the entire system of functions and their interrelations, given various anomalies. He demonstrated the necessity for a genetic analysis of systems;

first, with respect not only to the mental processes themselves, but also to their interrelations (that is, the changes in interfunctional relationships), and second, with respect to the examination of cause and effect in developmental characteristics and in all the deviations which can take place given a particular anomaly.

Vygotsky gave particular emphasis to the development of the higher mental processes and their interrelation with the more elementary processes in anomalous children. His research demonstrated the possibility of development and compensation for mental and sensory handicaps, given the prior development and perfection of the higher mental functions, instead of simple training in the elementary functions.

Vygotsky emphasized the necessity for studying not only the symptoms of a particular handicap, but also the essence of its changes and the character of new formations.

Vygotsky was the first to formulate, as basic to both the theory and the clinical practice for difficult children, the demand to move from studying symptoms in a particular handicap to studying the essence of the changes taking place in the developmental process, which manifest themselves as those symptoms. A transformation of the kind initiated by E. Kraepelin in psychiatry was near and dear to Vygotsky in that it surpassed the phenomenological approach and sought to discover the mechanism behind phenomena. But this was only the beginning for Vygotsky. Kraepelin's revolution actually consisted only in replacing symptoms with symptom-complexes and smaller complexes with larger ones.

The task Vygotsky offered researchers on difficult childhood was the transition from studying symptom-complexes as an end in themselves to studying the developmental process, "only manifested in these conditions." It is difficult to evaluate the novelty (early in the development of defectology) and the fruitfulness of this idea, which was directed at the discovery of internal regularities, the internal logic in a child's development process. With respect to anomalous childhood, one might call Vygotsky's task necessary for the clinical and psychological study of anomalous children or the discovery of the nature of the disorder characterizing various types of difficult child. Vygotsky showed that to create psychological clinics for difficult children means experimentally and theoretically separating and describing, in all their profusion, the causal-dynamic links in the basic types, mechanisms, and forms of development of both normal and abnormal children.

One of Vygotsky's most important attainments was his analysis of the relationship between the developmental processes and learning in childhood years. His consistently dialectical approach to this central issue resulted in the discovery of complex dynamic interrelationships between the processes of development and learning, in demonstrating the leading and stimulating role of instruction and the absence of parallelism between the two. He believed that instruction always leads development, and that a child has sensitive periods, during which he is particularly open to the influence of teaching, to absorbing a particular educational discipline, and during which various mental processes are particularly effectively formed in him.

Noting that, in human psychological development, the formation of various mental functions is characteristically neither simultaneous nor equal, Vygotsky, with his inherently dialectical thinking, showed that each mental function has an optimal stage of development during its formation, and that the period during which a function plays a leading role in activity occurs during that stage.

Distinguishing what a child has already attained (his actual developmental level) and his potential abilities (the zone of proximal development) proved spectacularly productive in understanding the mutual ties between learning and development. Vygotsky emphasized that instruction shou   based not so much on what the child has already achieved, as on the processes which   developing or which have not yet been formed. In differentiating what a child can atta   only in cooperation with adults from what he can attain personally through development, Vygotsky expressed one of his central ideas: The source of development in mental processes is always social. Only later do these processes acquire individual psychological characteristics.

The notion that early correction of abnormal development and taking account of the zones of proximal development were necessary in diagnostics for anomalous children was posited and based on the results of research into the processes of learning and development and into the sensitive (optimal) period in the development of mental functions.

The conception of actual levels and potential zones for development is based on the notion of broadening the proximal zones of development and broadening the child's potential possibilities. Vygotsky's introduction of these concepts had an invaluable significance in determining mental developmental conditions, tempi, and prospects in both normal and anomalous children. This idea, which shows the dialectical nature of the developmental process, has entered our practice and continues to serve in the study and teaching of anomalous children and in the analysis of the effectiveness of pedagogical processes. Its propositions have led to a new understanding of the problems of interrelations among special, self-timed, and differentiated learning and development in anomalous children; they have likewise permitted new understandings of problems in the diagnostics, compensation, and correction of various handicaps. In this respect, Vygotsky marked a new stage in the development of defectology: He elevated it to the level of a dialectical-materialist science. By giving a theoretical basis to the directions, principles, and methods of research and diagnostics about anomalous children, he imposed on the universal criticism which existed around those methods a basis which required the accommodation of handicaps and which indicated a path for restructuring special educational methods.

Lev Semenovich pointed out that the content of anomalous children's education acts as a powerful factor in correcting shortcomings in their development and in development in general. It is altogether obvious that this position has great significance not only for defectology, but for psychology and pedagogy as a whole.

A specific change in the structure of the handicap, unique in every case, takes place during the process of the development of anomalous children under the influence of instruction and education for work.

During the development of the higher mental processes, a restructuring of the relationships among them takes place; first, perception takes the leading role, then memory, then logical verbal thought, and likewise with the ever-growing inclusion of purposefulness and the use of varying amounts of mediation. In connection with this, there are new corrective tasks which arise in the teaching of anomalous children. Vygotsky saw the possibility of advancing and improving children's cognitive activities in the active formation of their higher mental processes.

Vygotsky's position on the law of "interiorization" (that is, the change from external processes using tools, supports, and methods of cognitive activity and behavioral forms, to internal ones) is extremely important for the instruction of anomalous children for communicating in the process of their cultural development. This communication takes place by first externally mastering the mediation to purposeful higher mental functions then mastering them internally.

In the area of defectology, we cannot bypass the f▮▮▮▮▮▮▮▮tion of the problems of speech formation in deaf children could not have▮▮▮▮▮▮▮▮ without Vygotsky's comments on every-day notions and scientific conc▮▮▮▮▮▮▮w that the deaf child, deprived as he is of the opportunity to form speech b▮▮▮▮▮▮▮n his environment, has no worldly concepts. Every concept, with all its mod▮▮▮▮▮▮▮grammatical changes, is absorbed by a deaf child as a learned concept. But the▮▮▮▮▮▮of such worldly concepts, which have such a decisive significance in a child's▮▮▮▮▮▮, in a child's mastery of the bases of instruction, do not and cannot appear as a▮▮▮▮▮ct of the curriculum in either mass or special schools; it would be impossible ▮▮▮▮▮nasize the need to introduce a discipline of a sort of practical-subject study or o▮▮▮▮▮ted activity into schools for the deaf.

In considering the possibilities for mentally r▮▮▮▮▮and other categories of anomalous children (those who are deaf, blind, or unmana▮▮▮▮▮ Vygotsky spoke of the possibility and necessity of extensively using practical, ob▮▮▮▮riented activity, first as a foundation for practical intellect and, then for the development of more complex forms of logical thinking. He believed that efficiency, based on practical work activity, activity which raises the ability to pose goals, plan, and think, is the basic principle of instruction and the only solid ground for the formation of thought and language with real content. This idea, later put into practice in teaching deaf children (by S. A. Zykov[*]), proved highly productive in developing speech in such children. Practical, object-oriented instruction was introduced into the curriculum of schools for the deaf as an independent discipline in 1972, after protracted and profound research.

Vygotsky was a deep and merciless critic of the fundamentally pessimistic pedological theory which relied on training (that is, educating the conditional reflexes) as the general method for educating and raising mentally retarded children. He countered this view with his conviction that, by mastering the rudiments of thinking during elementary forms of work, an anomalous child can acquire something more valuable that simply a fund of rote skills.

Vygotsky attached great significance to collective activity, collaboration, and interaction for the formation of the mentality of both normal and anomalous children. The role of the collective in anomalous childhood was revealed to him in a variety of ways: in speech development, in the formation of the child's personality, in the development of higher mental functions, and so on. He wrote: "The basic principle and fulcrum for all our pedagogy for the abnormal child requires us now to be able to understand anew, in the light of real, natural phenomena, the links between collaboration [interaction] and the development of higher mental functions; between the development of the collective and the abnormal child's personality." These positions, which continue even now to be important, were particularly significant in the first days of Soviet power, when the principles and organizational bases of special schools were still being framed.

It was Vygotsky himself who worked out the basic similarities in normal and abnormal children's personality formation, who uncovered the mutual, dialectic links and conditionality in thought and language; who indicated the significance of these higher mental functions as individual means of regulating activity, their place and role in establishing self-consciousness. He showed that it was not only the mental functions that form in the process of development, but also complex mutual ties and relationships amongst them which lead to

[*] S. A. Zykov heads the Institute of Defectology's laboratory for instruction in schools for the deaf in the former Soviet Union. [Transl.]

systemic and mea.   ent of *business, develop*   .ole. Developmental
levels in the conscic   r, det *pathological, however*   pment of each mental
process (including th   *psychological)* at   nscious activity.
    The fundamental   *dhood led him to*   vered in analyzing normal
and pathological chil.   *ity.*   elopment for an anomalous
child's whole personal.   *fferent variants*
    While analyzing di   *d intellect, of the*   searcher discovered the unique
relationship of affect an   *igins, and demo*   her mental functions. He revealed
the regularities in their of   *sequence of p*   possibility of preventing secondary
disorders which are the cor   *arise, in his ob*   s and are tied in turn to the diseased
organ. Secondary disorders ;   m, when there is inappropriately timed or
incorrect pedagogical activity.   *ositions on*
    Vygotsky formulated his p.   *ing*   *the*   development process as though they consti-
tuted the making of the human be *ing*   aking of the human personality. This process
takes place through the constant appe   ce of new characteristics, new ties, and new
formations. New formations, as Vygotsky indicated, are prepared throughout preceding
development, but they are not entirely contained in a prepared form nor simply weaker in
the preceding stages; once they have put in an appearance, new forms undergo qualitative
changes and exercise a regularized influence on subsequent psychological changes.

    Along with the appearance at each developmental stage of new formations and along
with the restructuring of interfunctional links, Vygotsky showed that there are particular
changes in the structure of a handicap which are specific to each developmental anomaly
and which anomalous children undergo during the development process under the influences
of instruction and labor education. Vygotsky substantiated the proposition that an anomalous
child's personality has a complex structure, and that various difficulties in interaction within
the social sphere lead to movement in and restructuring of the child's personality. Vygotsky
documented the significant and unusual unevenness of development of mental functions in
the presence of various kinds of handicaps. In connection with the disruption of sensory,
intellectual, affective, and volitional processes, the interrelationship of the mental functions
changes: One function may fail or be severely delayed in the developmental process while
others may develop compensatorily under the influence of individual exercises and special
instruction, and may, in their turn, influence other sides of an anomalous child's mental
activities and personality.

    Prior to Vygotsky, defectology was based on ideas about isolating the mental functions
and attaining purely descriptive pathological characterizations of individual functions and
symptoms. Vygotsky's teachings about the restructuring of the personality during the
compensatory process shattered the traditional psychological notion of separate functions,
more or less independent of one another, since he showed the dialectical nature of changes
in those functions and that these lead to qualitative changes in the whole consciousness and
personality.

    Vygotsky's theory of development categorically required the individualization of its
object: Understanding the internal essence of the pathological process cannot, according to
Vygotsky, be separated from a precise knowledge of the patient's personality.

    In examining the essence of the compensatory processes, Vygotsky reached a conclu-
sion, basic to research, about the two-sided nature of a handicap's consequences: On the one
hand, the result is an underdevelopment of functions, which is directly linked to the
pathogenic factor; on the other, adaptive compensatory mechanisms arise. In opposition to

the biologizing concept of the compensatory process in anomalous development as a mechanical automatic substitution for the suffering function, Vygotsky understood it as the sequel to the weakened function's independent exercise and as the result of the education of the remaining facets of the anomalous child's mind and personality. Vygotsky also demonstrated that the outcome of this compensation depends not only on the severity of the defect, but to a great degree also on the adequacy and efficacy of the methods of activity used during the formation of the compensatory processes; depending on the success of compensation and correction, the structure of the handicap changes.

In his works, Vygotsky first discovered the complex structure of handicaps with respect to the uneven development of mental functions (the uneven stages and severity of disruptions in various psychological processes, which was very important for the correction of developmental handicaps in children) and the unique nature of intercompensatory processes in anomalous children. Next he reinterpreted the concepts of primary and secondary symptoms and the peculiar relationship between primary and secondary disorders during anomalous development, given inappropriately timed or incorrect pedagogical action. As Vygotsky indicated, the structure of a handicap cannot be reduced to a symptom which is directly linked to the damaged biological systems (such as organic lesions of the analyzers [sensory organs] or central nervous system), and which Vygotsky referred to as primary symptoms of the disorder. The underdevelopment of the higher psychological functions (such as speech and thought in the deaf, mediated cultural memory in retarded children, perception and spatial orientation in the blind, and so on) and the social aspects of behavior were phenomena which Vygotsky called secondary problems and which he held were not directly linked with the basic, primary defect, but conditioned by it. He showed how this relationship among primary, secondary, and subsequent overlying defects in anomalous development complicates the structure of a handicap and the accurate understanding of its nature. He analyzed these same circumstances with a view to foreseeing and overcoming these developmental deviations. According to his observations, correct teaching and education help to overcome the causes which generate secondary, tertiary, and further deviations. Given this, Vygotsky believed that the central focus for compensation should be the intensification of cultural development: the development of the higher psychological functions, of the scope of communication, and of social and labor relationships within collectives.

According to Vygotsky's data, the further the disorder is from the affected organ and the primary deviations associated with it the more easily the disorder will respond to correction ("therapeutic pedagogical action").

Posing the problem of primary and secondary disorders and their differentiation in an anomalous (difficult) child's development led Vygotsky to reexamine the most important questions in the diagnostics of anomalous development. He insisted on a qualitative, and not a purely quantitative, approach to studying children with handicaps and demanded an explanation of such children's characteristics with a reasoned, causal, dynamic, positive, but not symptomatic, examination of their development. In connection with this, he sharply criticized the contemporary state of the pedagogy of difficult childhood, which he compared to the condition of psychiatry prior to Kraepelin, when psychoses were classified according to their external appearances, much as if internal illnesses could be classified according to the presence of a cough or a headache.

In Vygotsky's work on anomalous children, he paid a great deal of attention to the relationship between intellect and affect in the presence of various developmental abnormalities for example, the changing relationship of intellectual and affective disorders during the development of a mentally retarded child. Thus, the cornerstone on which the study of the mentally retarded should be built, Vygotsky believed, was the unity of intellect and affect, examined while taking into account the characteristics of development as a whole. If the affective processes first influence the cognitive ones, then, during development, the higher psychological functions begin to have, in their turn, an organizing influence on the affective processes which lie at their base.

In discussion of K. Lewin, Vygotsky noted that understanding the uniqueness of a retarded child does not mean only moving the center of gravity from the intellectual handicap to handicaps in the affective sphere. Rather it implies, first of all, the necessity of rising completely above the isolated and metaphysical vision of the intellect and affect as self-sufficient entities and recognizing their internal links and unity. It also means freeing oneself from seeing the tie between intellect and affect as a one-sided mechanical dependence of thought on feeling.

In Vygotsky's work on handicaps, especially in his book *Developmental Diagnostics and the Pedological Clinic for Difficult Childhood*, which was published posthumously (1936), he offered a critique of the antiscientific nature of contemporary pedology, a critique which was exceptional in its depth.

It is worth pausing, in particular, on Vygotsky's relationship with contemporary pedology.

At that time, in Soviet psychology, children's psychology had not yet been established as an independent branch of psychological knowledge; its foundations were only beginning to be laid, including Vygotsky's work. His works on child psychology were published as pedology, special science about children, of which child psychology was a part. Vygotsky saw child psychology precisely as one of pedology's branches, one of the pedological disciplines (cf. *Pedology of the Adolescent*, Volume 4 [Rus. edit.]). His contemporaries, the remarkable Soviet psychologists M. Ia. Basov and P. P. Blonskii, shared approximately the same opinion.

Vygotsky's psychological research on children bore the title of pedological research. Vygotsky himself wrote about the necessity of having a special science relating to children, a science which, during the period of his scientific creativity, was called pedology. But we should emphasize that he approached critically both pedological methods of research on children and the interpretation of the results derived by these methods.

From his first entry into defectology, and in almost all his subsequent works, including *Developmental Diagnostics* [this volume], he felt, as a scientist, that intellectual psychometric tests, which were intended to separate children out of general schools on the basis of negative indicators, were scientifically untrustworthy. In criticizing methods based on measurement through tests, he asserted that selection based on negative indicators separates children into groups where they have nothing in common with each other which is quite different what would happen if they were examined from a positive perspective. He wrote that traditional research methods are based on a purely quantitative conception of development and on a negative characterization of the child. Vygotsky spoke out against the primitive classification of children into normal, socially neglected, and handicapped. In Vygotsky's words, an antiscientific, scholastic vision lies at the basis of such a schematic structure. Even today, his criticism of methods using tests and the two-factor concept lying at the basis of pedological research has not lost its force.

The search for the positive capacities and qualitative characteristics in the development of anomalous children is a leading feature of all Vygotsky's work, and in particular of his work dealing with development diagnostics.

Thus, he made brilliant discoveries in a number of areas while working on the problems of difficult childhood: the general psychological idea of development, the idea of qualitative changes in children's developmental processes, the Vygotskian exposition of the laws of development in the higher psychological processes, the social conditioning of development, and the leading role played by instruction during development. At the same time, these also enriched general, child, and pedagogical psychology, and acted as a source of new hypotheses and a greater depth in general theoretical conceptions. Vygotsky's defectological work, such as *Developmental Diagnostics and Pedological Clinic for Troubled Childhood* and *Problems in Mental Retardation* (1935), were direct and immediate contributions to general psychological theory.

It is impossible to understand Vygotsky's profound interest in the problems of child and age-group psychology without taking into account the fact that he was both a theoretician and, particularly importantly, a practitioner in the area of anomalous mental development. For many years, he acted as the scientific director of a whole series of research projects undertaken at the Experimental Defectological Institute, and he systematically participated in consultations about children, even here filling a directing role. Hundreds of children with the most various of mental developmental anomalies passed through his consultations.

For conferences organized by Vygotsky, children of all ages were selected and thoroughly studied. Their medical histories, the histories of their development, their studies and education, and the results of complex research were analyzed in detail by Vygotsky. There were supplementary data from his personal investigations. Such a wealth of material permitted him to establish not only the reasons for deviation, but also the potential capacities for development in anomalous children. Through these studies, he showed how the well-timed and correctly organized teaching of anomalous children changes the appearance of a handicap, how possible additional consequences of a handicap can be foreseen and forestalled, and how the higher psychological functions develop. These ideas attracted the attention of a large number of doctors (psychiatrists and neuropathologists), psychologists, and other specialists, as well as students in pedagogical and medical institutes of higher education. Not only did these ideas derive from profound and careful analyses of data about patients, but they also allowed one to step beyond the limits of a concrete situation to support various general theoretical propositions.

All of Vygotsky's work in this field is permeated with the idea that specifically human psychological characteristics are socially conditioned. In contrast to the biological views, which argued that anomalous children are doomed, Vygotsky, while taking into account the biological bases for developmental deviations, was more optimistic: He emphasized the role of social factors which were capable of influencing a child's fate as he emphasized the possibility of compensation for and correction of a handicap.

Vygotsky saw the analysis of each case of any given anomaly as a concrete expression of some general problem in defectology.

By working with data from clinical research to solve theoretical and practical research questions about children, Vygotsky marked the course of the basic questions about diagnostics through a concrete application of the dialectical method.

Many of Vygotsky's theoretical ideas were finally demonstrated by his students: L. V. Zankov who studied the memories of retarded children; I. M. Soloviev through research into psychological saturation in profoundly retarded children; M. S. Pevsner by studying oligo-phrenia and other developmental anomalies. The organization of the education-and-study process in special schools for deaf and hearing-impaired children was based on a theoretical elaboration of Vygotsky's ideas about the characteristics of thought, memory, and other mental processes in these children (by R. M. Boskis, F. F. Rau, I. M. Soloviev, L. I. Tigranova, Zh. I. Shif, and others).

Vygotsky's ideas acted as the scientific basis of the system of education, teaching, and labor training for those attending auxiliary schools (work associated with G. M. Lul'nev, V. G. Petrova, Zh. I. Shif., and others), which helped overcome the tradition of "medical pedagogy," with its adaptation to the handicap during the education of mentally retarded children.

All the work of the Scientific-Research Institute of Defectology, attached to the Academy of Pedological Sciences of the USSR (involving R. M. Boskis, T. A. Vlasova, M. I. Zemtsova, S. A. Zykov, K. G. Korovin, Iu. A. Kulagin, R. E. Levina), is built on Vygotsky's theoretical bases: Differentiated instruction for various categories of anomalous children, which take into account Vygotsky's positions on the existence of primary and secondary formations in the development of handicap structures in such children. Thanks to this, ten types of special schools have been created in the USSR (in addition to auxiliary schools) in which children are given a complete or incomplete middle-level education in accordance with the program used in mass schools and in labor-production training.

Vygotsky's scientific heritage is to be found at the basis of the elaboration of problems about children with so-called delayed psychological development (DPD), carried out at the Institute of Defectology (by T. A. Vlasova, V. I. Lubovskii, K. S. Lebedinskiia, and M. S. Pevsner). A new kind of special school was established for such children in 1981. It is for a special category of children, which includes children with complicated forms of infantilism, cerebral asthenia, and other minor brain dysfunctions. These children consistently do not succeed in mass (general) schools; they often leave school in the early instructional stages and end up in schools for the mentally retarded, although they do not have oligophrenic handicaps.

L. S. Vygotsky was the first in the history of psychology and defectology to offer a profound psychological-pedagogical definition of the essence of infantilism—a breach of tempo in the qualitative restructuring of mental functions (thought, attention, memory, motor ability), in the presence of which a child's mind retains the organization of a younger age. Then, the formation of complex mediating behavioral forms is delayed and an underdevel-oped personality is formed; this leads to disruptions of all sorts of voluntary activities. Children with DPD, if placed in instructional and educational situations which take into account the etiopathogenesis and structure of their handicap, attain high educational levels, unlike retarded children.

The research which Vygotsky referred to as the "natural history of the sign," conducted by N. G. Morozova under his direction, lay at the base of work on the development of game activity in anomalous children, on mastery of word meaning, grammatical structure, and the significance and sense of the written word by deaf school children.

In this volume of the *Collected Works*, Vygotsky's theoretical works are laid out, as are the therapeutic principles which correspond with them, based on examples of mental retardation, blindness, and deafness. Works touching on other anomalies are not included in Vygotsky's published legacy. Still, it is known that I. I. Daniushevskii, with Vygotsky, initiated the beginnings of a speech clinic at the Experimental Defectological Institute, where they explored the preparation of a radical restructuring of speech therapy. That clinic became the prototype for a network of schools for children with severe speech impediments. Development in this area of defectology took place with the active involvement of R. E. Levina. A major part in establishing Soviet speech therapy was played, as Vygotsky had foreseen, by the role of phonological science in understanding the basis of speech pathology in children. In particular, it led to a reexamination of views on the nature of reading and writing disabilities. Vygotsky's ideas about the fundamental role of speech were productively used in constructing a theory of stammering.

Under Daniushevskii's direction at the Experimental Defectological Institute a complex study about unmanageable children, their instruction and education was organized and closely linked with Vygotsky's theoretical position. He undoubtedly participated in it, as did M. S. Pevsner, V. F. Shmidt, L. S. Geshelina, V. M. Torbek, and other members of the EDI. The theoretical analysis of the mental development process in anomalous children was always closely linked by Vygotsky to the problems of general and special pedagogy. The link joining psychology to pedagogy and defectology is unbroken in Vygotsky's work.

As a result of his creative approach to and particular interest in defectology, which he developed on the basis of his own theoretical positions and the experiments, Vygotsky concluded that the problems which defectology studies might also be key to a series of general psychological problems. He showed that, in the presence of a child's anomalous development and special education, essential links of psychological activity emerge, which in the normal case exist in undifferentiated form. Vygotsky believed that such natural experiments (the deviation of some psychological function in anomalous children) shed light on general laws about the formation of the normal child's mind and personality.

Using material from pathological development, Vygotsky confirmed the general laws of development that he had discovered and then showed their specific characteristics. All his propositions led toward a new understanding of the problem of special, differentiated, and appropriately timed teaching and development for anomalous children, and permitted a new understanding of the problem of diagnostics and compensation for a variety of handicaps. With this, Vygotsky initiated a new stage in the development of defectology and lifted it to the level of a dialectical-materialistic science. He introduced the genetic principle to the study of anomalous children and showed that the anomalous child is, above all, a child, one who develops like any other, though his development is unique. He demonstrated the whole complexity of the structure of a handicap and the specific characteristics of the developmental stages in children with various handicaps, while maintaining an optimistic perspective about these children's capabilities. He subjected the existing methods of special teaching to stringent criticism and indicated the how they might be restructured. This work served as the scientific basis for building special schools and as the theoretical basis of principles and methods of study in the diagnostics of difficult (anomalous) children. Vygotsky left a legacy of inescapable scientific significance, which has entered into the body of Soviet and worldwide psychology, defectology, psychoneurology, and other related sciences.

Lev Semenovich's research into general psychology, which in many respects determined the path of its further development, was always unwaveringly conducted from the position of a Marxist-Leninist theory of knowledge, swept clean of the old and petrified mantle of idealism and of other anti-scientific layers during the struggle for a new Soviet psychology.

On the difficult road toward creating a Marxist psychology, where Lev Semenovich acted as one of the vanguard, there could, of course, be incompleteness and imperfection, but no one could deny that he always struggled passionately for a Marxist science of children. Here it is appropriate to say, in his own words, "We well know that, in taking the first step, we cannot avoid many, perhaps even serious, errors. But the whole point lies in the fact that the first step has been taken, and in the right direction. The rest will follow. The false will drop away, and that which is lacking will be added."

NOTES TO THE RUSSIAN EDITION

Part I: General Problems of Defectology

Introduction: the Fundamental Problems of Defectology

1. This article was written on the basis of a report made by L.S. Vygotsky in the defectology section of the Institute of Scientific Pedagogy at the second Moscow State University. It was published in the book *Works of the Second Moscow University* (Moscow, 1929, v. I). Guided by the teachings of dialectic materialism on development, Vygotsky defines defectology as a branch of knowledge about qualitative developmental diversity in abnormal children, about the diversity of the kinds of this development. On this basis he outlines the main theoretical and practical tasks facing Soviet defectology and the special school.

2. *Kruenegel, Max* (?) When studying the level of motor development in mentally retarded children, he used N.I. Ozeretskii's metric scheme of motor giftedness.

3. *Binet, Alfred* (1857–1912), a French psychologist. He was interested in questions of oligophrenia (mental retardation) he established work principles for mentally retarded children. Along with Simon, he was one of the first to work out a system of testing methods for measuring the level of children's mental development and for studying individual differences. Vygotsky critically evaluated this purely quantitative system of methods and pointed out its limited diagnostic significance because it could guarantee the solution of only negative problems,— i.e., "weeding out children according to negative signs."

4. *Rossolimo, Grigorii Ivanovich* (1860–1926), a well-known Russian doctor, psychiatrist and neuropathologist. He also worked in the area of child psychology and defectology. For the study of children's individual psychological characteristics he elaborated the method known as psychological profiles. Vygotsky mentions this method in a critical analysis of the different quantitative methods for studying the psychology of a child.

5. *Lipmann, Otto* (1880–?), a German psychologist and psychotechnician, an advocate of the theory of special giftedness. Vygotsky indicated that, contrary to the widely used quantitative methods, Lipmann advanced the idea of the qualitative character of a child's intellectual growth, which is extremely important from the point of view of compensation. Vygotsky also interpreted Lipmann's position in relationship to the problem of practical intellect and in an analysis of the concept of general giftedness.

315

6. *Griboedov, Andrian Sergeevich* (1875–?), a Soviet defectologist, director of the Leningrad Children's Diagnostic Institute, the author of a series of works on the instruction and education of children in the special school. Vygotsky criticized his views on handicapped children.

7. Stern, William (1871–1938), a German psychologist who worked in the area of differential child psychology. Vygotsky noted both Stern's approach to child development, which is consonant with his own views, as well as the productivity of Stern's ideas about the "twofold role of a defect." Vygotsky also agreed with Stern's approaches both to the interrelationship between language and thought and with his conclusions about the role of exercise (drill and practice) in developing the sense of touch in the blind. At the same time, Vygotsky pointed out that philosophically, Stern proceeded from positions of idealistic philosophy (the philosophy of value).

8. Guertler, R. (?) Vygotsky spoke positively about Guertler when analyzing the quantitative uniqueness which characterizes the type of development present in a defective child. At the same time Vygotsky criticized Guertler's methodological primitiveness (the "lesson with the handkerchief") and advocated common goals for the normal and the auxiliary (special) school. Vygotsky also stressed the point that Guertler drew a basis for defectology from idealistic philosophy.

9. *Rickert, Heinrich* (1863–1936), see [Rus] Volume. I, p. 468. where he is identified as a German idealist philosopher and a founded of the so-called Baden-school of neo-Kantianism.

10. *Lipps, Theodor* (1851–1914), a German philosopher and psychologist. He worked out the problem of compensation from the point of view of the law advanced by him—the "law of psychological damming up." Vygotsky gave a positive evaluation to this notion of Lipps about the possibility of an increase of psychological energy, which overcomes emerging obstacles, and delays in the developmental process.

11. *Adler, Alfred* (1870–1937), an Austrian doctor-psychiatrist and psychologist who created the school of individual psychology (the psychology of personality). He detached himself from the school of S. Freud, with whom he broke off ties because of differing political and social views. Vygotsky accentuated the dialectical character of Adler's teachings and views about the social basis of personality development, putting him at odds with Freud [see Note 4 for Chapter 1] and Kretschmer [see Note 8 for Chapter 1]. Vygotsky gave special significance to Adler's notion that compensation is the dynamic force in the abnormal child's development. The idea of a "future perspective," which Adler introduced into this psychological analysis of the developmental process, was also given a positive assessment by Vygotsky from the point of view of defectology. Vygotsky did not assign the same value to Adler's individual positions. A more and more critical attitude toward a series of Adler's positions emerged in Vygotsky's writings: He criticized the limited and erroneous reductions of the environment's effect on child development to a "feeling of inferiority," the philosophical unfoundedness of the concept of *overcompensation* and other notions. In his concluding statements Vygotsky points out that Adler's teachings "are guided by a mixed and complex philosophical bases; his doctrine lacks its own "philosophical consistent methodology." From Vygotsky's point of view Adler's theories on the whole reflect the basic characteristics of an epoch of "psychological crisis."

12. *Pavlov, Ivan Petrovich* (1849–1936), an outstanding Soviet Russian physiologist, and academician. Pavlov's discoveries had great significance not only for physiology and medicine, but also for psychology and pedagogy. Vygotsky, especially in the early years of his work in the area of defectology, repeatedly cited the ideas of Pavlov (cf., for example, his use of Pavlov's concept *goal-oriented reflex* in analyzing problems of compensation). Vygotsky was one of the first psychologists and defectologists to highly value Pavlov's teachings as a materialistic base of psychology.

13. *Shcherbina, Aleksandr Moiseevich* (1874–1934), a Soviet psychologist, pedagogue and defectologist (for the blind), a philosopher, and a social activist. From a progressive standpoint, he worked out questions and methods of instruction and education for the blind. The data of his self-observations were used by Vygotsky in his analysis of the uniqueness of the abnormal developmental process. In 1920, he participated in the creation of a pedagogical technical school in Priluki, where for the first time a course of education for the blind was developed and introduced.

The most important goals were the creation of a solid scientific basis for the education of the blind and their inclusion in the labor work force (a life of work).

14. *Buerklen, Karl* (?), a German psychologist and educator of the blind, and director of the Institute for the Blind in Zuckerdorf, near Vienna. His book *The Psychology of the Blind* was translated into Russian (edited and with a Preface by E. A. Gander) in 1934 under the guidance and advice of Vygotsky. Vygotsky critically judged certain positions by the author, who underevaluated the possibilities for the blind from the point of view of compensation and the social conditionality of an abnormal child's development.

15. *Friedmann, A.* (?), a German pedagogue and defectologist who elaborated upon questions of individual psychological therapeutic pedagogy from the positions of Adler's school. He devised the interesting educational technique known as *systematic [methodological] dialectics.*

16. *Blonskii, Pavel Petrovich* (1884–1941), a Soviet psychologist and pedagogue. He was one of the first Soviet authors to begin to develop a theory of the vocational school and many questions of child psychology from the position of dialectical materialism. Given the proof of the impossibility of reducing the concept of a defect and defectology to phenomena of purely biogenic nature, Vygotsky supported the theoretic views of Blonskii. Vygotsky is in agreement with Blonskii's fundamental assessment of the notion *moral defectiveness,* but criticized him for making common cause with the conception of character, advocated by E. Kretschmer.

17. *Zalkind, Aron Borisovich* (1888–1936), a Soviet pedagogue and psychologist. Vygotsky stressed the correctness of Zalkind's critical evaluation of the majority of studies favoring "absolute biological statism in an approach to character."

18. *Lindworsky, Johannes* (1875–1939), a German psychologist. He developed an original conception of intellect, on the basis of which he examined intellectual defects resulting from the loss of one of the factors for perceiving relationships. Vygotsky highly valued the possibility, underscored by Lindworsky, of various qualitative types of intellectual inadequacy.

19. The First Congress of Therapeutic Pedagogy took place in Germany in 1923.

20. *Wertheimer, Max* (1880–1943), a German psychologist. He was one of the theoreticians of Gestalt psychology. Vygotsky agreed with his evaluation of role of the social milieu in the genesis of the so-called "innate psycho-pathology in children."

21. *Gurevich, Mikhail Osipovich* (1878–1953), a Soviet psychiatrist and the author of many fundamental works on child and general psychology. He described the impaired development of children's motor skills. He emphasized that motor defects in children do not always match mental skills.

22. *Dupré,* (?), the author of the first generally interesting work on motor defects.

23. *Heller, Theodore,* assigned the term *motor idiocy* to those cases where children have a marked motor deficiency which sharply contrasts with their strong intellect.

24. *Jacob, K.* (?), concerned himself with motor disorders of pyramidal and extrapyramidal [brain cell] origin (motor infantilism).

25. *Nadoleczny, M.,* perceived the essence of stuttering to be a functional disorder (of central origin) of the muscles needed for speech and at the same time noted that the character of a stutterer was differentiated from the norm. Nadoleczny recommended treatment with breath and speech exercises, psychotherapy, and psychoanalysis.

26. *Ozeretskii, Nikolai I.* (1894–1955), a Soviet psychiatrist. He created a method, graded by age level, for defining a child's motor development; this method became widespread both in our country and abroad.

27. *Spearman, Charles* (1863–1967), an English psychologist. He developed the fundamentals of factor analysis in psychology. Vygotsky set forth Spearman's positions in connection with a discussion of the problem of giftedness.

28. *Yerkes, Robert* (1876–1956), cf. [Russian] Volume 2, p. 485. [English Volume 1, p. 380.]

29. *Koehler, Wolfgang* (1887–1967), a German psychologist, one of the founders of Gestalt psychology. From 1935 he lived in the United States. His basic works are written about research on the intellect of anthropoid apes. He did not make a fundamental distinction between the intellect of a human and that of anthropoids. Koehler's data on the existence of not one, but many types of giftedness were of interest to Vygotsky. Koehler considered the mere recognition of the complexity and multiformity in the structure of the intellect to be the basis for the study of a qualitative specificity of types of mental deficiency.

30. *Thorndike, Edward* (1874–1949), an American psychologist and pedagogue. He introduced experimental research on behavior with the help of objective methods. He was one of the first representatives of behaviorism. He underestimated the value of the qualitative specifics of the human *mind* (human psychology). According to his philosophical views, he stood nearest to pragmatism showing that the education of normal and abnormal children has the same goals. Vygotsky agreed with Thorndike's statement about the necessity of combining educational influence with the natural drives of the child.

31. *Lindemann, E.* (?), conducted research on the practical intellect of mentally retarded children and proved their aptitude for rational activity.

32. *Petrova, Anna Evgen'evna* (1888–?), a Soviet psychologist and pedagogue. She worked in the Moscow psychoneurological and pedological school and sanatorium of NKZ (The People's Commissariat for Health Protection). Investigating child primitiveness, she demonstrated its distinction from genuine mental retardation. Vygotsky highly valued the research on child primitivism introduced by Petrova, because it coincided with his theory of cultural-historical development and certain problems in defectology. He considered that data on the possibility of delay in cultural development raise the issue of "a reexamination of many questions of children's vocational trainability and of their deficiencies."

33. *Ribot, Theodule A.*(1839–1916), a French philosopher and psychologist. He was a specialist in pathopsychology and general psychology. His major works are dedicated to problems of memory, voluntary attention and feelings. Ribot's distinction between two types of attention—natural-involuntary and artificial-involuntary—was used in Vygotsky's examination of a child's mastery of "cultural psychological tools" in the course of development and of the disruption of this process in an abnormal child. Vygotsky criticized Ribot's "static" approach to the essence of child character, connected with an erroneous conception of innateness and constancy of a child's character traits.

34. *Braille, Louis* (1809–1852), known world-wide as the French educator of the blind, the inventor of a reading and writing system of raised dots for the blind. He was blind from the age of three. Vygotsky held that the process of reading, according to Braille, differs psychologically from reading for normal children.

35. *Ach, Narciss* (1871–1946), a German philosopher and psychologist who belonged to the Wuerzburg School of Psychology. He conducted research on the use of "psychological tools" (for example, words as means or tools for developing a concept in abnormal children).

36. *Bacher, A.* (?), a German philosopher and psychologist, who belonged to the school of N. Ach. He applied Ach's method to his research on feebleminded (learning-disabled) children (debiles).

37. *Rimat, Franz* (?)[sic], German psychologist and specialist in the psychology of thinking. [note from L. S. Vygotsky *Collected Works*, (Rus.) Vol. 2, p. 486. (Engl.) Vol. 1. p. 380 to which this volume refers.

38. *Kerschensteiner, George* (1854–1932), a reactionary German pedagogue. Vygotsky mentioned him in connection with the differentiation between the concepts of primitiveness and feeblemindedness (a learning disability).

39. *Eliasberg, Wladimir* (?), a specialist in the area of cognitive psychology. In the context of his theory of cultural-historical development, Vygotsky upheld Eliasberg's notion of the role of artificial means ("psychological tools") in overcoming a defect and their differential significance in the assessment of feeblemindedness. He agreed also with Eliasberg when he cautioned against the dominance of visual methods in the auxiliary school since they were held to impede the development of abstract thought in mentally retarded children.

40. *Dewey, John* (1859–1952), a reactionary American philosopher, a pedagogue and theoretician, one of the leading representatives of pragmatism. He developed the concept of *instrumentalism*. He was an ideologue of bourgeois liberalism, the creator of the so-called pedocentric (child-centered) theory and instructional methods. Vygotsky mentioned Dewey's definition of the significance of words as "intellectual tools."

41. *Troshin, Peter Iakovlevich* (?). Vygotsky noted the productivity of Troshin's ideas about the absence of major differences between normal and abnormal children and about the erroneous tendency of examining them only from the point of view of "illness." Vygotsky also used Troshin's opinion about the characteristics of the senses in abnormal children to prove the falsity of traditional views which put primary emphasis on the development of the sense organs just as they are. All this serves to affirm one of Vygotsky's fundamental ideas about the social, and not the biological, nature of the process of compensating a defect.

Chapter 1: Defect and Compensation

1. Written in 1924. Vygotsky gave a report on this theme at the Second Congress for the Protection of Social Rights of Minors (SPON). This chapter was first published in the form of an article entitled "Defect and Overcompensation" in the collection *Retardation, Blindness and Deafness* (1927). In great detail, Vygotsky critically analyzed the state of diagnostics at that time and outlined ways for its future development. The change in the title of this article during its revision into a chapter of a book reflected the author's growing critical attitude toward the teachings of A. Adler. On the whole, this chapter gives a summary and critical analysis of foreign literary sources on the problem of abnormality. The personal data gathered by the author during his clinical, psychological study of abnormal children at the Experimental Defectological Institute (EDI) are reflected in the later works (cf. the works of this volume).

2. *Ruele, Otto* (1874–1943), a German pedagogue and a Social Democrat. He criticized the system of instruction and education in German schools for their clearly bourgeois character. He attempted to demonstrate the educational significance of work. A decided opponent of S. Freud's characterology, he contrasted it with the teachings of A. Adler. Vygotsky quoted Ruele in connection with an analysis of character formation as a "socially directed progress."

3. *Keller, Helen* (1880–1968), a blind-deaf American. She received a university education, became a writer, a doctor of philosophy and a preacher. Vygotsky analyzed the history of Keller's development from the point of view of the process of overcompensation in the favorable social conditions especially created for her.

4. *Freud, Sigmund* (1856–1939), an Austrian doctor, psychiatrist and psychologist, creator of the theory of psychoanalysis. After occupying himself with neuropathology (aphasia and childhood paralyses), he switched over to the development of the theory of psychoanalysis. At the first formative stages of this theory, he characteristically distinguished the features of consciousness and of human behavior from their biological (chiefly sexual) base. Such an approach incited a negative response from the leading psychologists and neuropathologists of his epoch. Subsequently, however, the theory of psychoanalysis acquired a broad influence on the formation of scientific,

clinical, psychological and social concepts, turning into a complete world view on the order of reactionary idealism. Vygotsky's work advances a very complex attitude toward the ideas of Freud. While evaluating positively the main category of the unconscious, on which Freud's theory rests, Vygotsky, in contrast sharply negates the aforementioned "biologization" (i.e., the excessive exaggeration of the biological components) of human nature. We find no direct evidence of the significance of unconscious psychological processes in the analysis of the laws of abnormal development.

5. *Darwin, Charles* (1809–1882), a well-known English naturalist, creator of the theory of evolution, which had a great influence on the development of related disciplines. Taking exception to principles of former and contemporary characterology, Vygotsky noted that "it reminds us of the state of the biological sciences before Darwin." He also used the Darwin's evolutionary teachings in his criticism of certain ideas of S. Freud.

6. *Kretschmer, Ernst* (1888–1964), a German psychiatrist and one of the founders of the constitutional direction in psychiatry. Vygotsky decidedly objected to Kretschmer's basic assumption, that character (a type of human behavior) is wholly and completely dependent on an inherent constitution, i.e., on the specific features of the body's make-up and endocrine system. Vygotsky unfolded a many-sided system of proofs, which refutes the static approach to character as a stable formation, defined entirely by biological factors. At the same time, he selected from Kretschmer's investigation a series of assumptions which go beyond the boundaries of characterology and with which he fully agreed. Kretschmer's deductions about specific features of verbal memory in the blind are important for defectology, a basis for holding that secondary complications in the developmental process of a sick child give way to treatment. The relevance and methodological significance of the criticism which Vygotsky and other psychologists voiced in regard to Kretschmer's characterology in this early period of the formation of Soviet psychology are beyond all question.

7. *Nietzsche, Friedrich* (1844–1900), a reactionary German philosopher, spokesman of the irrational theory of will, one of the founders of the "philosophy of life."

8. *Petzeld A.* (?). Vygotsky fully shared Petzeld's conception of the vast possibilities for the development of a blind child under the appropriate educational conditions. Appraising Petzeld's book "as the best book on the psychology of the blind," Vygotsky shared his opinion that the acquisition of speech and social communication is the fundamental and deciding compensatory target of blindness ("its defeat").

9. *Sokolianskii, Ivan Afanas'evich* (1889–1960), a Soviet pedagogue and defectologist, and specialist in the area of special education for the deaf and the blind. The unique system for education and instruction of the blind-deaf created by him has special scientific and practical significance. Further, he worked out a method for teaching speech to deaf-mute children on the basis of an integral visual perception of images, words, and phrases by lip-reading and by motor sensations received through the hand in the process of writing. Vygotsky considered the merits of this method to lie in the importance assigned to reflexes, and the specifically prescribed order of instruction. He emphasized that such a method leads in the end to the development of logically connected speech in a deaf-mute child; this represents one of the main goals of education for the deaf. Sokolyaknskii also worked out important problems in education of the blind. On his initiative, the only scientific and educational institution in the world for the blind-deaf was established as a school and clinic in Khar'kov (1923). He worked out the plans for various technological devices to be used in teaching the blind-deaf, and for this work he was posthumously awarded a special prize from the government.

10. *Sherrington, Charles Scott* (1859–1952), an English physiologist and founder of a scientific school; an author of important discoveries in the area of neurophysiology; the creator of the doctrine of receptive fields.

11. *Bekhterev, Vladimir Mikhailov* (1857–1927), a Russian Soviet physiologist, neurologist, and psychologist. He analyzed personality on the basis of a composite study of the brain using physiological, anatomical and psychological methods. He was the founder of reflexology. Vygotsky used Bekhterev's concept of *associative activity* when examining the disrupted social interactions of abnormal children and also when trying to establish a

reflexological foundation for the processes of writing, reading and comprehending speech among the blind and the deaf.

12. *Protopopov, Victor Pavlovich* (1880–1957), a Soviet psychiatrist who facilitated the introduction of I. P. Pavlov's teachings on conditional reflexes into psychiatry. In his studies of the blind-deaf, Protopopov came to the conclusion that it is possible for them to acquire social communication.

13. A reference to *Bogdanov-Berezovskii, Mikhial Valer'anovich* (1867–1921), the Russian ear, nose and throat specialist. He worked as a doctor in a Petersburg School for the deaf-mute and took an active part in the struggle for the education of the deaf-mute and for the improvement of their position in Russia. From the moment of the creation of a subsidized agency to protect the deaf-mute he became a member of the committee; he edited the journal *Herald of the Guardianship of the Deaf-Mute*. His main works are *Restoration of the Hearing in the Deaf-Mute* (St. Petersburg, 1901) and *The Plight of the Deaf-Mute in Russia* (St. Petersburg, 1901). He was the author of the Foreword to the translations of Helen Keller's book *Optimism*.

14. *Rousseau, Jean Jacques* (1712–1778), the great French writer and sensualist philosopher who exerted an enormous influence on the development of bourgeois philosophy, sociology, and education. Concluding his examination of the problem of compensation and overcompensation in the light of social needs, required for development, Vygotsky objected to Rousseau's position which "erases the boundary between the training of young animals and the rearing of infants, between training and education."

15. *Frank, Semen Liudvigovich* (1877–1950), a Russian philosopher.

Chapter 2: Principles of Education for Physically Handicapped Children

1. The basis of this chapter is a report on the theme "The Principles of Education for Handicapped Children, which Vygotsky prepared for the Second Congress on the Social and Legal Protection of Minors (1924). In this chapter Vygotsky reviewed A. N. Graborov's book *The Auxiliary School* (1925). The basic aim of this chapter is to establish criteria for the educational and vocational programs in institutions for children with various developmental anomalies. This chapter expresses the principles of the organization and content of pedagogical work with abnormal children.

At the Second Congress on the Social and Legal Protection of Minors, fundamentally new views on the cognitive possibilities of handicapped children were expressed. The Congress reflected an optimistic line of development for defectology. Defectologists, psychologists and doctors participated in the Congress. The task put before the Congress was to analyze the state of special schools with respect to their organization, instruction and overall educational programs. The Congress resolutions put forth the goal of integrating special pedagogy for the physically handicapped and mentally retarded with the general principles and methods of the social education of all children in Soviet schools. These resolutions stressed the necessity of bringing socially useful work and self-sufficient, active life within the reach of this category of children. The SLPM (Congress of the Social and Legal Protection of Minors) recognized the inadmissibility of segregating children into categories of normal and so-called morally defective, aesthetically retarded and etc. Emphasis was placed on the fact that experiments in transferring so called-difficult children into a different environment illustrated the possibility of radical change in their behavior. Children lose their defensive reactions against social circumstances. Their deviations in behavior are overcome.

The great historical significance of this Congress lies in the fact that it promoted a radical reorientation and reorganization of the instruction and education in our country's special schools.

2. Analyzing the major direction of educational influences on the abnormal child (in connection with problems of compensation), Vygotsky expressed his opinion of the booklet, published in Switzerland "this year," evidently between 1924–1926. He emphasized its productive underlying notion that "a blind child must be treated in the same way as a seeing child."

3. The same question, Vygotsky noted, had been analyzed at the last congress in Stuttgart ("this year"). A debate arose between advocates of the German system of education, which focused on the child's shortcomings,

and the advocates of the American system, which concentrates on the healthy traits in a child's personality. The American system took the upper hand in this dispute.

4. *Vatter, Johann* (1842–1916), a famous German educator of the deaf, an advocate of the "oral method," which was widespread in many countries, and of speech therapy for the deaf, the essence of which meant work on pronunciation. Experience using this method had led to broad discussion among leading educators of the deaf, who emphasized the rift between this system of instruction and the active life of these children and their means of communicating, etc. Other methods of teaching deaf children speech (writing, finger spelling, etc.) were juxtaposed to Vatter's ideas. Vygotsky sharply criticized the cruel implementation of the oral method and its contradiction of the child's nature. In the resolution of his report at the 1938 All-Russian Conference on Deaf Education, the Director of the Experimental Defectological Institute, I. I. Daniushevskii, rejected Vatter's purely oral method for teaching the deaf as a method which impeded the children's development.

5. *Graborov, Aleksei Nikolaevich* (1885–1946), a Soviet defectologist. One of the organizers of the auxiliary school, he worked out problems of content and methods for the instruction and education of abnormal children. In an attempt to develop a system for cultivating the senses and motor skills in a socially meaningful context (play, manual labor, object lessons, excursions, etc.), Vygotsky, without giving a totally negative evaluation to Graborov's book, *The Auxiliary School*, did criticize the gap between this book's defectological principles and those of general (public) education. He also took exception to several fundamental mistakes in Graborov's definition of the concept of child defectology and in individual, isolated aspects of his proposed organization of the pedagogical process in the auxiliary school. Particularly strong criticism is given to Graborov's pedagogy for the abnormal child because of his over-emphasis on sensorimotor development and psychological orthopedy to the detriment of cultivation of social habits.

6. *Golovin, Sergei Selivanovich* (1866–1931), a physician and ophthalmologist. Vygotsky noted Golovin's successful experiments together with the engineer P. Perls, who proved the ability of the blind to work in heavy industry. Golovin emphasized the fruitfulness of expanding the formerly narrow circle of professions for the blind. Vygotsky linked the proof of the capability of the blind to participate in "the highest form of labor" with the most important problem: overcoming the general attitude of "social disdain" for abnormal children by a practical realization of social education. In the early period of establishing Soviet special schools, the preparation of pupils for qualified labor was, without a doubt, a really pressing issue.

7. *Perls, Pavel* (?), director of one of the divisions of Siemens-Schuckert Electrical plants (Berlin). He proved the ability of the blind to work in heavy industry. His motto was: "To work, but not to suffer."

Chapter 3: The Psychology and Pedagogy of Children's Handicaps

1. Published in 1924 in the collection *Questions of Education of the Blind, the Deaf-Mute and Mentally Retarded Children*," edited by L. S. Vygotsky. This chapter examines certain scientific aspects. It is devoted both to the interrelationship of defectology with other related branches of knowledge and to its boundaries with respect to these other branches. In this chapter Vygotsky also analyzes the problem of a methodologically correct understanding of the co-relationship between "the biological" and "the social" in the development of an abnormal child and its significance for defectology in practice. For a more detailed account of the influences of Vygotsky's ideas on the course of the development of defectology in the USSR, see T. A. Vlasova, *Psychological Problems in the Differentiation of the Education and Upbringing of Abnormal Children* (Psikhlogicheskie problemy differentskii obucheniia i vospitaniia anomal'nykh detei) (Moscow, 1972), L. V. Zalkov. *Vygotsky as a Defectologist*, (Vygotskii kak defektolog). *Special School* (Spetsial'naia skola), 4th ed., 1972.

2. *Korolenko, Vladimir Galaktionovich* (1853–1921), is a well-known Russian writer, publicist, and progressive social activist. Vygotsky employed the image of the literary hero from Korolenko's work "The Blind Musician" as an example of the different social interaction of abnormal children with those surrounding them and as a demonstration of those paramount problems which the social dislocation of such a child can pose for defectology.

In final analysis, Vygotsky concluded that the nature of the compensatory process in abnormally developed children is social, not biological.

3. *Birilev, Aleksandr Vasil'evich* (1871–1959), a Russian Soviet educator of the blind and a lawyer. Vygotsky cites Birilev in connection with evidence of a very important position which holds that an especially keen sense of touch in the blind, similar to a heightened sense of sight in the deaf, is not explained by a unique constitutional nature. The causes here are functional and are connected with the increased role of these organs which have taken over for the defective ones. Vygotsky agrees with Birilev in his assessment of the disagreement between Shcherbina and V. G. Korolenko about the inner life of a blind child.

4. *Lagovskii, Nikolai Mikhailovich* (1862–1933), an educator of the deaf. He was the author of works on the history, theory, and methods of teaching the deaf. He valued their cognitive possibilities highly. He based an extensive project on the preparation of cadres of specialists, attributing great significance to the personality of the educators of deaf children.

5. *Krogius, August Adol'fovit* (1871–1933), a Soviet psychologist and professor. He made a significant contribution to the study of various sides of the psychology of the blind and of their cognitive processes.

6. *Popov, N.A.*(?), one of the authors and editor-in-chief of *The Works of the Donskoi Pedagogical Institute*.

7. *Heidzig, Johann*, a German educator of the deaf. He developed the oral method for teaching speech to the deaf-mute. He protested the condemnation of mimicry, but later became its adversary.

8. *Werner, F.* (?), one of the staunch opponents of the oral method in teaching the deaf mute. He saw it as a "contradiction to a child's nature."

9. *De l' Epie, Charles Michael* (1712–1789), a French educator of the deaf. He established the Paris National Institute (1770), the first school in the world for the deaf-mute; he was the author of the mimicry (sign language) method for teaching deaf children speech.

10. *Forchhammer, George* (1861–1938), a Danish educator of the deaf, one of the proponents of the written method of teaching deaf children speech. Vygotsky speaks positively about Forchhammer who developed the hand-mouth system, i.e., the coupling of movements of the mouth and hand as the deaf-mute child pronounces words.

11. *Hill, Moritz* (1805–1874), a German educator of the deaf. The reformer of the German method for teaching deaf-mute children. Vygotsky introduces his assessment of the need to bridge the gap between the development of speech in the deaf-mute and the norms of normal speech development.

12. *Wende, Gustav* (1860–1924), a German educator of the deaf. Vygotsky agreed with Wende's position on the necessity of teaching the deaf-mute speech in conjunction with life, with the child's needs, and with his or her social upbringing as a whole.

Part II: Special Problems of Defectology

The Blind Child

1. The year this manuscript was written is unknown. It is published here for the first time.

2. *Wanecek, Otto* (?), an Australian pedagogue of the blind. He upheld the idea of requiring the introduction of Esperanto into Austrian schools for the blind. Such a resolution was accepted at the Seventh Austrian Congress

of Assistance for the Blind (September 24–25, 1920). According to Wanecek's suggestion, a rule demanding the knowledge of Esperanto, not French or English as before, was introduced into the program for testing and certifying teachers of the blind.

3. *Meumann, Ernst* (1862–1915), a German pedagogue, one of the founders of experimental pedagogy. Vygotsky introduced Meumann's data supporting the fact that in spite of the theory of "vicariousness of the sense organs," in the case of a defect in one sense organ the others are able to remain intact. Meumann also affirms the possibility of substituting for malfunctions in perception. From Vygotsky's point of view, all these data is important for the support of the basic notion that the nature of the compensatory process is social and psychological, and not biological.

4. *Wundt, Wilhelm* (1832–1920), a German psychologist, physiologist and philosopher idealist. The initiator of the development of experiments in psychology, which he named physiological psychology. Vygotsky brought in Wundt's point of view on the process of substituting for blindness, which he saw not only as a deficiency but also as a source of emerging compensatory strength.

5. *Hauey, Valentin* (1745–1822), a French specialist on education of the blind. He first organized the instruction of the blind in special institutions in France and in Russia. His book *Experience of Teaching the Blind* (1876) was at that time the only guide for educators of the blind. Hauey brought socially useful labor within the reach of the blind. Vygotsky highly valued the progressive role of this activist for the blind at the dawn of the development of education for the blind.

6. *Saunderson, N.* (1682–1739), a blind mathematician. He developed an apparatus for producing calculations of numbers with many digits without the need of sight. He created a geometry textbook for the blind. Vygotsky uses this fact as an example of a blind person's overcompensation.

7. *Stumpf, Karl* (1848–1936), a German psychologist, philosopher, idealist and spokesman of phenomenology, with an affinity with Gestalt psychology. He was the author of experimental works on psychology of the blind, of spatial sensations and of perceptions. Vygotsky analyzes the data from Stumpf's research on the processes of attention in the blind.

Principles of Social Education for the Deaf-Mute Child

1. This work was written in 1925. It is being published here for the first time.

2. *The term behaviorism* is derived from the English word behavior. Spokesmen for this movement which arose at the beginning of the 20th century in the United States considered that the object of psychological research should be physical reactions which can be externally observed. Their main task was to study the learning process as the acquisition of new forms of reactions. The behaviorists do not distinguish between those features which govern the learning process of animals and those governing human behavior. [This note taken from the Russian version of Vygotsky's *Collected Works*, Vl. 1, p. 460 to which the note in the present volume refers].

3. *Lessing, Gotthold Ephraim* (1729–1781), a German playwright, a theoretician of art, a literary critic, and the founder of German classical literature.

4. *Malisch, Konstantin* (1860–1925), an Austrian specialist in deaf education (an educator of the deaf). When analyzing the significance of the synthetic method of lip-reading whole words and phrases, Vygotsky underscored the notion that this process is sustained not by the child's conscious efforts, as is indicated according to the German analytical method, but by his unconscious imitation. This path of speech development approximates the natural development of normal children. In this connection, he addressed Malisch's system, which insists on the necessity of reflex imitation and automatic reflex imitation and automatism at the stage of early speech instruction. At the

same time Vygotsky criticized Malisch for certain inconsistencies in overcoming the short comings of the German analytical phonetic method.

5. *Rau, Natal'ia Aleksandrovna* (1870–1947), a Soviet specialist in deaf education and a social worker as well as the organizer of the first kindergarten for deaf children in Russia and Europe. She was the author of many articles and books for educators of the deaf and for the parents of deaf children. She had enormous input into the organization and methodology of preschool education of deaf-mute children. Vygotsky was in complete solidarity with Rau on the question of the new method of synthetic lip-reading for the development of live, logical, oral speech and verbal thought, and for the reinforcement of the bonds between deaf-mute children and the hearing world. On the basis of this method, a connection is formed between concepts and the picture of lip movement (in contemporary terminology, the "oral," mouthed image of the word) and of the movement of the tongue; this transforms into inner pronunciation. Thus, this new method creates those conditions which are necessary for speech to take root in a child's life.

6. *Golosov, Ivan Vasil'evich*, (?), a teacher of the Moscow Institute for the Deaf Mute. Golosov is credited for his first and original attempt at constructing a method for teaching oral speech to the deaf-mute on the basis of whole words (that is, he attempted to maximize the normal natural process of speech development in small children). What is most important, according to Golosov, is not the drilling of individual sounds but reading from the face (lip-reading). He believed that a satisfactory pronunciation could be achieved only by means of reflex activity. In this idea lies the difference between his method and the German analytical method, whereby principal attention is given to the techniques of pronunciation. Vygotsky emphasized the fact that Golosov was consistent in his search for new means for teaching deaf-mute children. During the years of the Revolution this method was fully worked out and put into practice. The basic characteristics of his method correspond to Malisch's method, although it arose independently.

7. *Leman, G.* (?), a Czech pedagogue of the deaf.

8. *Krupskaia, Nadezhda Konstantinovna* (1869–1939), wife and companion-in-arms of the great Lenin, a steadfast worker in the Communist Party and the Soviet government, an outstanding Marxist pedagogue and an organizer of the people's education in the Soviet Union. Vygotsky cited Krupskaia's position when he examined those common questions of polytechnical, labor-oriented education for the deaf, which are shared with the normal school program. In her pedagogical works, Krupskaia thoroughly and critically examined the notion of the "morally, defective child" ("On the Question of Morally Defective Children," *Pedagogical Works*, Vol. 2, Moscow, 1979) she exposed the non-lawful character of this concept from a philosophical, polytechnical and pedagogical point of view. Having pointed out the causes and essence of child vagrancy during the years of establishing Soviet power, Krupskaia in all her certitude states that the term *morally defective* sanctioned a criminal attitude toward homeless children. Krupskaia tied the unacceptability of this term in the eyes of Soviet pedagogy to the widespread struggle with child vagrancy and homelessness of that early period.

Compensatory Processes in the Development of the Retarded Child

1. A stenogram of a report given at a conference of workers from auxiliary schools on May 23, 1931. This work reflects the growing evolution of Vygotsky's interpretation of the theoretical problems of general and child psychology, his intensive research in the area of pathological psychology, and a concrete examination of the development of abnormal children. He conducted these research projects with his co-workers in the Medical-Pedagogical Consultation Unit and the clinics of the Experimental Institute of Defectology, and also in the Neurological Clinic of the First Moscow State University which studied the disintegration of psychological functions in cases of structural organic brain damage.

2. When analyzing the qualitatively new formations occurring in the process of a mentally retarded child's development, Vygotsky turned his attention to the concept of sublation (*sniatie*), important from the point of view of dialectics. He pointed out its twofold meaning (*aufheben*): not only "to bury" but also to "preserve" (see W. F. Hegel, *The Encyclopedia of Philosophical Sciences*, vol. 1, *The Science of Logic*, Moscow, 1977, p. 237–288).

Such a distinction, in the author's mind, allows us to realize the fact that primary symptoms (biological traits) at later stages of development turn out not to be eliminated but "sublated" under the influence of compensatory processes.

3. *DeGreef, E.* (?). Vygotsky praises DeGreef's research studies on one aspect of a mentally retarded child's emotional-volitional sphere, so-called self-esteem. He touches upon these questions in connection with an analysis of compensatory processes in a given category of abnormal children.

4. *Lewenstein, S* (?). Vygotsky's view is similar to the general rule set down by Lewenstein, which states that secondary complications during abnormal child development are more easily eliminated.

5. *Terman, Lewis M.* (1877–1956), an American psychologist and pedagogue, author of a basic variation of the Binet-Simon tests, intended for measuring intelligence.

The Difficult Child

1. A stenogram of a lecture given March 4, 1928. From the personal archives of L. S. Vygotsky. It is published here for the first time.

2. *Kruedelen* (?), a German psychologist and defectologist. Vygotsky introduces his experimental data in an analysis of the correlation between intellectual and motor delay in children who have been classified as "debile" (feebleminded). According to Kruedelen's data, the degree of motor delay in a "debile" may not be lower than the norm. According to Vygotsky, this fact is very important from the point of view of the compensatory process.

Moral Insanity

1. Manuscript from Vygotsky's personal archive. It is being published here for the first time.

2. *Molozhavyi, S. S.* (?), a Soviet psychologist and pedagogue. He worked out a scheme for studying the behavior of a child and of a children's collective, the problem of toys and work at preschool age. He objected to the reactionary understanding of moral defectiveness.

The Dynamics of Child Character

1. This essay appeared in the collection *Pedology and Education* (Moscow, 1928).

2. *Hippocrates* (ca. 460 ca. 370 BCE), a doctor of ancient Greece; a materialist. He inquired into questions of etiology, prognosis, and temperament.

3. *Bergson, Henri* (1859–1941), a French philosopher, writer, and psychologist; an idealist. He was one of the creators of the theory of intuition. Vygotsky, in examining the primary forces on the development of the human character, opposed Bergson's notion of "internal vitalistic elan" with the necessity of social processes for personal realization.

4. *Hall, Stanley* (1844–1924), an American psychologist whose main works are in the area of educational psychology. He advocated the application of the biogenetical law to the development of child behavior. [Note from the Russian version of Vygotsky's *Collected Works*, vol. 1, p. 470 to which the present volume refers.]

5. *Groos, Karl* (1861–1946), a German psychologist, who worked in the area of child psychology. Vygotsky pointed out that, in contrast to views on innate nature of child character, Groos in his well-known theory of play

examined it as a process of a child's natural self education. Hence, Vygotsky associated Groos's theory of play with exercise and with the natural compensation of insufficient inherent reactions.

Defectology and the Study of the Development and Education of Abnormal Children

1. *Piaget, Jean* (1896–1980), an outstanding French and Swiss psychologist. He was the author of numerous experimental and theoretical works in the area of child and genetic psychology and the creator of the operational concept of the intellect. In his article, "A Mentally Retarded Child," Vygotsky tells us how Piaget's experiment was modified for the purpose of clarifying the genesis and role of a child's egocentric speech. In one of his fundamental works, *Thinking and Speech*, Vygotsky gives an extensive critical analysis of Piaget's work *Speech and Thought in a Child*.

2. *Claparéde, Edouard* (1873–1940), a Swiss psychologist, spokesman for functional psychology. The author of a theory on play. Vygotsky emphasizes Claparde's work in relation to the problem of a child's cultural development, and the emergence of higher forms of behavior.

Part III: Questions at the Forefront of Defectology

The Study of the Development of the Difficult Child

1. "Outline," published in the book *The Fundamental Problems of Pedology in the USSR* (Moscow, 1928).

Bases for Working with Mentally Retarded and Physically Handicapped Children

1. Written for *The Pedological Encyclopedia* , vol. 2 (1928).

Fundamental Principles in a Plan for Pedological Research in the Field of "Difficult Children"

1. Published in the journal *Pedagogy*, 1929, no. 3.

2. Pedology is one of the directions taken by bourgeois pedagogy in the West in the late 19th and early 20th centuries; it was widespread in the United States, England, and other capitalist countries. IQ is based on the reactionary idea that the fate of a child depends on biological factors and on the influence of heredity and unchanged environment. With the aid of a set of special tests, pedologists measure quantitatively the so-called coefficient of intellectual development—IQ. It is as if the size of this IQ points out a child's potential. In the late 1920's and early 1930's it gained some currency in the USSR and was significantly harmful to general and special pedagogy and psychology. During these years, auxiliary schools began to grow quickly in number; they were filled not with the feeble-minded but with pedagogically neglected and undisciplined students who, for various reasons, were unable to deal with the tests. Vygotsky, in using the terms *pedology* and *pedological*, in fact, had in mind a "synthetic" science of children, or, even better, of child and pedagogical psychology. But the foundations for such a science worked out by him correspond at least externally, and by name, with the understanding of *pedology*. In many essays in this volume, the reader will encounter Vygotsky's consequent principled criticism of various pedological theories and of practices of the time (see, for example, the critique of pedological preformism, the purely quantitative perspective on problems of mental backwardness, and so forth). Vygotsky's opinions about contemporary pedology psychotechniques disclose their more vulnerable structures. Vygotsky's position in evaluating contemporary pedology didn't differ from that expressed in the resolution of the Central Committee of the Party: "About Pedological Misinterpretations in the Narkompros Sstem" in 1936. There was not another single psychologist who, from the very beginning of the 1930's, demonstrated so convincingly, the crisis, the unscientific nature, and the harmfulness of the then common practice of purely numerical measurement of the intellect, particularly as it applied

to the diagnostics of mental backwardness. This principally phenomenological perspective must inevitably lead us, as shown above, to the determination of false connections, to a distortion of the picture of "realities, to an inaccurate orientation toward actions, because this perspective judges reality and the connections that lay at its foundations, as though they were symptoms." Thus, the "principal task in investigating mental backwardness is the study of child development and the laws which direct that development."

3. The Institute of Methods for School Work was organized in 1922; it was part of the Narkompros (Narodnyi Komissariat Prosveshcheniia, or People's Commissariat of Enlightenment) system. The Institute of Non-School Work was organized in 1929. Shortly, the two institutes were united.

4. Institutes for the protection of healthy children and adolescents existed in Moscow and Leningrad from 1928 on; they were part of the Narkompros system.

5. The Moscow psychoneurological and pedological school-sanitarium was part of the Narkomzdrav system [Narkomzdrav = Narodnyi Komissariat Zdorovia or the People's Commissariat of Health.] [Transl.]

6. The Institute of Scientific Pedagogy was founded at the second MGU, in 1929. [MGU = Moskovskii Gosudarstvennyi Universitet or Moscow State University. [Transl.]

7. The Medico-Pedagogical Station (8, Pogodinskaia Str., Moscow) was organized from private teaching-training institutions for defective and abnormal children.

8. *Sepp, Evgenii Konstantinovich* (1878–1957), a famous Soviet neuropathologist.

9. The Children's Investigative Institute (DOBI) of the State Psychoneurological Academy was organized in Leningrad in 1918; in 1924, it was named after Professor. A. S. Griboedov.

The Collective as a Factor in the Development of the Abnormal Child

1. This work was published in the journal *Questions of Defectology* 1931, nos. 1–2.

2. Speaking of collectives with reference to defective children, Vygotsky had in mind uniting them into a general group according to some simple kind of characteristic (age, belonging to one category of abnormality or other, stage of development or retardation). Further, this unificiation implied a broad program of training or education. The broad goal—the direction of collaborative learning, working, and play-activity—would at first come from the pedagogue (teacher and trainer). Depending on the measure of development, that general goal would become also the goal of the children's activity, organization from without gradually becoming the self-organization of the children.

3. *Galton, Francis* (1822–1911), an English anthropologist and psychologist. He contributed significant input into the development of experimental and quantitative methods for psychology. He assigned a significant role to hereditary factors, not sufficiently crediting the influence of the social environment. [Note from L. S. Vygotsky, *Collected Works*, [Rus.] vol. 1, p. 470 to which this volume refers).

Introduction to Ia. Tsveifel's Book, *Essay on the Behavioral Characteristics and Education of the Deaf-Mute*

1. Tsveifel's book was published in 1931 (Moscow, Leningrad).

Introduction to E. K. Gracheva's Book, *The Education and Instruction of Severely Retarded Children*

1. E. K. Gracheva's book was published in 1932.

Gracheva, Ekaterina Konstantinova (1866–1934), was the first Russian pedagogue-defectologist; she worked with severely mentally deficient children; she was the instructor of the first courses for pedagogue-defectologists and was widely known in defectology under the name of Auntie Kati. In his introduction to her book, Vygotsky defended the progressive, but at the time disputed, position about the necessity, purposefulness, and effectiveness of teaching imbeciles and idiots. In connection with the description of Gracheva's work and the authentic facts and conclusions presented by the author, Vygotsky raised important theoretical and practical questions about the possibilities for advancement of severely retarded children. He also stressed the question of becoming human in a comparative developmental plan: on one side, the animal, and on the other, the normal, retarded, and severely retarded child. On the basis of facts introduced by Gracheva, he underlined the enormous role played by teaching and education, by the collective, and by the inclusion of children in social life.

The Problem of Mental Retardation

1. This article was printed in the collection The Mentally Retarded Child, edited by L. S. Vygotsky and I. I. Daniushevskii (Moscow, 1935).

2. L. S. Vygotsky apparently had in mind the sensitivity of a child's psychological processes, their flexibility under various influences, and, at the same time, the lack of stability and the still diffused character of the processes of the nervous system in the child. Moreover, Vygotsky noted that the concentration, effort, and intensity of any given process varies in abnormal children of different ages, developmental levels, and categories.

The Diagnostics of Development and the Pedological Clinic for Difficult Children

1. This work was written in 1931. It was first intended as an article for a proposed collection on the question of difficult childhood. After Vygotsky's death, on the initiative of the director of EDI, I. I. Daniushevskii, it was prepared for publication by R. E. Levina and released as a separate brochure in 1935. It actually appeared in 1936. Writing "Developmental diagnostics ..." preceded a lengthy methodological treatment by Vygotsky of the rich clinical and experimental material he had at his disposal. At the beginning of the 1930's Vygotsky had already demonstrated the bankruptcy of contemporary pedology, which had a very negative effect on progress toward establishing and understanding anomalous development in children. [E.D.I. is the Experimental Defectological Institute, a precursor to the current Scientific Research Institute of Defectology, Soviet Academy of Pedagogical Sciences. See translator's "Introduction."]

2. *Bumke, Oswald* (?), a German psychiatrist.

3. *Lewin, Kurt* (1890–1947), a German psychologist who later worked in the United States; a methodologist, a theoretician and an experimental psychologist. He worked in the area of psychology of personality where he attempted to apply principles of Gestalt psychology. He is the author of the so-called dynamic theory of psychological fields. During the last years of his life he worked in the area of social psychology. Today, this school occupies a leading position in American social pathology. Vygotsky closely studied the works of Lewin in the last years of his life, when he concerned himself with the problems of personality, emotions, and the like. Vygotsky rather extensively analyzed Lewin's works in the article "The Problem of Mental Retardation," [Note from L. S. Vygotsky's, *Collected Works* (Rus.) vol 2, p.487—(Engl. vol.1 p. 382). Additionally, the note in this volume refers to (Rus.) vol. 1, p. 464.]

4. *James, William* (1842–1910), an American physiologist, psychologist, and philosopher. He was a founder of functional psychology, which interprets the mental processes from the viewpoint of the role which they fulfill in the process of the organism's adaptation to its milieu. [Note from L. S. Vygotsky *Collected Works* (Rus.) vol. 1,

p. 465, to which the present volume refers.] He was the founder of the philosophy of pragmatism in which the criterion of truth is: that which answers practical success in action. The sole reality in pragmatism is that of direct sensory experiences. In the area of psychology James addressed problems of religion and the theory of "stream of consciousness." Vygotsky was familiar with the major works of James. James' methodological criticism of the traditional subjective empirical approach to consciousness produced a particular effect on Vygotsky (Cf. "Consciousness as a Problem for Behavioral Psychology," L. S. Vygotsky's, *Collected Works*, [Rus.] vol. 1. pp. 78–98.) [Note from L. S. Vygotsky *Collected Works* (Rus) vol. 2, p. 487/(Egl.) vol. 1, p. 382. to which the present volume refers.]

5. *Kraepelin, Emil* (1856–1926)—a German psychiatrist and psychologist. He worked out a taxonomy for psychic illnesses based on nosological principles.

6. *Gesell, Arnold* (1880–1961), one of the founders of American child psychology. [Note from L. S. Vygotsky *Collected Works* (Rus.) vol. 2, p. 486/(Egl.) vol. 1, p 381 to which the present volume refers.]

7. *Sukhareva, Grunia Efinovna* (1891–1981), a Soviet psychiatrist. She made a great contribution to the clinical elaboration of mental retardation. One volume of her clinical lectures about the psychiatry of children's ages is entirely devoted to clinical oligophrenia.

8. The First All-Union Conference on the Study of Human Behavior (January 25–February 1, 1930, Leningrad) was to have produced a general methodological course for all the behavioral sciences.

9. *Bleuler, Eugen* (1859–1939), a Swiss psychiatrist. He advanced the concept of autism as a condition whereby the patient loses contact with reality and completely focuses on his own internal world of thoughts, ideas, and interests. [Note from L. S. Vygotsky, *Collected Works* (Rus.) vol. 1, p. 486, to which the present volume refers.]
[Dates given as 1857–1939] ... Bleuler was close in spirit to the psychoanalytical tendency. Together with Karl Jung he developed the method of the associative experiment [Note from L. S. Vygotsky, *Collected Works* (Rus.) vol. 2, p. 482/(Engl.) vol. 1, p.376 to which the present volume refers.]

10. *Jung, Karl Gustav* (1875–1961), a Swiss psychologist who, in part, supported psychoanalysis but rejected its pansexualism. He advanced the reactionary theory of the collective subconscious and individually inherited archetypes of thought. [Note from L. S. Vygotsky *Collected Works*, (Rus.) vol. 1, p. 469 to which this volume refers.]

11. Jaspers, Karl (1883–1969), an outstanding German philosophic-existentialist and pathopsychologist. He first formulated the question about distinguishing between psychopathological processes and pathological personality development. Clinical descriptions of psychological peculiarities in hysterical psychopaths were his idea.

12. *Lashley, Carl* (1890–1958), an American psychologist and a proponent of behaviorism. He studied the dependence of behaviour on the construction of the brain. [Note from L. S. Vygotsky *Collected Works*, vol.1, p. 467 to which this volume refers.]

13. *Ivanovskii, Vladimir Nikolaevich* (1867–1931), a Russian philosopher and psychologist. He concerned himself with the history associationism. He criticized the concepts of mental activity and apperception proposed by H. W. Leibneitz and F. Herbart and most significantly by W. Wundt from the point of view of associationism. He took an active part in the development of Russian educational psychology. [Note from L. S. Vygotsky *Collected Works*, (Rus.) vol. 1, p. 460 to which this volume refers.]

[The commentary notes for the section "From Addresses, Reports, etc." have been included adjacent to each of these short pieces of text.]

REFERENCES TO VOLUME 1 OF THIS SERIES

Marx, Karl and Frederick Engels. Sochenenie [Works].
Lenin, V.I. Polnoe sobranoe sochenenie [Complete Collected Works], v. 29.

*   *   *

Bleuler, E. Autisticheskoe myshlenie [Autistic Thinking], Odessa, 1927.
Borovskii, V.M. Vvedenie v sravnitel'nuiu psikhologiiu [Introduction to Comparative Psychology], Moscow, 1927.
Buehler, K. Dukhovnoe razvitie rebenka [The Spiritual Development of the Child], Kiev, 1916.
Gezell, G.A. Pedologiia rannego vozrasta [Pedology of the Early Ages], Moscow- Leningrad, 1932.
Groos, K. Dushevnaia zhizn' rebenka [The Mental Life of the Child], Kiev, 1916.
Dostoevskii, F.M. Dnevnik pisatelia [Diary of a Writer], Leningrad, 1929.
Krechmer, E. "Meditsinskaia psikhologiia myshleniia" [The Contemporary Psychology of Thinking], in: *Novye idei v filosofii* [New Ideas in Philosophy], 1914, No.16.
Levy-Bruhl, L. Pervobytnoe myshlenie [Primitive Thinking], Moscow, 1930.
Plekhanov, G.V. Izbrannye filosofskie proizvedeniia v 5-ti tom [Selected Philosophical Works in Five Volumes], Moscow, 1956, Volume 1.
Sakharov, L.S. "O medotakh issledovaniia poniatii" [On Methods of Studying Concepts], *Psikhlogiia*, 1930, Volume III.
Tolstoi, L.N. Pedagogicheskie stat'i [Pedagogical Articles], Moscow, 1903.
Tolstoi, L.N. Sobrannie sochinenie v 11-ti t. [Collected Works in 11 Volumes], Moscow, 1983, Volumes 10 and 11.
Uznadze, D.N. Psikhologicheskie issledovaniia [Psychological Investigations], Moscow 1966.
Uspenskii, G.I. Izbrannye proizvedeniia [Selected Works], Moscow, 1949.
Watson, J. Psikhlogiia kak nauka o povedenii [Psychology as the Science of Behavior], Moscow, 1926.
Folkelt G. Eksperimental'naia pskhologiia doshol'nika [Experimental Psychology of the Preschooler], Moscow, 1930.
Shif, Zh.I. Razvitie zhiteiskikh i nauchnykh poniatii [The Development of Everyday and Scientific Concepts], Dissertation, Moscow, 1933.
Shif, Zh.I. Razvitie zhiteiskikh i nauchnykh poniatii [The Development of Everyday and Scientific Concepts], Moscow, 1935.
Stern, William. Psikhologiia rannego detstva do shestiletnego vozrasts [The Psychology of Early Childhood Prior to the Age of Six], 1922.
Buehler, C. Soziologische und psychologische Studien uber das erste Lebenjahr. Leipsiz, 1927.

Buehler K. Abriss der geistigen Entwicklung des Kindes. Leipxig, 1923.

Delacroix H.S. Le langage et la pensée. Paris, 1924.

Frisch K. Die Sprache der Bienen. Wein, 1928.

Hempelmann F. Tierpsychologie vom Standpunktedes biologen. 1926.

Kafka G. Handbuch der vergleichenden Psychologie. Munchen, 1922.

Koffka K. Grundlagen der psychischen Entwicklung. Berlin, 1925.

Kohler W. Aus Psychologie des Schimpanzen. Psuch. Forschung, 1921, No.1.

Kohler W. Intelligenzprufungen und Menschenaffen. Berlin, 1921.

Learner W.S. A School System as a Educational Library. Cambridge, Mass., 1914.

Lemaitre A. Observations sur le langage interieur des enfants. Achives de Psychologie, 1905, N. 4.

Levy-Bruhl L. Les fonctions mentales dans les societés primatives. Paris 1922.

Meumann E. Die Entstehung der ersten Wortbedeutung beim Kinde. Philosophische Studien, 1928, v. XX.

Piaget, Jean. Le Langage et la pensée chez l'enfant. Paris, 1923.

Piaget, Jean. La causalité physique chez l' enfant. Paris, 1926.

*Piaget, Jean. Judgement and Reasoning in the Child, New York, Harcourt, Brace, & Company, 1928.

*Piaget, Jean. The Language and Thought of the Child, London, Routledge & Kegan Paul, 1932a.

Piaget, Jean. Rech' i Myshlenie Rebenka [The Speech and Thinking of the Child], Moscow–Leningrad, 1932b.

Piaget, Jean. Psychologie de l'enseignement de l'histoire. Bulletin trimestriel de la Conference Internationale pour l'enseignement de l'histoire, 1933, N.2.

*Piaget, Jean. The Construction of Reality in the Child, New York, Basic Books, 1927.

*Piaget, Jean. The Child's Conception of Physical Causality, Totowa, New Jersey, Littlefield, Adams & Co., 1966.

Rimat F. Intelligen zu Untersuchungen anschliessend und die Ach'sche Suchmethode, Leipzig, 1925.

Smidt B. Die Sprache und andere Ausdruchformen der Tiere. Berlin, 1923.

Stern W. Person und Sache, I Band. Leipzig, 1905.

Stern C., Stern W. Die Kindersprache. Berlin, 1928.

Thorndike E.R. The Mental Life of Monkeys.N.Y., 1901.

Yerkes R.M. The mental life of monkeys and apes. Behavior Monographs, 1916, III-I.

Yerkes R.M., Learned E.W. Chimpanzee Intelligence and Its Vocal Expression. Baltimore, 1925.

---

* The bulk of Vygotsky's discussions of Piaget are based on a Russian translation that combined The Language and Thought of the Child and Judgement and Reasoning in the Child into a single volume (e.g., Piaget, Jean. Rech' i Myshlenie Rebenka [The Speech and Thinking of the Child], Moscow-Leningrad, 1932). As a consequence, when reading Vygotsky, it is often difficult to know which of these two books by Piaget he is discussing or citing. To facilitate attempts by readers to analyze Vygotsky's discussion of Piaget, we have used the English rather than the Russian translations of Piaget's works for quotations and citations in this volume. The few significant discrepancies between the English and Russian translations are discussed in footnotes.

REFERENCES TO THIS VOLUME

Notes to References

The reference list provided here is derived from the Literatura (reference list or bibliography) provided in the Russian edition. It was found to contain listings of works not cited in the volume. These were retained in the list below.

Many works cited by Vygotsky in the volume were also found to be missing from the list. Some of these were found to be cited in other volumes of the Collected Works and were transferred to this list. Other citations—or their authors—are discussed in the Notes (Komentaria) which were provided by the Collegium for the Russian edition. Efforts were made by the translators and editors to provide references of English-language versions for those citations which were not supplied. Nevertheless, a fair number of Vygotsky's citations in the text remain unreferenced and undocumented.

The Soviet practice of citing works by Marx, Lenin and Engels at the head of the reference list was retained in the list below. However, the separate lists of Russian works and works written in languages using the Latin alphabet were combined. Citations (supplied by Soviet Collegium) of Russian translations of works from other languages (e.g. Dewey, Freud) are given with transliterations of the Russian titles and English versions of those titles.

Marx, K. and Engels F., *Collected works,* vols. 20, 25. Part II.

*   *   *

Ach, N., *Ueber die Begriffsbildung: eine experimentelle Untersuchung* (On concept formation: an experimental examination). Bamberg, 1921. [?]
Adler, A., *Praxis und Theorie der Individualspsychologie* (The practice and theory of individual psychology). Munich, 1927.

Adler, A., *Ueber den nervoesen Charakter* (The neurotic constitution). Munich, 1928.

Bacher, Die Ach'sche Suchmethode in ihrer Verwendung zur Intelligenzpruefung. *Unters. zur Phil., Psych, u. Paedag.,* B. 4. H. 3/4, 1925. (Ach's search-method in its application to testing intelligence. *Papers in Philosophy, Psychology and Pedagogy.* Vol 4. Nos. 3–4, 1925.

Baldwin, D., *Psikhologiia v ie primenenii k vospitaniyiu.* (Psychology and its application to education.) Moscow, 1904. [from Rus Vol. 4]

Baldwin, D., *Dukhovnoe rasvitie detskogo individuuma i chelovecheskogo roda.* (The spiritual development of the child's individuality and the human species.) Moscow, 1911, Vol, 1; 1912, Vol. 2. [from Rus. Vol. 4]

Basov, M. Ia., *Metodika psykhologicheskikh nabliudenii nad det'mi* (Methods for psychological observation of children) Moscow, 1926.

Bekhterev, V. M., *Obshchie osnovy refleksologii cheloveka* (The broad bases of human reflexology). Moscow and Leningrad, 1928.

Bekhterev, V. M., and Vasil'ev, L. L., *Refleksologiia truda* (The reflexology of work) Moscow and Leningrad, 1926.

Binet, A., *Psychologie des grands calculateurs et jouers déchecs.* (The psychology of great calculators and chess players). Paris, 1894.

Birilev, A. V., *Ob osiazanii slepykh* (On touch in the deaf). Kazan', 1901.

Birilev, A. V., "Svet dlia slephykh i nekotorye voprosy metodiki prepodovaniia slepym," v kn., *Voprosy vospitaniia slephykh, glukhonemykh, i umstvenno otstalykh,* pod red. L. S. Vygotsky ("Light for the blind and some methodological questions in teaching the blind," in L. S. Vygotsky, Questions in the education of the blind, deaf-mute, and mentally retarded), Moscow: 1924.

Blonskii, P. P., *Pedologiia* (Pedology) Moscow, 1925.

Buehler, K. *Ueber das Sprachverstaendnis vom Standpunkt der Normalpsychologie aus.* (Language comprehension from the viewpoint of normal psychology.) (Collected reference): *Monograf. exp. Psych. 3,* 1908 [from Rus. Vol. 4]

Buehler, K., *Dukhovnogo razvitie rebenka.* (The development of the psyche of the child.) Moscow, 1924. [from Rus. Vol. 4.]

Buehler, K. *Abriss der geistigen Entwicklung des Kindes.* (Outline of the development of the psyche of the child.) Leipzig, 1927 [from Rus. Vol. 2]

Buehler, K., *Die Krise der Psychologie.* (The crisis in psychology.) Jena, 1927. [from Rus. Vol. 1]

Buehler, K., *Ocherk dukhovnogo razvitie rebenka.* (Outline of the development of the psyche of the child.) Moscow, 1930. [from Rus. Vol. 1, 2, 4]

Buerklen, K. *Blindenpsychologie* (Psychology of the blind). Leipzig, 1924;

Buerklen, K. *Der Blindenfreund* (Friend of the blind). 1926, N 3. [sic]

Decker, G., *Biologiia organov chustv* (Biology of the sensory organs) Moscow and Prague, 1923.

Dewey, J. *Shkola i obshchestvo* (School and society), Moscow, 1907.

Dushevnaia zhizn' detei, pod red. A. F. Lazupskogo, A. P. Nechaeva (Children's mental life, edited by A. F. Lazupskii and A. P. Nechaev), Moscow, 1910.

Eliasberg, W. *Psychologie und Pathologie der Abstraktion* (The psychology and pathology of abstraction). 1925. [sic]

Frank, S. L., *Filosofiia i zhizn'* (Philosophy and life), St. Peterburg, 1910.

Freud, S., "Kharakter i anal'naia erotika," *Psikhologicheskaia i psikhoanaliticheskaia biblioteka* ("Character and anal eroticism," Psychological and Psychoanalytical Library), 15th ed.,1923.

Frolov, Iu. P., *Fiziologicheskaia priroda instinkta* (The physiological nature of instinct). Leningrad, 1925.

Gerhardt, F., *Materialien zur Blindenpsychologie* (Materials for [the study of] the pscyhology of the blind). 1924.[sic]

Gesell, A., *Pedologiia rannego vozrasta* (Pedology for early age groups), Moscow and Leningrad, 1932.

Gesell, A., *Umstvennoe razvitie rebenka* (The mental development of a child). Moscow and Leningrad, 1930.

Golovin, S. S., *Sovremennaia postanovka sotsial'noi pomoshchi slepym* (The current situation with respect to social help for the blind). Moscow, 1924.

Grabarov, A. N., *Vspomogatel'naia shkola* (The auxiliary school). Leningrad, 1925.

Griboedov, A. S. "Pedologicheskaia rabota i vspomogatel'naia shkola," v kn.: *Novaia shkola* ("Pedological work and the auxiliary school," in *The New School*). Moscow and Leningrad, Issue No. 2, 1926.

Griboedov, A. S., *Sovremennaia problemyi vspomogatel'nogo obucheniia.* v kn. *Voprosy izucheniia i vospitaniia lichnosti: Pedologiia i defektologiia,* pod red. B. M. Bekhtereva. (Contemporary problems in auxiliary education. in B. M. Bekhterev, ed., *Questions in personality study and education: Pedology and defectology*) Nos. 1–2, Leningrad, 1927.

Groos, K., *Dushevnaia zhizn' rebenka* (The mental life of children) Kiev, 1916.

Gruman, A., *Podgotovitel'noe i dopol'nitel'noe obuchenie glukhonemykh* (Preparatory and auxiliary teaching for the deaf-mute). Saint Petersburg, 1910.

Guertler, R., Das primitive Bewusstsein. *Bericht ueber den dritten Kongress fuer Heilpaedagogik in Muenchen 2–4 August 1926*. (The primitive consciousness. Report on the Third Congress for Therapuetic Pegagogy in Munich, August 2–4, 1926). Berlin, 1927.

Gurevich, M. O., "O formakh dvigatel'noi nedostatochnosti," v kn. *Voprosy pedologii i detskoi pshikhonevrologii pod red. M. O. Gurevicha* (On the forms of motoric inadequacies, in M. O. Gurevich, (Ed)., *Questions in pedology and child psychoneurology*), 2nd ed. Moscow, 1925.

Gurevich, M. O. (Ed), *Questions in pedology and child psychoneurology*), 2nd ed. Moscow, 1925.

Head. H., *Aphasia and kindred disorders of speech*. London, University of Cambridge Press, 2 vols., 1926 [revised reference]

Herbart, J. F., *Izbrannye pedagogicheskie sochinenniia*. (Selected pedagogical works.), Moscow, 1906. [from Rus. Vol. 4]

Homburger, A., *Psychopathologie des Kindes und Jugendalter* (Psychopathology of children and youth). Berlin, 1926 (a)

Homburger, A., *Psychologie des Kindesalters* (Psychology of childhood). Berlin, 1926(b)

Intelligenzleistungen hochgradig Schwachsinniger. *Ztschr. f. d. ges. Neurologie und Psychologie*. B. 104, 1926, H. 4/5. (Intellectual abilities of high grade retardates. *Journal for the Study of Neurology and Psychology*) Vol. 104, Issue 4/5, 1926. [sic: apparently a journal article, with no author given or unsigned. Ed.]

Internationale Zeitschrift fuer Individualpsychologie (International Journal for Individual Psychologie). 125, N. 5. [sic]

Internationale Zeitschrift fuer Individualpsychologie (International Journal for Individual Psychologie). Vol. 1, No. 1., 1914.

Ivanovskii, V. N., *Metodologicheskoe vvedenie v nauku i filosofiiu* (A methodological introduction to science and philosophy). Minsk, 1923.

Jaensch, E. R. *Einige allgemeinere Fragen der Psychologie und Biologie des Denkens*. (Some rather general question of the psychology and biology of thought.) Leipzig, 1920. [from Rus. Vol. IV]

Jaensch, E. R., *Ueber den Aufbau der Wahrnehmungswelt und ihere Struktur im Jugendalter*. (On the construction of the perceived world and its structure during adolescence.) Leipzig, 1925. [from Rus. Vol. IV]

Jaensch, E. R. , *Ueber den Aufbau der Wahrnehmungswelt und die Grundlagen des menschlichen Erkentnis*. (On the construction of the perceived world and the bases for human recognition.) Leipzig, 1927. (Vol. 1). [from Rus. Vol. IV].

Jaensch, E. R. *Ueber Eidetick und die typologische Forschungsmethode*. (On eidetic [imagery] and the typological research method.) *Zeitschr. Psychol.*, 1927, 102. [from Rus. Vol. IV]

Jaensch, E. R. *Eidetic imagery*. New York, 1930. [from Rus. Vol. 4]

Janet, P. *L'evolution psychologique de la personnalit*. (The psychological evolution of personality) Paris, 1930 [from Rus. Vol IV].6

Kanitz, O. F., Volkstuemliche individualpsychologische Literatur. *Die Sozialistische Erziehung*. Wein, 1926. H. 7/8. (Literature on individual psychology for the general public. Socialist Rearing No. 7/8). Vienna, 1926.

Keller, H., *Optimizm* (Optimism) Saint Petersburg: 1910.

Keller, H. *Die Geschichte meines Lebens*. (The story of my life) Stuttgart, 1920.

Kerschensteiner, G., *Das Grundaxiom des Bildungsprozess*. (The basic axiom of the process of education). 1924. [sic]

Koffka, K., Introspection and the method of psychology. *The British Journal of Psychology*, 1924, V. 15. [from Rus. Vol. 1]

Koffka, K., *Die Grundlagen des psychischen Entwicklung*. (The foundations of mental development.) Osterwieck am Harz, 1925. [from Rus. Vol. 1, 2]

Koffka, K., *Samonabliudennie i metod psykhologii*. (Introspection and method in psychology.) *B. Sb.: Problemy covremmenoi pskhologii*. (In Anthology: Problems of contemporary psychology.) Leningrad, 1926. [from Rus. Vol. 1]

Koffka, K., *Protiv mekhanizisma v vitalisma b sovremennoi psykhologii*. (In opposition to mechanism and vitalism in contemporary psychology.) *Psykhologiya*, [no place] 1932. [from Rus. Vol. 1]

Koffka, K., *Osnovi psikhicheskogo rasvitiia* (The foundations of mental development.) Moscow, Leningrad, 1934. [from Rus. Vol. 4]

Kompeire, G., *Otrochestvo, ego psikhologiia i pedagogiia*. (Adolescence: Its psychology and pedagogy.) St Petersburg, 1910. [from Rus. Vol. 4]

Kompeire, G. *Umstvennoye i nravstvennoye rasvitiye rebenka*. (The intellectual and moral development of the child.) Moscow, 1912.[from Rus. Vol. 4]

Kotel'nikov, M. N., " Na novom puti: (chtenie s gub kak osnova obucheniia glukhonemykh ustnoi rechi)," v kn. *Puti vospitaniia fizicheski defektivnogo rebenka* pod red. S. S. Tizanova, P. P. Pochapina ("On new paths—lipreading as the basis for the deaf-mute learning of verbal speech," in S. S. Tizanov and P. P. Pochapin, eds., Paths toward the education of physically handicapped children). Moscow, 1926.

Kretschmer, E., *Ob isterii* (On hysteria). Moscow and Leningrad, 1928.

Kretschmer, E., *Stroenie tela i kharakter* (Body structure and character). Moscow and Leningrad, 1932.

Krogius, A. A., "Shestoe chuvstvo u slepykh," *Vestnik psikhologii* ("Sixth sense in the blind," *Psychology Bulletin*. Issue 1, Saint Petersburg, 1907.

Kruenegel, M., Grundfragen der Heilpaedogogik zu ihren Grundlegung und Zielstellung. *Ztschr. f. Kinderforschung, B. XXXII, 1926*. (Basic questions for establishing and setting the goals of a therapeutic pedagogy. *Journal for Research on Children*.) Vol 32, 1926.

Kruenegel, M., Die motorische Befaehigung Schwachsinniger Kinder im Lichte des Experiments. *Ztschr. f. Kinderforschung*, B. 33, 1927., H. 2. (Enabling the motoric competence of feeble minded children in light of the experiment. *Journal for Research on Children*.) Vol 33, No. 2. , 1927.

Krupskaia. N. K., *Sistema narodnogo obrazovaniia v RSFSR* (The public education system in the Russian Soviet Federated Socialist Republics), vol. 2. Moscow, 1928.

Kuelpe, G. I., "Metod tselykh slov i fraz Malisha" v kn. *Puti vospitaniia fizicheski defektivnogo rebenka*, pod red. S. S. Tizanova, P. P. Pochapina (" Malisch's whole word and phrase method," in S. S. Tizanov, and P. P. Pochapin, eds., Paths toward the education of physically handicapped children). Moscow, 1926.

Lagovskii, N. M., *Skt-Peterburgskoe uchilishche glukhonemykh, 1810-1910* (The St. Petersburg school for the deaf-mute, 1810-1910). Saint Petersburg, 1910.

Lagovskii, N. M., *Obuchenie glukhonemykh ustnoi rechi* (Teaching the deaf-mute verbal speech). Aleksandrov, 1911.

Lashley, C. S. *Brain mechanisms and intelligence*. Chicago, Chicago Univ. Press, 1929. [revised reference]

Leman, G., "Tezisy sodokladchika," v kn., *Puti vospitaniia fizicheski defektivnogo rebenka* pod red. S. S. Tizanova, P. P. Pochapina. ("The thesis of a co-presentor" in S. S. Tizanov and P. P. Pochapin, Paths toward the Education of Physically Handicapped Children). Moscow, 1926. [See citation of K. Malish, below, which was the co-presentation. {Ed., Rus. edit.}]

Lindworsky, J., *Der Wille* (The will). Leipzig, Barth, 1919. [revised reference]

Lipmann, O. and Bogen, H., *Naive Physik* (Naive physicist) Jena, 1923.

Lipmann, O. Ueber Begriff und Formen der Intelligenz. *Zeitschr. f. ang. Psychol.* (On the concept and forms of intelligence. *Journal for Applied Psychology*) Vol 24, 1924.

Lipps, T. *Rukovodstvo k psikhologii* (Leadership toward psychology). Saint Petersburg, 1907.

Malish, K., "Sushnost' i tsennost' metoda tselovykh slov pri pervonachal'nom obuchenii glukhonemykh detei ustnoi rechi: tezisy," v. kn. *Puti vospitaniia fizicheski defektivnogo rebenka* pod red. S. S. Tizanova, P. P. Pochapina ("The essence and value of the whole word method in the initial teaching of verbal speech to the deaf-mute: theses," in S. S. Tizanov and P. P. Pochapin, eds., Paths toward the education of physically handicapped children). Moscow, 1926. [See citation of G. Leman, above, which was the co-presentation. {Ed., Rus. edit.}]

Messer, A., Experimentell-psychologische Untersuchung ueber das Denken (The experimental-psychological study of thought), *Archiv. gen Psychol. (Archive of General Psychology)*, Vol 8, 1906.

Messer, A., *Empfindung und Denken* (Sensation and thought), Leipzing, 1908.

Meumann, E., *Vorlesungen zur Einfuerung in die experimentelle Paedogogik under ihre psychologischen Grundlagen* (Introductory lectures on experimental pedagogy and its psychological foundations). Leipzig, 1911–1914.

Nathorp, P., *Sotsial'naia pedagogika* (Social pedagogy). Saint Petersburg, 1911.

Noell, H., Die Bedeutung der Vollendungstendenc im Arbeitsunterricht der Hilfsschule, *Ztschr. fuer d. Behandlung Schwachsinniger*. (The implication of 'closure' [the tendency toward completion] in vocational instruction in auxiliary schools. *Journal for the Treatment of the Feeble Minded*), 7–10, 1927

Novoe v refeksologii i fiziologii nervnoi sistemy pod red. V. M Bekhterev (*New studies in the reflexology and physiology of the nervous system*, V. M. Bekhterev, Ed.). Leningrad, Moscow, 1925.

Pavlov, I. P. "Dvadtsatiletnii opyt ob'yektivnogo izucheniia vysshei nervnoi deiatel'nosti (povedenia) zhivotnykh" *Poln sobr. soch.* t. 3. (A Twenty year experiment in the objective study of the higher nervous activity of organisms. *The Complete Collected Works*, Vol. 3. Moscow, Leningrad, 1951.

Petrova, A. E. Deti-primitivy. V. kn.: *Voprosy pedologii i detskoi psikhonevrologii* . Pod. red. M. O. Gurevicha ("Primitivity in children," in M. O. Gurevich, (Ed.) *Questions of pedology and childhood psychoneurology*). Moscow, 1925.

Petzeld, A. *Konzentration bei Blinden. Eine psychologisch-paedagogische Studie* (Concentration among the blind: A psychological-pedagogical study). Leipzig, 1925.

Poyer, D., *La psychologie des caracters-Trait de pscyhologie par. G. Dumas,* t. 11, (The psychology of character: Treatise on psychology by G. Dumas), Vol. 11, 1924.

Programmy vspomogatel'noi shkoly (dlia umstbenno otstalykh detei) (*Programs of auxiliary schools (for mentally retarded children*). Moscow, Leningrad, 1927.

Protopopov, V. P. "Materialy k izucheniiu; fiziologii reaktsii sosredotocheniia (vnimaniia) i gipnoidnykh sostoianii," *Ukrainskii visnik reflesologii ta eksperimental'noi pedagogiki*, No. 1. (in Ukranian). (Materials for study: Physiological reactions in concentration (of attention) in hypnotic states," *The Ukranian bulletin of refloxology and experimental pedagogy*), Vol. 1. Khar'kov, 1925.

Protopopov, V. P., "Refleksologiia i pedagogika," *Ukrainskii visnik refleksologii ta eksperimental'noi pedagogiki* No.2. (in Ukrainian) ("Reflexology and pedagogy," *The Ukrainian bulletin of reflexology and experimtental pedagogy*), Vol. 2.[?] Khar'kov, 1925.

Psikhologiia i marksizm (Psychology and Marxism) Moscow, Leningrad, 1925.

Rau, N. A., "Doshkoln'oe vospitanie gukhonemykh," v kn. *Puti vospitaniia fizicheski defektivnogo rebenka* pod red. S. S. Tizanova and P. P. Pochapina. ("Preschool education for the deaf-mute," in S. S. Tizanov and P. P. Pochapin, eds., *Paths toward the education of physically handicapped children*). Moscow, 1926.

Ribot, T., *Psikhologiia vnimaniia* (The psychology of attention). Prague, 1892.

Rimat, F., Intelligenzuntersuchungen anschliessend an die Ach'sche Suchmethode, *Unters. zur Phil., Psych. u. Paed.*, B. 5, 1925, H. 3/4. (Experiments on intelligence connected with Ach's search-method, *Papers on Philosophy, Psychology and Pedagogy.* Vol. 5, No. 3/4, 1925.

Ruele, O., *Psikhika proletarskogo rebenka* (The psychology of the proletarian child). Moscow, Leningrad, 1926.

Segen, E., *Vospitanie, gigiena i nravstvennoe lechenie umstvenno nenormal'nykh detei* (The rearing, hygiene, and moral treatment of mentally abnormal chidren). Saint Petersburg, 1903.

Shcherbina, A. M., *Slepoi muzykant' V. G. Korolenko kak popytka zriachikh proniknut' v psikhologiiu slepykh v svete moikh sobstvennykh nabliudenii* (V. G. Korolenko's 'The blind musician:' As an attempt by the seeing to penetrate the psychology of the blind, in the light of my own observations). Moscow, 1916.

Sokolianskii, I. A., "Pro tak zvana chitaniia z gub glukhonimi," *Ukrainskii visnik refleksologii ta eksperimental'noi pedagogiki* (in Urkrainian, "About so-called lip-reading among the deaf-mute," *The Ukrainian bulletin of reflexology and experimental pedagogy*) No. 2.[?] Khar'kov, 1926.

Spielrein, J. N., *Professional'nyi otbor* (*Professional selection*), Moscow, 1924.

Stern, W. *Die differnzielle Psychologie in ihren methodischen Grundlagen* (The methodological foundations of differential psychology). Leipzig, 1921.

Stern, W., *Psikhologiia rannego detstva do shestiletenego vozrasta* (The psychology of early childhood before six years of age). Prague, 1922.

Stern, W., *Die menschliche Persoenlichkeit* (Human personality). 1923.

Stern, W., *Person und Sache. System des kritischen Personalismus* B. 11 (Person and thing: The system of critial personalism). Vol. 11 [sic]. Leipzig, 1923.

Stumpf, K., "Davleniia psikhicheskikh funktsii," *Novye idei v filosofii* 1913, No. 4. ("The presssure of psychological functions," *New ideas in philosophy).* No. 4, 1913

Sukhareva, G. E., "K probleme struktury i dinamiki detskikh konstitutsionnykh psikhopatii (skhizoidnye formy)," *Zhurnal nevropatologii i psikhiatrii* ("On the problem of structure and dynamics in children's constitutional psychopathy (schizoid forms)," *Journal of Neuropathology and Psychiatry*), No. 6, 1930.

Thorndike, E. L., *The measurement of intelligence.* [sic]

Troshin, P. Ia., *Sravnitel'naia psikhologiia normal'nykh i nenormal'nykh detei.* tom. 1. (Comparative psychology of normal and abnormal children, Vol. 1). Prague, 1915.

Trudy Donskogo pedagogicheskogo instituta pod red. N. A. Popova (N. A. Popov, ed., *Works of the Donskoi Pedagogical Institute*), No. 1, Novocherkassk, 1920.

Vygotsky, L. S., Soznanie kak problema psikhologii povedeniia. *Sobr. Soch.* tom. 1 (Consciousness as a problem in the psychology of behavior. *Collected Works*, Vol. 1), Moscow, 1982. [In *Questions in the Theory and History of Psychology*, forthcoming in the English *Collected Works*]

Wanecek, O. Der Blinde in der Sage, im Maerchen und in der Legende, *Ztschr. f. d. oest. Blindwesen*, (The blind in sagas, fairy-tales and legends, *Journal for the Blind of Austria*,.1915. [sic]

Werner, F., *Psikhologicheskie osnovy nemetskogo metoda obucheniia glukhonemykh* (The psychological bases of the German method for teaching the deaf-mute), Saint Petersburg, 1909.

White, W. *Foundations of Psychiatry*, 1921.

Wittel, F., *Freid, ego lichnost', uchenie, i shkola*. (Freud, his personality, his teachings, and his school), Leningrad, 1925.

Zalkind, B., *Voprosy sovetskoi pedagogiki* (Questions of Soviet Pedagogy), Leningrad, 1926. [Citation from Volume 4 of the Russian edition.]

AUTHOR INDEX

SUBJECT INDEX